NINETY-SIX SERMONS

BY THE

RIGHT HONOURABLE AND REVEREND FATHER IN GOD,

LANCELOT ANDREWES,

SOMETIME LORD BISHOP OF WINCHESTER.

PUBLISHED BY HIS MAJESTY'S SPECIAL COMMAND.

VOL. V.

WIPF & STOCK · Eugene, Oregon

Wipf and Stock Publishers
199 W 8th Ave, Suite 3
Eugene, OR 97401

Ninety-Six Sermons by the Right Honourable and Reverend Father in God,
Lancelot Andrewes, Sometime Lord Bishop of Winchester, Vol. V
By Andrewes, Lancelot
ISBN 13: 978-1-60608-121-1
Publication date 01/23/2009
Previously published by James Parker and Co., 1884

SERMONS.

EDITOR'S PREFACE.

THE present volume completes the "Ninety-six Sermons," the only authentic Sermons of Bishop Andrewes which had been so far finished under his own hand as to be considered by those to whom his papers were entrusted, Bishops Laud and Buckeridge, in a fit state for publication.

The Funeral Sermon, preached by one of these, his friend Bishop Buckeridge, is appended in the place which it has usually occupied in former editions of the Ninety-six Sermons, being as it were the seal of their authenticity, and marking the boundary between Andrewes's finished and authenticated and his imperfect and less authenticated Sermons and Lectures.

Of this latter class are the Sermons on the Lord's Prayer and on the Temptation, The Exposition of the Moral Law, and the Orphan Lectures on Genesis; of which it is as certain from their matter and manner that they had no other author than Bishop Andrewes, as it is from other circumstances that they were not, strictly speaking, from his pen.

The account to be given of these publications is probably this.—In a Preface to the first edition of the work on the Moral Law, which was printed in a very negligent imperfect way in the year 1642, it is said that " he was scarce reputed a pretender to learning and piety in Cambridge (during Andrewes's residence there) who made not himself a disciple of Bishop Andrewes by diligent resorting to his lectures, nor he a pretender to the study of divinity who did not transcribe his notes;" and that these "had ever after passed from hand to hand in many hundreds of copies."

To the labours of these "disciples" and students, whether they were transcripts surreptitiously made from his MSS. or notes taken down in short-hand from his lips as he delivered them, we owe the imperfect and unauthenticated Sermons and Lectures of Bishop Andrewes.

It is on record that King Charles the First, with his characteristic reverence for holy subjects, and a tender jealousy for the reputation of the Bishop, gave his special charge to the Bishops of London and Ely, on confiding his papers to their care, that none should be committed to the press but such as they found perfected by his accurate hand. It seems to have been his desire to put a stop perhaps to the currency of those imperfect draughts or broken notes which had already crept into print, and to prevent a style at once so striking and so familiar from becoming, in less delicate and reverent hands, unlike itself. At the same time it seems to have been evident all along, nor indeed is it denied by those most concerned, that in the "undigested chaos" put forth in 1642, there were many good materials, and those originally from the mind of Andrewes. It is only insisted upon, that they were but ruins and fragments.

With these remarks, and this caution as to the probable amount of their authenticity, it has seemed desirable to print the Sermons on the Lord's Prayer and on the Temptation, both of which are early works, the former most probably to be assigned to the period during which Andrewes occupied the office of Catechist at Pembroke Hall. They were both appended to the above-mentioned edition of the work on the Moral Law, but had both appeared before, and had been uniformly ascribed to him.

The Sermons on the Lord's Prayer had been published originally in a small 12mo. in 1611, under the title of

"Scala Cœli," and subsequently, in a very improved state, in 1641, an edition extremely rare.

Of those on the Temptation, there does not appear to have been more than one original edition, and that as early as 1592, marked A in the present edition.

In the Prefaces to both the early editions of the Sermons on the Lord's Prayer, it is assumed that though the Author's name is concealed, they could hardly fail to be identified. In that prefixed to those on the Temptation, which was sent to the publisher "by a gentleman, a friend of his, for publication," it is said that "he was driven to let these pass without name, desiring the reader to suspend his judgment, whose they were, yet not doubting but that in printing them he had done God good service, and pleased many who had happily heard them preached."—Elsewhere he supposes that "the tree from which this heavenly fruit was gathered, would be discovered both by the beauty and taste." They are considerably less perfect than those on the Lord's Prayer, and the figure here employed, "*fruit gathered*," seems to imply the way in which they were obtained.

The edition of the Exposition of the Moral Law, published in 1642, had both these series appended to it. But in the new and improved edition of it, which appeared in 1650, retouched and perfected after the Author's own copy, we do not find them, nor were they directly or indirectly alluded to in it ; from which it may perhaps be inferred, either that the Editor of the improved edition rejected them altogether as the Bishop's works, which can scarcely be imagined, or that, as these had appeared before, he had the less occasion to make particular reference to them, and more especially if he had not the means by him of correcting their errors or of supplying their deficiencies. At all events he left them alike unnoticed and untouched.

The differences between the existing editions are in some instances such as might render it doubtful whether they were not originally obtained from different transcripts : but on the whole it may be perhaps rather concluded that they were from the same. This doubt has induced the Editor where the improvement seemed certain, in the Sermons on the Lord's Prayer, to correct by the improved edition of 1641, but in others to mark the differences as various readings.

The particulars above stated have determined him to collate carefully and reprint in the best form in which he could obtain them, these valuable remains, if no more, as completing the Sermons of Bishop Andrewes.

CONTENTS.

SERMON III.

SERMON IV.

SERMON V.

SERMON VI.

THE LORD'S PRAYER.

SERMON VII.

SERMON VIII.

SERMON XVII.

(Page 460.)

But deliver us from evil.

SERMON XVIII.

(Page 470.)

For Thine is the Kingdom, Power, and Glory, for ever and ever.

SERMON XIX.

(Page 480.)

Amen.

———

SEVEN SERMONS

UPON THE TEMPTATION OF CHRIST IN THE WILDERNESS.

SERMON I.

(Page 493.)

MATTHEW iv. 1.

Then was Jesus led aside of the Spirit into the wilderness, to be tempted of the devil.

SERMON II.

(Page 504.)

MATTHEW iv. 2.

And when He had fasted forty days, and forty nights, He was afterward hungry.

SERMON III.

(Page 515.)

MATTHEW iv. 4.

But He answering said, It is written, Man shall not live by bread only, but by every word that proceedeth out of the mouth of God.

SERMON IV.

(Page 527.)

MATTHEW iv. 5, 6.

*Then the devil took Him up into the holy city, and set Him on a
pinnacle of the Temple,*

*And said unto Him, If Thou be the Son of God, cast Thy-
self down; for it is written, that He will give His Angels
charge over Thee, and with their hands they shall lift Thee
up, lest at any time Thou shouldst dash Thy foot against a
stone.*

SERMON V.

(Page 540.)

MATTHEW iv. 7.

*Jesus said unto him, It is written again, Thou shalt not tempt
the Lord thy God.*

SERMON VI.

(Page 552.

MATTHEW iv. 8, 9.

*Again, the devil taketh Him up into an exceeding high moun-
tain, and sheweth Him all the kingdoms of the world, and the
glory of them;*

*And saith unto Him, All these things will I give Thee, if Thou
wilt fall down and worship me.*

SERMON VII.

(Page 565.)

MATTHEW iv. 10, 11.

*Then Jesus saith unto him, Get thee hence behind Me, Satan;
for it is written, Thou shalt worship the Lord thy God, and
Him only shalt thou serve.*

*Then the devil leaveth Him, and behold the Angels came, and
ministered unto Him.*

CERTAIN SERMONS

PREACHED AT

SUNDRY TIMES, UPON SEVERAL OCCASIONS.

["St. Mary's Hospital was founded by Walter Brune, citizen of London, and others, 1197; in whose yard was a pulpit-cross of equal celebrity with that of St. Paul's. At the latter 'some special learned man,' says Mr. Newcourt, 'by appointment preached on Good-Friday a Sermon treating of Christ's Passion; and on the three next Easter days the like learned men, to wit, on Monday a Bishop, on Tuesday a Dean, and on Wednesday a Doctor of Divinity used to preach in the forenoons, at the Spittle, on the Resurrection.' After the fire of London the Spital Sermons were preached at St. Bride's in Fleet Street, and the Good-Friday Sermon in the choir of St. Paul's.

On the south of the pulpit was a house of two stories, the first of which was for the Mayor and Aldermen when they came to the Spital Sermons, the second for the prelates who might attend." Gent.'s Mag. lxix. p. 590.]

A SERMON

PREACHED

AT ST. MARY'S HOSPITAL,

ON THE TENTH OF APRIL, BEING WEDNESDAY IN EASTER WEEK,
A.D. MDLXXXVIII.

1 TIMOTHY vi. 17, 18, 19.

Charge them that are rich in this world, that they be not high-
minded, that they trust not in the uncertainty of riches,
but in the living God, Which giveth us all things to enjoy
plenteously;
That they do good, be rich in good works, ready to distribute
and to communicate;
Laying up in store for themselves a good foundation against the
time to come, that they may lay hold of eternal life.

[*Divitibus hujus sæculi præcipe non sublime sapere, neque sperare*
in incerto divitiarum, sed in Deo vivo, Qui præstat nobis omnia
abunde ad fruendum;
Bene agere, divites fieri in bonis operibus, facile tribuere, communi-
care;
Thesaurizare sibi fundamentum bonum in futurum, ut apprehendant
veram vitam. Lat. Vulg.]

[*Charge them that are rich in this world, that they be not high-*
minded, nor trust in uncertain riches, but in the living God, Who
giveth us richly all things to enjoy;
That they do good, that they be rich in good works, ready to dis-
tribute, willing to communicate;
Laying up in store for themselves a good foundation against the time
to come, that they may lay hold on eternal life. Eng. Trans.]

THE commendation of the word of God is, that " Every 2 Tim. 3.
Scripture is profitable for our instruction." " Every Scrip- 16.
ture is profitable;" yet not " every Scripture," in every place

B 2

SERM.
I.

alike. For the place and auditory have great interest in some Scripture, and a fit Scripture hath a greater and fuller force in his own auditory. And God in so excellent a manner hath sorted His Scriptures, as there lie dispersed in them several texts seasonable for each time, and pertinent to each place and degree ; for Prince, for people, for rich, for poor, for each his peculiar Scripture in due time and place to be reached them.

This Scripture which I have read, whose it is, and to whom it speaketh, is at the very reading straightway evi-

[Ps. 41. 1.] dent. As one saith of the forty-first Psalm, "Blessed is he that judgeth rightly of the poor," that it is *Scriptura pauperum,* 'the poor man's Scripture;' so of this it may be rightly said, that it is *Scriptura divitum,* ' the rich man's Scripture.' And if this be the Scripture for rich men, this place is the place of rich men ; and therefore, if this Scripture have his place, no where so fit as in this place. For no where is there

Isa. 23. 3. such store of riches by the "harvest of the water," which far

Ezek. 28. surpasseth the harvest of the ground; no where are the like
12.
Deut. 33. "sums sealed ;" no where do they "suck the abundance of
19.
the sea and the treasures hid in the sand," in like measure ;

Isa. 23. 8. no where are the merchants noblemen's fellows, and able to lend the Princes of the earth, so much as here. Therefore when as I gave all diligence to speak, not only true things but also seasonable, both for this time and this place, I was directed to this Scripture. I need not to say much in this point, to shew it concerneth this audience. I will say as the Fathers say upon the like occasion : *Faxit Deus tam commoda, quam est accommoda,* ' I pray God make it as profitable as it is pertinent,' as fruitful to you as it is fit for you.

The divi-
sion.

1. This whole Scripture hath in his name given it even

I. in the first word : " Charge," saith he, " the rich," &c. It is a charge.

2. It is directed to certain men, namely, to " the rich of this world."

3. It consisteth of four branches ; whereof two are negative, for the removing of two abuses.

II. 1. The first, " Charge them, that they be not highminded."

2. The second, "Charge them that they trust not in their riches."

The reason is added, which is a maxim and a ground in the law of nature, that we must trust to no uncertain thing : "Trust not in the uncertainty of riches."

The other two are affirmative, concerning the true use of III. riches.

1. The first : "Charge them that they trust in God :" The reason : because "He giveth them all things to enjoy plenteously."

2. The second : "Charge them that they do good;" that is the substance. The quantity, that "they be rich in good works;" the quality, that they be "ready to part with," (and a special kind of doing good) "to communicate," to benefit the public.

And all these are one charge. The reason of them all doth follow ; because by this means they shall "lay up in store," and that "for themselves, a good foundation, against the time to come." The end; "that they may obtain eternal life."

Præcipe divitibus, "Charge the rich of this world," &c. I. 1.

Beloved, here is a charge, a *Præcipe,* a precept or a writ, A Charge. directed unto Timothy, and to those of his commission to the world's end, to convent and call before him ; he the rich men of Ephesus, and we the rich men of this city, and others of other places of the earth, and to give them a charge.

Charges, as you know, use to be given at assizes in courts from the bench. From thence is taken this judicial term Παράγγελλε, as it appeareth, Acts the fifth chapter and twenty-eighth verse : "Did not we charge you straitly?" [Acts 5. saith the bench in the consistory judicially assembled. 28.] Whereby we are given to understand that in such assemblies as this is the Lord of heaven doth hold His court, whereunto all men, and they that of all men seem least, the rich and mighty of the world, owe both suit and service. For as earthly princes have their laws, their commissions, their ministers of the law, their courts, and court-days, for the maintenance of their peace ; so hath the King of kings His laws and statutes, His precepts and commissions by authority delegate, *Ite prædicate,* "Go preach the Gospel ;" Mat. 28. 19.

His counsellors at law, whom Augustine calleth *divini juris consultos;* His courts *in occulto conscientiæ,* 'in the hid and secret part of the heart and conscience,' for the preservation of His "peace," which the world can neither give nor take away, to the end that none may offend or be offended at it.

This we learn. And with this we learn, all of us, so to conceive of and to dispose ourselves to such meetings as this, as men that are to appear in court before the Lord, there to receive a charge, which when the court is broken up we must think of how to discharge.

In which point, great is the occasion of complaint which we might take up. For who is there that with that awe and reverence standeth before the Lord at His charge-giving, that he receiveth a charge with at an earthly bar? Or with that care remembereth the Lord and His charge, wherewith he continually thinketh upon the judge and his charge? Truly, the Lord's commission is worthy to have as great reverence and regard attending on it as the charge of any prince, truly it is. Weigh with yourself; is not God's charge with as much heed and reverence to be received as an earthly judge's? *Absit ut sic,* saith St. Augustine, *sed utinam vel sic;* God forbid, but with more heed and reverence; well, I would it had so much in the mean time; and, which to our shame we must speak, I would we could do as much for the Bible as for the statute-books, for heaven as for the earth, for the immortal God as for a mortal man. But whether we do or no, yet as our Saviour Christ said of St. John Baptist, "If ye will receive, this is that Elias which was to come;" so say I of this precept, If ye will receive it, this is the charge the Lord hath laid on you. And this let me tell you farther; that it is such a charge as it concerneth your peace, the plentiful use of all your wealth and riches, in the second verse of my text, "Which giveth us all things to enjoy plenteously," &c. Which may move you. Or if that will not, let me add this farther; it is such a charge, as toucheth your estate in everlasting life—the very last words of my text. That is, the well or evil hearing of this charge is as much worth as your eternal life is worth. And therefore, "he that hath ears to hear, let him hear."

It is a charge then, and consequently to be discharged. 2.
To be discharged? where? "Charge," saith he, "the rich." To "the rich."
He speaketh to "the rich;" you know your own names, you
know best what those "rich" men are. Shall I tell you?
You are the "rich," he speaketh unto you. It is the fashion
and the fault of this world to exercise their authority on
them most that need it least; for rich men to feast them
that least need it, for mighty men to prefer them that least
deserve it. It is an old simile, we have oft heard it, that
the laws are like cobwebs; that they hold fast the silly flies,
but the great hornets break through them as oft as they
list. And as there are cobweb-laws which exempt mighty
men, so the same corruption that was the cause thereof
would also make cobweb-divinity. For notwithstanding the
commission runneth expressly to the rich, "Charge," &c.;
notwithstanding they be in great danger, and that of many
"snares," as the Apostle saith in this chapter, and there- 1 Tim. 6. 9.
fore need it greatly; yet I know not how it comes to pass,
whether because they think themselves too wise to receive
a charge, any charge at all; or because they think themselves too good to receive it at the hands of such mean men
as we be—and, if they must needs be charged, they would
be charged from the council, from men more noble and
honourable than themselves—they would not gladly hear it,
surely they would not; and because they would not gladly
hear it, we are not hasty they should hear it. And great
reason why, as we think; for as it is true which is in the
Psalm, "So long as they do good to themselves, men will Ps. 49. 18.
speak good of them," so it is true backward too; so long as
we speak well of them, spare them, call not on them, they
will do good to us. And otherwise, if we spare them not,
but prosecute our charge, then cometh *Odi Michæam filium* 1 Kings
Jemla, "I hate Micaiah the son of Imlah." And who would 22. 8.
willingly live in disgrace and sustain, I say not the fierce
wrath but the heavy look of a man in authority? That
makes this office of giving a charge a cold office, and therefore to decay, and be shunned of all hands; that makes us,
if we cannot of the eunuch learn to "speak good to the 1 Kings
King," yet to follow Balak's counsel at the least, "neither 22. 13.
Num. 23.
to bless nor curse;" that makes that though for shame of 25.

Isa. 58. 1.
[¹ i. e. put
them to
pain.]

the world we will not set up for upholsters and stuff cushions and pillows to lay them under their elbows, yet for fear of men we shun the prophet Esay's occupation to take the " trumpet" and disease¹ them, lest we lose Balak's promotion, or Ahab's friendship, Esau's portion, or I wot not what else, which we will not be without. In a word, this maketh that Jonah was never more unwilling to deliver his message at Nineveh, than is Timothy to give his charge at Ephesus.

1 Tim. 6.
13.

The Apostle saw this and what it would come to, and that you may see that he saw it, you shall understand he hath besides this of yours directed another writ to us, verse the thirteenth, " I charge thee, &c." running in very rigorous and peremptory terms, able to make any that shall consider them aright to tremble ; straitly commanding us in the name of God the Father and of the Lord Jesus Christ ; laying before us the Passion of Christ, if there be any grace, and the day of judgment, and there be any fear, that we fulfil every part of our charge, and immediately after nameth this your charge for one. And knowing that we are given to fear princes and lords, he telleth us of the " Prince" of

1 Tim. 6.
15.

1 Tim. 6.
16.

all princes, and " Lord of all lords ;" knowing that we are given to fear and be dazzled with the glittering of their pomp, which yet a man may abide to look on, he telleth us of Him Whose brightness no eye may once abide. Knowing that we fear honour and power though it last but for a small time, he feareth us with One Whose honour and power lasteth for ever.

Beloved in the Lord, I beseech you weigh but the place ; weigh it, and have pity on us. For, *Nunquid nos recipimus, nunquid nos delere possumus ? Si delemus, timemus deleri,* saith St. Augustine. We writ not this charge, our pens dealt not in it ; it was not we that writ it, and it is not we that can blot it out, unless we ourselves will be blotted out of the book of life.

Such is our charge, as you see, to charge you ; and but for this charge, but that we are commanded, but that we are threatened, and that in so fearful manner threatened, we should never do it ; of all men, we should never deal with the " rich." For who would not choose to hold his peace and to seek his own ease from this charge, many times chargeable, sometimes dangerous, evermore unsavoury, but for this process that is out against us? For myself I profess that, in the same words that St. Augustine did sometime, *ad istam otiosissimam securitatem nemo me vinceret,* 'in this discreet kind of idleness no man shall go beyond me,' if St. Paul would be content; if order might be taken to have these verses cancelled, if we could deliver, I say not yours, but our own souls with silence. But this standing in force, *Cogit nos Paulus iste,* ' we are enforced by this Paul;' his *Præcipio tibi,* "I charge you," drives us to our *Præcipe illis,* "to charge them;" we charge not you, but when we are charged ourselves; we terrify not you, but when we are first terrified ourselves. And I would to God we knowing this terror might both fear together this day at the charge-giving, that so we might both rejoice together in the great day at the charge answering. This may serve, and I beseech you let it serve to stand between us and your displeasure in this behalf; and seeing the commission is penned to our hand, and that "rich" men are in it *nominatim,* (except the leaven of affection shew itself too evidently in us,) to think we cannot otherwise do; and that therefore it is, because the commandment of our God is upon us, is heavy upon us. The charge itself followeth.

"Charge the rich," &c. This is the first point of the charge, "that they be not highminded." 1. First against that which, if it come with all the riches, yea all the virtues in the world, it spoileth them all; that is, against pride. 2. Secondly, against that which is the root of this bitter branch, and the prop and stay of a high-raised mind, namely, a vain trust in our riches. Both these forbidden by means of their uncertainty, ἀδηλότης· such, as a man cannot tell where to have them, therefore not to be boasted of, therefore not to be trusted in.

II. 1. The first point of the charge: not to be "highminded."

Ever since our first fathers by infection took this *morbum sathanicum,* this devilish disease, pride, of the devil, such tinder is our nature, that every little spark sets us on fire; our nature hath grown so light, that every little thing puffeth us up, and sets us aloft in our altitudes presently. Yea indeed, so light we are, that many times when the gifts are low, yet for all that the mind is as high as the bramble; Jud. 9. 15.

low in qualities, God knoweth, yet had his mind higher than the highest cedar in Lebanon. But if we but of mean stature once, but a thought higher than others our fellows, if never so little more in us than is in our neighbours, presently we fall into Simon's case, we seem to ourselves as he Acts 8. 9. did, to be τις μέγας, no doubt " some goodly great thing." But if we come once to any growth indeed, then presently Esther 6. 6. our case is Haman's case: who but he? " Who was he that the King would honour more than him?" Nay, who was there that the King could honour but he? he, and none but he. Through this aptness in us that we have to learn the devil's lesson, the devil's *Discite a me,* for I am proud— Mat. 11. 29. for so it is, by opposition of Christ's lesson, which is *Discite a Me, quia mitis sum,* " because I am meek and gentle"— we are ready to corrupt ourselves in every good gift of God; in wisdom, in manhood, in law, in divinity, in learning or eloquence: every and each of these serveth for a stirrup to mount us aloft in our own conceits. For where each of the former hath, as it were, his own circuit—as wisdom ruleth in counsel, manhood in the field, law in the judgment-seat, divinity in the pulpit, learning in the schools, and eloquence in persuasion—only riches ruleth without limitation, riches ruleth with them all, ruleth them all, and overruleth them all, his circuit is the whole world. For which cause some think when he saith, " Charge the rich," he presently addeth, " of this world," because this world standeth altogether at the devotion of riches, and he may do what he will in this world that is rich in this world. So said the Wise Eccles. 10. Man long ago, *Pecuniæ obediunt omnia,* " all things answer 19. money," money mastereth all things; they all answer at his call, and they all obey at his commandment. Let us go lightly over them all; you shall see that they all else have their several predicaments to bound them, and that riches is only the transcendent of this world.

Wisdom ruleth in counsel—so do riches; for we see in the Ezra 4. 5. court of the great King Artaxerxes, there were counsellors whose wisdom was to be commanded by riches, even to hinder a public benefit, the building of the temple. Manhood ruleth in the war—so do riches, experience teacheth us it is so; it is said, it was they that won Daventer[1], and

[1] Daventer was be-

that it was they and none but they that drove the Switzers trayed to the Spaniards by Sir Thomas Stanley. 1587.] out of France, and that without stroke stricken. Law governeth in the seat of justice—so do riches ; and oftentimes they turn justice itself into wormwood by a corrupt sentence, but more often doth it turn justice into vinegar by long standing and infinite delays ere sentence will come forth. Divinity ruleth in the church and pulpit—so do riches ; for with a set of silver pieces, saith Augustine, they brought *Concionatorem mundi,* ' the Preacher of the world,' Jesus Christ, to the bar, and the disciple is not above his Master. Learning ruleth in the schools—so do riches ; and indeed there money setteth us all to school. For, to say the truth, riches have so ordered the matter there, as learning is now the usher; money, he is the master ; the chair itself and the disposing of the chair is his too. Eloquence ruleth in persuasion, and so do riches. When Tertullus had laboured a goodly flowing oration against Paul, Felix looked that another, a greater orator should have spoken for him, namely, that something " should have been given him ;" and if that Acts 24. 26. orator had spoken his short pithy sentence, *Tantum dabo,* Tertullus' oration had been clean dashed. *Tantum dabo* is a strange piece of rhetoric ; devise as cunningly, pen as curiously as you can, it overthrows all. *Tantum valent quatuor syllabæ,* ' such force is there in four syllables.' Though indeed some think—it being so unreasonable short as it is, but two words—that it cannot be the rhetoric of it that worketh these strange effects, but that there is some sorcery or witchcraft in them, in *Tantum dabo.* And surely a great sorcerer, Simon Magus, used them to Peter; and it may well Acts 8. 19. be so, for all estates are shrewdly bewitched by them. I must end, for it is a world to think and tell what the rich of the world may do in the world.

So then riches seeing they may do so much, it is no marvel though they be much set by. *Et divites cum habeant quæ magni fiunt ab omnibus, quid mirum si ab omnibus ipsi magni fiant ; et cum magni fiant ab omnibus, quid mirum si et a se ?* ' Rich men having that which is much set by, no marvel though of all men they be much set by ; and if all other men set much by them, no marvel if they set much by themselves :' and to set much by a man's self, that is to be

SERM.
I.

[S. Aug.
Serm. 61.
10. *al.* 5.
de Verb.
Dom.]

1 Sam. 9.
21.

Ps. 62. 10.

Prov. 30.
8, 9.

highminded. It is our own proverb in our own tongue: 'As riseth our good, so riseth our blood.' And St. Augustine saith, that each fruit by kind hath his worm breeding in it; as the pear his, the nut his, and the bean his, so riches have their worm, *et vermis divitiarum superbia*, 'and the worm of riches is pride.' Whereof we see a plain proof in Saul, who while he was in a poor estate, that his boy and he could not make fivepence between them, was as the Scripture saith low in his own eyes. After, when the wealth and pleasant things of Israel were his, he grew so stern as he forgot himself, his friends, and God too; and at every word that liketh him not was ready to run David, Jonathan, and every one through with his javelin. It is very certain where riches are, there is great danger of pride. I desire you to think there is so, and not to put me to justify God's wisdom herein, in persuading and proving that this charge is needful for you that be "rich;" that it was needful for the Prophet to preach under the law, "If riches increase, set not your heart on the top of them," let not that rise as they rise; nor for the other Prophet, "Give me not riches, lest I wax proud;" nor for the Apostle Paul under the Gospel to say, "Charge them that be rich in this world that they be not highminded." I beseech you, honour God, and ease me so much as to think there was high cause it should be in charge, and that if a more principal sin had been reigning in the rich this sin should not have the principal place as it hath.

How then? what, are you able to charge any here? will some say; it is not the manner of our court, nor of any court that I know. To us it belongeth only to deliver the charge, and to exhort, that if none be proud none would be, and if any be they would be less; and if any be not humble they would be, and if any be humble they would be more. You that are the court, your part is to enquire, and to present, and to indict; and that, every one in his own conscience, as in the presence of God, unto Him to approve your innocency, or of Him to sue for your pardon. You will find none, you will say; I would to God you might not.

When a judge at an assize giveth his charge concerning treason and such like offences, I dare say he would with all

his heart that his charge might be in vain, rather than any
traitor or offender should be found. A physician, when he
hath tempered and prepared his potion, if there be in him
the true heart of a physician, desireth I know that the potion might be cast down the kennel, so that the patient
might recover without it; so truly it is the desire of my
heart, Christ He knoweth, that this charge may not find
one man guilty amongst all these hearers, amongst so many
men not one highminded man. I wish it might be in vain.
The best sessions, and potions, and sermons are those which
are in vain. I say not in vain, if there be cause of reproof
and no amends; but if there be no cause, and so it be in
vain, " I joy therein, and will joy." But if it be far unlikely, [Philip. 1.
amongst so great riches as is here, to find no pride at all, ^{18.]}
very unlikely; then hear the charge, and present yourselves,
and find yourselves guilty here in our office this day, while
you may find grace, lest you be tried and found so in that
day when there shall be no hope of grace, but only a fearful
expectation of judgment.

Which that you may do the better, so many as God shall
make willing, as some I hope He doth, I will inform you
how to try yourselves, referring you to the several branches
in our statutes, in the high court of parliament in heaven,
laying them out unto you as I find them in the records of
the Holy Ghost.

The points are three in number. First, if the mind of [1.]
any man be so exalted that he looketh down on his brethren
as if he stood on the top of a leads, and not on the same
ground they do, that man is highminded. St. Augustine
saith well: *Excipe pompatica hæc et volatica,* they are the
same that you are. They have not *vestem communem,* the
same coat, but they have *cutem communem,* the same skin;
and within a few years when you die, if a man come with
a joiner and measure all that you carry with you, they
shall carry away with them as much; and within a few
years after, a man shall not be able to discern between the [Vid. S.
shoulder-blade of one of them and one of you. Therefore Aug. Ser.
no cause why you should *incedere inflati, insericati,* and from 61. 9.]
a high mind betraying itself by a high look contemn them,
as many of you do. I say then, if any of you be a child of

SERM.
I.
Num. 13.
33.
Prov. 30.
13.
Ps. 101. 5.

1 Sam. 20.
27.

[Lu. 18.11.]
Hab. 1. 14.

Ezek. 11. 3.

Zeph. 3. 3.
[Gen. 4.
23.]

1 Sam. 2.
15, &c.

1 Kings
21. 7.

Jam. 2. 6.

Anak, and look down so upon another as in his sight his brethren seem as " grasshoppers :" 1. whether it appear in the countenance, in drawing up his eyebrows, in a disdainful and scornful eye, such an one as David, though he found no penal statute to punish it, could never abide, and David was a man after God's own heart, and therefore neither can God abide it : 2. or whether it appear in a proud kind of dialect of speech, as was that of Saul's, *Ubi nunc est iste filius Ishai ?* where is this son of Jesse ? that he come to the Pharisee's *Non sum sicut :* 3. or whether it be in the course of their life, that they be like to the great fishes, to pikes, that think all the little fishes in the stream were made for them to feed on. So that it appeareth they care not what misery, what beggary, what slavery they bring all men to, so they may soak in the broth of the caldron, and welter in their wealth and pleasure ; who are in their streets and parishes as " lions," a great deal more feared than beloved, as implacable as Lamech to bear any injury, and will have for one drop of blood no less than a man's life. What speak I of bearing injury ? which will do injury, and that for no other reason but this : Thus it must be, for Hophni will have it not thus but thus, and except they may do thus, what they will to whom they will, when and how they will, forsooth they do not " govern," their authority is nothing ; in this sort overbearing all things with their countenance and wealth, and whosoever standeth but up, drawing him before the " judgment-seats," and wearying him out with law. These men who do thus from a high in-bearing of the head, in phrase of speech, and in the order or rather disorder of their dealing, overlook, overcrow, and overbear their brethren of mean estate, it is certain they be highminded. Enquire and look whether any be so.

[2.]   Secondly, if any mind climb so high that the boughs will bear him no longer, by exalting himself above either his ability, condition or calling—a fault which hath like to cost our times dear—that man's footing will fail him, he will down, he and his mind are too high a great deal. The late treasons and conspiracies came from such kind of minds. For when the minds of men will overreach their abilities, what must be the end, but as we have seen of late to prove

traitors? Why? because they have swollen themselves out
of their skin. Why so? because they had lashed on more
on their pleasure than they had. For so doing, when they
had overreached themselves, they became προπετεῖς, they
must take some heady enterprise in hand. What is that?
to become προδόται, that seeing their credit is decayed in 2 Tim. 3. 4.
this state, they may set up a new, and that is by overturning
the old.

And not only this passing the ability is dangerous to the
overturning of a commonwealth, but the passing of a man's
condition too; and tendeth to the impoverishing, and at last
to the overthrow of the estate also. 1. Whether it be excess
of diet; as when being no magistrate, but plain Master
Nabal, his dinner must be "like to the feast of a King."
2. Or whether it be in excess of apparel, wherein the pride 1 Sam. 25.
of England now, as "the pride" of Ephraim in times past, Hos. 5. 5.
"testifieth against her to her face." 3. Or whether it be Prov. 17.
"in lifting up the gate too high," that is, in excess of build- 19.
ing. 4. Or whether it be in keeping too great a train, Gen. 32. 6.
Esau's case, that he go with "four hundred" men at his
tail, whereas the fourth part of the fourth part would have
served his father well enough. 5. Or whether it be in perk-
ing¹ too high in their alliance; the bramble's son in Le- [¹ i. e. lift-
banon must match with the cedar's daughter. These are their
evidences and signs set down to prove a high mind: see and 2 Kings
search into yourselves, whether you find them or no. 14. 9.

There is yet of this feather another kind of exalting ourselves above that we ought, much to be complained of in
these days. St. Paul calleth it "a stretching of ourselves 2 Cor. 10.
beyond measure." Thus if a man be attained to any high 14.
skill in law, which is the gift of God; or if a man be grown
wise, and experienced well in the affairs of this world, which
is also His good blessing; presently by virtue of this they
take themselves to be so qualified as they be able to overrule
our matters in divinity, able to prescribe Bishops how to
govern and Divines how to preach; so to determine our
cases as if they were professed with us; and that, many
times affirming things they know not, and censuring things 1 Tim. 1 7.
they have little skill of. Now seeing we take not upon us 10.
to deal in cases of your law, or in matters of your trade, we

S E R M.
I.
Hosea 4. 4.
1 Thes. 5.
12.
Rom. 12.
3.
[' i. e.
drunken.
Bailey.]

[Prov. 13.
10.]

Hosea 6. 5.

2 Cor. 10.
5.

1 Sam. 25.
17.
2 Sam. 3. 7.

1 Kings 22.
27.

take this is a stretching beyond your line; that in so doing you are a people that control the Priest; that you are too high when you set yourselves over them that " are over you in the Lord ;" and that this is no part of that sober wisdom which St. Paul commendeth to you, but of that cup-shotten[1] wisdom which he there condemneth. Which breaking compass and outreaching is, no doubt, the cause of these lamentable rents and ruptures in the Lord's net in our days. For " only by pride cometh contention," saith the Wise Man. Which point I wish might be looked upon and amended. Sure it will mar all in the end.

3.   Thirdly, if any man lift up himself too high, any of both these ways, God hath taken order to abate him and take him down, for He hath appointed His Prophets to " prune those that are too high," and He hath ordained His word to " bring down every imagination that shall be exalted against it." Now then, if there be any man that shall seek to set himself without the shot of it, and is so highminded as that he cannot suffer the words of exhortation, and where God hath said, " Charge them that be rich," he cannot abide to hear any charge—and such there be ; sure that man without all question is very highminded, and if he durst he would tear out this leaf, and all other where like charge is given, through the Bible. Of Nabal it is recorded, " He was so surly, a man might not speak to him ;" of Abner, a great man, and a special stay of the house of Saul, that upon a word spoken of his adulterous life with one of Saul's minions, he grew to such choler that he forgot all, and laid the plot that cost his master Ishbosheth his kingdom. Micaiah prophesied good things, that is to say, profitable to Ahab—the event shewed it ; yet because he did not prophesy good things, that is, such as Ahab would hear, he spared not openly to profess he hated him ; and whereas the false Prophets were fed at his own table, and fared no worse than he and the Queen, he took order for Micaiah's diet, that it should be the " bread of affliction" and the " water of trouble," and all for a charge-giving. These were, I dare boldly affirm, highminded men in their generations : if any be like these, they know what they are. If then there be any that refuse to be pruned and trimmed by the word of

God; 1. who either when he heareth the words of the charge, blesseth himself in his heart and saith, Tush, he doth but Deu. 29. 19. prate, these things shall not come upon me, though I walk still according to the stubbornness of mine own heart; 2. either in hearing the word of God, takes upon him (his flesh and blood, and he) to sit on it, and censure it, and say to himself one while, This is well spoken, while his humour is served ; another while, This is foolishly spoken, now he babbleth, because the charge sits somewhat near him ; 3. either is in the Pharisees' case, which after they have heard the charge do, as they did at Christ, ἐκμυκτηρίζειν, jest and Lu. 16. 14. scoff, and make themselves merry with it, and wash it down with a cup of sack, and that because they " were covetous :" Lu. 16. 14. if in very deed " the word of God be to them a reproach," Jer. 6. 10. and they take delight in both, and well were they if they might never hear it ; and to testify their good conceit of the word, shew it in the account of the ephod, which is a base and contemptible garment in their eyes, and the word in it and with it—this is Michal's case. Whosoever is in any of [See 2 Sam. 6. these men's cases is in the case of a highminded man, and 20, &c.] that of the highest degree ; for they lift themselves up, not against earth and man, but against Heaven and God Himself. O beloved, you that be in wealth and authority, love and reverence the word of God. It is the root that doth bear you, it is the majesty thereof that keepeth you in your thrones, and maketh you be that you are; but for *Ego dixi*, Ps. 82. 6. *Dii estis*, a parcel-commission out of this commission of ours, the madness of the people would bear no government, but run headlong and overthrow all chairs of estate, and break in pieces all the swords and sceptres in the world, which you of this city had a strange experience of in Jack Straw and his meiny[1], and keep a memorial of it in our city scutcheon, [¹ i.e. re- how all had gone down if this word had not held all up. And from a therefore honour it I beseech you; I say, honour it. For Saxon word signi- when the highest of you yourselves, which are but " grass," fying a multitude. and your lordships' glory and worship, which is " the flower" *Bailey.*] of this grass, shall " perish and pass away, this word shall Isa. 40. 6, continue for ever." And if you receive it now, with due re- ⁷, ⁸. gard and reverence, it will make you also to continue for ever.

This is your charge, touching the first branch. I beseech

SERM.
I.

you, enquire of it, whether there be any guilty in these points; and if there be, suffer us to do our office, that is, to humble you, or else sure the Lord will do His, that is, pull down riches and mind, and man and all: *Patimini falcem occantem, ne patiamini securim extirpantem.* God will not

Deu. 17. 20.

suffer it certainly; He would not suffer it in a king, He

Jude ver. 6.

would not suffer it in an Angel, He cannot bear it to rise in

2 Cor. 12.7.

an Apostle, "for the greatness of revelations;" therefore He will not bear it in any man for any cause whatsoever. Let this be the conclusion of this point.

2.
The second point: "not to trust in uncertain riches."

We shall never have pride well plucked up, so long as the root of it sticks still; that is, a vain confidence in riches. For if we doubted them, we would not trust in them, we would not boast of them. But we trust in them, and that inordinately, as countermeans against God; not subordinately, as undermeans unto God; and in so doing, we translate God's office unto us, and our homage unto Him, to a plate of silver or a wedge of gold. And that is, St. Paul

Col. 3. 5.

saith, the worldly man's "idolatry." And indeed there is little difference, it is but turning the sentence of the Pro-

Ps. 135. 15.

phet David: of idolaters, to say thus, "Their idols are silver and gold;" and of the worldly men thus, Silver and gold are their idols.

We may examine ourselves in this point of the charge,

Prov. 11.
28.

namely, whether our trust be in our riches, by two ways; for it being a received ground that our strength is our confidence, where we take our chief strength to lie, that is it certainly which we trust to. Now what that is, we shall soon find: 1. if we can certify ourselves in our need, among all means, what doth first offer itself in our intention; 2. and again, when all our means forsake us, and fail us, what is our last succour in execution.

1.

By course of nature, every thing when it is assaulted ever rouseth that part first wherein his principal strength lieth: if it be in his tusks, them; or in his horns, or whatsoever it is, that. To a poor man, if he have a cause in hand, there is nothing cometh to mind but God and innocency, and the goodness of his cause; there is his strength, and that is the

[Ps. 18. 2.]

"horn of his salvation." But the rich, saith Amos, hath

Amos 6. 13.

"gotten him horns in his own strength;" and not "iron

orns," as were Zedekiah's, but golden horns, with which [1 Kings 22. 11.]
he is able to "push" any cause, till he have consumed it.
For indeed if he be to undertake aught, the first thing
that cometh to his head is, Thus much will despatch it,
such a gift will assure such a man, and such a gift will stop
such a man's mouth, and so it is done: "neither is God in [Ps. 10. 4.]
all his thoughts."

Tell me, then, in your affairs what cometh first to mind?
nay, tell yourselves what it is. *Aures omnium pulso,* saith
St. Augustine, *conscientias singulorum convenio:* tell yourselves what it is, and by this try and know wherein your
trust is; whether this charge meet with you or no, whether
your riches be the strength of your confidence.

Now lightly, what we first think of, that we last fly to. 2.
It is so. Solomon saw it in his time, and said, "The rich 11.
man's wealth is his castle;" that even as men, when they
are foiled in the field and beaten from the city walls, fly last
of all into the castle, and there think themselves safe as in
their place of chief strength, so it falleth out with "the rich
of this world" in many of their causes; when justice and
equity, and truth and right, and God and good men, and a
good conscience and all forsake them—and yet yield they
will not, in the pride of a high mind—they know, when all
other have forsaken them, their purse will stand to them;
and thither as to their strongest salvation they fly, when
nothing else comforts them. So that when they cannot in
heart say to God, Thou art my hope, their matter is so bad;
they do say—it is he in Job—to their wedge of gold, Well Job 31. 24.
yet, "thou art my confidence." And surely, he that de-
viseth or pursueth an unrighteous cause because his hand
hath strength, that man may be arraigned of the point. As Mic. 2. 1.
again, if any say, and say within, truly, (*Dic, dic, sed intus
dic,* saith Augustine)—With all my riches, with all my
friends, and all the means I can make, I can do nothing
against the truth. When a man is so rich that he is poor
to do evil; so wise, that he is a fool to do evil; so trusteth
in his riches that he dare not take an evil cause in hand,
no more than the poorest commoner in the city; I dare
discharge that man the court for this point. Oh beloved,
think of these things, and secretly betwixt God and you,

c 2

Prov. 18.

SERM.
I.

use yourselves to this examination; sure if God be God, and if there be any truth in Him, you shall find great peace and comfort in it at the last.

The reason.
"The uncertainty of riches."

"Charge the rich, that they be not highminded, nor trust," &c. And, why not "highminded?" and why "not trust?" Inclusively the reason is added in these words, because of "the uncertainty of riches." It is Paul's reason, and it is Solomon's too, who knew better what belonged to riches than Paul or any other. "Travail not too greedily for them, bestow not all thy wisdom upon them," saith he, "for they have the wings of an eagle, and will take their flight of a sudden." Such is St. Paul's word here, the very same. We behold them, we hold them, they are here with us; let us but turn ourselves aside a little, and look for them, and they are gone. It is as if he should say, Indeed, if we could pinion the wings of our riches, if we could nail them down fast to us, then were there some show or shadow why we should repose trust in them; but it is otherwise, they are exceeding uncertain, even the harvest of the water much above all trades. Yea, I take it the merchants confess so much before they be aware; for by this he claimeth to be allowed an extraordinary gain, because he ventureth his traffic as uncertain, and that he is driven to hazard and put in a venture his goods continually, and many times his person, and, to make him a right venturer, many times his soul too. And if they be not uncertain, how cometh it then to pass that rich men themselves are so uncertain? that is, that they that were but the other day even a little before of principal credit, within a while after, and a very short while after, their bills will not be taken? And if riches be not uncertain, what need they upon a night of foul weather any assurances upon the exchange? What need the merchants have security one of another? What need they to have their estates sure, and so good? such assurances and conveyances, so strong, yea more strong than the wit of man can devise, if both riches and men be not uncertain? I know they pretend the man's mortality; but they know they mean many times the mortality of his riches rather than himself, or at the least of the one as of the other. I will be judged by themselves.

Prov. 23, 4, 5.

Prov. 27. 24.

I would have you mark St. Paul's manner of speech. Before, he called them not rich barely; but with an addition, "the rich of this world." Sure it is thought of divers of the best writers both old and new—I name of the new Master Calvin, and of the old St. Augustine—that this [Calvin. in loc. Vid. addition is a diminution, and that it is as it were a bar in S. Aug. the arms of all rich men; and that even by that word he Ser. 36. 3.] means to enthwite them, and as I may say to cry them down, so to make an entrance to his charge that men should not be too proud of them. For being "of this world" they must needs savour of the soil, be as this world is, that is, transitory, fickle, and deceitful. And now he comes in with riches again, and will not put it alone, but calleth it "the uncertainty of riches." And I see it is the Holy Ghost's fashion, not in this place only but all along the Scriptures, to speak nothing magnifically of them, as the manner of the world is to do. St. Paul calleth them not rich, but the "rich of this world;" St. John likewise calleth them not goods simply, but "this world's goods." St. Paul calleth 1 Joh. 3. 17. them not riches, but the "uncertainty of riches;" our Saviour Christ calleth them not riches, but the "deceitfulness Mat. 13. 22. of riches." So David, the plate and arras and rich furniture of a wealthy man, calleth it of purpose, "the glory of a Ps. 49. 16. man's house," not his glory, but the glory of his house— that is St. Chrysostom's note[1]. And Solomon calleth them, [1 In Ps. sup. cit.] as they be indeed, God's blessing of His left hand. For [See Prov. immortality, eternal life, that only is the blessing of His 3. 16.] right hand. All to learn us not to boast ourselves or stay ourselves, or as Christ calleth it to "rejoice"—I say not, as He to His Disciples, that a few devils, but—that a few [Lu. 10. minerals be subject unto us, but that by our humbleness of 20.] mind, trust in God, dealing truly with all, and mercifully with our poor brethren, we are assured that our names are written in the book of life. This then is the uncertainty of our riches, because they are the riches of this world—the world and they are all within the compass of our text—that is, you must leave them to the world, they are none of yours. *Denique si vestra sint,* saith Gregory, *tollite ea vobiscum,* 'If they be yours, why do you not take them with you, when you go?' By leaving them behind you to the world, you confess they are not yours, but the world's. But indeed they are the riches of this world : *hîc enim acquiruntur, hîc vel amittuntur, vel dimittuntur ;* 'here you get them and here you may lose them, here you get them and here you must leave them.' And in this disjunctive you have the certainty of riches : the very certainty is losing or leaving, that is, foregoing; so the very certainty is an uncertainty. Leave them or lose them we must, leave them when we die, or lose them while we live. One end they must have, *finem tuum,* or *finem suum,* 'thy end,' or 'their own end.' You must either leave them when you die, or they will leave you while you live—this is certain; but whether you them, or they you, this is uncertain. Job tarried himself, his riches

Lu. 16. 22. went; the rich man's riches tarried, but he himself went. One of these shall be we know; but which of them shall be, or when, or how, or how soon it shall be, that we know not.

Let us briefly consider this double uncertainty :

1. Of our riches staying with us, first;

2. And then, of our staying with them.

1. In the second of Corinthians, eleventh chapter, thirtieth verse, when as he would glory, he saith " he will glory in
[2 Cor. 11. his infirmity;" which when he would recount as a principal
30.]
[2 Cor. 11. part of it, he reckoneth that he " had been in perils of waters.
26.] in perils of robbers, of his own nation, among the Gentiles, in the city, in the wilderness, in the sea, and amongst false brethren." If this were frailty, then sure frail and weak are riches. And sure if the rich will glory they must glory with St. Paul, for they are in all, and in more, and greater than the Apostle ever was. He was " in perils of water," they in peril both of water and fire; he was " in peril of robbers," they in peril of rovers by sea, and robbers by land; he " in peril of his own nation," they are in peril of our own nation and of other nations, both removed as the Moor and Spaniard, and near home as the Dunkirker; he " in peril of strangers," they not of strangers only but of their own household, their servants and factors; he " in peril of the sea," they both of the tempest at the sea, and the Publican on land ; he " in peril of the wilderness," that is, of wild beasts, they not only of the wild beast called the sycophant, but of the tame beast too called the flatterer; he

in danger " of false brethren," and so are they in peril of
certain false brethren called wilful bankrupts, and of certain
other called deceitful lawyers : for the one their debts, for
the other their estates and deeds can have no certainty.

Musculus on that place where Christ willeth " our trea- Matt. 6.
sure to be laid where no moths come," saith his auditors ¹⁹, ²⁰.
did laugh in conceit at Christ That frayed them with moths;
their maids should deal with the moths well enough.   Saith
he, You think He meant the poor silly flies; tush, you are
deceived, what say you to *tineæ urbanæ*, 'evil creditors?'
You must needs credit, you can have no vent for your merchandise; and what say you to a second kind of moths
called *tineæ forenses*, 'Westminster Hall moths?'—for I
trust I may speak of the corrupt lawyer, with the favour of
the better sort—you must needs credit them with your
evidences and estates, it is not certain what wealth these
two moths do waste, and in what uncertainty men's riches
are by their means.

These are out of St. Paul's " perils," he was free from these
moths.   But many rich men might be brought forth in a
fair day and shewed, whose substance hath by these moths
been fretted to pieces.   Thus little certainty have we of
their staying with us.

2. But grant, let it be that they were certain ; yet except
we ourselves were sure to stay with them also, it is as good
as nothing.   That there may be a certainty between two
things, as a man and his wealth, to continue together, they
must either of them be sure; else if the one fail, where is
the other's assurance?   Grant then we were certain of them,
we are not certain of ourselves, and in very deed we are no
more certain of them than they of us.   Leases of them we
have for sixty years, but they have no leases of us for three
hours ; if they might take leases of us too, it were somewhat.
Now when the lease is taken, nay when the fee simple is
bought, and the house and the warehouse filled, and the
purse too, if God say but *hâc nocte*, it dashes all.   For which Lu. 12. 20.
cause, I think, St. James speaking in two several places of
our life and our riches—our riches he compareth to " the Jas. 1. 11.
grass," of no certainty, it will either wither or be plucked
up shortly; but this is a great certainty in respect of that

SERM.
I.
[Jam. 4.
14.]
of our life, which he resembleth to "a vapour" which we
see now, and by and by we turn us to look for it, and it is
vanished away. To us then that are uncertain of ourselves,
they cannot be but riches of uncertainty.

But let us admit we were sure of both these, what is it
to have riches and not to enjoy them? And the enjoying
of riches dependeth upon two uncertainties more.

1. First, a man's uncertainty, which hangeth upon the
favour of a Prince, which is many times wavering and uncertain. I know not whether I shall make you understand
it, because of the want of examples in our time, by means of
the mild and blessed government that we live in. For a
practice it hath been, and many records do our chronicles
afford in the days of some Princes of this realm, when a
man was grown to wealth, to pick holes and make quarrels
against him, and so seize his goods into the Prince's hand ;
to use wealthy citizens as spunges, to roll them up and down
in moisture till they be full, and then to wring all out of
them again. God wot, an easy matter it is, if a Prince
stand so minded, to find matter of disgrace against a subject
of some wealth ; and then he might fare never a whit the
better for his wealth, for fine and forfeiture whereof, rather
than any fault else, the business itself was made against him.
We cannot tell what this meaneth, we may thank the gracious government we live under, so that I think I do scarce
speak so that I am understood. But such a thing there is,
such an uncertainty belonging to riches, whether we conceive it or no.

2. Again, if the times which we live in happen to prove
unquiet and troublesome, then again comes another uncertainty. For the days being evil and dangerous, a man can
have no joy, and indeed no certainty neither of riches. For
[¹ i. e.
trouble,
disturb-
ance.
Bailey.]
Job 8. 14.
if there fall an invasion or garboil¹ into the state by foreign
or civil war, then if ever is Job's simile verified, that riches
are like "a cobweb ;" that which a man shall be weaving all
his life long, with great ado and much travail, there comes
me a soldier, a barbarous soldier, with his broom, and in the
turning of a hand sweeps it clean away. How many in our
neighbour countries, during their misery, have tasted this
uncertainty ! How many have gone to bed rich, and risen

poor men in the morning! Great troubles are looked for, and great troubles there must be and will be, doubtless. The world now " knoweth his Master's will and doeth it not; [Lu. 12. it must therefore certainly be beaten with many stripes," 47.] with many more than the ignorant world was. And therefore this word—" of this world" in this text, we may with an emphasis pronounce and say, " Charge them that are rich in this world, that they trust not in the uncertainty of riches."

There are but three things in riches; 1. the possessing, 2. the enjoying, 3. and last the conveying of them. Little assurance is there in the two former, and what shall we say of the conveyance? If our pomp cannot descend with us, well yet if we were certain to whom we should leave them, somewhat it were for the certainty of them. These considerations oft had in mind would loosen both our assurance in and our liking of them.

What for the conveyance? do we not see daily that men make heritages, but God makes heirs; that many sons roast not that their fathers got in hunting? that they that have been in chief account for their wealth, their sons should be driven even " to flatter the poor," and have nothing in their Job 20, 10. hands, no not bread? that never snow in the sun melted faster, than do some men's riches as soon as they be gone?

These things are in the eyes of the whole world. O beloved, these are the judgments of God! Deceive not yourselves with vain words; say not in your hearts, This is the way of the world, some must get and some must lose. No, no, it is not the way of the world, it is the way of God's judgment. For to the reason of man nothing can be alleged, but that considering the infinite number of infinite rich men in this place, the posterity of them these many years should by this time have filled the whole land, were it much bigger than it is, with their progeny, even with divers both worshipful and honourable families from them descended; and it is well known it is otherwise, that there is scarcely a handful in comparison. This is not the way of the world, for we see divers houses of divers lines remain to this day in continuance of the same wealth and worship which they had five hundred years since. It is not therefore the way of the

world, say not it is so, but it is a heavy judgment from the
Lord. And these uncertainties, namely this last, came upon
some of them for their wicked and deceitful getting of them;
upon some of them for their proud and riotous abusing them;
upon some of them for their wretched and covetous retaining them. And except ye now hear this the Lord's charge,
look unto it, howsoever you wrestle out with the uncertainties yourselves, assuredly this last uncertainty remaineth for
Isa. 59. 1. your children. " The Lord's hand is not shortened." I
shall never get out of this point if I break not from it.

These are but three fruits of all your getting: 1. the
tenure, 2. the fruition, 3. the parting with. See whether
the Lord hath not laid one uncertainty on them all: 1. uncertainty in their tarrying with us, and uncertainty in our
tarrying with them; 2. uncertainty of enjoying, by reason of
the danger of the time; 3. uncertainty of our leaving them,
by reason of the danger of our children's scattering. The
estate in them, the enjoying of them, the departing with
them, all being uncertain, so many uncertainties, might not
St. Paul truly say, "the uncertainty of riches?"

There is yet one behind worse than them all. I will add
no more but that; and that is, that our riches and our worship they shall leave us, because they be uncertain, but the
pride of our minds and the vain trust in them, them we shall
be certain of, they shall not leave us. And this is *grave
jugum*, a heavy misery upon mankind : the goods, the lordships, the offices that they got, them they shall leave here ;
the sin that they commit in getting and enjoying them, they
shall not leave behind them for their hearts, but that shall
cleave fast unto them. This is a certainty, you will say;
it is indeed a certainty of sin, but therefore an uncertainty of the soul: so doth Job reckon it amongst the uncer-
Job 27. 8. tainties of riches. For "what hope hath the hypocrite when
he hath heaped up riches, if God take away his soul?" where
is his hope or his trust then? Never will they shew them-
Isa. 36. 6. selves in their own kind to be a " staff of reed," as then ;
both deceiving them which lean on them, and besides going
into their souls and piercing them. For very sure it is, many
of that calling die in great uncertainty this way, wishing
they had never seen that wealth which they have seen, that

so they might not see that sin which they then see. Yea some of them, I speak it of mine own knowledge abroad, wish they had never come further than the shovel and the spade; crying out at the hour of death, both of the uncertainty of their riches and of the uncertainty of the estate of their souls too.

This point, this is a point of special importance, to be spoken of by me, and to be thought of by you. I would God you would take it many times, when God shall move you, into sad consideration. With a great affection, and no less great truth, said Chrysostom, that Heaven and earth and all the creatures in them, if they had tears they would shed them in great abundance, to see a great many of us so careless in this point as we be. It is the hand of the Lord, and it is His gracious hand, if we could see it, that He in this manner maketh the world to totter and reel under us, that we might not stay and rest upon it, where certainty and steadfastness we shall never find, but in Him above, where only they are to be found. For if riches, being so brittle and unsteady as they be, men are so mad upon them, if God had settled them in any certainty, what would they have done? What poor man's right, what widow's copy, or what orphan's legacy should have been free from us?

Well then, if riches be uncertain, whereto shall we trust? If not in them, where then? It is the third point: "Charge them that be rich in this world, that they be not highminded, neither trust in the uncertainty of riches, but that they trust in God." It is the third point of the charge in general, and the first of the affirmative part; and containeth partly a homage to be done for our riches to God, and that is, trust in him; and partly a rent-charge laid upon our riches, which is doing good. And indeed, no other than David had said before, "Trust in the Lord and be doing good." *Ps. 37. 5.*

III.
The third
point:
"trust in
God."

St. Paul will batter down and lay flat our castle, but he will erect us another wherein we may trust. Yea indeed, so as Solomon did before, setteth up a tower against the tower, the "tower of the righteous, which is the name of the Lord," *Prov. 18. 10.* against the rich man's tower, which is as you have heard before, his riches. Instead of the worldling's faith, which is to make money an article of his faith, teacheth us the faith of a

Christian, which is to vouchsafe none but God that honour. Even so doth the Apostle here, and that for great reason; *nam qui vult securus sperare, speret in Eo Qui non potest perire,* 'he that will trust and be secure in his trust, let him trust in Him Who Himself never failed,' and never failed those that put their trust in Him; in Whom is no uncertainty, no not so much as any shadow of uncertainty.

Trust in Him, by looking to Him first ere we admit any else into our conceit; and by looking to Him last and not looking beyond Him to any, as if we had a safer or trustier than He.

And that because He is "the living God:" as if He should say, That you fancy to yourselves to trust in, is a dead idol, and not a "living God," and if ever you come to any dangerous disease, you shall find it is an idol dead in itself, not able to give itself life, much less to another; not able to ransom the body from the death, much less the soul from hers; not able to recover life when it is gone, nay not able to preserve life when it is present; not to remove death, nay not to remove sickness, not any sickness, not the gout from your feet, not the palsy from your hands, nay not so much as the ache from your teeth; not able to add one hair to your head, nor one hair's breadth to your stature, nor one hour to your days, nor one minute to the hours of your life. This moth-eaten god, as our Saviour Christ calleth it, this canker-eaten god, this god that must be kept under lock and key from a thief, trust not in it for shame. O let it be never said the living trust in the dead. Trust in "the living God" That liveth Himself, nay That is life Himself; in His Son That was able to quicken Himself and is able to quicken you, of Whose gift and inspiration you have already this life, by Whose daily Spirit and visitation your soul is preserved in this life, in this mortal and corruptible life, and of Whose grace and mercy we look for our other immortal and eternal life.

Who not only liveth but also "giveth you," &c. A living and a giving God, that is, That liveth and That giveth; of Whose gift you have not only your life and term of years, but even also your riches themselves, the very horns that you lift so high, and wherewith unnaturally many times you push against Him That gave them. He giveth, for "the earth was the Lord's, and all that therein is," till "the earth He gave unto the children of men;" and "silver and gold" were ^{Haggai 2. 8.} the Lord's, till not by a casual scattering but by His appointed giving, not by chance but by gift, He made them thine. He gave them; thou broughtest none of them with thee into the world, thou camest naked. He gave them, and when He gave them He might have given them to thy brother of low estate, and made thee stand and ask at his door as He hath made him now stand and ask at thine. He giveth you riches, you get them not, it is not your own wisdom or travail that getteth them, but His grace and goodness that giveth them. For you see many men of as great understanding and foresight as yourselves, want not only "riches" but even "bread." It is not your travail; ^{Eccl. 9. 11.} except the Lord had given them, all the early uprising and late down-lying had been in vain. It is God That giveth: make your recognizance it is so, for fear lest if you deny *Dominus dedit,* you come to affirm *Dominus abstulit.* God ^{Job 1. 21.} teacheth it was He That gave them, by taking them away.

This is St. Paul's reason: let us see how it serves his conclusion to the overthrow of our vain pride and foolish trust in them. If it be gift, *si accepisti quid gloriaris?* be not ^{1 Cor. 4. 7.} proud of it. And if it be gift, He That sent it can call for it again; trust not in it.

"Who giveth us all things," &c. All things, spiritual or corporal, temporal or eternal, little or great; from the least, and so upward; from the greatest, and so downward; from *panem quotidianum,* ' a morsel of bread,' to *Regnum cælorum,* ^[Mat. 6. 11, 13.] ' the kingdom of heaven.' He giveth us all, even unto Himself; yea He giveth us Himself and all, and more we cannot desire.

Why then, if He give all, all are donatives, all that we hold we hold in frank-almoigne¹; and no other tenure is ^[1 i. e. a tenure by divine service.] there at God's hands, or in our law. For *quid habes quod non accepisti?* " what is there?" that is to say, name one ^{1 Cor. 4. 7.} thing thou hast that thou hast not received; and if there be any one thing, boast of that and spare not. But if that be nothing, then let Cyprian's sentence take place, so much commended and so often cited by St. Augustine, *De nullo* ^[S. Cyp. Te-t. l. 3. c. 4.] *gloriandum est, quia nullum est nostrum;* and add unto it,

De nullo fidendum est, quia nullum est nostrum, 'We must glory of nothing, for that we have nothing of our own; neither must we trust any thing, for that we have nothing of our own.'

"That giveth us all things to enjoy." Not only to have, but " to enjoy." For so to have them, that we have no joy of them; so to get all things, that we can take no part of them when we have gotten them; so to possess the labours of our hands, that we cannot eat the labours of our hands,

Eccl. 6. 2.
3.
as good be without them. This is a great "vanity" and vexation, and indeed, as Solomon saith, " an untimely birth were better" than so to be. But blessed be God That besides these blessings to be enjoyed giveth us healthful bodies to enjoy them with, the favour of our Prince to enjoy them under, the days of peace to enjoy them in, whereby our souls may be satisfied with good things, and every one may eat his portion with joy of heart.

"That giveth all things to enjoy;" that is, dealeth not with you as He hath dealt with the poor, hath given you things not only of use and necessity, but things also of fruition and pleasure; hath given you not only manna for

Ps. 78. 30.
your need, but also quails for your "lust;" hath given you out of Ophir, not only linen cloth, and horses, for your ser-

[1 Kings
10. 22.]
vice, but also " apes, ivory, and peacocks," for your delight. Unto them He giveth *indumenta,* 'covering for their naked-ness ;' but unto you *ornamenta,* 'clothing for your comeli-ness.' Unto them He giveth *alimenta,* 'nourishment for their emptiness;' unto you *delectamenta,* 'delicious fare for daintiness.' Therefore you above all men are to rejoice in Him, (there is great cause) that He may rejoice over you, unto whom He hath given so many ways so great cause of rejoicing.

"That giveth us things to enjoy plenteously." " Plente-ously" indeed, may Israel now say, said the Prophet; may England now say, say I, and I am sure upon as great cause.

Ps. 147. 20.
He hath not dealt so with every nation, nay " He hath not dealt so with any nation." And " plenteously" may Eng-land now say, for it could not always; nay, it could not ever have said the like. " Plenteously" indeed, for He hath not sprinkled, but poured His benefits upon us. Not only,

"blessed be the people whose God is the Lord," that bless- Ps. 144. 15.
ing which is highly to be esteemed if we had none besides it,
but "blessed be the people that are in such a case." That Ibid.
blessing He hath given us, "all things to enjoy plenteously;"
we cannot, nay our enemies cannot but confess it. O that
our thankfulness to Him, and our bounty to His, might be
as plenteous as His gifts and goodness have been plenteous
to us!

To move us from the two evils before, the Apostle used
their uncertainty, which is a reason from law and the course
thereof. So he might now have told us, if we trusted not
in God we should have the table turned, and His giving
changed to taking away; our all things into want of many
things, and having nothing near all; our plenty into penury; and our enjoying more than we need into no more
than needs, nor so much neither. Thus he might have dealt,
but he is now in a point of Gospel and therefore taketh his
persuasion from thence. For this indeed is the evangelical
argument of God's goodness, and there is no goodness to that
which the consideration of God's goodness worketh in us.

The argument is forcible, and so forcible, as that choose
whether this will move us or no. Sure if this will not prevail with us, we shall not need Moses nor Christ, to sit and
give sentence upon us, the devil himself will do it. For as
wicked as he is, and as wretched a spirit, yet thus he reasoneth upon Job: "Doth Job fear Thee for nought?" As if he Job 1. 9.
should say, Seeing Thou hast dealt so plenteously, yea so
bounteously with him, if he should not serve Thee, if he
should so far forget himself, it were a fault past all excuse,
a fault well worthy to be condemned. A bad fault it must
be, that the devil doth abhor; yet so bad a fault it is, you
see, that the devil doth abhor it. When men receive blessing plenteously from God, and return not their homage back
again, unthankful rich men shall need no other judge but
the devil, and then, as you see, they are sure to be condemned. For if God will not do it, the devil will.

Let me then recommend this third part of the charge to
your careful remembrance and regard. It concerneth your
homage, which is your trust in Him, that you trust in Him
with your service of body and soul, Who hath trusted you

SERM.
I.

Jas. 1. 5.

The fourth
part:
"that they
do good."
1.
Ps. 37. 3.

with His plenty and store, and hath made you in that estate that you are trusted with matters of high importance both at home and abroad. For it is the argument of all arguments to the true Christian : because God hath given him, saith St. James, " without exprobration;" and given " all things," without exception of any ; and that " to enjoy," which is more than competency; and that " plenteously," which is more than sufficiency ; therefore, even therefore, to trust in Him only. If there be in us the hearts of true Christians, this will shew it, for it will move us ; and so let it, I beseech you. Let us not as men under the law be tired with the uncertainty of the creatures, but as men under grace have our hearts broken with the goodness of our God. In that God to place our trust, Who beyond all our deserts giveth ; if we respect the quantity, " all things ;" if the manner, very " plenteously :" if the end, " to joy" in them ; yet so, that our joy and repose end in Him—a very blessed and heavenly condition.

" Trust in the Lord and be doing good," said David. St. Paul saith the same : " Charge the rich of this world that they do good." The last was a very plausible point, which we have dwelt in with great delight. What ? the plenty of all things, that we enjoy—and long may enjoy, I beseech God ; who is not moved with joy to hear it reported ?

But little know they what a consequent St. Paul will infer upon this antecedent. For thus doth Paul argue : God hath done good to you by giving you, you also are bound to do good to others by giving them. If He hath given you " all things," you ought to part with something—and the more you part with, the liker ye become to Him That giveth " all things." If He have given you " to enjoy," you ought to receive others into the fellowship of the same joy ; and not to think that to do others good is to do yourselves hurt. If " plenteously" He have given you, you ought to be plenteous in giving; and not when the Lord hath His ephah great, wherein He hath meted to you, to make your hin small, whereby you measure to the poor, turning the plenty of Heaven into the scarcity of earth.

Thus doth the Apostle fetch the matter about, and thus doth he infer your doing good to these little lambs and such like, out of God's doing good unto you.

And that which he inferreth he doth exceedingly fitly, and sheweth great art and learning in it. For, speaking of enjoying, his very last word, he is carried in a very good zeal and affection to " the rich of this world," to desire of God, and to entreat of them that they may not have only πρό-σκαιρον ἀπόλαυσιν of them, that is, " enjoy them for a sea- Heb. 11. 25. son," but that they may enjoy them for ever; not only for a few years, or weeks, or days, we cannot tell well which, but from everlasting to everlasting. And that is, by doing " good." So " enjoy," that we may do " good," too.

To say truth, St. Paul could not better devise than here to place it. For our too much enjoying eateth up our well-doing, clean. Our too much lashing on in doing ourselves good, maketh that we can do good to none but ourselves. Our present enjoying destroyeth our well-doing utterly, and consequently the eternal enjoying we should have of our riches. As Pharaoh's lean kine devoured the fat, and it was Gen. 41. 4, not seen on them, so doth, saith St. Basil, our ἐφ' ἃ μὴ δεῖ, 21. our riotous mis-spending, where we should not, eat up our ἐφ' ἃ δεῖ, our Christian bestowing, where we should; and a man cannot tell what is become of it. Very well and wisely said that Father, 'Ακόνη γὰρ τῆς ἀσωτίας ἡ φιλοτιμία, ' Pride is prodigality's whetstone,' and it sets such an edge upon it in our enjoying, that it cuts so deep into our wealth, and shares so much for our vain and riotous enjoying, that it leaves but little for our well-doing.

Look how the trust in God and the trust in riches are set one against another here by the Apostle; so are our high minds, and our doing good. One would not think it at the first, but sure so it is; we must have lower minds and less pride, if we will have more good works and greater plenty of well-doing. You may therefore enjoy your wealth, that is true; but you must also take this with you, you must do good with it, and learn of the Apostle there be two uses of your riches, and that therefore God hath given them : 1. to enjoy, 2. to do good ; not to enjoy only, but to enjoy and to do good.

Enjoying is doing good, but to ourselves only; but by doing good here St. Paul meaneth to do it to others, that they may be better for us. The very same two doth Solomon in very fit terms set down; that water is given into our "cistern," 1. that we may drink of it ourselves, 2. that our fountains may flow out, and they that dwell about us fare the better for them. The very same two doth "a greater than Solomon," our Saviour Himself, count of too; for of His purse we read He had these two uses, to "buy" that He had need of Himself, and to "give something to the poor." It is good reason, that man consisting of two parts, the soul and body, the body only should not take up all, but the soul should be remembered too. Enjoying is the body's part, and well-doing is the soul's; your souls are suitors to you to remember them, that is, to remember well-doing, which is the soul's portion.

Remember this second; the other, I doubt not but you will remember fast enough. This was the use of our Saviour Christ's purse, and if yours be like His this must be the use of yours also. For surely it is greatly to be feared that many rich at this day know not both these; indeed know no other use of their wealth than an ox or an ass or other brute beasts would know, to have their crib well served, sweet and clean provender of the best in the manger, and their furniture and trappings fit and of the finest fashion. No other than the glutton did, to go in soft linen and rich silk and to fare deliciously every day. Or than the other his pew-['i. e. boon companion. Pew
sometimes
is used for
an ale-
house
bench.
See Hist.
of Pews:
Camb.
Camd.
Soc.] fellow[1], that professed it was all the use he counted of; and therefore we see he saith to his soul, Eat thy fill, soul, and drink thy fill, fill and fat thyself, and enjoy this life, never look to enjoy any other.

We must learn one use more, one more out of our charge, and consequently. When we look upon our sealed sums, our heaps of treasure, and continual comings in, thus to think with ourselves: This that I see here hath God given me "to enjoy," but not only for that but to "do good" with also. The former use of my riches I have had long, and daily still have, but what have I done in the other? The rich men in the Gospel they had the same, they did enjoy theirs, but now it is sure little joy they have of them. Why? for want of this other. Abraham, he did both; he enjoyed his riches here, and now another, an eternal joy of them. Yea, he received Lazarus into his bosom. Why? he received him into his bosom and cherished him, and did good here on earth. And so did Job, and so did Zaccheus. Now good [Job 29. Lord, so give me grace so " to enjoy" here, that I lose not ${}^{11,\ \&c.}_{Luke\ 19.}$ my endless joy in Thy heavenly kingdom. Let me follow 8, 9.] their steps in my life, with whom I wish my soul after death. These things are good and profitable for the rich oft to think on.

Well then, if to " do good" be a part of the charge, what is it to " do good ?" It is a positive thing, " good ;" not a privative, to do no harm. Yet as the world goeth now, we are fain so to commend men. He is an honest man, he doth no hurt : of which praise any wicked man that keeps himself to himself may be partaker. But it is to do some good thing; what good thing? I will not answer as in the schools, I fear I should not be understood, I will go grossly to work. These that you see here before your eyes, to do them good, to part with that that may do them good ; use the goods that you have to do but that which sundry that have heretofore occupied those rooms where you now sit— whose remembrance is therefore in blessing upon earth and whose names are in the book of life in Heaven—have done before you in divers works of charity, to the maintenance of the Church, the benefit of learning, and the relief of the poor of the land. This is to " do good." This I trust you understand.

This know, that God hath not given sight to the eye to enjoy, but to lighten the members; nor wisdom to the honourable man, but for us men of simple shallow forecast; nor learning to the divine, but for the ignorant; so neither riches to the wealthy, but for those that want relief. Think you Timothy hath his *depositum,* and we ours, and you have [1 Tim. 6. none? it is sure you have. We ours in inward graces and ${}^{20.]}$ treasures of knowledge; you yours in outward blessings and treasures of wealth. But both are *deposita,* and we both are feoffees of trust. I see there is a strange hatred and a bitter gainsaying every where stirred up against unpreach- ing Prelates, as you term them, and pastors that feed them- selves only : and they are well worthy. If I might see the same hatred begun among yourselves, I would think it sin- cere. But that I cannot see. For that which a slothful

SERM.
I. divine is in things spiritual, that is a rich man for himself
and nobody else in things carnal: and they are not pointed
at. But sure you have your harvest as well as we ours, and
that a great harvest. Lift up your eyes and see the streets
Mat. 9. 37. round about you, "the harvest is verily great and the labourers few." Let us pray both that the Lord would thrust
out labourers into both these harvests, that the treasures of
knowledge being opened they may have the bread of eternal
life; and the treasures of well-doing being opened they may
have the bread of this life, and so they may want neither.

I will tell you it another as easy a way. St. Augustine
making it plain to his auditory, somewhat backward as it
should seem, was fain to tell them thus, thus to define doing
good: *Quod non vultis facere, hoc bonum est,* said he; 'that
that you will not do, that that I cannot get you to do, that is
to do good.' Shall I say so to you? No indeed I will not,
I hope better things, and partly I know them. But this I
will say; that which the Papists with open mouth, in all
their books, to the slander of the Gospel, that which they
say you do not, nay you will not do, that is to "do good."

One of them saith that our religion hath comforted your
force attractive so much, and made it so strong, that nothing
can be wrung from you. Another, he saith that our religion
hath brought a hardness into the bowels of our professors,
that they pity little, and the cramp or chiragra into their
hands, that they give less. Another, that our preaching
hath bred you minds full of Solomon's horseleeches, that
[Prov. 30.
15.] cry "Bring in, bring in," and nothing else. All of them say
that your good works come so from you, as if indeed your
religion were to be saved by faith only. Thus through you,
and through want of your doing good, the Gospel of Christ
is evil spoken of among them that are without. They say,
we call not to you for them; that we preach not this point,
that we leave them out of our charges. *Libero animam meam,*
'I deliver here mine own soul.' I do now call for them, I
have done it elsewhere ere now. Here I call for them now,
I take witness, I call you to record, I call heaven to record;
Domine scis quia dixi, scis quia locutus sum, scis quia clamavi,
'Lord, thou knowest I have spoken for them, I have called
for them, I have cried for them,' I have made them a part

of my charge, and the most earnest and vehement part of
my charge, even the charge of doing good.

Unto you therefore that be rich be it spoken; hear your
charge, I pray you. There is no avoiding, you must needs
seal this fruit of well-doing, you must needs do it. For
having wealth and wherewithal to "do good," if you do it
not, *inprimis*, talk not of faith, for you have no faith in you;
if you have wherewith to shew it and shew it not, St. James
saith you have none to shew. Nor tell me not of your re- [Jas. 2. 17.]
ligion, there is no religion in you; "pure religion is this,"
as to very good purpose was shewed yesterday, "To visit the [Jas. 1. 27.]
fatherless and widows;" and you never learned other religion of us.

Secondly, if you do it not, I warn you of it now, you shall
then find it when you shall never be able to answer the ex-
acting of this charge in the great day; where the question
shall not be of the highness or lowness of your minds, not of
your trust and confidence, or any other virtues, though they
be excellent, but of your feeding, clothing, visiting, harbour-
ing, succouring, and in a word, of your well-doing only.
This I say to you, bear witness I say it.

Now to them in your just defence I say—for God forbid
but while I live I should always defend this honourable city
in all truth—to them whom the mist of envy hath so blinded
that they can see no good at all done but by themselves, I
forbid them, the best of them, to shew me in Rheims or in
Rome, or any popish city Christian, such a show as we have
seen here these two days. To-day but a handful of the heap,
but yesterday and on Monday the whole heap, even a mighty
army of so many good works as there were relieved orphans,
"the chariots" of this city, I doubt not, and "the horsemen 2 Kings 13,
thereof." 14.

They will say it is but one, so they say; be it so, yet it is
a matchless one. I will go further with them, spoken be it
to God's glory, *Non nobis Domine, non nobis, sed Nomini Tuo* P. 115. 1.
da gloriam: "Not unto us, not unto us, O Lord, but unto
Thy Name give the praise, for Thy loving mercy and for Thy
truth's sake which we profess." I will be able to prove that
learning in the foundation of schools and increase of revenues
within colleges, and the poor in foundation of almshouses,

and increase of perpetuities to them, have received greater
help in this realm within these forty years last past, since not
the starting up of our Church as they fondly use to speak,
but since the reforming ours from the error of theirs, than it
hath I say in any realm Christian, not only within the self-
same forty years, (which were enough to stop their mouths,)
but also than it hath in any forty years upward, during all
the time of popery, which I speak partly of mine own knowledge, and partly by sufficient grave information to this behalf. This may be said, and said truly.

And when we have said this, what great things have we
said? that time for time, so many years for so many, thirty
years of light have made comparison with thirty years of
trouble. But this is not as we would have it, we would have
it out of all comparison. This that hath been said is strange
to them I know, and more than they reckoned of. But I
would have you in these times of peace and truth so far

1 Pet. 2.
15.

beyond them, as that you might φιμοῦν, "snaffle" them
in this. So they durst not once offer to enter into this
theme with us, or once to mention it more. So it should
be, I am sure, so the Gospel deserves to have it.

2. The
quantity:
"be rich
in good
works."

You have the substance of that you must do, to "do good."
Now here is the quantity : "Be rich in good works;" that
seeing you are rich indeed, you would not be poor men, but
"rich in good works."

"Good works," St. Paul saith, not good words. "Good,"
with the goodness of the hand, not with the goodness of the
tongue, and tongue only, as many now are—well therefore
resembled to the tree that Pliny speaketh of, the leaves of
it as broad as any target, but the fruit is no bigger than a
bean—to talk targets and to do beans. It were better re-

2 Tim. 3.
17.

versed, if we were, as St. Paul saith, "perfect in all good
works," than perfect in certain curious and quaint terms and
set phrases, wherein a great part of many men's religions do
now-a-days consist ; plain speech and sound dealing, plain
speech and good works, best.

[Lu. 12.
18.]

And "rich" in them. The rich man in the Gospel, would,
as he said, build his barns bigger to put in them πάντα
ἀγαθὰ, "all his goods" he had ; no good out of his barn.
Yes, yes, some "in good works" too. St. Paul hath here

within the compass of this text two rich men; his desire is they may both meet together in every rich man. " Rich," ἐν τῷ νῦν αἰῶνι, "in the world that now is ;" so ye are : rich in the world that shall be after this; be that too. Rich in coffer; so ye are : rich in conscience; be so too. Your consciences you shall carry with you, your coffers you shall not. Thus you are valued in the Queen's books; what are you in God's books? So much worth in this land of the dying; how much worth in the land of the living? St. Paul's advice is, that you strive for both; which you shall be, if ye be " rich in good works." The true riches are the riches of " His glorious inheritance." They be the true riches, which Ephes. 1. except a man can assure himself of after the lease of his life ^{18.} is out, he shall be in a marvellous poor case, as was the rich man ; and beg of Lazarus there, that begged of him here. La. 16. 24. Those riches must be thought of, marry then you must be " rich in good works." Not to give something to somebody at some time. Why? who doth not so? That is not to be " rich." To give φειδομένως, " sparingly," a piece of bread [2 Cor. 9. or a draught of drink, and that only, that belongeth to him ^{6.]} whom God hath sparingly blessed, to the brother of low estate ; it is not your work.

In the law, to the building of the Tabernacle the poor gave Exod. 35. goats' hair and badgers' skins; that was for them, and that ^{23, 27.} was accepted : the rich, they gave purple, gold, and jewels, to the Tabernacle, they were " rich in good works." And in the Gospel, " To whom much is given, of him" proportionably Lu. 12. 48. " much shall be required." That is, in a word, As you are sessed in the Queen's books so are you in God's books, each one according to his ability. And God will look, that according to that sessment they should be done; that you 2 Cor. 9. 8. should περισσεῦσαι, " abound" in good works as you do in wealth, that you should προΐστασθαι, " go before" and sit [Tit. 3. 8.] highest and have a precedence in works as you have in your places. And in a word, that you should be lords, knights, aldermen, masters, wardens, and of the livery in good works, as you be in your several wards and companies. And indeed to say the truth, to commit so many sins as no auditor can number them, and to afford so few good works as a child may tell them ; to receive such profits as great count-books will not hold them ; and to yield so small store of good works as a little paper not so broad as my hand may contain them; to lash out at a banquet you know what, and to cast to a captive's redemption all the world knows what; to cast your pride with pounds and your good works with pence, what coherence is there in these? This is not to be " rich." But that is a part of the charge too. I pray you remember it, remember to be " rich;" not only to do good, but to be " rich" in doing good. That will make you in case well to die, as now, God be thanked, you are well to live.

3. The quality: " ready to distribute." [2 Cor. 9. 7.]
And with the quantity take the quality too, I pray you: for the quantity, richly; for the quality, readily. Ἐξ ἀνά-γκης, "with compulsion," not willingly ; and ἐκ λύπης, " with grudging," not cheerfully, these are the faults contrary to this virtue. God must have it done with a facility, with a readiness, easily. And good reason easily, for easily you may. We that want, cannot without difficulty ; we would, and we cannot; we have a heart without a hand ; though we be willing, nothing is done. Why? we are not able. You are able, God be thanked ; if you be well willing, there is no more to do, it is done. This readiness is a necessary virtue in our days, where ere a benefit come, nay many times ere a debt, so much ingenuity is spent, so many

Prov. 3. 28. *rogo*s, such a *Vade et redi*, "go and come" such a time ; such a dancing on the threshold, such a failing of the eyes ere it can be seen, such a cleaving to the fingers ere it will come off, such instillation by now a drop and then a drop, as to a liberal nature when it cometh it is like to bread full of gravel; for hunger a man must needs have it, and but for needs must a man had as lief be without it. O beloved, mar not all you do before God and man for want of this one thing. You love a fair seed-time, all of you: *Hilaris datio, serena satio,* 'cheerful giving is like a fair seed-time.' As you for your seed, to bury it wish a seasonable time, so and no less God desireth for His, that His seed may not be sown with an overcast mind, but with the gladness of heart and cheerfulness of countenance. Even as He doth Himself, Who what He bestoweth, bestoweth so as He taketh as much yea more delight in giving than we of receiving. So do, and then this charge is at an end : " Be ready to communicate."

There is of this word some difference among writers, but such as you may easily reconcile. Some think the Apostle would have rich men to be εὐπροσόδους, ' easy to be spoken with,' and to be spoken to. Some, that he would not only have them give readily, but lend freely, and not practise the devil's alchemistry, as they do, by multiplication in lending. Some, that they should not think their beneficence to be a taking from them without receiving back, inasmuch as there is an intercourse of the giver's grace, and the receiver's prayer. Some, that his mind is, that they should not do good to some few, but even to a multitude. All are good and godly, and agreeable to the analogy of faith; and you by doing all may verify and agree all, and make of a discord in opinions a harmony in practice. St. Hierome, methinketh, saith best, that *Communicare est communitati dare, aut ad aliquid commune,* ' to be beneficial to a society, or to bestow to some common use.'

[Vid. Corn. a Lap. in loc.]

This is the perfection or pitch of well-doing, " that most plenteous grace, by the thanksgiving of many, may redound to the glory of God." The Apostle therefore is a further suitor to you that be rich, and will not end his charge till he hath laid this on you too, to do good to societies and foundations, either necessary to be erected, or more than necessary to be maintained, lest through our evil-doing our fathers' well-doing perish. It is not for every man to reach unto them, there is no hope to have them upholden but by you; that you would therefore have them in remembrance, and to think upon them to do them good.

2 Cor. 4. 15.

But alas, what hope is there to hear that good will be this way done, since it is thought that many may be indicted for seeking to eat up companies, and to convert that which was the good and making of many into their own *singulare commodo,* by out-buying and out-bidding all besides themselves, that they alone may appropriate civil livings, turn common into private, the whole body's nourishment into one foregrown member, and in the end " dwell alone" upon the earth.

Jer. 49. 31.

That the world is toward an end, other men may be persuaded by other reasons; none more effectual to persuade me than this one, that every man doeth what in him lieth to discommon communities, and to bring all to the first priva-

SERM.
I.

tion. For the world being itself a main society, these men by dismembering under-societies seek and do what they can to dissolve the whole. So that God must needs come to make an end of the world, or else if this hold on we should shortly make an end of it ourselves.

It is further complained, that whereas there hath been and is given charitably to the poor and their maintenance, that the poor themselves want, and they that have the receiving of the profits do yet increase mightily. Had not these things need to be put in the charge? Are they not in the ears of the Lord? Is it not a sin crying to Heaven? Shall He not visit for these things? for this discredit of His Gospel, for this unexcusable, unfaithful dealing, in the ears of Jew and Gentile, of Turk and Christian, of God and man? I beseech

[Heb. 13.
22.]

you still, "suffer the words of exhortation;" it is good for you to know what things are said abroad. For my part, in God's presence I protest, I know none; and if there be none, present none. It is that I desire ; the charge is now given, may be given in vain.

1. To the
Church.

Now if you enquire to whom your doing good should stretch itself, St. Paul himself will tell you. To them that

Gal. 6. 6.

instruct you—they are to "communicate" with you in all

Rom. 12.
13.

your "goods," that is, the Church; and "to the necessity of the Saints," or to the Saints that be in necessity, that is, to the poor.

Esther 4.
14.
Neh. 1. 11.

The Church first : for this end came Esther "to the kingdom," and Nehemiah to his great favour with the prince, even to do good to the Church; and for this end hath Tyrus, that rich city, that abundance bestowed on her, even to be

Ezek. 28.
14.

"a covering cherub" to the Church of God, and to stretch out her wings over it. The Prophet's meaning was, that rich men must be a shadow of maintenance and defence to the ark, to divinity ; their riches must serve them as wings to that end, they must be covering cherubs on earth to the Church militant, if ever they will be singing cherubs in Heaven with the Church triumphant.

And much good might be done, and is not, in this behalf; and that many w—— I will name but one, that is, that with their wings stretched out they would keep the filth and pollution of the sin or sins whereof you heard so bitter complaint

both these days, of simony and sacrilege, from falling on the
ark, and corrupting and putrifying it, which it hath almost
already done. That seeing the Pope do that he doth—howsoever some have alleged the Papists' great detestation of this
sin, and of us for this sin, for a motive, it is all but dis-
sembling, their hand is as deep in this sin as any man's—I
say, seeing the Pope doth as he doth : that is, as he hath dis-
pensed with the oath and duty of subjects to their Prince
against the fifth commandment; with the murder, both
violent with dags[1], and secret with poison, of the sacred
persons of Princes, against the sixth; with the uncleanness of
the stews, and with incestuous marriages, against the seventh;
so now of late, with the abomination of simony against the
eighth ; having lately—as it is known by the voluntary confession of their own Priests—by special and express warrant
of the See Apostolic sent hither into this land his licence dis-
pensative to all patrons of his mark to set up simony, and to
mart and make sale of all spiritual livings which they have or
can get to the uttermost penny, even if it were possible by
the sound of the drum ; and that with a very clear conscience, so that some portion thereof be sent over to the relief
of his seminaries, which by such honest means as this come
to be now maintained ; seeing thus do the Papists, and we
loath to be behind them in this gain of blood make such merchandise with this sin, of the poor Church and her patrimony, as all the world crieth shame of it ; to redeem the
orderly disposing them to the Church's good, were a special
way for you rich men to do good in these days. Neither, as
these times are, do I know a better service, nor which I am
persuaded will please God better than this, or be better accepted at His hands.

This for the Church ; you must have a wing stretched
abroad to cover it. And for the poor, you must have a bosom
wide open to receive them. Lazarus in a rich man's bosom
is a goodly sight in Heaven, and no less goodly in earth.
And there shall be never a rich man with Lazarus in his
bosom in heaven, unless he have had a Lazarus in his bosom
here on earth.

The poor are of two sorts ; such as shall be with us "always,"
as Christ saith, to whom we must do good by relieving them :
such is the comfortless estate of poor captives, the succour-

[1 Dag sig-
nifies both
a dagg.r,
and also a
pistol.]

2. To the
p. or.

Joh. 12. 8.

less estate of poor orphans, the desolate estate of the poor widows, the distressed estate of poor strangers, the discontented estate of poor scholars ; all which must be suffered and succoured too.

There are others, such as should not be suffered to be in Israel, whereof Israel is full ; I mean beggars and vagabonds able to work; to whom good must be done, by not suffering them to be as they are, but to employ them in such sort as they may do good. This is a good deed no doubt; and there being, as I hear, an honourable good purpose in hand for the redress of it, God send it good success. I am as one, in part of my charge, to exhort you by all good means to help and further it.

Methinketh it is strange that the exiled Churches of strangers which are harboured here with us, should be able in this kind to do such good as not one of their poor is seen to ask about the streets ; and this city, the harbourer and maintainer of them, should not be able to do the same good. Able it is no doubt, but men would have doing good too good-cheap. I know the charges will be great ; but it will quit the charges, the good done will be so great. Great good to their bodies in redeeming them from divers corrupt and noisome diseases, and this city from danger of infection. Great good to their souls in redeeming them from idleness, and the fruit of idleness, which is all naughtiness, nowhere so rife as among them; and this city from much pilfering, and loss that way. Great good to the commonwealth in redeeming unto it many rotten members, and making them men of service, which may hereafter do good in it to the public benefit, and redeem this city from the blood of many souls which perish in it for want of good order. Last of all, great good to the whole estate, in bringing the blessing of God upon it; even that blessing that there shall not be a beggar in all Israel. So much for doing good.

Deu. 15. 4.

The last points. The reason.

"Laying up in store," &c. That is, your work shall not be in vain in the end, but receive a recompense of reward ; which is a prerogative, the which God's charges have above all other. In man's there is death to the offender ; but if any have kept his charge, he may claim nothing but that he hath. Only the Lord's charges are rewarded.

So that, besides the two reasons which may be drawn out

of the former, 1. one of the uncertainty, 2. the other of
God's bounty : 1. of the uncertainty, *Da quod non potes re-
tinere,* 'that we would part with that that we cannot keep
long,' that we must part with ere long whether we will or
no ; 2. of the bounty of God, *De Meo peto, dicit Christus,*
'that God Which gave asketh but His own,' but of that He
gave us a part to be given Him, and we—if there be in us
the heart of David—will say, *quod de manu Tuâ accepimus ;* 1 Chr. n. 29.
3. besides these a third : Though God might justly challenge ^{14.}
a free gift without any hope of receiving again, He will not ;
but tell us His meaning is not to impoverish or undo us,
but to receive these which He gave us, and came from Him
every one, and those that within a while forego we must, to
give us that we shall never forego. That is that He teacheth
us, commandeth not our loss, but commendeth to us a way
to lay up for ourselves, if we could see it; not to lease and
leave all, we know not to whom.

Well said Augustine, preaching on these very words: At
the very hearing these words " part with and distribute" the
covetous man shrinks in himself, at the very sound of parting with ; as if one should pour a basin of cold water upon
him, so doth he chill and draw himself together and say,
Non perdo ; he saith not I will not part with, but I will not [Vid.
lose, for he counteth all parting with to be losing. And Serm. 85.
will ye not lose, saith St. Augustine ? yet use the matter 5; 61. 9,
how you can, lose you shall ; for when you can carry nothing ii.]
away of all you have, do you not lose it ? But go to, saith
he, be not troubled ; hear what follows, shut not thy heart
against it.

" Laying up" for yourselves. I know Judas was of the "Laying
mind that all that went besides the bag was, *Utquid per-* your-
ditio ? and so be all they that be of his spirit. But St. Paul selves.
is of that mind, that ἀγαθοεργεῖν, " to lay out to good uses,"
is to lay up to our own uses ; that in parting thus with it,
we do not *dimittere* but *præmittere ;* not lose it by leaving it
here from whence we are going, but store it up by sending
it thither before whither we are going. And indeed one of
the two, we must needs either leave it behind and lose it for
ever, or send it before and have it our own for ever. Now
choose whether you will hold of Judas' or Paul's.

For indeed it is not the laying up St. Paul findeth fault with, but the place where; not building or obtaining or purchasing, all which three are specified, and the Apostle speaketh in your own terms, and the things you chiefly delight in; but the laying up in the flesh which will rot, and with it whatsoever is laid up with it; or in the world, which is so variable now, and will be consumed all to nought, and with it whatsoever is laid up in it. But he would have us to lay it up in Heaven; which, besides that it is our own country, and this but a strange land, is the place whither we pass, leaving this place behind, and from whence we [*probably there.*] must never pass but stay here[1], and either for ever want or have use for ever of that we part with here. And to say truth, *Ut quid respicimus?* With what face can we look up, and look upon heaven where we have laid up nothing? or what entertainment can we hope for there, whither we have sent no part of our provision, but for aught of our sending the place is clean empty?

You will say, how can one reach heaven to lay any thing there? I will ask you also another question. How can a man being in France reach into England to lay any thing there? By exchange. And did you never hear of our exchange, *cambium cœleste?* You know that to avoid the danger of pirates and the inconvenience of foreign coin not current at home, it is the use of merchants to pay it there, to receive it here. Such a thing is there in this "laying up." We are here as strangers; the place where we wish ourselves is our country, even paradise—if so be we send our carriage thither before; if not, I fear we intend some other place, it is not our country. When we shall take our way thither through the way of all flesh, through death, certainly we lose all; he strips every one he lays hold of. And put case we could get through with all our bags; here it is current, for it is the coin of the world, but there it is base, and goeth for nought: what shall we then do? *Quare non facis?* Why deal you not with exchange, paying here so much to have so [*Mat. 25. 27.*] much repaid you there. *Adites trapezitas,* 'you should go to the bankers:' who be those ' *Cum quæsiveris,* 'when you have sought all,' *pauperes sunt campsores,* 'they be the poor.' *Da pauperibus, et accipies thesaurum.* Where is our bill? *Quod, vel quantum uni.* Who will repay it? *Ego resolvam: nec repetit mercedem sed dat mercedem.* What? refuse you to take Christ's bill? if you dare trust your servants without fear of losing, if you trust your Lord fear you to lose? If them of whom you receive nothing but they of you, what, not Him of Whom erst you professed to receive all things? If Christ be of credit and heaven be not Utopia, if we think there is such a life after this, we shall ever have to do there, lay up here. Think it is a "laying up:" upon the believing of this one word, the weight of doing and not doing, all the text lieth.

When we recount our good deeds we commonly say, For him and not for him we have done this and that. It is true, saith St. Paul. That good you do you do for them, and for yourselves too; but more for yourselves than for them. To lay up and to do good, yea to others, nay to do your-selves good, to lay up for yourselves. Before, you thought it scattering, it was indeed laying up. Now you think it is for them, it is for you and your sakes God commandeth it.

God hath no need of you to feed the poor, no need of the widow to feed Elias; He could still have fed him by ravens, and as He fed Elias by one, so could He them by others or [1 Kings 17. 4, 9, &c.] other means, and never send them to Sarepta among you. He could have created sufficient for all men, or so few men as all should have been sufficient for them. He would not. He ordered there should ever be "poor" in the "land." Why? Deu. 15. 11. To prove them, and to prove you by them; that He Which feedeth you might feed them by you, that your superfluities might be their necessaries; that they of their patience in wanting, and you of your liberality in supporting, might both together of Him That made you both receive reward. They with you in your bosoms there, as here; a good sight in hea-ven, and a good sight in earth. For sure there shall never be a rich man in heaven without a Lazarus in his bosom. Therefore we have need of them as they have need of us, yet that we make theirs remaineth ours still.

It liketh the Holy Ghost, as to term our preaching our 2 Cor. 9. 6. seed, so to term your wealth your seed. The seed, the hus-bandman casts it, the ground receives it. Whose is it? the ground's? no, the husbandman's. And though it be cast

S E R M.
I.
out of his hands and rot in the bowels of the earth and come to nothing, and there becomes of it no man can tell what, yet this count he maketh, it is his still, and that every grain will bring him an ear at time of the year, and so that he hath in casting it from him stored it up for himself. Whereas, in foolishly loving it—as many do their wealth—he might have stored it up for worms and mustiness, and by that means indeed have lost it for altogether. The seed is your alms, the ground is the poor, you are the sowers. When it is therefore sown among them, how it is spent, or what becomes of it, you know not; yet this you know, and may
[See Mat. 13. 39.]
reckon, that at the fulness of time, at the harvest of the end of the world, for every grain of temporal contribution, you shall receive an ear of eternal retribution. Whereas, storing it up here, it may after your decease be stored for harlots and gamesters and rioters, in whose hands it shall corrupt and putrify, and yourselves lose the fruit thereof for ever. By this comparison you may know, that when you are dealing for the poor, it is your own business you intend; that not forgetting them, you remember yourselves; pitying
1 Cor. 15. 58.
them, you have pity on your own souls, and that "your labour shall not be in vain in the Lord."

Men use to reason with themselves: It will not always be health, let us lay up for sickness; it will not alway be youth, for age; and why not, saith St. Paul, it will not alway be this life, nor alway present life, lay up for yourselves against the life to come. In this place here we shall not be always, but in another of our eternal abode. This time, that is, will not be always, but such a time will come, as in which that
Ps. 90. 4.
[2 Pet. 3. 8]
we "call a thousand years, shall be no more than a day now." That place and that time would be thought of; and good wisdom it will be for a man to forget what he is, and to weigh what he shall be. Surely for any present matter God did not make us, *sed ad nescio quid aliud,* 'to some further matter yet to come.' Not yet present: as yet in promise, not yet in performance; as yet in hope, not in possession. I know that even in this place the Lord doth re-
[Lu. 6. 38.]
ward, and sheweth us plainly that *Date* and *Dabitur* are two twins: we ourselves have by good trial found it true, when our careful *Date* and provision for the poor last year save

one was requited *in presenti* with a great *Dabitur* of the last
year's increase. This is but an &c., making nothing to the
main promise which is to come, which our Saviour would
never have out of our eye : *Habetis hîc,* 'here you have' Lu. 6. 24.
your comfort ; *habete illic,* 'have it there' too, for here you
cannot ever have it. For the present time, you have officers
and servants to wait on you ; in the time to come, none will
accompany you, all will leave you, when to the grave they
have brought you, save mercy only ; none will wait or make
room but *opera eorum,* your works which you have laid up
for the time to come.

The Scripture speaketh of this life, and all the felicity Heb. 11. 9.
therein, as of a tent or booth, spread for a day and taken ^{2 Cor. 5. 1.}
down at night. Even like Jonas' gourd for all the world, [Jonah 4.
fresh in the morning, and stark withered ere evening. But ^{6, 8.]}
of the life to come, as of a groundwork, never to remove
itself, or we from it ; but to abide therein, ἐν τῇ φυλακῇ or
ἐν τῇ βασιλικῇ, 'in the prison' or 'the palace' for evermore.
We shall not therefore lose, but lay up in store : not for
others, but for ourselves ; not for a few days now, but for
hereafter ; not a tent to be taken down, but a foundation
never to be removed.

Of all the words in the text, not one was meet for the teeth
of the Rhemists save this only ; here you have a perilous
note close in the margin : *Good works are a "foundation."*
"A foundation"—very true. Who denies it ? but whether
a "foundation" in our graces, as Christ is without us, that
is the point. The ground whereon every building is raised,
is termed *fundamentum.* The lowest part of the building
immediately lying on it is so termed too. In the first sense,
Christ is said to be the only "foundation ;" yet the Apostles, 1 Cor. 3. 11.
because they are the lowest row of stones, are said to be
"foundations" in the second. So among the graces within Ephes. 2.
us, faith is properly in the first sense said to be the founda- ^{20.} [Rev. 21.
tion ; yet in the second, do we not deny but, as the Apostle ^{14.]} Col. 1. 23.
calleth them, as the lowest row, next to faith, charity, and Ephes. 3.
the works of charity may be called foundations too. Albeit ^{17.}
the margin might well have been spared at this place ; for
the note is here all out of place. For being so great schoolmen as they would seem, they must needs know it is not the

E

SERM.
I.

drift of the Apostle here in calling them "a foundation" to carry our considerations into the matter of justifying, but only to press his former reason of uncertainty there, by a contrary weight of certain stability here, and so their note comes in like *Magnificat* at Mattins.

Thus reasoneth St. Paul: This world is uncertain, of a sandy nature; you may rear upon it, but it is so bad a soil, as whatsoever you raise will never be well settled, and therefore ever tottering; and when "the rain," and "the wind,"

Mat. 7. 27.

and the waves "beat" against it, it cometh down on your heads. Therefore to make choice of a faster soil, build upon God's ground, not upon the world's ground; for πάντα ἐκεῖνα

Chrysost. in locum Hom. 18. [circa med.]

βέβαια, μεταβολὴ οὐδεμία, saith Chrysostom, 'there all is firm, there you may build and be sure:' fall the rain upon the top of it, blow the wind against the side of it, rise the waves against the foot of it, it stands irremovable. Wherein the Apostle, saith Chrysostom, doth teach a very goodly and excellent art, how to make of our fugitive riches a trusty and fast friend, how to make gold of our quicksilver, and of the uncertainty of riches a sure and certain groundwork.

Assurance and security are two things, we know, that rich men many times buy dear. Here they may be had; not for thus much, or thus long, but for as much as you list, and as long as eternity is long, that never shall have end. The meaning is, that if you lay out or lay on that you have on these earthly things—the plot which the world would fain commend unto you—with this life, or at the furthest with this world, they shall be shaken in pieces and come to nought; and you possibly in the hour of death, but most certainly in the day of judgment, shall shake, when the world your groundwork shakes, and be in trembling fear and perplexed agony, touching the estate of your soul; knowing there is nothing coming to you but the fruit of this world which is ruin, or the fruit of the flesh which is corruption. But if you shall have grace to make choice of God's plot, which He hath here levelled for you to raise upon, *O quanto dignum pretio!* that will be worth all the world in that day; the perfect certainty, sound knowledge, and precious assurance you shall then have, whereby you shall be assured to be received, because you are sure you are Christ's, because you are sure you have true faith, because you are sure you have framed it up into good works. And so shall they be a foundation to you-ward, by making evident the assurance of salvation ; not *naturá* to God-ward, in bringing forth the essence of your salvation.

Look you how excellent a groundwork here is! (not for a cottage) whereon you may raise your frame to so notable a height, as standing on it you may lay hand on, and lay hold of, eternal life. O that you would mind once these high things, that you would be in this sense high-minded! St. Paul's meaning is to take nothing from you, but give you a better to requite it by far. He would have you part with part of your wealth to do good; he will lay you up for it "treasure in Heaven" for your own use. He would have [Mat. 6. 20.] you forsake the world's sand and uncertainty, wherein you cannot trust; but therefore he marks you out a plot out of the rock, whereto you may trust. He would not have you highminded in consideration or comparison of aught on this earth, but he would have your minds truly exalted to reach up to heavenly things higher than the earth. And last, instead of this world, the lusts and riches thereof, to match that if you will lay hold of it, he holdeth out eternal life and the glory thereof.

To take a short prospect into "eternal life." Life itself, first, you know, is such a thing as, were it to be sold, would be stapleware; if it stood where hold might be laid on it, some would thrust their shoulders out of joint but they would reach it. It was a great truth out of a great liar's mouth—"skin and all." And I mean not "eternal," but [Job 2. 4.] this "life," and therefore some readings have, "to lay hold [1 Tim. 6. 19.] of true life," as if in this were little truth. Indeed, St. Augustine saith, it is nothing but a disease. We say of [Vid. S. Aug. Ser. 80. 2.] dangerous sicknesses, he hath the plague, he is in a consumption, sure he will die; and yet it fails, divers die not ; whereas, saith he, of life itself it may be said and never fails : *He lives, therefore he will certainly die.*

Well yet, this life such as it is, yet we love it, and loath we are to end it; and if it be in hazard by the law, what running, riding, posting, suing, bribing, and if all will not serve, breaking prison is there for it! Or if it be in danger

SERM.
I.

of disease, what ado is there kept, what ill-savoured drugs taken! what scarifying, cutting, searing! and when all comes to all, it is but a few years more added ; and when they are done, we are where we should have been before ; and then, that which is now life, shall be then no life. And then, what is it the nearer ? What, if Adam had lived till this morning, what were he now the nearer ? Yet for all that, as short and frail as it is, we do what possibly man can do to eke it still; and think ourselves jolly wise men when we have done, though we die next year after for all that. If then with so great labour, diligence, earnestness, endeavour, care and cost, we busy ourselves sometimes to live for a while, how ought we to desire to live for ever? if for a time to put death away, how to take death away clean ?

Ps. 91. 16.

You desire life I am sure, and " long life ;" and therefore a long life, because it is long, that is, cometh somewhat nearer in some degree to eternal life. If you desire a long-lasting life, why do you not desire an everlasting life ? If a life of many years, which yet in the end shall fail, why not that life whose years shall never fail ? If we say it is lack of wit or grace when any man runs in danger of the law of man, whereby haply he abridges himself of half a dozen years of his life, what wit or grace is there wilfully to incur the loss of eternal life? For indeed, as in the beginning we set down, it is a matter touching the loss of eternal life we have in hand; and withal, touching the pain of eternal death. It is not a loss only, for we cannot lose life and become as a

['i. e. lose.]

stone, free from either. If we leese[1] our hold of this life, eternal death taketh hold upon us; if we heap not up the

Rom. 2. 5.

treasure of immortality, we heap up the treasure of "wrath against the day of wrath." If your wealth be not with us

Acts 8. 20.

to life, *pecunia vestra vobiscum est in perditionem.* We have not far to seek for this. For if now we turn our deaf ear to this charge, you shall " fall into temptations :" fear ye not

1 Tim. 6. 9.

that ? Into many " foolish and noisome lusts :" nor fear ye that neither? Yet fear whither these lead ; " which drown men in perdition and destruction" of body and soul. Fear ye not these? doth the Lord thunder thus, and are ye not moved? *Quibus verbis te curabo?* I know not how to do you good. But let eternal life prevail. Sure if life come

not, death comes. There is as much said now, not as I have
to say, but as the time would suffer; only let me in a few
words deliver the charge concerning this, and so I will break
up the court for this time.

And now, Right honourable, beloved, &c., albeit that according to the power that the Lord hath given us, I might
testify and charge you "in the presence of God" the Father, [1 Tim. 6.
"Who quickeneth all things;" and of the Lord Jesus, Who 2 Thess. 1.
shall shew Himself "from Heaven with His mighty Angels 7, 8.]
in flaming fire, rendering vengeance to them" not only "that
know not God," but to them also "that obey not the Gospel
of our Lord Jesus Christ," that ye think upon these things
which you have heard, to do them; yet *humanum dico,* "for [Rom. 6.
your infirmity I will speak after the manner of men," the 19.]
nature of a man best loveth to be dealt withal, and even
beseech you by the mercies of God, even of God the Father,
Who hath loved you, and given you an everlasting consolation, and a good hope through grace, and by the coming of
our Lord Jesus Christ, and our assembly unto Him, that
you receive not this charge in vain; that ye account it His
charge, and not mine; received of Him, to deliver to you.
Look not to me, I beseech you; in whom whatsoever you
regard, countenance or learning, years or authority, I do
most willingly acknowledge myself far unmeet to deliver
any; more meet a great deal to receive one myself, save
that I have obtained fellowship in this business in dispensing
the mysteries and delivering the charges of the Lord. Look
not on me, look on your own souls and have pity on them;
look upon Heaven, and the Lord of Heaven and earth from
Whom it cometh, and of Whom it will be one day called
for again. Surely there is a Heaven, surely there is a hell;
surely there will be a day when enquiry shall be made how
we have discharged that we have received of the Lord; and
how you have discharged that you have received of us in the
Lord's name. Against which day your consciences stand
charged with many things at many times heard. "O seek Wisd. 1. 12.
not death in the error of your life," deceive not yourselves;
think not that when my words shall be at an end, both
they shall vanish in the air and you never hear of them
again. Surely you shall, the day is coming when it shall

be required again at your hands. A fearful day for all those that for a little riches think basely of others; upon all those that repose in these vain riches—as they shall see then, a vain confidence; upon all those that enjoy only with the belly and the back, and do either no good, or miserable sparing good, with their riches; whose riches shall be with them to their destruction. Beloved, when your life shall have an end, as an end it shall have; when the terror of death shall be upon you; when your soul shall be cited to appear before God, *in novissimo;* I know and am perfectly assured all these things will come to mind again, you will perceive and feel that which possibly now you do not. The devil's charge cometh then, who will press these points in another manner than we can; then it will be too late. Prevent his charge, I beseech you, by regarding and remembering this now. Now is the time, while you may, and have time wherein, and ability wherewith; think upon it and provide for eternal life; you shall never in your life stand in so great need of your riches as in that day; provide for that day, and provide for eternal life. It will not come yet it is true, it will be long in coming; but when it comes, it will never have an end.

This end is so good that I will end with "eternal life," which you see is St. Paul's end. It is his, and the same shall be my end, and I beseech God it may be all our ends. To God immortal, invisible, and only wise, God Who hath prepared this eternal life for us, Who hath taught us this day how to come unto it, Whose grace be ever with us, and leave us not till it have thereto brought us, the Father, the Son, and the Holy Ghost, be all glory, power, praise, and thanksgiving, now and for ever. Amen.

ONE OF THE SERMONS

UPON THE

SECOND COMMANDMENT,

PREACHED IN THE

PARISH CHURCH OF ST. GILES, CRIPPLEGATE,

ON THE NINTH OF JANUARY, A.D. MDXCII.

———

ACTS ii. 42.

*And they continued in the Apostles' doctrine, and fellowship,
and breaking of bread and prayers.*

[*Erant autem perseverantes in doctrinâ Apostolorum, et communicatione fractionis panis, et orationibus.* Lat. Vulg.]

[*And they continued steadfastly in the Apostles' doctrine and fellowship, and in breaking of bread, and in prayers.* Eng. Trans.]

*There had been, two sundry days before, Sermons concerning
the positive outward worship of God, out of this Text, consisting of these four parts :*

*1. The Apostles' doctrine; 2. their society or fellowship;
3. breaking of bread ; 4. prayers.*

*The effect of this last was to acquaint the auditory with
sundry imaginations by divers erected, which many unstable
persons do run after and worship instead of those four, the
Apostles' doctrine, &c. The order was to begin with the doctrine first, and so after through the rest as they stand.*

THAT such imaginations there are, Solomon complaineth ɪ.
of *ratiocinia plurima*, whereby men were withdrawn from the Eccl. 7. 29.
simplicity of their creation. And under the Gospel, St. Paul
likewise of *venti doctrinarum*, whereby Christian people

began to be blown and carried about from the steadfastness of the truth.

But especially under the Gospel. For that, as St. Augus-
tine saith, *Videns diabolus templa dæmonum deseri, et in nomen Christi currere genus humanum, &c.* Seeing idolatrous images would down, he bent his whole device in place of them to erect and set up divers imaginations, that the people instead of the former might bow down to these and worship them. Since which it hath been and is his daily practice,
either to broach *doctrinas novas et peregrinas,* " new imaginations never heard of before," or to revive the old and new dress them. And these—for that by themselves they will not utter—to mingle and to card with " the Apostles' doctrine," &c., that at the least yet he may so vent them.

And this indeed is the disease of our age, and the just complaint we make of it : that there hath been good riddance made of images ; but for imaginations, they be daily stamped in great number, and instead of the old images set up, deified and worshipped, carrying the names and credit of " the Apostles' doctrine," government, &c.

Touching these imaginations then, to find some heads of them. They be, in respect of the devil who inspireth them,
called *doctrinæ dæmoniorum.* In respect of the instruments,
by whom he breathes them out, *doctrinæ hominum ;* as " the doctrine of the Pharisees," " the doctrine of the Nicolaitanes."

These men were of two sorts, as St. Paul sorteth them :
1. " wolves " which from without entered into the Church ; 2. " men arising from among themselves," teaching " perverse things."

1. Those which from without entered, were philosophers from the Gentiles, Pharisees from the Jews. Both which bred many imaginations in Christian religion.

Against them both St. Paul giveth a double *caveat :* not to be seduced by " philosophy," meaning, as he sheweth, the
" vain deceit" of that profession—that is the former ; 2. nor with the human traditions and rudiments of the Pharisees—
that is the latter. To avoid " oppositions of science falsely so called"—there is the first. To avoid " Jewish fables" and traditions—there is the second. For from these two forges came a great part of the imaginations which ensued.

Each of these sects esteeming his "old wine" good, and consequently brewing it with the "new wine" of the Gospel. ^{Lu. 5. 37, 8, 9.}

Imaginations by philosophy. First, by the course of the ecclesiastical history it appeareth that Simon Magus—who of a heathen philosopher became a Christian, and was baptized—after, through "the gall of bitterness" wherein he was, fell away again and proved the first of all heretics. He first, and after, Valentine; and then, Basilides devised many strange speculative fancies. And indeed, whosoever they be that dote about unprofitable curious speculations, from this kind they sprung first. ^{1. By Philosophy. [Vid. Tertull. adv. omn. Hæret. Libel. c.c. 2. et sq. inter Routh. Opusc.] Acts 8. 23.}

After these, those two main heresies that so mightily troubled the Church: first, that of the Manichee, who brought a necessity upon all things by means of his *duo principia*, making men secure how they lived, because it was ordained what should become of them; secondly, the other of the Pelagian, who ascribed to man's free will and ability to keep God's law, and thereby made void the grace of Christ. Both these were but two bastard slips of corrupt philosophy: the former, an imagination issuing from the sect of the Stoics and their fatal destiny; the latter, from the sect of the Peripatetics, and their pure naturals.

Imaginations by Judaism. As the curious speculations came from the philosophers of the Gentiles, so whatsoever superstitious observations were imagined, came from the Pharisees and sects of the Jews. As Simon Magus is reckoned the first heretic, so Ebion the Jew is the second. And from him sprang the opinion of the necessity of Jewish observances, which was the occasion of the council in Acts, the fifteenth chapter; and the opinion of "worshipping angels" as mediators, as Theodoret testifieth upon the second chapter of Colossians, the eighteenth verse. And for those ceremonies, as at the first they desired to retain those very same that were Judaical, so when it was withstood by the Apostles they did after but turn them, and new varnish them over into others like, and with them so clogged the Church as the Jews' estate was much more tolerable than the Christians'—St. Augustine's complaint. ^{2. By Judaism.}

Now from these two sorts of persons proceeded those two several means whereby, as it were in two moulds, all imagi- ^{Ep. 119. [al. 55. s. 55. ad finem.]}

S E R M.
II.

Mat. 9. 16.

Mark 7. 4.
2 Pet. 3, 16.
nations have been cast, and the truth of God's word ever perverted. 1. From the Pharisee, that piecing out the new garment with old rags of traditions, that is, adding to and eking out God's truth with men's fancies, with the phylacteries and fringes of the Pharisees, who took upon them to observe many things beside it. 2. From the philosopher, that wresting and tentering of the Scriptures, which St. Peter complaineth of, with expositions and glosses newly coined, to make them speak that they never meant; giving such new and strange senses to places of Scripture, as the Church of Christ never heard of. And what words are there or can there be, that—being helped out with the Pharisees' addition of a truth unwritten, or tuned with the philosopher's wrest of a devised sense—may not be made to give colour to a new imagination? Therefore the ancient Fathers thought it meet that they that would take upon them to interpret "the Apostles' doctrine," should put in sureties that their senses they gave were no other than the Church in former time hath acknowledged. It is true the Apostles indeed spake from the Spirit, and every affection of theirs was an oracle; but that, I take it, was their peculiar privilege. But all that are after them speak not by revelation, but by labouring in the word and learning; are not to utter their own fancies, and to desire to be believed upon their bare word—if this be not *dominari*

[See 1 Pet.
5. 3.]
fidei, 'to be lords of their auditors' faith,' I know not what it is—but only on condition that the sense they now give not a feigned sense, as St. Peter termeth it, but such a one as hath been before given by our fathers and forerunners in

[1 Cor. 9.
8.]
the Christian faith. "Say I this of myself," saith the Apostle, "saith not the law so too?" Give I this sense of mine own head? hath not Christ's Church heretofore given the

['strictly.
ed. 1661.]
like? Which one course, if it were straitly[1] holden, would rid our Church of many fond imaginations which now are stamped daily, because every man upon his own single bond is trusted to deliver the meaning of any Scripture, which is many times nought else but his own imagination. This is the disease of our age. Not the Pharisee's addition, which is well left; but, as bad as it, the philosopher's gloss, which too much aboundeth. And I see no way but this to help it.

2. From
within by
Christians.
Imaginations from the Christians. Secondly, from among

the Christians themselves arose men "speaking perverse [Acts 20. 30.] things," whom St. Paul well calleth *fratres subintroductos;* Gal. 2. 4. who also by their imaginations mainly corrupted the Apostles' doctrine, which we heretofore divided

into the { 1. matter, in which 2. manner, } { 1. The substance, and therein 2. The ceremony. } { 1. the foundation. 2. the building upon it. }

concerning all which, imaginations have risen.

Imaginations touching the foundations. Which are two— 1. In the matter and substance. so called by the name of foundations, first laid by our Saviour Christ, and after kept by the Apostles—even "repentance" Touching the foundation. and "faith." Heb. 6. 1.

Imaginations touching "repentance." Nicolas, one of the Mark 1. 15. seven, as Eusebius testifieth, became a man of imaginations, Acts 6, 5. Acts 20. 21. and began the sect of "the Nicolaitanes, whom God hateth." Rev. 2. 15. After whom arose Carpocrates in the same, of whom came the sect of the Gnostics—a sect that blew up that part of "the [Heb. 6. 1.] foundation" which is called "repentance from dead works." Repentance. For, as Epiphanius testifieth, they held that all other things [Epiphan. besides "faith" were indifferent, "repentance" and all; and Hær. 88. 5. sive 25; that so a man knew and embraced certain dictates and posi- 6. sive 26; tions, they would deliver him; live how he list, he could not 27. sive 47; choose but be saved. And of these high points of knowledge 41. sive 61.] they entitled themselves Gnostics, that is, men of knowledge. And all other Christians that could not talk like them, *simplices,* 'good simple souls.' Such is the imagination in our days of carnal Gospellers; that, so he forget not his creed, he cannot miscarry. These be the Gnostics of our age.

Imaginations touching "faith." On the other side against [Faith.] the other part of "the foundation," "faith," Latinus a Christian and a great learned man cast his mine, of whom was the sect of the Encratites, who offended at the licentious lives of the Gnostics fell into the other extreme, that *Non est curandum quid quisque credat, id tantum curandum est quid quisque faciat;* 'that the Creed might be cancelled well enough, for an upright and straight course of life God only regarded,' and in every sect a man might be saved that lived well. These, for their sober and temperate kind of life, termed themselves Encratites, that is, strict livers; and all other Christians that lived not in like austerity *Psychicos*, that is, carnal men. Such is in our days the imagination of the civil Christian; who, so his conversation be blameless and honest careth not for religion and faith at all, but for the most part lives and dies in brutish ignorance. We may call these the Encratites of our age.

2. Touch-
ing the
Building.
Imaginations touching the building; a secondary part of the Apostles' doctrine, and not of like necessity with the former. Epiphanius writeth, they were a sect, a branch of the old *Cathari* or Puritans, as he saith, which called themselves *Apostolici, propter exactum disciplinæ studium, &c.* For an extraordinary desire they had above other men to have discipline and all things to the exact pattern of the Apostles' days; which is itself an imagination.

1.   For it were *cacozelia*, 'an apish imitation,' to retain all in use then, seeing divers things even then were but *temporaria*.
Gal. 6. 16.
For beside their canon in matters of knowledge, they had their *dogmata* or *decreta*, not of equal importance; as was
Acts 15. 20.
that of eating "things strangled, and blood;" which no man now thinketh himself bound to abstain from. And, besides
1 Cor. 7. 10.
their *epitaxes*, 'commandments' in matter of practice, they had their *diataxes*, 'injunctions,' not of equal regard with
Jude ver.
19.
1 Cor. 11.
20, 21.
the former. Such were their *agapæ*, "love-feasts" after the Sacrament; and their celebrating the Sacrament after supper, which no Church at this day doth imitate. Therefore to press all that was in that time, is an imagination.

2.   And as to press all, so of these things that remain to press all alike, or think an equal necessity of them, which was a parcel of the imagination of the Donatists. For some things
1 Cor. 7. 10.
the Apostles peremptorily commanded; some things they had
1 Cor. 7. 25.
no commandment for, but only gave counsel; some things
1 Tim. 4.
11; 6. 2.
they commanded and taught; some things they taught and exhorted, whereof each was to be esteemed in his own value and worthiness; neither to dispense with the commandment, nor to make a matter of necessity of the counsel. Both which have not a little harmed the Church.

Lastly, for these matters of counsel, which for the most part are things indifferent, they also fall upon two imagina-
1 Cor. 10.
23.
tions: 1. some say, *Omnia mihi licent*, and so it be not con-

demned as unlawful, make no bones of it; which tendeth to all profaneness. Others say, "Touch not, taste not, handle Col 2 21. not;" which speak of things indifferent as merely unlawful, which imagination ends in superstition. A mean way would be holden between them both, that neither "a snare be cast" 1 Cor. 7. 35. on men's consciences, by turning *Non expedit* into *Non licet,* nor our "liberty" in Christ be made an "occasion to the Gal. 5. 13. flesh," by casting *Non expedit* out of doors. For the Spirit of Christ is the spirit of ingenuity, which will freely submit itself to that which is expedient, even in things of their own nature lawful. The not observing whereof with good heed and discretion, hath in old time filled the world with many a superstitious imagination; and in our days hath healed the imagination and superstition and hypocrisy with another of riot and licentious liberty, as bad as the former, yea a great deal worse.

Imaginations touching the ceremony. First, I take it to 2. Imagin-be a fancy to imagine there needs none; for without them the cere-neither comeliness nor orderly uniformity will be in the mony. Church. Women will "pray uncovered" (an uncomely sight) 1 Cor. 11. unless the Apostle enjoin the contrary: therefore, "Let 1 Cor. 14. everything be done decently and in order." Now, to advise 40. what is comely and orderly in each age and place, is left in the power and discretion of the governors of each Church: *Visum est Spiritui Sancto et nobis.* And the custom of each [Acts 15. Church is peaceably to be observed by the members of it. 28.] In a matter ceremonial, touching the veiling of women—after some reasons alleged, which yet a troublesome body might quarrel with—thus doth St. Paul determine the matter defi-nitively: "If any list to be contentious," *Nos non habemus* 1 Cor. 11. *talem consuetudinem, nec Ecclesiæ Dei.* As if he should say, 16. In matters of that quality each Church's custom is to over-Ep. 28. rule; as from that place St. Hierome and St. Augustine do finem.] both resolve. Ep. 86. [al. 36. s. 2.]

It hath been ever thought meet, saith St. Gregory, that 118. [al. 54. there should be *in unitate fidei consuetudo diversa;* that is, [S. Greg. the diversity of customs should be in divers Churches, all in al. 61. circ. the unity of one faith, to shew the Church's liberty in those med.] matters. And therefore the "eating of things offered to 1 Cor. 10. idols," wholly restrained the Churches of Syria and Cilicia, 27.

S E R M.
II.
  seemeth in some sort permitted the Church of Corinth, in
case no man did challenge it.

    And as for divers Churches this hath been judged requi-
site, so hath it likewise been deemed no less requisite that
every person should inviolably observe the rites and customs of his own Church. Therefore those former ordinances
which were not urged upon the Corinthians—upon the Galatians within the compass of the regions where they took place
as we see they were urged (as the Fathers interpret those

Gal. 1. 9. places) under the pain of Anathema, which censure is due
Gal. 5. 12. to all those that " trouble" the Church; as those do who for
setting light by the customs and orders of the Church are
1 Cor. 11. by St. Paul concluded within the number of persons " con-
16. tentious" and troublesome.

2. In the   Imaginations touching the manner of delivery. For even
manner of
delivery. in it also, for failing, men must imagine something, that
when they can take no exception to the matter yet they may
itch after a new manner, and hear it after such and such a
sort delivered, or they will not hear at all, and therefore

2 Tim. 4. 3. after their own liking " get them a heap of teachers."
    1. They must hear no Latin, nor Greek; no, though it be
interpreted. A mere imagination. For the Apostle writing
to the Corinthians which were Grecians, hath not feared to
use terms as strange to them, as Latin or Greek is to us—

1 Cor. 16. " Maranatha," " Belial," " Abba." All which he might easily
22.
2 Cor. 6. 15. enough have expressed in their vulgar, but that it liked him
Rom. 8. 15. to retain his liberty in this point.

    2. Nor none of the Apocrypha cited. Another imagina-
Jude ver. tion; for St. Jude in his Epistle hath not feared to allege out
14. of the book of Enoch, which book hath ever been reckoned
Apocrypha. And by his example all the ancient writers are
full of allegations from them; ever to these writings yielding
the next place after the canon of the Scriptures, and pre-
ferring them before all foreign writers whatsoever.

    3. Nor anything alleged out of the Jews' Talmud; a third
imagination. For, from their records, St. Paul is judged to
have set down the names of the sorcerers that " withstood

2 Tim. 3. 8. Moses" to be " Jannes and Jambres;" which in Exodus, or
the whole canon of Scriptures, are not named. As many
other things in the New Testament from them receive great

light. And the Jews themselves are therein clearly confuted.

4. But especially no heathen example or authority—for with allegation of the ancient Fathers I have often dealt—a matter which the Primitive Church never imagined unlawful. For Clemens Alexandrinus, by allusion to Sarah and Agar, teacheth the contrary. So doth Basil, in a set treatise; and Gregory Nyssen, out of the twenty-first chapter of Deuteronomy, by the rites touching the marrying of heathen women taken captive: and last of all, St. Augustine most plainly. And these all reckoned of the contrary, as a very imagination. Which they did the rather, for that besides divers other places not so apparent, they find St. Paul in matter of doctrine alleging Aratus a heathen writer, in his Sermon at Athens. And again, in matter of life, alleging Menander, a writer of Comedies, in his Epistle; and thirdly, in matter of report only, without any urgent necessity, alleging Epimenides, or, as some think, Callimachus.

And surely, if it be lawful to reason from that which "nature teacheth," as St. Paul doth against men's wearing long hair, it is not unlawful neither to reason from the wisest and most pithy sayings of natural men. Especially, with the Apostle, using them—as in a manner they only are used—thereby to provoke Christian men to emulation, by shewing them their own blindness in matter of knowledge, that see not so much as the heathen did by the light of nature; or their slackness in matter of conversation, that cannot be got so far forward by God's law, as the poor pagan can by his philosophy. That if grace will not move, shame may.

Imaginations touching "the Apostles' fellowship." For this doctrine received doth incorporate the receivers of it into a fellowship or society, which is called the fellowship or corporation of the Gospel; and they that "bring not this doctrine," are no ways to be received thereto. Which fellowship is not to be forsaken, "as the manner of some is," — men of imagination — in our days, either because there be heresies, for *oportet esse;* or, for that many at communions "come together, not for the better, but for the worse," for so did they in Corinth; or lastly, for that many and many "Christians walk" — which St. Paul wrote with

In Strom. 7. [for. 1. 5.]
De Legendis Ethnicorum Scriptis.
De Vitâ Mosis.
De Doc. Christ. 2. 40.
Acts 17. 28.
1 Cor. 15. 33.
[Tit. 1. 12.] [Vid. Wet. Not. in loc.]
1 Cor 11. 14.
II. Touching "the Apostles' fellowship."
2 John 10.
Heb. 10. 25. 1 Cor. 11. 19.
1 Cor. 11 17.
Phil. 3. 18.

SERM.   tears—"as enemies to the cross of Christ;" for so it was
II.   in the Church of Philippi.

1 Cor.12.28. Now it is plain, there can no society endure without government, and therefore God hath appointed in it governors
and assistants, which seeing they have power from God to
1 Tim.5.19. reject or "receive accusations," and to "judge those that
1 Cor. 5. 12. are within" and of the fellowship, it is an idle imagination
Mat. 18. 17. that some have imagined, to hold "the Church" hath not
her judgment-seat, and power to censure her disobedient
children.   It hath ever been holden good divinity that the
Church from Christ received power to censure and separate
wilful offenders.   Both, with the heathen man's separation,
who might not so much as enter into the Church door,
Acts 21. 28. (which is the greater censure); and with the publican's
separation, (which is the less,) who might enter and pray in
Lu. 18. 10. "the temple," but was avoided in common conversation, and
in the fellowship of the private table, and therefore much
more of the altar.   Of which twain, the former the Apostle
Gal. 5. 12. calleth "cutting off;" the latter, "abstaining from."   The
2 Thess. 3. Primitive Church calleth the former *excommunicatos*, the
6.   latter *abstentos*.   So that, to fancy no government, is an
imagination.   A government there is.

Touching the form of which government many imaginations have lately been bred, in these our days especially.
Acts 2. 42. At the writing of this verse, it is certain that the government
of Christian people consisted in two degrees only—of both
Lu. 9. 1; which our Saviour Christ Himself was the Author : 1. of the
10. 1.   Twelve, 2. of the Seventy ; both which were over the people,
in things pertaining to God.

These two were, one superior to another, and not equal.
And that the Apostles established an equality in the Clergy,
is, I take it, an imagination.   No man could perish in the
[Jude ver. "gainsaying of Korah" under the Gospel, which St. Jude
11.]   saith they may, if there were not a superiority in the Clergy ;
for Korah's mutiny was, because he might not be equal to
Nu. 16. 10. Aaron, appointed his superior by God.   Which very humour,
observe it who will, hath brought forth most part of the
heresies since the time of the Gospel ; that Korah might not
be Aaron's equal.   Now of these two orders, the Apostles
have ever been reckoned the superior to the other, till our

times; as having, even under our Saviour Christ, a power to forbid others. And after, exercising the same power; Silas, one of the Seventy, receiving a commandment, ἐντολὴν, from St. Paul an Apostle to come unto him. As the auditory had their "room" by themselves, so among the persons ecclesiastical the Apostles had a higher seat, as may be gathered; and in the very place itself were distinguished. Now in the place of the Twelve, succeeded Bishops; and in the place of the Seventy, *Presbyteri,* Priests or Ministers, and that by the judgment of Irenæus, who lived immediately upon the Apostles' age, of Tertullian, of St. Augustine. And this, till of late, was thought the form of fellowship, and never other imagined.

But not long since, some have fancied another, that should consist of Lay-elders, Pastors, and Doctors, and whether of Deacons too is not fully agreed yet. Which device is pressed now upon our Church, not as a form of more convenience than that it hath, but as one absolutely necessary, and of our Saviour Christ's own only institution, which maketh it the less sufferable. I know that by virtue of St. Peter's wrench before mentioned some places may be brought which may seem to give it colour, but that is if we allow those new glossed senses. But if we seek what senses the Primitive Church gave of them, not one of them but will suffer it to fall to the ground. And finding it a stranger to them, I know not how to term it but an imagination. To touch it briefly in a word.

If we ask Scripture for it, and where we may find it, they pass by the two most evident places in appearance, the twelfth chapter of the first Epistle to the Corinthians, the twenty-eighth verse, because there are no Pastors; and the fourth chapter of Ephesians, the eleventh verse, because there are no Lay-elders; and lay it upon the twelfth chapter of Romans, the sixth, seventh, and eighth verses. And there, by a strange and unheard of exposition, they will find them all four; but not except that exposition be allowed them, nor if the ancient writers may be heard, what the true sense of it is. There is no Epistle on which so many of them have written. Six only I will name: Origen, Chrysostom, Theodoret, Ambrose, Hierome, Œcumenius; all which have en-

Side notes:
Lu. 9. 49.

Acts 15. 30.
32; 17. 15.
1 Cor. 14.
16.

Lib. 3. c. 3.

De Præscript.
[32.]
In Ps. 44.
[32.]

[2 Pet. 3.
16.]

[1 Cor 12.
28; Eph.
4. 11;
Rom. 12.
6, 7, 8.]

F

SERM.
II.

treated of it. Let their commentaries be looked on upon that place. Not one of them applieth it to the Church government—which by any likelihood cannot be imagined but they would, if it were the main place for it—or findeth those offices in those words, which they in good earnest tell us of, as that Διάκονον in the seventh verse is not the deacon, but the distributer in the eighth verse is he; or that *qui miseretur* is Latin for a widow, or such like.

But if jointly they find them not, let us see how severally they warrant their offices. 1. Of Elders, some both preach and govern, some govern only; and there they imagine they have found their Lay-elder, by implication that there are *Presbyteri* that labour not in preaching. Hear St. Chrysostom on the first Epistle of the Corinthians, the first chapter and seventeenth verse. You shall find a far other sense : *Evangelizare*, saith he, *perpaucorum est ; baptizare autem cujuslibet, modo fungatur Sacerdotio.* And a little after : *Siquidem Presbyteris quidem qui simpliciores sunt hoc munus tradimus ut baptizent, verbum autem ut doceant non nisi Sapientioribus, hic sapientia est* [*et*] *labor. Quamobrem et alibi inquit : Qui bene præsunt Presbyteri, duplici honore digni sunt, maxime qui laborant in verbo.* Whereby it is plain that in St. Chrysostom's time it was not reckoned meet that every one that ministered the Sacraments, should also preach. That the meaner sort dealt with the Baptizing, and they only that were of the more wise sort with the word. And to prove it should thus be, he citeth this their Scripture, as if in the Apostles' days the like had been thought wisdom. But as for lay-elders, he nor any that writeth on it can find in this verse ; nor any such in all antiquity ever understood by the name of Presbyter.

The elders preachers they divide into pastors and doctors, and these they sever in function, limiting the one to his exhortation only, the other to point of doctrine only. An imagination which none of the Fathers would ever acknowledge ; search their writings. St. Chrysostom upon this verse (Ephesians 4. 11.) taketh them both for one, and maketh no difference. So St. Hierome in both his Commentaries upon that Epistle : *Omnis enim pastor doctor est.* But St. Augustine may serve for all, to shew how unknown this was

1 Tim. 5.
17.

[Hom. 3.]

[ἐκεῖ γάρ
ἐστιν ὁ
πόνος καὶ ὁ
ἱδρώς.]

Aug. Ep.
59. [*al.* 149,
c. 11.] ad
Paulinum.

then. Who being purposely written to by Paulinus to assign a difference between them, thus answereth : *Pastores autem et Doctores, quos maxime ut discerneremus voluisti, eosdem puto esse, sicut et tibi visum est, ut non alios Pastores, alios Doctores intelligeremus, &c. Hos enim sicut unum aliquid duobus nominibus complexus est.*

Lastly, for their deacons too : that they should be men of occupation and trade to deal with the Church-stock and care of the poor only, is also I doubt not an imagination ; seeing all antiquity hath ever reckoned of that calling as of a step or degree to the ministry, out of the first of Timothy, the third chapter, and thirteenth verse. And that the Church's practice hath been always to employ them in other parts and functions besides that, is plain by Justin Martyr who Apol. 2. lived in the Apostles' days, namely, to distribute the Com-ad Antoninum. munion ; by Tertullian, to baptize ; by Cyprian and divers [ad fi-nem.] De others. So that to conclude, these are imaginations touch-Bapt. [c. ing "the Apostles' fellowship," howsoever a great number of Ser. 6. de deceived people bow down to them and worship them. lapsis. [Ed. Ba-

Imaginations touching the "breaking of bread ;" which is luz. p. 189.] joined to that "fellowship" as the chiefest badge of that III. Imagina-"fellowship." For by it is gathered the Communion, as tions may be gathered by conference with the twentieth chapter the of the Acts, the seventh verse, and as the Syrian text trans-"breaking of bread." lateth it. For that as by the other Sacrament in the verse immediately going before they are "received into the body of the Church," so by this they are made to "drink of the Spirit," and so perfected in the highest mystery of this 1 Cor. 12. society. 13.

Concerning which, as the Church of Rome hath her ima-ginations ; first, in that she many times celebrateth this mys-tery *sine fractione,* 'without any breaking' at all. Whereas, as heretofore hath been shewed out of the tenth chapter of the first of Corinthians, the eighteenth verse, it is of the nature of an Eucharist or peace-offering ; which was never [Comp. Levit. 3. 3; offered but it was eaten, that both there might be a repre-7. 15.] sentation of the memory of that sacrifice, and together an application to each person by partaking it. And secondly, in that she hath indeed no "breaking of bread" at all. For it being broken ever after it is consecrated, there is with

F 2

SERM.
II.

them no bread remaining to break; and the body of Christ
is now impassible, and cannot be broken; so that they are
fain to say they break accidents, and indeed they well know
not what.   Contrary to St. Luke here, who calleth it *frac-*
1 Cor. 10. *tionem panis,* and to St. Paul who saith, *Panis quem frangi-*
16.
mus.   As these are their imaginations, so we want not ours.
For many among us fancy only a Sacrament in this action,
and look strange at the mention of a sacrifice; whereas we
not only use it as a nourishment spiritual, as that it is too,
but as a mean also to renew a " covenant" with God by
Ps. 50. 5.   virtue of that " sacrifice," as the Psalmist speaketh.   So our
Saviour Christ in the institution telleth us, in the twenty-
second chapter of Luke and twentieth verse, and the Apostle,
in the thirteenth chapter of Hebrews and tenth verse.   And
the old writers use no less the word sacrifice than Sacrament,
altar than table, offer than eat; but both indifferently, to
shew there is both.

And again too, that to a many with us it is indeed so
fractio panis, as it is that only and nothing beside; whereas
1 Cor. 10.   the " bread which we break is the partaking of Christ's"
16.
true " body"—and not of a sign, figure, or remembrance of
it.   For the Church hath ever believed a true fruition of the
true body of Christ in that Sacrament.

Further, as heretofore hath been made plain, it is an ima-
Acts 2. 46.   gination to think that this " breaking of bread" can be
Isa. 58. 7.   severed from the other, which is Esay's breaking of " bread
to the needy."   Whereby as in the former Christ communi-
cateth Himself with us, so we in this latter communicate
ourselves with our poor brethren, that so there may be a
perfect communion.   For both in the sacrifice which was
Deut. 16.   the figure of it it was a matter of commandment, insomuch
10.
Lu. 21. 4.   as the poorest were not exempt from God's offerings; and
Joh. 13. 29.   our Saviour Christ's practice was, at this feast, to command
somewhat " to be given to the poor."   And last of all the
agapæ or love-feasts of the Christians for relief of the poor,
do most plainly express that I mean.   In place of which,
when they after proved inconvenient, succeeded the Christian offertory.

And lastly, whereas we continue in the doctrine and
prayers of the Church, we do many times discontinue this

action a whole year together. These long intermissions—so that if it be *panis annuus*, once a-year received, we think our duty discharged—are also, no doubt, a second imagination in our common practice. For sure we should continue also in this part and the frequenting of it, if not so often as the Primitive Church did—which either thrice in the week, or at the furthest once, did communicate—yet as often as the Church doth celebrate; which, I think, should do better to celebrate more often. And those exceptions which commonly we allege to disturb ourselves for that action, make us no less meet for prayers than for it. For except a man abandon Ps. 66. 18. the purpose of sin, and except he be in charity, he is no Mat. 6. 14, more fit to pray than to communicate, and therefore should ^{15.} abstain from the one as well as from the other; or, to say the truth, should by renewing himself in both these points, make himself meet for both, continuing no less in the "breaking of bread" than in "prayers" and "doctrine."

Imaginations touching "prayers." As the former was the IV. most special exercise of a Christian and chiefest in dignity, tions so this is the most general and chiefest in use. Therefore "prayers." he puts it in the plural number; as if both in preaching, censuring, and communicating, it had his use (as indeed it hath) "before all things," "in all things," after all things. 1 Tim. 2. 1. And in this also we want not fancies; in this age especially, 18. wherein an idle conceit is taken up that never came into Eph 6. 18. the heads of any of the old heretics (though never so brain-sick) once to imagine. Our Saviour Christ thus willeth us: "When ye pray, say, Our Father," &c. A most fond imagi- Lu. 11. 2. nation is started up in our times, never once dreamed of before, that telleth us in no case we must say "Our Father," &c., with which form, if St. Augustine be to be believed as Ep. 59. a witness of antiquity, the universal Church of Christ hath [al 149. ever used to begin and end all her prayers, as striving indeed Ep. 121. by divers other forms more largely to express the sense of 21, 22.] that prayer; but not being able to come near the high art and most excellent spirit of perfection in that pattern, they always conclude with it, as being sure, howsoever they may for divers defects not attain to the depth of it, and ¹by it [¹*perhaps* they shall be sure to beg all things necessary at God's hands. ^{that.}] This I named first because it is appropriate to our times.

Besides, as the Church of Rome hath her imaginations touching prayers; first, against St. Paul's *Orabo et mente*, in setting the people to pray they wot not what, and so making their "understanding unfruitful." And again, against our Saviour Christ's *caveat*, in setting them to go over whole rosaries and Psalters, as if much babbling after the heathen manner were acceptable to God. So likewise do others also among us err in their imaginations no less, and that even against the same places. First, against *Orabo spiritu*, in the same verse, by finding fault with a set Liturgy, which they call stinted prayers, and giving themselves to imagine prayers at the same instant; whereby, it is plain, they so occupy their minds with devising still what to say next, their spirit is "unfruitful," no less than the others' "understanding;" and both these, 1. the understanding of the mind, 2. and the affection of the spirit, are there necessarily required. And again, that instead of rosaries and a number of prayers, they bring in the Pharisee's imagination of "long prayers," that is, a prayer as long as a whole rosary. And this they take to be a great part of holiness, but indeed it is nothing but the former superstition drawn in backward. In which whoso marks them, shall find they commit both faults : that of the Pharisee, in tedious length, procuring many times *nauseam spiritûs*, a dangerous passion ; and the other of the heathen, in fond repetitions, tautologies, inconsequences, and all the absurdities that may fall into such manner of speech. St. Cyprian saith, It was ever in Christ's Church counted an absurd thing, which some count their glory, *ventilare preces inconditis vocibus*. The absurdity whereof would better appear if—seeing under prayers here Psalms and spiritual songs are contained, both being parts of invocation—they would have no stinted Psalms, but conceive their songs too upon the present out of the spirit, and so sing them. For to say truth, there is no more reason for the one than for the other. But God's Church hath ever had, as a form of doctrine, both of faith in the Creed, and of life in the Decalogue, so of prayer too. Which, from the thirteenth chapter of Acts, the second verse, the Fathers in all ages have called a Liturgy or service of God.

These are of many imaginations, some set up and magni-

1 Cor. 14.
14.

Mat. 6. 7.

1 Cor. 14.
15.

Mat 23. 14.

[De Orat.
Domin.
init.]

fied by some, and by others adored and worshipped, under the names of the 1. Apostles' Doctrine, 2. Government, 3. Sacraments, and 4. Prayers.

St. Stephen telleth us, out of the fifth of Amos, that if we [Amos 5. do thus make to ourselves tabernacles and figures to worship ^{25, 26, 27.]} them, our punishment shall be " to be carried away beyond Acts 7. 43. Babylon." And good reason, for these idle fancies are not from Christ's Church, from Sion, but from Babylon they came, and if we delight in them thither shall we be carried.

And sure we are in a good way thitherward, for of Babel St. Augustine saith, *Civitas illa confusionis indifferenter ha-* De Civit. *buit philosophos inter se diversa et adversa sentientes ;* 'In ^{Dei. 18.} ^[51.] God's city it was never so, there was ever correction for coiners, but in Babel, the city of confusion, every philosopher might set up, as now every sect-master may broach any imagination that taketh him in the head without punishment. For in Babel it is reckoned but an indifferent matter.' Sure the Prophets tell us that if Babylon's confusion go thus before, the captivity of Babylon is not far behind. From which Almighty God deliver us, and make us careful, as to continue " the Apostles' doctrine," &c., so neither to engrave nor to bow down and worship any of these imaginations. Amen.

ONE OF THE SERMONS

UPON THE

THIRD COMMANDMENT,

PREACHED IN THE

PARISH CHURCH OF ST. GILES, CRIPPLEGATE,

ON THE ELEVENTH OF JUNE, A.D. MDXCII.

JEREMIAH iv. 2.

And thou shalt swear, The Lord liveth, in truth, in judgment, and in righteousness.

Et jurabis, Vivit Dominus, in veritate, et in judicio, et in justitiâ.
Lat. Vulg.

[*And thou shalt swear, The Lord liveth, in truth, in judgment, and in righteousness.* Eng. Trans.]

SERM.
III.

OF this commandment there are two main propositions: 1. Thou shalt take "the name of God"—else it should have been, Thou shalt not take it at all; 2. Thou shalt take it orderly, and not "in vain." Of the first : Thou shalt take it to those ends and uses to which God lendeth it. Of which one is "Thou shalt swear by it;" which is limited by two ways.

First, by what : "The Lord liveth."

Secondly, how : "In truth, judgment, justice." As in the former Commandments so in this, there be two extremes. 1. The one of the Anabaptists, which hold all swearing unlawful, contrary to the first, "Thou shalt swear." 2. The other of the licentious Christian, which holds, at least in practice, A man may swear how and in what sort he list : by creatures, &c. contrary to "The Lord liveth," &c. falsely, rashly, lewdly ; contrary to "In truth, judgment, justice."

That it is lawful to swear, it appeareth by the Law, Deuteronomy the sixth chapter, and thirteenth verse: by the Prophets—Jeremy here. Esay more earnestly: "I have sworn by Myself, the word is gone out of My mouth and shall not return, That every knee shall bow to Me, and every tongue shall swear by Me." David: *Laudabuntur omnes, qui jurant per Eum.* By the practice of the saints not only under Moses, but under the law of nature. Abraham sweareth, Isaac sweareth, Jacob sweareth. Now our Saviour Christ came "not to destroy the law and the Prophets" in those things wherein they agree with the law of nature: therefore, not to take away an oath. I. "Thou shalt swear." Isa. 45. 23.
Ps. 63. 11.
Gen. 21. 24.
Gen. 26. 31.
Gen. 31. 53.
[Mat. 5.
17.]

Whereas they object first, that it standeth not with Christian profession, but was tolerated as an imperfect thing under the law:

We answer, it cannot be reckoned an imperfection to swear. For that not only Abraham, the pattern of human perfection, both sware himself and put his servant to an oath, but even the Angels, nearer than we to perfection, "sware" both under the law, and under the Gospel. And not only they, but even God Himself in Whom are all perfections, so that it cannot be imagined an imperfection. Gen. 21. 24.
Gen. 24. 3.
Dan. 12. 7.
Rev. 10. 6.
Gen. 22. 16.
Ps. 110. 4.

Besides, the holy Apostles, the most perfect Christians have in urgent causes done the like: "I call God for a record against mine own soul;" and, "By our rejoicing which I have in Christ Jesus our Lord;" which place cannot be avoided, having in the Greek the word *Nὴ* never used but in an oath only. 2 Cor. 1. 23.
1 Cor. 15.
31.
[S. Aug.
Serm.
180. 5.]

Whereas secondly they object our Saviour's saying, "I say unto you, Swear not at all," the ancient writers answer, that our Saviour Christ in the very same place, not reproving the other part, *Reddes autem Domino juramenta tua,* meant not to take all oaths away, but must be understood according to the Pharisees' erroneous gloss of this commandment, which He intendeth to overthrow by opposing to *Dictum est antiquis, Ego autem dico;* which was of two sorts: 1. for first, it seemeth they understood it of perjury alone; so that if a man forsware not himself, he might swear any oath. And so Christ reproveth not only false, but all rash and unadvised swearing. [Mat 5.
34, 33.]

S E R M.
III.

2. Secondly, it seemeth they had this conceit: so a man sware not by the great name of God all was well, he might swear by any creature at his pleasure; and so Christ willeth not to swear at all by any creature.

Though indeed we hold in divinity that *jurare* of and by itself considered is an act forbidden no less than *occidere*, and that as it is an absolute countermand, *Non occides*, and yet the magistrate by due course of justice executing a malefactor is commended, so is it likewise, *Non jurabis ;* and yet Ps. 63. 11. being, as we term it, *vestitum debitis circumstantiis, Laudabuntur omnes qui jurant per Eum,* as King David saith.

Lastly, there is also a bar in the word *jurare.* For God in His law, ever putting it passively, that is rather, Thou shalt be sworn, or called to an oath, than Thou shalt swear, actively ; our Saviour Christ here utterly condemneth the active voluntary swearing of men of their own heads, which was indeed never permitted, howsoever the Pharisees glossed the matter if the matter were true and so it were by Jehovah.

So that an oath is lawful ; but with this condition limited, [Vid.
S. Aug.
Serm. 180.
10.] that the party do therein *habere se passive,* come to it not of his own accord, but pressed, as St. Augustine well saith, *vel authoritate deferentis, vel duritie non credentis,* as to the lift- Num. 30.
2, 3. ing of a burden, as to the entering of " a bond."

1. Limita-
tion. " Thou shalt swear, The Lord liveth ;" or, as Moses saith, " The Lord
liveth."
Deut. 6. 13.
Jer. 5. 7.
Exod. 23.
13. Josh.
23. 7.
Amos 8, 14.
Zeph. 1. 5.
Mat. 5. 34–
36. by " God's Name." Which clause first doth limit by what we are to swear, and doth exclude 1. swearing by those which are " no gods ;" either idols forbidden in the law, (either to swear by them alone, or to join God and them together) 2. or creatures, which our Saviour Christ forbiddeth.

And sure, as to swear by them is derogatory to ourselves, seeing thereby we make them our betters, for that every one Heb. 6. 16. that sweareth " sweareth by a greater than himself ;" so it is highly injurious to the Majesty of God, seeing to swear by a creature is to ascribe unto it power to see and know all things, and to do vengeance on perjury : which in divinity to think or say, is manifest blasphemy.

Howbeit yet the Fathers—well weighing that speech of 1 Cor. 15.
31. St. Paul's, where he speaketh on this wise, " By our rejoicing which we have in Christ Jesus our Lord," &c. wherein

his oath is not immediately by the name of God, but by a secondary thing issuing from it—have thought it not absolutely necessary that in every oath the name of God should be expressly mentioned, but sufficient if *reductive*. It is ruled in divinity that such things as presently are reduced to God will bear an oath. In which respect, to swear by the Holy Gospel, considering our rejoicing will bear an oath, and that in the Gospel our matter of rejoicing is principally contained, hath in the Primitive Church been holden lawful. As in the Council of Constantinople. Especially seeing there is no direct contestation used, but rather by way of oppignoration, engaging unto God our salvation, faith, rejoicing, part in His Gospel and promises, the contents, &c. if we utter an untruth. [Con. Const. III. Lab. Tom. 11. Col. 578. E l. Florent. 1765.]

Secondly, the form and manner of swearing. Which is of three sorts: 1. Either by contestation as here, "The Lord liveth," "Before God," or, "God knoweth" it is so, "God is my witness." 2. Or by a more earnest asseveration; "As sure as God liveth." 3. Or by detestation and execration, as in other places. And that again is of two sorts: 1. by imprecation of evil; "God be my Judge," "God behold it and rebuke it," "God do so and so unto me," "I call God a record against my soul." 2. Or by oppignoration or engaging of some good which we would not lose: as, "Our rejoicing in Christ," our salvation, God's help, &c. II. The manner, or second limitation. Gal. 1. 20. 2 Cor. 11. 11. 1 Thes 2. 5. Judg. 8. 19. Gen. 31. 53. 1 Chron. 12. 17. 1 Sam. 14. 44. 2 Cor. 1. 23. 1 Cor. 15. 31.

Both are oft and may be joined together, if it be thought meet. "God is my witness" that thus it is, and "God be my Judge" if thus it be not. Wherein as in prayer when all means fail, we acknowledge that God can help as well without as with second causes, so we confess that He can discover our truth and falsehood, and can punish the same by ways and means to Him known, though no creature in the world beside know the thing or can take hold of us.

"Thou shalt swear, in truth, judgment, justice." The three enclosures and companions of a Christian oath are

In { Truth / Judgment / Justice } against { Falsehood / Lightness / Unlawfulness } the { matter. / matter and manner both. / end. }

"In truth:" "Ye shall not swear by My name falsely." 1. In truth. Levit. 19. 12.

S E R M. Which vice forbidden we call perjury. Each action, we say,
III.

——— is to light *super debitam materiam*. The due and own matter
of swearing is a truth. If it fall or light *super indebitam ma-*
teriam, as falsehood, it proveth a sin.

Eph. 4. 25. At all times are we bound "to speak truth to our neighbour;" but because men are naturally given to have their

Ps. 144. 11. "mouth" fraught with "vanity," in solemn matters to be
sure to bring the truth from us God is set before us. If

Josh. 7. 19. then when we confess the truth we "give glory to God,"
so if when God being set before us we testify an untruth,
it is exceeding contumelious to Him; it is to make Him
one that knoweth not all things, or that can be deceived,
or that if He know cannot do any harm, or, which is worst,
which will willingly be used to bolster out our lies. *Peje-*
rare est dicere Deo, Descende de Cælo, et assere mecum men-
dacium hoc.

1. Of Pro-   In an oath of promise, we are to swear "in truth." "He
mise.
Num. 30. 2. that sweareth an oath, and by it bindeth his soul with a bond,
shall not violate his word, but do according to all that proceedeth out of his mouth:" *Reddes autem Domino juramenta.*

Mat. 5. 33. Yea, by the very light of nature Pharaoh willeth Joseph,
[Gen. 50. "Go and bury thy father, seeing he made thee swear to do
6.]
so." Against which oath men are two ways faulty: 1. if at

Ps. 119. 106. the swearing, they purpose not, as David saith, "I have
sworn and am utterly purposed"—such is the nature of an
oath; 2. if they then purpose, but after a damage being

Ps. 15. 4. likely to ensue, they disappoint their former oath. Touching which we see that when Joshua and the Israelites had

[Jud. 9.   sworn to the men of Gibeon, though that oath cost them
3, &c.]
four great and fair cities, which should otherwise have come
to their possession, they would not break through. As con-

2 Chron.   trariwise, Zedekias having given his oath of allegiance to the
3.. 13.
King of Babylon, when he regarded it not but rose against

Ezek. 17. him notwithstanding, God sendeth him word, "he shall
15.
never prosper for so doing." And to say truth, there is
nothing more forcible to move us herein, than to consider

Ps. 110. 4. God's own practice; Who having "sworn" for our benefit,
though by many our unkindnesses and hard usages pro-

Ps. 89. 34. voked, yet, as Himself saith, "will not break His covenant,
nor alter the thing that is gone out of His lips." Which

is it that keepeth us all from perishing; even the immutable truth of God's oath, that we the rather may take it to imitation.

In an oath of proof, the charge ought to be that we speak "nothing but that which is true in the name of the Lord." That "we say the truth and lie not, our consciences bearing us witness in the Holy Ghost;" which if we do not being charged by a judge, we "bear" our own "iniquity." *2. Of Proof. 1 Kings 22. 16. Rom. 9. 1. Levit. 5. 1.*

Against which oath men are two ways faulty : 1. if either they swear to that which they know to be false; as if a man find and deny it, "swearing falsely." 2. Or if they presume to swear directly in a matter wherein themselves are doubtful, or have no sure ground of. As if a man swear, and "the thing be hid from him." *Levit. 6. 3. Levit. 5. 4.*

The breach of these two sorts of oaths, in regard of the truth, is called perjury, and both in old time and now we greatly complain of it in two places : 1. the one they call *Juramenta Officinarum,* when men in their shops, so they may utter to their gain, care not how untruly they abuse the name of God, men which, as the Wise Man saith, reckon our life "as a market," wherein they "must be getting on every side," though it be by evil means ; or, as the Apostle saith, that do in practice seem to hold that "gain is godliness;" for all the world as the profane man in the comedy, *juramentum rei servandæ non perdendæ conditum,* that 'oaths were made to thrive by.' Full little knew those men that whatsoever is gotten by false swearing, must by God's law both be restored in the whole sum, and add an overplus beside ; else no atonement can be made for them. And if that atonement be not made, that God by His Prophet hath denounced that their gain shall not prosper. For He will send the flying book into their house, a curse appropriate to those that both swear and steal—that is, steal by swearing—which shall consume both the goods, and the very stone, timber and all, of the house itself. *Wisd. 15. 12. 1 Tim. 6. 5. Levit. 6. 5. Zec. 5. 1—4.*

2. The other they call *Juramenta Tribunalium,* much more fearful and heinous than the former ; when a man—or rather as St. Augustine calleth him, *detestanda bellua,* no man, but 'a detestable beast'—shall so far presume as in "the judgment" itself which is God's, before the magistrates which are *2 Chron. 19. 8. Ps 82. 6. Eccl. 8. 2.*

"gods" to profane "the oath of God," even as it were to come into God's own place, and there to offer Him villainy to His face. A crime so grievous as no nation, were it never so barbarous, but have thought it severely to be punished; some with loss of tongue, some of fingers, some of ears, and some of life itself. And howsoever they escape man, the Prophet saith, the very book of the law which they have touched in testifying an untruth shall have wings given it, and shall pursue them, and cut them off on this side and on that side, till they and their name be rotted from the earth. It is a fearful thing to fall into God's hands on this wise; and of no one sin more dreadful examples. For it is indeed, *facere Deum mendacii consortem.* We hold it worse in divinity, to lay upon God that evil which we call *malum culpæ*, than the other which we term *malum pœnæ*, which hath been inflicted on many an innocent good man. Consequently a less evil to crucify Christ by any bodily pain than to draw Him into the society of sin, which every perjured person doth as much as in him lieth. Yea, we say that the name of God being fearful to the devils themselves, and bringing them to tremble, that that party that treadeth that most glorious and fearful name under his feet is in worse estate not only than the wickedest of men, the murderers of Christ, but even than the devil himself. And all this, that we conceive aright of *in veritate.*

2.
"In judgment."
Mat. 5. 20.

In judicio. For thus far the Pharisees themselves come, to think perjury condemned. But our "righteousness" is to "exceed" theirs, and therefore we must seek yet farther.

This clause, we say, standeth against a double vanity, 1. as well in matter, if for a vain, light, trifling matter we swear; 2. as in manner also, if with a vain, light, unadvised mind or affection. For both the matter is to be weighty, grave, and judicial, and we are with due advice and judgment to come to the action.

Against which judicial swearing we complain of two evil kinds: 1. the one *juramenta platearum*, such as going through the streets, a man shall every day hear—yea, even out of the mouths of children—light, undiscreet, frivolous oaths; 2. the other *juramenta popinarum*, much worse yet than they, when men in tabling-houses, at their game, blaspheme

the name of God most grievously; not content to swear by
Him whole, dismember Him and pluck Him in pieces, that
they may have oaths enough. And that Person of the Holy
Trinity, to Whom and to His Name, for taking our flesh
upon Him, and performing our redemption, even by God's
own charge, a special regard is due; and that action of His,
which among the rest is most venerable of all others, which
is His death, Passion, and shedding His blood.

For the matter. The very words of the Commandment 1. For the
teach us it is to be weighty, which speak of God's name ^{matter.}
as a thing to be lifted up with strength, as if it were heavy;
and we use not to remove things heavy but upon good
occasion.

The nature of an oath is as of a bond, which none that is
wise will easily enter; it is to be drawn from or pressed out
of a man, upon necessary cause. Yea it is no further good
than it is necessary. For so is our rule : *Necessarium extra
terminos necessitatis non est bonum* ; as, purging, blood-let-
ting, which are no longer good than needful. The name of
God is as a strong castle, which men fly not to but when
they have need. These shew that for every frivolous matter,
and of no importance, we are not vainly to take up God's Ps. 111. 9.
name. God's name is said to be " holy," and " holy things" Num. 18.
may not be put to common and vulgar uses. And in plain Levit. 22.
words, " Ye shall not pollute My Name." Polluting, by ^{32.}
God's own word, being nothing else but to make " common." Acts 10. 15.
Therefore they to be condemned that, no man urging them,
upon no sufficient ground make it common.

For the manner, with great " regard ;" we must swear to 2. For the
the Lord with all our heart. They are highly praised that Eccl. 8. 2.
did so; that is, when they are to take an oath, they are 2 Chron.
to call together the powers of their soul, and with sad and 15. 15.
serious deliberation to undertake it; that is, to do it *in
judicio*. Therefore in the law, God maketh it the entry,
" Thou shalt fear the Lord thy God, and shalt swear by [Deut. 6.
His Name ;" that is, with due fear and reverence thou shalt ^{13.]}
swear. For, as God's name is " holy," not for every common
matter ; so is it also "reverend," not with an unregarding [Ps. 111.
affection to be taken in our mouths. 9.]

To this end is it that the Church of God excludeth such

persons from oaths as are presumed that in "judgment" they cannot or will take them : as persons already convict of perjury, that they will not; those that are under years, that they cannot. To this end also there have ever been used ceremonies, that by that means there might be a reverend regard stricken into the mind of the swearer. Therefore the very Angels, when they swear, do it not without ceremony, but with lifting up their hands "to Heaven." The Patriarchs, under the law of nature, not without ceremony, but laying their "hand" on "the thigh," therein have reference to the incarnation of the blessed Seed. The people of God under the law came into the temple, and before "the altar," and in the presence of the priest, uncovered, so took their oath; all these serving to stir up their reverence, that what they did they might do in "judgment."

Therefore, they are to be condemned that passionately swear—which passion always bereaveth men of judgment— either in anger as David, which "he repented of," or in desire as Saul, which proved prejudicial to him and his people. And they, that as not of any passion, so without all manner of respect, to avow any idle fond fancy of their own, even as it were water, pour out the name of God.

And they yet more that not only unadvisedly sometimes, but continually as it were by a custom make it an interjection of filling for all their speeches, and cannot utter one sentence without it; yea, which thereby come to a *diabetica passio* of swearing, that oaths run from them and they feel them not.

But above all they that are come to that pitch, that even in contempt they swear, and will swear, and the rather because they be told of it. These persons the Church of God hath so detested, that they are excommunicate without sentence of any judge or canon, and Christian people forbidden to have any fellowship with them.

In justitiâ. As the matter of the oath is to be true and weighty, and the manner with due advice and "judgment," so is it to be taken also to a good and just end. And of this there is to be had chief regard, for that divers times both false and rash oaths are not hurtful save to the swearer only.

Dan. 12. 7.
Rev. 10. 5.
Gen. 24. 2,
3; 47. 29.
1 Kings 8.
31.
Deut. 12. 8.
Num. 5. 18,
19.

Eccl. 5. 4, 5.
1 Sam. 25.
32, &c.
1 Sam. 14.
28

I.
"In justice."

But these tend alway to some mischief beside the sin of the swearing.

An oath is of the nature of a bond, and bindeth a man to do what he sweareth. Now it is sin enough to do evil of itself, but to bind himself to do evil, and to make the name of God the bond, that is sin out of measure sinful. God hath ordained that only for truth and right His name should be used: to abuse it, to uphold falsehood, and to enforce men to evil dealing, is to change a sanctuary and to make it a brothel house. These we call *latronum juramenta,* such oaths as thieves and such kind of persons take one of another; for they do not only "join hand in hand," as Solo- Prov.11.21. mon telleth us, but do also by oath bind themselves to do mischief. Tobiah the special hinderer of the temple had "many in Judah" his "sworn" men. Neh. 6. 18.

That an oath may be "in justice," it is required that it be I. Not of of a thing possible. No man ever required an oath to an impossi- impossibility apparent. So Abraham's servant saith, "What ble. Gen. 24. if I cannot possibly get any maiden to come with me?" 5. 8. Abraham's answer is, then "he shall be free from the oath." So that if at the present it seem possible—otherwise not to be sworn to—and after there do *emergere impossibile,* the party is innocent. The same is observed touching our know-ledge, for so the law saith: A man shall testify that only Levit. 5. 1. which he hath seen, heard or known, and more shall not be required of him. So the law of nature, only *de quibus sciam poteroque.*

Now because as Joseph well telleth us that we only "can [2.] do" that which lawfully we can, and Christian possibility fulne-s. implieth lawfulness, that is the second point of *injustitia,* Gen. 39. 9. and the second caveat, *Ne illicitum;* which is either *primâ* 1 Sam. 28. *facie,* as Saul's oath, or it is likewise *emergens,* as in Herod's [Mar. 6. oath, at the first no harm being understood, but after the 23.] demand made it was sin to keep it. So saith Ezra in the Ezra 10. 5. law, *Secundum Legem fiat,* and St. Paul in the Gospel. They Acts 23. 3. sit to judge *secundum id quod in Lege est.*

Put these together, that we be required to swear nothing but the truth, *in veritate;* that we do it upon due advice and consideration, *in judicio;* that we do it but of those things we know and can tell, and of those whereto law bind-

G

eth us; there is no more required in a Christian oath. This

to be remembered, because divers which will be accounted

Christians refuse in our days the oath which hath all her

attendants. If the magistrate, either civil or ecclesiastical*.
1. Either by a curse, where the party is not known, 2. or by
tendering an oath, and that again double: 1. either by way
of adjuration, 2. or by way of swearing them. Where the
party is accused by complaint, detection, presumption, common fame, he is bound to purge himself, and satisfy the people, in adultery, theft, or any crime.

But what if it tend to his damage, or to the prejudice of
his liberty? Our rule is, *Qui potest ad pœnam, potest ad quæ
pœna consequitur.* Therefore in a matter of life and limb we
admit not the oath, because no man can lawfully swear to
cast away or maim himself. But a man may directly swear
to his loss in his goods, and to become a prisoner, as Shimei
did. Therefore swear, and be sworn in those causes and
questions whereto law doth bind to give answer, though fine
and commitment do ensue upon them.

This question remaineth, If a man have sworn without
those, what he is to do? when an oath binds, when it doth
not?

We hold, no man is so straitened between two sins,
but without committing a third he may get forth. Herod
thought he could not; and therefore being in a strait betwixt murder and perjury, thought he could have no issue
but by putting St. John Baptist to death. It was not so;
for having sworn, and his oath proving unlawful, if he had
repented him of his unadvisedness in swearing, and gone no
further, he had had his issue without any new offence.

1. If then we have sworn to be simply evil, the rule is, *Ne
sit sacramentum pietatis vinculum iniquitatis.*

2. If it hinder a greater or higher good, the rule is, *Ne sit
sacramentum pietatis impedimentum pietatis.*

3. If it be in things indifferent, as we term them, *absque
grano salis,* it is a rash oath, to be repented not to be executed.

4. If the oath be simply made, yet, as we say, it doth
subjacere civili intellectui; so as God's oath doth, and there-

fore those conditions may exclude the event, and the oath remain good.

5. If in regard of the manner it be extorted from us, the rule is, *Injusta vincula rumpit justitia.*

6. If rashly, *Pœnitenda promissio, non perficienda præsumptio.*

7. If to any man for his benefit or for favour to him, if that party release it it bindeth not.

A SERMON

PREACHED AT WHITEHALL,

UPON THE SUNDAY AFTER EASTER, BEING THE THIRTIETH OF MARCH, A.D. MDC.

JOHN xx. 23.

Whosesoever sins ye remit, they are remitted unto them ; and whosesoever ye retain, they are retained. The Conclusion of the Gospel for the Sunday.

Quorum remiseritis peccata, remittuntur eis; et quorum retinueritis, retenta sunt. Lat. Vulg.

[*Whosesoever sins ye remit, they are remitted unto them ; and whosesoever sins ye retain, they are retained.* Eng. Trans.]

SERM.
IV.

THEY be the words of our Saviour Christ to His Apostles ; a part of the first words which He spake to them at His Epiphany, or first apparition after He arose from the dead. And they contain a commission by Him granted to the Apostles, which is the sum or contents of this verse.

Which commission is His first largess after His rising again. For at His first appearing to them it pleased Him not to come empty but with a blessing, and to bestow on them and on the world by them, as the first fruits of His resurrection, this commission ; a part of that commission which the sinful world most of all stood in need of, for remission of sins.

The summary proceeding in it.
[Joh. 20. 21.]

To the granting whereof He proceedeth not without some solemnity or circumstance, well worthy to be remembered.

For first, verse the twenty-first, He saith, "As My Father sent Me, so send I you ;" which is their authorizing, or giving them their credence.

Secondly, verse the twenty-second, He doth breathe upon [Joh. 20. them, and withal inspireth them with the Holy Ghost; which 22.] is their enabling or furnishing thereto.

And having so authorized and enabled them, now in this verse here He giveth them their commission, and thereby doth perfectly inaugurate them in this part of their office.

A commission is nothing else but the imparting of a power which before they had not. First therefore He imparteth to them a power, a power over sins; over sins, either for the remitting or the retaining of them, as the persons shall be qualified.

And after, to this power He addeth a promise (as the lawyers term it) of ratihabition, that He will ratify and make it good, that His power shall accompany this power, and the lawful use of it in His Church for ever.

And very agreeably is this power now bestowed by Him The de-pendence upon His resurrection. Not so conveniently before His death, in respect because till then " He had not made His soul an offering for of the time. sin;" nor till then He had not shed His "blood, without Why not before? which there is no remission of sins." Therefore it was Isa. 53. 10. Heb. 9. 22. promised before but not given till now, because it was con- Mat. 16. 19; venient there should be *solutio* before there was *absolutio.* 18. 18. Not before He was risen then.

And again, no longer than till He was risen, not till He was ascended. First, to shew that the remission of sins is Why now? the undivided and immediate effect of His death. Secondly, to shew how much the world needed it, for which cause He would not withhold it, no not so much as one day—for this was done in the very day of His resurrection. Thirdly, but especially, to set forth His great love and tender care over us, in this, that as soon as He had accomplished His own resur-rection, even presently upon it, He sets in hand with ours, and beginneth the first part of it the very first day of His rising.

The Scripture maketh mention of a first and second death, and from them two of a first and second resurrection. Both expressly set down in one verse : " Happy is he that hath Rev. 20. 6. his part in the first resurrection, for over such the second death hath no power." Understanding by the first the death of the soul by sin, and the rising thence to the life of grace; by the second the death of the body by corruption, and the rising thence to the life of glory.

Christ truly is the Saviour of the whole man, both soul and body, from the first and second death.

But beginning first with the first, that is with sin, the death of the soul and the rising from it. So is the method Mat. 23. 26. of Divinity prescribed by Himself: first, to cleanse that which is within—the soul; then that which is without— the body. And so is the method of physic, first to cure the cause, and then the disease. Now the cause or, as the 1 Cor. 15. Apostle calleth it, "the sting of death, is sin." Therefore 56. first to remove sin, and then death afterwards. For the cure of sin being performed, the other will follow of his [Rev. 20. own accord. As St. John telleth us, "He that hath his 6.] part in the first resurrection," shall not fail of it "in the second." The "first resurrection" then from sin is it which our Saviour Christ here goeth about, whereto there is no less power required than a divine power. For look what power is necessary to raise the dead body out of the dust, the very same every way is requisite to raise the dead soul out of sin. For which cause the remission of sins is an article of faith, no less than the resurrection of the body. For in very deed a resurrection it is, and so it is termed no less than that.

To the service and ministry of which divine work a commission is here granted to the Apostles. And first, they have here their sending from God the Father, their inspiring from God the Holy Ghost, their commission from God the Son; that being thus sent from the Father, by the power of the Holy Ghost, in the person of Christ, they may perform the office or, as the Apostle calleth it, the embassage of re-2 Cor. 5. 20. conciling sinners unto God, to which they are appointed. And so much for the sum and dependence of this Scripture.

The division. The points of special observation are three: 1. first, the power that is granted; 2. the matter or subject, whereon the power is to be exercised; 3. the promise of ratifying the exercise of that power.

I. The power itself: in which cometh first to be entreated, 1. what is meant by remitting and retaining; 2. after in general, that there is a power to "remit" and "retain," but first to "remit," and after to "retain;" 2. then in particular, of that power as it is set down in both words, *Remiseritis* and *Remittuntur.*

The matter or subject: which is also two ways to be con- II. sidered, either as it is sin in itself, which is the matter at large, or as it is the sin of some persons—for it is not *Quæ peccata* but *Quorum*—which is the immediate or proper matter of this power.

The ratifying or promise of concurrence, to assure the con- III. science of the sinner of the certainty and efficacy of the Church's act, that what the Apostles do in the person of Christ by the instinct of the Holy Ghost, He that sent them will certainly make good and effectual from heaven. And of these three in order.

The terms of remitting and retaining may be taken many I. ways. To the end then that we may the more clearly con- The terms ceive that which shall be said, it will be expedient that first under- of all we understand in what sense especially and according stood. to what resemblance those terms are to be taken.

This may we best do out of our Saviour Christ's own com- The origi- mission. For this of the Apostles' is nothing else but a Christ's branch out of His, which He Himself as man had here upon sion. earth. For as man He Himself was sent and was anointed with the Spirit, and proceeded by commission.

His commission we find in the fourth chapter of Luke, Lu. 4. 18. which He Himself read in the synagogue at Nazareth at Isa. 61. 1. His first entering on it; which is originally recorded in the sixty-first chapter of Isaiah. Wherein among others this power is one; to preach ἄφεσιν, that is, "remission," as it is turned here, or "deliverance," as it is turned there; but the word is one in both places, and that respectively to "captives;" and, as it followeth in that place of Esay, "to them that are bound the opening of the prison."

Which very term of "captives," or such as are in prison, Sin and doth open unto us with what reference or respect this term ment. of remitting, or letting go, is to be conceived. And as it was in His, so must it be understood here in this, since this is but derived from that of Christ's.

The mind of the Holy Ghost then, as in other places by divers other resemblances, so in this here, is to compare the sinner's case to the estate of a person imprisoned. And

SERM. indeed, whoso well weigheth the place, it cannot well be
IV.
—— taken otherwise. For not only here but elsewhere, where
this power is expressed, it seemeth ever to be with reference
Mat. 16. 19. as it were to parties committed. The very term of "the
keys"—wherein it was promised, and wherein it is most
usually delivered—the terms of opening and shutting, seem
to have relation as it were to the prison-gate. The terms
Mat. 18. 18. of binding and loosing, as it were, to the fetters or bands.
And these here of letting forth or still detaining, all and
every of them seem to have an evident relation to the
prisoner's estate, as if sin were a prison, and the case of
sinners like theirs that are shut up.

Verily, as sin at the first in committing seemeth sweet,
Job 20. 12, that men cannot be got to spit it out (saith Job) but hold it
13.
close under their tongues till they have swallowed it down;
but after it is committed, the sinner findeth then that it is
Jer. 2. 19. *malum et amarum dereliquisse Dominum*, saith the Prophet;
that it turneth to a bitter and choleric matter, of which
Isa. 66. 24. there breedeth "a worm" which never leaveth gnawing;
even so doth sin at the first also seem a matter of liberty.
For a liberty it is not to be restrained, not to be, as the
Gal. 3. 23. Apostle speaketh, committed to Moses, to be "kept and
Gen. 3. 2, shut up under the law;" not to be forbidden any "fruit,"
3.
under which very term the serpent did persuade it; but
when it was done and past, then shall a man feel a pinching
Rom. 2. 9. or straitness in his soul, termed by the Apostle στενοχωρία,
which properly signifieth the pain which they suffer that are
shut up in a narrow room or some place of little ease.
Prov. 5. 22.   So speaketh Solomon of sin: "His own wickedness shall
attach the sinner, and he shall be holden or pinioned with
the cords of his own sin. So St. Peter to Simon Magus:
Acts 8. 23. "I perceive thou art (to express the former resemblance) in
the gall of bitterness, and (to express the latter) in the bond
of iniquity." And St. Paul; that sinners instead of having
2 Tim. 2. 26. Moses to their keeper become the devil's captives, and are of
him holden and taken "at his will" and pleasure.

Truly some have felt as much as I speak of, and have in
Ps. 88. 8. pregnant terms complained of it. "I am so fast in prison,"
Ps. 142. 7.
Ps. 119. 32. saith David, "that I cannot get out." And, "Bring my
soul out of prison and I will praise Thee." And, "I will

run the way of Thy commandments, when Thou shalt set
my heart at liberty."

Peradventure all feel not this presently as soon as they
have sinned, nor it may be a good while after. So God told
Cain at the beginning: his "sin should lie at the door," Gen. 4. 7.
that is, while he kept within he should not be troubled
with it perhaps, but at his coming forth it should certainly
attach him. But, saith Moses, let every one that sinneth
be sure that "his sin" at last "will find him out;" for he Nu. 32. 23.
shall no sooner be under arrest of any trouble, sickness,
cross, or calamity, but he shall be shut into his στενοχωρία
and feel it presently. As the brethren of Joseph for very Gen. 42. 21.
many years after they had of envy and without all pity sold
him to be a bondservant seemed at liberty, no sooner fell
they into danger and displeasure in a strange country, but it
came to mind and they were served with it straightway. Even
as in Job it is said : The sins of our youth shall let us go up Job 20. 11.
and down quietly all our youth time, but when we come to
years we shall feel them pinch us in our very " bones."

Yea though many, even then when they feel this straitness in their soul make means to put it away for the time,
and seem merry and light enough, as many times prisoners
be in the gaol till the very day of the assizes come; yet
when it is come to that, that *judex est præ foribus,* when Jas. 5. 9.
the terror of death cometh, and with it " a fearful expect- Heb. 10. 27.
ation of judgment," then certainly, then without all doubt,
the "anguish" St. Paul speaketh of shall be "upon every [Rom. 2.
soul of every one that doeth evil." Then, there is no man 9.]
never so wicked, that with his good will would "die" in Joh. 8. 24.
his "sins," but would have them released while he is yet
in viâ, yet "in the way." Then we seek help at such Mat. 5. 25.
scriptures as this, and call for the persons to whom this
commission belongeth. And those whom we have gone by
seven years together and never said word to about it, then
we are content to speak with, when the counsel and direction they give we are scarce able to receive, and much
less to put in practice. As if all our lifetime we believed
the permission of sins, as if that were the article of our
faith all our life long, and the article of remission of sins
never till the point of death.

And this may serve shortly to set forth unto us this
prison of the soul; which if any conceive not by that
which hath been said, I must say with the Prophet to
Jer. 30. 24. them, that sure there is such a thing, and that *in novis-
simo intelligetis hæc plane*, "at their latter end (I wish before, but sure then) they shall very plainly understand that
such a thing there is."

Good tid-
ings that
there is
remission.
But now they that have either felt or believed that such
an imprisonment there is, will be glad to hear that there
is a power whereby they may be enlarged; and this very
tidings in general, that there is a *Remittuntur*, that men
may have deliverance from these fetters, this prison, this
straitness or anguish of the soul, must needs be very acceptable and welcome tidings to them. For which very
point, even that there is a *Remittuntur*, what thanks are
we eternally bound to render unto God! For I tell you,
Heb. 2. 16. *nusquam Angelos apprehendit*, "the Angels never found the
Jude ver. 6. like." For "the Angels, which kept not their first estate,
hath He reserved in everlasting chains of darkness to the
judgment of the great day." Their chains everlasting, their
imprisonment perpetual; no commission to be sued for them,
no *Remittuntur eis*. But with man it is not so. To him
deliverance, to him loosing of the chains, to him opening of
the prison is promised. For his sins a commission is granted
out, his sins have a *Remittuntur*. This is a high and special
privilege of our nature, to be had by us in an everlasting
thankful remembrance. So that no man needeth now
Jer. 18. 12. abruptly to say with those in Jeremiah, *Desperavimus*, "we
are desperate now," we never shall be forgiven, let us now
Ezra 10. 2. do what we list. No, but as it is said in Ezra, "Though
we have grievously sinned, yet there is hope for all that;"
Ezek. 18.
30.
and, as in Ezekiel, that we may so use the matter that *peccata nostra non erunt nobis in scandalum*, "our sins shall not
be our destruction." Which very point is both an especial
stay of our hope, and a principal means of manifesting unto
us the great goodness of God.

Remission
first before
retention.
Which goodness of God, as it doth shew forth itself in
this first, that such a power there is, so doth it secondly
and no less in the order, that—where both acts are mentioned, as well retaining as remitting—He placeth the power

of remitting first. Which very sorting of them in that order
doth plainly shew unto us whereunto God of His goodness
is most inclinable, and which of them it is that is the principal in His intent. That to "remit" is more proper to
Him, and that He is more ready to it, and that it is first;
first in His purpose, first in His grant; and that to the Isa. 28. 21.
other He cometh but secondarily, but by occasion, when
the former cannot take place. For of remitting sin He
taketh the ground from Himself and not from any other,
and therefore that more naturally; but of retaining it, the
cause is ministered from us, even from our hardness, and
heart that cannot repent. And as Himself doth use this
power, so giveth He it to them, "to edification and not to 2 Cor. 10. 8.
destruction." I say, not first or principally "to destruction," nor of any, save only of the wilful impenitent sinner.
Thus much of the remitting and retaining in general, and
of their place and order. Now of the power itself in particular.

Of this power there is here in my text twice mention; Of remis-
1. one in *Remiseritis*, and 2. again in *Remittuntur*. Which particular.
two words do plainly lead us to two acts, of which two acts The power
of it two-
by good consequence are inferred two powers. Which two fold.
powers, though they be concurrent to one end, yet are they
distinct in themselves. Distinct in person, for *Remiseritis* 1. *Re-*
is the second person, and meant of the Apostles, and *Remit-* 2. *Remit-*
tuntur is the third person, and meant of God Himself. And *tuntur.*
as distinct in person, so distinct in place : for the one is
exercised in earth, which is the Apostles'; the other in
heaven, which is God's. *Quicquid solveritis in terrâ, solu-* Mat. 16. 19.
tum erit in cœlo.

Now where two powers are, and one of them in God, the
other must needs be subordinate and derived from it. For
duo principia, 'two beginnings' there are not. Therefore
none other from whence it can proceed, but from God and
from the power in Him alone.

Of these two then. *Remittuntur,* though latter in place, 1.
yet indeed is by nature and order first, and from it doth *tuntur,*
proceed the other of *Remiseritis;* which, howsoever in the God's
sentence it stand before it, yet without all question it is de- first in
rived from it and after it. So that thus the case stands be-

S E R M.
IV. tween them : *Remittuntur,* which is God's power, is the primitive or original ; *Remiseritis,* which is the Apostles' power, is merely derived. That in God sovereign, this in the Apostles dependent. In Him only absolute, in them delegate. In Him imperial, in them ministerial.

The power of remitting sin is originally in God, and in God alone. And in Christ our Saviour, by means of the union of the Godhead and manhood into one person ; by virtue whereof " the Son of man hath power to forgive sins upon earth."

This power being thus solely invested in God He might without wrong to any have retained and kept to Himself, and without means of word or Sacrament, and without Ministers, either Apostles or others, have exercised immediately by Himself from heaven.

But we should then have said of the remission of sins, saith St. Paul : " Who shall go up to heaven for it, and fetch it thence ?" For which cause, saith he, " the righteousness of faith speaketh thus, Say not so in thy heart. The word shall be near thee, in thy mouth, and in thy heart, and this is the word of faith which we preach."

Partly this, that there should be no such difficulty to shake our faith, as once to imagine to fetch Christ from heaven for the remission of our sins.

Partly also, because Christ, to Whom alone this commission was originally granted, having ordained Himself a body, would work by bodily things ; and having taken the nature of man upon Him, would honour the nature He had so taken. For these causes, that which was His and His alone He vouchsafed to impart ; and out of His commission to grant a commission, and thereby to associate them to Himself—it is His own word by the Prophet—and to make them συνέργους, that is, *co-operatores,* " workers together with Him," as the Apostle speaketh, to the work of salvation both of themselves and of others.

From God then it is derived ; from God, and to men.

To men, and not to Angels. And this I take to be a second prerogative of our nature. That an Angel must give order to Cornelius to send to Joppa for one Simon, to speak words to him by which he and his household should

Marginal notes:
- Isa. 43. 25.
- Mark 2. 10.
- Rom. 10. 6.
- [Rom. 10. 8.]
- [Zech. 13. 7.]
- [1 Cor. 3. 9 ; 2 Cor. 6. 1.]
- 2. *Remiseritis.* God's power derived to men, and not to Angels.

be saved, but the Angel must not be the doer of it. That [Acts 10. 5, 6. 32.]
not to Angels, but to men, is committed this office or embassage of reconciliation. And that which is yet more, to To sinful men. sinful men, for so is the truth, and so themselves confess it.
St. Peter: "Go from me, Lord, for I am a sinful man." [Lu. 5. 8.]
St. James: "In many things we offend all;" putting himself in the number. And, lest we should think it to be but [Jas. 3. 2.]
their modesty, St. John speaketh plainly: "If we say we [1 Joh. 1. 8.]
have no sin"—what then? not, we are proud, and there is
no humility in us, but "we are liars, and there is no truth
in us." And this is that which is wonderful in this point,
that St. Paul who confesseth himself "a sinner" and "a 1 Tim.1.15.
chief sinner," *quorum primus ego;* the same concerning
another sinner, the incestuous Corinthian, "I forgive it
him," saith he, ἐν προσώπῳ τοῦ Χριστοῦ, "in the person 2 Cor. 2. 10.
of Christ."

Now if we ask to what men? the text is plain. They to To the Apostles. whom Christ said this *Remiseritis*, were the Apostles.

In the Apostles, that we may come nearer yet, we find
three capacities, as we may term them: 1. as Christians in
general; 2. as Preachers, Priests, or Ministers, more special;
3. as those twelve persons, whom in strict propriety of speech
we term the Apostles.

Some things that Christ spake to them, He spake to them
as representing the whole company of Christians, as His
Vigilate. Mark 13. 37.
Some things to them, not as Christians, but as preachers
or Priests; as His *Ite prædicate Evangelium,* and His *Hoc* Mat.28.19. *facite,* which no man thinketh all Christians may do. Lu. 22. 19.

And some things to themselves personally; as that He
had appointed them "witnesses" of His miracles and resur- Acts 1. 8.
rection, which cannot be applied but to them, and them in
person. It remaineth we enquire, in which of these three
capacities Christ imparteth to them this commission.

Not as to Apostles properly. That is, this was no personal
privilege to be in them and to die with them, that they
should only execute it for a time, and none ever after them.
God forbid we should so think it. For this power being
more than needful for the world, as in the beginning it was
said, it was not to be either personal or for a time. Then

those persons dying, and those times determining, they in the ages following, as we now in this, that should light into this prison or captivity of sin, how could they or we receive any benefit by it? Of nature it is said by the heathen philosopher, that it doth neither *abundare in superfluis,* nor *deficere in necessariis.* God forbid but we should ascribe as much to God at the least, that neither He would ordain a power superfluous or more than needed, or else it being needful would appropriate it unto one age, and leave all other destitute of it ; and not rather as all writers both new and old take it, continue it successively to the world's end.

And as not proper to the Apostles' persons, so neither common to all Christians in general, nor in the persons of all Christians conveyed to them. Which thing, the very Joh. 20. 21, circumstances of the text do evict. For He sent them first, 22. and after inspired them ; and after both these, gave them this commission. Now all Christians are not so sent, nor are all Christians inspired with the grace or gift of the Spirit that they were here. Consequently, it was not intended to the whole society of Christians. Yea I add, that forasmuch as these two, both these two, must go before it, 1. *Missio,* and 2. *Inspiratio,* that though God inspire some laymen, if I may have leave so to term them, with very special graces of knowledge to this end, yet inasmuch as they have not the former of sending, it agreeth not to them, neither may they exercise it until they be sent, that is, until they have their calling thereunto.

To them, as Ministers. It being then neither personal nor peculiar to them as Apostles, nor again common to all as Christians, it must needs be committed to them as Ministers, Priests, or Preachers, and consequently to those that in that office and function do succeed them, to whom and by whom this commission is still continued. Neither are they that are ordained or instituted to that calling, ordained or instituted by any other words or verse than this. Yet not so that absolutely without them God cannot bestow it on whom or when Him pleaseth, or that He is bound to this means only, and cannot work without it. For, *Gratia Dei non alligatur mediis,* ' the grace of God is not bound but free,' and can work without means either of word or Sacrament; and as without means, so without Ministers, how and when to Him seemeth good. But speaking of that which is proper and ordinary in the course by Him established, this is an Ecclesiastical act committed, as the residue of the ministry of reconciliation, to Ecclesiastical persons. And if at any time He vouchsafe it by others that are not such, they be in that case *Ministri necessitatis non officii,* 'in case of necessity Ministers, but by office not so.'

Now as by committing this power God doth not deprive or bereave Himself of it, for there is a *Remittuntur* still, and that chief, sovereign, and absolute; so on the other side where God proceedeth by the Church's act as ordinarily He doth, it being His own ordinance, there whosoever will be partaker of the Church's act must be partaker of it by the Apostles' means; there doth *Remiseritis* concur in his own order and place, and there runneth still a correspondence between both. There doth God associate His Ministers, and maketh them "workers together with Him." There have they their parts in this work, and cannot be excluded; no more in this than in the other acts and parts of their function. And to exclude them is, after a sort, to wring the keys out of their hands to whom Christ hath given them, is to cancel and make void this clause of *Remiseritis,* as if it were no part of the sentence; to account of all this solemn sending and inspiring, as if it were an idle and fruitless ceremony; which if it may not be admitted, then sure it is they have their part and concurrence in this work, as in the rest of " the ministry of reconciliation." *Of God's sovereign power still.*

Zech. 13. 7.
1 Cor. 3. 9.
[2 Cor. 6.
1.]

[2 Cor. 5.
18.]

Neither is this a new or strange thing; from the beginning it was so. Under the law of nature, saith Elihu in Job speaking of one for his sins in God's prison, " If there be with him an ambassador, commissioner, or interpreter"— not any whosoever, but—" one among a thousand to shew unto him his righteousness, then shall God have mercy upon him and say, Let him go, for I have received a propitiation." The act of the Church ordinary. Job 33. 23, 24.

Under Moses it is certain the " covenant of life and peace" was made with Levi, and at the sacrifices for sin he was ever a party. Mal. 2. 5. Levit. 4. 5, 6.

Under the Prophets. It pleased God to use this concurrence towards David himself, Nathan the Prophet saying

unto him, *Transtulit Dominus peccatum tuum.*

The ne-
cessity of
the Priest
therein.
[2 Cor. 5.
19.]
Which course so established by God till Christ should come—for neither covenant nor Priesthood was to endure any longer—was by Christ re-established anew in the Church, in that calling to whom He hath " committed the word of reconciliation." Neither are we, the ordinance of God thus standing, to rend off one part of the sentence. There are here expressed three persons : 1. the person of the sinner, in *quorum ;* 2. of God, in *Remittuntur ;* 3. of the Priest, in *Remiseritis.* Three are expressed, and where three are expressed three are required ; and where three are required,

two are not enough. It is St. Augustine that thus speaketh of this Ecclesiastical act in his time : *Nemo sibi dicat, Occulte ago pœnitentiam, apud Deum ago. Novit Deus qui mihi ignoscat, quia in corde ago. Ergo sine causá dictum est, Quæ solveritis in terrá, soluta erunt in cœlo ? ergo sine causá, Claves datæ sunt Ecclesiæ Dei ? Frustramus Evangelium Dei, Frustramus verba Christi ?*

Which may suffice for the distinguishing of these two powers, the deriving of the one from whom, and to whom the continuance and concurrence of them.

The remission of sins, as it is from God only, so is it by the death and blood-shedding of Christ alone ; but for the applying of this unto us, there are divers means esta-

blished. There is *multiformis gratia,* saith St. Peter, " variety of graces" whereof we are made the " disposers." Now all and every of these means working to the remission of sins which is the first and greatest benefit our Saviour Christ hath obtained for us, it resteth that we further enquire what that means is in particular which is here imparted.

For sure it is, that besides this there are divers acts instituted by God and executed by us, which all tend to the remission of sins.

1. In the institution of Baptism there is a power to that end. " Be baptized every one of you for the remission of

sins," saith St. Peter to three thousand at once. " Arise and

be baptized," saith Ananias to Paul, " and wash away thy sins." And to be short, I believe one baptism for the remission of sins, saith the Nicene Creed.

2. Again there is also another power for the remission of sins, in the institution of the holy Eucharist. The words are exceeding plain : " This is My blood of the New Testament for the remission of sins." 2. By the Eucharist. Mat. 26. 28.

3. Besides, in the word itself there is a like power ordained. " Now are you clean," saith Christ, no doubt from their sins, *propter sermonem hunc.* And the very name giveth as much, that is entitled, " The word of reconciliation." 3. By preaching. Joh. 15. 3. 2 Cor. 5. 19.

4. Further, there is to the same effect a power in prayer, and that in the priest's prayer. " Call for the priests," saith the Apostle, " and let them pray for the sick person, and if he have committed sin it shall be forgiven him." 4. ¹ y prayer. Jas. 5. 14.

All and every of these are acts for the remission of sins ; and in all and every of these is the person of the minister required, and they cannot be despatched without him.

But the ceremonies and circumstances that here I find used, prevail with me to think that there is somewhat here imparted to them that was not before. For it carrieth no likelihood, that our Saviour bestowing on them nothing here but that which before He had, would use so much solemnity, so diverse and new circumstances, no new or diverse grace being here communicated. None of these meant here.

1. Now for Baptism, it appeareth plainly that the Apostles baptized in a manner from the beginning, which I make no question they did not without a commission. Joh. 4. 2.

2. And for the power of administering the holy Sacrament, it was granted expressly to them by *Hoc facite* before His passion. Lu. 22. 19.

3. The like may we say of the power of preaching, which was given them long before, even when He sent them, and commanded them to preach the kingdom of God, which was done before this power was promised which here is bestowed ; as will evidently appear, the one being given, (Mat. 10. 7.) the other after promised, (Mat. 16. 19.) Mat. 10. 7. Lu. 9. 2.

4. Neither can it be meant of prayer. There is no partition in prayer : " Prayers and supplications are to be made for all men." But here is a plain partition. There is a *quorum* whose sins are remitted, and another *quorum* whose sins are retained. 1 Tim. 2. 1.

Seeing then this new ceremony and solemn manner of But the power of Absolution.

SERM.
IV.
proceeding in this are able to persuade any, it was some
new power that here was conferred, and not those which
before had been, (though there be that apply this, others
to some one, and others to all of them,) I take it to be a
power distinct from the former, and, not to hold you long,
to be the accomplishment of the promise made, of the power

Mat. 16. 19. of "the keys," which here in this place and in these words
is fulfilled, and have therein for me the joint consent of the
Fathers. Which being a different power in itself, is that
which we all call the act or benefit of absolution, in which,
as in the rest, there is in the due time and place of it a use

Joh. 20. 21, for the remission of sins. Whereunto our Saviour Christ,
22.
by His sending them, doth institute them and give them
the key of authority; and by breathing on them and inspiring them doth enable them, and give them the key of
knowledge to do it well; and having bestowed both these
upon them as the stewards of His house, doth last of all
deliver them their commission to do it, having so enabled
them and authorized them as before. So much for the
power.

II.
*Quorum
peccata.*
The sub-
ject of
this power.
Every power is not everywhere to be exercised, not upon
every matter, but each power hath his proper subject.

The matter or subject whereon this power is to be exercised, is sin: to be considered first in itself, as the matter
at large; and then, as qualified with the person, (for it is
quorum, and not *quæ peccata*) as the nearer and more proper
subject.

Peccata,
at large.
First then, the subject are sins—sins in themselves, no
ways restrained or limited; no sins at all, either for number
or greatness, being excepted.

Without
exception
of number.
Mat. 18. 22.
Not for number. For Christ teaching us that we ourselves should forgive until "seventy times seven times," doth
thereby after a sort give us to understand that He will not
stick with us for the like number in ours. For God forbid
we should imagine He taught us to be more merciful or of
greater perfection than He will be Himself. That number
amounteth to ten jubilees of pardon; for so many sins may we
then hope for pardon at His hands. If those be not enough,

Ps. 40. 12.
Orat. Ma-
nas.
we have example of one whose sins were "more in number
than the hairs of his head," and of another whose were more

" than the sands of the sea ;" both which give us hope, for
they both obtained pardon.

But that which followeth in the place of Matthew, maketh Or great-
both parts plain. For there a debt is remitted not only of ness.
" five hundred " but of " ten thousand," and those—not as Mat. 18. 24.
in Luke " pence," but—" talents ;" a great and huge sum, Lu. 7. 41.
yet for that hath He remission in store. So that no man
shall need to say his " sin is greater than can be remitted," Gen. 4. 13.
as Cain did, since that assertion is convinced to be errone- [Vulg.]
ous ; for his sin may be forgiven that slew Abel though his
brother, seeing St. Peter saith that theirs was not greater Acts 31. 15,
than might be forgiven that slew the Son of God. For no 19.
man but will conceive that the betraying and murdering
Jesus Christ was far a more heinous offence than that of
Abel's killing: but that might, saith St. Peter ; therefore
this much more may be forgiven. And, to end this point,
whereas it is affirmed, and that most truly, by the Apostle, 1 Cor. 1. 25.
that " the weakness of God is stronger than men," if there
were any sin greater than could be remitted, the weakness
of man—for of that cometh sin—should be stronger than
God ; which neither religion nor reason will admit. In respect of the sin itself therefore, there is no exception.

But because it is not *quæ peccata,* but *quorum,* it sheweth Quorum,
that in the act of remission we are to respect not the sin The proper imme-
so much as the person. So that, though all sins may be d ate subject.
remitted, yet not to all persons, but to a *quorum,* as we
see. For there is another *quorum* whose sins are retained ;
so that this limiteth the former, and sheweth indeed what
is the *materia propinqua,* or ' immediate subject ' of this
power committed.

Our Saviour Christ Himself at the reading of His commission, whereof this is a branch, in effect expresseth as
much. For He telleth them, " There were many lepers in
the days of Elisha, and many widows in the days of Elias ; Lu. 4. 18.
25—27.
yet none cleansed but Naaman, nor to none was Elias sent,
but to the widow of Sarepta." And so the case standeth
here. Many sinners there be, and many sins may be remitted, but not to any, except they be of this *quorum.* In
which point there is a special use of " the key of know- [Lu. 11.
52.]
ledge," to direct to whom, and to whom not ; since it is

SERM. not but with advice to be applied, nor "hands hastily to
IV.
————— be laid on any man," as the Apostle testifieth; which place
1 Tim. 5. 22.
Cypr. 3. 16. is referred by the ancient writers to the act of absolution,
[Epist.]
Pacian. in and the circumstance of the place giveth no less. But
Paræn. 16. discretion is to be used in applying of comfort, counsel,
[circ.
med.] and the benefit of absolution. Whereby it falleth out
Aug. de
Bapt. 5. 20, sometimes, that the very same sins to some may be re-
23. [Vid.
Ham- mitted, being of the *quorum*, that to some others may not,
mond. in
loc.] that are out of it.

The quali- To see then a little into this qualification, that thereby
fication of
the per- we may discern who be of either *quorum*. The conditions
sons. to be required, to be of *quorum remittuntur*, are two :

That, First, that the party be within the house and family
in the
Church. whereto those keys belong, that is, be a member of the
Exod. 26. Church, be a faithful believing Christian. In the law,
34. the propitiatory was annexed to the ark and could not be
severed from it; to shew that they must hold of the ark,
that is, be of the number of the people of God, or else
could they not be partakers of the propitiation for their
Ps. 87. 7. sins. So saith the Psalmist, in the Psalm of the Church :
Omnes canales mei erunt in te; "All the conduit-pipes of
all my spiritual graces are conveyed into thee," and are no
where else to be had. And namely, of this benefit of re-
Ps. 85. 1, 2. mission of sins : "Thou hast, saith he, O Lord, been gracious unto Thy land, &c.; Thou hast forgiven all their
Isa. 33. 24. iniquity and covered all their sin." But the Prophet Esay
most plainly : "The people which dwelleth in her," that is,
the Church, "they shall have their iniquity forgiven." And
to end this point, the Angel when he interpreteth the name
Mat. 1. 21. of Jesus, extendeth it no further than thus, that "He shall
save His people from their sins." To them then is the
benefit of remission of sins entailed and limited; it is *sors
Sanctorum*, and *dos Ecclesiæ*. And they that are of this
quorum, have their certain hope thereof. They that are out
of it pertain to the second sort, of them that have their sins
retained. The power of the keys reacheth not to them :
1 Cor. 5. 12, "What have I to do with them that are without," saith
13. the Apostle? "Them that are without, God shall judge."
Therefore all Pagans, Infidels, Jews, and Turks are without
the compass of this *quorum*. For whoso believeth not in

Christ, whoso is not a faithful Christian, "shall die in his Joh. 8. 24.
sins."

But are all that are within this house thereby partakers of That,
this remission? is there nothing else required? Yes indeed, repentant.
there is yet another condition requisite, whereby many are
cut off that are within the *quorum* of the Church. And that
is, as our Saviour Christ Himself setteth it down, repentance. For He willeth "repentance and remission of sins to Lu. 24. 47.
be preached in His name;" both these, but repentance first,
and then remission of sins to follow after. So that the sinner
that is a member of the Church, if he want this, is not of
the former but of the latter *quorum.*

To repentance there go two things, as heretofore hath That is,
been entreated more at large. To insist upon the resem- feel the
blance here made. First, that he feel his chains and im- remission,
prisonment, and be grieved with them, and therefore would it.
gladly be let loose, and discharged from them. And no
otherwise doth our Saviour Christ proclaim it; that none
shall come to Him, but such as are "weary and heavy Mat. 11. 28.
laden." For, *sentiat onus qui vult levari, et sentiat vincula
qui vult solvi.* And no reason there is means should be
made for his enlargement that is well enough already, and
had rather be where he is than at liberty abroad.

Out of which groweth this division of sinners, which make
this double *quorum;* for there are sinners that are weary of
their commitment, and would gladly be enlarged. Such as
he was: "O bring my soul out of prison, that I may praise Ps. 142. 7.
Thee." And as he: "Wretched man that I am, who shall Rom. 7. 24.
deliver me?" And to these belongeth the first clause of
remission, even *pœnitentibus et petentibus,* to them that
are weary of their durance, and that desire and sue for
deliverance.

Again there are sinners which care not greatly for their
present estate, but are as it were without sense of their
misery. The prison grieveth them not; being in it, they
reckon themselves well enough, either because they have
drunken of the slumbering "cup," which is the very Isa. 51. 22.
"dregs" of God's wrath, having their hearts "as brawn," Ps. 119. 70.
and "their consciences seared with a hot iron," that is, 1 Tim. 4. 2.
as the Apostle doth interpret it, "being past all feeling" [Eph. 4.
19.]

S E R M. or remorse of sin; or else a worse sort of people that not
IV. only have no sense of their present wretched case, but do
even take delight and pleasure in the place, and, to choose,
Prov. 2. 14. will not be out of it. *Qui lætantur cum malum fecerint, et
exultant in rebus pessimis,* that scorn the denouncing of
God's judgments, and when they hear the words of this
Deut. 29. curse absolve themselves and say, "I shall have peace" and
19, 20. do full well for all that. Of such, *Dominus ne ignoscat illis,*
saith Moses, "let not God be merciful unto them." Pity it
is they should be let go, or the key once turned to let them
out. Sense and sorrow is required of their restraint, and an
earnest desire of enlargement, else they pertain not to the
first but to the latter *quorum.*

In which very point, of sorrow for sin, there is an especial
[Lu. 11. good use of "the key of knowledge," for counsel and direc-
52.] tion. 1. For, inasmuch as repentance itself is an act of cor-
Ezek. 33.
14. [marg.] rective justice, and to repent is to "do judgment," as the
1 Cor. 11. Prophet; and to "judge ourselves," as the Apostle calleth
31.
Ezek. 36. it. 2. To which there belongeth not only a sentence, but
31.
2 Cor. 7. 11. also ἐκδίκησις, "a revenge," or punishment. And because
it is not a fruitless repentance which must serve the turn,
Lu. 3. 8. but it must have "fruits," saith St. John Baptist, and "fruits
worthy of repentance;" that is more plainly, as St. Paul
Acts 26. 20. saith he was charged to preach even from Heaven, that men
Dan. 4. 27. must not only "repent and turn to God," but also "do
Joh. 3. 8.
Acts 8. 22. works worthy of repentance." 3. And for that the works
of repentance, all of them, are not meet and suitable to
every sin, but as the sins are divers, so are the works to
be also. 4. For that also, as a man may go too far in them
2 Cor. 2. 7. —as appeareth in the case of the Corinthian—so may one
Nu. 12. 14.
Rev. 3. 2. fall too short, as appeareth in the case of Miriam; and a
proportion or analogy is to be kept, according as the case
of the sin requireth. In both these to advise both what
works are meet and also what measure is to be kept, "the
[Lu. 11. key of knowledge" will help to direct, and we may have use
52.] of it if we mean to use it to that end.

The other condition which must be joined to the former is
an unfeigned purpose and endeavour ourselves to remit or let
go those sins which we would have by God remitted. For
it is not enough to be sorry for sin past, or to seek repent-

ance, no though it be "with tears;" this will not make us Heb.12.17.
of the first *quorum* if there be nothing but this, if there be
in our hearts a purpose ourselves to retain and hold fast our
old sin still. Esau lifted up his voice with a "great cry and Gen. 27.
bitter out of measure, and wept," yet even at the same time ³⁴·³⁸·
vowed in his heart so soon as his father was dead, to make
away his brother. And this purpose of mind, for all his
bitter crying and tears, cast him into the latter *quorum*, and
made his sins to be retained still. And such is the case of
them that would be let go out of prison, but would have
liberty to go in and out still to visit the company there,
when and as often as them list. So do not the Saints that
be of the first *quorum*, to whom God, as "He speaketh Ps. 85. 8.
peace," so He speaketh this too, "that they turn not thither
again," that they fall not again to their former folly.

But these latter would have their sins let go by God,
but themselves would not let them go, but keep fast their
end still. They would *quoad reatum* hear that saying from
Christ's mouth, "Thy sins are forgiven thee;" but *quoad* Lu. 7. 48.
actum would not willingly hear that other, " Go and sin no Joh. 8. 11.
more." But we must be willing to hear them both; willing
to have our sins remitted by God, and willing too ourselves
to remit our sinning, or from thenceforth *remissius peccare*,
' to sin more remissly,' and nothing so licentiously as before.
To the former sorrow, sentence, and revenge, we must, saith
St. Paul, join a desire, ἐπιπόθησιν; and to that desire an
endeavour, σπουδὴν, and that such an endeavour as may be
able to allege for itself ἀπολογίαν, an honest defence, that we 2 Cor. 7. 11.
have used all good means to do that which on our parts is to
be performed, that we may be of the first *quorum*.

In which point no less than the former there may be use
of "the key of knowledge" to advise and direct ourselves, [Lu. 11.
no less in the cure of sin than in the sorrow for it. They ³²·]
in the second of the Acts, which were "pricked in their Acts 2. 37.
hearts," knew of themselves that somewhat they should do,
as by their question appeareth; but what it was they should
do they knew not. Sometimes men have good minds, but
know not which way to turn them or set themselves about
it. Sometimes they are scrupulous and doubtful whether
they do as they should, because one may *propitius esse sibi*, [See Mat.
16. 22.]

favour himself too much, and be over partial in his own case, neither so careful to use the means to good, nor to avoid the occasions of evil, as he ought. Wherein it were good for men to make sure work and to be fully resolved. For most usual it is for men at their ends to doubt, not of the power of remitting of sins, but of their own disposition to receive it; and whether they have ordered the matter so that they be within the compass of God's effectual calling, or, as the text is, of the *quorum* to whom it belongeth. So much for the matter, or subject, whereto this power is to be applied.

And here I should now speak somewhat of the applying or use of it, but the time hath overtaken me and will not permit it. Now only a word of the third part, of the efficacy, or, as the lawyers term it, of God's ratihabition, and so an end.

III.
Of the rati-
habition.
Wherein God willing more abundantly to shew to them that should be partakers of it the stableness of His counsel, He hath penned it exceedingly effectually, and indeed strangely to them that deeply consider of it; which He hath so done to the end that thereby such poor sinners as shall be partakers of it might have strong consolation and perfect assurance, not to waver in the hope which is set before them.

And to that end, even for comfort, I will only point at four things in the inditing of it, all expressing the efficacy of it in more than common manner.

Super ver-
bis Esaiæ
" Vidi Do-
minum."
Homil. 5.
[init.]
1. The order in this, that *Remiseritis* standeth first, and *Remittuntur* second. It is St. Chrysostom's note, that it beginneth in earth, and that heaven followeth after. So that whereas in prayer and in other parts of religion it is *sicut in cœlo, sic in terrâ*, here it is, *sicut in terrâ, sic in cœlo. A terrâ judicandi principalem authoritatem sumit cœlum. Nam judex sedet in terrâ : Dominus sequitur servum, et quicquid hic in inferioribus judicârit, hoc Ille in supernis comprobat*, saith he.

2. The time in this, that it is *Remittuntur* in the present tense; there is no delay between, no deferring or holding in suspense, but the absolution pronounced upon earth, *Remittuntur*, presently they are remitted; that He saith not, hereafter they shall be, but they are already remitted.

3. The manner, in setting down of the two words. For it is so delivered by Christ as if He were content it should be accounted their act and that the Apostles were the agents in it, and Himself but the patient and suffered it to be done. For the Apostles' part is delivered in the active, *Remiseritis,* and His own in the passive, *Remittuntur.*

4. The certainty; which in the identity of the word, in not changing the word, but keeping the selfsame in both parts. For Christ hath not thus indited it : Whose sins ye wish or ye pray for; or, Whose sins ye declare to be remitted; but "Whose sins ye remit;" using no other word in the Apostles' than He useth in His own. And to all these in St. Matthew He addeth His solemn protestation of "Verily, verily," or "Amen, amen," that so it is, and shall Mat. 18. 18. be. And all to certify us that He fully meaneth with effect to ratify in heaven that is done in earth, to the sure and steadfast comfort of them that shall partake it.

A SERMON

PREACHED AT WHITEHALL,

UPON THE TWENTY-THIRD OF NOVEMBER, A. D. MDC.

JEREMIAH xxiii. 6.

This is the Name whereby they shall call Him, The Lord our righteousness.

Hoc est nomen, quod vocabunt Eum, Jehova justitia nostra. Lat. Vulg.

[*This is His Name whereby He shall be called, The Lord our righteousness.* Eng. Trans.]

SERM.
V. THE former points, which the Prophet pointeth us to with his *Ecce*, and willed us to behold, we then were so long in beholding that we had no time to take a view of this last; which I take to be the chiefest part of his *Ecce*, and the point of all points most worthy our beholding. *Hoc est Nomen, &c.*

1. The chief, because His Name is given Him from this, and not from any of the rest. For commonly, from his chiefest title doth every man take his denomination. In Jer. 23. 7. the verse next following God saith, He will no more be called their deliverer from Egypt, because He will vouchsafe them a greater deliverance from Babylon; and so from thence, as from the greater, have His Name given. And as God, so men. What title of honour is highest in their style, that of all other doth each person delight to be termed by.

Now those in the former part of this verse, of salvation and peace which He will procure them, be great and excellent titles, and they be no less verified of Him than this of righteousness: "The Lord is my light and my salvation," by Ps. 27. 1. the Prophet; and, "He is our peace," by the Apostle; yet of Ephes. 2. 14. neither of these doth He take His Name. But from this of righteousness He doth. And that, both His former Name, in metaphor and figure, "The branch of righteousness;" Jer. 23. 5. and this His latter, in propriety and truth His royal Name, *Jehova justitia nostra.* This therefore is chief in his account.

2. Again, the chief because it is His peculiar. And every man reckoneth of that as his chiefest title that is not common to him with others, but proper to him alone, as wherein he hath a prerogative above all. He, and none but he.

Now those in the former verse—of " executing judgment and justice"—are such as are also given to other kings. King David is said to have " executed judgment and justice 2 Sam. 8. to all his people;" so is king Solomon likewise, the queen of 15. 1 Kings 10. Sheba giveth him that title. To do justice is the title also 9. of others—and not many neither, but yet of some others; but to be justice, to be righteousness, that is the name of none but Christ only. His, and His only, is that title. Therefore as well in this regard as in the former, this is the very chief part in the *Ecce,* the Name of " Jehovah our righteousness."

Which, because it is nothing but a name, may seem to some a matter of no great importance. The Deputy of Achaia, Gallio, in the Acts, seemeth of that mind : " If it Acts 18. 14, were some weighty matter, I would sit the hearing," saith 15. he; " but if it be a matter of names, I take it not worth the while;" hear it who will, for I will not. And to say the truth, if it were a name of men's giving he said not much amiss. Their names are not greatly to be looked after. The argument taken from them, the heathen philosopher confesseth, is μάρτυς ἀλαζὼν, an argument that setteth a good face upon it, but no great substance in it. The reason whereof is, because with men there be nominals and there be reals, names and things are many times two. There is, *quædam dicuntur de, et non insunt.* There is learning, saith the Apostle, ψευδώνυμος, " falsely so called." And as learn- 1 Tim. 6.20. ing, so many things beside. The churl is named liberal, and Isa. 32. 5. they worshipful that have nothing worthy worship in them. Yea it falleth out that some have a name " that they live and Rev. 3. 1. yet are dead;" and many things besides, *quæ dicuntur de, et non insunt in.* Whereof we need not seek far; we have an example here in the Prophet of king Zedekiah that reigned

S E R M.
V.

Ezek. 17.
16. 18, 19.

at the time of this prophecy, one that had neither truth nor righteousness in him, a breaker of his league and covenant, a falsifier of his oath, and yet his name is Zedekiah, God's righteous one, or the righteousness of God. Men's names for the most part are false.

2. And when they be true, empty, and no great weight in them. For what are men's titles but men's breath; but a blast of air, but wind. If they be popular titles, the wind of a common pair of bellows. If of those of the better sort, as the heathen man well said, ἐπιχρύσου φυσητῆρος, the wind ' of a gilt or wrought pair of bellows,' but both of them wind.

But the names of God's imposition are not so. They ever carry truth in them. For seeing God cannot away with

Job. 32. 21, 22.

those that are title-givers, as saith Elihu, He will give none Himself. With Him is not the division that is with us, of nominals and reals ; of *quædam dicuntur de, quædam insunt*

1 Joh. 3. 1, 2.

in. If we be named " the sons of God," we " are" so, saith St. John : and therefore from His Name a sound and sub-stantial argument may be drawn, as we see the Apostle

Heb. 1. 4.

doth ; proving the excellency of Christ's nature above the Angels, from the excellency of His Name above theirs.

And as they are free from falsehood, so are they not empty

Prov. 18. 10.

sounds, but have ever some virtue in them. " The Name of God," saith Solomon, " is a strong tower." So that, when

Ps. 20. 8.

" some trust in chariots and horses," and other some " in the Name of God ;" they that trust in chariots and horses, they " go down ;" they that in that Name, " stand upright." And this not only in the dangers of this life, but there is also in the Name of God a saving power for the life to come. A

1 Cor. 6. 11.

power to justify : " Ye are justified in the Name of Christ," saith St. Paul. A power for remission of sins : " Your sins

1 Joh. 2. 12.

are forgiven you, for His Name's sake," saith St. John. A

Acts 4. 12.

power to save : " In this Name you have salvation," saith St. Peter.

And such is the Name here named, " Jehovah our right-eousness." " Our righteousness," to justify, to forgive us our sins, to give us salvation. Such is this " Name :" and " there

Acts 4. 12.

is not under heaven any Name given to men, wherein they may be saved, beside it."

The Di-vision.

In the *Ecce,* or beholding whereof, two things present

themselves to our view : I. The "Name itself; II. The calling Him by it. The Name in these words : *Hoc est Nomen.*
The calling in these : *quo vocabunt Eum.*

In either of which, two others. In the Name, these two : I.
1. the parts of it, and the reason of them; 2. the sense
of it.

In the calling Him by it, likewise two : 1. as it is our II.
duty so to call Him; 2. as we have an use or benefit by so
calling Him. The duty and the use.

To God Himself, as the Psalmist telleth us, all the service I.
we can perform reacheth not. The perfection of His nature $\overset{\text{The}}{\text{"Name,"}}$
is such, as it can from us receive nothing. But two things of Ps. 16. 2.
His there are which He hath left to express that duty which
we owe and bear to Himself. Which two are in one verse
set down by the prophet David : "Thou hast magnified, Ps. 138. 2.
1. Thy Name, and 2. Thy word above all things ;" 1. His
Name, and 2. His word. His Name for our invocation, His
word for our instruction. And these two, as they are the
highest things in God's account, so are they to be in ours.
Not the word only, which carrieth all away in a manner in
these days, but His Name also no less. For in the setting
them down, the Holy Ghost giveth the first place to the
Name. Our very assembling, and coming together, is in this Mat. 18. 20.
" Name." And then, " before all things, supplications are to 1 Tim. 2. 1.
be made" in this Name. And the very hearing of the word
itself is, that we may call upon His Name. How shall they Rom. 10.
call upon His Name Whom they have not heard? "How $\overset{14.}{}$
shall they hear without a preacher ?" So that preaching and
hearing of the word are both ordained for the calling on of
this Name.

Which being so high in God's account, of very civility, if
there were nothing else, we are not to be ignorant what His
Name is that He is to be called by. No man that maketh
any, yea but common, account of a party, but he will learn
by what name to call him. And so requisite doth Solomon
hold this, as he affirmeth there is little more in that man Prov. 30. 2.
than in a beast, yea there is not " the understanding of a
man" in him; of God—of Him That stretcheth out the
heavens, and " gathereth the winds in His fist, bindeth the [Prov. 30.
waters in a garment, establisheth all the ends of the earth" $\overset{4.]}{}$

—not to know "what is His Name, or what is His Son's Name," that His Name is Jehovah, and His Son's Name *Jehova justitia nostra.*

This were we bound to get notice of if it were but civility, or, as Solomon reckoneth it, even humanity. But that is not all. For seeing, as the heathen man confesseth, Πάντη δὲ Διὸς κεχρήμεθα πάντες, 'we all either have or may have need of God' in our necessities of this life, but specially in our last need, of very necessity it will stand us in hand to know how to call unto Him. There is no client but will be sure to learn his advocate's name, nor no patient but will tell his physician's. Nor, in a word, any of them of whom we are to have any special use, but we will be careful as to learn his true name, that we miss not in it; so, if he have divers names, and love to be called by any one rather than other, to be sure to be perfect in it, and ready to salute him by it. And such is this Name here; and we therefore not to be to seek in it, seeing not only courtesy but very necessity commendeth it to us.

Which Name, as you see, is compounded of three words. 1. *Jehova*, 2. *justitia*, 3. *nostra*; all of them necessary, all of them essential. And they all three concurring, as it were three twists, they make "a threefold cord," like that which the preacher mentioneth, "that cannot be broken." But except it be entire, and have all three, it loseth the virtue, it worketh nothing. For sever any one of them from the rest, and the other are not of moment. A sound, but not a name; or a name, but not *hoc Nomen*, "this Name," a Name qualified to save them that call on it. Take *Jehova* from *justitia nostra*, and *justitia nostra* is nothing worth. And take *justitia* from *Jehova*, and though there be worth in *Jehova*, yet there is not that which we seek for. Yea, take *nostra* from the other two, and how excellent soever they be they concern us not, but are against us rather than for us. So that together we must take them or the Name is lost.

To see this the better, it will not be amiss to take it in sunder, and to see the ground of every part in order. Why, 1. *Jehova*, 2. why *justitia*, 3. why *Jehova justitia*, 4. why *justitia nostra*, 5. both *nostra* and *justitia*.

Jehova. Touching which word, and the ground why it must be a part of this name, the prophet David resolveth us: *Memorabor,* saith he, *justitiæ Tuæ solius.* Because His Ps. 71. 16. righteousness, and only His righteousness, is worth the remembering, and any other's beside His is not meet to be mentioned. For as for our own "righteousness" which we have without Him, Esay telleth us " it is but a defiled cloth," Isa. 64. 6. and St. Paul that it is " but dung." Two very homely com- Phil. 3. 8. parisons, but they be the Holy Ghost's own ; yet nothing so homely as in the original, where they be so odious, as what manner of defiled cloth, or what kind of dung, we have not dared to translate.

Our own then being no better, we are driven to seek for it elsewhere. " He shall receive His righteousness," saith the Ps. 24. 5 Prophet ; and " the gift of righteousness," saith the Apostle. Rom. 5. 17. It is then another, to be given us, and to be received by us, which we must seek for. And whither shall we go for it ? Job alone despatcheth this point. Not to the heavens or stars ; for they are " unclean in His sight." Not to the Job 15. 15; Saints ; for in them He found " folly." Nor to the Angels ; 4. 18; 25. 5. for neither in them found He any steadfastness. Now if none of these will serve, we see a necessary reason why *Jehova* must be a part of this Name. And this is the reason why Jeremy here expressing more fully the Name given Him before in Esay—" Immanuel, God with us"— [Isa. 7. 14.] instead of the name of God in that Name, which is *El,* setteth down by way of explanation this Name here of *Jehova.* Because that *El,* and the other Names of God are communicated to creatures. As the name of *El* to Angels, for their names end in it ; Michael, Gabriel, &c. And the name of *Jah* to Saints, and their names end in it ; Esaiah, Jeremiah, Zachariah[1]. To certify us therefore that it is [¹ So written here.] neither the righteousness of Saints nor Angels that will serve the turn, but the righteousness of God and very God, he useth that Name which is proper to God alone; ever reserved to Him only, and never imparted by any occasion to Angel or Saint, or any creature in heaven or earth.

Justitia, "righteousness." Why that ? If we ask, in re- 2. *Justitia.* gard of the other benefits which are before remembered, salvation and peace, why " righteousness" and not salvation

S E R M.
V.
[Jer. 23. 5.]
nor peace? it is evident. Because—as in the verse next before, the Prophet termeth it—" righteousness" is the "branch;" and these two, salvation and peace, are the fruits growing on it. So that, if this be had, both the other are had with it. Of " righteousness" and " salvation,"

Isa. 45. 8.
Esay saith " they grow both together," as it were out of one stalk. And of peace, that *opus justitiæ pax*, " the very work"

Isa. 32. 17.
or proper effect " of righteousness is peace." For which cause the Apostle interpreting the name of Melchisedek,

Heb. 7. 2.
" King of Salem;" first, saith he, " King of Righteousness;" and after, " King of Peace." Even as on the contrary part, sin which is nothing else but ἀνομία, iniquity or unrighteous-

1 Joh. 3. 4.
ness, as saith St. John, is that root of bitterness from whence shooteth forth both perdition of the soul contrary to salvation, and unquietness of the conscience opposite to peace. And both they and all other miseries are, as Job termeth

Job 5. 7.
them, " sparks" of this brand of hell; as health and peace, and all blessings, are the fruits of this " branch of righteousness." Now because there is *vana salus*, " a vain salvation,"

Ps. 60. 11.
as saith David; and a peace falsely so called, " a peace which

Jer. 6. 14.
is no peace," as saith Jeremy; to the end therefore that our salvation might be substantial, and our peace uncounterfeit, it behoveth us to lay a sure ground-work of them both, and to set a true root of this branch, which is the Name Jehovah. For such as the root of this branch is, such will salvation and peace, the fruits thereof, be. If it be man's righteousness which is vain, it will be also *vana salus hominis*, vain and soon at an end; and the peace, like the world's peace, vain and of no certainty. But if " Jehovah" be " our righteousness," look how He is so will they be, everlasting salvation,

[Phil. 4. 7.]
a " peace which passeth all understanding."

3. *Jehova
justitia.*
Jehova justitia. We are now to seek the reason why *Jehova* is in this Name *per modum justitiæ*, by the way or under the term of " righteousness," rather than of some other attribute, as of power or mercy; that it is not *Jehova misericor-*

[Isa. 7. 14.]
dia, or *Jehova potentia*, but *Jehova justitia*. " God with us," saith Esay; with us, saith Jeremy, of all His properties, by that of " righteousness" chiefly and above other.

Not of power, as in Esay, by His name *El*; which is His name of power. For in power there is no true comfort with-

out justice be joined to it. For what is power, except righteousness go before? We see it is a thing very agreeable to
our nature to have that we shall have by justice, to choose;
and that way do even the mightiest first seek it, and when
that way it will not come they overbear it with power.

Nor of mercy; not *Jehova misericordia,* by which name Ps. 59. 17.
David calleth Him. For though it be a name of special comfort, and St. Augustine saith of it, *O Nomen sub quo nemini* [S. Aug.
desperandum! yet if we weigh it well of itself alone, we shall ^{in loc.}]
find there is no full or perfect comfort in it except this also
be added, for that we have in us two respects : 1. one, as
persons in misery ; 2. the other, as persons convict of sin.
And though Mercy be willing to relieve us in the one, for
her delight is to help those in misery, yet what shall become
of the other, how shall that be answered? We have in the
verse before, mention of a King ready to " execute judgment [Jer.23.5.]
and justice." Now justice is professed enemy to all sin;
and justice in her proceeding may not admit of any respect,
either of the might or of the misery of any, to lead her from
giving sentence according to law.

True it is, mercy is ours, ours wholly there is no doubt ;
but justice is against us, and except justice may be made
ours too, all is not as it should be. But if justice, if that
in God which only is against, might be made for us, then
were we safe. Therefore all our thought is to be, either how
we may get mercy to triumph over justice with the Apostle ; Jas. 2. 13.
or how, at the least, we may get them to meet together and Ps. 85. 10.
be friends in this work. For except justice be satisfied, and
do join in it also, in vain we promise ourselves that mercy of
itself shall work our salvation. Which may serve for the
reason why neither *Jehova potentia,* or *Jehova misericordia*
are enough, but it must be *Jehova justitia,* and *justitia* a
part of the Name.

Nostra: and neither may this be left out; for without 4. *Nostra.*
this *Jehova* alone doth not concern us, and *Jehova justitia*
is altogether against us. But if He be righteousness, and
not only righteousness but ours too, all is at an end, we
have our desires ; verily this last, this possessive, this word
of application, is all in all. By it we have interest in both
the former, and without it our case is as theirs, *Quid nobis*

I

SERM.
V.

Mat. 8. 29.

et Tibi? "what have we to do with Thee," *Jehova justitia?* which is most fearful, and nothing but terror and torment in the consideration of it. Therefore we must make much of this; for if once He be *nobiscum,* 'with us,' and not against us, and not only *nobiscum,* with us, but *noster,* 'our own,' all is safe. Otherwise it falleth out oft there be many *nobiscum* that be not *nostri;* 'with us,' talk with us, eat with us, sit with us, which yet are not 'ours' for all that. And in this point also doth this name of Jeremy more fully express the name of Esay's Immanuel no less than in the two former: first of *Jehova,* which is more than *El,* and then of *justitia,* which is more agreeable than that of *potentia;* and now in this here, that there it is *nobiscum,* which is well, and here it is *noster,* which is better, and more sure by a great deal. For if He be, as the Apostle saith, *factus*

1 Cor. 1. 30. *nobis,* "made unto us righteousness," and that so as He becometh ours, what can we have more? What can hinder

Serm. 3. in
Missus est,
&c. [ad
finem.]

us, saith St. Bernard, but that we should *uti Nostro in utilitatem nostram, et de Servatore salutem operari,* 'use Him, and His righteousness, use that which is ours to our best behoof, and work our salvation out of this our Saviour.' So that *nostra* may not be spared, no more than the other part of the name. For all is in suspense, and there is no complete comfort without it.

5. *Justitia*
nostra.

To which comfort this may be added for a conclusion of this part, no less effectual than any of the former. That it is *justitia nostra* in the abstract, and not in the concrete *Justificans,* or *Justificator noster;* "our justice or righteousness" itself, not 'our Justifier or Maker of us righteous.' For thus delivered, I make no doubt it hath much more efficacy in it; and more significant it is by far to say "Jehovah our justice," than Jehovah our Justifier. I know St. Paul saith much; that our Saviour Christ shed His blood

Rom. 3. 26.

"to shew His righteousness, that He might not only be just, but a justifier" of those which are of His faith. And much more again in that when he should have so said, To him

Rom. 4. 5.

that believeth in God, he chooseth thus to set it down, "To him that believeth in Him That justifieth the ungodly;" making these two to be all one, God, and the Justifier of sinners. Though this be very much, yet certainly this is

most forcible, that "He is made unto us by God" very 1 Cor. 1. 30.
"righteousness" itself. And that yet more, that He is
made "righteousness to us, that we be made the righteous- 2 Cor. 5. 21.
ness of God in Him." Which place St. Chrysostom well [S. Chrys.
weighing, this very word δικαιοσύνη, saith he, the Apostle in loc.]
useth, δεικνὺς τὸ ἄφατον τῆς δωρεᾶς, 'to express the unspeakable bounty of that gift,' that He hath not given us
the operation or effect of His righteousness, but His very
righteousness, yea His very self unto us. Mark, saith he,
how every thing is lively, and as full as can be imagined.
Christ, one not only That had done no sin, but "That had
not so much as known any sin, hath God made (not a
sinner, but) sin" itself; as in another place (not accursed,
but) "a curse" itself; "sin" in respect of the guilt, "a [Gal. 3.
curse" in respect of the punishment. And why this? To 13.]
the end "that we might be made (not righteous persons; [2 Cor. 5.
that was not full enough, but) righteousness" itself; and 21.]
there he stays not yet—and not every righteousness, but
the very "righteousness of God" Himself. What can be
further said, what can be conceived more comfortable? To
have Him ours, not to make us righteous but to make us
"righteousness," and that not any other but "the righteousness of God;" the wit of man can devise no more.
And all to this end, that we might see there belongeth a
special *Ecce* to this name, that there is more than ordinary
comfort in it; that therefore we should be careful to honour
Him with it, and so call Him by it; "Jehovah our righteousness."

There is no Christian man that will deny this Name, but 2.
will call Christ by it, and say of Him that He is *Jehova* The sense
justitia nostra, without taking a syllable or letter from it. "Name."
But it is not the syllables, but the sense that maketh the
Name. And the sense is it we are to look unto; that we
keep it entire in sense as well as in sound, if we mean to
preserve this name of *justitia nostra* full and whole unto
Him. And as this is true, so is it true likewise that even
among Christians all take it not in one sense; but some, of
a greater latitude than other. There are that take it in that
sense which the Prophet Esay hath set down: *In Jehovâ* Isa. 45. 24.
justitia mea, that all "our righteousness is in Him; and we [marg.]

116 *Of Justification*

SERM.
V.
[Philip.
3. 9.]
2 Cor. 5. 21.

to be found in Him, not having our own righteousness," but being "made the righteousness of God in Him." There are some other, that though in one part of our righteousness they take it in that sense, yet in another part they shrink it up, and in that make it up a proposition causal, and the interpretation thereof to be, *A Jehova justitia mea.* Which is true too, 1. whether we respect Him as the cause ex-

Rom. 8. 29.

emplary, or pattern—for we are to be made "conformable to the image" of Christ; 2. or whether we respect Him as the cause efficient; for of all his righteous works the Pro-

Isa. 26. 12.

phet truly protesteth, *Domine, universa opera nostra Tu operatus es in nobis;* and the Apostle when he had said

1 Cor. 15. 10.

Ego, correcteth himself presently and saith, *Non ego sed gratia Dei mecum;* "Not I, but the grace of God." This meaning then is true and good, but not full enough. For either it taketh the Name in sunder, and giveth Him not all, but a part of it again, or else it maketh two senses, which may not be allowed in one name.

1. "Righteousness" accounted.
2. "Righteousness" done.
Rom. 3. 21.
Rom. 4. 1.

For the more plain conceiving of which point we are to be put in mind that the true righteousness, as saith St. Paul, is not of man's device, but hath his witness from "the law and prophets;" which he there proceedeth to shew out of the example first of Abraham and after of David. In the Scripture then there is a double righteousness set down, both in the Old and in the New Testament.

Gen. 15. 6.

In the Old, and in the very first place that righteousness is named in the Bible: "Abraham believed and it was accounted unto him for righteousness." A righteousness

Gen. 18. 19.

accounted. And again, in the very next line, it is mentioned, Abraham will teach his house to do righteousness. A righteousness done. In the New likewise. The former, in one chapter, even the fourth to the Romans, no fewer

[* Rom. 4. 3, 5, 6, 8, 9, 10, 11, 16, 22, 23, 24.]
[¹ Not in the exact words.]
1 Joh. 3. 7.

than eleven times*, *Reputatum est illi ad justitiam*¹. A reputed righteousness. The latter in St. John: "My beloved, let no man deceive you, he that doeth righteousness is righteous." A righteousness done. Which is nothing else but our just dealing, upright carriage, honest conversation.

Of these, the latter the philosophers themselves conceived and acknowledged; the other is proper to Christians only, and altogether unknown in philosophy. The one is a quality of the party. The other an act of the judge, declaring or pronouncing righteous. The one ours by influence or infusion, the other by account or imputation.

That both these there are, there is no question. The question is, whether of these the prophet here principally meaneth in this Name?

This shall we best inform ourselves of by looking back to the verse before, and without so looking back we shall never do it to purpose.

There the Prophet setteth one before us in His royal judicial power in the person of a King, and of a King set down to execute judgment; and this he telleth us, before he thinks meet to tell us His name. Before this King, thus set down in His throne, there to do judgment, the righteousness that will stand against the law, our conscience, Satan, sin, the gates of hell and the power of darkness; and so stand that we may be delivered by it from death, despair and damnation; and entitled by it to life, salvation, and happiness eternal; that is righteousness indeed, that is it we seek for, if we may find it. And that is not this latter, but the former only; and therefore that is the true interpretation of *Jehova justitia nostra.* Look but how St. Augustine and the rest of the Fathers, when they have occasion to mention that place in the Proverbs, *Cum Rex justus sederit in solio, quis potest dicere, Mundum est cor meum?* Look how they interpret it then, and it will give us light to understand this Name; and we shall see that no Name will serve then but this Name. Nor this Name neither, but with this interpretation of it. *[Cont. Cres. 4. [3. c. 80. Ed. B.] Prov. 20. 8, 9.]*

And that the Holy Ghost would have it ever thus understood, and us ever to represent before our eyes this King thus sitting in His judgment-seat, when we speak of this righteousness, it is plain two ways. 1. By way of position. For the tenor of the Scripture touching our justification all along runneth in judicial terms, to admonish us still what to set before us. The usual joining of justice and judgment continually all along the Scriptures, shew it is a judicial justice we are to set before us. The terms of 1. A judge: " It is the Lord That judgeth me." 2. A prison: Kept and *[1 Cor. 4. 4. Gal. 3. 23.]*

S E R M.
V.
2 Cor. 5. 10.
Rom. 8. 33.
Rev. 12, 10.
Rom. 2. 15.
Deut. 27.
26.
Jas. 2. 10.
Rom. 3. 19.
[Mat. 6.12.]
Col. 2. 14.
1 Joh. 2. 1.
Gal. 4. 4.
[Heb. 7.
22.]
[Acts 13.
39.]

shut up under Moses. 3. A bar: "We must all appear before the bar." 4. A proclamation: "Who will lay any thing to the" prisoner's "charge?" 5. An accuser: "The accuser of our brethren." 6. A witness: Our "conscience bearing witness." 7. An indictment upon these: "Cursed be he that continueth not in all the words of this law to do them." And again, he that breaketh one "is guilty of all." A conviction that all may be ὑπόδικοι, "guilty" or culpable "before God." Yea the very delivering of our sins under the name of "debts," of the law under the name of a "handwriting," the very terms of "an advocate," of "a surety" "made under the law;" of a pardon, or "being justified from those things which by the law we could not;" all these, wherein for the most part this is still expressed, what speak they but that the sense of this Name cannot be rightly understood, nor what manner of righteousness is in question, except we still have before our eyes this same *coram Rege justo judicium faciente.*

2. And again by way of opposition. For usually where 'justifying' is named, there 'condemning,' which is a term merely judicial, is set against it. In the law: "When there shall be strife, and the matter shall come before thee, and sentence to be given, see the righteous be justified and the sinner condemned." "To justify the wicked and condemn the innocent, both are alike abominable before God." "If man cannot judge, hear Thou from heaven, condemn the wicked and justify the righteous."

Deut. 25. 1.

Prov. 17.15.

1 Kings 8.
32.

Mat. 12. 37.
Rom. 8. 33,
34.
Rom. 5. 16.

In the Gospel: "By thy words shalt thou be justified, and by thy words condemned." "It is God that justifieth, who shall condemn?" Grace to "justification," as sin to "condemnation." All these shew manifestly we must imagine ourselves standing at the bar, or we shall never take the state of this question aright, nor truly understand the mystery of this Name.

For it is not in question whether we have an inherent righteousness or no, or whether God will accept it or reward it; but whether that must be our righteousness, *coram Rege justo judicium faciente.*

Which is a point very material, and in no wise to be forgotten. For without this, if we compare ourselves with ourselves, what heretofore we have been; or if we compare ourselves with others, as did the Pharisee; we may take a fancy perhaps, and have some good conceit of our inherent righteousness. Yea, if we be to deal in schools by argument or disputation, we may peradventure argue for it, and make some show in the matter. But let us once be brought and arraigned *coram Rege justo sedente in solio,* let us set ourselves there, we shall then see that all our former conceit will vanish straight, and righteousness in that sense will not abide the trial.

Bring them hither then, and ask them here of this Name, and never a Saint nor Father, no nor the Schoolmen themselves, none of them but will shew you how to understand it aright. In their commentaries it may be, in their questions and debates, they will hold hard for the other. But remove it hither, they forsake it presently, and take the Name in the right sense. " Hast thou considered My servant Job," saith Job 1. 8. God to Satan, " how just and perfect he is?" This just and perfect Job standing here, "Though I be just," saith he, " I Job 9. 15; will not hold up my head"—or as they say, *Stare rectus in* 10. 15. *curiá*—will never plead it or stand upon it, but put up a supplication to be relieved by *Jehova justitia nostra.*

David hath the witness to have been " a man according 1 Sam. 13. to God's own heart." For all that he dareth not stand here, 14. but desireth God would not " enter into judgment with him;" for that *in conspectu Tuo,* in His sight, not he, " nor Ps. 143. 2. any other living" — which St. Bernard extendeth to the [De Verb. Esa. *Vidi* Angels— " shall be justified." But if he must come—as Dom. Ser. 5.] thither we must come all — then *Memorabor justitiæ Tuæ* Ps. 71. 16. *solius,* he will never chant his own righteousness, but make mention only of this Name, *Jehova justitia nostra.*

Daniel, *Vir desideriorum,* as the Angel termed him, even Dan. 9. 23. he that " man so greatly beloved," after he saw the " An- Dan. 7. 9. cient of days" set down in His throne, and the books open before Him, then *Tibi Domine justitia, nobis autem confusio* Dan. 9. 7. *faciei. Non in justificationibus nostris,* " not in our righte- Dan. 9. 18. ousness"—yet was that righteousness *a Jehová,* but here it would not serve; he must wait for the Messias, and the " everlasting righteousness" which He bringeth with Him. Dan. 9. 24.

And Esay likewise, at the vision of the Lord *sedentis super* Isa. 6. 1, 2.

thronum, and the Angels covering their faces before Him, crieth out, *Væ mihi*, "Wo is me, I am a man of polluted lips;" wo is me, for I have held my peace; and there he seeth the very sins of his lips, and the very sins of omission will be enough to condemn him, though he had never in act committed any.

To end this point. St. Paul, "a vessel of election"—so God Himself doth name him—saith plainly, if it were before the Corinthians, or any assize of man, he would stand upon

his righteousness; but, seeing *Qui me judicat est Dominus*, he will give it over and confess that though *Nihil mihi conscius sum* (and so had *justitia a Domino*), yet for all that *in hoc non sum justificatus;* it is another righteousness, and not that must acquit him.

Thus do the Saints, both of the Old and of the New Testament, take this Name. And do not the Fathers the

like? St. Augustine's report it is of St. Ambrose, that being now at the point of death he alleged that the cause why he feared not death was, *quia bonum habemus Dominum;* and doth he not give this note upon it, that he did not presume *de suis purgatissimis moribus*, 'of his conversation, though most holy and clean,' but only stood on the goodness of the Lord, "the Lord our righteousness."

And doth he not in his own case fly to the same against Cresconius the Donatist? Then he shunned not to have his life sifted to the uttermost by any Donatist of them all. Yet in the eyes of God, *cum Rex justus sederit in solio*, (these very words he allegeth,) he saith plainly he dare not justify himself; but rather waited for the overflowing bounty of His grace, than would abide the severe examination of His

judgment. And Bernard, in his three hundred and tenth epistle, the very last he wrote, a little before his death, to the Abbot of Chartres, concludeth he not, *Calcaneum vacuum meritis curate munire precibus?* Abandoneth he not then his *justitia a Domino*, and confesseth his heel, meaning the end of his life, is bare of all merits, and desireth to have it by prayers commended to *Jehova justitia nostra*. Thus do the Fathers conceive of it.

Yea, the very schoolmen themselves, take them from their questions, quodlibets, and comments on the sentences, let them be in their soliloquies, meditations, or devotions, and specially in directing how to deal with men in their last agony, *quando judex præ foribus est;* then take Anselm, take Bonaventure, take Gerson, you would not wish to find *Jehova justitia nostra* better or more pregnantly acknow-ledged than in them you shall find it. But this is by virtue of this *Ecce Rex faciet judicium;* out of whose sight when we be, we may fall into a fancy, or as the Prophet saith, we may have a dream of *justitia nostra a Jehova.*

Anselm. interrogat. Bonaventura in Brevilo-quio.
Gers. in Agone.

Jer. 23. 16.

But framing ourselves as before Him, we shall see it is not that righteousness will consist there; but we must come to *justitia nostra in Jehová.* It is the only way how to settle the state of this controversy aright, and without this we may well miss of the interpretation of this Name. And this, they that do not, or will not now conceive, the Prophet telleth them after, at the twentieth verse, *quod in novis-simo intelligetis plane,* " at the end they shall understand" whether they will or no.

And indeed, to do them no wrong, it is true that at this judgment-seat, so far as it concerneth the satisfaction for sin and our escaping from eternal death, the Church of Rome taketh this Name aright; and that term which a great while seemed harsh unto them, now they find no such absurdity in it; that Christ's righteousness and merits are imputed to us. So saith Bellarmine: *Et hoc modo non esset absurdum, si quis diceret, nobis imputari Christi justitiam et merita, cum nobis donentur et applicentur, ac si nos ipsi Deo satisfecisse-mus.* And again: *Solus Christus pro salute nostrá satis-facere potuit, et re ipsá ex justitiá satisfecit, et illa satis-factio nobis donatur et applicatur et nostra reputatur, cum Deo reconciliamur et justificamur.* So saith Stapleton: *Illa sane justitiá quá satisfecit pro nobis per communicationem sic nostra est, ut perinde nobis imputetur ac si nos ipsi suffi-cienter satisfecimus:*—in as full terms as one would wish. So that this point is meetly well cleared now. Thus they understand this Name in that part of righteousness which is satisfactory for punishment; and there they say with us, as we with Esay, *In Jehova justitia nostra.*

De Justif. 2.10; 2.11.

De Justif. 7. 9. [post med.]

But in the positive justice, or that part thereof which is meritorious for reward, there fall they into a fancy they may

give it over, and suppose that *justitia a Domino,* 'a righteousness from God' they grant, yet inherent in themselves,
without the righteousness that is in Christ, will serve them;
whereof they have a good conceit that it will endure God's
justice, and standeth not by acceptation. So by this means
shrink they up their Name, and though they leave the full
sound, yet take they half the sense from it.

Now as for us, in this point of righteousness, if we both go
no further than the former, of taking away sin, then as much
as we strive for they do yield us. And therein we think we
have cause to blame them justly, for not contenting them-

Isa. 27. 9. selves with that which contented the Prophet: *Hic est omnis
fructus*—mark that *omnis*—*ut auferatur peccatum.* Which

Joh. 1. 29. contented St. John Baptist: *Ecce Agnus Dei, Qui tollit pec-*
Mat. 1. 21. *cata mundi.* Which contented the Angel: *Hic servabit
populum Suum a peccatis eorum.* Which contented the Fa-
De verb. thers: St. Augustine, *Puto hoc esse, Justus sum, quod pec-*
Apost. 16.
[c. 4.] *cator non sum.* St. Bernard : *Factus est nobis justitia, sapi-*
In Cant.
22. [circ. *entia, &c. Sapientia in prædicatione, justitia in peccatorum
med.] absolutione.* So that to be absolved from sin with him is
our righteousness. And yet more plainly in his hundred
[ad fi- and ninetieth epistle to Innocentius the Pope himself, *Ubi
nem.] reconciliatio, ibi remissio peccatorum, et quid ipsa nisi justifi-
catio?* Which the very name and nature of a judgment-
seat doth give, which proceedeth only in matters penal.

And as we blame them for that, so likewise for this no
less, that if they will needs have it a part of justice, they
allow not Christ's name as full in this part as in the former.
For there they allow imputation, but here they do not.

For I ask, What is the reason why in the other part of
satisfaction for sin we need Christ's righteousness to be ac-
De Justif. counted ours? The reason is, saith Bellarmine, *Non acceptat
2. 5. Deus in veram satisfactionem pro peccato nisi justitiam infi-
nitam, quoniam peccatum offensa est infinita.* If that be the
reason, that 'it must have an infinite satisfaction, because
the offence is infinite,' we reason *a pari,* there must also be
an infinite merit, because the reward is no less infinite.
Else by what proportion do they proceed, or at what beam
do they weigh these twain, that cannot counterpoise an infinite sin but with an infinite satisfaction, and think they

can weigh down a reward every way as infinite with a merit, to say the least, surely not infinite? Why should there be a necessary use of the sacrifice of Christ's death for the one, and not a use full as necessary of the oblation of His life for the other? Or how cometh it to pass, that no less than the one will serve to free us from eternal death, and a great deal less will serve to entitle us to eternal life? Is there not as much requisite to purchase for us the crown of glory, as there is to redeem us from the torments of hell? What difference is there? are they not both equal, both alike infinite? Why is His death allowed solely sufficient to put away sin, and why is not His life to be allowed like solely sufficient to bring us to life? If in that, the blessed saints themselves—were their sufferings never so great, yea though they endured never so cruel martyrdom—if all those could not serve to satisfy God's justice for their sins, but it is the death of Christ must deliver them; is it not the very same reason, that were their merits never so many, and their life never so holy, yet that by them they could not, nor we cannot, challenge the reward; but it is the life and obedience of Christ that *de justitiâ* must procure it for us all? For sure it is, that *Finiti ad infinitum nulla est proportio.* Especially if we add hereunto, that as it cannot be denied but to be finite, so withal that the ancient fathers seem further to be but meanly conceited of it; reckoning it not to be full but defective, nor pure but defiled; and if it be judged by the just judge, *districte* or *cum districtione examinis*—they be St. Gregory's and St. Bernard's words—indeed, no righteousness at all. [S. Greg. Mor. 9. 14.] [S. Bernard. in Fest. om. S. S. Serm. 1. post.]

Not full, but defective. So saith St. Augustine: *Neque totam neque plenam, in hac vitâ, justitiam nos habere, confitendum nobis est.* If neither whole but a part, nor full but wanting, then imperfect and defective. Now[1] which must be weighed in God's balance, must not be found *minus habens;* and this is *minus habens,* saith St. Bernard in express terms. [med.] [1 [that.]] [S. Bernard. supra.]

Not pure, but defiled. *Nostra recta forsan, sed non pura justitia,* saith Bernard, *nisi forte meliores sumus quàm patres nostri, quorum illa vox, Omnes justitiæ nostræ sicut pannus* [De verb. Esa. Vidi Dom. Ser. 5.]

SERM.
V.

[S. Chrys. in 2 Cor. 5. 21.]

menstruatæ. Mala nostra, pura mala; bona nostra, pura nequaquam, saith Gregory. Now κηλίδα ἀνάγκη τινὰ μὴ εὑρεθῆναι, saith St. Chrysostom; 'necessary it is that the righteousness that shall present itself there, have not a spot in it.' As for ours, as pope Adrian the Sixth said, the case standeth thus, that *stillamus quotidie super telam justitiæ nostræ saniem concupiscentiæ nostræ,* and so it is defiled.

Mor. 9. 2.
[Ib. 9. 36.]

[Ib. 9. 18.]

And last of all, if it be straitly examined, indeed no righteousness. *Sancti viri omne meritum vitium est, si ab Æterno Arbitro districte judicetur.* And again : *Quousque pœná corruptionis astringimur, veram munditiam nequaquam apprehendimus.* And, *Omnis humana justitia injustitia esse invenietur ; si districte judicetur, injusta invenietur omnis justitia nostra.* And thus we see the conceit these Fathers have of our righteousness inherent ; that if it be dealt with according to righteousness, *in illo examine etiam justorum*

Mor. 9. 14.

vita succumbet, 'in that examination it will sink and cannot stand before it.' Yea, they themselves of the Church of Rome also, upon better examination, have begun to cry it down ; and I doubt not but the longer and further they look into it, the easier account they will make of it.

Disp. 8.
Quæst. 6.
p. 4.
[de effect.
Grat.]

Gregory de Valentia, after long debating the matter, thus resolveth : that, *Seclusá promissione diviná, non suppetit aliquis sufficiens titulus, cur opera nostra debent compensari.* And thus he expresseth his meaning, touching their value ; that they be like to base money (as princes have sometime made leather money current) wherewith plate is bought or other wares far exceeding the coin in value, which is no way in respect of itself, but because it pleased the prince so to allow of it. And what is this but a proclaiming our righteousness base, or as I said before, a crying it down ?

De Just.
6. 8.
[init.]

Stapleton, in his seventh proposition, how the matter standeth in our justification, at length is fain to resolve thus : *Facitque indulgendo, ut perinde simus coram Deo justi ac si universa ad amussim omnia mandata eademque perfectissime fecissemus.* Now indulgence, we know, belongeth unto sin, and righteousness, if it be true, needeth none. Therefore he telleth us it is *perinde ac si justi;* it is not *justi,* as they defend it. So that he confesseth their righteousness needeth an indulgence; and it is but *perinde ac si,* and not that neither in justice but acceptation, which is mere matter of favour and not of judicial proceeding.

And, to conclude, Bellarmine after his long disputation in the end taking upon him to answer a case of conscience, whether a man may repose any trust in that he had so long argued for, and how far, compriseth the matter in three propositions well worth the noting. 1. For first, very stoutly he setteth down, *Fiducia non ex fide solá nascitur, sed ex bonis meritis.* 2. Then in the second he falleth somewhat: *In meritis (quæ vere talia compertum est) fiducia aliqua collocari potest.* Not unless it be *compertum* they be *talia*—a case with them impossible; and not in them neither, but only *aliqua fiducia.* _{De Just.}

De Just. 5. 7.

3. And yet there is some; but after better bethinking himself, it may be, of the Judge sitting in His throne, he spoileth all in the third, which is, that *Propter incertitudinem propriæ justitiæ* (against his *compertum est*) *et periculum inanis gloriæ, tutissimum est fiduciam totam in solá Dei misericordiá reponere.* Mark that same *totam in solá,* which is clean contrary to his *aliqua* a little before. Mark his *misericordia;* and that he declineth the judicial proceeding. And mark his reason, because his righteousness is such as he is not sure of it, nor dare not put any trust in it, nor plead it *coram Rege justo judicium faciente.* Which is enough, I think, to shew when they have forgot themselves a little out of the fervour of their oppositions, how light and small account they make of it themselves, for which they spoil Christ of one half of His Name.

This is then the interpretation or meaning of this Name, that as well in the one sense as the other Christ is "our righteousness;" and as the prophet Esay putteth it down, in the plural number, *in Domino justitiæ nostræ,* as it were prophesying of these men, "All our righteousness," this as that, that one as well as the other "are in the Lord." No abatement is to be devised, the Name is not to be mangled or divided, but entirely belongeth to Christ full and whole, and we to call Him by it, *Jehova justitia nostra.* [Isa. 45. 24.]

We to call Him by it; this is our duty first: and that so to call Him by it, as by His Name. And a name is a note

II. The calling Christ

126 *Of Justification*

SERM.
V.
by this
"Name."
1.
Our duty.

Isa. 42. 8.

Ps. 115. 1.

Phil. 2. 9,
10.

Isa. 45. 23,
24, 25.

[Rom. 3.
27.]

1 Cor. 1. 30,
31.

De Justif.
5. 3.

of distinction, and we therefore so to use it; to apply it to Him and to none other whatsoever, as the nature of a name is; the nature of all names, but chiefly of those which be titles of honour. For howsoever we dispense with others, those we will not in any wise divide with any. *Gloriam meam alteri non dabo,* saith God by the Prophet; which maketh the Prophet to protest he will not meddle with it. *Non nobis Domine :* and again more vehemently, *Non nobis, sed Nomini Tuo da gloriam.* And such is this Name. For that very place in the New Testament where it is said, that "God hath given Him a Name which is above all names, that in His Name all knees should bow, and all tongues confess;" that place is taken out of the Prophet Esay, where the very same is said, that "all knees shall bow, and all tongues" shall acknowledge this Name; and that thus, by saying *In Jehová justitiæ meæ ;* and so acknowledging concludeth, that all the whole "seed of Israel," as they shall be "justified," so shall they "glory in the Lord." It is the very question which the Apostle of purpose doth propound, *Ubi ergo est gloriatio tua?* as if he should admonish us that this Name is given with express intent to exclude it from us, and us from it. And therefore in that very place where he saith, He is "made unto us from God, righteousness;" to this end, saith he, He is so made, *ut qui gloriatur, in Domino glorietur.* All which I put you in mind of to this end, that you may mark that this nipping at this Name of Christ is for no other reason but that we may have some honour ourselves out of our righteousness.

Bellarmine doth disclose as much, and doth not stick in plain terms to avow it. For in answer to that argument which is alleged by us, that after we are acquit of our sins at this bar, and that only for Christ our only righteousness, we are received into God's favour, and made His children by adoption, and then have heaven by way of inheritance; he answereth directly, Their meaning is not to content themselves with that single title of inheritance, but they mean to lay claim to it *duplici jure.* That is, not only *titulo hæreditatis,* but *jure mercedis* too. And therefore he giveth this reason; *Quoniam magis honorificum est habere aliquid ex merito,* 'for that it is more for their honour to have it by merit.' For so, saith he, Christ had it, and they must not be behind Him, but go even as far as He did. So that it seemeth he is resolved that rather than they will lose their honour, Christ must part with a piece of His Name, and be named *justitia nostra* only in the latter sense. Which is it the Prophet after, in the twenty-seventh verse of this chapter, setteth down as a mark of false prophets; that by having a pleasant dream of their own righteousness, they make God's people to forget His Name. As indeed, by this means, this part of Christ's Name hath been forgotten. And so much doth Pighius confess: *Dissimulare non possumus, hanc vel primam doctrinæ Christianæ partem obscuratam quam illustratam magis a scholasticis spinosis plerisque quæstionibus,* 'that this being the very chief part of a Christian doctrine, hath rather been obscured than received any light by the Schoolmen's questions and handling of it.' As much to say, as they had made the people in a manner to forget His Name.

[Jer. 23. 16, 27.]

[De Fid. et Just. Cont. f. 64. Ed. Ven. 1541.]

Now as to call Him by this Name is a duty, so to call Him by it is a use likewise, and a benefit there is which we receive by it. For calling Him by that Name which God hath prescribed, and which therefore is to Him most acceptable, we shall not do it for nought, for He will answer us; answer us, and answer for us; for us, as an advocate in our cause. So calleth Ezekias to Him: *Domine vim patior, responde pro me.* So king David reposeth himself: "Thou shalt answer for me, O Lord my God." And this shall He in all things wherein we shall need Him; but above all in that which concerneth His Name in particular, to be "our righteousness" against sin, and that before "the righteous Judge." And even so doth Jeremy teach us to pray unto Him: "O Lord our misdeeds testify against us, yet deal Thou with us according to Thy Name," which is *Jehova justitia nostra.* In Thy "Name" we are "justified:" deal Thou with us according to Thy Name, and justify us. Our sins are forgiven for Thy Name's sake: deal Thou with us according to Thy Name, and forgive us our sins. *Et noli ita reminisci peccatum nostrum, ut velis propterea oblivisci Nomen Tuum;* 'Let not the remembrance of our sins make Thee forget Thine own Name.' And this if we do, thus if

2. Our benefit.

Isa. 38. 14.

Ps. 38. 15.

Jer. 14. 7.

1 Cor. 6. 11.

we call on Him, *fidelis et justus est,* " He is faithful," saith St. John, "and just to forgive us our sins," to justify us and to be "our righteousness." For so is His Name, and He beareth not His Name for nought.

And this if we do, and if He be "our righteousness," as we may say in respect of His other Name with the Prophet, Ps.119.132. " Look Thou upon us and be merciful unto us, as Thou usest to do unto those that love Thy Name ;" so may we in respect of this go further and safely say, *Esto justitia et fac justitiam, esto justitia et intra in judicium cum servo Tuo.* For with this advocate, with this righteousness, with this Name, we may without fear appear before the King executing judgment and justice.

So for that duty which we are bound to acknowledge, we have this benefit which we shall be sure to receive; the greatest benefit that can be received for importance in itself, and the greatest in respect of the most dreadful place and time wherein we shall need to receive it, wherein heaven and earth and all in them shall not be able to stand us in stead, but "Jehovah our righteousness" only. And this is the view of His Name whereby we are called to Him, as well for our duty to it as for our benefit by it, which is that the Prophet by his *Ecce* willeth us to behold, and the sum of this Scripture.

A SERMON

PREACHED AT WHITEHALL,

UPON THE FIFTEENTH OF NOVEMBER, A.D. MDCI.

MATTHEW xxii. 21.

Give therefore to Cæsar the things which are Cæsar's; and to God those things which are God's.

Reddite ergo quæ sunt Cæsaris Cæsari; et quæ sunt Dei Deo. Lat. Vulg.

[*Render therefore unto Cæsar the things which are Cæsar's; and unto God the things that are God's.* Eng. Trans.]

WHICH twenty-second of Matthew in effect is nothing else but a chapter of controversies: with the Sadducee, verse twenty-three; with the Pharisee, verse twenty-two; with the Scribe, verse thirty-four; and here with the Herodian. With the Pharisees, of the great Commandment; with the Scribes, of the Messias. All worthy to be weighed; and all at other times commended by the Church to our consideration. This here in this.

The Herodian was a politic, and his question according, about a secular point; *Licetne solvere?* The case standeth not in this as it did in the other. The Pharisees and Sadducees had no further end but to set Him on ground, and so to expose Him to the contempt of the people. The Herodians had laid a more dangerous plot: they came with this mind, saith St. Luke, *ut caperent Eum, &c.*, "to catch Him;" by Lu. 20. 20. catching somewhat from Him, whereby they might lay Him fast, and draw Him within danger of the state. It stood our Saviour upon, to be well advised, to escape this snare thus

K

laid for Him, which accordingly He doth; leaving them in a
muse, and withal under one leaving us a pattern, that He is
no enemy but a friend to Cæsar, and a friend in this special
point of his receipt. That there is no duty, no not in this
kind, but Christ saith of it, *Reddite;* willeth and commandeth it to be rendered. That so, knowing what Christ held,
we may make it our tenet, and both hold it in opinion and
hold us to it in practice for ever.

At or about the birth of Christ this came to be first a
question, and so from thence still remained. So that it was
Lu. 2. 1. very meet Christ should resolve it. At His birth was the
great tax of the world under Augustus; which being a new
imposition, and never heard of before, fell out to breed much
matter of question, two sorts of men taking two several parts
about it. There is in the fifth chapter of Acts mention of
Acts 5. 37. " Judas of Galilee," that rose in the days of tribute. He
it was that held touching the tax, *Quod non.* The people
of God, Abraham's seed, free born, they to be charged with
taxes by a stranger, a heathen, an idolater? No, rather
rise and take arms, as Jeroboam did. The people's ears
itched after this doctrine. The best religion for the purse
is the best for them, and they ready to hold with Jeroboam, or Judas, or any that will abrogate payments. And
now, though Judas was taken and had as he deserved, and
after his execution pay it they did, though with an ill will,
yet the scruple of this question remained in men's minds
still; they continued irresolute touching the right of it. As
indeed in no one thing men are ever so long in resolving.
Still there were that muttered in corners Judas was right;
tribute was but a mere exaction. Men indeed of tumultuous
spirits, but in show zealous preservers of the people's liber-
ties, whom they called Gaulonites.

On the other side, Herod and they that were toward him
being all that they were by Cæsar, to make the tribute sure
work, they held that not only tribute but whatsoever else
was Cæsar's. His *quæ* was *quæcunque;* he could not have
enough, not till he had *quæ Dei* too. The Roman monarchy
[Vid. Hor. pricked fast towards this point; *Divisum imperium cum Jove*
Od. 1. 12.
50. et seq.] was received at this time with great applause. Cæsar and
Jupiter at halves; half God. Not long after, full out a

God; *Edictum Domini, &c.,* 'the edict of our Lord God Domitian.' And this was not a piece of poetry; but we find in the Jewish story Petronius in good earnest sought to bring in Caligula's image into the temple of God, and called for not only tribute but sacrifice for Cæsar. Now them that thus in derogation of the people's liberty held this part they termed Herodians, as it were men of Herod's turn. And thus held this question : thus have we both sides, and both their abettors. Of which the people inclined to the Gaulonite, and liked them better; the statesmen and officers took part with the Herodian.

Now come they to Christ to receive His resolution, which part He will take to. It is, for them, a very *quodlibet.* If to retain the people's favour, to avoid their outcry, he speak but doubtfully of Cæsar's tribute, *habetur propositum,* 'they have what they would;' it is that they came for, to bring Him in disgrace with the state, and in danger of His life. Thus would they fain have had it; and therefore, when truly they could not, as by this answer it is too plain, untruly they suggested, "We found this man denying to pay tri- Lu. 23. 2. bute unto Cæsar." But if this hit not, if He be for the tribute, yet will it not be from the purpose; they shall set the people (as good as a wasp's nest) upon Him; they shall subject Him to their clamour and obloquy. He that must be their Messias must proclaim a jubilee, must cry, No tribute; otherwise He is not for them. If He betray them to the servitude of tolls and taxes, away with Him; not Him, but Judas of Galilee. So have they Him at a dangerous dilemma, imagining He must needs take one part. But that was their error. For Christ took a way between both. For as neither part is simply true, so is there some truth in both. Therefore He answers not absolutely, as they fondly conceived He needs must, but with a double *quæ,* as indeed He should, which was not the answer they looked for. But it was such as they missed their purpose, and knew not how to reprove it.

The sum whereof is, that Christ is neither Gaulonite nor Herodian; nor no more are Christians Gaulonites to deny Cæsar his *quæ,* nor Herodians to grant him God's, and leave God none at all. But ready to acknowledge what

K 2

S E R M. due is to either, both of faith to God and allegiance to
VI.   Cæsar; and that in every point, and even in this here of
Licetne solvere?

The substance of which answer is the main ground of all
[Rom. 13. justice, *Suum cuique*, "Let every one render to each that
7.]   which is his." And if to every one, then to these two great
ones, Cæsar and God. To Cæsar Cæsar's due, to God God's.
Upon which two duties, by virtue of this text, there go forth
[Lu. 2. 1.] two decrees "for all the world to be taxed." The first tax-
ing to be for Cæsar and his affairs; 2. the like tax to be
levied for God and for His. For though many other duties
be due to both, and to be rendered to them both, yet the
[Mat. 22. matter of principal entendment in this place is, *Ostende mihi
19.]   numisma*, matter of payment.

The di-   These be the two capital points. Wherein I. of the joint
vision.
    I.   and mutual consistence of Cæsar and of God.
    II.   II. That there are, among the things we have, certain of
them things of Cæsar's; certain others things of God's.
    III.   III. That these things are to be rendered and given.
    IV.   IV. What these things are that are Cæsar's in this kind,
and what those that are God's, that we may pay each his
own.

    I.   From this happy conjunction of these two great lights,
Cæsar and
God jointly. Cæsar and God, here met together, linked with this copulative, *Cæsari* and *Deo*, and both in compass of one period;
against the Gaulonite of our age, the Anabaptist, who thinketh they are in opposition, the whole heaven in sunder,
and that God hath not His due unless Cæsar lays down
his sceptre; that Cæsar and God, Christ and a Christian
magistrate, are ἀσύστατα, 'incompatible,' that they stand
aloof and will not come near another; here is a *systasie*, a
consistence, they will stand together well—both they and
their duties—as close as one verse, one breath, one period
can join them.

To see then this pair thus near, thus coupled, thus as it
were arm in arm together, is a blessed sight. Not here only
to be seen, but all the Scriptures through with like aspect.
Exod. 20. Here in one Gospel, Cæsar and God; before in one law, God
providing as for His own worship, so for their honour that
are set over us. In one verse the Prophet joineth them

" My son, fear God and the King;" and in one verse the Prov. 24.
Apostle sorteth them, " Fear God, honour the King." So 1 Pet. 2. 17.
God and Christ, the Law and Gospel, the Prophets and
Apostles, fetch not their breath, come not to a full point, till
they have taken in both. Sure it is Christ and Belial agree
not, and as sure that they are the children of Belial that
" have no part in David," that is, the lawful magistrate— 2 Sam.
by Sheba's case. 20. 1.

This is enough to shew God impeacheth not Cæsar, nor
God's due Cæsar's right. Either permitteth other's interest,
and both of them may jointly be performed. That as God's
law supporteth the law of nations, so doth Christ plead for
Cæsar; His religion for Cæsar's allegiance, His Gospel for
Cæsar's duty, even to a penny. It was but a penny was
shewed ; not so much as a penny of Cæsar's, but Christ will
speak, he may have it. This against the Gaulonite, that
steps over *quæ Cæsaris*, the first part, and is all for *quæ Dei*,
the latter. And against the Herodian too, by whom *quæ
Cæsaris* is stood on alone, and *quæ Dei* slipped over. Two
duties are set forth ; there is a like regard to be had of both,
that we make not Christ's answer serve for either alone. I
know not how an evil use hath possessed the world ; commonly one duty is singled out and made much of, without
heed had of the other. *Quæ Cæsaris* audibly and with full
voice, *quæ Dei* drowned and scarce heard. And it is not in
this alone but in many others ; we cannot raise the price of
one virtue but we must cry down all the rest. Not canonize
preaching, but prayer must grow out of request. Not possible to bring up alms and works of mercy, but offerings and
works of devotion must be laid down. But by sale of Christ's [Mat. 26.
ointment no way to provide for the poor. Sensible in others, 9.]
and this too dull.

God is not entire thinks the Gaulonite, unless Cæsar's
image and superscription be blotted out. Cæsar hath not
enough till God have nothing left, thinks the Herodian.

Christ's course is the best, to hold the mean between
both ; either to be preserved in his right. Not to look so
much on one, as we lose sight of the other. Not to give
so good an ear to one, as we care not though the other
be never spoken of. God hath coupled them here ; and

SERM.
VI.
[Mat. 19.
6.]
since God hath coupled them, let not man sever them. To Cæsar and to God; not to Cæsar only, but to Cæsar and God. And again, not to God only, but to God and Cæsar.

Cæsar and God then will stand together : descend yet one degree further, we may put the case harder yet. For I demand, What Cæsar was this for whose interest Christ here pleadeth? To quicken this point somewhat more; it is certain it was Tiberius, even he under whom our Saviour was (and knew He was to be) put to death ; a stranger from Israel, a heathen man, uncircumcised, an idolater, and enemy to the truth. So were Augustus and the rest you will say ; but even in moral goodness he nothing so good as they. The Roman stories are in every man's hand ; men know he was far from a good prince or good man either, as good went even among the heathen. Yet even this Cæsar, and such as he ; any Cæsar will stand with God, and God with them for all that.

[Mat. 22.
21.]
Rom. 13. 7.
1 Pet. 2. 13.

1 Sam. 26.
9.
1 Chron.
16. 22.
Dan. 3. 1.
Dan. 5. 1,
&c.
Baruch 1.
11.
Not only to Cæsar, but to this and such as this, *Reddite,* saith Christ, *Solvite,* saith Paul, *Subjecti estote,* saith Peter, for all that ; so was the old divinity. Though an "evil spirit sent from God vex Saul," yet, saith David, " Destroy not," it is his word ; nay, "Touch not the Lord's anointed." Though Nebuchadnezzar set up a great idol in the field Dura, and Belshazzar his son rather worse than his father, yet " pray for Nebuchadnezzar," saith Jeremy, " and for Belshazzar his son," and for the peace even of that state. From these examples might Judas of Galilee have taken his directions. Christ did, and His Apostles after Him willed duties to be paid and obedience to be yielded, and yielded it themselves to such Cæsars as Claudius, Caligula, 1 Pet. 2. 18. and Nero ; *dyscolis dominis,* as St. Peter's term is, if ever there were any. Which sheweth they were all of mind, that Cæsar (though no better than these) and God will stand together well enough. Yea that though Cæsar gave not God His due, as these did not certainly, yet are we to give Cæsar that is his notwithstanding.

I know, we all know, if this Cæsar be Constantine, or Theodosius, the case is much the stronger, and the duty Rom. 13. 1. toucheth us nearer. But whether he be or no, "the powers that are are ordained of God," though Tiberius or Nero have

the powers. It is not the man, it is "the ordinance of God" Rom 13. 2.
we owe and perform our subjection to. We yield it not to
Tiberius, but to Cæsar; and Cæsar is God's ordinance, be
Tiberius what he will. This for the consorting of God and
Cæsar, and even of this Cæsar.

That point established, we come to the second; out of
these words *quæ Cæsaris et quæ Dei,* this may we infer,
that among the things we have, we all and every of us have
certain things of Cæsar's, and certain other things of God's.
That all the things we have are not our own, inasmuch as
out of them there belong some things to either of these. It
is as if Christ would make all we have not to be fully and
wholly ours, but three persons to be interested in them;
Cæsar to have a right to some, God to other some, and the
remainder only clearly to be ours—weigh the words *quæ*
Dei—so that His meaning is, every man should thus make
account with himself of that he hath, that there is in his
hands somewhat that pertaineth to either of these two.
That there is our substance, a portion whereto they have
as good right and title as we to the rest. That what we
have is ours, God's part and Cæsar's part first deducted.
Quæ Dei et quæ Cæsaris (it is the case possessive) do carry
thus much. Therefore saith the true Israelite, when he
tendereth his offering to God, *Sustuli quod sanctum est e* Deu. 26. 13.
domo meâ; I had a holy portion due to God amongst my
goods, I have severed it from the rest, I have brought it
and laid it upon the altar. So they in the first of Samuel,
the tenth chapter, to Saul their lawful magistrate presented
that was his. They that did so, *Tetigit Deus cor eorum,* 1 Sam. 10.
"God had touched their hearts." Consequently in their 26, 27.
hearts that did it not, there was the print of the devil's
claws, not the touch of the finger of God. This may serve
for the second, of the duty; for we shall strike the same nail
home in the third of *Reddite.*

For from this right thus imported in the words *quæ*
Cæsaris, quæ Dei, without any straining naturally doth follow the *Reddite.*

That theirs it is, and so, being theirs, to be paid them.
Not of courtesy, but of duty; not as a free legacy, but as a
due debt. Not *Date* but *Reddite,* 'Απόδοτε. As if our

Marginal notes: II. Certain things Cæsar's. Certain things God's. III. These to be rendered.

Saviour should say, You ask Me whether it be lawful to
pay, I tell you it is as lawful to pay it as it is unlawful to
withhold it; you would know whether you may, I say unto
you you not only may but must answer it. Nor *dare*, as
a matter of gift, but *reddere*, as a matter of repayment or
restitution. St. Paul maketh this point yet more plain,
[Rom. 13. indeed past all controversy, where he addeth to 'Ἀπόδοτε
7.] the other, ὀφειλὰς, to the word of rendering the plain term
of "debts;" expressly calling them "debts," both "tribute"
and "custom."

Then what is paid to the prince or to God is not to be
termed a donative, gratuity, or benevolence, but of the
nature of things restored, which though they be in our
keeping are in very deed other men's. And they that
reckon of them as matters merely voluntary, must alter
Christ's *Reddite* needs, and teach Him some other term.
But they that will learn of Him, must think and call them
Rom. 13. 7. "debts," must account themselves debtors; and that God
and Cæsar are as two creditors, and they indebted to them
both, and thereby as truly bound to discharge themselves
of these as of any debt or bond they owe. That if they
render not these duties, they detain that which is none of
theirs; and so doing are not only hard and illiberal, but
unrighteous and unjust men.

This from *Reddite*, but this is not all. There is yet a further matter in it, which giveth a great grace to this rendering.

For in that He willeth them *'Ἀπόδοτε*, His meaning is
withal it should not be ἀπότισις, a 'forced yielding,' but
ἀπόδοσις, 'a rendering,' and that willingly; for so the nature
of the word doth import, and so the Grecians distinguish
ἀποτίσαι and ἀποδοῦναι. Our translation readeth "Give to
Cæsar," no doubt with reference to this; that it should,
though duly, yet so willingly be paid, as it were even a frank
gift. In our speech we say, What is more due than debt?
And again, What is more free than gift? Yet both these
may meet, as in another case the Apostle coupleth them,
[1 Cor. 7. ὀφειλομένην εὔνοιαν, duty, yet benevolent; "benevolence"
3.] and yet "due," the one respecting the nature, the other
the mind; so both translations not amiss, both readings reconciled.

That is, not therefore to pay them because it will no better be. Cæsar hath *vim coactivam.* Hophni hath a flesh-hook, and can say, *Date vel auferetur a vobis;* and therefore to part with it as one delivereth a purse, or to bear it as a porter doth his load, groaning under it, that is not the manner of rendering it that is here required. But we must offer it as it were a gift, voluntarily, willingly, cheerfully, ἐκ χάριτος, ἐκ ψυχῆς· not ἐξ ἀνάγκης, ἐκ λύπης. Διὰ τὸν Κύριον, saith St. Peter, Διὰ τὴν συνείδησιν, saith St. Paul; even "for the Lord," even "for conscience sake;" though Hophni had no flesh-hook, though Cæsar had no Publican to take a stress. *1 Sam. 2. 16.*

Col. 3. 23. 2 Cor. 9. 7. 1 Pet. 2. 13. Rom. 13. 5.

To pay it with grudging and an evil eye, to say *Vade et redi cras,* to put off, to pay it after often coming and sending; this is not Ἀπόδοτε, these the heathen man termeth *viscata beneficia,* when they hang to the fingers like birdlime, and will not come away. *Prov. 3. 28.*

Nay, *Ecce venio,* saith Christ, so to pay it, even with love and good-will : an "offering of a free heart," as the Prophet, "a blessing" and "a grace," as the Apostle termeth it. The manner is much, and much to be regarded. The willing-ness of the mind is ever the fat of the sacrifice, and without it all is lean and dry. It holdeth here, which the Apostle saith, "If I preach," saith he—if we pay, say we—"we have no great cause to rejoice," necessity lieth on us so to do. But if we do it with a good will, there is then a reward. A reward at His hands, Who, as His Apostle telleth us, *hila-rem datorem diligit.* Not *datorem,* "any that giveth;" but *hilarem,* "him that giveth it cheerfully." That gift best pleaseth God; and that service, *Læti serviemus Regi,* is ever best pleasing and most acceptable. *Ps. 40. 7.*

[Ps. 110. 3. P.B. vers.] 2 Cor. 9. 5, 8.

1 Cor. 9. 16.

2 Cor. 9. 7.

Gen. 47. 25. [Vulg.]

Render then and give *quæ Cæsaris Cæsari,* that is, the right duty to the right owner; as dutifully and willingly, so to do it wisely. In *Suum cuique* there is not only justice but wisdom, to know and to preserve to every one that is his own, the right *quæ* to him that of right it belongeth to. *IV. What are Cæsar's, what God's.*

Not to shuffle them together—Cæsar's to God, God's to Cæsar—it skills not which to which, (" God is not the author of confusion,") but to know and discern what to each per-taineth; and what pertaineth, that to be answered. As before *1 Cor. 14. 33.*

SERM.
VI.
Mat. 19. 6.
Leu. 19. 14.

we pleaded, "What God hath joined," man should not sever, so now we plead again, What God hath severed, man should not confound. The Prophet calleth it "removing the landmark" which God hath set to distinguish the duties, that neither invade the other's right, but keep the partition which He hath set up. Not to stand as here they do straining at a penny which was Cæsar's without question, and do as after they did, receive the Roman eagle into their temple, which was God's right, and but slightly of them looked to. *Ægerrime pendere tributum, promptissime suscipere religionem;* 'with much ado to pay any tribute at all, with little ado to receive one religion after another.' God forbid Cæsar should so readily receive God's duties at their hands, as he might easily have them if he would.

To the end then we may know which to render to which, it remaineth we enquire what is either's due, that we may tender it accordingly. And first, what is Cæsar's.

If we ask then, What is Cæsar's? our answer must be, what God hath set over to him. For though *quæ Dei* stand last in place, yet sure it is the former *quæ* cometh out of the latter, and *quæ Cæsaris* is derived out of *quæ Dei.*

1 Chron.
29. 11, 12.

Originally in the person of all kings doth King David acknowledge that "All things are of Him," and "all things are His." But the sovereign bounty of God was such as He would not keep all in His own hands, but as He hath vouchsafed to take unto Himself a secondary means in the government of mankind, so hath He set over unto them

[¹perhaps
omit.]

a part of His own duty, that so one man might be one[1] another's debtor, and after a sort, *homo homini deus.* To the conveyance then of divers benefits He hath called to Himself divers persons, and joined them with Himself: as our parents, to the work of our bringing forth; our teachers, in the work of our training up; and many other, in their

Rom. 13. 4.

kinds, with Him and under Him, His means and ministers, all for our good.

And in the high and heavenly work of the preservation of all our lives, persons, estates, and goods, in safety, peace, and quietness, in this His so great and divine benefit, He hath associated Cæsar to Himself; and in regard of his care and travail therein hath entitled him to part of His own right, hath made over this *quæ*, and made it due to Cæsar, and so cometh he to claim it.

In which point we learn, if we pay tribute, what we have for it back in exchange; if we give, what Cæsar giveth us for it again, our penny and our pennyworths; even this, *Ut sit pax et veritas in diebus nostris.* This is it to which Isa. 39. 8. we do *debitum reddere*, as he calleth it. This to which we 1 Tim. 5. 4. do *mutuam vicem rependere*, as he speaketh, καὶ διὰ τοῦτο, Rom. 13. and even "for this cause pay we tribute." For this, that ⁶, ⁷. Rom. 13. 6. while we intend our private pleasures and profits in particular, we have them that study how we may safely and quietly do it, that counsel and contrive our peace, while we intend every man his own affairs; that wake while we sleep securely, and cark and care while we are merry and never think of it. Persons by whose providence a happy peace we long have enjoyed, and many good blessings are come to our nation. In which respect we owe them a large *quæ*, larger than I now can stand to recount.

1. We owe them honour inward, by a reverent conceit; 2. and outward, by an honourable testimony of the virtues in them and the good we receive by them. And sure I am this we owe, "not to speak evil" of them that are in authority; 2 Pet. 2. 10. and if there were some infirmity, not to blaze, but to con- Jude ver. 8. ceal and cover it; for that the Apostle maketh a part of "honour." 3. We owe them our prayers and daily devout 1 Cor. 12. remembrances; for all, saith St. Paul, but by special pre- 23. 1 Tim. 2. 2. rogative for princes. 4. We owe them the service of our bodies, which if we refuse to come in person to do, the Angel of the Lord will "curse" us, as he did Meroz. And Judg. 5. 23. in a word, to say with the Apostle, *Non recuso mori.* Acts 25. 11.

All these we owe, and all these are parts of *quæ Cæsaris*, but these are without the compass of this *quæ* here. These be not the things here questioned. It is the coin with Cæsar's stamp, it is a matter of payment. Let us hold us to that.

I say then, to be safe from the foreign enemy, from the wolf abroad, is a very great benefit. The sword holdeth him out; *propter hoc* we owe to the sword. To be quiet from the inward violent injurious oppressors, the fat and foregrown rams within our own fold, is a special blessing; the sceptre holds them in, *propter hoc* we owe to the sceptre. That by means of Cæsar's sword we have a free sea and safe port and harbour; *propter hoc* we owe to Cæsar our custom. That by means of his sword we have our seed-time to ear the ground, our harvest to inn the crop quiet and safe; *propter hoc* we owe to Cæsar our tribute or tax. That by means of his sceptre we have right in all wrongs, and are not overborne in our innocence by such as never cease to trouble such as are quiet in the land; *propter hoc* we owe to Cæsar the fees due to his courts of justice.

These are *quæ Cæsaris;* and not one of these but hath his ground in the word of God. The custom, Luke 3. 13; the tax, 1 Sam. 17. 25; the fines, Ezra 7. 26; the confiscation, Ezra 10. 8.

These then are *quæ Cæsaris.* But these are current and ordinary; but extraordinary occasions cannot be answered with ordinary charges. Though in peace the set maintenance of garrisons which is certain (the ordinance of Josaphat) is enough; yet when war cometh, πόλεμος οὐ τεταγμένα ζητεῖ, war admits no stint, but as occasions call for it supply must be ready.

There is no safety or assurance of quietness except the enemy fear. There is no fear without power, except we be able to hold our own, maugre the malice and force of the enemies. There is no power but by preparation of soldiers and furniture for war. Nor that without pay, the sinews of all affairs; nor pay without contribution. And *propter hoc,* διὰ τοῦτο, besides those other ordinary, the indictions for war, which we call subsidies, are part of *quæ Cæsaris* too.

And warranted by the Scripture; Amaziah levying a hundred talents at one time against Edom, Menahem levying a thousand talents at another against Assur, a great contribution of fifty shekels a man. Indeed so it was, but such were the occasions; and the occasions being such, done, and done lawfully.

Then as generally we are bound to render all *quæ Cæsaris,* so in particular by this text and at this instant this *quæ,* when the times make it requisite, and it is orderly required.

Christ That willeth us to render it, rendered it Himself, and very timely He did it. For He went "to be taxed,"

2 Chron. 25. 6.
2 Kings 15. 19, 20.

Lu. 2. 5.

being yet in His mother's womb, as Levi is said to "pay Heb. 7. 9, tithe in his father's loins." And He was born under the 10. obedience of paying this duty. This may haply be said not to be His own act: therefore after at full years, then also, though He might have pleaded exemption as He telleth Peter, yet paid He His stater; though not due, yet to avoid Mat. 17. 27. the offence of refusing to pay to Cæsar, *Conditor Cæsaris censum solvit Cæsar.* Seeing then Cæsar's Creator paid Cæsar his due, will any deny to do it? Especially seeing He paid Cæsar his due, yea even then when Cæsar did not render to God His due, but to idols; and what colour then can any have to deny it?

So have we His example, whereof we have here His precept; doing that before us which He willeth us to do after Him, and calling to us for no more than He did Himself. And ensuing His steps, His Apostle presseth the same point, telling us custom and tribute are ὀφειλαὶ, "debts;" shewing Rom. 13. 7. us why they be debts, διὰ τοῦτο, for the good we receive; and willing us therefore to depart with them, even *propter* [Rom. 13. 5.] *conscientiam,* "for very conscience sake."

Let me add but this one. The forefathers of these here that move this doubt, they forsook David's house only because they thought much of paying the tax which Solomon had set, and they revolted to Jeroboam: what got they by it? By denying *quæ Cæsaris* they lost *quæ Dei,* the true religion, and besides enthralled themselves to far greater exactions, which the erecting of a new estate must needs require. Even these not obeying this advice, this *Reddite* of our Saviour's, but mutinying for the Roman tribute after, under Florus and Albinus, deputies for Cæsar; besides that they lost their temple, sacrifice, and service, their *quæ Dei;* upon this very point overthrew their estate clean, which to this day they never recovered. Therefore *Reddite quæ Cæsaris* is good counsel, lest *quæ Dei* and all go after it.

To conclude then, 1. Cæsar and God will stand together; yea Tiberius Cæsar and God. 2. To these, so standing, there are certain things due of duty belonging. 3. These things so due are to be rendered; not given as gratuities, but rendered as debts. And again, with good will to be rendered, not delivered by force; and as willingly so wisely,

SERM.
VI.

Cæsar to have his, God His; in distinction, not confusion, but each His own. 4. Cæsar such duties, all such duties as pertain to him at large; but, as this text occasioneth, the duty of tribute and subsidy. This is the sum.

[¹ Queen Elizabeth.] And if Tiberius Cæsar, much more that Prince¹ that every way Christ Himself would recommend before Tiberius, whom it were an injury once to compare with Tiberius, above any Cæsar of them all; who hath exalted Him Whom Tiberius crucified, and professed Him with hazard of her estate and life, Whom they persecuted in all bloody manner.

Who hath preserved us in the profession of His holy Name and truth many years, quietly without fear and peaceably without interruption; and so may still, many and many times many years more. To this, to such a one, by special due, *Reddite* more, and more willingly, and more bounteously, than to them. The conclusion is good, the consequent much more forcible. This for *quæ Cæsaris* now. For *quæ Dei* at some other time, when like text shall offer like occasion.

A SERMON

PREACHED BEFORE

THE KING'S MAJESTY AT HAMPTON COURT,

ON SUNDAY THE TWENTY-EIGHTH OF SEPTEMBER, A. D. MDCVI.

NUMBERS x. 1, 2.

Then God spake to Moses, saying,
Make thee two trumpets of silver, of one whole piece shalt thou
make them.   And thou shalt have them (or *they shall be for* והיו לך
thee) to assemble (or *call together) the congregation, and to* למה רא
remove the camp. העדה

[*Locutusque est Dominus ad Moysen, dicens,*
Fac tibi duas tubas argenteas ductiles, quibus convocare possis multi-
tudinem quando movenda sunt castra.   Lat. Vulg.]

[*And the Lord spake unto Moses, saying,*
Make thee two trumpets of silver, of a whole piece shalt thou make
them ; that thou mayest use them for the calling of the assembly,
and for the journeying of the camps.   Eng. Trans.]

AMONG divers and sundry commissions granted in the Law A Grant.
for the benefit and better order of God's people, this which I
have read is one ; given, as we see, *per Ipsum Deum,* 'by God From God.
Himself,' and that *vivæ vocis oraculo,* by express warrant
from His own mouth : " Then God spake to Moses, saying."

And it is a grant of the right and power of the trumpets, Of the
and with them of assembling the people of God.   A right calling as-
and power not to be lightly accounted of, or to be heard of semblies.
with slight attention ; it is a matter of great weight and of this
consequence, the calling of assemblies.   There is yearly a matter of
solemn feast holden in memory of it, and that by God's own Nu. 29. 1.
appointment, no less than of the Passover or of the Law

itself, even the "feast of the trumpets," much about this
time of the year, the latter equinoctial. And God appointeth
no feast but in remembrance of some special benefit. It is
therefore one of His special benefits and high favours vouchsafed them, and to be regarded accordingly.

In whose
hands this
power was
before.
This power hitherto, ever since they came out of Egypt
and that God adopted them for His people, unto this very
day and place had God kept in His own hands, as to Him
alone of right properly belonging. For unto this very day
and place the people of God, as they had assembled many
times and oft, so it was ever—they be the very last words

Nu. 9.
18, 20, 23.
of the last chapter, which serve for an introduction to these
of ours—ever all their meetings and removings were by
immediate warrant from God Himself. But here now God
no longer intending thus to warn them still by special direction from His own self, but to set over this power once for

Exod. 19.
13.
all, here He doth it. This is the primary passing it from
God and deriving it to Moses, who was the first that ever
held it by force of the Law written. For to this place they
came by the sound of God's, and from this place they dis-
lodged by the sound of Moses' trumpet.

The time
and place
of the
granting.
And it is a point very considerable what day and place
this was; for it appeareth they were yet at Sinai, by the
twelfth verse, yet at the very mount of God by the thirty-
third verse of this chapter, even then when this commission
came forth; so that this power is as ancient as the Law. At
no other place nor no other time delivered than even the
Law itself; when the two tables were given, the two trumpets
were given; and Moses that was made keeper of both the
tables, made likewise keeper of both the trumpets; both at
Sinai, both at one time, as if there were some near alliance between the Law and assemblies. And so there is,
assemblies being ever a special means to revive the Law, as
occasions serve, and to keep it in life. As if the Law itself
therefore lacked yet something, and were not perfect and
full without them; so till this grant was passed, they stayed
still at Sinai, and so soon as ever this was passed, they presently removed.

To entreat then of this power. The story of the Bible
would serve our turn to shew us who have had the exercise

of it in their hands from time to time, if that were enough. But that is not enough. For the errors first and last about this point, from hence they seem to grow, that men look not back enough, have not an eye to this, how it was "in the Mat. 19. 4. beginning," by the very law of God. Being therefore to search for the original warrant by which the assemblies of This the God's people are called and kept, this place of Numbers is original generally agreed to be it; that here it is first found, and here it is first founded; even in the Law, the best ground for a power that may be.

In Lege quid scriptum est? quomodo legis? saith our Saviour, "What is written in the Law? how read you there?" Lu. 10. 26. as if He should say, If it be to be read there it is well, then must it needs be yielded to; there is no excepting to it then, unless you will except to Law and Lawgiver, to God and all. Let us then come to this commission.

The points of it be three; first, "two trumpets of silver," The parts to be made out of "one whole piece" both. Secondly, with of the these trumpets "the congregation" to be called, and "the grant. camp" removed. Thirdly, Moses to make these trumpets, and being made to use them to these ends. These three; 1. the instrument, 2. the end for which, 3. the party to whom.

Now, to marshal these in their right order. 1. The end is to be first; *Sapiens semper incipit a fine,* saith the philosopher. 'A wise man begins ever at the end,' for that indeed is *causa causarum,* as logic teacheth us, 'the cause of all the causes,' the cause that sets them all on working. 2. Then next, the instrument, which applieth this power to this end. 3. And so last, the agent who is to guide the instrument, and to whom both instrument and power is committed.

1. The end for which this power is conveyed is double, as the subject is double whereon it hath his operation; 1. the camp, and the 2. congregation. On either of these a special act exercised; to "remove the camp," to "call together the congregation." One for war, the other for peace.

That of the camp hath no longer use than while it is war. God forbid that should be long; nay, God forbid it should be at all. The best removing of the camp is the removing of it quite and clean away. But if it be not possible, if it lie Rom. 12. not in us, to have peace with all men, if war must be, here 18.

L

is order for it. But the calling of the congregation, that is it; that is to continue, and therefore that which we to deal with.

The calling of the congregation, as in the two next verses, either in whole or in part; either of all the tribes, or but the chief and principal men in them. A power for both these. And in a word, a power general for calling assemblies; assemblies in war, assemblies in peace, assemblies of the whole, assemblies of each or any part.

2. This power to be executed by instruments : the instruments, to be trumpets, two in number; those to be of silver, and both of one entire piece of silver.

3. This power, and the executing of it by these instruments, committed to Moses. First he to have the making of these trumpets, *Fac tibi ;* then he to have the right to them being made, *Et erunt tibi ;* then he to use them to " call the congregation," and if need be to " remove the camp." None to make any trumpet but he ; none to have any trumpet but he. None to meddle with the calling of the congregation or removing the camp with them but he, or by his leave and appointment.

Wherein as we find the grant full, so are we further to search and see whether this grant took place or no. Whether as these trumpets were made and given to " call the congregation," so the congregation from time to time have been called by these trumpets. And so first of the granting this power to be executed, and then of the executing this power so granted.

So have we two subjects, " the camp" and " the congregation." Two acts, to " assemble" and to " remove." Two instruments, the " two silver trumpets." Two powers : to make them, to own them being made for the two acts or ends before specified ; first for calling the assembly, and then for dislodging the camp. And all these committed to Moses. The sum of all this is, the establishing in Moses the prerogative and power of calling and dissolving assemblies about public affairs.

Then God spake to Moses, &c.

If we begin with the end, the end is assembling. Assembling is reduced to motion ; not to every motion, but to the very chiefest of all, as that which draweth together all, and so at once moveth all. For as in the soul when the mind summoneth all the powers and faculties together, or in the body when all the sinews join their forces together it is *ultimum potentiæ ;* so in the body politic when all the estates are drawn together into one, it is *nixus* rather than *motus,* a main sway rather than a motion ; or if a motion, it is *motus magnus,* no common and ordinary, but an extraordinary great motion. Such a motion is assembling, and such is the nature of it.

Yet even this, great and extraordinary as it is, such and so urgent occasions may and do daily arise, as very requisite it is such meetings there should be ; very requisite, I say, both in war and in peace, both for " the camp" and for " the congregation." The ground whereof seemeth to be, that power dispersed may do many things ; but to do some, it must be united. United in consultation ; for that which one eye cannot discern, many may. United in action ; for many hands may discharge that by parts, which in whole were too troublesome for any. But action is more proper to war : that is the assembly of fortitude. And consultation rather for peace : that is the assembly of prudence. And in peace, chiefly for making of laws ; for that every man is more willing to submit himself to that whereof all do agree. The whole " camp" then when it is assembled, will be the more surely fortified ; and the whole " congregation," when it is assembled, will be the more soundly advised. And hereby it cometh to pass, that there ever hath and ever will be great use of calling assemblies.

Let me add yet one thing further, to bring it home to ourselves. There is no people under heaven may better speak for the use of assemblies than we ; there was nothing that did our ancestors the Britons more hurt, saith Tacitus[a] of them, nothing that turned them to greater prejudice than this one, that they met not, they consulted not in common, but every man ran a course by himself of his own head ;

Marginal notes:
Yet necessary.
For " the camp."
For " the congregation."
Especially for this land of Britain.

[a] Nec aliud adversus validissimas gentes pro nobis utilius, quam quod in commune non consulunt. Rarus ad pro- pulsandum commune periculum con- ventus. Ita dum singuli pugnant, uni- versi vincuntur. In vitâ Agric. [c. 12.]

and this was the greatest advantage the Roman had of them, they were not so wise as to know what good there was in public conventions. Therefore great use of assemblies, may we say of all others.

Now if they be needful for "the camp," and for "the congregation" as it is a civil body, I doubt not but I may add also every way as needful for "the congregation" properly so Necessary called, that is, the Church. The Church hath her wars to fight, the Church hath her laws to make.

Necessary for the Church.

Wars with heresies, wherein experience teacheth us it is matter of less difficulty to raze a good fort than to cast down a strong imagination, and more easy to drive out of the field a good army of men than to chase out of men's minds a heap of fond opinions, having once taken head. Now heresies have ever been best put to flight by the Church's assemblies, that is, councils, as it were by the armies of *De vitâ* God's Angels, as Eusebius calleth them; yea, it is well *Constantini, lib. 3.* known some heresies could never be thoroughly mastered *cap. 6.* or conquered but so.

De vitâ Constantini, lib. 3. cap. 6.

Then for the Church's laws, which we call canons and rules, made to restrain or redress abuses, they have always likewise been made at her assemblies in councils, and not elsewhere. So that as requisite are assemblies for the congregation in this sense, as in any other. By this then that hath been said it appeareth that God's *Fac tibi* here is no more than needs, but that meet it is the trumpets be put to making. And so I pass over to the instruments, which is the second part.

2.
Instruments.
Assembling we said is reduced to motion. Motion is a work of power. Power is executed *organice,* that is, by instrument; so an instrument we must have, wherewithal to stir up or to begin this motion.

Trumpets.
1. That instrument to be the trumpet. It is the sound that God Himself made choice of, to use at the publishing or proclaiming His Law. And the same sound He will have continued and used still for assemblies, which are, as hath been said, special supporters of His Law. And the very same He will use too at the last, when He will take account of the keeping or breaking of it, which shall be *1 Cor.* 15. done *in tubâ novissimâ,* by the sound of "the last trump."
52.

And He holdeth on, or continueth one and the same instrument, to shew it is one and the same power that continueth still; that whether an Angel blow it as at Sinai, or whether Moses as ever after, it is one sound, even God's sound, God's voice we hear in both.

2. They are to be twain, for the two assemblies that follow in the next verses; either of the whole tribes, *coagmentative*, or of the chief and choice persons of them only, *representative*. And for the two tables also. For even this very month, the first day, they are used to a civil end; the tenth day to a holy, for the day of expiation; of which this latter belongeth to the first, that former to the second table. Two.

3. They are to be "of silver" (not to seek after speculations) only, for the metal's sake, which hath the shrillest and clearest sound of all others. 3. "Of silver."

4. They are to be "of one whole piece" both of them, not of two diverse; and that must needs have a meaning, it cannot be for nothing. For unless it were for some meaning, what skilled it else though they had been made of two several plates? but only to shew that both assemblies are *unius juris*, both 'of one and the same right;' as the trumpets are wrought and beaten out, both of one entire piece of bullion. 4. "Of one entire piece."

3. But it will be to small purpose to stand much upon the instrument; I make way therefore to the third point, how they shall be bestowed, who shall have the dealing with them; for on them depends, and with them goeth the power of calling assemblies.

First, to whom these trumpets, to whom this power was granted, "to call the congregation;" and then whether "the congregation" were ever after so called by this power and these trumpets. To whom committed.

1. Where first it will be soon agreed, I trust, that every body must not be allowed to be a maker of trumpets; nor when they be made, that they hang where who that list may blow them; that is, that every man hand over head is not to be in case to draw multitudes together: there will be, saith St. Luke, *turbatio non minima*, "no small ado," if that may be suffered. If Demetrius getteth together his fellow-craftsmen, they may of their own heads rush into the common hall, and there keep a shouting and crying two hours to- Not to all. Acts 19. 23.

SERM. gether, not knowing most of them why they came thither
VII. —and yet thither they came. There is not so much good
in public meetings, but there is thrice as much hurt in such
as this; no commonwealth, no not popular estates could ever
[1 Cor. 14. endure them. Nay πάντα κατὰ τάξιν, say both Scripture
40.]
Acts 19. 39. and nature, "Let all be done in order;" let us have ἔννο-
μον ἐκκλησίαν, "lawful orderly assemblies," or else none at
all. Away then with this confusion, to begin with, away
with Demetrius' assemblies.

But some.   To avoid then this confusion some must have this power,
for and in the name of the rest. Shall it be one or more?
for that is next. Nay, but one, saith God, in saying, *Tibi*.
Some, not Where I wish you mark this, That as at the first He took
many, but this power into His own hands and called them still together
one.
Himself, so here He deriveth this power immediately from
Himself unto one, without first settling it in any body col-
lective at all.

It is from our purpose to enter the question, whether the
power were in the whole body originally? seeing though it
were, it is now by the positive ordinance of God otherwise
disposed. The reason may seem to be partly, necessity of
expedition; the trumpets may need to be blown sometimes
suddenly, sooner than divers can well meet and agree upon
it too. Partly, avoiding of distraction; the two trumpets
may be blown two divers ways, if they be in two hands,
1 Cor. 14. 8. and so shall the "trumpet give an uncertain sound," and
how shall the congregation know whither to assemble?
Nay, a worse matter yet than all that, so may we have
assembly against assembly; and rather than so, better no
assembly at all.

Therefore as God would have them both made of one
piece, so will He have them both made over to one person;
1. for *Tibi* implieth one. Who is that one? It is to Moses
That one, God speaketh, to him is this *Tibi* directed; him doth God
Moses.
Moses to nominate, and of his person make choice first to make these
be maker
of them. trumpets. No man to make, no man to have the hammering
of any trumpet but he.

And there is no question but for Aaron, and his sons the
priests; they are to call the Levites, to call the people together to their assemblies; how shall they warn them to-

gether, unless they make a trumpet too? But if there be any question about this, God's proceeding here will put all out of question. For to whom giveth He this charge? וְהָיוּ לְךָ Not to Aaron is this spoken, but to Moses; Aaron receiveth And owner of them. no charge to make any trumpet, never a *Fac tibi* to him, neither in this nor in any other place. To Moses is this charge given. And to Moses; not, "Make thee" one, one for secular affairs—that they would allow him, but *Fac tibi duas,* "make thee two," make both.

2. Well, the making is not it. One may make and another may have, *Sic vos non vobis;* you know the old verse. [In vitâ When they be made and done, then who shall own them? Virg.] It is expressed, that too: *Et erunt tibi,* "they shall be for thee." They shall be, not one for thee and another for Aaron; but *erunt tibi,* "they shall be both for thee," they shall be both thine. A third if they can find, they may lay claim to that; but both these are for Moses.

We have then the delivery of them to Moses to make, which is a kind of seizin, or a ceremony investing him with the right of them. We have beside, plain words to lead their possession, and those words operative, *Erunt tibi;* that as none to make them, so none to own them being made but Moses. And what would we have more to shew us, *cujus sunt tubæ,* 'whose the trumpets be,' or whose is the right of calling assemblies? It is Moses' certainly, and he by virtue of these stands seized of it.

To go yet further. But was not all this to Moses for his That time only, and as it began in him so to take end with him? power to continue after Moses. Was it not one of these same *privilegia personalia quæ non trahuntur in exemplum,* 'a privilege peculiar to him, and so no precedent to be made of it?' No, for if you look but a little forward, to the eighth verse following, there you shall see that this power which God here conveyeth, this law of the silver trumpets, is a "law to last for ever," even throughout all their generations, not that generation only. And there is great reason it should be so, that seeing the use should never cease, the power likewise should never determine.

Being then not to determine but to continue, it must Moses received it as chief magistrate. descend to those that hold Moses' place. I demand then,

What place did Moses hold? Sure it is that Aaron was now the High-Priest, anointed and fully invested in all the rights of it ever since the eighth chapter of the last book. Moses had in him now no other right but that of the chief magistrate. Therefore as in that right, and no other, he received and held them, so he was made *custos utriusque tabulæ;* so he is made *custos utriusque tubæ.* But who can tell us better than he himself, in what right he held them? He doth it in the fifth verse of the thirty-third chapter of [Deut. 33. 5.] Deuteronomy, read it which way you will: *Erat in Jishrune Rex,* or *in rectissimo Rex,* or *in rectitudine Rex,* or *in recto Regis, dum congregaret Principes populi, et tribus Israel.* All come to this, that though in strict propriety of speech Moses were no King, yet in this he was *in rectitudine Rex,* or *in recto Regis;* that is, in this had, as we say, *jus regale,* that he might and did assemble the tribes and chief men of the tribes at his pleasure. Herein he was *Rex in rectitudine.* For this was *rectitudo Regis,* a power regal. And so it was holden in Egypt before Moses, even in the Gen. 41. 44. law of nature; that without Pharaoh no man might "lift up hand or foot in all the land of Egypt"—suppose to no public or principal motion; and so hath it been holden in all nations, as a special power belonging to dominion. Which maketh it seem strange, that those men which in no cause are so fervent as when they plead that Churchmen should not καριεύειν, that is, 'have dominion;' do yet hold this power, which hath ever been reputed most proper to dominion, should belong to none but to them only. Our Sa-Mat. 20. 26. viour Christ's *Vos autem non sic,* may, I am sure, be said to them here in a truer sense than as they commonly use to apply it.

The chief magistrate to succeed in it.   To conclude then this point, if Moses as in the right of chief magistrate held this power, it was from him to descend to the chief magistrates after him over the people of God, and they to succeed him, as in his place so in this right, it being by God Himself settled in Moses and annexed to his place, *lege perpetuâ,* by an estate indefeasible, "by a perpetual law," throughout all their generations. Therefore ever after by God's express order, from year to year, every year on the first day of the seventh month were they blown by Moses first, and after by them that held his place, and the feast of the trumpets solemnly holden; as to put them in mind of the benefit thereby coming to them, so withal to keep alive and fresh still in the knowledge of all, that this power belonged to their place, that so none might ever be ignorant to whom it did of right appertain to call assemblies.

And how then shall Aaron's assemblies be called? with what trumpet they? God Himself hath provided for that in the tenth verse following, that with no other than these. There is in all the Law no order for calling an assembly, to what end or for what cause soever, but this and only this; no order for making any third trumpet; under these two therefore all are comprised. This order there God taketh, that Moses shall permit Aaron's sons to have the use of these trumpets. But the use, not the property. They must take them from Moses, as in the thirty-first chapter of this Book Phinehas doth; but, *Erunt tibi*—God's own words, *Erunt tibi*—must still be remembered; his they be for all that, Moses the owner still, the right remains in him; their sounding of them deprives not him of his interest, alters not the property; *Erunt tibi*, must still be true, that right must still be preserved. It may be, if we communicate with flesh and blood, we may think it more convenient, as some do, that God had delivered Moses and Aaron either of them one. But when we see God's will by God's word what it is, that Moses is to have them both, we will let that pass as a revelation of flesh and blood, and think that which God thinketh to be most convenient.

Now then, if the trumpets belong to Moses, and that to this end, that with them he may "call the congregation," these two things do follow: first, that if he "call," "the congregation" must not refuse to come; secondly, that unless he "call" they must not assemble of their own heads, but keep their places. Briefly thus: "the congregation" must come when it is called; and it must be called, ere it come. These are the two duties we owe to the two trumpets, and both these have God's people ever duly performed.

And yet not so, but that this right had been called in

[margin: Aaron's assemblies, how called. Nu. 10. 10.]

[margin: Nu. 31. 6.]

[margin: למקרא העדה The two duties.]

question, yea even in Moses' own time, (that we marvel not if it be so now) and both these duties denied him even by those who were alive and present then, when God gave him the trumpets. But mark by whom, and what became of them.

1.
To come
when they
be called.
The first duty is to come when they be called; and this was denied, in the sixteenth chapter following, the twelfth verse, by Korah, Dathan, and their crew. Moses sounded his trumpet, sent to call them; they answer flatly—and that not once, but once and again — *Non veniemus,* they would not come, not once stir for him or his trumpet, they. A plain contradiction indeed; neither is there in all that chapter any contradiction *veri nominis,* 'true and properly so to be called,' but only that. You know what became of them, they went quick to hell for it; and wo be to them,

Jude ver.
11.
even under the Gospel, saith St. Jude, that perish in the same contradiction, "the contradiction of Korah."

2.
To be call-
ed ere
they come.
The second duty is, to be called ere they come; this likewise denied, even Moses himself, (that they in this place may not think strange of it) in the twentieth chapter of this very book. Water waxing scant, a company of them grew mutinous, and in tumultuous manner, without any sound of the trumpet, assembled of themselves. But these are

Nu. 20. 13.
branded too: the water they got is called "the water of Meribah;" and what followed you know. None of them

[Ps. 95.
11.]
that drank of it, came into the land of promise. "God swore they should not enter into His rest."

Called,
and came
not.
Came un-
called.
Now as both these are bad, so of the twain this latter is the worse. The former, that came not being called, do but sit still, as if they were somewhat thick of hearing; but these latter that come being not called, either they make themselves a trumpet without ever a *Fac tibi,* or else they offer to wring Moses' trumpet out of his hands, and take it in their own. Take heed of this latter; it is said there to be *adversus Mosen,* "even against Moses himself." It is the very next forerunner to it, it pricks fast upon it. For they that meet against Moses' will, when they have once thoroughly learned that lesson, will quickly perhaps grow capable of another, even to meet against Moses himself, as these

Acts 19. 40.
did. *Periclitamur argui seditionis,* saith the town-clerk, " We

have done more than we can well answer;" we may be indicted of treason for this day's work, for coming together
without a trumpet; and yet it was for Diana, that is, for
a matter of religion.

You see then whose the right is, and what the duties be
to it, and in whose steps they tread that deny them. Sure
they have been baptized or made to drink of the same water,
"the water of Meribah," that ever shall offer to do the like,
to draw together without Moses' call.

And now to our Saviour Christ's question: "In the Law
how is it written? How read you?" Our answer is: There
it is thus written, and thus we read, that Moses hath the
right of the trumpets, that they to go ever with him and his
successors; and that to them belongeth the power of calling
the public assemblies.

This is the Law of God, and that no judicial Law, peculiar Agreeable
to that people alone, but agreeable to the Law of nature and to the Law
of nature.
nations, two Laws of force through the whole world. For
even in the little empire of the body natural, *principium
motus*, 'the beginning of all motion' is in and from the
head. There all the knots, or as they call them all the
conjugations of sinews, have their head, by which all the
body is moved. And as the Law of nature by secret in- To the Law
stinct, by the light of the creation, annexeth the organ to of nations.
the chiefest part, even so doth the Law of nations, by the
light of reason, to the chiefest person; and both fall just
with the Law here written, where, by *Erunt tibi*, the same
organ and power is committed to Moses, the principal person
in that commonwealth. The Law of nations in this point,
both before the Law written and since, where the Law
written was not known, might easily appear if time would
suffer, both in their general order for conventions so to be
called, and in their general opposing to all conventicles
called otherwise.

Verily the heathen Laws made all such assemblies unlawful which the highest authority did not cause to meet,
yea though they were *ἱερῶν Ὀργίων ἕνεκα*, say Solon's
Laws; yea though *sub prætextu religionis*, say the Roman
Laws. Neither did the Christian Emperors think good to
abate any thing of that right. Nay, they took more straight

order; for besides the exiling of the person, which was the Law before, they proscribed the place where under pretence of religion any such meetings should be. But I let them pass, and stand only on the written Law, the Law of God.

We have Law then for us, that Moses is ever to "call the congregation." But though we have Law, *Mos vincit Legem*, 'Custom overruleth Law.' And the custom or practice may go another way, and it is practice that ever best betrayeth a power. How then hath the practice gone? It is a necessary question this, and pertinent to the text itself. For there is a power granted; and in vain is that power that never cometh into act. Came then this power into act? It is a power to "call the congregation together." Were the congregations called together by it? A grant there is that *Erunt tibi*, so it should be: did it take place? Was it so, *Erantne illi?* Had he it? did he enjoy it? Let us look into that another while, what became of this grant, what place it took. And we shall not offend Moses in so doing. It is his advice and desire both, that we should enquire into the days past that were before us, and ask "even from one end of heaven to the other," to see how matters have been carried. So that, as our Saviour Christ sendeth us to the Law by His *In Lege quid scriptum est?* so doth Moses direct us to the use and practice by his *Interroga de diebus antiquis*. I do ask then, these trumpets here given, this power to "call together the congregation," how hath it been used? Hath "the congregation" been called accordingly in this, and no other manner? by this and no other power? It hath, as shall appear; and I will deal with no assemblies, but only for matters of religion.

The practice or use of this power among the Jews.

Deut. 4. 32.

Of Moses, first, there is no question; it is yielded that he called them, and dismissed them. And even so did Joshua after him no less than he, and they obeyed him in that power no less than Moses. And as for that which is objected concerning Moses, that he for a time dealt in matters of the Priest's office, it hath no colour in Joshua and those that succeeded him.

By Moses.
Joshua.
Josh. 1. 17.

The covenant and the renewing of the covenant are matters merely spiritual; yet in that case did Joshua (Joshua, not Eleazar) assemble all the tribes, Levi and all, to Sichem

—Joshua the twenty-fourth—called the assembly at the first Josh. 24. 1, 28.
verse, dissolved it at the twenty-eighth. For if Joshua may
call, he may dissolve too; Law, reason, sense, teach that
cujus est nolle, ejus est et velle. That calling and discharging belong both to one power. Nay, Demetrius' assembly,
though they had come together disorderly, yet when the
town-clerk that should have called them together did discharge them, they added not one fault to another but went
their ways, every man quietly, Demetrius himself and all;
that they are worse than Demetrius, that deny this.

But I pass to the Kings, that estate fitteth us better.
There doth David call together the Priests and other per- David.
sons ecclesiastical, and that even with these trumpets. And 1 Chron. 15. 4.
for what matters? Secular? Nay, but first, when the ark
was to be removed. And again, when the offices of the 1 Chron. 23. 2, 3, 6.
temple were to be set in order; things merely pertaining to
religion? and as he calleth them, 1 Chron. 15. 4. so he dis-
misseth them, 1 Chron. 16. 43.

The like did Solomon, when the temple was to be dedi- Solomon.
cated; called the assembly 2 Chron. 5. 2, dissolved the assembly in the tenth verse of the seventh chapter following.

The like did Asa: when religion was to be restored, and Asa.
a solemn oath of association to be taken for the maintaining 2 Chron. 15. 14.
of it, with the sound of these trumpets did he it.

Jehoshaphat used them, when a public fast to be pro- Jehosha-phat.
claimed. Jehu used them, when a solemn sacrifice to be 2 Chron. 20. 3. Jehu.
performed. Joash in a case of dilapidations of the temple, 2 Kings 10. 20.
a matter merely ecclesiastical. Josias when the temple to Joash.
be purified, and a mass of superstitions to be removed. 2 Chron. 24. 5.
In all these cases did all these Kings call all these con- Josias.
ventions of Priests and Levites for matters of religion. I 2 Chron. 34. 29, 30.
insist only on the fact of Ezekias. He was a King, he gave Ezekias.
forth his precept for the Priests and all their brethren to as- 2 Chron. 29. 15.
semble. Wherefore? *Ad res Jehovæ,* 'for the affairs of the
service of God,' yea, God Himself. There are fourteen chief
men of the Priests set down there by name, that by virtue
of that precept of the King, came together themselves, they
and their brethren, all *ex præcepto Regis ad res Jehovæ,*
by the King's authority for matters merely of the Church.
I know not what can be more plain: the matters spiritual,

SERM.
VII.

the persons assembled spiritual, and yet called by the King's trumpet.

Mordecai.
Est. 9. 20.

Thus till the captivity. In the captivity there have we Mordecai, when he came in place of authority, appointing the days of Purim, and calling all the Jews in the province together, to the celebrating of them.

Nehemias.

After the captivity Nehemias kept the trumpet still; and

Neh. 7. 39,
&c. 64, 65.
Neh. 13. 11.

by it first called the Priests to shew their right to their places by their genealogies, and after reduced them also to their places again, when they were all shrunk away in time of his absence.

The Maccabees.

These lead the practice till you come to the Maccabees, and there it is but too evident; they profess there expressly to Simon, made then their ruler, that it should not be lawful

1 Mac. 14.
41.

for any ἐπισυστρέψαι συστροφὴν, "to call any assembly in the land," ἄνευ αὐτοῦ, "without him." A plain evidence that so had ever gone the course of their government; else how should it come to pass, that the altering of religion is still termed the deed of the King? that his disposition, godly or otherwise, did always accordingly change the public face of religion? which thing the Priests by themselves never did, neither could at any time hinder from being done. Had the Priests without him been possessed of this power of assembling, how had any act concerning religion passed without them? In them it had been to stop it at any time, if they had of themselves had this power of assembling themselves to set order in matters of religion.

Thus, from Moses to the Maccabees, we see in whose hands this power was. And what should I say more? There was in all God's people no one religious king but this power he practised; and there was of all God's Prophets no one that ever interposed any prohibition against it.

Would Esay, shall we once imagine, have endured Ezekias him to call, or the Priests to come together only by his pre-

Isa. 58. 1.

cept, *ad res Jehovæ;* and not "lift up his voice like a trumpet" against it, if it had not been in his knowledge the King's right to command, and their duty to obey? Never, certainly.

What shall we say then? were all these wrong? shall we condemn them all? Take heed. In all that government,

God hath no other children but these: if we condemn these, we "condemn the whole generation of His children." Yet Ps. 73. 15. to this we are come now, that either we must condemn them all, one after another; the Kings as usurpers, for taking on them to use more power than ever orderly they received, and the Prophets for soothers of them in that their unjust claim; or else confess they did no more than they might, and exceeded not therein the bounds of their calling. And indeed that we must confess, for that is the truth.

This then may serve for the custom of God's own elect people. But they were Jews, and we would be loath to judaize; and it may be this was one of the clauses of "the Law of commandments, consisting of ordinances" which Eph. 2. 15. Christ came to abrogate.

I demand therefore, when Christ came how was it then? The practice or use of this power among Christians. will the like appear in the assemblies since Christ? The very like every way, as consonant to that of the Old Testament as may be. For Christ giveth a promise of His assistance to such meetings; but sets no new order for calling of them, Mat. 18. [15, &c.] other than had been taken in the Old. Therefore the same order to be kept still.

A time there was you know after Christ, when they were infidels, Kings and kingdoms both. A time there followed when Kings received religion; and no sooner received they it, but they received this power of the trumpets with it. This to be made manifest: 1. By general councils; 2. By national and provincial councils that have been assembled, 3. under Emperors, 4. and under Kings, by the space of many hundred years.

1. And for general councils, this first to begin with; that In General councils. if those assemblies be not rightly called that by this power are called, we have lost all our general councils at one blow. The Church of Christ hath to this day never a general council; *unâ liturâ*, 'with one wipe' we dash them out all, we leave never a one, no not one. For all that ever have been, have been thus called and kept. Yea, those four first, which all Christians have ever had in so great reverence and high estimation, not one of them a lawful council if this new assertion take place. This is a perilous inconvenience, yet this we must yield to, and more than this, if we seek to disable

assemblies so holden. For sure it is, all the general councils were thus assembled, all, all seven—for more are not to be reckoned, the eighth was only for a private business. The rest were only of the West Church alone, and so not general; the East and West together make a general; the East and West together never met but in one of those seven, for public affairs, unless it were once after in that of Ferrara.

And it is well known, that was in hope of help on the East Church's part, which they never had, and so the council never kept but broken, even as soon as it was broken up.

Briefly then to survey those seven. And I will not therein allege the reports of stories, (they write things they saw not many times, and so frame matters to their own conceits, and many times are tainted with a partial humour) but only out of authentical records in them, and out of the very acts of the councils themselves, best able to testify and tell by whose authority they came together. And it is happy for the Church of Christ, there are so many of them extant as there are, to guide us to the truth in this point, that so the right may appear.

[tom. 1.
563.]
First, then, for the great Nicene council, the first general congregation of all that were called in the Christian world. The whole council in their synodical epistle[b] written to the Church of Alexandria witness they were assembled, the holy Emperor Constantine gathering them together out of divers cities and provinces. The whole letter is extant upon record in Socrates i. 9. and Theodorit i. 9. Give me leave to make here a little stand; for here at this council was the pale first broken, and the right (if any such were) here it went first away. At Nice there were then together three hundred and eighteen bishops, *totius orbis lumina,* as Victorinus well termeth them, 'the lights of the whole world;' the chiefest and choicest men for holiness, learning, virtue, and valour, that the Christian religion ever had before or since; men that had laid down their lives for the testimony of the truth. Did any of them refuse to come, being called by him, as not called aright? or, coming, was there any one

---

[b] Συνεκροτήθη τοῦ θεοφιλεστάτου Βασιλέως Κωνσταντίνου συναγάγοντος ἡμᾶς ἐκ διαφόρων πόλεών τε καὶ ἐπαρχίων.

of them that did protest against it? or pleaded the Church's interest, to meet of themselves? Not one.

What was it then? want of skill in so many famous men, that knew not their own rights? Or want of valour, that knowing it for such would not so much as speak a word for it, but sit still, and say nothing all the while? There were then and there present, Spyridion, Paphnutius, Potamon, and divers besides, but these I name that had not long before for their constancy had their right eyes bored out, their right ham-strings and the strings of their right arm-pits cut in sunder. Did these want courage, think we? Were they become so faint-hearted that they durst not open their mouth, for their own due?

Verily, that council of Nice which is and ever hath been so much admired by all Christians, cannot be excused before God or men, if they thus conspired, all, to betray the Church's right, and suffered it contrary to all equity to be carried away, leaving a dangerous precedent therein, for all councils ever after to the world's end. But no such right there was; if there had been, they neither wanted wit to discern it, nor courage to claim it. But they knew whose the trumpets were, to whom *Erunt tibi* was spoken; and therefore never offered to lay hold on either of them and say, This is ours.

And yet, to say the truth, there is no man of reason but will think it reasonable, if this were the Church's own peculiar, if appropriate unto it, and so known to them to be, there ought to have been plain dealing now at the very first council of all; that if Constantine would embrace religion, he must needs resign up one of his trumpets, and forbear from thence to meddle with their assemblies. Was there so? No such thing. Why was there not? Belike, because none were there that had ever been present at any assembly, holden under persecution, to know the Church's order and manner of meeting then. Yes, there was Hosius bishop of Cordova, who had held the council of Elvira in Spain, even in the time of persecution. Hosius for the West. And for the East there was Eustathius bishop of Antioch, had held the like at Ancyra then too—both the councils yet extant to be seen—and these two, presidents of them. Yet were these

Concil. Eliberit. t. 1. 602. Concil. Ancyra. t. 1. 446.

M

SERM.
VII.

twain, two that came first, and sat foremost at the council of Nice; and neither of them pleaded or knew of any such right, but that their power then ceased, and that Constantine's trumpet now took place. Sure, if but this first council be well considered, it is able to move much. And the example of this first was of great consequence; for all the rest followed it, and as this went so went they. And this for the first.

2. The second general council at Constantinople; who called that congregation? Their own letter to the Emperor[c] is yet to be seen, professing they were thither assembled by his writ.

[Lab. 3. 5.7.]

3. For the third at Ephesus, let the acts of the council, now set out in Greek, be looked on. Four several times they acknowledge they were thither summoned by the Emperor's oracle[d], beck[e], charge[f], and commandment[g].

4. For the fourth at Chalcedon, look but upon the very front of the council, it proclaimeth itself to be there assembled, *Facta est Synodus ex decreto piissimorum, et fidelissimorum Imperatorum, Valentiniani et Martiani.* And it is well known it was first called at Nice, and then recalled from thence and removed to Chalcedon, all wholly by the disposing of the Emperor.

tom. 2. 129.

5. So saith the fifth at Constantinople : *Juxta pium jussum a Christo amati, et a Deo custoditi Justiniani Imperatoris.* They be their own words[h].

tom. 2. 579.

6. And so the sixth at Constantinople : *Secundum imperialem sanctionem congregata est ;* and, *pro obedientiá quam debuimus.* They be the express words of Agatho, bishop of Rome, in the same council[i].

tom. 3. 237.

7. And even so the seventh at Nice, *quæ per pium Imperatorum decretum congregata est* — meaning Constantine and Irene.

tom. 3. 453.

---

[c] Συνελθόντες κατὰ τὸ γράμμα τῆς σῆς εὐσεβείας.
[d] Συγκροτηθεῖσα ἐκ θεσπίσματος τῶν εὐσεβεστάτων βασιλέων. [Lab. 4. 1123-4.]
[e] Νεύματιτοῦ ὑμετέρουκράτουςσυναχθεῖσα. [ibid. 1235-6.]
[f] Συναχθῆναι τὸ ὑμέτερον προσέταξε κράτος. [ibid. 1301-2.]
[g] Συναχθῆναι ἐκέλευσεν ἡ ὑμετέρα εὐσέβεια. [ibid. 1235-6.]

[h] Conveniente Concilio secundum sacram præceptionem. Tom. 2. 579. Imperator Justin. quintam œcumenicam Synodum Episcopis Ecclesiarum evocatis coegit. Tom. 2. 266.
[i] Secundum piissimam jussionem mansuetudinis vestræ. Iis . . . . quæ per mansuetissimæ fortitudinis vestræ Sacram dudum præcepta sunt efficaciter promptam obedientiam exhibere. Tom. 3. 244.

And these be all the general. In all which the force of
the truth presenteth itself so clearly, that Bellarmine is even De Concil.
dazzled with it; for, as one dazzled, he sets down divers lib. 1. cap.
13.
reasons why the Emperors were to call them, in that very
place where he taketh upon him to prove the Emperors were
not to call them.

2. But it may be general councils have a fashion by themselves. Those congregations may be called thus: but National or Provincial, such as ours, how? Even so too, and
no otherwise. Constantine began with them first, before he
proceeded to the general at Nice. His *tractoria,* or writ, is
extant to be seen in Eusebius; whereby he called the first
provincial council in France. For sure by no canon could
the bishop of Syracuse in Sicily, or Restitutus bishop of
London in Britain, be lawfully summoned to a Synod in
France, which they were, but, as it was indeed, by the Emperor's writ only. But this he did at the beginning of his
reign, perhaps while he was yet an imperfect Christian.
Nay, even first and last he did the same: as at the beginning, he called this, so in the end of his reign, the thirtieth
year, the year before his death, called he the council at Tyre,
and from thence removed it to Jerusalem, and from thence
called them to appear before himself in Constantinople. The
letters are to be seen by which they were called. The like
after him did Constans at Sardis, Valentinian at Lampsacus,
Theodosius at Aquileia, Gratian at Thessalonica.

It is too tedious to go through them all; only for that of
Aquileia thus much. St. Ambrose, a man of as much spirit
and as high a courage as ever the Church had, and one
that stood as much as ever did any for the Church's right,
he was there present and president both. Thus writeth he
from the council to the Emperor in his own name, and in
the name of all the rest[k] : *Juxta mansuetudinis vestræ statuta* tom. 1. 718.
convenimus, 'Hither we are assembled by the appointment
of your clemency.' And there is no one council more plain
than that of St. Ambrose for this purpose. Yea, I add this,
which is a point to be considered, that even then when the
Emperors were professed Arians, even then did the bishops

Margin notes:
In Na-
tional and
Provin-
cial; from
Constan-
tine to
Justinian.

Euseb. 10.
5.

Socrat.
1. 28. 33.
34, 36.
Theodor.
2. 8.
Sozom.
6. 7.
Συνοδ. 453.
[ubi Leo.]

---

[k] Qui ad removendas altercationes congregare studuistis sacerdotale Concilium. Tom. 1. 718.

SERM.
VII.

acknowledge their power to call councils ; came to them being called ; sued to them that they might be called. Came

tom. 1. 680.
Socrat. 2.
29.
Lucifer.
oper. [Vid.
Baron.
Annal. an.
354.] Leon.
Epist. 9.
[*id.* 23.]

to them as Hosius to that of Arimine, Liberius to that of Sirmium and that of Seleucia.   Sued for them as Liberius to Constantius, as Leo to Theodosius for the second Ephesine council, Innocentius to Arcadius.   And sometimes they sped, as Leo ; and sometimes not, as Liberius and Innocentius ; and yet, when they sped not, they held themselves quiet, and never presumed to draw together of their own heads.

Under
Kings
from Justinian to
Charles
the Great.

But it may be this was some imperial power, and that Emperors had in this point more jurisdiction than Kings. Nor that neither ; for about five hundred years after Christ, when the empire fell in pieces, and these western parts came into the hands of Kings, those Kings had, held, enjoyed, and practised the same power.   In Italy[1], Theodoric at

¹tom. 2 470.
²tom. 2.503.
³tom. 2.510.
⁴tom. 2.557.
⁵tom. 2.551.
⁶tom. 2.817.
⁷tom. 2.810.
⁸tom. 2 851.
⁹tom. 3.208.
¹tom. 3.437.
²tom. 3.439.

Rome[1] ; Alaric at Agatha[m2].   In France, Clovis, the first Christian king there, Childebert, Theodobert, and Cherebert ; at Orleans[3] the first, Auverne[4], Orleans[5] the second, Tours[6].   And after that again by Gontran, Clovis, Carloman, and Pepin : at Mascon[7], first and second[8], Châlon[9] ; that which is called Francica[1], and that which is in Vernis[2]. Twenty of them at the least in France.

³tom. 2.825.
828.
⁴tom. 2.
546. 859.
tom. 3. 65.
79. 83. 181.
184. 204.
216. 374.
⁵tom. 2.551.
⁶tom. 3. 67.
⁷.om. 3. 83.
⁸tom. 3.237.
⁹tom. 3.391.
¹tom.2.840.
²tom. 2.857.
³tom. 3.208.
⁴tom. 2. 504.
⁵tom. 3.216.
⁶tom. 3.682.

In Spain by ten several Kings ; in two councils at Braccara[3], and in ten at Toledo[4], by the space of three hundred years together.   And how ? under what terms ?   Peruse the councils themselves, their very Acts speak : *Ex præcepto*[5], *imperio*[6], *jussu*[7], *sanctione*[8], *nutu*[9], *decreto*[9] ; *ex evocatione*[1], *dispositione*[2], *ordinatione*[3] *Regis*.   One saith, *Potestas*[4] *permissa est nobis ;* another, *Facultas*[5] *data est nobis ;* a third, *Injunctum*[6] *est nobis a Rege*.   See their several styles ; nothing can be more pregnant.   And now we are gone eight hundred years after Christ.

From
Charles
the Great
to Arnulphus.

4. Then arose there a kind of empire here in the West under Charles the Great.   And did not he then take the trumpets as his own, and use them six several times, in calling six several councils, at Frankfort[1], Arles[2], Tours[3], Châlon[4], Mentz[n5], and Rheims[6]?   And what saith he in

¹tom. 3.635.
²tom. 3.679.
³tom. 3.682.
⁴tom. 3.686.
⁵tom. 3.693.
⁶tom. 3.700.

¹ Synodus ex præcepto glorosissimi Regis Theodorici congregata.
[ᵐ Oppidum provinciæ Narbonensis. ibid.]   [ⁿ Mayence.]

them? Rheims I named last, take that; *In conventu more priscorum Imperatorum congregato a piissimo Domino nostro Carolo.* That he called that convention by no other right than as the manner of the ancient Emperors had been to do. Expressing under one both what his was, and what the usage had ever been before him.

The like after him did Ludovicus Pius, Lotharius, Ludovicus Balbus, Carolus Calvus, Carolus Crassus, and Arnulphus, at the several councils holden at Aken[o1], Mentz[2], Melden[p3], Worms[4], Cologne[5], and Tribur[6]; and so held it till nine hundred years; for about that year, a year or two under or over, was holden the council at Tribur in Germany[7], *cum concilium sacrum continuari decrevisset;* and *præsidente pio Principe Arnulpho,* by the Emperor Arnulphus' decree, himself then president of it [q].

[1]tom. 3.703.
[2]tom. 3.832.
[3]tom. 3.865.
[4]tom. 3.977.
[5]tom. 4. 17.
[6]tom. 4. 26.
[7]tom. 4. 41.

And if it be excepted there are of the councils which carry in their acts no mention how they were called, for them we are to understand that after the decrees of the first Nicene Council were by Constantine's edict confirmed, wherein (as likewise in the Council of Chalcedon) it was ordered each province should yearly hold their Synods twice, but specially after Justinian had made the decrees of the four first general councils to have the nature and force of imperial laws, a law being thus passed from them, we are to conceive the Emperor's authority was in all afterward, habitually at least; that is, if not, as in the other, by express and formal consent, yet by way of implied allowance, as passed by a former grant.

Nicen. Can. 5.

Chalced. Can. 19.
Authent. 131.

Well, thus far the trumpet giveth a certain sound. Now after this there is a great silence in the volumes of the councils in a manner for the space of two hundred years, until the year 1180 or thereabout, when the Council of Lateran was; and then, indeed, the case was altered. By that time had the bishop of Rome, by his skill and practice, got one of the trumpets away, and carried it with him to Rome, so leaving princes but one; but so long they held it.

tom. 4. 101.

One of the trumpets gotten away.

Truly three times so much time as we are allowed would

[o Aix-la-Chapelle.]
[p Meaux.]
[q The Chronology of History by

Sir H. Nicolas, p. 201—258, may be consulted with advantage on the subject of these councils.]

not serve for this one point of the councils, but even barely to recite them, and to cite them, they are so many. You remember how Abraham dealt with God for the saving of the five cities, how he went down from fifty to ten : I might well take a course the other way, and rise from ten to fifty, nay sixty, nay seventy, nay eighty, not so few, of councils general, national, provincial, called by Emperors, by Kings ; Emperors of the East, of the West; Kings of Italy, France, Spain, Germany; as before from Moses to the Maccabees, so here from Constantine to Arnulphus, for so many hundred years together, extant all, to be shewed and seen, all clear and evident, all full and forcible for this power; as indeed it is a cause that laboureth rather of plenty than penury of proof. And this was the course that of old was well thought of in the Christian world. Thus was the congregation so long called, neither is there yet brought any thing to force us to swerve from the way wherein so many and so holy ages have gone before us.

How in the time of persecution for three hundred years before Constantine.
Yes, something; for what say you to the three hundred years before Constantine? How went assemblies then? who called them all that while? for divers were holden that while : in Palestine, about Easter ; at Carthage, about heretics' baptism; at Rome, about Novatus; at Antioch, about Paulus Samosatenus. How assembled these?

1.
As in Egypt.
Truly even as these people here, of the Jews, did before in Egypt under the tyranny of Pharaoh; they were then a Church under persecution, until Moses was raised up by God, a lawful magistrate over them. The cases are like for all the world. No magistrate did assemble them in Egypt. And good reason, they had then none to do it. Pharaoh, we may be sure, would not offer to do it; nor for any conscience I trust or fear to encroach upon the Church's right, but because he hated both assembly and congregation, and sought by all means to extinguish both. But this was no bar but that when Moses arose, authorized by God, and had the trumpets here by God delivered him, he might take them, keep them, and use them to that end for which God gave them, "to call the congregation." And none then but he could do it, because to none but him then was this power conveyed. They could not say to him now as before

one of them did in Egypt: "Who made you a commander Exod. 2. 14.
over us," to call us together? nor plead in bar of the trumpets, and say, Nay, but we will meet still of ourselves, even
as we did before in Egypt, we will still keep our old manner
of conventions. No, for God had now taken another order;
God I say had now done it, and God shall I trust be allowed
to translate this power to the principal member of the body,
and to dispose of it as it best pleaseth Him.

The very same case fell out again after in the captivity of   2.
Babylon, and again, after that, in the persecution under As under
 the cap-
Antiochus; and these three are all the patterns we have in tivity.
 3.
the Old Testament. As before in Egypt, so then they had As under
 Antiochus.
meetings, but they were all by stealth; yet meetings then
they had. For Moses ceasing, and his right with him, the
power devolved to the body, to gather itself, as is usual in
such cases. But then, when Nehemias after the captivity,
and Simon Maccabeus after the fury of Antiochus, were
raised them by God; when God had set them in Moses'
place, they might lawfully do as Moses before had done, and
take the silver trumpets into their hands again. So soon
as they had a lawful governor, the right returned to him
straight; and the congregation, none of them might then
plead, Nay, but as we did in Babylon, or as we did under
Antiochus, so and no otherwise will we assemble still. No,
we see the contrary rather; even of themselves they profess 1 Mac.
 14. 44.
to Simon plainly, now they have a lawful governor, no meeting should be from thenceforth in the land without him, his
privity and permission.

And even as these two Nehemias and Simon, even by the   4.
 So before
same right Constantine; by Moses' right all, all by the com- Constan-
mission here penned. By it did Constantine resume the tine.
trumpet, and enjoy and exercise the power of calling the
congregation; for even Moses' pattern and practice five
sundry times at least doth Eusebius allege, in the life of
Constantine, to justify his proceedings still by Moses' example. True it is therefore that before Constantine's time
they met together as they durst, and took such order as
they could. They must venture then, there was no Moses,
they had no trumpet; and if they had, they durst not have
blown it. But when Constantine came in place, in Moses'

place, it was lawful for him to do as Moses did; and so he did, and they never said to him, Nay, spare your trumpet, look how we have done hitherto, we will do so even still; meet no otherwise now than in former times we have, by our own agreement. As before it was said, this had been plain dealing; thus, if rightly they might, they should have done. Did they so? No, but to him they went, as to Moses, for their meetings, at his hands they sought them, without his leave or liking they would not attempt them; yea, I dare say they blessed God from their hearts, that they had lived to see the day they might now assemble by the sound of the trumpet.

To conclude this point then. These two times or estates of the Church are not to be confounded; there is a plain difference between them, and a diverse respect to be had of each. If the succession of magistrates be interrupted, in such case of necessity the Church of herself maketh supply, because then God's order ceaseth. But God granting a Constantine to them again, God's former positive order returneth, and the course is to proceed and go on as before. When the magistrate and his authority was at any time wanting to the Church, forced she was to deal with her own affairs within herself; for then was the Church wholly divided from princes, and they from it. But when this wall of partition is pulled down, shall Moses have no more to do than Pharaoh, or Constantine than Nero? Congregations were so called under them; must they be so still under these too? No, no more than their manner of meeting in Egypt—for all the world like this of the primitive Church persecuted—was to be a rule, and to overrule these trumpets here in the text, either God for giving them, or Moses for taking them at His hands. This rather, if ever the Church fall into such bloody times, they must meet as they may, and come together as they can; they have no Moses, no trumpet to call them. The times of Pharaoh and Nero are then their pattern. But if it be so happy as to find the days of peace, Moses and Constantine are patterns for the days of peace; they have a Moses then, from that time forward they must give ear to the trumpet. In a word, none can seek to have the congregation so called as before

Constantine, but they must secretly and by implication con‑ fess they are a persecuted Church as that then was, without a Moses, without a Constantine.

The times then before Constantine are no bar, no kind of impeachment to Constantine's, no more than the times in Egypt were to Moses' right. And indeed no more they were; for Constantine and his successors had them and held them till a thousand years after Christ, and then one of them (by what means we all know) was let go by them, or gotten away from them; it was then gotten away, and carried to Rome. But that getting hath hitherto been holden a plain usurping, and an usurping (not upon the congregation, but) upon princes and their right, and that they in their own wrong suffered it to be wrung from them. And why? Because not to Aaron, but to Moses it was said, *Et erunt tibi.*

1. To draw to an end, it was then gotten away and with some ado it was recovered not long since. And what, shall we now let it go, and destroy so soon that which so lately we built again? You may please to remember there was not long since a clergy in place that was wholly *ad opposi‑ tum*, and would never have yielded to reform ought; no‑ thing they would do, and in eye of law without them no‑ thing could then be done, they had encroached the power of assembling into their own hands. How then? how shall we do for an assembly? Then, *Erunt tibi* was a good text, it must needs be meant of the prince; he had this power, and to him of right it belonged. This was then good divi‑ nity, and what writer is there extant of those times but it may be turned to in him? And was it good divinity then, and is it now no longer so? Was the King but licensed for a while to hold this power till another clergy were in, and must he then be deprived of it again? Was it then usurped from princes, and are now princes usurpers of it themselves? And is this all the difference in the matter of assemblies, and calling of them; that there must be only a change, and that instead of a foreign they shall have a domestical, and instead of one, many; and no remedy now, but one of these two they must needs admit of? Is this

The re‑ covery of the trum‑ pets.

Now sought to be gotten away.

1. *By the Presbytery.*

now become good divinity? Nay, I trust, if *Erunt tibi* were once true, it is so still; and if *Tibi* were then Moses, it is so still. That we will be better advised and not thus go against ourselves, and let truth be no longer truth than it will serve our turns.

2. *By the people themselves. Penry, Barrow, &c.* 2. And this calleth to my mind the like dealing of a sort of men not long since here among us. Awhile they plied prince and parliament with admonitions, supplications, motions, and petitions. And in them it was their duty, their right to frame all things to their new-invented plot; and this, so long as any hope blew out of that coast. But when that way they saw it would not be, then took they up a new tenet straight; they needed neither magistrate nor trumpet they, the godly among the people might do it of themselves. For confusion to the wise and mighty, the poor and simple must take this work in hand, and so by this means the trumpet prove their right in the end, and so come by devolution to Demetrius and the craftsmen. Now, if not for love of the truth, yet for ₁very shame of these shifting absurdities, let these fantasies be abandoned, and that which God's own mouth hath spoken, let it be for once and for ever true; that which once we truly held and maintained for truth, let us do so still; that we be

Lu. 19. 22. not like evil servants, judged *ex ore proprio,* "out of their own mouths."

The conclusion. Let me not over-weary you, let this rather suffice. 1. We have done as our Saviour Christ willed us, resorted to the Law, and found what there is written, the grant of this power to Moses "to call the congregation;" 2. we have followed Moses' advice, enquired of the days before us, even from one end of heaven to the other, and found the practice of this grant in Moses' successors, and the congregation so by them called. It remaineth, that as God by His Law hath taken this order, and His people in former ages have kept this order, that we do so too; that we say as God saith, *Erunt tibi,* this power pertaineth to Moses.

[Num. 16. 14.] And that neither with Korah we say, *Non veniemus;* nor with Demetrius run together of ourselves, and think to

[Acts. 19. 28.] carry it away with crying, "Great is Diana." But as we

see the power is of God, so truly to acknowledge it and
dutifully to yield it; that so they whose it is may quietly
hold it, and laudably use it to His glory that gave it, and
their good for whom it was given: which God Almighty
grant, &c.

The edition of the Councils here alleged, is that of Venice, by Dominicus
Nicolinus, in five tomes.

A SERMON

THE KING'S MAJESTY AT WHITEHALL,

ON THE TWENTY-FOURTH OF MARCH, A.D. MDCVI.[a]

JUDGES xvii. 6.

In those days, there was no King in Israel, but every man did
that which was good in his own eyes.

Vel, *Quod*
rectum
videbatur
in oculis
suis.

In diebus illis non erat Rex in Israel; sed unusquisque, quod sibi
rectum videbatur, hoc faciebat.

[*In those days there was no King in Israel, but every man did that*
which was right in his own eyes. Eng. Trans.]

SERM.
VIII.

THIS chapter, the seventeenth of Judges, is the chapter
which by the course of the calendar is proper to this very
day. Not as now it is, for now by reason this day God
sent us a King in Israel it hath a select service, both of
Psalms and of chapters. But by order of the Church-service
this chapter is for this day; and so it was this time four
years, I am sure we all that then heard it have good cause
to remember it. And though we have got us a new, it will
not be amiss to call ourselves back to our old chapter, being
this day come hither to render our thanks even for this very
thing, that in these days it is not with us as in those days it
was with them, but that to the joy and comfort of us all
there is a King in Israel.

This, how great a benefit it is, it is not it may be the best
way simply to inform ourselves, by *Non erat Rex.* Not
simply, but sure to us as our nature is, to us I say, there
is no way better. It is an old observation, but experience
daily reneweth it, that of *Carendo magis quam fruendo;*

a [The anniversary of the King's accession.]

' What is it to have, no better way to make us truly to value, than by feeling awhile how great a plague it is to be without.' Our nature surely is more sensible that way, and never taketh perfect impression of that we enjoy, but by the privation or want; nor understandeth thoroughly, *in his diebus est,* now there is one, but by those, *in illis non erat.* And that is our verse.

Of which this is the occasion. The book of the Judges, and the estate of the Judges now growing to an end, the Holy Ghost here beginneth to make a passage to the estate and books of the Kings. To which state this chapter (and so to the end of the book) is a preparative or introduction, to shew that now the time was at hand.

There should be Kings of his race, God first told Abra- Gen. 17. 6. ham by way of promise. That those Kings should come of Judah and the sceptre be his, Jacob foretold by way of pro- Gen. 49. phecy. The duty of those Kings against the time came, was ^10. set down by Moses by way of provision long before. This Deut. 17. shewed, Kings there should be. [14—20.]

But all things have a time, saith Solomon; and time hath Eccles. 3. 1 a "fulness" saith St. Paul. And till that time, it is not Gal. 4. 4. only a folly but a fault to press things out of season. We see, offer was twice made to Gideon to take it; by Abime- Judg.8.22; lech, to get it: both came to nothing, the time was not yet ^9. 2. come. But still as the time drew near every thing did co-operate, every thing made way and gave occasion to the purpose of God.

And now here, in this chapter, is set down the very first The sum. occasion on which God first misseth Kings; that for all the Judges one Micah, a private man of Mount Ephraim, he Judg. 17. 2. and his old mother, it took them in the heads they would have a new religion by themselves, and that was plain ido-latry; and up with an idol they went. And because they Judg. 17. 5. lacked a priest, it came into Micah's head to give orders, and so he did. Why, could he be suffered? It was, and then cometh in this verse, This was all for want of a King. And when he had done with this, he goeth to another; and when with that to a third, disorder upon disorder. And still at the end of every one this cometh in, All these, be- Judg. 18. 1; cause there was no King. Which all is nothing else but a 19. 1. ^21. 25;

SERM. preparative against the time came that God should give
VIII. Kings; that they might with joy receive that His gift, and
with thanks celebrate it from year to year, do as we do
now. And this is the sum.

The divi- Three points there are in it. Two are *ad oculum,* ' appa-
sion. rent,' the third by necessary inference. 1. The want of a
King. 2. For want of a King what mischief ensued, " Every
man did what he thought good ;" this in general. And
thirdly, every man, but namely Micah ; he went up with
idols. For Micah's fact it was begat this verse, and so of
necessity falleth into it. Those two, both general and particular disorder, are linked to the first as to the efficient cause,
or rather deficient. For evil it is, *et malum non habet effi-
cientem, sed deficientem causam,* ' evil hath a deficient but no
efficient cause.' For the want of some notable good, as here
a King, is the cause of some notorious evil, as greater evil
cannot possibly come to a people than to be in this case,
every one to do what he lists.

For the handling of these, though in nature the cause be
first (and so standeth it ever) to us, the effect first offereth
itself, and through it as through the veil we enter into the
[Mat. 19. cause; and so *erunt novissimi primi,* " the last shall be first."
30.] 1. First then, of *Fecit quisque;* 2. and then, of *Non erat Rex.*

I. In the former of these we have two parts : 1. The eye,
rectum in oculis; 2. the hand, *Fecit quisque;* 3. and then
together, that what seemed to the eye the hand did, and that
was mischief enough.

II. In the latter likewise three. 1. There was no King—in
opposition to other estates : they had judges and priests, but
no King. 2. No King in Israel, with reference to other
nations. Not in Canaan, nor in Edom, but not in Israel;
even there it is a want to want a King. 3. And then out
of these, *Quid faciat nobis Rex,* ' what a King hath to perform.' To repress all insolencies, not only in general, but
particularly this of Micah. Where will fall in, that the
good or evil estate of religion doth much depend on the
having or not having a King. For it is as if he should say,
Had there been a King, this of Micah had never been endured. Now because there was not, religion first, and after
it all went to wrack.

And last, we shall see how far all this doth touch us III. in matter of our bounden duty of thanks to God for this day.

"In those days when," &c. What "days" were those? were they good or evil days? And this whole verse, is it set down by way of liking or complaint? At the first one would think that it were a merry world, if every man might do what he listed, that there were no harm in the world; they be fair words all. Right, and doing right, and the eye, the fairest member, not an evil word amongst them.

I.
Of the
effect,
Fecit quis-
que, &c.

But yet sure those days were evil. This a complaint. *Quasi ingemiscit super hæc Scriptura,* 'the Scripture doth as it were fetch a deep sigh so oft as it repeateth this verse,' and saith thus in effect; *Tanta mala conciliat non habere Regem,* so much mischief cometh there in Israel, or any where where there is no King, saith Theodoret.

To let you see then what a monster lurketh under these smooth terms, "doing that which is right in our eyes." Two parts there be, 1. the eye, 2. and the hand. To begin with the eye, and that which is right in the eye. There began all evil in the first tentation; even from this persuasion, they should need no direction from God or from any, their own eye should be their director to what was right, they should do but what was "right in their own eyes."

1.
Quod rec-
tum in
oculis,
The eye.

Three evils are in it. It is not safe to commit the judgment of what is right to the eye; and yet I know it is our surest sense, as that which apprehendeth greatest variety of differences. But I know withal, the optics, the masters of that faculty, reckon up twenty several ways, all which it may be and is deceived. The object full of deceit; things are not as they seem. The medium is not evenly disposed. The organ itself hath his suffusions. Take but one; that of the oar in the water. Though the oar be straight, yet if the eye be judge it seemeth bowed. And if that which is right may seem crooked, that which is crooked may seem right; so the eye no competent judge. The rule is the judge of right: if it touch the rule and run even with it, it is right; if it vary from the rule, let it seem to the eye as it will, it is awry. God saw this was not good; an express countermand we have from Him in Deuteronomy, "You shall not do every

Three
evils in it.
1. Quod
in oculis.

Deu. 12. 8.

SERM.
VIII. man that which is right in his eyes;" that is, you shall have a surer rule of right than your eyes.

2. *Quod quisque.* But admit we will make the eye judge, yet I hope not *quisque*, not every man's eye ; that were too much. Many weak and dim eyes there be, many goggle and mis-set, many little better than blind : shall all and every of these be allowed to define what is right ? Some it may be, perhaps the eagle's ; but shall the owl and all ? I trow not. Many misshapen kinds of right shall we have if that be suffered ; yea, otherwhile, divers of them contrary one to the other.

3. *Quod in suis.* To go yet further. Say we would allow every eye his privilege—it were great folly to do it, but say we should— if we would allow it every one, yet not every one *in suis.* Not his own eye to direct his own doings, or as we say to sit judge in his own right. No not the eagle, not the best eye to be allowed to right itself. The judge himself cometh down from the bench, when his own right is in hearing. We all know, self-love, what a thing it is, how it dazzleth the sight; how every thing appeareth right and good, that appeareth through those spectacles. Therefore, 1. not right by the eye; 2. at least, not every man's eye ; 3. nay, not any man's right by his own eye.

We shall never see this so well in the general, as if we look in some few examples upon it, *in individuo.* And that can we no where better than in this chapter, and those that follow it to the end of the book. They be nothing else but a commentary at large upon these words, " Right in every man's eyes," &c.

Exod. 20. 4, 5. 1. What say you to making and worshipping a graven image? Lay it to the rule: the rule is, *Non facies, non adorabis.* Then it is crooked and nought. Yet to Micah's eyes, and his mother's, a goodly graven image sheweth fair and well.

2. Go to the next chapter. What say you to burglary, robbing and rifling of houses, yea whole cities of harmless poor people, and cutting all their throats? Fie upon it, it is crooked. Put it to the men of Dan, they saw nothing but it was right enough.

3. Go to the next to that. How think you by ravishing of women, and that to death? How? away with that, let

it not be once named ; no man will think that right. Yes,
they of Gibeah, in the nineteenth chapter, did, and stood to
maintain it. You see a good gloss of this text. Upon the
matter, there are no worse things in the world than these
were : if these seem straight, there is nothing but will seem
so to the eye. There is no trusting *in oculis*.

But this is not all. I now pass to the next point ; here is
a hand too, *Fecit quisque*. *Fecit* is but one word ; but there
is more in this one than in all the former. For here at this
breaketh in the whole sea of confusion, when the hand followeth the eye, and men proceed to do as lewdly as they
see perversely. And sure the hand will follow the eye, and
men do as it seemeth right to them, be it never so absurd
that so seemeth. To die for it, Eve if her eye like it, her
hand will have it : and Eve's children that have no other
guide but their eye, if their eye rove at it, their hand will
reach at it ; there is no parting them. Therefore if a bad
eye light upon a hand that hath strength, and there be not
Rex, or the stronger bar, it will be done. You will see it in
all the former. 1. Micah liked an idol well, Micah had a
good purse ; he told out two hundred shekels, and so up
went the idol. 2. The men of Dan liked well of spoiling ;
they were well appointed, their swords were sharp, *fecerunt*,
'they did it.' 3. They of Gibeah : to their lust, rape seemed
a small matter ; they were a multitude, no resisting them ;
and so they committed that abominable villainy.

By this time we see what a mass of mischief there is in
these few words. For sure if these all seemed right, and
so seeming were done, then are we come to *quidlibet a quo-
libet*, any man do any thing ; which is the next door to
confusion, nay confusion itself. For so no man's soul shall
be safe, if idolatry go up. Alas, what talk we of the soul !
they have least sense of it ; talk to them of that they have
feeling. No man's goods, or wife, or life, in safety, if this
may go on thus. If robbery, rape, and murder be right,
what is wrong ?

See then now, what a woeful face of a commonwealth is
here ! Idols and murder seen and allowed for good, done and
practised for good. Again, Micah a private man, Gibeah a
city, Dan a whole tribe ; tribes, cities, families, all out of

2.
*Fecit quis-
que.*
The hand.

course. Out of course in religion, and not in religion alone but in moral matters; and so that the like never heard of, no not among the heathen.

Last, this was now not in a corner, but all over the land. Micah was at mount Ephraim, in the midst; Gibeah was at one end, and Dan at the other. So in the midst and both ends, all were wrapped in the same confusion.

But what, shall this be suffered, and no remedy sought? God forbid.

First, the eye; error in the eye is harm enough, and order must be taken even for that. For men do not err in judgment but with hazard to their souls; very requisite therefore that men be travailed with, that they may see their own Rev. 3. 18. blindness. Then that the counsel be followed that "eyesalve" be bought of Him and applied to the eyes, that that may seem to them right that is so indeed. This, if it may be, is best.

But if they be strongly conceited of their own sight, and marvel at Christ, (as they, John 9. 40, "What, are we blind trow?") and will not endure any to come near their eyes; if we cannot cure their eyes, what, shall we not hold their hands neither? Yes, in any wise. So long as they but see, though they see amiss, they hurt none but themselves, it is but *suo damno*, "to their own hurt;" and that is enough, nay too much, it may be as much as their souls be worth; but that is all, if it stay there, and go no further than the eye. But when they see amiss, and that grossly; what, shall their hand be suffered to follow their eye? their hand to be as desperate in misdoing as their eye dark in mistaking, to the detriment of others, and the scandal of all? That may not be.

We cannot pull men's eyes out of their heads, nor their opinions neither; but shall we not pinion their hands, or bind them to the peace? Yes, whatsoever become of *rectum in oculis*, order must be taken with *fecit*, or else farewell all. Foul rule we are like to have, even for all the world such as was here in Israel.

II.
The cause.
1. *Non erat Rex.*
We see then the malady; more than time we sought out a remedy for it. That shall we best do, if we know the cause. The cause is here set down, and this is it, *Non erat*

Rex. Is this the cause? We would perhaps imagine many causes besides, but God passeth by them all and layeth it upon none but this, *Non erat Rex.* And seeing He hath assigned that only for the cause, we will not be wiser than He, but rest ourselves in it. The rather, for that *ex ore inimici* we have as much. For these miscreants whom he sets on work to bring realms to confusion and to root out religion, that "every one may do that is good in their own eyes," to this point they all drive, *ut ne sit Rex.* Away with the King, that is their only way. Heaven and hell both are agreed, that is the cause.

To make short work then. If the cause be, There is no King, let there be one, that is the remedy: A good King will help all. If it be of absolute necessity, that neither Micah for his wealth, nor Dan for all their forces, nor Gibeah for all their multitude, do what they list; and if the miss of the Kings were the cause that all this were amiss; no better way to cease it, no better way to keep religion from idolatry, men's lives and goods in safety, their vessels in honour, than by Kings. No more effectual bar to *Fecit quisque quod rectum in oculis,* than *Rex in Israel.*

This will better appear if we take it in sunder: "There was no King." He doth not charge them with a flat anarchy, that there were no estates, no kind of government among them; but this only, "There was no King." What then? There were Priests: would they not serve? It seemed they would not. Phinehas was to look to their eyes: but somewhere there be some such as Osee speaks of; *Populus hic* Hosea 4. 4. *quasi qui contradicit Sacerdoti,* This people will look to Phinehas' eyes; set their priests and preachers to school, and not learn of them but learn them divinity. The judges are to look to their hands: but there are too somewhere such as he speaketh of, *Devorabunt judices;* such as, if it Hosea 7. 7. take them in the head, will not stick to sup up, and swallow down their judges; specially, *inter arma.* How then, shall we have military government? Nay, that is too violent; and if it lie long, the remedy proves as ill as the disease. To me a plain evidence, that although all these were, all these were not perfect. There was one yet missing, that was to do this to better purpose than yet it had been done; and till he were had, they were not where they should be.

This is then God's means. We cannot say His only means, in that we see there are states that subsist without them. But this we may say, His best means. The best, saith the philosopher, for order, peace, strength, steadiness, and proves them all one by one. But best, say the Fathers, for that had there been a better than this, God would not last have resolved on this. This is the most perfect He last brought them to. Hither till they came, He changed their government: from Joshua a captain, to the Judges; from the Judges, to Eli and Samuel, Priests. But here when He had settled them, He changed no more. And this act of God in this change is enough to shew, where it is not, there is a defect certainly, and such a state we may repute defective.

Besides, you shall observe; of those three estates, which swayeth most, that in a manner doth overtop the rest, and like a foregrown member depriveth the other of their proportion of growth. The world hath seen it in two already, and shall daily more and more see it in the third. Requisite therefore there be one over all, that is, none of all, but a common Father to all, that may poise and keep them all *in equilibrio*, that so all the estates may be evenly balanced.

This act then of God in this change is enough to teach, that this *Non erat Rex* is a defect certainly; and where there is not one, we may report the estate for deficient. At least thus far, that God yet may change it into a more perfect, as He did His own. And again this, that it is not conformed to the government, simply the most perfect of all, the government of the whole; when as the inferior bodies are ruled by the superior, so a multitude by unity, that is, all by one. Thus far on these words, "There was no King," howsoever other states there were.

2.
Non Rex in Israel. The next point is, "No King in Israel." That this is not noted as a defect in gross or at large, but even in Israel, God's own chosen people. It is a want, not in Edom or Canaan, but even in Israel too, the want of a King. Truly Israel being God's own peculiar might seem to claim a pre-

rogative above other nations in this, that they had the knowledge of His laws, whereby their eyes were lightened and
their hands taught, and so the most likely to spare one.
Others had not like light; yet this, *non obstante* their light
and their law, and that they were God's own people, is no
supersedeas for having a King. Of which there needeth no
reason but this, that a King is a good means to keep them
God's Israel. Here, for want of a King, Israel began and
was fair onward to be no longer Israel, but even Babel;
when Micah, and by good reason any other as well as he,
might set up religions and give orders themselves, as it
were in open contempt of God and His law. So that the
people of God can plead no exemption from this, since it is
His own ordinance to make them and keep them the people
of God.

Was it thus here in the Old Testament, and is it not so
likewise in the New? Yea, even in the New too. For
there St. Peter willeth them, that they be subject to "the 1 Pet. 2. 13.
King," as to the sovereign, or most excellent. And St. Paul
goeth further, and expresseth it more strongly, in the style
of parliament, and like a law-giver saith, ὑποτασσέσθω, Be it Rom. 13. 1.
enacted that they submit themselves. And when St. Paul
there had in his act said, *omnis anima*, that this act reacheth
to "every soul," which was enough, yet because that seemed
too general, St. Peter came after, and goeth to the very
point and saith, *gens sancta* must do thus too; that is, there 1 Pet. 2. 9.
must be a King even in God's Israel. And what would
we more?

I come to the third part. And to what end a King? *Quid faciet*
Quid faciet nobis? "What will a King do unto us?" It *nobis Rex.*
hath been said already; he will look that every one do not *3.]*
that which is good in his own, and evil in God's eyes. He
will in his general care look to both parts, the eye and the
hand. The eye, that men sin not blindly, for want of direction. The hand, that men sin not with a high hand, that
is wilfully, for want of correction. He will there be good
ophthalmists with right eye-salve, that the sight may be
cured, and things seem as they be, and not be as they seem.
At the hardest, *Si noluerunt intelligere*, but the eye will
rove and run astray, that the hand be bound to the good

abearing¹. That they do it not; or if they do it, as do it they will, yea though there be a King, yet that they may not do it *impune*, do it and nothing done to them for it, and scape the punishment due unto it. For that is the case, when there is no King in Israel. And if when there is one that be the case too, where have we been all this while? For if so, *etiam non est Rex cum est Rex*, 'then when there is a King there is no King,' or one in name but none in deed. Which as it is not good for the state, so neither is it safe for themselves. To this, special regard will be had.

Non enim frustra, saith St. Paul, "for they bear not the sword in vain."

2. That every one do not thus. Every one, but namely, which is the occasion of this text, that not Micah. For Micah's fact brought forth this first sight; that they were now come to this pass, that he or any such as he was might set up in his house any religion he would, and no man control him for it. To look to every one therefore, but specially to Micah; and to care for all, but above all the matter of religion. *Ne quisque videat quod rectum est* there, that every one be not allowed to see visions there; at least, *Ne quisque faciat*, that see what they list they be not suffered to set them up; but if the eye will not be rectified, the hand be restrained.

And sure, no where doth the eye more miss, nor the hand swerve, than in this; and therefore no where more cause to call for a King than for this. One would think this were impertinent, and we were free enough from Micah. We are not. Even to this day do men still cast images or imaginations (all is one) in the mould of their conceits, and up they set them, at least for their own household to adore. And then if they can get such a fellow as is hereafter described, a Levite for ten shekels and a suit, (or because now the world is harder, ten pounds,) they are safe, and there they have and hold a religion by themselves.

3. For evident it is by this text, setting up of false worship is the cause why Kings were missed, and the redress of it the cause why they were placed. The cause I say, and the first cause of their placing; and therefore this a part,

and a principal part of this charge. I will touch them severally. 1. A part, to look to Micah and his false worship: Why this is matter ecclesiastical? It is so, and thereby it appeareth I think, that Kings have, and are to have a hand in matters of that nature; if religion were at a fault because there was no King, and that one there must be to set it right again. For is it once to be imagined that the cause of corrupt religion is laid on the want of a King, and yet when there is one he should not meddle with it? Rather the consequence is strong on the other side. Micah thus did, because there was then no King; therefore when there is one, he will look better to it, that never a Micah of them all shall do the like. Thus it went when there was no King; after, when there was one, I find again the not taking away the high places, which were places merely religious, where the people did sacrifice, imputed still to the King as his fault; and yet shall he have nothing to do with high places, or sacrificing either there or any where else?

Very strange it were, that they who are by God Himself, by an express *Ego dixi,* termed "gods," should yet have Ps. 82. 6. nothing to do with God's affairs! And no less, that being termed by Esay *nutritii,* "foster-fathers," to whose care the Isa. 49. 23. Church is committed, to cherish and bring up, should yet be forbidden to intermeddle with the Church, in that which is of all fostering the principal part! Verily, when the Apostle speaketh of the service that Kings do unto God, he doth not only use the term of λειτουργὸς, that is, "public Rom. 13. officer," but διάκονος too, as it were God's "deacon" or 6, 4. servitor, by a name peculiar to the Church offices; and this he useth twice for one other. It can therefore neither be denied nor doubted of, in that idolatry came up by defect of Kings, but that Kings were placed to pull down idolatry, and to plant and preserve the true service of God. In a word, there is a King in Israel that there may not be a Micah in Israel.

But this is not all, the text carrieth us yet further; that it is not only the charge of the King, but the very first and chief article in his charge. For this mark I pray you, that this is the first place in all the Scripture where, and the first cause why, Kings were missed; this the very first occasion, that drew this complaint from God. Being to set down the disorders that then multiplied, other there were besides this; yet this He beginneth with, not with the outrage of Gibeah, or the riot of Dan, but with Micah's idolatry; as that which He chiefly misliked, and therefore would have first and chiefest care to see it reformed. This with God is first, and God was not well pleased it was not so with them.

Hos. 10. 9. It is that wherewith God upbraideth them, Osee the tenth, with their hot taking the matter of Gibeah. Why were they to blame for it, being so villainous an act? No indeed, it was so good a piece of justice. This only it is God findeth fault with, that they could be so forward and fervent in the case of wrong offered to a woman, and so cold and careless when His worship received so great a wound; so sensible of their own wrong, so past all feeling in His. For when injury

Judg. 19. 30. was offered one of their concubines, they cry, "The like was never seen in Israel." They were all up in arms, and upon the point to root out the whole tribe of Benjamin. But when idolatry was set up, first here in a house, after in a whole tribe, even as it were in open defiance of God and His law, no man drew a sword; nay, no man so much as spake

ibid. a word in reproof of it; not cry then, "The like was never seen in Israel." Their fathers were more tender in this point. They, upon the erecting of a thing but like an altar, but no

Josh. 22. 11. altar indeed, were all ready to have bidden battle, till they were sufficiently satisfied that no such thing was meant. Here there is not a show of an altar, but (past a show) very idols, a whole house full of them, and no man saith to Micah so much as, What doest thou? This is that He blameth them for there. This it which He taketh in evil part and saith, He will trust them no longer with His worship; He will have one who shall look better to His worship than they had done.

One, that seeing that was the first cause that made God think of setting up Kings, will therefore think it his first duty, *primum et ante omnia*, to have regard of that point.

To conclude, if the want of Kings, Kings in Israel, be evil, as evil it is, being the cause of so much evil, it is God's will there should be remedy for it. That remedy is a King;

it is God's will therefore there be Kings. St. Peter speaketh
it *totidem verbis,* This is the will of God, that ye be subject 1 Pet. 2.
15.
to your Kings.

Then secondly, being evil, it is God's will that Israel be
not only kept from it at sometime, but at all. Evil is not to
be allowed any, though never so short a time; but it agreeth
well with His pleasure, that once and ever it be kept from
Israel. Consequently, that there never be a time wherein
it may be said, *Non erat Rex.* That there be not only Kings,
but a succession of Kings; not only *Rex,* but *sanguis, semen,
stirps Regis,* (they be all in Scripture) "the blood," the 1 Kings
11. 14.
"seed," the "race." It is among other one, of the differ- Jer. 41. 1.
ences of the state of Kings and Judges; and a main incon- 2 Chron.
22. 10.
venience of the state of Judges, (and so is it of all elective
kingdoms) the *interregna* as we term them; times between
the old judge's death and the raising up a new; in which
times all ran to riot, and much disorder got head. To the
end then there be no such inconvenience, no *interregna* at
all, not so much as a minute of time wherein it may be said,
Non est Rex in Israel, it agreeth with His will there be not
only Kings but a race of Kings; that so soon as the breath
is gone from one, instantly it may be rested in another;
that so the good may ever be, and the evil never, found in
Israel.

Thus have we gone through the matter of instruction, III.
Our duty.
and now come to the matter of our own thanksgiving rising
out of it.

As there cannot be a greater plague to a land than to be
in that case, so is there not a higher benefit that God bestoweth on any people, to be fairly blessed from in it, than
for the removing from us so many mischiefs, and for the preserving to us the opposite blessings; for freeing us from that
misery, and not only conveying, but entailing to us and ours
this happiness. For this are we all now met here, in His
presence every man to put in his thanks into one common
stock, and so all jointly to offer it up unto God That as this
day sent us a King in Israel.

We come not for this alone to thank Him, (yet well might
we come for this, if there were none but this) but there is
more besides; and even seven times are we bound this day

SERM.
VIII.

Nu. 23. 21.

Hos. 10. 3.

Jer. 29. 7.

Hos. 13. 11.

Ezek. 37.
22.

to praise God for so many benefits, and yet go not out of the text.

1. Our first thanks then shall be for this first, the ground of all the rest, for a King. This very thing, that there is one, and that this defect, *Non erat Rex*, hath not taken hold on us. "The shout of a King" is a joyful shout, was a true saying out of the mouth of a false prophet, Balaam, but forced thereto by God. That a joyful shout, and this a woeful cry, *Nonne ideo nobis nullus Rex, quia non timemus Dominum?* "Are we not therefore without any King at all, because we feared not God?" And our fear to God was not such, but He might justly have brought us to that miserable plight. The more cause have we to thank Him that we have one. And when I say *one*, I mean first, have any one. For be he Nebuchadnezzar, yet must we pray for him; or be it Jeroboam, him though "God gave in His wrath," yet "He took away in His fury," the worst wrath of the twain. Or, be he who he will, to have one, though but such an one, is a matter of thanksgiving. For better any than an anarchy; better any one a King, than every one a King; and every one is more than a King, if he do what he lists. It calleth to mind the cry of the beasts in the fable when they were in consultation, to submit themselves to the lion as to their king. For when it was alleged, it was like enough he would do they knew not well what, what he listed which they had cause to fear, they all cried, *Præstat unum timere quam multos,* 'Better one lion do so than all the bears and wolves and wild beasts of the forest, as before they did.' First then for this, that there is a King.

Secondly for this, that *a* King, not many. For to have many, is a plague for the people's sins. Not many, nay not two, as of late, but now *Rex* indeed, one King over all Israel. We know when there were two Kings, one in Judah and the other in the ten tribes, two in one territory, it was a maim and a blemish both; that there were not *Rex*, one entire King, but two diverse Kings, as it were, over two halves of a country. The like imperfection was it, even the dividing this one island under two sovereigns. The reducing of both those under one, was promised Israel as a high favour. The same to us performed can be no less,

even that now there is a King indeed. *Rex*, one King; one,
and no more, absolute entire King over all the tribes, over
all Israel. Let this be the second.

And this our third. That not only over Israel, but, as
the words are, "in Israel." These are two different things.
To speak as the Prophet doth, that this King is not Ashur.
"For this cause Ashur shall be your King," is a fearful Hos. 11. 5.
threat God useth to His people for their unkindness. To
have a mere alien, one from beyond the water, as Nebuchadnezzar was, out of a people whose speech they did not
understand. One not *in* but *extra Israelem*, that is, over
Israel, but neither in it nor of it. That this is not our
case, as it is well known some would have had it. Therein
then must we also acknowledge, God hath dealt graciously
with us, sending us such an one as by more than one or
two, before this very last of all, is come of the race royal,
and is by due and undoubted right a King, not only over,
but in and of Israel. Is not this a third?

And sure this fourth. That as He sent us not Ashur a
stranger, so neither sent He a Jeroboam. No stranger in
birth he, but one addicted to strange worship, a stranger
in religion; (and it was even Micah's religion just; as
Micah's countryman he was, for both were of Ephraim)
who did that which was evil in God's eyes, by doing that
which was good in his own, and so "made Israel to sin." 1 Kings
Such an one He hath not sent us, but one that knoweth 15. 26.
God; doth neither favour Micah nor Micah's worship, since
that was a principal cause why there is a King in Israel,
that Micah's idols might not be set up.

And then, fifthly. As not a Jeroboam favouring Micah,
not a Rehoboam neither, who was indeed well for his religion, but otherwise not able to advise himself, and so ready
to be advised for the worse. One that was full of great 2 Chron.
words, but so faint-hearted as not able to resist ought; that 10. 14.
under him every one did what he would, for all the King. 2 Chron.
It was, as in another case the Prophet speaketh, *Rex, Rex,* 13. 17.
et non est Rex. It is otherwise where princes are intelligent,
learned, and as David was, both religious and wise; wise as
"an angel of God," to discern good and evil. Such a King 2 Sam. 19.
27.

SERM.
VIII.
as David, a special blessing; not *omnibus data*, not 'given to every people,' nay many times not to Israel itself. May we not report this for a fifth.

And for a sixth, this. That not as David neither, though he were both gentle and wise, which Rehoboam was not. For though he were both, yet was he so entangled with wars all his time, and forced still by continual effusion of blood, first to recover and then to maintain his right, as that he was rather *Dux* than *Rex in Israel*, a General of an army rather than a King. No, but (that which addeth still to the heap of our blessings) like Solomon, more happy than his father, as one that procureth to his people peace with all the nations round about. Of him, of such an one as he, [1 Kings 10. 9.] saith the Queen of Sheba, "Because the Lord thy God loved Israel, to establish it for ever, therefore hath He set thee King over them, to bring them to, and to preserve them in, the happy days of peace." That is indeed the right Heb. 7. 2. King, to be as Melchisedek "King of Salem, that is, King Isa. 9. 6. of peace." To be as the great King of Israel, Whose style is *Princeps pacis*.

And last of all, which is the complete perfection of all, that in and by him God hath not only sent us a King, but a race and succession of Kings. A blessing yet further, a greater hope, by blessing him, and in him us all, with an issue of such hope, and with hope still of more. Who shall (we trust, and pray they may) stretch their line to the world's end, and ever keep this land from this plague here mentioned, from days whereof it may be said, *Non erat Rex in Israel*. Even so Lord Jesus, so be it.

And thus seven times this day praise we God for this His sevenfold goodness. 1. For a King, 2. an absolute entire King, 3. a King both in and of Israel, 4. a King neither favouring nor favoured by Micah, 5. a King too wise to endure *Fecit quisque quod rectum*, 6. a King of peace, 7. a King who hath already by himself, and shall for ever by his seed preserve this land from the evil days wherein Israel was without a King. There is not any one of these seven but we owe our special thanks for it; but for them all, all that ever we have or can make.

And these now we offer and present to the Divine Majesty, all; and together with our thanks a commixtion of prayers, that this blessing of a King in Israel, and of this King in Israel, may to us and our posterity long and many years, yea many times many be continued, and we or they often see the renewing of this blessed day. Which Almighty God grant, &c.

A SERMON

THE KING'S MAJESTY AT GREENWICH,

A.D. MDCVII.

JAMES i. 22.

*And be ye doers of the word, and not hearers only, deceiving
your own selves.*

*Estote autem factores verbi, et non auditores tantum, fallentes vosmet-
ipsos.*

[*But be ye doers of the word, and not hearers only, deceiving your
own selves.* Eng. Trans.]

SERM.
IX.
[James
1. 21.]

AN advice or caution of St. James to those that "receive
the word engrafted." And that so necessary an advice, as
without which all our receiving the word, or hearing sermons, is nothing else, saith he, but a very cozening or deceiving ourselves.

Which I therefore thought very meet to attend upon the
former verse so lately handled. That being a commandment
to do it, this a caution to do it well.

There is not any time, but this caution of St. James is
needful; but the special time for it is, when hearing of the
word is growing into such request, as it hath got the start
of all the rest of the parts of God's service. So as, but that
sure we are the world will not like any one thing long, it
might justly be feared lest this part eating out the rest
should grow indeed the sole and only worship of God;
which St. James by no means would have it.

Now if this be a proper text for such times, our times
are such; this way our age is affected, now is the world of

sermons. For proof whereof, as if all godliness were in hearing of sermons, take this very place, the house of God, which now you see meetly well replenished; come at any other parts of the service of God, (parts, I say, of the service of God no less than this) you shall find it in a manner desolate. And not here only, but go any whither else ye shall find even the like.

And this, to speak with Solomon, "is an evil disease Eccl. 5. 13. under the sun," which hath possessed the world; or, with St. James, a strong illusion of our ghostly enemy. Who, when he cannot draw us wholly from the service of God, maketh us single out some one part of it from all the rest, and to be superstitiously conceited of that part, to make much of it, and to magnify it highly, nay only, with neglect and even as it were with some disgrace to all besides it.

Of which I may well say with St. James, the third chapter following, at the tenth verse, "My beloved, these things ought not so to be;" nor they cannot so be, without manifest impeachment of the wisdom of God, who hath appointed all the rest as well as this, and would have us make a conscience of all the rest no less than of this. And we cannot so sever out one as we do, but this will follow, that God did well and wisely in appointing that one, but not so in the rest. For as for them, they might well have been spared; we can serve God without them well enough.

Truly, though we cannot turn the stream or torrent of the time, (for that men will not hear of ought against hearing) yet sure it is this is "utterly a fault;" hearing is not the 1 Cor. 6. 7. only thing, and so much we must and do testify unto you, Joh. 3. 32. though our witness be not received.

But this is not properly St. James' only; this rather, that in hearing, when we have made it the only thing, we so carry ourselves as, when we have heard and heard only, though we do nothing else but hear and only hear, we think we have done enough, we stand discharged before God, no further thing can be required at our hands. This, saith St. James, is certainly an illusion, or "deceiving" ourselves. For if all other parts be neglected for this, and then in this so great an error be committed, if all we do be hearing, and even in that we be deceived too, what shall become of us?

SERM.
IX.

The sum.
Jas. 1. 19,
21.

Mar. 4. 24.
Lu. 8. 18.

Ezek. 33.
31.

The division.

I.

For remedy then of this doth St. James give us this item, "See that ye be," &c. In effect as if he should say, You are "swift to hear," you receive the word with all gladness, you will not miss a sermon; all this I allow of, and like well. But then "see," that is, do it not blindly: to hear the word is not a blind man's work; he had need not only have his ears but his eyes too, that shall do it to purpose; yea both his eyes, for there is work for both; *videte quid audiatis,* "to see what he hears;" *videte quomodo audiatis,* "to see how he hears." In any wise to see he be not a "hearer only," and nothing but a "hearer," and when he hath done that think he hath nothing else to do.

Yet such there were in Ezekiel's time (which place in the Old Testament matcheth this in the New) that called one to another, Come, let us go to the sermon; *Et audiunt,* saith he, *sed nihil faciunt,* and heard but did nothing.

Such in St. James' time; else was his caution without cause. And such in our time; not *in dogmate,* for they maintain it not, but their practice plainly discovers as much; that so they hear, they care neither what, nor how; *ipsum audire,* 'very hearing' serves their turn.

Well, whosoever so doth, how sure soever he makes himself, how well and wisely soever he thinks he carries the matter, it is sure saith St. James, if he see not to it, he is fallen into *deceptio visûs.* And if he hear no otherwise, into *deceptio auditûs.* His receiving of the word is nothing but a deceiving himself.

So have we two principal parts of this text. 1. First his advice or caution: "See that ye be doers of the word, and not hearers only." 2. And secondly, that which giveth an edge to this advice, which is a main inconvenience we fall into if we follow it not: Lest we deceive ourselves.

The former of the advice thus we put in order: "Be not hearers only of the word, but doers." So is the true placing of the words, though it stands otherwise in the text. Now he that saith, "Be not hearers only," saith two things: 1. Be ye hearers; 2. but not hearers only. So that the points grow to be three: 1. an allowing us to be hearers, first; 2. but "not hearers only," but somewhat else, the second; 3. thirdly, what that is, namely, to be "doers of

the word;" which is nothing else but the fruit of that graft Jas. 1. 21.
which so lately ye heard of. And this is the caution.

Then secondly, he giveth it an edge by saying, If we II.
follow not his caution, we fall into a flat paralogism, we
make a false conclusion or fallacy. Yea, a double edge:
1. first, that we are deceived; 2. the second, that we deceive ourselves.

We begin with this, that St. James in saying, "Be not I.
hearers only," this he saith, Be hearers, but not only hear- The ad-
ers, be ye doers too; but be hearers still. 1. Be
hearers.

For in dealing with Scriptures that consist of negatives by
comparison, "not hearers but doers," and such like, we had
need walk warily; and, as the schoolmen say, resolve them
cum grano salis, lest we cast out one devil with another, as Mat. 12. 24.
the manner of some is; the devil of hearing only with the
devil of not hearing at all, and so "the last error prove worse Mat. 27. 64.
than the first." We must take heed we preserve both, both
hearing and doing, each in their several right; and so do
the former, that the latter we "leave not undone." Mat. 23. 23.

For St. James, by opening our hands to do, hath no
meaning to shut our ears to hear; by wishing us to fall
to doing, he willeth us not to give over hearing; by bringing in the latter, taketh not away the former. But, as I
said, to hold on our hearing still, only with this caution,
that we reckon not that for all, or to be the thing solely
or wholly to be intended by us. This being seen unto, to
hear on as we did.

For he that had, two verses before, willed us to be "swift Jas. 1. 19,
to hear;" he that, the very next verse before, "meekly to 21.
receive the word;" he could not possibly so soon forget
himself, as to have any such meaning. No certainly, he
had given it the honour of the first place, and his purpose
is not to take it away again.

God from heaven so began His law with hearing: "Hear Deu. 4. 1.
O Israel." God from heaven too so began His gospel:
"This is My beloved Son, hear Him." So God began, and Mat. 17. 5.
so must we begin, or else we begin wrong.

And not begin only, but continue still hearing; for so
doth the Apostle comment on the place of the Psalm, Ps. 95. 7.
"To-day if you will hear His voice," that by "to-day" is

o

SERM.
IX.

Heb. 3. 7.

Lu. 10. 42.

Lu. 11. 52.

Rom. 10.
13, 14.

Acts 9. 6.
Joh. 14. 6.

2 Pet. 3. 1.

Mat. 12. 42.

meant *donec cognominatur hodie,* "while it is called to-day." And to-morrow and every day, when it comes, is called "to-day;" so that "to-day" is all the days of our life.

The reason of which our continual being hearers is the continual necessity of hearing of the word of God. Which necessity our Saviour Christ Himself setteth down; in express terms speaking of Mary's choice to sit and hear His words, *Unum est necessarium,* one of the necessary things it is, and for such we may boldly affirm it.

What that necessity is He tells us, when He calls it "the key of knowledge." That there is a door shut, this is the key; no opening, no entrance without it, none at all. For *Quomodo possunt,* saith St. Paul, How can they possibly be saved, except they call upon God; or call upon Him, except they hear? It seems he knew not how, and if not he not any man else. For if we must be "doers of the word," as by and by he tells us we must, we must needs hear first what to do before we can do it.

At the first, we are in his case that said, *Domine quid me vis facere?* We know not what to do: then it is necessary to teach us.

After we know, we forget again: then it is necessary to call us to remembrance.

When we remember, we grow dull in our duty: then it is necessary "to stir up" and quicken us. So every way it is necessary, and we cannot be quit of it, *donec cognominatur hodie,* "while it is called to-day."

As the philosopher said of the celestial bodies and lights, that they were *dignum et idoneum spectaculum, si tantum præterirent,* (it is Seneca,) 'if they only passed by over our heads,' and we received not the benefit of their motion and influence, which we do, yet were they a spectacle worth the beholding; so may we justly say of the word, though it only disclosed the high and admirable treasure of wisdom and knowledge it doth, yet were it worth the while to hear it. For the "Queen of the south" came a great long journey only to be partaker of Solomon's wisdom, and for nothing else; *et ecce major Solomone hîc,* and He That was the Author of this word "is greater than Solomon."

How much more then, when besides this excellency we

have further so necessary use of it. It serves us first as a
key, or special means, whereby we may escape the place of
torments. So saith Abraham to him that was in them: If
your five brethren would not come where you are, "they
have Moses and the Prophets," *audiant ipsos*, "let them hear Lu. 16. 29.
them;" that shall quit them for ever coming there.

And it serves us not only as a "key" to lock that place, Lu. 11. 52.
but to open us another, even the kingdom of heaven. For
not so few as twenty times in the Gospel is the preaching of
the word called the kingdom of heaven, as a special means
to bring us thither. It is that which St. James in the verse
before saith, "It is able to save our souls." The very words Jas. 1. 21.
which the Angel used to Cornelius, that when St. Peter
came he should speak words by which he and his household Acts 11. 14
should be saved. Such and so necessary is the use of hearing the word both ways.

I conclude then with St. Peter, *Cui bene facitis attendentes,* 2 Pet. 1. 19.
"that ye do well in giving heed to it;" as St. James here
saith, not as ἀκουσταὶ, 'bare hearers,' but as ἀκροαταὶ, "attentive hearers;" that in so doing you do well.

But St. Paul is so far carried with this desire to have us
hear that he saith, Let the word be preached, and let it be Phil. 1. 18.
heard; be it sincerely, or be it pretensedly, so it be done, it
is to him, and should be to us, matter (not only of content-
ment, but also) of rejoicing. As much to say as, Let them
come and be hearers, though it be but to mock; let them
come and be hearers, though it be but to carp, so they come
and be hearers. And it is not amiss. They that came to Acts 2. 6,
mock the Apostles, as men gone with drink, were caught by 13.
their hearing. They that came to take our Saviour Christ, Joh. 7. 32,
were taken themselves by their hearing. Therefore, *Quo-* 46.
cunque modo saith St. Paul, and though it be more than
St. James seems to warrant say we, Howsoever and with
what condition soever it be, be ye hearers of the word,
still.

Hearers, but hearers of the word. For it should be the Hearers;
word we hear. Words we hear, every foot; but I dare not but of the
say, *the* word always. Much chaff is sown instead of right
grain; many a dry stick engrafted, instead of a scion with
life and sap in it. This was it our Saviour Christ willed us

to look to; *quid*, "what" we heard, as well as *quomodo*, "how." And indeed, for all our hearing, few have exercised senses to discern this point. Whatsoever it be that we hear out of the pulpit, it serves our turn, it is all one: there is much deceit in this point. But a point it is that would not be saluted afar off, or touched lightly, but the very core of it searched, if it were dealt with as it should. But indeed it is not so pertinent to St. James' purpose in this place; therefore I will not enter into it, but go on to the second.

2. "Not hearers only."
Hearers of the word; but "not hearers only," for all the matter is in the word "only." The more hearers the better; the more "hearers only," the worse. We cannot say so much good of hearing, as we must speak evil of such as content themselves with hearing only.

And why not "only?" Because to hear is somewhat, but it is not all. A part it is, but in no wise the whole. It is one thing, but not the "only" one thing. And therefore we must not stay in it, there is a *plus ultra;* when we have done hearing, somewhat else is to be done.

This appeareth plainly from our Saviour Christ's own mouth, even in that very place where He so much commendeth hearing, and so setteth out the necessity of it. He commendeth it by saying, "Mary hath chosen the better part:" the better part is but a part yet; therefore not the whole then. He setteth out the necessity of it by saying, *Unum est necessarium. Unum* He saith, not *unicum;* that "one thing" it is, but not 'the only one thing' that is, "necessary," nor so to be reputed.

Lu. 10. 42.

But of all other St. Paul doth best shew the absurdity of them that so esteem it. What, saith he, is all the body an ear? Is all hearing? As if he should say, That is too gross. Yet thither they must come, even to make all the senses hearing, and all the body an ear, that place all religion in lectures and sermons.

1 Cor. 12. 17.

This then being but a part only, being but one thing, we must not stay here; we must not stay, for the Scripture itself (mark it where you will) never maketh a stay at this of hearing. Ever the sentence is suspended; ever there followeth a copulative, an *and* in the neck of it. It never cometh to a pause or full point, till somewhat else be supplied.

"This people hath well said," saith God in Deuteronomy. Deut. 5. 28.
What was that, that we may say so too? This it was; they
said to Moses, "Bring thou God's word to us, and we will [Deut. 5. 27.]
hear it, and do it." Not hear it only, for then it should not
have been commended, but "hear it and do it." And so it
is "well said," and not otherwise. I will tell you, saith our
Saviour Christ, who is a wise builder; "He that heareth Mat. 7. 24
My words and"—no period there, but "and doeth them."
And to the woman that heard His words with a great passion, "Blessed are they that hear the word of God, and Lu. 11. 28.
keep it." And not to trouble you with many allegations,
so concludeth he in the Revelation : "Blessed is he that Rev. 1. 3.
readeth, and they that hear the words of this prophecy, and
keep the things written therein." Mark it well; never a
pause, a breath, a full point, or stay at hearing, but still
an "and;" "*and* do," "*and* keep," "*and* fulfil," "*and*"
somewhat else. To shew it is neither the sole nor the
whole thing, there remaineth still for us some further
duty behind.

Inasmuch then as it is never put alone, but still coupled
with some other, and it is a rule—not only for marriage,
but for all things else—"What God hath coupled, let no Mat. 19. 6.
man put asunder," let us see what that other thing is which
God hath coupled, and St. James supplieth to be joined
with it.

What is that? Is it to be moved a little with that we 3. But "doers of the word."
hear? Upon our hearing to say with Agrippa, ἐν ὀλίγῳ,
Somewhat I was, I was a little moved with it? No, this Acts 26. 28.
is to suffer, not to do. St. James speaketh of doing.

What is it then? Is it to cry, *Magister bene dixisti*,
"Sir, you well said," you have made us a good sermon? Lu. 20. 39.
Nay then, what say you to *Nunquam quisquam*, "we never Joh. 7. 46.
heard a better :" is not that it? No, for this is to say and
not to do. St. James speaketh of doing.

What say you to conferring of it by the walls of our
house, and making that we have heard matter of discourse
or question? I can tell what I would say, if our questions
and discourses tended to that of St. James here, to doing;
that then we were in a good way. But ye shall observe for
the most part they be about some pretty speculative point,

SERM.
IX.
some subtle objection; somewhat ever tending to curiosity of knowledge, rather than conscience of practice. But if we did so, yet it were but to talk of doing, not to do. Still we are short of St. James, who whatsoever we do to satisfy him besides, will not leave us till we be doers of it. And sure any that observeth it shall find those that I have named, 1. to hear, 2. to be moved with it a little, 3. to commend it, 4. to spend a little talk about it, this is all. And that all these be but bye-ways which the enemy of our souls seeketh to lead us into, so to divert us from the true end, that we may rest in these as in our final conclusion, and never come to this of St. James, which is the point indeed, to be doers.

We see then what the other part is; to hear that we may do, to receive that we may bring forth, to be grafted that we may fructify.

And that our care of it may be according, I add that this Lu. 10. 42. is not only a part, but far "the better part" of the twain. For though Mary's part was better than Martha's—Mary's in hearing, than Martha's in entertaining—yet Mary's part in doing, that is, in anointing Christ, was better than her part in hearing Christ, and hath a greater praise and pro-
Mat. 26. 13. mise from Christ's own mouth: "This that she hath done shall be spoken of through the world." It is our rule: *Unumquodque propter quid, et illud magis.* In that doing is the *propter quid*, the end of hearing, and we therefore hear what to do that we may do what we hear; in that, as the schoolmen say, *Scire est propter ire,* we know the way to go the way, doing must needs be the worthier of the twain; worthier in itself, and consequently worthier our care and intendment.

To make it plain, do but take them in sunder, and sever
Rom. 2. 13. them: St. Paul saith plainly then, *non auditores,* hearing is nothing, *sed factores,* but doing is all. And when they be joined, still there is a mark set upon this part, to shew it for the chief. As here, at the twenty-fifth verse following,
[Jas. 1. 25.] he saith plainly, *Beatus erit in opere suo,* he that shall be blessed "shall be blessed in his work," not in any thing else. Our Saviour Himself saith the same in express terms:
Joh. 13. 17. "If ye know these things"—How then? "blessed shall ye

be if ye do them." Mark, "Blessed, if ye do them." Otherwise, if ye know them never so much, never the more blessed. Never the more blessed? Nay, *scienti et non facienti,* saith Jas. 4. 17. St. James, "knowing and not doing" is an increase of our sin, and consequently a greater heap of our condemnation. This therefore is the principal part, to be doers.

If then we would fain be doers, and ask what that is, it is a material point to know. There are two kinds of doers; 1. ποιηταὶ, and 2. πρακτικοὶ, which the Latin likewise expresseth in 1. *agere,* and 2. *facere. Agere,* as in music, where, when we have done singing or playing, nothing remaineth ; *facere,* as in building, where, after we have done, there is a thing permanent. And ποιηταὶ, *factores,* they are St. James' doers. But we have both the words in the English tongue : actors, as in a play ; factors, as in merchandise. When the play is done, all the actors do vanish ; but of the factors' doing there is a gain, a real thing remaining.

To be a doer of the word is, as St. Gregory saith well, *convertere scripturas in operas,* to change the word which is audible into a work which is visible, the word which is transient into a work which is permanent.

Or rather not to change it, but, as St. Augustine saith, [Conf. S. Aug. Ser. 179.] *accedat ad verbum,* unto the word that we hear let there be joined the element of the work, that is, some real elemental deed ; *et sic fit magnum sacramentum pietatis,* and so shall you have "the great mystery" or sacrament "of godliness." 1 Tim. 3. For indeed godliness is as a sacrament ; hath not only the 16. mystery to be known, but the exercise to be done; not the 1 Tim. 4. 7. word to be heard, but the work also to be performed : or else, if it be not a sacrament it is not true godliness.

Which very sacrament of godliness is there said to be the manifesting of the word in the flesh ; which itself is livelily expressed by us when we are doers of the word, as it is well gathered out of our Saviour Christ's speech to them which interrupted Him in His sermon, and told Him His mother was without. "Who is My mother?" saith He. These Mat. 12. 50. here, that hear and do My words are My mother, they "tra- Gal. 4. 19. vail" of Me till I am fashioned in them. Hearing, they re- 1 Pet. 1. 23. ceive the immortal seed of the word ; by a firm purpose of

SERM. doing they conceive, by a longing desire they quicken, by
IX. an earnest endeavour they travail with it; and when the
Joh. 1. 14. work is wrought, *verbum caro factum est*, they have incarnate
Lu. 11. 27. the word. Therefore to the woman's acclamation, "Blessed
be the womb that bare Thee;" True, saith Christ, but that
blessing can extend but only to one, and no more. I will
tell you how you may be blessed too; blessed are they that
so incarnate the written word by doing it, as the blessed
Virgin gave flesh to the eternal Word by bearing It.

Jam. 2. 18. It is that which St. James meaneth in the next chapter,
Rom. 10. where he saith, *Ostende mihi fidem*, "Faith cometh by hear-
17. ing;" "shew me thy faith" and thy hearing, saith he in the
person of a heathen man. The Christian faith is, *quando
creditur quod dicitur*; the heathen saith, *quando fit quod
dicitur*; for so they define it in their books of offices. Ye
shall never shew them your faith, *cum creditur quod dicitur*,
but by that they understand, that is, their own faith, *cum
fit quod dicitur*, by doing the word. Enough to shew what
is meant by "doers of the word."

And lest we excuse ourselves by this, that all sermons are
not *de theologiá practicá*, 'entreat not of matters of action,'
and so not to be done, by this that hath been said of the
sacrament of godliness we may easily understand that there
is no article of faith or mystery of religion at all, but is as
a key to open, and as a hand to lead us to some operative virtue; even those mystical points being by the Holy
Ghost's wisdom so tempered, that they minister every one
1 Tim. 4. 7. of them somewhat to be doing with, somewhat pertaining
to the exercise of godliness no less than the moral points
themselves. So that if we would dispose ourselves to keep
St. James' caution, I make no question we might well do
it through all. At least when the points are plainly prac-
tical, mere *agends*, then to make a conscience of doing them,
and to call ourselves to account of what we have heard, what
we have done, till as St. James' term is we find ourselves to
be "doers of the word;" till as St. James' term was the
verbum insitum, "the engrafted word," have his fruit in a
work suitable to the seed or scion it came of. And this is
the sum of his caution.

II. What if we do thus, what then? So doing, saith St. James,
The edge
of the cau-

we shall do wisely and make sure work, in saying that not tion, or the
doing so, we shall but beguile ourselves. For indeed, those inconvenience.
are the only hearers that are doers too; the other that are 1. "Deceiving."
"hearers only," as good not hear, for when all is done doing
must do it. That is plainest that Scripture telleth us, how
it shall go at last : " They that have done good shall go into Joh. 5. 29.
life everlasting, and they that have done evil" go—I need
not tell you, you know whither well enough.

This very thing had David said long before of the word :
" A good understanding have all they that do thereafter." Ps. 111. 10.
And so had our Saviour Christ, Who saith of him that
heareth and doeth, that he approveth himself for a wise Mat. 7. 24.
builder. Which is that and nothing else which St. James
here implieth, that they make a sound conclusion or true
syllogism.

As, on the other side, supposing they do it not, they be Mat. 7. 26.
foolish builders, "foolish virgins," saith Christ; saith St. Mat. 25. 2.
James, they fall into a flat fallacy or paralogism, are deceived by a piece of the devil's sophistry.

And the Apostle could not possibly devise to speak more
fitly, or to give his caution a better edge. For these great
hearers, nothing so much nettles them as to be accounted
men deceived, unwise, or overseen. Men are deceived for
want of knowledge : they reckon themselves the only people,
as if knowledge should " die with them." And being men [Job 12. 2.]
of knowledge, consequently freest from error of any men
alive. They pity much the blindness of the former times ;
but as for them they see light clearly, and are not deceived
you may be sure. Therefore this seemeth very strange to
them, and in evil part they must needs take it, to be holden
for men deceived. The more it moveth them, the liker it
is to work with them, and therefore St. James the rather
chooseth it.

It is the course the Holy Ghost still keeps with them.
For such were, in our Saviour's time, the Pharisees. None
such men of knowledge as they, they were knowledge all
over; in their forehead, at their wrists, down to the very
fringe and skirts of their garment. Notwithstanding, upon
this very point of *non faciunt*, our Saviour Christ lets not
to call them " fools and blind," though they took themselves [Mat. 23. 17.]

SERM.
IX.

[Ps. 95.
10.]

2 Tim. 3.
7.

1 Tim. 6.
20.

Gal. 6. 7.

Isa. 49. 4.

Isa. 55. 10,
11.

2 Cor. 2.
15.

[Ezek. 33.
32.]

to be the only eagles of the world. Even so were those in the Psalm, when they had heard the Law, sabbath after sabbath, forty years together, yet saith He, "It is a people that do err in their hearts," for all that; and though they have heard so long, yet "they know not My ways." And even so St. Paul, with some in his time, whom though he terms "always learning," continually hearing, still at sermons, yet for all that he saith they never came to the "knowledge of the truth;" not the true knowledge which consisteth in the practice, but a kind of jangling knowledge, and holding of "opposition," which he calleth "knowledge falsely so called." Therefore for all their sermons and all their lectures, a deceit there is certainly.

For let us examine it. If that which is heard be therefore heard that it may be done, and it be not done, a deceit there is; somebody there is deceived, light where it will. Now there be but three in all that be parties to it; 1. God, 2. the preacher, 3. and the hearer. One of these it must be.

"Be not deceived," saith the Apostle, "God is not mocked:"—no deceiving of Him. It is not He sure.

Then it is we. So one would think, so thought Esay. "Alas," saith he, "I have laboured in vain, I have spent my strength in vain," I find I am deceived. But he receives answer of God it was not so. That neither he had preached the word, nor the word he had preached had been or should be in vain. For himself, that his reward was with God, whether the hearer profited or no. For the word, that as the rain or snow going forth, it "should not return empty" without his effects.

Which answer to Esay was it which put comfort in St. Paul; that were his preaching the savour of life or of death, both ways it was in him a sweet smelling savour, accepted of God. And if neither God nor the preacher, then must the deceit fall on the hearer, and he it is that is deceived.

Deceived? Wherein, or how? Many ways. And first, in grossly mistaking the very nature of sermons. Upon *audiunt et non faciunt*, Ezekiel saith plainly of those in his days, they seemed to reckon of sermons no otherwise than of songs; to give them the hearing, to commend the air of them, and so

let them go. The music of a song, and the rhetoric of a
sermon, all is one. A foul error, even in the very nature
of the word; for that is a law, a testament, and neither
song nor sonnet. A law, enacted to be done. For it shall
not serve the three children to say of Nebuchadnezzar's law, Dan. 3. 8,
they had heard it proclaimed from point to point; but do it &c.
they must or into the furnace, for such is the nature of a
law. A testament; which "though it be but a man's," as Gal. 3. 15.
St. Paul saith, must be executed, and we are compellable to
the execution of it; and to God's much more.

To speak but according to the metaphor in the verse be- Jas. 1. 21
fore. It is a plain mistaking of the word—which is as seed
in a soil, or as a scion in a stock—to take it for a stake in
a hedge, there to stick and stand still, and bring forth nothing. Or according to the metaphor in the verse next Jas. 1. 23.
after, where it is termed "a glass," which we should look
in to do somewhat by; to take away some spot, to mend
somewhat amiss, to set somewhat right; and it is plainly to
mistake it, to look in it and look off it, and forget our chief
errand to it.

As this is a manifest mistaking in the nature, so is there
a like in the end. For whereas they hear to do, and to do
is the end why they hear, these *auditores tantum* do, even
as St. Paul saith, *requiescunt in lege,* "make the law their Rom. 2. 17.
pillow," lay them down upon it, and there take their rest;
never seek farther, and so miss their mark quite.

But a worse error yet than this is, that they which when
they have heard have done, seem to think that hearing and
doing is all one, inasmuch as all they do is only that they
hear, and so grossly confound the two parts that are plainly
distinguished. For hearing is a sense, and sense is in suffering; but the hearing of the word is so easy a suffering, as if
we look not to ourselves we often fall asleep at it. Now
suffering and doing are plainly distinguished; and not only
plainly distinguished, but as we see flatly opposed by St.
James in the text, either to other.

Not to hold you over long, seeing the Apostle borrowed
his term of paralogism from the schools, to speak in school
terms. In hearing only and not doing, there is, first, the
clench, *A sensu composito ad divisum;* which they fall into

that, where two things are required, rest in one. And again, the elench, *A dicto secundum quid ad dictum simpliciter;* wherewith they are deceived, that having a part think that part shall serve them instead of the whole. Which two are a piece of the devil's sophistry ; and so you see, both 1. that they are deceived, 2. and how they are deceived that rest upon hearing only.

But to be deceived simply, is no so great matter ; wise men, many of them, are so, and any of them may be. This is that which edgeth it yet more, which giveth it a double edge, that they deceive themselves.

1. In which point, first, certain it is there is no man that willingly would be deceived, can endure to be deceived himself. Saith the first and greatest deceiver to Eve, even then when he came purposely to deceive her, אַף כִּי, " Is it for a truth, that God hath forbidden you to eat of all the trees ?" As if he should say : I would not have you deceive me, tell me true, whether it be so or no. Lo, he would not be deceived himself, though he came merely about deceit.

2. But then, secondly, if deceived we must be, of all men we would not be deceived of such as we trust; that grieves
us exceedingly. Saith David : " He hath beguiled me whom I trusted ; my guide, my counsellor, my familiar friend." He can never say enough of it, for it is a grief above all griefs to be so deceived.

3. Thirdly then, if not by one we trust, least of all by that party whom most of all we trust, that is, by ourselves ; for we trust none better, I suppose. It we must be deceived, of another, of any other rather than of ourselves. For he that deceiveth himself, is both the deceived and the deceiver too. The deceived may be pitied, the deceiver is ever to be blamed ; therefore he is utterly without excuse, that is the author of his own deceiving. And there is no man pitieth him, but every one mocketh him, and takes up proverbs over him of, Self do self have, and I wot not what. So that this of all other is the worst. 1. To be deceived, 2. to be deceivers, 3. to be their own deceivers.

Will ye see an example of this, that they do but deceive themselves that build upon *auditores tantum?* You may, Luke the thirteenth, where you shall see some that upon

their bare hearing bare themselves very confidently, as if
they could by no means be deceived in it, and yet they were.
Christa saith to them, *Nescio vos.* They think very strange of Lu. 13. 25, 26.
that speech, and reply, Lord, why hast not Thou preached
in our streets, and have not we heard Thee daily, and never
missed? Well for that, for all their hearing, He telleth
them again, *Nescio vos.* Though He had seen them at never
so many sermons, He taketh no notice of them by their
being or hearing there, but by their doing afterward. By
which it appeareth, that upon this very point they promised
themselves very much, but found at last they had but deceived themselves.

And, which is worst of all, found it then when it was too
late; when no writ of error could be brought, when it was
past time, and they no way to be relieved.

And yet to go further. If this deceit of themselves were
in some light matter, of no great importance, it were so
much the more tolerable; but so it is not here. The last
words of the last verse are, as you remember, *salvare animas
vestras;* so that it is a matter of saving our souls, a matter
as much as our souls or salvation are worth. Life or death,
heaven or hell, no less matters, depend upon our being deceived here; things which most of all it concerneth us not
to be deceived in.

One point more, and so an end. They will be hearers of
the word, and not do it: what say you to this, that when
they have been " hearers only" all their life long, they shall
in the end be forced to be doers, and doers of that word
which least of all others they would do. Is not this evidently to deceive themselves? In the Prophet Jeremy, they Jer. 18. 18.
say, they will give God the hearing, but not do any of His
words. But they shall not go away with it so; for when
they have done what they can, they shall find themselves
deceived in that too. A word there is they shall not hear
only, but hear and do, whether they will or no. And what
is that word? Even, *Discedite maledicti in ignem æternum.* Mat. 25. 41.
For they that will do none else, that they shall do, and fulfil
that commandment that break all the rest. And who is able
to fulfil, nay to abide that word? Who can endure to go
whither that will send him? Of all words, that is *durus* Joh. 6. 60.

sermo, nay *durissimus,* the hardest to do of all; better do any, yea, better do all than do that.

You see then what an edge the Apostle hath set upon his advice, how great an inconvenience they run themselves into that be "hearers only." Which if it be intolerable, as sure it is, it will import us to take heed to the caution, that so we may avoid this double edge.

First then, that we do as we do, hear still. For, *bene-facitis attendentes.*

Yet not to be carried away with the common error, that sermon-hearing is the *consummatum est* of all Christianity ; and so we hear our sermons duly, all is safe, more needs not. But to resolve with ourselves that only will not do it, somewhat there must be besides. And when all is done, it must be *factores verbi.*

Lastly, that we may, if we please, entertain other opinions touching this point, but they will deceive us, and we in holding them be deceived. And that in a matter of great weight and consequence, which then we shall find and feel when it will be too late to help it.

Then, that hearing and not doing, we shall in the end be forced both to hear and to do a word, the heaviest to be heard and the worst to be done of all others. Therefore, that we see to it in time, and keep the caution, that we may avoid the penalty. Which Almighty God open our eyes that we may see, &c.

A SERMON

PREACHED AT

THE OPENING OF THE PARLIAMENT,

A.D. MDCXXI.

PSALM lxxxii. 1.

Deus stat in synagogâ deorum : in medio deos judicavit.

The Greek, word for word, the same.

God standeth in the congregation of Princes[1]. *Or, in the assembly of gods*[2]. *Or, of the mighty*[3].

In the midst will He judge the gods.

[1] The Psalter.
[2] The Geneva.
[3] The new translation

Which was the Psalm for the day, viz. the sixteenth day of the month, on which day the Parliament was first begun.

"GOD standeth in the congregation of Princes," &c. Of a "congregation of Princes" is this Psalm, as you have heard. And behold here such a congregation, and God, I trust, standing in it. And who then can doubt but this Psalm is for this day?

The words, sure, seem to favour it; the use much more, which hath ever gone with it.

For standing the policy of the commonwealth of Israel, their writers tell us, when ought was to be done, for choosing their rulers, for placing them and giving them their charge; but specially when there was any meeting of them in their *synagoga magna,* their 'great congregation,' this was ever the Psalm before they sat down. Purposely set, as it seemeth, for the assembly, to set them in tune. For that end set, and to that end ever used.

It was Moses the man of God that by special direction from God Himself began and brought up this order first, of making men's duty into music: putting it into their mouths, that so with the sweetness of melody it might be conveyed into their minds. And David since continued it and brought it to perfection, as having a special grace and felicity; he for a song, and his son Solomon for a proverb; by which two—the unhappy adage and a wanton song—Satan hath ever breathed most of his infection and poison into the mind of man.

Now in this holy and heavenly use of his harp he doth by his tunes, as it were, teach all sorts of men how to tune themselves. And there is no estate whatsoever, but in this Book he sweetly singeth their duty into them. Into his court, Psalm the hundred and first, and so severally into the rest. And here now in this Psalm, how to preserve harmony in a congregation.

Of which Psalm this is the first verse, the key and the compendium of the whole. And thus we divide it: 1. into two parties first; 2. into two acts, second. Two parties: 1. the first word of it is God, God in the singular; 2. the last is gods, gods in the plural. These two parties are distinct; 1. one from another, 2. one above another.

1. God That standeth, from the congregation He standeth in. 2. God that judgeth, from and above the gods whom He will judge.

The gods we consider two ways, as the word is twice repeated: 1. *deorum*, and 2. *deos*. 1. *In synagogâ deorum*, and 2. *in medio deos*. 1. *Deorum* in the congregation, 2.
I. *deos* out of it. If you will, thus: into the 1. gods of the
II. congregation, and the 2. congregation of the gods.

Now of the first God in and upon the last gods, and in
III. and upon the congregation of them, two acts there are set
IV. down; 1. His standing, 2. His judgment.

1. In the congregation He stands: *Stat in synagogâ deorum.*

2. Out of it, the gods He will judge: *deos judicabit*, that is, call them to account, every god of them; and even upon this very point, how they carried themselves before Him standing in the congregation. 1. This He will do; and do

ıt *in medio,* not in a corner, but bring them forth into the midst, and do it in the view of all. *In medio deos judicabit.*

The order lieth plain. 1. Of the gods first: 2. then of the congregation of them. After of God; 1. His standing, and 2. His judging. Standing now, *Deus stat;* judging hereafter, *Deus judicabit.* Judging, 1. even the gods themselves. And that 2. *in medio,* that all the world may see it. 1. In the whole course of our lives we may have good use of these two; 2. but the Psalmist seemeth to think not at any time so good as at this.

Therefore whatever else slip you, my desire is these two may stick with you, and be ever in your minds all the session long. Two they be, and short ones and plain ones they be; but two words apiece. 1. *Deus stat,* 2. *Deus judicabit;* 1. "God doth stand," and 2. "God will judge." 1. "Doth stand" for the present; 2. and "will judge," will take a time to call each party to a reckoning, for every thing shall here pass.

1. The taking to heart, a true impression there of these two, cannot but do much good, keep all in true measure, time, and tune. 2. The *ignorantibus* or *non recordantibus* of it, as it is at the fifth verse, like enough to put all out of course; while men run on and carry things away before them, as if there were no *judicare* in the creed, as if they should never come to account again.

It hath been thought there needeth no more to make a good Parliament, but the due recording of this verse. It will serve as a rest to tune, and to set all right. To set God, 1. first standing, and then 2. judging, before our eyes.

But specially, standing; for if we shall regard Him well when He stands, we shall never need to fear Him when He judges; and then I shall never need to trouble you with that part. The regard then of God's standing to be our only care for the present, and we to commend it to your care, and so to conclude.

Of the gods first. And first, on our parts that be men; after, on theirs that be the gods.

On our parts. When we read, and weigh well with ourselves this high term and title of gods, given to them that are in authority, we learn to hold them for gods, to owe and

V.

I.
The two
parties.
The gods
of the con-
gregation.
1. The duty
of infe-
riors to the
gods.

SERM. to bear all reverend regard to their places and persons. And
  X.
——— above all, highly to magnify such assemblies as this. So
taught by the Prophet here, who once and twice, over and
over again, so styleth them, their persons themselves, *deos*,
their assembly, *synagogam deorum*. In the congregation they
are so, out of it they are so. Add to these two a third yet,
more authentical, and it is in this Psalm too. The Pro-
Ps. 82. 6. phet speaketh here, God Himself there; *Ego dixi dii estis*.
Joh. 10. 35. This, saith our Saviour, is *sermo Dei*. The other two may
seem to drop out of the Prophet's pen, but this came from
God's own mouth : the more, say I, to be regarded. And
this is not Old Testament, as say our Anabaptists. Our
blessed Saviour in the New comments upon these words—
the best Commentor that ever was—and two things He tells
us.   1. One, we thought it to be but a Psalm, He tells us
Joh. 10. 34. it is a law, *Nonne scriptum est in Lege?* and so gives it the
force of a law.   2. The other, that it is a binding law still;
Joh. 10. 35. so binding, that *Non potest solvi*, (they be His own words,)
"it cannot be loosed." Was not by Him, nor can by any
other ; and so is in full force still.

These then, *dii*, *deorum*, and *deos*, are not St. Peter's
2 Pet. 2. 18. ὑπέρογκα ματαιότητος, " swelling words of vanity." This is
not to give titles, but of God's own giving; not to say one
syllable more than God hath said before us. Said it must
be that God hath said, Who never gives *titulum sine re*.
So they are by Him intituled, and so they are.

Yet not to   But I take it my duty not to keep from you that all that
hold all
the gods   are comprised here under *dii, deorum*, and *deos*, are not all
equal.   gods alike. No : in this godhead some are before or after
other, some are greater and lesser than another. There are
some higher than other, saith Solomon. And there are others
Eccl. 5. 8. yet " higher than they." For " the powers that are, are
Rom. 13. 1. by God" both " ordained" and set in order, saith St. Paul.
1 Pet. 2. 13. So in order, saith St. Peter, as there is one ὑπερέχων, and
that he saith is " the King" by name, supereminent above
the rest, and the rest *ab eo missi* have their mission and commission from him. Many superiors, but one sovereign.

Ego dixi was said to all, but not to all at once. To some
2 Sam. 23. one before the rest; even to David, to whom before the
3.   writing of this Psalm, " God," saith he, " even the strength

of Israel, spake to me and said, Thou shalt bear rule over
men." Nor did all the "sons of the Most High," as they
are after called at the sixth verse, come into the world at
one time. There was *primogenitus inter fratres;* of whose
primogeniture or birthright this was a part, "Be thou Lord Gen. 27.
over thy brethren, and let thy mother's sons bow unto 29.
thee." And take even the word *synagoga;* never was there
a synagogue heard of, but there was an *archisynagogus,*
a ruler of it.

Nazianzen, speaking of Magistrates as of the images of
God, and sorting them, compareth the highest to a picture
drawn clean through down to the feet; the middle sort, to
half pictures drawn but to the girdle; the lowest, to those
same Idyllia, no farther but to the neck and shoulders.
But all in some degree carry the image of God, as all have
the honour to be called by His Name. This for our parts.
Now for theirs, the gods.

What infer we of this? Nothing, but that what they are 2.
they would be; "having obtained so excellent a name," they The duty of the
would be even what their name bodeth. They that wear gods: to be as they
God's name, hold God's place, represent His person, "what be called,
manner persons" ought they to be? Choice persons they gods in-deed.
would be, taken as the fat from the sacrifice, having more Heb. 1. 4.
2 Pet. 3. 11.
sparks of the Deity, a larger portion of the Spirit of God,
more lively expressing the image and similitude whereto Gen. 1. 26.
man was made, than the rest. If it were possible, such as
of them might be said in the Lycaonian tongue, "Gods are Acts 14. 11.
come down to us in the likeness of men." Sure they that
are styled gods, somewhat more than men they would be;
as like, come as near *rem nominis,* 'the truth of that they
are named,' as human frailty will permit.

But have they been ever so? I cannot say it. Assemblies Yet have
there have been; Abimelech had one, and Rehoboam his, they not always
and Jeroboam his. But Abimelech with his needy indigent been such.
Shechemites, Rehoboam with his youth that never stood be- Judg. 9. 4.
1 Kings 12.
fore Solomon, Jeroboam with his crew of malcontents, "sons 8.
2 Chron.
of Belial," shall I call any of these *synagoga deorum?* I can- 13. 7.
not, I see no lineaments, no resemblance at all, nothing for
which this name should once be vouchsafed them, of Gods.
Nay, nor scarce of *synagoga* neither; as deserving not only

SERM.
X.

to be left out of the list of gods, but even to be put *extra synagogam.* Scarce a synagogue, much less of gods.

After, in this Psalm, at the fifth verse, they are told as much, when by their *ignorantibus*, or *non intelligentibus*, things were grown "out of course." And told it by God Himself, and that with a kind of indignation, that He had said they were gods, and they carried themselves scarce like men; gone from their names quite.

But ours we wish to be such.

But I leave them, and come to this of ours. There is not in the world a more reasonable request than this, what you would be, that to be; what you would be in name, that to be in deed; to make good your name. Every one to be *homo homini Deus*, by doing good; specially that good which is the good of all, that is, the good of this assembly. This the time and place for it. And so my wish is you may, and my trust is you will. And so I leave *deorum*, the gods of the congregation, and come to *synagoga*, "the congregation" itself.

II.
"The congregation of the gods."
Ezek. 1. 20.

For when we consider these gods each apart, they are as in Ezekiel, every spirit on his wheel, and every wheel in his own course, when they are at home in their several countries. But when as in a congregation, then are they to come and to be together.

God alloweth such congregations, when there is cause.
Num. 10. 3, 4.

And this, if cause be, God alloweth well of. 1. For He hath to that end left with His lieutenant a power to blow the trumpets, one or both, to call together a part or the whole congregation. By the trumpets, while they were all within the trumpets' sound; but after, when they were settled all Canaan over, to call them by "the pen of the writer," that is, by writ; of which we have a fair example, Judges the fifth chapter and fourteenth verse. 2. For

Judg. 5. 23.

secondly, He hath willed the Angels of His Church, by the Angel's example, to lay Meroz's curse to them that come not to it. 3. For thirdly, He here calleth their meeting by the name of synagogue, which is a holy place, a sanctuary, a high place, or court of refuge:—עדה signifies all these. 4. For fourthly, He hath to that end spared them a piece of His own Temple to have their meetings

1 Chron. 26. 15, 16.

in, on the south side of it, called twice by the name of Asuppim — which was to them as the Parliament-house is to us—that so their feet might stand on holy ground. And they knew themselves to be no קהל, common or profane, but עדה, a sacred assembly to Him. 5. For fifthly, He hath set them here a monitory Psalm of this, to put them in mind how to bear themselves in it, like gods, that is, divinely. 6. For last, when they are together, He comes Himself in person and stands among them. All which shew He favours and likes well such assemblies as this.

But then there must be a cause; and indeed else, it is *concursus atomorum* rather than *congregatio deorum.* Thus many, so goodly a company to meet to no end, God forbid. If the Apostle had not, nature doth teach us, "when we come together, to come together for the better, not for the worse." And nothing is worse than to come together for nothing. Better, as Deborah saith well, stay at home, and "hear the bleating of their flocks." This be far from any assembly, especially the assembly of the gods, who are herein to imitate God, Who doth nothing in vain, or without a cause. The cause
of the
meeting of
such con-
gregations.
1 Cor. 11.
17.

Judg. 5. 16.

If you ask me the cause, the two words themselves, *syna-goga* and *deorum,* contain either of them a cause of it. As a congregation, for the good of the congregation; as gods, *cœtus deorum cœtus Dei,* saith St. Hierom, 'the congregation of gods is God's congregation.' As His, for Him, for His honour, Who gave them theirs; to the high pleasure of that God Whose *Ego dixi* goded them all. And so, as I remember, it is written *in capite libri,* the first page or front of your Acts, To the high pleasure of Almighty God—there lo, is God; and for the weal public—there is the congregation. Not this only here, the congregation of gods, but the congregation of men (I know not how many) all the land over, even the great congregation. This cause
double.
1. One
from *syna-
goga.*
2. The
other from
deorum.

Learn a parable of the natural body. If there be no other cause, each member is left to look to itself; but if there be any danger toward the whole body, presently all the parts are summoned as it were to come together, and every vein sends his blood, and every sinew his strength, and every artery his spirits, and all draw together about the heart for awhile, till the safety of the whole be provided for, and then 1. From
synagoga
when it is
in danger.

SERM.
X.

The danger of two sorts.
1. Ordinary.
2. Or upon special occasion.
1. Ordinary, by *synagoga vitiorum.*
2. *Ex malis moribus.*
Ps. 82. 5.

return back every one to his place again. So is it with the body civil, in case of danger; and never but in it.

But is there any danger then towards? There is, and that to both. To the synagogue first, and that from a twofold synagogue, and of two sorts: 1. one continual or ordinary; 2. the other not so, but special and upon occasion. The danger this Psalm expresseth thus, that "things are brought out of course," yea "foundations" and all. Thus, there be (I may call them a synagogue, for they be many) of these same *mali mores*, that like *tubera terræ* shoot out daily, no man knows whence or how; never heard of before. These, if they be suffered to grow, will bring all "out of course." And grow they do; for even of them, some that have penalties already set (I know not how) such a head they get as they outgrow their punishments; that if this congregation grind not on a new and a sharper edge, they will bring things yet further "out of course."

3. *Ex legibus depravatis.*
[Rev. 2. 9.]

Besides, those that should keep all in course, the laws themselves are in danger too. There be a sort of men (I may well say of "the synagogue of Satan") that give their ways and bend their wits to nothing, but even to devise how to fret through the laws as soon as they be made, as it were in scorn of this congregation, and of all the gods in it. These go to the foundations, (for so are the laws,) undermine them, and in a sort, though after another manner, seek to blow up all. Great pity but this congregation here should look well to the foundations of all. Great pity that it should be "overcome of their evil," but that "their evil should be overcome of our good," and this of yours go beyond them.

Rom. 12. 21.

1 Sam. 11. 5.

These to be helped with good laws.

It is not to go through all. Generally, *Quid populo quod flet?* what the congregations of men have just cause to complain of, the congregation of gods sit to redress. Whatsoever *synagoga Satanæ per malos mores* doth put out, *synagoga deorum per bonas leges* is to set in joint again. And that is the proper work of this assembly, to make laws. And that is properly the work of God, His work at Sinai and at Sion both. And in truth that "there is but one lawgiver," and that is God, saith St. James; as till *Ego dixi*, till then, there was but one God, but together with His name He imparted

Jas. 4. 12.

also His power, and made you a congregation of lawgivers
and of gods, both at once. A high power, the highest in
earth save one; next to the "sceptre" in Judah's hand is Gen. 49.
the "lawgiver between his feet," even with Jacob. And so $\frac{10.}{\text{Prov. 8.}}$
with Solomon. After *Per Me Reges regnant*, presently fol- 15.
lows *Et legum conditores justa decernunt*. To this so high a
work a whole synagogue of wisdom is little enough, to bring
into course that is out, to set the foundations fast against
this synagogue of Satan. And this, lo, is the ordinary and
continual danger I spake of.

But for all this danger, we might well enough stay a 2. Upon
longer time and not come together, there is no such pre- $\frac{\text{special oc-}}{\text{casion.}}$
sent haste to meet with that. There is another I take it $\frac{\text{By syna-}}{\text{goga ini-}}$
more pressing, as I said before, upon a more special and *micorum.*
present occasion. Will you but look over into the next
Psalm following, into the beginning of it? There you will
find another congregation, a second, "casting their heads Ps. 83. 5.
and confederate together," able to put "foundations" and Ps. 82. 5.
all "out of course." And then he reckons up a rabble of
them. Edomites: the Edomites first, and you know what
they cried, *Exinanite usque ad fundamenta*, "Up with all, Ps. 137. 7.
foundations and all." "The Edomites and Ishmaelites, and [Ps. 83. 6,
Moabites and Hagarenes, Gebal and Ammon and Amalek." 7.]
And at last "Ashur also was joined with them;" Ashur [Ps. 83. 8]
that even then purposed, and after did eat them all up one
after another; yet he was then "joined with them." Such
a congregation, it is said, there is now abroad; and what
will they do? No harm, bring nothing "out of course,"
they say. But it will be the wisdom of this congregation
to be provided for them, if they should not do as they say.
This Psalm stands before that, that this congregation may
be beforehand with that.

Peace and perfect amity to be wished before all; no man
doubts of that. "If it be possible, as much as in us lieth, Rom. 12.
peace with all men." But peace will be had with never the 18.
less assurance, and with never the worse conditions, if the
congregation be well appointed that seek it.

And this is the second work of this congregation, if not
the first. Therefore (it may be thought) at this time called
together that there may be *multitudo consilii*, soundly to ad-

SERM. vise of it, and *multitudo auxilii*, roundly to go through with
  X.
—————— it. The text intends this of help specially, for in some translations it is "the congregation of the mighty;" but howsoever, the very name is taken from אל, that name of God that
is given Him for His strength and power. Of those that are
mighty and so can shew themselves, of those is this congregation. Ever remembering this, that they who assemble for
an end assemble also to devise how to furnish means to compass that end; and indeed of the end properly we consult
Lu. 14. 31. not, but of the means rather. Our Saviour Christ spake
with His own mouth, Who will ever resolve upon war but
they will sit down first and set down what forces will be
needful? and how much they will stand in? and how that
Eccl. 10. is to be had or levied that, as the Wise Man saith, *respondit*
19. *omnibus*, "answers, takes order for all."

1. From   Thus for the synagogue. What for God? There is no
deorum. doubt, blessed be God for it, but what Moses said of Judah
Deut. 33. ("His own hands shall be sufficient for him, if Thou, Lord,
7. help him against his enemies") may be said of this our land:
if God help us, "sufficient" enough. And He will help us,
if we help Him. Help God? what a word is that? Even
the very word the Angel used, when he had laid a curse
Judg. 5. 23. upon Meroz, for not coming "to help the Lord." Again,
lest we might think it scaped him, upon deliberation he
saith, "to help the Lord against the mighty," that is Sisera
and Jabin's mighty preparations. Ever where the right is,
there God is; when that in danger, God in danger; they
that help that help Him, and He will help them. If the
Judg. 5. 20. congregation God, God the congregation. "They will fight
from heaven then, the stars in heaven will fight in their
courses for us," and then it will be an auxiliary war right.
And in sign that He will so, when they are met together
about these matters God comes Himself here in person, and
stands among them. God in the congregation of gods, what
more proper and kindly? And so much for the gods and for
their congregation.

III.   Now for the two acts of God, in and upon this congrega-
The two tion: 1. His standing, and 2. judging; first jointly, after
acts.
  1. apart. 1. Jointly. They are thought to be set first, these
Jointly.
1. To cor- two, as two correcters of the two former, *deorum* and *deos*,

lest the gods of the congregation should be exalted above rect the word measure with this deifying revelation. Secondly, as two "gods." marks of difference between the first God and the last gods, so to let them see what manner of gods they be indeed, how differing from Him.

"God stands :" this may well refer to that in the seventh verse, "but you shall fall." A standing God; He Who only stands, and will stand, when they all shall fall, and fall even to dust, every god of them. And this could not be told in a fitter place : the place where we stand is compassed about with a congregation of these fallen gods, these same *dii caduci;* with monuments of the mortality of many a great Elohim in their times. And let me tell you this, that in the Hebrew tongue the grave is called a synagogue as well as the Church. All shall be gathered, even the gods, even the whole synagogue of them, into this synagogue at last. So this first shews them their godships give them no immortality. Gods; but mortal, temporal gods they be.

The other is of judging. That as they have no exemption from the first statute, *Statutum est omnibus semel mori,* so neither from the second, *Et post mortem judicium.* They be *dii sub judice;* they be not gods *absque aliquo computo reddendo.* When they have done judging others, they shall come to be judged themselves. *Dii caduci, dii judicandi,* 'gods that shall fall, gods that must come to judgment.' From neither of these shall their godhead excuse them.

These two then sever them from the first God, the eternal God, and the sovereign Judge of all. And shew, the one, their judging, that their glory is not equal; the other, their falling, that their majesty is not co-eternal, that so they may understand themselves aright.

And now to standing and judging, either of them apart by itself. Standing first. The members of man, the eye, hand, and foot; and the acts of them, seeing, doing, standing, are not in God—to speak properly; only by them is noted in God the efficacy of those acts and members. By the eye His knowledge, by the hand His power, by the foot His presence. The meaning then is first, that God is present. It is not enough for Him to look down from heaven and behold us afar off, but He comes and stands here. And not,

S E R M.   as in the Canticles, "behind the wall," and looks in by the
X   grates, but it is even in the assembly itself, even in the place
Cant. 2. 9.   where the gods are.

Not as   Present? Why what great matter is that? Where is He
every   not present? Heaven and earth He fills, "the earth is His
where.
Jer. 23. 24.   footstool:" where then stands He not? Indeed God is pre-
Isa. 66. 1.   sent in all places; yet not in all alike. In some by a more
special presence than in other some. And among all, and
above all, there where the gods are together.

But in a   For though God be both in heaven and earth, yet we say
more spe-   "Which art in heaven;" intending that there He is with a
cial man-
ner.   far more high and glorious presence. And so here is He
Mat. 6. 9.   in a more eminent sort. For nowhere on earth doth His
glory shine and shew forth itself so, as in a well-ordered
assembly.

Mat. 18. 20.   And if "where two or three" common Christians "be together in His name, there is He in the midst of them," when
three or four hundred, and those no common ordinary persons but of His own name, "gods," even a whole "congregation" of them—of His name and in His name too—are
together, in most solemn manner assembled, and to do His
work; shall He not much more be there, and in a much
more excellent manner of presence, to assist them? Yes
sure, it toucheth His providence in the highest degree.

2. God's   Present then. And secondly, the manner of His pre-
attention.   sence; standing. And that is a word of site. Standing
is a site, and it is a site of attention. When we sit and
hear ought that we would listen better to, up we stand and
leave sitting. So do we, without the occasion, usually; even
to stir up ourselves, for sitting we may fall on sleep. This
to shew we shall not need to say to Him here, as in another
Ps. 44. 23.   Psalm they do, "Up Lord, Why sleepest Thou?" For He
stands, and they never sleep. The truth is, to be present,
as good be absent if we do not intend. This then sheweth
God is so present, as He is also attentive; nothing passes
but *Deo astante et attestante,* but He is an ear, nay an eye-
witness, nay more than that, a heart-witness of all.

3. God's   Stands then. And thirdly, the manner of His standing.
per sever-   Which is, as is observed, נצב; and that is not the ordinary
ance.   word for standing when one flits, so stands as he will re-

move; no, but as one fixed, not to start. It is *statio mili-taris* this, that pitch about their standard not to remove thence, but still to maintain and keep their standing. So He, where you leave Him, you shall be sure to find Him. He makes it His rest, means to stand it out to the very last.

These three, 1. presence, 2. attendance, 3. perseverance, be in this standing of His. Present, for He stands; and standing, marks; marks, and will mark from the beginning to the end. So we not to conceive of Him, 1. as if He were away, 2. or here stood and noted not, 3. or did for a time, but would leave off and give over and not stand it out. This for standing.

And so long as it is but standing and no more, it is no great matter, so He suffer them to go on quietly and trouble them not. And indeed so long as God doth no more, He may be said to stand, and but even to stand. But saith the text, when He hath done standing He hath not done. Stay a while, you shall see He so stands as He will judge also before He have done. IV.
2. The
latter act.
God's
judging.
He not
only
stands
(the act),
but "will
judge"
also.

The congregation will not always sit, nor God always stand. When that is over and past, the Prophet here begins to set Him up a seat, to erect Him a throne to sit down and judge in. And then lo, the courses will change. We sit now, and He stands; He will sit then, and we all shall stand. All, *omnes stabimus ante tribunal,* "before His judg-ment-seat." His first act, standing, then to take an end; and His latter act, *judicabit,* to have his turn too. 2 Cor. 5.
10.

But by this we see, as before I told you, while He stood He stood attentive; He stood not like an idol, was all the while no idle stander by or looker on, but as the writing was on the wall, "Mene, Mene," He told and numbered; and "Tekel," *Stetit cum staterâ,* He weighed and pondered well every motion that was made, every bill that was read, every consent or otherwise passed upon it. And weighed withal whence every of them proceeded, whether from a dutiful regard of Him and His presence, or otherwise for some by-respect of our own. *Stetit ut testis,* 'as a witness He stood;' *Sedet ut judex,* 'now sits as a judge,' and will give His doom accordingly. And upon whom will He give it? Not upon So while
He stood,
He stood
attentive.
Dan. 5. 25.

The per-
sons. He

SERM.
X.

will judge
the gods,
deos.

Ps. 50. 1.
[Vulg.]
the meaner sort, upon inferior persons, but even upon the greatest; upon *deos*, the gods themselves. For even to them doth this His judgment extend. They that sit and judge others, shall then stand and be judged themselves. They be gods, but He is *Deus deorum*. They are judges, but He *Judex judicum; Judex judicum* and *judiciorum* 'both Judge of judges and of courts,' and even of this High Court and all. Men may not, God may and will convent even the conventions themselves, if they forget themselves. Yea even the rather, for that they are gods, shall He judge them. And namely, how they used themselves in their deity, when they sat in His place and went under His Name.

And not for any fault they ever have made, as for those they have made here, *in synagogâ*. Above all, for them; for not regarding His presence and standing here.

The differ-
ence of the
persons ;
*deorum in
synagogâ,*
and *deos
judicabit.*
And because there is here a double mention of *deorum* and *deos, deorum in synagogâ* and *deos in judicio*, it will not be amiss to set them before us both at once. Now when they sit *in synagogâ*, how glorious; but when *in judicio* they shall stand to be judged, how poor then ! When God but stands and looks on, how secure; when He shall sit down to His sentence, how full of fear then ! Specially when He shall take, and they shall give account of abusing His presence here. For a special *judicabit* belongs to that, and remains for them that so do. They that despise God's long-suffering when He stands here, shall find and suffer His severity, and suffer it long, when He sits to judge there.

But I cannot say this will be presently, or out of hand. It may be, it will be deferred yet for a while; it is not *judicat* in the present, but *judicabit* in the future, "He will judge;" *Cum accepero tempus*, as he saith Psalm the seventy-

The time.
fifth, and second verse, "He will take a time for it."

This judg-
ment will
not be pre-
sent. It
is *judicabit*
the future.
But take a time He will, and judge He will. Even the heathen, that have written *de serâ numinis vindictâ*, are clear for this point, that you may well account of it, He that stands will sit, and sitting judge; judge, and never a god of them all shall escape Him.

The place.
He will
judge *in
medio.*
And *in medio* He will do it; in the midst it shall be. The midst, either inwardly of the gods' ownselves, even of their own hearts—בקרב will bear it, and so it is taken, Jeremiah

the thirty-first chapter, and thirty-third verse. There in the midst, in their heart, their conscience accusing them, and a worm there gnawing, when they shall see the evil that doth follow of their carrying matters unduly; see any foundation shaken by it. _{1. Of themselves.}

Or in the midst, that is, openly; as openly He hath ever made it appear that evil counsel, first or last, shall prove worst for them that gave it. _{2. Of the world.}

Or *in medio*, referring it to the parties; that is, in the midst between them both. Those that regard, and those other that never looked after nor cared for Him nor His standing. _{3. Of them that regard, and them that regard not.}

And it is well for us it is *judicabit;* for so we have a time to bethink us of it, and to prevent it. And again it is well for us that it is *in medio*, for so we may yet choose our side, which side we will fall on; for indeed, *judicare* is *actus in medio*, it may be for, and it may be against. It is not necessary it should be against, God forbid. We may not prejudice it then. _{The future *judicabit*, and *in medio*, are two favours to us.}

All is as we carry ourselves here. For as we here, so He there. They that saw Him standing, and demeaned themselves accordingly, a *judicabit* for them. Those other that ran on their own courses (His standing. there notwithstanding) a hard judgment will they have, they that be loath to endure it. And this for God, His standing and His judging.

And now to ourselves, and to our duty to God, thus standing and judging. _{v. Our own duty to the text. To regard God's standing. 1 Cor. 11. 31.}

To avoid God's judgment, the Apostle tells us there is but one way, To "judge ourselves." And here now in this, not upon many, but upon this one point only of God's standing—for I will be bold to cut off the other, His judging —regard His standing, and you shall never need to fear His judging.

To regard that, do but these four: 1. Set down this and believe it, that He is present. 2. So behave yourselves, as if you did so believe. 3. To do that, shew yourselves well affected to His standing. 4. To shew that, procure but those means that He may take pleasure in His standing. These four. _{Four things to be done.}

SERM.
X.

1. To believe God is present.
Job 9. 11.

Joh. 1. 26.

Heb. 11. 27.

2. To behave ourselves as if present.

Mat. 21. 37.

First, never imagine this, that God is far enough off, or hath otherwise to busy Himself than to have a hand or foot in these assemblies, but with Job believe He is hard by us though we perceive Him not; or, as the Baptist said of Christ, *Medius vestrûm stetit Quem vos nescitis,* "He standeth in the midst of us, though we know not so much." To see Him so standing with the eyes of faith, with which, the Apostle saith, "Moses saw Him That was invisible."

Then will it follow of itself, to do all we do *tanquam Deo stante et inspectante,* 'as if God stood and beheld us.' This we behove to think: when He comes thus to stand among us, He will say as much for Himself as He did for His Son in the Gospel, *Certe reverebuntur Me,* 'Surely they will yet reverence Me;' My standing, My being there, will make them the more careful; if I come and stand among them, all will go the better, if it be but because I am there. Not any thing at all shall I trust, but if ought should be moved against His good liking, shall not our own hearts smite us, and tell us straight, What, God standing and looking on, shall we offer this? What, give Him an affront in His own presence, to His own face? *Nonne judicabit super hoc?* what, will He never judge for this gear? And when He doth, shall it go for nought? Thus, to behave ourselves as in His presence.

3. To stand well affected to God's standing.

Mat. 8. 34.

But yet, I know not how, this is not it, to do it for fear of Him or of His *judicabit;* but to do it willingly, that is it. For as if some were not willing to allow Him a place not so much as to stand in, with a kind of irony, some think, he saith: Well yet howsoever, God stands in the congregation, though against somebodies' will, that would be content if they durst to say with them in Esay the thirtieth chapter, and eleventh verse, "Cause the Holy One of Israel to cease from us," get Him away; or with them in the Gospel, the Gergesites, not only give Christ good leave, but even to pray Him fair to be gone and take His ease somewhere else, their matters would speed better if He were out of the way.

Never speak of that: there He stands and there He will stand; He ought not, cannot be excluded. To endure Him, that is not it. The point is, how we stand affected to His standing: whether we be willing with it; whether it be the

desire of our hearts that He should, and the joy that He
doth stand and will stand there.

Put case He stood not; would we earnestly entreat Him
to vouchsafe us His presence, to take up His standing among
us? If He made as if He would be gone — as Luke the
twenty-fourth chapter, and twenty-eighth verse—would we [Lu. 24.
be instant with *Mane nobiscum Domine,* "Stay with us still, 28, 29.]
good Lord?" Moses said, "If Thou go not with us, carry Ex. 33. 15.
us not hence:" would we say, If Thou, Lord, stay not with
us, what do we here? If God be gone, *migremus hinc,* 'let
us be gone too,' and never hope for good of that assembly
where He is not.

Now fourthly, if we be willing and glad, if we take com- 4. To pro-
fort in His standing, hereby shall we be tried; if we use cure the
means that
all means as will procure Him to stay in our assembly the God may
be willing
more willingly, as will make His standing pleasant and not to stand.
grow tedious to Him. And such things there are, and these Those be
four.
they are.

One special thing that gives Him content, is a place 1. To be
where there is concord and unity. "At Salem," that is, mind.
where peace is, *In pace factus est locus Ejus*—so read the Ps. 76. 2.
Fathers—there "is His tabernacle;" and that tabernacle is
the tabernacle of the congregation; His feet and our feet
both stand willingly in the gates there. The reason; for it
is "at unity within itself." There loves He to stand; and Ps. 122. 3.
there His Spirit, where "they were all with one accord in Acts 2. 1.
one place." *Qui facit unanimes habitare in domo,* if He
make "all of one mind that are in one house," if "brethren Ps. 68. 6.
to dwell together in unity," O how good, O how pleasing is Ps.133.1,2.
that standing to Him! It passes Aaron's perfume, his ointment is nothing to the delight of it.

And in very deed, if we consider it well, it is the virtue
(this of concord) that is most proper, nay essential then,
to a congregation: without it, a gregation it may be, but
no *con*gregation. The *con* is gone; a *dis*gregation rather.
Enough to make Him to be gone, that. For if there "spring Heb.12.15.
up a root of bitterness," if the "evil spirit" get in that was Judg. 9. 23.
"sent upon Abimelech and the men of Shechem;" if "the Judg. 5.15,
divisions of Reuben do make great thoughts of heart," there 16.
God stands upon thorns. But where the "hearts of all the 2 Sam. 19.
14.

congregation are bowed as the heart of one man," there
stands God, and there He delights to stand.

To use no
cunning
but plain
dealing.
Ps. 51. 6.
Another: He takes pleasure to stand among them that are
good and true of heart. Where He finds "truth in the inward parts;" where without art or artificial glossing or cunning carrying of things under-hand men go plainly to work,
every one in the sincerity and singleness of an honest upright meaning. And the more plainness, ever the more
pleasure God takes there to stand. Truth, as it is the
mightiest, so is it the wisest thing, when all is done. They
that love it not, but to cover and colour and carry all by
Ps. 15. 1.
cunning, they shall never stand in God's "tabernacle."
Neither they in His, nor He in theirs.

To look to
idipsum.
One more. There is a word, and it is a great word in
this book, ἐπὶ τὸ αὐτὸ, *in idipsum;* that is, to look to the
thing itself, the very point, the principal matter of all; to
have our eye on that, and not off it upon *alia omnia,* any
Neither to
bye mat-
ters; nor to
personal
respects.
thing but it. So say I again, upon the thing itself, not
upon some persons or personal respects: God accepts no
person, nor loves them that do. The very first thing that
in the very next verse He finds fault with and charges them
with, is this: when men are for or against a thing, be it
what it will be, and neither for itself, but only because it
proceeds from such or such persons, neither of these is *in
medio. Idipsum,* that is the centre, that the middle, that
place is God's place. To go to the point, drive all to that;
as also to go to the matter real, without declining from it
this way or that, to the right hand or to the left, for any
personal regard.

To do that
we do,
cheer-
fully.
And last of all, that which pleaseth Him best of all; and
that is, where He finds a ready well-willing mind, His heart
is upon such. And where His heart is, ever His feet stand
at ease; *Calcat rosas,* 'He treads upon roses' there. In the
Song of Deborah it is thought there is set down a pattern of
the virtues or faults of an assembly. In that Song there are
two Hallelujahs, two *Benedicite*s for it. First, at the very
Judg. 5. 2.
beginning, "Hallelujah, praise the Lord." Why? for the
"people" that came off, and "offered themselves" so "wil-
Judg. 5. 9.
lingly." And again seven verses after, "My heart is upon
the governors that offered themselves," and made the people

to offer so willingly, " Hallelujah, praise the Lord." Hallelujah for the princes, Hallelujah for the people; blessed be God for both.

Then have you again after those, two verses together; in Judg. 5. 23, the one Meroz cursed for their backwardness, and Jael for ^{24.} her forwardness blessed and blessed again. For this indeed is the marrow of the sacrifice, the fat of the offering; and without this all is poor and lean.

This is sure, God loves not to dwell in Mesech; that is And reainterpreted, *prolongatus est.* And His Son calling on *Serve* _{Ps. 120. 5.} *nequam et piger,* shews He loves *piger* as evil as He does Mat. 25. 26. *nequam.* And His Spirit cannot skill of these same *tarda molimina.* In a word, none of them to be wearied with standing I know not how long.

And see the very next word of all, the next that follows these immediately is, " How long?" So He begins His com- [Ps. 82. 2.] plaint the first word of the next verse, which shews He loves it not.

Not that He can be weary. It is an infirmity that, and so is grief, and so is repentance, and they cannot fall into God; they are attributed to Him though. And God is said as to repent and to be grieved, so to be stark " weary," in Gen. 6. 6. no other sense but this, that if He be not weary no thanks Eph. 4. 30. to us; for if it were possible, if the divine nature were or Jer. 6. 11. could be subject to it, if God could be weary, if " His feet" Rev. 1. 15. were not " of brass," we would put Him to it; we do even what in us lieth to tire Him outright, to make Him cry, *Usquequo,* " How long?"

But 1. where there is accord without " Reuben's divisions;" 2. where plain meaning and dealing without, as Esay calls them, these same deep-digged devices; 3. where Isa. 29. 15. the eye is upon *idipsum,* and no *ipsum* else; 4. where God is not constrained to dwell in Mesech, but the people and their governors offer willingly; there stands God, and there will He ever stand. Of that place He saith, *Hæc est requies mea,* " This is My rest, here will I stay, for I have a delight Ps. 132. 14. therein."

Thus doing then, thus procuring, our assembly thus qualified, we perform our duty to God and to His standing. And this done we shall never need to fear *judicabit,* come when it will.

SERM.
X.

To have regard what will be said abroad.

Ps. 26. 5.
[Ps. 42. 3, 10.]

1 Cor. 14. 25.

Mat. 25. 23.

To have regard of our present use of Him against our enemies.

And now to conclude. Mine unfeigned hearty prayer to God is, and daily shall be, that if ever in any, He would stand in this congregation; and if ever any used the means so to procure Him, we may use them. The rather that *ecclesia malignantium,* " the malignant synagogue" may not ask with derision, Where was then their God? Where stood He? Behind the wall sure, not in the assembly; such proceedings and His standing will never stand together.

But rather that all may say, Verily God was among them, of a truth God stood in that congregation, where with so good accord so good things so readily were passed. Christ was in the midst of them, His Holy Spirit rested on them.

Yet I know, what men say off or on is not it; what God saith, that is all in all. To men we do not, to God we stand or fall, Whose *judicabit* we cannot escape either the one way or the other; but have a *judicabit* for us that we may, if we yield His standing all due respect, even *Euge serve bone, intra in gaudium Domini,* which in the end will be worth all.

But if any shall say, O the time is long to that—peradventure not so long though as we reckon—well yet in the mean time, now for the present, it stands us in hand to use Him well, and ourselves well to Him. For if He stand not to us we shall not subsist, we shall not stand but fall before our enemies. This time is now, this danger is at hand.

Use Him well then; stand before Him thus standing, with all due reverence and regard; that as by His presence He doth stand among us, so He may not only do that, but by His mercy also stand by us, and by His power stand for us. So shall we stand and withstand all the adverse forces, and at last (for thither at last we must all come) stand in His judgment, stand there upright; to our comfort, for the present, of His standing by us, and to our endless comfort, for the time to come, of His judging for us [a].

[a] [The King's speech at the opening of this Parliament, together with the proceedings of the two houses, may be seen in Rapin, ii. 202—212. Fol. 1743.]

A SERMON

PREACHED

AT CHISWICK IN THE TIME OF PESTILENCE.

ON THE TWENTY-FIRST OF AUGUST, A.D. MDCIII.

Ps. cvi. 29, 30.

Thus they provoked Him to anger with their own inventions, and the Plague was great (or, brake in) among them.

Then stood up Phinehas and prayed (or, executed judgment), and so the Plague was ceased (or, stayed).

[*Et irritaverunt Eum in adinventionibus suis, et multiplicata est in eis Ruina.*

Et stetit Phinees et placavit, et cessavit Quassatio. Lat. Vulg.]

[*Thus they provoked Him to anger with their inventions, and the Plague brake in upon them.*

Then stood up Phinehas and executed judgment, and so the Plague was stayed. Eng. Trans.]

THERE is mention of a Plague, of a great Plague, for there died of it "four and twenty thousand." And we complain Nu. 25. 9. of a Plague at this time. The same axe is laid to the root of our trees. Or rather, because an axe is long in cutting down of one tree, the "razor is hired" for us, that sweeps Isa. 7. 20. away a great number of hairs at once—as Esay calleth it— or a scythe that mows down grass, a great deal at once.

But here is not only mention of the breaking in of the Plague in the twenty-ninth verse, but of the staying or ceasing of the Plague in the thirtieth.

Now "whatsoever things were written aforetime, were Rom. 15. 4. written for our learning;" and so was this text. Under one to teach us how the Plague comes, and how it may be stayed.

Q 2

SERM. XI.

The division.

The Plague is a disease. In every disease we consider the cause and the cure : both which are here set forth unto us in these two verses. In the former the cause, how it comes. In the latter the cure, how it may be stayed. To know the cause is expedient, for if we know it not our cure will be but palliative, as not going to the right. And if knowing the cause we add not the cure when we are taught it, who will pity us? For none is then to blame but ourselves.

I. Of the cause first, and then of the cure. The cause is set down to be twofold ; 1. God's anger, and 2. their inventions.

God's anger by the which, and their inventions for the which, " the Plague brake in among them."

II. The cure is likewise set down; and it is twofold, out of two significations of one word, the word *palal* in the verse. " Phinehas prayed," some read it ; " Phinehas executed judgment," some other ; and the word bears both. Two then, 1. Phinehas' prayer, one ; 2. Phinehas' executing judgment, the other ; by both which " the Plague ceased." His prayer referring to God's anger, his executing judgment to their inventions. God's wrath was appeased by his prayer : prayer refers to that. Their inventions were removed by his executing of judgment: the execution of judgment refers to

Ps. 99. 8.

that. If His anger provoked do send the Plague, His anger appeased will stay it. If our inventions provoke His anger, the punishing of our inventions will appease it. The one worketh upon God, pacifieth Him ; the other worketh upon our soul, and cures it. For there is a cure of the soul no

Ps. 41. 4.

less than of the body, as appeareth by the Psalm, " Heal my soul, for I have sinned against Thee."

We are to begin with the cause of the Plague in the first verse, and so to come to the cure in the second.

1. Of the cause.

Of the cause. 1. First, that there is a cause ; 2. and secondly, what that cause may be.

A cause there is.

1. That there is a cause, that is, that the Plague is a thing causal, not casual ; comes not merely by chance, but hath somewhat, some cause that procureth it.

Mat. 10. 29, 31.

Sure if a sparrow " fall not to the ground" without the providence of God, of which " two are sold for a farthing," much less doth any man or woman, which are " more worth than many sparrows."

And if any one man comes not to his end as we call it by
casualty, but it is God that delivers him so to die, how Ex. 21. 13.
much more then when not one but many thousands are
swept away at once? The Philistines, in their plague, put 1 Sam. 6. 9.
the matter upon trial of both these ways: 1. whether it
were God's hand, 2. or whether it were but a chance. And
the event shewed it was no casualty, but the very handy-
work of God upon them.

And indeed the very name of the Plague doth tell us as
much. For *deber* in Hebrew sheweth there is a reason,
there is a cause why it cometh. And the English word
Plague, coming from the Latin word *plaga*, which is properly ' a stroke,' necessarily inferreth a cause. For where
there is a stroke there must be one that striketh. And in
that both it and other evil things that come upon us are
usually in Scripture called God's judgments, if they be judgments it followeth there is a judge they come from. They
come not by adventure, by chance they come not. Chance
and judgment are utterly opposite. Not casually then, but
judicially. Judged we are; "for when we are chastened, we 1 Cor. 11.
are judged of the Lord." 32.

There is a cause: now, what that cause is. Concerning 1.
which if you ask the physician, he will say the cause is in is. That cause
the air. The air is infected; the humours corrupted; the 1. Natural.
contagion of the sick, coming to and conversing with the
sound. And they be all true causes.

The air. For so we see by casting ashes of the furnace 1. The air
towards heaven in the air the air became infected, and the Ex. 9. 8. infected.
Plague of botches and blains was so brought forth in Egypt.

The humours. For to that doth King David ascribe the 2. The hu-
cause of his disease; that is, that his " moisture" in him was rupted. mour cor-
corrupt, dried up, " turned into the drought of summer." Ps. 32. 4.

Contagion. Which is clear by the Law, where the leprous 3. Conta-
person for fear of contagion from him was ordered to cry gion.
that nobody should come near him; to dwell apart from Lev. 13.
other men; the clothing he had worn to be washed, and 45, 46, 52,
in some case to be burnt; the house walls he had dwelt [Lev. 14.
in to be scraped, and in some case the house itself to be 41, 45.]
pulled down.

In all which three respects, Solomon saith, " A wise man Prov. 14.
16.

SERM. feareth the Plague and departeth from it, and fools run on
XI. and be careless." A wise man doth it, and a good man
too. For King David himself durst not go to the altar of
God at Gibeon, to enquire of God there, because the Angel
that smote the people with the Plague, stood between him
and it; that is, because he was to pass through infected
places thither.

1 Chron. 21. 30.

2. Super-
natural,
by which
God.

But as we acknowledge these to be true, that in all diseases
and even in this also there is a natural cause, so we say there
is somewhat more, something divine and above nature. As
somewhat which the Physician is to look unto in the Plague,
so likewise something for Phinehas to do—and Phinehas was
a priest. And so some work for the priest as well as for the
physician, and more then it may be.

[2 Chron. 16. 12.]

It was King Asa's fault. He in his sickness looked all to
physicians, and looked not after God at all. That is noted
as his fault. It seems his conceit was, there was nothing
in a disease but natural, nothing but bodily; which is not
so. For infirmity is not only a thing bodily, there is "a
spirit of infirmity" we find, Luke the thirteenth chapter,
and eleventh verse. And something spiritual there is in all
infirmities, something in the soul to be healed. In all, but
especially in this, wherein that we might know it to be spiritual, we find it ofttimes to be executed by spirits. We see

Ex. 12. 13. an Angel, a destroying Angel, in the Plague of Egypt; an-
Isa. 37. 36. other in the Plague in Sennacherib's camp; a third in the
1 Chron. 21. 16. Plague at Jerusalem under David; a fourth pouring "his
Rev. 16. 2. vial upon earth, and there fell a noisome plague upon man
and beast." So that no man looketh deeply enough into
the cause of this sickness, unless he acknowledge the finger
of God in it, over and above any causes natural.

God "pro-
voked to
anger."

God then hath His part. God? but how affected? God
"provoked to anger;" so it is in the text. His anger, His
wrath it is, that bringeth the Plague among us. The verse
is plain: "They provoked Him to anger, and the Plague
brake in among them."

Job 5. 6, 7.

Generally, there is no evil, saith Job, but it is a spark of
God's wrath. And of all evils, "the Plague" by name.
"There is wrath gone out from the Lord, and the Plague
is begun," saith Moses, Numbers the sixteenth chapter, and

forty-sixth verse. So it is said God was displeased with David, and "He smote Israel" with the Plague. So that if there be a Plague God is angry, and if there be a great Plague God is very angry. Thus much for, By what? for the anger of God, by which the Plague is sent. Now, For what? 1 Chron. 21. 7.

There is a cause in God, that He is angry. And there is a cause for which He is angry. For He is not angry without a cause. And what is that cause? For what is God angry? What, is God angry with the waters when He sends a tempest? it is Habakkuk's question. Or is God angry with the earth when He sends barrenness? Or with the air when He makes it contagious? No indeed, His anger is not against the elements, they provoke Him not. Against them it is that provoke Him to anger. Against men it is, and against their sins, and "for them cometh the wrath of God upon the children of disobedience." For which? Sin in general. Hab. 3. 8. Eph. 5. 6.

And this is the very cause indeed. As there is *putredo humorum,* so there is also *putredo morum.* And *putredo morum* is more a cause than *putredo humorum.* The corruption of the soul, the corruption of our ways, more than the corrupting of the air. "The Plague of the heart," more than the sore that is seen in the body. The cause of death, that is, sin, the same is the cause of this kind of death, of the Plague of mortality. And as "the balm of Gilead," and the "physician there," may yield us help when God's wrath is removed; so, if it be not, no balm, no medicine will serve. Let us with the woman in the Gospel spend all upon physicians, we shall be never the better till we come to Christ, and He cure us of our sins Who is the only Physician of the diseases of the soul. Micah 7. 3. Gen. 6. 12. 1 Kings 8. 38. Rom. 5. 12. Ps. 38. 5. Jer. 8.22. Jer. 46. 11. Mark 5. 26.

And with Christ the cure begins ever within. First, "Son, thy sins be forgiven thee;" and then after, "take up thy bed and walk." His sins be first, and his limbs after. As likewise when we are once well Christ's counsel is, "Sin no more, lest a worse thing come unto thee." As if sin would certainly bring a relapse into a sickness. Mark. 2. 9. [Joh.5.14.]

But shall we say, the wrath of God for sins indefinitely? That were somewhat too general: may we not specify them, or set them down in particular? Yes, I will point you at three or four. Particular sin.

SERM.
XI.

1. Forni-
cation.
[Ps. 106.
28.]
Num. 25.
6, 14.

First, this Plague here, as appeareth by the twenty-eighth verse, the verse next before, came for the sin of Peor, that is for fornication, as you may read. And not every fornication, but fornication past shame, as was that of Zimri there with a daughter of Moab. And indeed if we mark it well, it fits well. For that kind of sin, fornication, doth end in ulcers and sores, and those as infectious as the Plague itself : a proper punishment, such sore for such evil.

2. Pride.

1 Chron.
21. 14.

Secondly, David's Plague of "seventy thousand" (which we mention in our prayer) that came for pride plainly ; his heart was lifted up to number the people. And that seems somewhat kindly too, and to agree with this disease. That pride which swells itself should end in a tumour or swelling, as for the most part this disease doth.

3. Blas-
phemy.
Isa. 37. 23,
36.
Num. 16.
46.

Thirdly, Sennacherib's Plague, it is plain, came from Rabshakeh's blasphemy ; blasphemy able to infect the air, it was so foul. In which regard Aaron's act might be justified, in putting odours into his censer to purify the air from such corruption.

4. Neglect
of the Sa-
crament.
1 Cor. 11.
30.

And last, the Apostle sets down the cause of the Plague at Corinth : " For this cause," saith he, that is, for neglect of the Sacrament, either in not caring to come to it, or in coming to it we care not how ; " For this cause is there a mortality among you, and many are sick, and many are weak, and many are fallen asleep." And this is no new

Ex. 4. 24.

thing. Moses himself, his neglect of the Sacrament made him be stricken of God, that it was like to have cost him his life. And he saith plainly to Pharaoh, if they neg-

Ex. 5. 3.

lected their sacrifice, God would "fall upon them with the pestilence :" which appeareth by this, that the Sacrament of the Passover, and the blood of it, was the means to save them from the Plague of the destroying Angel in Egypt.

The phrase
for sin,
" their in-
ventions."

A little now of the phrase, that their sins are here called by the name of " their inventions." And so, sure, they are ; as no ways taught us by God, but of our own imagining or finding out. For indeed our inventions are the cause of all sins. And if we look well into it, we shall find our inven-

In matters
of religion.
Deut. 12. 8.

tions are so. By God's injunction we should all live, and His injunction is, " You shall not do every man what seems good in his own eyes" (or finds out in his own brains), but

whatsoever I command you, that only shall you do. But
we setting light by that charge of His, out of the old disease
of our father Adam (*Eritis sicut Dei, scientes bonum et ma-* [Gen. 3. 5.]
lum) think it a goodly matter to be witty, and to find out
things ourselves to make to ourselves, to be authors and inventors of somewhat, that so we may seem to be as wise as
God, if not wiser; and to know what is for our turns as well
as He, if not better. It was Saul's fault. God bade destroy [1 Sam.
Amalek all, and he would invent a better way, to save some 15. 9.]
forsooth for sacrifice, which God could not think of. And
it was St. Peter's fault, when he persuaded Christ from His Mat. 16. 22.
passion, and found out a better way as he thought than
Christ could devise.

This is the proud invention which will not be kept in,
but makes men even not to forbear in things pertaining to
God's worship; but there to be still devising new tricks,
opinions and fashions, fresh and newly taken up, which Deut. 32. 17.
their fathers never knew of. And this is that which makes
men that have itching ears to " heap to themselves teachers 2 Tim. 4. 3.
according to their own lusts," which may fill their heads
full with new inventions.

And this is that that even out of religion, in the common In the
life, spoils all. The wanton invention in finding out new common
meats in diet, in inventing new fashions in apparel, which life.
men so dote on—as the Psalm saith at the thirty-ninth verse
—as they even "go a whoring" with them, " with their own
inventions," and care not what they spend on them. And
know no end of them : but as fast as they are weary of one,
a new invention is found out; which whatsoever it cost,
how much soever it take from our alms or good deeds, must
be had, till all come to nought. That the Psalmist hath
chosen a very fit word, that for our " inventions" the Plague
breaks in among us; for them, as for the primary or first
moving cause of all. Indeed for them, as much and more
than for any thing else.

We see then, 1. first, that a cause there is; 2. that that
cause is not only natural, but that God Himself hath a hand
in it; 3. God, as being provoked to anger; 4. to anger for
our sins in general—and for what sins in special—for our
sins proceeding from nothing but our inventions. Which

SERM. cause if it continue, and yet we turn not to the Lord, as
XI.
[Amos 4.
6-12.]
[Isa. 9. 12.]

Amos the fourth, "then will not His anger be turned away, but His hand will be stretched out still," as Esay the ninth. And no way to avoid the one but by appeasing the other.

II.
Of the cure.

For the cure now. One contrary is ever cured by another. If then it be anger which is the cause in God, anger would be appeased. If it be inventions which is the cause in us of the anger of God, they would be punished and removed. That so the cause being taken away, the effect may cease. Take away our inventions, God's anger will cease. Take away God's anger, the Plague will cease.

Two readings, we said, there were: 1. "Phinehas prayed," or 2. "Phinehas executed judgment." *Palal*, the Hebrew word, will bear both. And both are good; and so we will take them both in.

Against
God's
anger.
1. Prayer.
Num. 25. 6.
2 Sam. 24.
17.

Prayer is good against the Plague, as appeareth not only in this Plague in the text, wherein all the congregation were "weeping" and praying "before the door of the tabernacle," but in King David's Plague also, where we see what his prayer was, and the very words of it.

Isa. 38. 2, 3.

And in Hezekiah's Plague, who "turned his face to the wall, and prayed unto God"—and his prayer is set down: God heard his prayer, and healed him. And, for a general

1 Kings 8.
37, 38, 39.

rule, if there be in the land any pestilent disease; whatsoever Plague, whatsoever sickness it be, the "prayer and supplication" in the temple made by the people, "every man knowing the plague of his own heart," God in heaven will hear it, and remove His hand from afflicting them any further.

Num 16.
47, 48.

And it standeth with good reason. For as the air is infected with noisome scents or smells, so the infection is removed by sweet odours or incense; which Aaron did in the Plague, "put sweet odours in his censer, and went between the living and the dead." Now there is a fit resemblance

Ps. 141. 2.

between incense and prayers: "Let my Prayer come before Thy presence as the incense." And when the priest was

Lu. 1. 10.

within, burning incense, "the people were without at their

Rev. 5. 8.

prayers." And it is expressly said, that "the sweet odours" were nothing else but "the prayers of the Saints."

2. Phi-
nehas'

Prayer is good, and that, Phinehas' prayer. Phinehas was

a priest, the son of Eleazar, the nephew of Aaron. So as prayer, as there is virtue, as in the prayer, so in the person that did a priest. pray, in Phinehas himself.

As we know, the office of a serjeant being to arrest, the office of a notary to make acts, the act that is done by one of them is much more authentical than that which is done by any common person. So "every priest being taken from Heb. 5. 1. among men, and ordained for men, in things pertaining to God," that he may offer prayers ; the prayers he offereth, he offereth out of his office, and so even in that respect there is, *cæteris paribus*, a more force and energy in them, as coming from him whose calling it is to offer them, than in those that come from another whose calling it is not so to do.

To this end God saith to Abimelech : " Abraham is a Gen. 20. 7. prophet, and he shall pray for thee and thou shalt live." So that the prayer of a prophet, in that he is a prophet, is more effectual.

And in the Law, you shall find it all along; when men come to bring their sacrifice for their sins it is said, " The [Lev.4.20.] priest shall make an atonement for them before the Lord, and their sins shall be forgiven them."

And in the Prophets, we see plainly, in time of distress, Hezekiah sent unto the Prophet Esay, to entreat him " to [Isa. 37. 4.] lift up his prayer for the remnant that were left :" and so he did, and was heard by God.

And in the New Testament, St. James' advice is in time [Jas. 5. of sickness to " call for the priests," and they to " pray over" 14, 15.] the party, and that prayer shall work his health ; " and if he have committed sins, they shall be forgiven him." For where the grace of prayer is, and the calling both, they cannot but avail more than where no calling is but the grace alone.

The prayer of Phinehas, and of Phinehas standing. What need there be any mention of Phinehas standing? Was it not enough to say, Phinehas prayed ? It skills not whether he sat or stood, for praying itself was enough.

No; we must not think the Holy Ghost sets down any thing that is superfluous. Somewhat there is in that he stood. Of Moses it is said before in this Psalm, that he " stood in the gap to turn away the wrath of God." In [Ps. 106. 23.] Jeremy it is said, " Though Moses and Samuel stood before [Jer. 15. 1.]

SERM.
XI. Me :" so there is mention made of standing also. And the Prophet himself puts God in mind, that he "stood before

Jer. 18. 20. Him to speak good for the people" and to turn away His wrath from them, that is, put God in mind of the very site of His body.

Joh. 4. 24. For though "God be a Spirit," and so "in spirit to be worshipped," yet inasmuch as He hath given us a body, 1 Cor. 6. 20. with that also are we to worship Him, and "to glorify Him in our body and spirit, which both are God's;" and to "pre- Rom. 12. 1. sent," or offer, "our bodies" to God "as a holy and accept- able sacrifice," in the "reasonable service" of Him.

1 Cor. 14. 40. And to present them "decently." For that also is re- 1 Cor. 11. 13. quired in the service of God. Now "judge in yourselves," is it comely to speak unto our betters, sitting? *Sedentem* [Vid. Ter- tull. de Orat. 12.] *orare extra disciplinam est,* saith Tertullian, To pray sitting or sit praying is against the order of the Church. The Church of God never had, nor hath any such fashion.

[S. Cyp. de Orat. Dom. init.] All tendeth to this, as Cyprian's advice is, *Etiam habitu corporis placere Deo,* 'even by our very gesture and the carriage of our body to behave ourselves so as with it we may please God. Unreverent, careless, undevout behaviour, pleaseth Him not.

Job 1. 6. Isa. 6. 2. Dan. 7. 10. It is noted of the very Angels, that they were standing before God. If them it becomes, if Phinehas, if Moses, if Samuel, and Jeremy, it may well become us to learn our gesture of them.

Against "their in- ventions." 1. Execu- tion of judgment. Prayer is available to appease God's wrath, and so conse- quently to remove the Plague : but not prayer alone. For though it abate the anger of God (which is the first), yet it goeth not high enough, takes not away the second cause, that is, our inventions, which are the cause of God's anger. We see it plain in Numbers the twenty-fifth chapter and sixth verse; they were all at prayers, and Phinehas among Num. 25. 7, 8. them, he and the rest. But yet the Plague ceased not for all that ; till in the verse following Phinehas took his javelin, wherewith in the very act of fornication "he thrust them both through," Zimri and his woman, "and then the Plague was stayed from the children of Israel." For as prayer re- ferreth properly to anger, so doth executing judgment to sin or to our inventions, the cause of it.

Prayer then doth well; but prayer and doing justice, both these together, jointly, will do it indeed. And if you disjoin or separate them, nothing will be done. If we "draw near to God with our mouths, and honour Him with our lips," Isa. 29. 13. it will not avail us if judgment be turned back, or justice stand afar off.

There are two persons. Both of them were in Phinehas. 2. By Phinehas, as a prince in his tribe, and a magistrate. For as he was a priest, so he was a prince of his tribe. So then both these must join together, as well the devotion of the priest in prayer, which is his office, as the zeal of the magistrate in executing judgment, which is his. For Phinehas the priest must not only stand up and pray, but Moses the magistrate also must stand in the gap, to turn away the wrath of God, that He destroy not the people. No less he, than Aaron with his golden censer, to run into the midst of the congregation, to make atonement for them when the Plague is begun.

Moses, he gave in charge for the executing of them "that Num. 25. 5 were joined to Baal-Peor :" Phinehas, he executed the charge. Moses stood in the gap, when he gave the sentence: Phinehas stood up, when he did the execution. And these two are a blessed conjunction. One of them without the other may miss, but both together never fail. For when Zimri was slain, and so when Rabshakeh perished, and so when the incestuous Corinthian was excommunicated, in all three the Plague ceased.

But what, if Moses give no charge; what, if Phinehas do 3. By every man upon himself. no execution, as oft it falleth out? How then? In that case every private man is to be Phinehas to himself; is not only to pray to God, but to be wreaked, do judgment, chasten his 2 Cor. 7. 11. own body, and so judge himself that he may not be judged 1 Cor 9. 27. 1 Cor. 11. of the Lord. For every one, for his part, is a cause of the 31. judgments of God sent down; and so may be, and is to be, a cause of the removing them. Somewhile the King, as David, 1 Chron. by the pride of his heart. Otherwhile the people, by their 21. 1, 8. murmuring against Moses and Aaron. So that King and Num. 16. people both must judge themselves; every private offender, 3. himself. Zimri, if he had judged himself, Phinehas should not have judged him. The incestuous Corinthian, if he had judged himself, St. Paul had not judged him. For either by [1 Cor. 5. 5]

SERM.
XI.
ourselves, or by the magistrate; or if by neither of both, by God Himself. For one way or other sin must be judged. Zimri by his repentance, Phinehas by his prayer or doing justice, or God by the Plague sent among them.

Now then these two, 1. "Phinehas stood up and prayed," 2. and "Phinehas stood up and executed judgment," if they might be coupled together, I durst undertake the conclusion would be, "and the Plague ceased." But either of them wanting, I dare promise nothing.

To conclude then. 1. The Plague comes not by chance, but hath a cause. 2. That cause is not altogether natural and pertains to physic, but hath something supernatural in it, and pertains to divinity. 3. That supernatural cause is the wrath of God. 4. Which yet is not the first cause; for the wrath of God would not rise, but that He is provoked by our sins—and the certain sins that provoke it have been set down. 5. And the cause of them our own inventions. So our inventions beget sin, sin provokes the wrath of God, the wrath of God sends the Plague among us. To stay the Plague, God's wrath must be stayed; to stay it, there must be a ceasing from sin; that sin may cease, we must be out of love with our own inventions, and not go a whoring after them. Prayer, that assuageth anger; to execute justice, that abateth sin; to execute justice, either publicly as doth the magistrate, or privately as every man doth or may do upon himself. Which joined with prayer, and prayer with it, will soon rid us of that we complain; and otherwise, [Isa. 9. 12.] "His anger will not be turned away, but His hand stretched out still."

A SERMON[a]

PREACHED BEFORE TWO KINGS[b].

ON THE FIFTH OF AUGUST, A.D. MDCVI.

Ps. cxliv. 10.

It is He That giveth salvation unto Kings, Who delivereth David His servant from the perilous, or malignant, sword.

Ipse est Qui dat salutem Regibus, Qui eruit Davidem servum Suum de gladio maligno. [*Qui* das *salutem. . . . Qui* redemisti. . . . Vulg.]

[*It is He that giveth salvation unto Kings, Who delivereth David His servant from the hurtful sword.* Eng. Trans.]

SCARCE any that hear this verse rehearsed, but sees that it fits both to this our purpose and time. The time. Here is mention of Kings, of salvation given to Kings, of one a matchless King; David in danger and delivered; from the sword, in danger and delivered: all most apposite.

For behold Kings, Kings to whom God hath given salvation; hath given salvation, and doth give salvation, and I pray God He may ever give it, much salvation for many years. Behold our King His servant, whom this day now six years since, I say this very day, God delivered, wonderfully delivered from the hurtful sword. Verily these agree; whilst at once we hear the words of the text, we have as it were a commentary thereof before our eyes.

But for our purpose. This meeting, and this not only honourable but also sacred assembly, what means it, what intends it? What else than to give thanks to God for salvation given to the King? And what else, I pray you, doth

---

[a This Sermon is not one of the Ninety-six, nor does it occur in some of the earlier editions. It is given in that of 1661 between the last on the Gunpowder Treason and the Occasional Sermons.]

[b James I. and Christiern IV. King of Denmark, the brother of the Queen, who paid a visit to the English court during this summer.]

this verse sound forth, than thanks also to God for salvation given to David.

For in the preceding verse the Psalmist took his harp, tuned the strings, promised a song, a new song. And behold the contents of this new song in this verse. The sum of this verse (for the next verse is a prayer, neither hath it any song in it) and the argument is giving of thanks, and of thanks for no other benefit (although there were many more, yet for no other benefit) than the King's deliverance. That namely, the Saviour of Kings, to wit God—for this is God's periphrase, " Who gives salvation to Kings" that this Saviour of Kings had delivered His servant David from some eminent danger; yet from no other danger than " the hurtful sword," that is, the traitor's.

And thus surely doth this verse, and thus then also the people of Israel praised Him for their King's deliverance : " It is He that giveth salvation unto Kings, who delivereth David His servant from the hurtful sword."

And we indeed here to-day sing the very same thing, every way the same, one only word a little changed : " It is He that gives salvation unto Kings, it is He who hath delivered" James " His servant from the perilous sword." It is He That hath done this, it is He Whom for this delivery all of us have met here to-day to praise in a festival, an assembly, a song.

And this verily is usual with God, and surely no new thing, to give " salvation to Kings." This is His ancient goodness ; yet of this ancient and no new goodness ever and anon He shews new examples, yea in our age He hath shewn them ; nor doth He cease to shew them even to this day. For this very thing which to-day we celebrate, although it be new, and surely new it is, yet it is not the last. For since God hath vouchsafed us him, one and again another hath befallen us, wherewith God hath lately blessed us. Twice or thrice hath God given deliverance, twice or thrice hath God delivered him ; and (to let pass other, surely those most admirable) He That six years since hath " delivered him from the hurtful sword," very lately, this year, this very year, hath delivered him from the perilous gunpowder. Thus yearly He heaps upon us new deliverances. It shall be our duty here to imitate David, and for several new precedents to sing new songs; for several new deliverances, new thanksgivings. So shall He every year heap upon us new deliverance: rehearsing old, He will enrich us with new; nor shall there ever be wanting new matter for a song, if a new song be not wanting. If old ones be not forgotten, a new harvest of thanksgiving shall yearly increase unto us.

And thus briefly, touching the scope of this verse. It is an easy task to divide it. It falls asunder of its own accord, and severs into two parts. The one a thesis, the other an hypothesis. The thesis is concerning His care of Kings in general: "It is He Who gives salvation to Kings." The hypothesis is touching His care of David in particular: "It is He Who delivereth David His servant from the hurtful sword." Or indeed, because we have to do with music, and are to treat of a song, His general care of Kings is as the *cantus, cantus firmus;* His particular care of David is as the *discantus,* or *cantus figuratus.* Yet for David, although God hath diversely delivered him both many ways and times, notwithstanding he insists on this alone, which is proper both to this season and to us, because "He delivered him from the perilous sword."

I will first speak of the safety of Kings in general, and also I. both of the cause of it, and manner of giving it.

Next of King David's deliverance. II.

Lastly of our King. III.

Quæ ego dum sic singula complectar, &c.

It is He That giveth salvation unto Kings, &c.

I promised first to speak of the thesis. I.

"Who gives salvation,"

"Who gives it to Kings."

To give salvation: so well it agrees to the Divine nature to shew Himself a deliverer, that God doth challenge that as native, proper, and peculiar to Himself: "I, even I am the Is. 43. 11. Lord, and besides Me there is no Saviour." Thus He is a Saviour; save therefore He will.

And indeed God will "save both man and beast," so wonderful is His mercy, saith our Prophet. Even thus also the Ps. 36. 6, 7.

R

SERM.
XII.

1 Cor. 9. 9,
10.

Job 7. 20.

[Vid.
Hom. Il. 1.
175, 176.]

Ps. 18. 50.

Ps. 28. 8.

1.
2.
3.

Ps. 147. 10.
Ps. 48. 7.

Ps. 33. 17.

Ps. 60. 11.

Ps. 3. 8.

Ps. 35. 3.

nature of beasts is partaker of this saving power in God; it is He Who gives salvation even to brute beasts.

Yet even to brute beasts; yet so, that nevertheless the Apostle doubts not to demand and ask, "Doth God take care for oxen? doth He not rather say it for our sake?" As though His care for them, in respect of that to us, might be esteemed no care at all. Neither is it. For we are His chief care; thence Job speaks unto Him on our behalf, as it were by a peculiar title, "I have sinned, what shall I do unto Thee, O Thou preserver of men?" He it is Who gives salvation unto men. He is the preserver of men, but especially of Kings, μάλιστα διοτρεφέων Βασιλήων, as the heathen poet sings not amiss, for they more than all kind of men are God's delight and care; the name θεοφυλάκτου agrees to the King more than others. For "great deliverance giveth He to the King," saith our Psalmist. He also saith, "He is the saving health of His anointed." In whomsoever He shews Himself wonderful, "He is wonderful in the Kings of the earth," as he saith, Psalm the seventy-sixth, and twelfth verse. 1. He is surely wonderful in them, in preserving them. 2. In none more. 3. In none so wonderful. Thus by these three steps we ascend to our thesis; "It is He that giveth salvation unto Kings."

To Kings I say, in general; for touching Kings, God's servants, I shall discourse more fully when I come to the hypothesis concerning David His servant.

"It is He Who gives salvation unto Kings;" He it is. Therefore let Kings know to Whom they ought to ascribe their deliverance, even to Him. There is no safety for them "in the strength of a horse," namely, not in their cavalry; "not in the legs of man," namely, not in their infantry; not in "the ships of Tarshish," namely, not in their naval forces. "A horse is a vain thing to save a man." A ship is a weak vessel, and cannot save. Finally, "Vain is the help of man," "salvation belongeth to the Lord." His it is; look up thither unto Him. He it is Who tells you from heaven, "I am your salvation." Let Kings know this.

Let the people also know whither, when all is done, they ought to lift up their eyes, whom to implore when they would have their King safe; namely, to the Lord to whom salvation belongs. "O Lord save the King." "Hosanna in the highest." _{Ps. 20. 9. [Vulg.] Mat. 21. 9.}

Hence let rebels amongst the people know, that God hates those who labour to snatch that salvation from Kings which God gives them ; let loyal people know, that they are God's friends, and God theirs, who desire the salvation of Kings. For God desires the very same thing. "It is He That gives salvation unto Kings."

I come nearer. "Who gives salvation." What salvation? Surely each kind, whether that of physicians, of a sound and healthful body against diseases; namely, as they are mortal. For, as Daniel's image may teach us, every Kingdom stands _{Dan. 2. 33.} upon feet of clay. Kings also are the very same treasures of their people; but yet "treasures in earthen vessels." _{2 Cor. 4. 7.} Therefore they need this salvation.

True therefore it is should we mean this, for God gives this also. True indeed, but not proper to this place. For this salvation, as our text tells us, is from the sword, not sickness; rather from malignant manners than malignant humours; from external force, not from internal distemper. δυσκρασία. I therefore apply myself to that. "He gives salvation," He gives this salvation "to Kings;" to Kings before others.

I now demand the cause, and more near and inwardly search God's will. Why to them before others? Is it because Kings have need of safety, and the donor of safety more than others? Yes verily, because they have; forasmuch as to them, more than others, that malignant one shews himself more malicious; (for thus κατ᾽ ἐξοχὴν, St. John _{1 Joh. 2. 13, 14; 5, 18.} in his first Epistle often calls that wicked spirit) he it is that destroys Kings, namely, the angel of the bottomless pit, of whom the same John speaks. "His name in Hebrew is _{Rev. 9. 11.} Abaddon; in Greek Apollyon," that is, a destroyer. A destroyer; a name directly opposite to God's name. His name is Saviour. And the name of His Son, Jesus, a Saviour also _{Mat. 1. 21.} —an Angel interpreting it. They give salvation. But he is Abaddon, he is a destroyer who chiefly desires this, to snatch away, to take, wholly to overthrow this salvation, all the salvation of all. And mark with me how earnestly he endeavours it.

We said this formerly: God saves even beasts, much

SERM.
XII.
_____

Mat. 8. 32.

Job 1 12;
2. 4.

Esther 2.
21.

Deut. 12. 8.

Judg. 17. 4.

more men. And Princes most of all. This Abaddon sets up himself against God, and is only bent to destruction. Yea, rather than not destroy, he is busied in destroying brute beasts; which very thing is evident in the silly swine, which Christ permitting him he carried headlong and choked in the sea. Thus he it is who takes away safety even from brute beasts.

But he covets rather to destroy any man, any one man, than whole flocks and herds of cattle, as Job witnesseth. Thus he it is who takes away salvation from men.

But to Kings especially, beside and above other mortals, he is most hatefully malicious; and if any King be eminent in piety, as David, him he chiefly hates. He indeed always meditates on mischief against Kings, he desired to destroy even Ahasuerus, a heathen King, only because he was a King, by his eunuchs. Yea, David also! For how often was he "thrust at," yea overthrown that he might perish; and now at the very point of destruction unless God had delivered him, as he speaks of himself, Psalm the hundred and eighteenth, and thirteenth verse. He it must be, in every respect, Who can give salvation to them. It is the other who takes it away.

But why doth that Abaddon so zealously devise to bring destruction upon Kings, to take away their safety? What have they only done? Surely because there is none who can be to him, who can be to his kingdom, a more capital enemy than Kings. For it is by their power and authority, that what likes may not be lawful to every one—I will use the words of Scripture—that "every man may not do (unpunished) whatsoever is right in his own eyes;" which every one both might and did do, when there was no King in Israel. Now for every man to have power to do whatsoever seems right in his own eyes unpunished, this verily that Abaddon earnestly desires; it must needs please him well, his kingdom may well prosper, if things go thus.

For then it will seem right to the eyes of Micah to make, and set up, an idol for himself in his private house. And what is lawful for Micah, why not for another also? Thus, look, how many families, so many new prodigious idols. And that is indeed a miserable Church where this is suffered.

It will also seem right to the Danites to rob, to steal, not
only to break through the walls of Micah's house, but also as
Laish, even to pillage and spoil whole cities, to destroy all,
not save a man. Then ravishings of women, and whoredoms Judg. 18.
not to be named, will seem right in the eyes of the men of [15—27.]
Gibeah. Lamentable indeed is the face of that kingdom Judg. 19.
where there is such work. That these and such like things
may be done, this surely he wills earnestly, and that Abaddon would purchase this at a high rate. But that these and
such things as these may not be done, Kings doubtless are
his hinderers. Wherefore he labours by all means to take
them away, to take their safety from them, and in this he is
wholly employed.

First, and before all things, he desires anarchy. If that Ἀναρχίαν.
may not be, then would he incontinently destroy Kings one
after another. That so kingdoms might shake "as a reed
in the water," which usually happens in often change of 1 Kings 14.
Kings, never enjoying a settled rest. Whereby, being always [15.]
under one new King or another, they can never get strength
against evil manners and wicked men.

We have already seen for what reason: it will be worth
our labour to know, by what means also that Abaddon seeks
to destroy Kings. And this is plain from the same chapter,
in the ninth of the Apocalypse. For there he hath his emis-
saries, "locusts ascending out of the smoke of the pit," whose [Rev. 9. 2,
king he is, and those also, as well as their king Abaddon, are 3.]
sworn enemies to Kings. He suborns these for this attempt.
But who are these locusts? A kind of creatures who have a
man's face, women's hair, but lions' teeth, and their tails the
stings of scorpions. No others surely, if Fathers which interpret this place are to be heard, than those very same
which our Prophet David twice in this Psalm calls "strange Ps. 144. 7,
children," whom St. John afterward perceived to be locusts. [11.]
These did David call "strange children" long before. For
that kind of people was neither unknown to David, neither
yet are they unknown to us. Even our age brings forth
"strange children." Strange indeed. A kind of men which
style themselves ———— Of the society of Jesu. But Jesus,
as is aforesaid, is a Saviour. Wherefore these also, if from
Him they have their name, if they be not "strange chil-

dren," they ought to minister salvation. But is not this a
strange thing, a monster-like, that these who from Jesus
a Saviour have made a name for themselves, are accounted
most wicked, even the ambassadors of Abaddon, traitors to
Kings, the overthrow of kingdoms in what state soever they
get footing? Are not these verily "strange children," who
under a strange Jesu by name every where attempt practices
most estranged from the nature of JESUS; namely, destruc-
tions, treasons, seditions? And that you may know that
these also of ours are of the same lineage with those of

[Ps. 18. 45.] David, their marks are every way alike: *Filii alieni*, saith
David, *mentiti sunt mihi*. Even the same thing which he

[Ps. 144. 11.] saith twice in this Psalm: "Their mouth speaketh a lie,
their right hand is a right hand of iniquity." And are not
these of ours just like them? only except what David calls
lying, that they call equivocation. A diverse title, no different things. For "their right hand" is equally wicked.
Because, whether they engage their hand for faithful dealing,
or lay their hand on those sacred Evangels to win belief by
religious oaths, "their right hand" is wicked and deceitful
in both; both ways, both mouth and right hand is estranged
from their mind, their mind estranged from God, at least

[2 Cor. 4. 4.] from the true God; for from an equivocal god, that is, "the
god of this world," it is not perchance estranged. And now
he employs the helps and assistance of these, whether if
you please to call them "locusts," or "strange children," to
whet these perilous swords, to mingle poisons, to give fire
to powder-plots. To whom their king Abaddon gives in
strict charge, these being his chieftains, that which formerly

[1 Kings 22. 31.] the King of Syria commanded his captains: "Fight neither
with small nor great, save only against the King." But de-

[1 i. e. dagger. See Nares' Gloss.] stroy him with sword, with fire, with poynado[1], with poison,
with powder; despatch him what way soever:

[Virgil. Georg. 4. 212.]
Nempe
—— *Rege incolumi mens omnibus una,*
Amisso rupere fidem.

(as the poet very elegantly) I conclude. Though One there
be Who would give salvation, there is another who would
take it away; though One there be Who would stretch
forth a gracious shield, there is another who brandisheth

a " perilous sword." Though there be true-born children
which desire their safety, there are "strange children" which
wish their ruin. Though there be a Jesus Who can save,
there is Abaddon who would destroy. Though there be
Christ Who would favour them, there is an Antichrist —
neither is he only called Antichrist because he is an adversary to Christ the Lord, but also because he is an enemy
to the anointed of the Lord—I say there is an Antichrist,
who would be mischievous and quickly destroy them, either
with "the perilous sword" or else a powder-plot.

You have now already seen both why and how that Abaddon would destroy Kings. Next, you shall briefly hear both
wherefore and by what means God would give them salvation. First wherefore, wherefore doth God give salvation to
Kings? Namely, because they are His vicegerents upon
earth; because they are in God's place, because they represent His person; because they are His "ministers," His Rom. 13.
chief ministers. Whereby is shewn that there is a kind of 4, 6.
necessity for God to save those, namely, because they are
His ambassadors. Surely those that are Kings' legates into
foreign countries, those who are viceroys and presidents in
provinces here at home, it hath always been accounted part
of princely wisdom by all means to protect them, to vindi-
cate them from contempt. For the honour of an ambassador
is his honour that sends him, and the viceroy's dishonour
redounds upon the King. Even our Prophet David, when 2 Sam. 10.
those were reproachfully handled whom he sent instead of 4; 12. 31.
himself to rejoice with King Hanun, he judged himself to
be violated in them. The disgrace, as though it had been
proper to himself, he severely revenged. Thus it is with the
supreme King, to Whom our Kings are viceroys; His own
honour, except Kings be safe who are His viceroys, His
own honour cannot stand safe and inviolate. Even for
His own honour He will preserve them safe. For "by Him Prov. 8. 15.
they reign," by Him they "are ordained." By Him they Rom. 13. 1.
are what they are. All come to this point, that it belongs
to Him, in some sort behoves Him, that whom He makes,
them He should also favour; and whom He favours, that
they may not be wronged; He is also their revenger if they

be violated. This is one reason why He should give salvation unto them.

Further, to this I also add another.

God desires His people's safety, He desires all our safety; for the benefit of salvation the more general it is, the more [Jonah 4. 10, 11.] heavenly it is. The Lord said to Jonas, Is it meet that thou shouldest desire the preservation of the gourd? "And should not I spare Nineveh, that great city, wherein are a hundred and twenty thousand persons which cannot discern between their right hand and their left?" Now He gives salvation to Kings, thereby to derive it to the people, fitly to them, that by them it may extend to all. For thence it is Ps. 82. 6. that He not only calls the magistrates gods—"I have called you gods"—but also saviours. For so it is in the book of Judges, as often as mention is made of the supreme magis- Judg. 3. 9, trate. God, saith he, hath raised up a saviour for them, 15. [See the Vulgate.] Othniel, Gideon, Jephthah, and others. Therefore they save many thousands. Finally, it is most agreeable, fit, and a thing well beseeming God, to save the saviours of so many thousands; that is, to give salvation to them in whose safety our safety, yea all our safety, is placed. That place [1 Tim. 2. 1, 2.] of St. Paul is remarkable: "Let prayers," saith he, "be made for all men." But this is boundless, it is too long to run through all. Will you therefore confine it in brief? Let them be made "for Kings." Because if for them, for all. If it be well with them, it will be well with all. In which place the Apostle pleads powerfully. Mark his gradations. "For Kings," saith he, that they may be safe: thence it is, that whilst they are safe, the peace is safe; in a safe peace there is a knowledge of God; from the knowledge of God an honest and godly life; from a godly and honest life comes the safety of the whole world. Do you not see that the safety of Kings, and prayers for it, is laid as the very corner-stone to all men's safety?

But why seek I for these examples abroad, seeing we have them growing at home here in our Psalm, and surely far more abundantly? In this verse are thanks to be given for the deliverance of Kings; in the next verse are prayers to [Ps. 144. 12, 13, 14.] be made. Why, I pray you? namely, the twelfth verse, that

so it might go well with "our sons," "our daughters;" the
thirteenth verse, that *so* it might be well with "our store-
houses," our "flocks;" the fourteenth verse, that *so* all
might go well with our "oxen;" that there be no "breaking
in nor going out," or "complaining in our streets." None
of these shall be, we shall have all these safe, if the King be
safe. By account indeed there are eight—which the Fathers
from the words of the Psalm, "Blessed are the people who [Ps. 144.
are in such a case," have called them the eight felicities of 15.]
this life, the eight earthly beatitudes—all depending upon
the safety of Kings. Nor only these eight, but also—which
last remains and is worth all, "Blessed are the people whose [Ps. 33.
God is the Lord"—this also, that God may be our Lord, 12.]
that is, that our religion may be safe, doth certainly very
much depend on the Prince. For surely he that reads of
six Kings of Judah successively in the books of Kings,
or the five Emperors successively in the ecclesiastical history; or he that here at home hath seen amongst us four
Princes successively by turns altering religion, and as the
Kings so the people also changing in religion; will discern
that it is of great consequence that salvation be given to
Solomon, lest when he is dead Jeroboam "make Israel 1 Kings 15.
to sin." Therefore that He may give salvation to the 30.
people, He "gives salvation unto Kings;" both for His
own honour's sake, and even for all our sakes He gives
salvation to Kings. Why He should give salvation I have
already made known. How He gives it, that yet remains.
I haste unto it.

First, by sending His word that He may save them; but 1.
if that be a small thing, by stretching forth His hands also,
that He may set them in safety.

First, by the word of salvation. For, lest any should overthrow that salvation which God hath given, He hath provided in a triple charge, wherewith as with a triple trench
He hath fortified the safety of Kings.

1. "Touch not Mine anointed:" whereby He secures Ps. 105. 15.
them from violent hands.

2. "Curse not the ruler of thy people:" whereby He Exod. 22.
secures them from the poison of the tongue. 28.

3. "Curse not the King, no not in thy thought:" whereby Eccl. 10.
20.

He secures them against the bold and boundless thoughts of the soul itself.

And if they be safe enough from these three, all would be well; the safety of Kings would be abundantly provided for. Thus God provides by His triple saving word, that their safety may not come in danger.

But if these are not enough, and often they are not enough, but this triple bulwark being cast down, "strange children" dare sit in counsel and mutter ill words, nay verily even lift up their hand against God's anointed; yet then, as it is in the seventh verse, "He will send His hand from [Ps. 144. 7.] heaven," He will send His hand from heaven and will deliver them from the midst of danger. This truly and indeed He will do, by opposing Himself both against their counsels and against them.

Against their counsels, partly by detecting them whilst yet they are scarcely ripened; partly by scattering them, even then when they are digested, finished; even then, when all is in a readiness.

And verily, for to detect their counsel He saith in another Ps. 132. 17. place, that He "hath ordained a lantern for His anointed." "A lantern" surely, that is, faithful counsel; and those that are His ministers, they being the lamps of Kings, whom it concerns thoroughly to know their inmost designs; but when the King's lamp is too dim, then God's lightning gives light. For so it is in the sixth verse; when the light of the lamp Ps. 144. 6. sufficeth not, by Him, *misso a se de cœlo fulgure*, is the whole Esth. 2. 22. plot discovered. The King's lantern I say, as when Mor-2 Kings 6. decai brought the accusation against the traitorous eunuchs; 9. [¹ the as when Elisha revealed the plot concerning Aram's lying in King of Syria's wait¹ for the King of Israel. lying in wait.] But it was *fulgur Dei*, when, as Solomon saith, "A bird of Eccl. 10. the air shall carry the voice," namely, when by some strange 20. means and by no human assistance things are brought to Ps. 64. 8. light. When "their own tongues shall make them fall," as it is Psalm the sixty-fourth, and eighth verse. That is, when by their own whisperings, their own writings, they betray themselves. That all that see it may be astonished; [Ps. 109. who see it to be the hand of God, and that "Thou, Lord, 27.] hast done it." And doubtless He is wonderful in the Kings

of the earth, but in no one thing more than in sending this
His lightning, whereby the most secret counsels of traitors
are often revealed.

Yet suppose it to be so; grant that nothing be suspected,
not a word spoken, every thing concealed till all be in readiness, and now the treason brought to the very last cast; yet,
even then He will scatter them notwithstanding, and as it
is in the fifth verse, "He will touch the mountains and they Ps. 144. 5.
shall smoke," every one. Absalom now having usurped a
kingdom grew as big as a mountain. God will but touch
Absalom, He will smite his brain with madness that he 2 Sam. 17.
might reject that very counsel which was most conducing 14.
to his design. Thus in a moment God scattered them all.
Adonijah also swelled into a mountain. God will but touch
Adonijah, He will smite his heart with a causeless fear, [1 Kings
that then, when he was almost fully enthroned, he durst 1. 50.]
neither go on forward nor stir: thus they all vanish into
smoke. "All of them are become," even when all was as Ps. 62. 3.
sure as bird in hand, "as a bowing wall and tottering
fence;" they either fall with their own accord, or with
the least enforcing are cast down; they are touched, turn
into smoke, and vanish.

And thus God sets up Himself against their conspiracies, and shews that He will assert the salvation of Kings.
Moreover, He undertakes this very thing against the traitors themselves, "by making ready the strings of His bow Ps. 21. 12.
against the face of them," as it is Psalm the twenty-first;
and as it is here, the sixth verse, by consuming them with
His "arrows." That men seeing their most unhappy ends,
might tremble at their accursed deeds. Moses hath rightly
comprised the whole matter, then when Korah first of all
withstood him. Hereby, saith he, shall ye know that magistrates are from God, that God takes care for their safety:
"If these men die the common death of all men, or if they Num. 16.
be visited after the visitation of all men," then ye may make 28, 29, 30.
a doubt whether it be He; "but if God do a new thing"
and bring all of them forth, every one to punishment, all
of them to fearful ends; if Divine justice follow them at the
heels and suffer them not to be carried to their graves in
peace, morte vel maturâ vel siccâ, hereby shall ye plainly

SERM.
XII.
know that it is the Lord Himself "Who gives salvation unto Kings," because the hand of the Lord is gone forth against them. And verily so it is; for what is become of those who boldly essayed to cast down that triple bulwark of which I lately spake? What is become of Sheba, who durst lift up
2 Sam. 20. 1, 22.
his hand and sound a trumpet against David? "His head is thrown down from the wall." And what become of Shimei, who durst open his mouth and curse the anointed of the
1 Kings 2. 9, 46.
Lord? "His hoar head went down to the grave with blood." What also became of the eunuchs who only thought in their minds how they might lay hands on the King?
Esth. 2. 21, 23.
2 Sam. 4. 12.
2 Sam. 15. 10, 12.
[1 Kings 1. 7.]
[1 Kings 16. 9]
[2 Kings 12. 21.]
[2 Chron. 25. 3.]
Ps. 18. 2.
"They were both hanged on a tree." And what should I say more? The time would fail me to speak of Baanah and Rechab, of Absalom and Ahithophel, of Adonijah and Joab, of Zimri and Jehozabad; and all the rest, all who have sought the destruction of their Kings, they have all perished and are gone to their grave by some shameful death. All these cry out as it were with one voice, From our example let no mortal men dare to take that salvation from Kings which God hath given unto them. David called God "the horn of his salvation;" he said truly. For by pouring out oil from the horn, out of the lowest and hollow part of it, God anointed him. And with the same horn, the end of it being sharpened, God scattered his enemies and brake them all in pieces. Thus with one end He anointed him King, with the other He gave him deliverance. Thus is God indeed a "horn of salvation" to His anointed.

But I may not keep you too long in the thesis; ye have seen, I suppose, already both why it should be just with God to give salvation unto Kings. 1. Because there is a wicked one who would destroy them. 2. Kings are in God's place. 3. God's honour is concerned in saving them. 4. In their safety the safety of many nations consists. You have also seen how God brings this to pass, by His word, and by His work. 1. He reveals it by His lightning. 2. He touches them, and turns their counsels into smoke. 3. The contrivers themselves, He shoots them through with His arrows. And thus He works salvation for Kings in the middle of the earth.

II. The thesis now finished, I descend to the hypothesis.

"It is He who hath delivered David His servant," &c. But I begin with this. God "is the Saviour of all men, but especially those that believe." It is St. Paul's saying. Let me add, He is the Saviour of all Kings, but especially of those that believe. For there is like reason in both. Thus I infer it. If Divine Providence rest upon Kings, Kings indefinitely, Kings in general, what shall it do upon Kings who also themselves believe, and are the rulers of them that believe? If God be wonderful in the Kings of the earth, what is He in Kings who are both sons and "nursing fathers" of the Church? If in Ahasuerus a heathen, what is He in David, a religious and pious Prince. For, as the son of Sirach spake wisely of him, "Even as fat is parted from the flesh of the sacrifice, so is David from the Kings of the earth;" that look what Kings are amongst men, such is David amongst Kings: what will God therefore do for him? What will He do for them that are to Him faithful as David in all his house? For surely what you may find severally in other Kings are here in David conjoined; namely, a King and a servant of God. Wherefore, both because he is a King "He will give salvation unto him," and because he is His servant "He will deliver him from the perilous sword." That he is a king, he hath that in common with other Kings of the heathen; for whom that God should thus provide, there is no cause but only this, because they are Kings. That he is God's servant, this is peculiar to him above others.

And God will surely save all His servants, of whatsoever, even of the meanest, condition; but Kings that are His servants, above others, both because as Kings by Him they reign, and because as servants they are governed by Him. "O Lord save the King:" this is his prayer, Psalm the twentieth, and ninth verse. "O God save Thy servant:" this is his prayer, Psalm the eighty-sixth, and second verse. This is one petition, and yet not one. One in David; not one in all, for all are not servants. Yes verily, all are His servants, all the Kings of the earth. And so it is indeed; all are, for all although unwitting, although unwilling, yet all do His will. All are; but, which is for our purpose, all do not so acknowledge themselves, all carry themselves

1 Tim. 4. 10.

[Isa. 49. 23.]

Eccl. 47. 2.

Ps. 20. 9.

Ps. 86. 2.

SERM.
XII.
Jer. 27. 6.

like servants. Nebuchadnezzar was His servant. For so God spake by Jeremiah: "Behold, I have given all these lands to Nebuchadnezzar My servant;" yet notwithstanding he did not acknowledge this. He acknowledged not either himself to be a servant, or Him his Lord. For he

Dan. 3. 15.

said as much to the three children: "Let us see who is that God Which will deliver you out of my hands?"

Exod. 5. 2.

Neither indeed did Pharaoh acknowledge it. "Who is the Lord? I know not the Lord, neither will I let Israel go." Our David did not so (no surely) but he acknowledged himself a servant. Hear him speak for himself:

Ps. 116. 16.

"Behold, O Lord, how that I am Thy servant; I am Thy servant, and the son of Thy handmaid." Neither is he this in word and speech alone, but also in deed and in truth; not, as they, doing it neither wittingly nor willingly, but of set purpose, doing all His will. Being so careful in

Ps. 132. 3, 4, 5.

the Lord's business, that he would not "climb up into his bed," would not "suffer his eyes to sleep," until he had found out a place for the ark of the Lord; and in bringing it back, being girt with a linen ephod, he so behaved him-

2 Sam. 6. 16, 20.

self amongst the servants of God, so I say, that he seemed to his wife to be too much a servant. But he could never be humbled enough before his Lord, never careful enough to do His will. David was a servant indeed, humble as

1 Sam. 13. 14.

a servant, faithful as a servant, a servant "after His own heart." Fitly therefore, and to the purpose is it said in this verse, "His servant David." Therefore God speaks so

Ps. 89. 21, 22, 23.

of him His servant: "My hand shall hold him fast, and My arm shall strengthen him; the enemy shall not be able to do him violence, the son of wickedness shall not hurt him." That is, in one word, "I will deliver him."

And what He said in His word, He fulfilled in deed: therefore God often delivered him, both from many—I do not say dangers; that word is too large for our present purpose—weapons (I do say, which is more apposite) from sharp arrows drawn and shot at him to destroy him. He delivered him from Goliath's spear; He delivered him from the javelin of Saul; and, which is proper to this place, He also delivered him from the sword.

From the sword, yet not from any man's at all in common and promiscuously, but as it is in the verse, "from the malignant sword." And is there indeed a "malignant sword?" Do I say a "malignant" one? Perhaps there is an evil one, perhaps a wicked one; but to call it a "malignant sword," that is too violent an expression. Indeed the sword is in no fault, there is no malignancy in the iron; all the malevolency is in him, and is diffused through his mind, at whose side it hangs. For in any other sense there is no "malignant sword."

Who therefore, I pray you, is that malignant one? Truly it is not he, who openly and in flat terms is mischievous or malevolent; not he, who as an enemy professeth open hostility. He is that malignant one, who covertly and in secret is malevolent. Who under a smooth forehead hath a festered mind; under a painted face, a rotten heart. Who, as Solomon skilfully describes him, speaks fair, but "there are seven [Pro. 26. abominations in his heart." Finally, he is that malignant $\begin{smallmatrix}25.]\\[1 \text{ Joh. 2.}\end{smallmatrix}$ one, and his sword, inasmuch as he is malignant, is malig- 13, 14.] nant, that is, it is like its master.

Those locusts which I lately mentioned, are the malignant ones; they have a woman's face, but behind, a scorpion's tail. Whom I lately called "strange children," they are those malignant ones; whose mouth is vain; but for their sword's point, that is not vain as we see, neither wounds it in vain, but gives a home, and more than that, a malignant wound.

And is it so? Are there such about David, who covertly wish him evil? Cannot so good a King, so faithful a servant of God, cannot he however, escape those malignant ones? Surely he might, and so he did. David had such, whom David did not satisfy. David had also his malignant ones, and they their swords; and by them and their swords he was in greatest peril. The King as yet met 1 Sam. 22. with no Doeg, and men of Keilah: now the King met 9; 23. 12. with Shimei and Sheba. He had to deal with his companions, his guide, and Ahithophel "his familiar friend." He had to do with "Absalom his son, his son" Absalom. Ps. 55. 14. He met with others, and those no few; for in many Psalms $\begin{smallmatrix}2 \text{ Sam. 18.}\\33.\end{smallmatrix}$ you may hear him complaining of the worst (for they are not the best) sort of men. Yea even in this our Psalm

SERM.
XII.
[Ps. 144.
8, 11.] twice he complains of some natives indeed by birth, but
in affection foreigners, that is, painted subjects, in whose
mouth there is no truth, nor trust in their right hand.
David had such as these; even he that is like David, if
any be like him, yet such as these he shall have. And
from these, namely, once at the eighth verse; nor there
once alone, but again also at the eleventh, that is, again
and again he prays to be delivered. For he knew how
perilous this sword was, that surely the enemy's sword in
respect of it was full of courtesy. For this sword was no
sword of war, nor of Goliath, nor of the Philistines, who
openly invade, which because he saw he might avoid. This
sword is the traitor's sword; Joab is a sword, even this
[2 Sam. 3.
27; 20. 9,
10.] sword, who friendly saluted Abner, kindly embraced Amasa;
yet thrust both of them into the belly, and that in such
sort, namely so perilously, that he needed not to give
them a second wound ; for with that alone both their
bowels gushed out upon the earth. Joab is a sword, a
perilous sword; the fault is in him.

Now, that all may know how good God is to David, God
delivered him from this sword, him I say ; for some there
are, yea some Kings, whom He delivers not; there are some
Kings whom He destroys, whom this "perilous sword" destroys; namely, over whom God doth not stretch forth His
2 Sam. 4. 5. helmet of salvation. He destroyed Ishbosheth, who "lay on
1 Kings 16.
9. his bed at noon." He destroyed Elah, as he was "drinking
himself drunk in his steward's house." He destroyed Joash,
2 Chron.
24. 25.
[Jer. 41. 2.] affrighted with the people's uproar. He destroyed Gedaliah,
fearlessly feasting with Ishmael his malicious murderer.
This sword destroyed all these; that is, God delivered them
not. But God delivered David, delivered him (whoever that
malignant one was) from his sword. And because God
delivered him, he sung this verse to God, as it were his
canticum, σωτήριον. And thus much for the hypothesis,
that is, concerning David.

III. I now come to ourselves.

For as God formerly delivered His servant David, so lately
He delivered His servant James; He delivered both, and
both from the sword, both from the "perilous sword;" so
that this verse may truly be applied to them both, that it

may be rightly sung, both on this day this year, and on this day for every year.

For now the first year is past since on this day, this very day, "strange children" lay in wait for him; "strange chil- ^{Ps. 18. 45.} dren dissembled with him." They enticed him home to their house, they entertained him with all seeming courtesy, moreover they promised some secret thing—vanities and lies all. And so at last, he that was not guilty of wickedness himself and therefore suspecting no evil, him they brought whither they desired, namely, to a place in the very inmost room in the house where that "perilous sword" was. There they set upon him, against the law of hospitality, their guest; nay against a far greater law, for subjects assaulted their King; his retinue was included, the doors bolted: thus they set upon him alone, unarmed, void of all defence and assistance. For then were "strange children" present, who brought forth that sword; true born children, who might interpose their buckler, and if need were, their body too, these were absent, all gone away. What could here be expected but a certain death? Surely my mind trembles to remember how near that sword was brandished, that he even felt its cold iron edge both applied, and more than that, dashed against that sacred breast. What, I say, but certain death, the sword being brandished so near unto him? Even then God freed and delivered him, God Who gives salvation unto Kings, to Kings His servants; even then God freed and delivered him, the King His servant, in the midst of danger, in the very jaws of death; from the midst of danger, from the very jaws of death He saved and delivered him. God Himself, I say, delivered him.

First, by striking that armed man with fear who was ready instructed and appointed to act this great wickedness, so that he neither durst nor could essay any thing. Moreover He changed the mind of that armed man so suddenly, that he who was appointed to do it held back his hand who appointed him thereto, when he would have acted this wickedness. Further yet, by giving present courage, both power and strength sufficient to the King, *ad feralem illam palæstram,* "that the enemy was not able to do him ^{Ps. 89. 22.} violence, that the son of wickedness could not hurt him."

SERM.
XII.

Ps. 37. 15.
Ps. 7. 16.

[Ps. 118.
23.]

2 Sam. 7.
19.

Lastly, by leading those the right way after a marvellous manner through unknown passages, that knew not the place, unacquainted with the way, and by guiding those men who being summoned by the King's outcry hasted on each side towards his relief—men, for this so happy and faithful service, worthy eternal memory; finally, by freeing him both from this first and also from that other sword of the other brother, yet more malignant than the perilous one; and so freeing him that "their sword went through their own heart," and "their mischievousness was turned on their own pate." Thus the King is saved, salvation given to the King, given from heaven, if ever salvation was given from heaven to any, as if God had sent His hand from heaven and brought him help, at once delivering him, and at once overthrowing those perilous cut-throats and killing them with their own "perilous sword." Surely this is no human assistance, not from man. "It is the Lord's doing, and it is marvellous in our eyes," in all men's eyes; and it is wonderful in our ears, in all men's ears; and for this cause, no posterity, no future age, shall pass it in silence.

But this also seemed "a small thing" to God, unless afterward often, and indeed very lately, He had delivered him—for yet it is not a year ago—from a like, yea from a greater, from a far greater danger, not of the sword, but of the perilous powder; an act so horrid, so black, so foul, so accursed, that it is to be cursed with all execrations, that it almost exceeds our belief who yet ourselves have seen it. Later ages sure enough, I think, will scarcely credit it, that ever there were in a man's shape such locusts from the nethermost hell who should devise so hellish practices. Such as was the magnitude of the danger, such shall be the measure of our thanksgiving. And verily that late powder-plot might make us forget this day's deliverance. But far be it from us, for as I said at first, new deliverances are so to be celebrated that old ones are also to be renewed. We shall sing Him His song for that in due season. Now it is enough to mention it.

I will no longer offend your patience, I will finish the remainder in few words.

Therefore as they then sung this song for their King, so

do we now for ours. For salvation is not so like salvation
as is theirs and ours. Nor verily is there any where an example whence we may take a pattern to ourselves, what it
behoves us now to do, so fit for us to imitate, as the manner
and method of this Psalm, nor (do I far digress) of this place
in the Psalm which we have now in hand. David doth two
things, which the Hebrews especially do elegantly express;
he mixes *tehilla* and *tephilla*; that is, petitions with thanks- תהלה
givings, prayers with a song. As soon as he had sung his תפלה
hymn, instantly, with one and the same breath, he said his
prayers. For in the foregoing verse he brought forth his song,
he tuned his strings, takes his lute, sings thus as ye have
heard: "It is He Who gives salvation to Kings; it is He
Who hath delivered David His servant from the perilous
sword." And behold immediately, namely in the following
verse, he lays his lute out of his hand, he falls down on his
knees, betakes himself to his prayers, and there dictates a
prayer for himself and for us in these words: "Save me, and [Ps. 144.
deliver me from the hand of strange children; whose mouth 11.]
talketh of vanity, and their right hand is a right hand of
iniquity." This was the best way for himself and for his
people, whilst he mixed these: and let us imitate his example.
And first, as the ground of our duty requires, let us praise
this preserver of Kings, the deliverer of His servant our King.
Let us praise Him with a new song, in singing with stringed
instruments, with pipes, with wind instruments; with the
best and choicest that our breath, voice, mind, hand, either
hath or can get. For even the best we have is due to this
favour, is due to God for this. Yea, all we have, even the
best things are less than this favour, less than He deserves
for this. But yet let us essay the best we can, to sing something. And herein let "all that is within us," all our "bones" Ps. 103. 1;
confess unto Thee, O Lord, that salvation is Thine, that Thou 35. 10.
givest it, that Thou givest it unto Kings, that Thou hast
given it to our King; and in him, to us all, even to three
kingdoms in one; to one in three. And now, what can we
"say more unto Thee?" For Thou, Lord, knowest Thy ser- 2 Sam. 7.
vants, though we express our minds unworthily; yet in- 20.
wardly in our minds and inmost thoughts we are eternally
bound unto Thee, for this the King's salvation.

SERM.
XII.

Rev. 12. 12.

Ps. 118. 25;
68. 28.

Ps. 17. 7.
P-. 44. 4.
[Ps.18.50.]

Ps. 102. 27.

2 Sam. 18.
32.

Judg. 5. 31.

But yet, because to have once delivered him, it is not enough, nor twice, or thrice, nor seven times, for as long as he lives so long is there this danger from those perilous ones, because all "strange children" are not in a strange land. Some there are in ours, even with us; in regard all the sons of Belial are not yet dead, at least their father Belial is not dead, but yet is alive, yet he devises his mischievous plots no less now than in David's time; no less than any time since David till this day. No less? yea certainly, and more, "because He hath but a short time." Let us also after the manner of our Psalm, lest we stay too long in the song, hang up our lutes a while, and lay them aside for a season; yea let us also kneel down and adjoin our prayers, yea let us also after his example make public prayers; no other than he himself doth make here and in other Psalms. Here, "Save him;" yea "deliver him from strange children;" from "their mouth," "right hand," their "perilous sword." And out of other Psalms, "Save now I beseech Thee, O Lord; O Lord, I beseech Thee send now prosperity." "O God, send forth Thy strength; stablish this good work that Thou hast wrought for us." "Shew Thy marvellous loving-kindness." "Shew great deliverance to Thy King." *Præcipe omnimodam salutem Jacobo.* It is Thou Who hast given salvation, it is Thou Who hast delivered; be Thou always "the same" that Thou art. Always deliver, always save him, always continue these blessings unto us.

But for those that remain — for I much fear that yet some remain — "strange children," what else pray we than as Cushi did for David also, when he was then in like sort delivered from the sword of a son, both his own and a strange one, Absalom : "The enemies of my lord the King and all that rise against him to do him hurt, let them be" as those brothers, brothers in iniquity, mischievous brothers. "So let all Thine enemies perish (the enemies of Thine anointed), O Lord. But those that love Thee (that love him) be as the sun when he goeth forth in his might." That thereby as we, so may our seed enjoy, who under the prosperous success of his reign have possessed, those eight earthly beatitudes in this Psalm, the eight felicities of this life; yea, that ninth also, worth all the rest, of pure religion; I pray God we may long and many years enjoy the same under him in safety, in health, in long life, (which this four years we have done,) yearly paying our vows on this day for this day's sake, for the salvation given on this day; always interlacing this verse in the beginning, in the midst, in the end : " It is He Who gives salvation unto Kings, it is He Who hath delivered" James " His servant from the perilous sword." To Him be honour, praise, glory, thanksgiving, for ever and ever. Amen.

A SERMON

PREACHED

AT THE FUNERAL

OF THE

RIGHT HONOURABLE AND REVEREND FATHER IN GOD

LANCELOT

LATE LORD BISHOP OF WINCHESTER,

IN THE PARISH CHURCH OF ST. SAVIOUR'S IN SOUTHWARK,

ON SATURDAY, BEING THE ELEVENTH OF NOVEMBER,

A.D. MDCXXVI.

BY THE RIGHT REVEREND FATHER IN GOD,

JOHN

LATE LORD BISHOP OF ELY.

A SERMON

PREACHED AT THE

FUNERAL OF THE RIGHT REVEREND FATHER IN GOD,

LANCELOT

LATE LORD BISHOP OF WINCHESTER.

Heb. xiii. 16.

To do good and to distribute forget not; for with such sacrifices God is well pleased.

[*Beneficentiæ autem et communionis nolite oblivisci; talibus enim hostiis promeretur Deus.* Lat. Vulg.]

[*But to do good and communicate forget not; for with such sacrifices God is well pleased.* Eng. Trans.]

In the tenth verse the Apostle saith, " We have an altar, of which they have no right to eat that serve the tabernacle." *Habemus altare,* " We have," that is, Christians. So it is *proprium Christianorum,* ' proper to Christians,' not common to the Jews together with Christians; they have no right to communicate and eat there, that " serve the tabernacle." And yet it is *commune altare,* ' a common altar' to all Christians, they have all right to eat there. And so it is *externum altare,* not only a spiritual altar in the heart of every Christian—then St. Paul should have said *habeo,* or *habet unusquisque,* ' I have,' and ' every Christian hath in private to himself '—but " We have an altar," that is, all Christians have; and it must be external, else all Christians cannot have it.

Our Head, Christ, offered His sacrifice of Himself upon the cross; *Crux altare Christi;* and ' the cross of Christ was the altar' of our Head, where He offered the *unicum, verum, et proprium sacrificium,* ' the only, true, proper sacrifice, propitiatory' for the sins of mankind, in which all other sacrifices are accepted, and applicatory of this propitiation.

1. The only sacrifice, one in itself, and once only offered, that purchased eternal redemption; and if the redemption be eternal what need is there that it should be offered more than once, when once is all-sufficient?

2. And the true sacrifice. All other are but types and representations of this sacrifice; this only hath power to appease God's wrath, and make all other sacrificers and sacrifices acceptable.

[Heb. 10. 5. Ps 40. 6.] 3. And the proper sacrifice : as the Psalm saith, *Corpus aptasti Mihi*, "Thou hast fitted Me with a body;" the Deity assumed the humanity, that It might *accipere a nobis quod offerret pro nobis;* being the Deity could not offer nor be offered to Itself, He took flesh of ours that He might offer for us.

Now as Christ's cross was His altar where He offered Himself for us, so the Church hath an altar also, where it offereth itself; not *Christum in Capite*, but *Christum in membris*, not 'Christ the Head' properly but only by commemoration, but Christ the members. For Christ cannot be offered truly and properly no more but once upon the cross, for He cannot be offered again no more than He can be dead again; and dying and shedding blood as He did upon the cross, and not dying and not shedding blood as in the Eucharist, cannot be one action of Christ offered on the cross, and of Christ offered in the Church at the altar by the priest by representation only, no more than Christ and the Priest are one person : and therefore, though in the cross and the Eucharist there be *idem sacrificatum,* 'the same sacrificed thing,' that is, the body and blood of Christ offered by Christ to His Father on the cross, and received and participated by the communicants in the sacrifice of the altar; yet *idem sacrificium quoad actionem sacrificii,* or *sacrificandi,* 'it is impossible there should be the same sacrifice, understanding by sacrifice the action of sacrifice.' For then the action of Christ's sacrifice, which is long since past, should continue as long as the Eucharist shall endure, even unto the world's end, and His *consummatum est* is not yet finished; and dying and not dying, shedding of blood and not shedding of blood, and suffering and not suffering, cannot possibly be one action; and the representation of an action cannot be the action itself.

And this conceit was unknown to antiquity. All the Fathers held it a sacrifice, only because it is a representation or commemoration of the true sacrifice of Christ upon the cross, even as our Saviour commanded, " Do this in remembrance of Me." St. Augustine saith, *Hujus sacrificii caro et sanguis, ante adventum Christi, per victimas similitudinum promittebatur; in passione Christi, per ipsam veritatem reddebatur; post ascensum Christi, per sacramentum memoriæ celebratur, &c.* And St. Chrysostom, *Hoc est exemplar illius, &c.* And Thomas Aquinas, giving the reason of the divers names given to this sacrament, saith that it hath a triple signification. 1. *Respectu præteriti,* one ' in respect of the time past,' inasmuch as it is commemorative of the Lord's passion, which is called a true sacrifice; and according to this it is called a sacrifice. 2. *Respectu presentis,* ' in respect of the present,' that is, of the unity of the Church, unto which men are gathered by this sacrament, and according to this it is named a communion, or *synaxis,* because by it we communicate with Christ, and are partakers of His Flesh and Deity. 3. *Respectu futuri,* ' in respect of that which is to come,' inasmuch as this sacrament is prefigurative of the fruition of God, which shall be in heaven; and accordingly it is called *viaticum,* because it here furnisheth us in the way that leads us thither. Again, it is called the Eucharist, that is, *bona gratia,* ' the good grace,' because " eternal life is the grace of God;" or else, because it really contains Christ, Who is full of grace. It is also called *metalepsis* or *assumptio,* because by it we assume the Deity of the Son. All this, Part III. Q. lxxiii. Art. 4. *In corpore.* And in his answer *ad tertiam* he addeth, That this sacrament is called a sacrifice inasmuch as it doth represent the passion of Christ; it is likewise called *hostia,* ' an host,' inasmuch as it containeth Christ Himself, who is *Hostia salutaris.*

Here is a representative, or commemorative, and participated sacrifice of the passion of Christ, the true sacrifice, that is past; and here is an eucharistical sacrifice; but for any external proper sacrifice, especially as sacrifice doth sig-

Margin notes:
[Lu.22.19.]
Contra Faustum, lib. 20. 21.
Ad. Hebr. Hom.
Rom. 6. 23.
Eph. 5. 2.

nify the action of sacrificing, here is not one word. And therefore this is a new conceit of latter men, since Thomas' time, unknown to him, and a mere novelism. And the cure is as bad as the disease; though Thomas gives no other reasons why it is called a sacrifice, yet say they, Thomas denieth it not. For that is plainly to confess that this is but a patch added to antiquity. And yet when he saith it is a representative or commemorative sacrifice, *respectu præteriti*, 'in respect of that which is past,' that is, the passion of Christ which was the true sacrifice, he doth deny by consequent that it is the true sacrifice itself which is past. And if Christ be sacrificed daily in the Eucharist, according to the action of sacrifice, and it be one and the same sacrifice offered by Christ on the cross and the priest at the altar, then can it not be a representation of that sacrifice which is past, because it is one and the same sacrifice and action present.

Therefore St. Paul proceeds in the fifteenth verse: "By Him therefore let us offer the sacrifice of praise to God continually, that is, the fruit of our lips giving thanks to His name." "Let us offer up to God." Christians then have an offering. And, "let us offer up to God continually:" this is the ground of the daily sacrifice of Christians, that answereth to the daily sacrifice of the Jews. And this sacrifice of praise and thanks may well be understood the Eucharist, in which we chiefly praise and thank God for this His chief and great blessing of our redemption. And this and all other sacrifices of the Church, external or spiritual, must be offered up and accepted *per Ipsum*, in, by, and through Christ. St. Paul saith not, *Ipsum offeramus*, 'Let us offer Him,' that is, Christ; but, "Let us offer and sacrifice" *per Ipsum*, "by Him," in Whom only we and our sacrifices are accepted. And Romans the twelfth, *Offerte corpora*, "Offer your bodies living sacrifices, holy and acceptable to God, which is your reasonable service." It is not *corpora sine animis*, not 'bodies without souls,' for in them without souls there is no life, no holiness, no accepting; and this is man's "reasonable service," all else is without reason. And St. Peter—the first Pope, as they reckon him, who I am assured had infallibility—saith, "Ye also as lively stones are

[Rom. 12.
1.]

1 Peter 2.
5.

built up a spiritual house, a holy priesthood, to offer up
spiritual sacrifices acceptable to God," *per Jesum Christum*,
" by Jesus Christ." And St. James tells us that to this
end God "begat us by His word of truth," that we might James 1.
be *primitiæ creaturarum;* not offer to God the first-fruits ^18.
of our fields or cattle, but that we might offer up ourselves
as "first-fruits" to God. So all the offerings of the Church
are the Church itself; and Christ the Head offered *corpus
naturale,* ' His natural body,' His soul and flesh for a sacrifice for the ransom and price of our sin, thereby purchasing
" eternal redemption," and by this "one offering He per- Heb. 9. 12.
fected for ever them that are sanctified." Neither doth Heb. 10. 14.
Christ there, that is, in heaven, where He " now appears in Heb. 9.
the presence of God," offer often, or any more for us, but ^24-26.
this once; there is appearing, but no offering. And the
Apostle gives the reason of it : " For then he must have
often suffered since the foundation of the world." He appears in heaven as our High Priest, and makes intercession Heb. 7. 25.
for us; but He offers His natural body no more but once,
because He suffers but once. No offering of Christ, by
St. Paul's rule, without the suffering of Christ : the Priest
cannot offer Christ's natural body without the suffering of
Christ's natural body.

So likewise the Church, which is Christ's mystical body,
offers not Christ's natural body; it hath no power to offer
the natural body, which is proper to Christ only, *Pono ani-* [Joh. 10.
mam et nemo tollit ; not the Church, nor they that are not ^17, 18.]
the Church. And there is no such thing in Scripture, nor
I presume can easily be shewed out of any of the probable
and undoubted Fathers; but the Church offers *corpus mysti-
cum,* ' Christ's mystical body,' that is, itself, to God in her
daily sacrifice.

First, all sacrifice is proper and due only to God. Be S. Aug.
men never so venerable, never so worshipful, yea *adorandi,* Dei, l. 10.
' to be adored' also, yet no man ever offered sacrifice to ^c. 4.
any, unless he knew him or thought him or feigned him
to be God. True angels would never accept sacrifice; and
wicked angels only sought it, because they also affected to
be deified.

In which respect never any priest at the altar, even *super corpus Martyris,* 'over the body or sepulchre of any martyr,' prayed thus, *Offero tibi sacrificium, Petre, Paule, Cypriane,* 'I offer sacrifice to thee, O St. Peter, St. Paul, or St. Cyprian.' All celebrities towards them, whether praises to God for their victories, or exhortations to their imitation, are

only *ornamenta memoriarum,* 'the ornaments of their memories,' not *sacra,* nor *sacrificia mortuorum, tanquam deorum,* 'not the sacred things or sacrifices of the dead, as if they were gods.'

And therefore St. Augustine often denies temples, altars, and sacrifices inward and outward, visible and invisible, to all martyrs and saints, as being proper and peculiar to God only. And I trust prayers and invocation be in this number. For as *orantes et laudantes,* 'praying and praising, we direct our signifying words to Him to Whom we offer the things signified in our hearts; so sacrificing, we know the visible sacrifice is to be offered to no other but to Him Whose invisible sacrifice in our hearts we ourselves ought to be,'

nos esse debemus. And then it followeth in the twentieth chapter: 'The true Mediator, inasmuch as taking upon Him the form of a servant the Man Jesus Christ became a Mediator of God and man, whereas in the form of God He takes sacrifice with His Father, yet in the form of a servant,' *maluit esse quam sumere,* 'He chose rather to be a sacrifice than to receive sacrifice, lest even by this occasion any man might think he might sacrifice to a creature. By this (nature) He is a Priest, the same the offerer, and the same the thing offered.' *Cujus rei sacramentum,* 'of which things He would have the daily sacrifice of the Church to be a sacrament,' *quæ cum Ipsius Capitis corpus sit, seipsam per Ipsum discit offerre;* 'which Church being the body of our Head Himself, doth learn to offer itself, that is, the Church by Him, that is, by Christ.' Here the body of the Head is the mystical body of Christ, and therefore the daily sacrifice of the Church is not the natural body of Christ, but the mystical body that offers itself to God by Christ. This made St. Augustine to say of angels, and elect and

glorious saints, *Nec illis sacrificemus, sed cum illis sacrificium Deo simus,* 'Let us not sacrifice to them, but let us be a sacrifice to God together with them.'

But a singular and full place we have in the same tenth [Lib. 10. book and sixth chapter. Where, having shewed what sacri-^{6.]} fice is, that is, every work which is performed, that we may cleave to God in a holy society, being referred to that end of good, by which we may be truly blessed; (as a man consecrated to the name of God, and dying to the world that he may live to God, is a sacrifice; as the body chastened by temperance, is a sacrifice, such as the Apostle calls for, "Offer up your bodies to be a living sacrifice;" and if the Rom. 12. 1. body, the servant and instrument of the soul, much more the soul itself is a sacrifice; as likewise works of mercy and the like;) hence, saith he, it cometh to pass, *ut tota ipsa redempta civitas societasque sanctorum universale sacrificium offeratur Deo, &c.,* 'that the whole redeemed city and society of the Saints is offered up an universal sacrifice to God by our great Priest; Who also offered Himself in His passion for us, that we might be the body of so great a Head, in the form of a servant. For this He offered, in this He was offered, because according to this He is our Mediator, in this our Priest, in this our sacrifice.' And then urging again the Apostle's words, of offering our "bodies a living Rom. 12. 1. sacrifice, holy and acceptable to God, which is our reasonable service" of Him, he adds, *Quod totum sacrificium ipsi nos sumus,* 'all which whole sacrifice we are;' we the members are this whole sacrifice, not Christ the Head. For as in the body there are many members, and many offices of those members, so "we being many, are one body in Christ, [Rom. 12. and every one members one of another," having "divers ^{5, 6.]} gifts according to the grace given us." *Hoc est sacrificium* [S. Aug. *Christianorum, multi unum corpus sumus in Christo,* 'this is ^{ubi sup.]} the sacrifice of Christians, many are one body in Christ.' This must necessarily be the mystical body of Christ, the natural body it cannot be: *Quod etiam Sacramento altaris* [Ibid.] *fidelibus noto frequentat Ecclesia; ubi ei demonstratur, quod in illá oblatione quam offert ipsa offeratur;* 'Which sacrifice the Church also frequents in the Sacrament of the altar, well known to the faithful, in which it is demonstrated to the Church, that in that oblation which the Church offers, the Church itself is offered.' I hope the Church is the mystical body of Christ, not the natural. *Ipsum vero sacri-* Lib. 22 c. 10.

ficium corpus est Christi, quod non offertur ipsis, quia hoc sunt et ipsi; denying temples, altars, and sacrifices to martyrs and saints, he saith, ' The sacrifice itself is the body of Christ, which is not offered to them, because they are also this sacrifice.' This may suffice to satisfy any reasonable man of the sacrifice of the Church in St. Augustine's judgment : yet give me leave to add one place more because it may stand for many, and that is, lib. 10. cap. 31. *Nec jubent, &c.* 'Neither do they command that we should sacrifice to them, but only to Him, Whose sacrifice we together with them ought to be'—a sacrifice, *ut sæpe dixi, et sæpe dicendum est,* ' as I have often said, and must often say.'

This then is the daily sacrifice of the Church in St. Augustine's resolute judgment, even the Church itself, the universal body of Christ, not the natural body, whereof the Sacrament is an exemplar and a memorial only, as hath been shewed. And when they shall prove the Church's sacrifice to be the natural body of Christ, and the same sacrifice with the sacrifice of the cross, as it denoteth the action of sacrificing, because the Fathers often use the word *corpus Christi,* ' the body of Christ,' they shall be further answered.

In the meantime the Church of England in her reformed Liturgy—offering " ourselves, our souls, and bodies to be a living sacrifice, holy and acceptable to God, which is our reasonable service of Him"—may truly and boldly say, that in this she hath far exceeded their canon of their Mass, in which there is not one syllable that mentions the sacrifice of ourselves and souls and bodies, which is the only thing that God looks and calls for at our hands, and in Christ our Head is most pleasing; nay more, only pleasing to Him, and in our power to offer properly.

We deny not then the daily sacrifice of the Church, that is, the Church itself, warranted by Scriptures and Fathers. We take not upon us to sacrifice the natural body of Christ otherwise than by commemoration, as Christ Himself and St. Paul doth prescribe. They rather that take a power never given them over the natural body of Christ, which once offered by Himself purchased eternal redemption allsufficient for sin, to offer it again and often, never thinking of the offering of Christ's mystical body, the Church, that is ourselves, our souls and bodies—they I say do destroy the daily sacrifice of Christians, which is most acceptable to God.

Now then that which went before in the Head, Christ, on the cross, is daily performed in the members, in the Church. Christ there offered Himself once for us; we daily offer ourselves by Christ, that so the whole mystical body of Christ in due time may be offered to God.

This was begun in the Apostles in their Liturgy, of whom it is said *Ministrantibus illis,* "While they ministered and prayed the Holy Ghost said unto them," &c. Erasmus reads it, *Sacrificantibus illis,* "While they sacrificed and prayed." If they had offered Christ's natural body, the Apostles would surely have made some mention of it in their writings, as well as they do of the commemorative sacrifice. The word is λειτουργούντων· so it is a Liturgical sacrifice, or a sacrifice performed or offered in our Liturgy or form of God's worship; so the offering of ourselves, our souls, and bodies, is a part of divine worship. Acts 13. 2.

Now as it is not enough to feed our own souls, unless we also feed both the souls and bodies of the poor, and there is no true fast unless we distribute that to the poor which we deny to our own bellies and stomachs; and there cannot be a perfect and complete adoration to God in our devotions, unless there be also doing good and distributing to our neighbours; therefore to the sacrifice of praise and thanksgiving in the Eucharist in the Church, mentioned in the fifteenth verse, we must also add beneficence and communication in this text; for, *Devotio debetur Capiti, beneficentia membris,* 'The sacrifice of devotion is due to our Head, Christ, and piety and charity is due to the members.' So then, offer the sacrifice of praise to God daily in the Church, as in the fifteenth verse: and distribute and communicate the sacrifice of compassion and alms to the poor out of the Church, as in this text.

Shall I say *extra Ecclesiam,* 'out of the Church?' I do not say amiss if I do say so; yet I must say also *intra Ecclesiam;* this should be a sacrifice in the Church, the Apostles kept it so in their time. *Primo die,* "the first day of the week," when they came together to pray and to break bread, St. Paul's rule was, *separet unusquisque,* "let every one set apart" or "lay by in store, as God hath prospered him, that there be no gatherings when I come." And our Liturgy in the offertory tenders her prayers and alms on the Lord's day or Sunday, as a part of the sacrifice or service of that day, and of God's worship; which I wish were more carefully observed among us. For this also is a Liturgy or office, so called by the Apostle, ἡ διακονία τῆς λειτουργίας, "the administration of this service," or "office," or "Liturgy;" there is the word "Liturgy" and "office." For the daily service and sacrifice not only supplieth the want of the saints, but is abundant also by many thanksgivings unto God. So the Lord's day, or Sunday, is then best kept and observed, when to our prayers and praises and sacrifices of ourselves, our souls and bodies, we also add the sacrifice of our goods and alms, and other works of mercy to make it up perfect and complete, that there may be *opus diei in die suo,* "the work of the day in the proper day thereof," and these two sacrifices of praise and alms, joined here by God and His Apostle, may never be parted by us in our lives and practice.

First then we see, that as our Saviour first preached in the mount, and then healed in the cities and towns, so when we have offered ourselves, our souls, and bodies, to be living and spiritual sacrifices in the Church unto God, by our High Priest Christ, we must not rest there, but must also offer our goods and alms, whether in the Church or out of the Church, to the relief of the poor members of Christ that are in want. And that these two, 1. the sacrifice of praise, 2. and the sacrifice of alms may appear to be indivisible and inseparable, insomuch that he that will give himself, his soul, and body to God, will never spare also to give his goods to those that suffer hunger, and thirst, and nakedness—see how our Apostle joins these two. 1. First, *Per Ipsum offeramus,* "By Christ our High Priest, let us offer ourselves;" 2. and lest that should be thought to be all the whole sacrifice that man is to tender to his God, He adds this second, with a *Nolite oblivisci,* by a kind of negative, which is many times more forcible than an ordinary affirmative, "To do good and to distribute forget not;" fearing,

as it were, lest when man had done his homage and fealty
to God, of whom he holds in chief, he might think that
were enough to sacrifice to God in the church on the Lord's
day, and then forget his brother all the week after, and
never to take compassion on him; whereas the truth is,
Unus amor, but *duplex objectum*, 'the love is but one' wherewith we love God for Himself, and our brother who is God's
image for His sake, as there be two eyes, yet but one visual
faculty. For as it is to no purpose to learn our duty at the
mouth of God's preachers on the Lord's day, and never to
put it in practice all our week or life following, as if it were
a matter only for the brain and understanding, whereas in
truth first it should edify our faith and then fructify in our
lives; so it is a very short love to profess to love God Whom
we have not seen, and starve our poor brethren, who lie at
our gates in such sort that we cannot choose but see them.

I. So then the words contain first, an act *beneficentiæ et* The divi-
communionis, " to do good and to distribute;" and that must sion.
needs be a great work, for it is " to do good," and nothing I.
is truly great but that which is good. II. A caveat, *Nolite* II.
oblivisci, it is a work of great consequence, very important
to our salvation, it may not be forgotten. III. How small III.
or vile it may seem in itself, yet it is of a high rate and
great esteem ; *sacrificia sunt, et talia sunt*, 'they are sacrifices, and sacrifices of much price,' though they be but
crumbs of bread or drops of water, and so much the more
precious because they are grateful to God. *Delectatur*, or
placatur Deus, " God is pacified," or " God is well pleased;"
and all the world is well given to appease and pacify His
wrath, and gain His favour.

Now the work is comprised in two words, *beneficentia et
communicatio*, " beneficence and distribution." Beneficence
or bounty, that is *affectio cordis*, 'the affection and compassion of the heart;' and communication and distribution,
that is *opus manuum*, 'the work of the hand.' And these
two may be no more divided than the two other sacrifices,
of devotion in the sacrifice of ourselves, and charity in the
relief of the poor; for beneficence is *ut fons*, 'as the fountain' and spring or cistern, whence all works of compassion
do arise, and distribution is *ut rivuli*, 'as the rivers' or chan-

nels or pipes, by which the waters of comfort and goodness are carried to hungry souls.

Beneficence is as the sun, distribution is as the light that proceeds from the sun. At the beneficence of the heart, there we must begin; and by the distribution and communication of the hand, there is the progress. And it is not enough that our heart is charitable and full of compassion, if we be cluster-fisted and close-handed, and give nothing. [Jas. 2. 15, 16.] " Go and be warm;" and, " Go and be fed;" and, " Go and be clothed;" they be *verba compassionis,* ' words of compassion;' but if we do not as well feed and clothe as our tongue blesseth, we may have gentle hearts like Jacob's voice, but our hands will be cruel and hairy like Esau's, that vowed to kill his brother.

And true religion is no way a gargleism only, to wash the tongue and mouth, to speak good words; it must root in the heart and then fructify in the hand, else it will not cleanse the whole man.

Now God only is good, and the universal good of all things, and goodness itself. If there be any good in man, it is particular, not universal, and it is *participatum;* man is not good in himself, but only by participation; goodness in God is *essentia,* ' essence and being,' and He is so goodness that He cannot be but goodness, good in Himself and good of Himself.

In man goodness is *accidens,* ' an accident,' and such an accident as most commonly he is devoid of it, but only by the grace and likeness of God; so that man is good *sola similitudine bonitatis divinæ,* ' only by the similitude and imitation of the divine good;' the nearer to God the nearer to goodness, and the further from God the more removed from all goodness. So that as in every good the greatest good is most desired, so in doing good that is ever best that joins us most to our greatest good.

1. All creatures are said to be good by the goodness of God, *ut principio,* ' as the principal and efficient cause' of all good;
2. 2. *ut exemplari,* ' as the pattern and exemplar,' and idea, ac-
3. cording to which all good things are fashioned; 3. *ut fine,* ' as the end and final cause' for which all things were made.

And the like is in this beneficence and doing of good.

For first, it must be good *a causâ,* 'in regard of the first 1. and efficient cause,' which is God, as the good fruit proceeds from the good tree, and the tree owes his goodness to God That transplants and waters it. 2. It must be good *in* 2. *fundamento,* 'in respect of the foundation,' as the house and the living stones and spiritual buildings are therefore good, because they are built upon the immoveable foundation, the rock Christ. And 3. it must be good *a fine,* 'from the end,' 3. to which it is referred ; it takes beginning from the Holy Ghost and the riches of grace, and it must be directed only to the supreme and grand end of all things, God's glory and the relief of the poor members of Christ.

And these two, beneficence and communication, the eminent and imperated acts of true religion, the mother of all virtue, they are also the acts of many other particular virtues. For first, they are the acts of charity, because they proceed 1. from the love of God ; 2. they are the acts of justice, because 2. relief and sustentation is the due debt that is owing to the poor ; 3. they are the acts of liberality and bounty, because 3. the free gift of men, not the merit of the needy ; 4. they 4. are the acts of mercy, because they participate with the wants and miseries of the afflicted.

So that as *impendere* is *bonitatis,* "to do good and distribute," and bestow is the act of goodness ; so likewise *rependere,* to pay them where we owe them is *justitiæ,* 'the work of justice.' And therefore our goods, they are not properly ours in such sort that we can carry them with us when we go hence, but they are *bona pauperum,* so our goods that they are also the goods of the poor, whereof we are rather stewards than proprietaries and lords; and he that so keeps and hoards them that he doth not expend them to buy the kingdom of heaven with them at the hands of the poor, (*Ipsorum est regnum,*) he doth indeed *detinere alienum,* he [Mat. 5. 3.] defrauds the poor, 'and detains that which is another's.' And therefore the Psalm saith, *Dispersit, dedit pauperibus,* Ps. 112. 9. *justitia ejus manet in æternum;* "He hath dispersed and given to the poor, His righteousness endures for ever ;" not His mercy only, but His justice also.

Where, by the way, observe that there it is first, *Dispersit, dedit,* "He dispersed and gave to the poor." Here in the text that lies before me this day it is *Dedit, dispersit,* He gave it, and then he dispersed it to the poor, in such sort that he did as it were study how to disperse it to all sorts of poor, even as many kinds of poor as he could devise and find fit to receive it, learned, old men, widows, children and prisoners, and the like.

And this goodness, whether we understand it plainly as the intention of the heart that doth the good, and the works of the hand that distributes and divides it ; or whether we understand it as some do, that there is *beneficentia in iis quæ dantur,* ' beneficence in those things that are given,' and *communicatio in iis quæ servantur,* ' communication in those things that we give not,' because in these times *omnia erant communia,* " all things were in common," and so they did communicate even those things which they did not communicate and distribute ; this goodness, I say, hath two properties of true goodness : first, it is *diffusivum sui,* ' diffusive of itself,' it imparts itself to as many as it can, it heaps not all upon one, as those do that rob all others that they may enrich their heir ; secondly, it is *unitivum Deo et proximo,* ' it is unitive, and unites us to God,' for whose sake we do it, ' and to our neighbour,' to whom we do it.

[Acts 2. 44.]

1.

2.

[Hor. Od. 3. 24. 35, 36.]
And surely as in the civil states, *Quid leges sine moribus vanæ proficiunt?* ' What will the best laws profit us, if there be no obedience, no manners ?' are they not altogether vain, of less force than spiders' webs ? And in Christianity, *Quid fides sine operibus?* ' What will faith and knowledge profit us, if it fructify not in life and works ?' what can devotion and justice profit, if alms follow not ? He that will send an embassage to God that shall surely speed, he must send sighs from his heart, tears from his eyes, prayers from his mouth, and also alms from his hands, and they will prove of that force that God cannot deny them.

And if we will take with us the resolution of the learned, out of the form of the last judgment, it will amount to thus much, that not only *peccata commissionis,* ' sins of commission,' or sins committed will condemn us, but also *peccata omissionis,* ' sins of omission,' or omission of doing good, as not feeding and clothing the poor, will cast us into hell ; and *auferre aliena et non dare sua,* ' to take other men's goods from them' either by force or fraud, 'and not to give our own' to the poor, both are damnable, though not in the same degree. And therefore our Saviour's counsel is well worth the learning: " Make you friends of unrighteous Lu. 16. 9. Mammon, that when you shall fail, they may receive you into everlasting tabernacles." And these external gifts, they are the *viaticum* or viands to carry us to heaven ; for though *non hîc cœlum,* 'heaven be not here' in this life, yet *hîc quæritur cœlum,* here in this life heaven is to be sought, and here it is either found or lost. So then, shall we fast from meat and not from sin ? shall we pray, and rob the poor ? shall our tongue praise charity, and our hands spoil those that need our charity ? God forbid !

And now, most glorious Bounty, and Communication, and Distribution, what shall I say of thee, but that thou art *vita sanctorum,* 'the very life, and joy, and delight of all saints ?' And when saints must leave this life, and all things else leave them, and they leave all things, yet thou leavest them not, but art *comes defunctorum,* ' the inseparable companion of the dying.' For of all that a man hath, there is nothing that shall accompany him to the tribunal of the great Judge of the quick and the dead but *peccata et bona opera,* 'sins and good works;' and then it will appear that the voice of a few good works, done for Christ's sake, will speak louder, and plead harder and more effectually for us, than all our glorious words and professions.

And this doing good and distributing is not only profit-able, but admirable also. For why ? By evils and wants of others itself is bettered, and it becomes beautiful by the uncleanness and nastiness of the wretched; it is enriched by others' poverty, by others' infirmities it grows strong, the bearing of burdens attols and lifts it up, and therein of all other it is happy, *de spinis colligit uvas;* it does that which Christ denies to be feasible, it gathers "grapes of thorns," [Mat. 7. and sweetest consolation out of greatest miseries; and that [16.] which is contrary to all nature and natural reason, *ex agro sterilissimo paupertatis messem copiosissimam colligit,* ' out of the most barren fields of poverty it reaps the most plentiful harvest.' And herein are these two virtues most to be ad-mired : *misericordia miseriam aliorum facit nostram,* 'mercy

makes other men's miseries and calamities to be our own;'
and *charitas facit bona nostra proximorum,* 'charity makes
our goods to be our neighbours'.'

If a travelling man were heavy-laden, were it not a great
and happy ease for him if his fellow-traveller would bear
part of his burden? And *divitiæ onus,* 'riches is a heavy
load,' it presses down many so much that they are never
able to climb up to heaven. What is then to be done?
Da partem comiti, 'give thy companion,' the poor man, 'a
part with thee,' thou shalt refresh him that is weary of
his wants, and thyself shalt run most lightly and nimbly
to heaven gates.

And now if thou wilt do as my text teacheth—that is,
"to do good and distribute"—yet take these few rules in
the way, they will make thee to make the more and better
1. speed. First, do it voluntarily, willingly, not by compulsion,
as if it were a grievous tax or seize; for God more regards
[Mark 12. 42.] thy affection than thy gift, the widow's two mites more
than great heaps of treasure. And why? God is *ponderator
spirituum, non panis aut monetæ,* 'God is a weigher of spirits
2. rather than of bread and money.' 2. Do it *hilariter,* 'cheerfully;' for thou well knowest what God loves most, that is,
[2 Cor. 9. 7.] "a cheerful giver." He doth not respect *quid,* what it is
that thou givest, but *ex quanto,* the cheerful heart it comes
3. from. 3. Do it *affabiliter,* 'with kind words and fair language,' not of a weariness to be rid of a beggar, as the un-
[Lu. 18. 3—5.] just judge righted the importunate widow, but out of compassion to relieve him. And certainly when there is *pietas
in re,* 'compassion and piety in the deed,' *non sit in verbis
contumelia,* 'though thou give him good counsel, yet load
him not with reproaches and contumelies,' upbraid him not
with his wants or diseases, for God might have turned the
tables, and made him as rich as Abraham and thee as poor
4. and infirm as Job or Lazarus. 4. Do it *festinanter,* 'speedily;'
[Ps. 41. 1.] for "blessed is he that considers the poor and needy," and
prevents his petition; for this is indeed to give twice, to give
quickly; to have his money or his bread prepared and ready
at his hand, as more ready to give than they to ask; and
this is indeed *quærere pauperes quibus benefacias,* 'to seek
and search for poor to whom thou mayest do good.' And

know withal, that Abraham's speed to entertain Christ and
His Angels made *sinum Abrahæ receptaculum Lazari,* 'Abraham's bosom to be the receptacle and place of rest to Lazarus,' as well as Lazarus' patience advanced him to Abraham's
bosom. And 5. do it *humiliter,* 'in all humility,' *ut eluas* 5.
peccatum, non ut corrumpas judicem, "to redeem thine own
sins by thine own alms," as Daniel said to Nebuchadnezzar, [Dan. 4.
but 'not to corrupt thy judge,' that thou mayest sin more ²⁷·]
freely, more securely. For God is like to hear the loudest
cry; and it may be the cry of thy sin may decry or cry
down thine alms, and the scale of sin may make thine alms
to be found too light.

Again, take I beseech you these things into your consideration. First, *Quis petit?* 'Who it is that asks an alms 1.
of thee?' Thou takest it to be the poor man, but thou mis-
takest it; it is *Deus in paupere, et Christus in paupere,* 'God
thy Creator, and Christ thy Redeemer in the poor man.'
And dost thou hoard up for thy wife, or thy child, or thy
servant, that will spend it in riot, *et negas Creatori vel Re-
demptori,* 'and dost thou deny to God thy Creator, and
Christ thy Redeemer' That bought thee with His own blood
and life?

Secondly, *Quid petit?* 'What it is that He doth ask?' 2.
In short, *Suum non tuum,* He asks not thine, thou hast only
the use and dispose of it, but He asks His own, and "what [1 Cor.
hast thou that thou hast not received," even to thyself, thy ⁴· ⁷·]
soul, and thy body, all the gifts of nature, and all the gifts
of grace? And when all is said, this is indeed all, *Da quod
dedi,* 'Give Me that I first gave thee,' a fruit of Mine own
tree, I bestowed it on thee; *Da et reddam,* 'Give Me' but
some crumbs, some drops out of thy heap, out of thy fountain, 'I will repay it;' nay, *Da et debitor ero,* 'Give Me any
part, I will become a debtor to thee' upon My word and promise to repay it in heaven.

Thirdly, *Ad quid,* 'To what purpose' doth God ask thee 3.
by the poor man? to gain it to Himself? No, *ad mutu-
andum,* only 'to borrow' of thee; and be assured He is
the best pay-master, He will restore to thee a hundred-
fold. And wilt thou lend to a Jew or a Turk for ten or
eight in the hundred, *et Deo non accommodas,* 'and wilt

thou not lend' to thy Creator and Redeemer, Who will give an "everlasting weight of glory" for thy crumbs and drops.

4. And fourthly, *Quid daturus Qui petit,* 'What will He give thee, That now begs of thee?' For thy broken bread and meat He will make thee partaker of the feast of the Lamb, and for a few drops of water He will crown thee in the kingdom of glory; *pro poculo aquæ frigidæ torrens voluptatis,* 'for a cup of cold water'—water, the common element, and cold water, that cost thee not the charge of a fire to warm it—'there is a torrent,' nay, a very sea of all pleasures provided for thee for all eternity.

"Do good then and distribute," but do it *manibus propriis,* 'with thine own hands,' if thou canst spare it; not by other men's hands, which may die soon after thee, or else deceive thy trust. *Lucerna in manibus, non a tergo,* 'Hang not thy light at thy back to shine after thy death, but carry it in thy hand;' be executor of thine own will. And do it *secreto,* 'in secret,' without a trumpet; the seed must be buried or harrowed under the earth, else it neither roots nor multiplies; which though *perdi videtur,* 'it seem to be lost,' yet, unless it be thus sowed and buried, *re verâ perditur,* 'it will be lost indeed;' and the more thou sowest the more thou shalt reap, for "he that sows sparingly shall reap sparingly."

II. And now, in the second place, mark the caution; *Nolite oblivisci,* "To do good and to distribute forget not." Offer the sacrifice of praise daily; and if daily, it is likely enough to be remembered, because it is never forgotten, never omitted in the Church, whither thou art put as to the school of memory. This is but lip-labour, or at the most but a heart-labour, it costs nothing but breath; but to give alms, to "do good, and to distribute," that costs more; it will put thee to the charge of bread and water, and clothes, and the like, which is chargeable and burdensome. Any thing but our purses. No, that must not be left out neither; to "do good, and to distribute," to rob thine own back and thy belly to feed the hungry and clothe the naked, *nolite oblivisci;* forget not to add this sacrifice of alms to that other of devotion and praise.

And surely I may call this the chapter of remembrances, or the remembrancer's chapter. In the second verse, *Memento hospitalitatis*, "Forget not to be hospitable;" Abraham entertained Angels, yea, the Son of God, the Lord of Angels, by his hospitality. In the third verse, *Memento vinctorum et afflictorum laborantium*, "Remember those that are in bonds and afflicted, being yourselves in bonds and adversity together with them;" for as *Christus pascitur in iis*, so *incarceratur*, as 'Christ is fed in the poor,' so 'He is imprisoned' with them that are in bonds, and exiled with His exiled members, and condemned to the mines with those that are chained in the mines; and it is an impossibility to banish the Head from His members, in whom He lives, and they in Him. In the eighth verse, *Memento præpositorum*, "Remember your governors, that have the rule over you;" you owe much to them that have sown in you the word of God, whose faith is a light or example to you. So here, "To do good and to distribute forget not." The rest are particulars, hospitality to strangers, visitation to prisoners, comfort to the persecuted, and sustentation to our spiritual governors; but this is general and extends to all, strangers, prisoners, persecuted, governors, and all other men in need in general, though with a *præcipue*, "chiefly, to the household of faith." For every man is our neighbour to whom charity is to be extended, but they are more nearly our neighbours to whom we stand bound by a double obligation and fraternity, of nature and grace.

[Heb. 13. 2.]

[Gal. 6. 10.]

Why then is our Apostle so solicitous that we "forget not" this "doing good and distributing?" A man would think the precept need not be so strictly urged and inculcated, and that in the negative which binds *semper et ad semper*, and therefore never to be forgotten. The moralist gives a good rule: *Homo in homine calamitoso misericors meminit sui*, 'That man that is merciful to a man in misery and calamity remembers himself;' he might have been in misery and need, as well as his afflicted neighbour, if God had so disposed. Is it such a matter to be so much and so often inculcated? Can a man forget himself? or can any man think that that which falls to another man might not fall upon him? Equal in nature and grace may also be equal in misery, if God will. Yes surely there is need, for he that beheld his face in the glass, he went away, *et statim oblitus est*, "straightway he forgetteth" his own shape, his own spots and deformities, amends none of them, never thinks on them more till he comes to the glass again; be the glass never so true, never so pure, even as pure as the word of God itself, yet so often as he comes so often he forgets: therefore nothing is more needful than this not forgetting.

And the truth is, most men are like to the young man that said to our Saviour Christ, "All these things," the commandments of God, *custodivi ab adolescentiâ*, "have I kept from my youth;" but yet he had not so strictly kept God's commandments but that withal *custodivit bona omnia a pauperibus*, 'he had more strictly kept all his goods from the poor;' and because he had great substance, and loved it greatly, he had need to be remembered with, *Nolite oblivisci*, "Forget not to do good and distribute;" for he was *custos pecuniæ potius quam præcepti*, he was a keeper, but 'a keeper of money,' and no keeper but a breaker of the commandments.

The rich man and all his fellows have need of this, "For-
get not:" he saw Lazarus "full of sores," from the crown of the head to the sole of the foot, and the very sight of him was *conflatorium pietatis*, 'the very bellows' and anvil 'of compassion;' and he lay at his gate, he could neither go in nor out but he must look upon him, yet *obliviscitur quod vidit*, 'he forgot him that he saw' and could not choose but
see him; nay, he saw the "dogs" more merciful in "licking his sores" than himself was in curing or feeding him; and therefore *non accepit guttam aquæ*, 'he received not one drop of water' "to cool his tongue." (He was a great but a most miserable professor, and therefore his tongue was most tormented, because therein consisted all his religion.) And the reason is, because *non dedit micam panis*, 'he would not give him' so much as he gave his dogs, 'not one crumb of bread.'

There be some that say, *Quando Te vidimus esurientem, nudum, &c.?* "When did we see Thee hungry or naked?" Peradventure they never saw Him in His own person, *in*

capite, as a particular man, 'the Head,' but they could not
but see Him *in membris,* 'in His members,' the poor; *vident
pauperem,* but *Christum in paupere non vident,* 'they saw the
poor man, but Christ they saw not in the poor man.' Here
is great need of this *Nolite oblivisci,* Forget not to put them
in mind, that they flatter not themselves with this ambiguity.
Te et Te totum, they see not the man Jesus, the Head alone,
but they cannot choose but see whole Christ, that is, Christ
the Head and the poor His members.

There is one, and I would there were but one, that re- Mat. 25. 18.
ceived a talent and hid it in a napkin under the earth: he
was worthy to hear, *Serve nequam,* "Evil servant," for he
knew his Master's will, That gave His talents to "receive
them with increase;" his memory failed and had need to be
rubbed with *oblitus tradere usurariis,* he forgot that which
he did not forget; he forgot not to take usury for his money,
and use upon use, but he forgot the true and lawful usury,
to "give it to the poor," and so to "lend it to the Lord," [Pro. 19.
Who would surely have paid both principal and interest also; 17.]
both the substantial reward of eternal life, and also the acci-
dental degree and measure of glory.

How many are there that forget the preacher's precept,
"Cast thy bread upon the waters." How many are there Eccl. 11. 1.
that say, "My barns are too little, I will pull them down Lu. 12. 18.
and build bigger." Who have been at the school of forget-
fulness, and do not remember, *quod ventres pauperum capiunt
quod horrea non capiunt,* 'that the bellies of the poor are
greater than the greatest barns,' and will receive and consume all that which the greatest barns cannot hold; yea
the poor do so multiply that the rich are not able to feed
them. The foolish rich man said in the Gospel, "Soul, Lu. 12. 19.
thou hast much goods laid up in store for many years;"
but when he said so he had not many hours to reckon, to
"eat and drink and take his pleasure." *Male recondita
melius erogata,* 'They were ill laid up, they had been much
better distributed and scattered abroad.'

It may be they may pass all the degrees of comparison:
male parta, 'ill gotten' by oppression and fraud and rapine;
and *pejus detenta,* 'worse kept and detained'—that which is
ill gotten may be worse kept; and so that is that is scraped

and extorted from all others, is denied to all others, and most of all to himself, and God, and Christ; and *pessime erogata,* 'expended worst of all,' in riot and excess, in pride and vanity, in cruelty and rebellion, in denying maintenance to the King and country, or to the poor.

But howsoever ill gotten, worse imprisoned and debarred the light of the sun; and worst of all so spent, that with them the soul and life and heaven itself is spent and lost; yet the truth is, they are then best kept when they are well expended, and never better than on the poor afflicted members of Christ, than in buying of heaven. But if you will make a true conjunction indeed, they are then *bene recondita* when *bene erogata,* 'well stored and laid up when they are well laid out.' *Reconde in sinu pauperum,* 'The best house to lay them up is to put them into the box and bosom of the poor,' for that indeed is the safest and surest treasury, safer than the temple itself, the living temples of God; a treasury *sine fure, sine verme,* 'without thief, without worm;' whatsoever is put there *defertur Deo,* the poor man 'will carry it to God,' out of Whose hands it can never be taken.

And this is indeed the art of arts. Not the gold-making juggling-art, which under the name of gold-making is the consumer of gold, but the art of turning earth into heaven, and earthly alms into celestial riches; *dando cœlestes fiunt,* 'these transitory earthly things procure us the unspeakable riches and treasures of heaven.' And now consider, Cornelius' "alms and prayers ascended as a memorial to God," and procured the great grace of the knowledge of Christ, and the gift of the Holy Ghost; and Dorcas' alms obtained her resurrection to life; God remembered them both, and shall we "forget to do good and distribute" our alms, which have that force that God will never forget them? Acts 10. 4. [Acts 9. 39—41.]

III. God cannot forget them, if we do remember and perform them; nay God holds them at a great rate, He accepts them as sacrifices, and such sacrifices as both pacify and please Him. *Talibus sacrificiis,* "with such sacrifices God is pleased;" *talibus,* with these of praise and alms, and with all those that are like or of the same nature with these. Not with the sacrifices of nature and Moses' law: such are both *mortua* and *mortifera,* 'dead' in themselves, and 'mor-

tiferous' and deadly to all that shall use them. These had
their time, and were accepted as types and figures of the
true sacrifice of Christ upon the cross, in Whom all sacrifices
were accepted; in which they were partakers of Christ, and
" did eat the same spiritual meat, and drink the same spiri- [1 Cor. 10.
tual drink," that we now eat and drink by faith, "and the ⁴·]
rock that followed them was Christ."

No more then to do with the sacrifice *pecoris trucidati*, 'of
the slain beasts'—that is past; but *cordis contriti*, with the
sacrifice of a broken and ' contrite heart'—that was from the
beginning, and so shall continue acceptable to God even to
the end; the spiritual sacrifice, or the sacrifice of the soul
and spirit, that is it which God ever accepted in the sacrifice
of His Son Christ, even from the first Adam to the last son
of Adam, the last man that shall live at the last day. And
God hath been and is weary of carnal and external sacrifice,
and neglected yea rejected it for default and want of the
inward sacrifice; but of this inward and spiritual sacrifice,
God will never be wearied with it.

In vocal prayer and fasting, and outward alms, and the
like, there may be *nimium*, ' too much,' but of inward prayer
and fasting from sin, and compassion and mercy, there can
never be *nimium*, ' too much;' nay not *satis*, not ' enough;'
for God calls for all, and all we are not able to perform
which we owe. So then the *sacrificia* must be *talia*, " such
sacrifices," that is, spiritual.

And they be *sacrificia*, in the plural number, " sacrifices:"
the sacrifice representative or memorial of Christ's sacrifice,
the Eucharist, which is truly the sacrifice of praise; and the
daily sacrifice of ourselves, our souls and bodies, in devotion
and adoration to God. And the sacrifice of mercy and alms
— both here recorded — these be the sacrifices here mentioned that please God; and all others not here mentioned
that are included in the *talibus*, in such like sacrifices God
is pleased.

And be the number of them as great as any man please
to make them, yet because they are all reducible to three, I
will comprise them in the number of three. First, *sacri*- 1.
ficium cordis contriti, ' the sacrifice of the contrite and broken
heart,' as before, which we tender to God in our repentance

FUNERAL and sighs and tears for our sins. The second, *sacrificium*
SERM.
2. *cordis grati,* 'the sacrifice of the thankful heart,' in praise
[Heb. 13. and thanksgiving to God, called here the "sacrifice of praise."
15.]
3. The third, *sacrificium cordis pii,* 'the sacrifice of a pious and
merciful heart,' in compassion and works of mercy and alms-
deeds, called here "doing good and distributing."

All these and every one of these, which are indeed but the
variations or divers affections of one and the same heart,
they are the *talia sacrificia,* "such sacrifices" which God
[S. Bern. accepts. St. Bernard was a skilful confectioner, he made
de divers.
87. al. 52. three rare and most odoriferous ointments of them, most
6.]
1. pleasing unto God Himself: the first, *unguentum contritionis,*
'the ointment of contrition,' made of the sighs of the heart
and the tears of the eyes, the confession and prayers of the
tongue, the revenge, the judgment and execution done upon
our own souls for our sins; and this compunction of heart,
though it be all made of bitter and sharp poignant ingre-
dients, yet the more sour it is the sweeter and more welcome
2. it is to God. The second is *unguentum pietatis,* 'the ointment of piety' and compassion, made up of the miseries and
the wants of the poor; wherein the greater is the misery the
greater is the mercy, and the more fellow-feeling and compassion of the pressures of the poor, the more odoriferous is
3. this sacrifice to pacify God's wrath. The third is *unguentum
devotionis,* 'the ointment of devotion,' which spends itself in
praise and thanksgiving by the remembrance of His manifold blessings and graces, which cannot but be acceptable
unto God, because though praise and glory be nothing unto
God Who cannot be increased by the breath of a mortal
man, yet because it is all the rent and tribute that man can
render to his God whereof to rob God is the greatest sacrilege, it is an ointment most welcome to God; the rather,
because man ever did himself the most hurt when he kept
glory back from God, and ascribed it to himself. In the
fifty-first Psalm, the ointment of contrition is accepted of
[Ps. 51. God with a *Non despicies;* "the sacrifice of the broken and
17.]
contrite heart God will not despise." The ointment of compassion in this place is accepted of God with *Delectatur
Deus,* "With such sacrifices God is pleased." The ointment
of praise goes somewhat higher, with an *Honorificat Me,*

"He that offers Me praise he honoureth Me." So the Ps. 50. 23.
contrite heart, the merciful heart, and the thankful heart
—*talibus sacrificiis,* "with such sacrifices God is pleased;"
all of these together, and every one of these severally, and
all others like unto these, they do pacify and please, and
delight God Himself.

Placatur or *conciliatur,* "God is pacified" or "reconciled,"
as some read; *Delectatur,* "God is pleased" or "delighted."
Hilarescit, or *pulchrescit,* 'God is cheered,' or 'looks upon
us with a serene or pleasant countenance;' but the Vulgar
will have it, *Promeretur Deus,* "God is promerited," in
favour of merits. I will not much stand upon the word;
be it *promeretur* in the Fathers' sense, in which merit is
via obtinendi, 'the way and means of obtaining,' the matter
is not great.

But the word in the proper sense signifies no more but
this, that "God is pleased," or at most "pacified with such
sacrifices;" and this is remarkable, that the same word,
Hebrews the eleventh chapter and sixth verse, signifies only
"God is well pleased" when it is spoken of faith. "For
without faith it is impossible to please God," εὐαρεστῆσαι·
but here εὐαρεστεῖται must be *promeretur,* as if works were
more meritorious than faith; when all the merits of works
proceed from grace and faith, as the goodness of the fruit
is from the root and the sap thereof. And so God may be
both pacified and pleased, and yet no merit in us, but acceptation in God; for the best works and sacrifices and
righteousness in man are so far from true merit, out of any
dignity or condignity of the work, that they cannot stand
before God without mercy and grace. The best and most
laudable life of the best man hath a *væ,* or 'woe,' lying
upon it, *si sine misericordiâ discutiatur,* 'if it come to be
discussed without mercy;' and in the district judgment
of God, no man, no not the "man after God's own heart," [1 Sam.
dares enter, but prays against it, *Ne intres in judicium* 13. 14.]
cum servo Tuo, "Enter not into judgment with Thy ser- Ps. 143. 2.
vant, O Lord." And why? For "no flesh is righteous in
Thy sight." No flesh, no man, righteous or justified: then
surely no true merit.

Brass or copper money may be made current by the King's

proclamation, but still it is but brass and copper, and wants of the true value of gold and silver; and good works, and "to do good and distribute," may go for current by God's promise, and receive a reward out of justice, but justice with mercy. For there is *justitia in reddendo,* 'justice in giving' the crown according to His promise; but there is *misericordia in promittendo,* 'mercy' that triumpheth over justice 'in promising' to give an infinite reward to a finite work, as heaven for a cup of cold water, or bread, or drink, or clothes, and the like; and between the kingdom of heaven and the crown of glory and eternal life which is infinite, and a few crumbs, or drops or rags which are scant so much as finite, there is no equality. *Inter finitum et infinitum nulla est proportio,* 'There is no proportion between that which is finite and that which is infinite.' So that as much as infinite doth exceed that which is finite, so much do God's infinite rewards exceed the best finite works of the best man. And the rule of the school in this is true: God punishes *citra condignum,* 'less than we deserve'—so there is mercy in God's justice and punishments; and God rewards *ultra meritum,* 'beyond our merit or desert,' and so eternal life is the grace and free gift of God.

1. Insomuch that we may thus resolve: first, *non tenetur Deus,* 'God is not bound' to give us any reward for any
2. dignity or worthiness of our works. Secondly, *non meremur nos,* 'we deserve nothing,' but are unprofitable servants, and our best works are imperfect, and fall short of that perfection
3. that law and justice do require. And thirdly, *non deerit tamen Deus,* 'though God be not bound, and man merits not, yet God never failed any man' that did do any good work, but he was sure of his reward. For though we be bound to good works *ex debito,* 'of duty,' God commands them and requires an account of them, yet God is not bound to reward them *ex debito,* 'out of any debt' owing to us for them, but only *ex pacto,* 'out of His promise and agreement.' For eternal life is not a reward which man may exact and require in justice at God's hands for his labour and hire, but it is His free gift; and therefore He calleth
[Mat. 20. it not *tuum,* 'thine,' but *Meum,* "Mine own:" "May I not
15.] do what I list with Mine own?"

What is the reason the Prophet saith, "O Lord," *memo-* Ps. 71. 16.
rabor justitiæ Tuæ solius, "I will remember Thy righteousness only," but because there is no other righteousness worth
the remembering but only "Thy righteousness only?" That
righteousness that is *a Domino,* inherent in us by sanctification of the gifts and graces of the Lord, is not worth the
remembrance, for it is "a defiled cloth," and dung in itself; Isa. 64. 6.
and were it never so good, God hath no need of it, nay
being offered to God He is nothing increased by it. If thou
do all good works, *Deus meus es, et bonorum meorum non
indiges,* "Thou art my God," saith David, "my goods"— Ps. 16. 2.
and therein are his good works also—"are nothing to Thee;"
God is not increased or enriched by them. If thou do commit all manner of sins with all manner of greediness, thou
canst not defile God nor take any thing from Him, thy
evil cannot decrease or diminish Him. But it is *justitia in
Domino,* "righteousness in the Lord," that is, Christ's right- [Isa. 45.
eousness communicated or imputed to us; for "Christ is ¹Cor. 1. 30.
made to us wisdom from God, and justice, or righteousness,
and sanctification and redemption;" and He doth not say
fecit nos, 'He made us righteous' in the concrete, but *factus
est nobis,* "He was made righteousness to us" in the abstract, because He communicates His righteousness to us
and thereby covers our nakedness, as Jacob clothed in his
elder brother's garments received the blessing. And therefore the name of the Son of God is *Jehova justitia nostra,* Jer. 23. 6.
"The Lord our righteousness."

Besides no man is accepted or well-pleasing to God for
his work's sake, but rather the work is accepted for the
workman's sake; as God first *respexit Abelem,* "He re- [Gen. 4.
spected or accepted of Abel's person;" and then follows, ⁴·]
et sacrificium ejus, "and then his sacrifice;" for God cares
not for Abel's lamb, but because Abel the lamb offered it,
his heart and willing readiness to offer a lamb was pleasing, and He accepted the sacrifice. As in the father of the
faithful, God could not accept the sacrifice of Isaac because he was not sacrificed *facto sed voto* or *voluntate,* not
'in deed but only in vow and will' and purpose, in him
voluntas reputatur pro facto, 'his will was accepted for the
sacrifice.'

And in Cain's sacrifice God made no difference between the lamb and the sheaf of corn, both which were after commanded equally in the law, and the *panes propositionis* were ever joined with a lamb. The difference was, he offered his ears of corn but not himself, and therefore the words be, *Ad*

[Gen. 4.
5.]
Cain vero et ad munera ejus non respexit, "But to Cain and to his offering God had not respect;" He accepted not his person, and therefore He regarded not his sacrifice. And

Rupert. in
Gen. lib. 4.
c. 2.
therefore the ancient say, that either of them offered *parem cultu et religione hostiam,* 'an equal sacrifice in respect of religion and the worship of God,' *sed non recte uterque divisit:* 'Cain made an ill division,' he offered the fruits of the earth to God; *cor retinuit sibi, seipsum non obtulit,* 'he reserved his heart to himself, and he offered not himself to God;' but Abel first offered himself to God, and then his lamb.

[Heb. 11.
4.]
And so St. Paul's words are true, "Abel offered a greater sacrifice to God than Cain." Greater first, *quia hostia copiosior,* 'because he offered a double sacrifice,' himself and his lamb, but Cain only offered his corn. Secondly, *quia excellentior,* he "offered a more excellent sacrifice," better chosen, because *de adipibus,* "of the fattest and best of the flock;" Cain carelessly took that came first to hand, *de fructibus,* "of the fruit," and no more. Thirdly, *quia ex fide,* "by faith he offered it;" and that faith justified him and his sacrifice, because he believed in the Seed of the woman That should bruise the serpent's head. And so it is true, *dignitas operantis,* 'the faith and piety of the sacrificer and worker,' *dignitatem confert operi,* 'confers all the worth to the work.' For if a heathen or Turk do the same work of alms or mercy that the faithful Christian doth, it shall pass without all regard, whereas the faithful heart and person makes the work of the hand acceptable to the Lord.

So then sacrifices of goodness and alms or distribution there must be, they are necessary to salvation in them that have time and opportunity and means; and therefore *sufficit ad pœnam meritis carere,* 'it is sufficient to punish us if we want good works.' But there can be no trust or confidence placed in them, for they are imperfect and defective and therefore merit nothing at God's hands out of justice, but only are accepted out of God's mercy and the infinite merit of Christ, which is equal to His Person That is infinite, as He is the eternal Son of God; and therefore, *sufficit ad præmium de meritis non præsumere,* the greatest part of the dignity of the best works of the best men, is to renounce all trust and confidence in ourselves and our best works, and to repose all our hope in the mercy and merits of Christ.

Now to return to the use of the word, *promeretur.* In antiquity I remember St. Cyprian useth it not for the dignity and merit of the best work, but only for the way or means of obtaining. For reading that place of St. Paul, "But I obtained mercy because I did it ignorantly in unbelief," he reads it thus: *Sed misericordiam merui,* "But I merited mercy." What was *merui* in St. Cyprian's sense but "I obtained mercy?" and so the Vulgar reads that place. 1 Tim. 1. 13. Epist. 73.

Again, speaking of those that were baptized and signed in the forehead with the sign of the cross, he saith of Ozias the leper that he was maculated with leprosy in that part of his body in which they are signed *qui Dominum promerentur,* 'which promerit the Lord'—so would our Rhemists read it; but the true understanding is, 'they that promerited the Lord,' that is, they that enter covenant with the Lord in baptism. And I presume, rather the keeping the covenant than the entering should be meritorious, if there be any merit at all. De unit. Eccles. [post med.]

And St. Augustine speaking of St. Paul saith: *Meritum fuit in Paulo sed malum,* 'In Paul there was no merit, but evil merit,' when he persecuted the Church and received good for it. And after, Let us return to the Apostle, whom we find 'without any good merits'—*sine ullis bonis meritis, immo cum multis malis meritis,*—'yea, with many evil merits,' to have obtained the grace of God; and then he adds, *ut post bona merita consequatur coronam, qui post mala merita consecutus est gratiam,* 'that after his good merits obtained the crown, who after his evil merits had obtained grace.' De Gratiâ, et Libero Arbitrio. cap. 5, 6.

1. Here first it is plain, merit is joined in both with obtaining. 2. Again, merits are good and merits are bad; the

word is common to both. 3. Merit signifies in St. Augustine's sense no dignity of work, but only a means of obtaining. For it is impossible that evil merit (that is, sin) out of the dignity of the work should merit grace; and by the same proportion and form of speech it is as impossible that the dignity of the work should merit a crown, since St. Augustine in the same place doth say, there would be none unto whom God the just Judge *redderet coronam,* 'should render a crown,' unless first as a merciful Father *donásset gratiam,* 'He had given His grace.' And then he adds, *Dona Sua coronat Deus, non merita tua;* 'God crowns not thy merit but His own gifts.' His reason is, For if they be such—that is, thine—they are evil, and if they be evil, God crowns them not; if they be good they are God's gifts, and He crowns them not as thy merits, but as His own gifts.

But I have troubled you too long with this school-doctrine and pulpit-divinity of magnifying man's merits before men, since their death-bed divinity recants it all; and then they are all forced, learned and ignorant, utterly to renounce it, and put all their trust in Christ's mercy and merits, as their sure anchor-head; of which I have only this to say, that merit may have some place in their science, but their own consciences, unless they be seared, tell them there is no true merit but Christ's only.

Application. I have now done with my text, and now I apply myself and my text to the present text that lies before us: *vir nec silendus, nec dicendus sine curâ,* 'a man whose worth may not be passed over in silence,' whom all ages with us may celebrate and admire, 'nor to be spoken of without great care and study;' of whom I can say nothing, but his worth and virtues will far exceed all men's words. Here I desire neither the tongue of man nor Angels: if it were lawful I should wish no other but his own tongue and pen; *ipse, ipse, quem loquar, loquatur,* 'let him speak of himself, none so fit as himself was, of whom I am to speak this day.' *Et jam loquitur,* 'and he now speaks,' he speaks in his learned works and sermons, and he speaks in his life and works of mercy, and he speaks in his death; and what he taught in his life and works, he taught and expressed in his death.

He is the great actor and performer, I but the poor cryer, *vox clamantis;* he was the *vox clamans,* 'he was the loud [Lu. 3. 4.] and great crying voice,' I am but the poor echo; and it is well with me, if as an echo of his large and learned books and works I only repeat a few of the last words.

No man can blame me if I commend him at his death, whose whole life was every way commendable; *justus sine mendacio candor apud bonos crimini non est,* 'just commendation without flattery is no fault in the opinion of the best men;' and the ancient custom of the Church did celebrate the memories of holy men to the praise of God That gave such eminent graces to them, and to stir up others by their example to the imitation of their virtues.

I speak my knowledge of him in many things; I loved and honoured him for above thirty years' space. I loved him I confess, but yet *judicio meo non obstat amor qui ex judicio natus est,* 'my love doth not blind or outsway my judgment, because it proceeded from judgment.' Of whom what can I say less, than that he was *vitâ innocentissimus, ingenio florentissimus, et proposito sanctissimus,* 'in his life most innocent, in his knowledge and learning most flourishing and eminent, and in his purpose and life most holy and devout;' whose carriage was so happy, *quem nemo vituperat nisi etiam laudet,* 'no man could ever discommend him but, will he, nill he, he must withal commend him.' And no man's words were ever able to disgrace him; *vera necesse est benedicant, falsum vita moresque superant,* 'they that spake truth of him could not but speak well of him, and if they spake falsely of him his life and manners did confute them.'

And if this text were ever fully applied in any, I presume it was in him; for he was *totus in his sacrificiis,* 'he wholly spent himself and his studies and estate in these sacrifices,' in prayer and the praise of God, and compassion and works of charity, as if he had minded nothing else all his life long but this, to offer himself, his soul and body, a contrite and a broken heart, a pitiful and compassionate heart, and a thankful and grateful heart, "a living sacrifice, holy and accept- [Rom. 12. able to God by Jesus Christ, which is our reasonable service" 1.] of Him.

He was born in this city of London of honest and godly
parents, who besides his breeding in learning left him a sufficient patrimony and inheritance, which is descended to his
heir at Rawreth in Essex. It is true, *Senum vita composita,*
'The lives of old men many times are orderly and well
composed,' and disposed, and staid, whereas in youth many
things that are in true judgment not altogether decent are
not so indecent in them, but that they well enough become
their younger years. In this he was happy, *Hujus vita composita a pueritiá,* 'His life was well composed and ordered
even from his childhood.' I may well say of him as the Prophet doth, *Bonum est portare jugum Domini ab adolescentiá,*

[Lam. 3.
27.]

"Herein was his happiness, that he took up and did stoutly
bear the yoke of the Lord even from his youth."

In his tenderest years he shewed such readiness and
sharpness of wit and capacity, that his teachers and masters
foresaw in him that he would prove *lumen literarum et
literatorum,* 'the burning and shining candle of all learning
and learned men.' And therefore those two first masters
that had the care of the first elements of his learning —

[¹ Master
of the
Coopers'
free
school.]

Master Ward of Ratcliffe,[1] and Master Mulcaster of the
Merchant-Taylors' School—contended for him, who should
have the honour of his breeding, that after became the
honour of their schools and all learning. Master Ward
first obtained of his parents that he should not be a prentice,
and at length Master Mulcaster got him to his school;
and from this time, *perit omne tempus quod studiis non im-
penditur,* 'he accounted all that time lost that he spent
not in his studies,' wherein in learning he outstripped all his
equals, and his indefatigable industry had almost outstripped himself. He studied so hard when others played, that
if his parents and masters had not forced him to play with
them also, all the play had been marred. His late studying
by candle, and early rising at four in the morning, procured
him envy among his equals, yea with the ushers also, because he called them up too soon; not like to our modern
scholars, *qui nondum hesternam edormiverunt crapulam,* who
at seven and eight of the clock have their heads and stomachs
aching, because they have not yet slept out their last night's
surfeits and fulness.

Their pains and care he so carefully remembered all his life long, that he studied always how to do good to them and theirs. In which gratefulness he promoted Dr. Ward to the parsonage of Waltham, and ever loved and honoured his Master Mulcaster during his life, and was a continual helper to him and his son Peter Mulcaster, to whom he gave a legacy of twenty pounds by his will; and as if he had made Master Mulcaster his tutor or supervisor, he placed his picture over the door of his study, whereas in all the rest of the house you could scantly see a picture.

From Master Mulcaster he went to Cambridge, to Pembroke Hall, and was there admitted one of Dr. Watts' [1571.] scholars; a notable grammarian, well entered in the Latin, Greek, and Hebrew tongues, and likewise in the geometry and some of the mathematics; and after a fellow there, [1576.] in which he passed over all degrees and places in such sort, *ut majoribus semper dignus haberetur,* 'he ever seemed worthy of higher and greater places,' and would in the end attain the highest; *virtutes enim ejus maturæ erant,* 'for his abilities and virtues were mature, and ripe for greater employments.'

And in this he owed little to his tutors, but most to his own pains and study. In which, give me leave to remember one thing which he hath often lamented himself to me and others, that he never could find a fit opportunity to shew his thankfulness to Dr. Watts, his patron, nor to any of his posterity; yet he did not utterly forget him in his will, having ordered that the two fellowships to be founded by him in Pembroke Hall, should always be chosen and filled out of the scholars of Dr. Watts' foundation, if they were found fit, of which himself had been one.

Being in holy orders he attended the noble and zealous Henry Earl of Huntingdon, president of York, and was employed by him in often preaching, and conference with recusants both of the clergy and laity, in which God so blest his endeavours that he converted some of the priests and many of the laity, with great success, bringing many to the Church, and seldom losing his labour, none ever converting so many as he did.

After this, Master Secretary Walsingham takes notice [About 1589.]

of him, and obtained him of the Earl, intending his preferment, in which he would never permit him to take any
country benefice, lest he and his great learning should be
buried in a country church. His intent was to make him
Reader of Controversies in Cambridge, and for his maintenance he assigned to him, as I am informed, the lease
of the parsonage of Alton in Hampshire, which after his
death he returned to his lady, which she never knew or
thought of.

After this he obtained the vicarage of St. Giles without
Cripplegate, London, and a Prebend Residentiary's place
[1589.] in St. Paul's, and was chosen Master of Pembroke Hall,
[1601.] and afterward was advanced to the Deanery of Westminster;
and all this without all ambition or suit of his own, God
turning the hearts of his friends to promote him for his
great worth.

When he took the degree of D.D. in Cambridge, one of
his questions was, that *Decimæ debentur jure divino;* which
he betrayed not, as some have done, but made it good by
Scriptures, and divine and natural reason, as will appear to
the reader when that among other of his works shall enrich
the English Church with a happy treasure of learning.

He was, as all our English world well knows, a singular
preacher and a most famous writer. He was so singular a
preacher, and so profound a writer, that you will doubt in
which he did excel; whose weapons in the mouths of the
adversary proved as stones in the teeth of dogs: while they
thought to withstand or answer them, they bit the stones
and brake their own teeth; and so it is true of him, *Re-
sponsa ejus sine responsionibus,* 'His answers were answer-
less.' Never durst any Romanist answer him; as their
common use is, that which they cannot answer and confute,
they slight it, and let it pass without any answer at all.

His admirable knowledge in the learned tongues, Latin,
Greek, Hebrew, Chaldee, Syriac, Arabic, besides other modern tongues to the number of fifteen as I am informed,
was such and so rare, that he may well be ranked in the
first place, to be one of the rarest linguists in Christendom;
in which he was so perfect and absolute, both for grammar
and profound knowledge therein, that he was so perfect in

the grammar and criticisms of them as if he had utterly neglected the matter itself, and yet he was so exquisite and sound in the matter and learning of these tongues as if he had never regarded the grammar.

Scientia magna, memoria major, judicium maximum, 'His knowledge was great and rare, his memory greater, and his judgment profoundest and greatest of all;' and over and above all these, *industria infinita,* 'his pains and industry was infinite;' for in the things the world hath seen, he used no man to read for him; as those great clerks, Bellarmine, and others' fashion is, to employ whole colleges and societies to study and read for them, and so furnish them; he only used an amanuensis to transcribe that which himself had first written with his own hand.

So that now I may propose him *ut exemplum sine exemplo maximum,* 'as a great example example-less;' *nec ante eum quem ille imitaretur, nec post eum qui eum imitari et assequi possit inventus est,* 'there was none before him whom he did imitate, nor none will come after him that will easily overtake him;' insomuch that his great gifts may well be taken a little to cloud and overshadow and obscure all men of his age and order; and surely the fame of this singular Bishop will become such a light to all posterity, *ut nec bona eorum nec mala latere patiatur,* 'it will not suffer neither their good nor their evil to lie hid.'

Was his fame great? *Major inventus est,* 'He was ever found to be greater than fame made him.' In which as he was a wonderful mirror of learning and learned men, so he was a singular lover and encourager of learning and learned men; which appeared in his liberality and bounty to Master Casaubon, Master Cluverius, Master Vossius, Master Grotius, Master Erpenius, whom he attempted with the offer of a very large stipend out of his own purse to draw into England, to have read and taught the Oriental tongues here; even as one well said, *Omnes quod in se amant in aliis venerantur,* 'Those gifts and knowledges which he loved in himself he honoured and rewarded in others.'

When the Bishoprics of Ely and Salisbury were void, and some things were to be pared from them, some overture being made to him to take them he refused them utterly. If it please you to give me leave, I will make his answer for him : *Nolo episcopari, quia nolo alienare,* 'I will not be made a Bishop, because I will not alienate Bishops' lands.'

[1605.]   After this by some persuasion he accepted of Chichester,
[1609.]   yet with some fear of the burden; and after, that of Ely;
[1619.]   and last, of this of Winchester, whence God hath translated him to heaven; in which he freed himself and his successor of a pension of four hundred pounds per annum, which many
[ᵃ 1605.]   of his predecessors had paid. He was Almonerᵃ, Deanᵇ of
[ᵇ 1619.]   the chapel, and a Privy Counsellor to King James and King Charles; in which he spake and meddled little in civil and temporal affairs, being out of his profession and element; but in causes that any way concerned the Church and his calling he spake fully and home to the purpose, that he made all know that he understood and could speak when it concerned him, as by those few speeches which are preserved you may judge, *ex ungue leonem,* a wise man by his works and deeds.

And herein he was like the ark of God, all places where it rested were blessed by the presence of God in it: so wheresoever he came and lived, they all tasted and were bettered by his providence and goodness. St. Giles' was reduced to him by a rate toward the better maintenance of the place, and the house repaired. He found nothing in the treasury in Pembroke Hall, he left in it in ready money a thousand pounds. Being Prebend Residentiary in St. Paul's, he built the house in Creed-lane belonging to his prebend, and recovered it to the Church. He repaired the Dean's lodging in Westminster. When he came to Chichester, he repaired the palace there, and the house in Aldingbourne. At Ely he spent in reparation of Ely-house in Holborn, of Ely-palace at Downham, and Wisbech Castle, two thousand pounds. At Winchester-house, at Farnham, at Waltham, and Wolversey, likewise two thousand pounds.

It seems plainly he loved the churches in which he was promoted and lived, better than he did his money or his own gain. For if we consider these expenses in his episcopal houses, and his most magnificent entertainment of his most gracious sovereign King James at Farnham, where in three days he spent three thousand pounds—as great and bountiful entertainment as ever King James received at a subject's hand—besides he refused to make some leases in his last years, which might have been very beneficial to him, for the good of his successor; his reason was, Many are too ready to spoil bishoprics, and few enough to uphold them: add to these the many alms he gave in his life, and now at his death, and we shall see he was free from all avarice and love of money. In him is true that word of St. John, [1 Joh. 2. *Nolite diligere mundum.* He doth not say, *Nolite habere,* 15.] but *Nolite diligere,* "Love not the world;" he doth not say, Have not, possess not the world, or goods of the world, but "love" them not. He had them, but he loved them not; *ut dispensator, ut erogator,* he had them but as a steward to dispose and expend them, to procure an everlasting tabernacle in the highest heavens.

He meddled little with them, but left the taking of his accounts from his officers to his brothers; and when he began his will at Waltham a year before his death, he understood not his own estate; nay, till about six weeks before his death, when his accounts were delivered up and perfected, he did not fully know his own estate; and therefore in his first draught of his will he gave but little to his kindred, doubting he might give away more than he had, and therefore in a codicil annexed to his will he doubled all his legacies to them, and made every hundred to be two hundred, and every two hundred to be four hundred; and yet notwithstanding this increase, he gave more to the maintenance of learning and the poor than to his kindred; his charity and love of God and the poor was greater in him than natural affection, and yet he forgot not his natural affection to them.

It was said of him that in his time was held to be *Deliciæ hominum* (Titus) *abstinuit alieno ut si quis unquam,* 'If ever any man abstained from that which was not his own he was the man.' This is as true of this most reverend Prelate; he never took any man's goods or right from him. Give me leave to add a little more of him: *Distribuit sua ut si quis unquam,* 'If ever any studied to disperse and distribute his own, either to kindred or to the poor, surely this is the man.'

Neither did he stay to do good and distribute till his death, that is, then gave his goods to the poor when he could keep them no longer. The first place he lived on was St. Giles': there, I speak my knowledge, I do not say he began, sure I am he continued his charity; his certain alms there was ten pounds per annum, which was paid quarterly by equal portions, and twelve pence every Sunday he came to church, and five shillings at every communion; and for many years, since he left that cure, he sent five pounds about Christmas, besides the number of gowns given to the poor of that parish when he was Almoner. And I have reason to presume the like of those other parishes mentioned in his will, to which he also gave legacies: to St. Giles' an hundred pounds, where he had been vicar; to All-hallows', Barking, where he was born, twenty pounds; to St. Martin's, Ludgate, where he dwelt, five pounds; to St. Andrew's in Holborn, where Ely-house stands, ten pounds. And to this parish of St. Saviour in Southwark where he died, twenty pounds; which parishes he hath remembered, for his alms to the poor, when the land shall be purchased for the relief and use of the poor.

When he came to Oxford, attending King James in the end of his progress, his custom was to send fifty pounds to be distributed among poor scholars. And the like he did at Cambridge, in his journey to Ely. And lest his left hand should know what his right hand did, he sent great alms to many poor places under other men's names, and he stayed not till the poor sought him, for he first sought them—as his servants employed in that service can witness—as appeareth at Farnham, at Waltham, and Winchester; and in the last year of great sickness he gave in this parish of St. Saviour a hundred marks. Besides, since the year one thousand six hundred and twenty, as I have my information from him that kept his books of accounts and delivered him the money, he gave in private alms to the sum of one thousand three hundred and forty pounds.

The total of his pious and charitable works mentioned in

his will, amounts to the sum of six thousand three hundred and twenty-six pounds. Of which, to Pembroke Hall, for the erection of two Fellowships, and other uses mentioned in the codicil, a thousand pounds, to buy fifty pound land per annum to that purpose. Besides a bason and ewer, like that of their foundress, and some books.

To buy two hundred pounds per annum, four thousand pounds : namely, for aged poor men, fifty pounds per annum; for poor widows, the wives of one husband, fifty pounds; for the putting of poor orphans to prentice, fifty pounds; to prisoners, fifty pounds.

He was always a diligent and painful preacher. Most of his solemn Sermons he was most careful of, and exact; I dare say few of them but they passed his hand, and were thrice revised, before they were preached; and he ever misliked often and loose preaching without study of antiquity, and he would be bold with himself and say, when he preached twice a day at St. Giles', he prated once : and when his weakness grew on him, and that by infirmity of his body he grew unable to preach, he began to go little to the Court, not so much for weakness as for inability to preach.

After he came to have an episcopal house with a chapel, he kept monthly communions inviolably, yea though himself had received at the Court the same month. In which, his carriage was not only decent and religious, but also exemplary; he ever offered twice at the altar, and so did every one of his servants, to which purpose he gave them money, lest it should be burthensome to them.

Now before I come to his last end, give me leave to tell you that privately he did much find fault and reprove three sins, too common, and reigning in this latter age. 1. Usury was one, from which, what by his Sermons, what by private conference, he withdrew many. 2. Another was simony, for which he endured many troubles by *Quare impedit,* and *duplex querela.* As for himself, he seldom gave a benefice or preferment to him that petitioned or made suit for it; he rather sent for men of note that he thought wanted preferment, and gave them prebends and benefices, under seal, before they knew of it, as to Master Boys and Master Fuller. 3. The third and greatest was sacrilege, which he did abhor as one principal cause among many of the foreign and civil wars in Christendom, and invasion of the Turk. Wherein even the reformed, and otherwise the true professors and servants of Christ, because they took God's portion and turned it to public profane uses, or to private advancements, did suffer just chastisement and correction at God's hand; and at home it had been observed, and he wished some man would take the pains to collect, how many families that were raised by the spoils of the Church were now vanished, and the place thereof knows them no more.

And now I draw to an end. God's house is truly called, and is indeed, *domus orationis*, "the house of prayer," it [Mat. 21. 13.] accompanies all acts done in God's house. Of this Reverend Prelate I may say, *Vita ejus vita orationis*, 'His life was a life of prayer;' a great part of five hours every day did he spend in prayer and devotion to God. After the death of his brother Master Thomas Andrewes in the sickness time, whom he loved dearly, he began to foretel his own death before the end of summer or before the beginning of winter. And when his brother Master Nicholas Andrewes died, he took that as a certain sign and prognostic and warning of his own death, and from that time till the hour of his dissolution he spent all his time in prayer; and his prayer-book, when he was private, was seldom seen out of his hands; and in the time of his fever and last sickness, besides the often prayers which were read to him, in which he repeated all the parts of the Confession and other petitions with an audible voice, as long as his strength endured, he did—as was well observed by certain tokens in him—continually pray to himself, though he seemed otherwise to rest or slumber; and when he could pray no longer *voce*, 'with his voice,' yet *oculis et manibus*, 'by lifting up his eyes and hands' he prayed still; and when *nec manus nec vox officium faciunt*, 'both voice, and eyes, and hands failed' in their office, then *corde*, 'with his heart,' he still prayed, until it pleased God to receive his blessed soul to Himself.

And so, *hujus mortalitas magis finita quam vita*, 'his mortality had an end,' and he died peaceably and quietly in the Lord, 'but his life shall have no end;' yea, then his life did begin, when his mortality made an end; that was *natalis*, 'his birth-day,' September the twenty-fifth, being Monday, about four of the clock in the morning. So died he *aliorum majore damno quam suo,* 'with greater damage to others,' even to all this English Church and all Christendom, 'than to himself.' And God grant that many ages may be so happy to bring forth and enjoy such a Prelate, so furnished with all endowments of learning and knowledge, with innocency and holiness of life, and with such piety and charity as he shewed in his life and death.

My conclusion is short. I have spoken somewhat of this most Reverend Prelate, but much short of his graces and worth. In sum thus much: In his life he was *concionator et scriptor potentissimus,* 'a most powerful preacher and writer;' in his deeds and actions, he was *potentior et diuturnior,* 'more powerful and lasting.' Death hath bereaved us of him; but his life, and his works of learning, and his works of piety and charity, I doubt not but God in His goodness will make them *monumentum ære perennius,* 'a [Hor. Od. monument more lasting than brass' and stone, even to the 3. 30. 1.] coming of our Lord Christ.

For no doubt while he lived he sowed the sincere word of life in the souls of men, and in his life and death, *posuit eleemosynam in sinu pauperis,* 'he put his alms into the bosom of the poor;' and shall I say, *Oravit pro eo,* 'It prayed for him,' and by it he procured himself a strong army, and *bellatores fortes,* 'valiant soldiers,' whose many prayers and blessings God could not resist, the rather because they knew him not? That is too short, and the text goes further, *Exorabit,* 'It shall pray and prevail too;' and he and they have prevailed, and he is now at rest and peace in heaven, and "follows the Lamb wheresoever He [Rev. 14. goes." 4.]

And after him let us all send this blessing, which the voice from heaven uttered, "Write, blessed are the dead which die Rev. 14. 13. in the Lord." For the Lord, there was no cause he should die; but he died "in the Lord" because he always lived to the Lord, and a happy death must needs accompany and crown such a life. "From henceforth, saith the Spirit, they rest from their labours;" all tears are wiped from their eyes, and all sighs from their hearts, and "their works follow

them;" *opera sequuntur et opera præcedunt,* 'their works go
before them.' So no doubt but his works have done, as the
prayer and alms and fasting of Cornelius did; they have procured a place for him in heaven, and his works shall follow
him, and the fame of them shall stir up many to follow his
example.

And so I end, beseeching God to give to us all, as He
gave to him, our parts in the "first resurrection" from sin
to grace; and to grant to him, and all the faithful and saints
departed, and us all with him, a joyful resurrection to everlasting life and glory in Jesus Christ. Amen.

NINETEEN SERMONS

UPON

PRAYER IN GENERAL,

AND

THE LORD'S PRAYER IN PARTICULAR.

A

PREPARATION TO PRAYER.

SERMON I.

2 Cor. iii. 5.

Not that we are sufficient of ourselves to think any thing as of ourselves; but our sufficiency is of God.

[*Non quod sufficientes simus cogitare aliquid a nobis, quasi ex nobis; sed sufficientia nostra ex Deo est.* Lat. Vulg.]

[*Not that we are sufficient of ourselves to think any thing as of ourselves; but our sufficiency is of God.* Eng. Trans.]

TOUCHING our hope which we have concerning the performance of God's promises the Apostle saith, that unto Heb. 6. 11. "the full assurance of hope" there must be "diligence" shewed, and that we are to prepare ourselves to receive Christ, and also having received Him with all His benefits to strive to hold Him fast, and never suffer our hope to be taken from us.

Upon which points, the doctrine that is to be delivered out of this Scripture doth follow by good consequence, for of these points of holding fast our faith in Christ two questions may arise, which may be answered by the Apostle's words in this place, where it may be demanded first, Whether we be able of our own strength to shew forth that diligence that is required to assure us of our hope. The Apostle resolveth us of that doubt in saying, "We are not able of ourselves to think any good of ourselves."

Secondly, because it may be objected, If we be not able of ourselves, from whence then may we receive ability? he addeth, that "our sufficiency is of God," from Whose goodness it cometh that we are able to do any good thing what-

SERM.
I.

Rev. 3. 20.

Mat. 7. 7.

Acts 14. 27.

Hosea 2. 15.

Rom. 3. 27.

2 Cor. 10. 5.

Gal. 6. 3.

1 Cor. 8. 2.

soever; to the end that when God stands without, knocking at the door of our hearts for the performance of such duties as please Him, we, in regard that of ourselves we cannot do the least thing that He requireth, should knock at the gate of His mercy, that He will minister to us ability to do the same according to His promise, " Knock, and it shall be opened to you." That as by the preaching of the Law there was opened unto us " the door of faith," and as the Creed is unto us " a door of hope," so the consideration of our own insufficiency might open unto us a door unto prayer, by which we may sue unto God for that ability which we have not of ourselves. So this Scripture hath two uses, first, to preserve us from error, that we seek not for that in ourselves which cannot be found in us; secondly, for our direction, that seeing all ability cometh from God, we should seek for it where it is to be found.

Both these things are matter very necessary to be known: the first serveth to exclude our boasting; we ought not to boast of our ability, because we have none. The second is a means to provoke us to call upon God by prayer, that from Him we may receive that which is wanting in ourselves.

To speak first of the negative part, both heathen and holy writings do commend to us that saying, Γνῶθι σεαυτὸν, but in a diverse sense. The heathen use it as a means to puff up our nature, that in regard of the excellency which God hath vouchsafed us above other creatures we should be proud thereof; but Christian religion laboureth by the knowledge of ourselves and of our misery " to cast down every high thing that exalteth itself against the knowledge of God, and to bring into captivity all imaginations to the obedience of Christ."

Whereas heathen philosophers will us to consider the excellent virtues wherewith man's nature is endued, the Scriptures all along put us in mind of our insufficiency and tell us, that " if any man seem to himself to be something when he is nothing, he deceiveth himself" in his own fancy. And " if any man thinketh that he knoweth any thing, he knoweth nothing yet as he ought to know."

Amongst the places of Scripture which the Holy Ghost useth to shew our insufficiency, none doth so much disable our nature as this place of the Apostle, which denieth unto us all power ever to conceive a good thought, so far are we off from fulfilling that good which we ought.

In this negative we are, first, to consider these words, whereby the Holy Ghost doth disable us: " We are not able to think any thing ;" secondly, the qualification in these words, " as of ourselves."

In denying our ability he setteth down three things : 1. "not able to think ;" 2. "any thing;" 3. this want of ability is imputed not to the common sort of men only, but even to the Apostles themselves, who of all other seemed to be most able. The Apostle to shew our insufficiency telleth us, " We are not able" so much as "to think any thing ;" therefore much less are we able fully to perform that good which is enjoined us. For whereas there are seven degrees to be considered in the effecting of any thing, to think that which is good is the least and lowest degree ; which being denied unto us, doth plainly shew what is our imperfection.

The first thing to be observed in undertaking any good, is the accomplishing of it ; secondly, the working or doing of the thing required ; thirdly, the beginning to do it ; fourthly, to speak that which is good ; fifthly, to will and desire it; sixthly, to understand ; seventhly, to think. But the Scripture doth deny all these unto us. The perfecting or bringing to pass of that which is good, is not in ourselves. " To will is present with us," *sed bonum perficere non invenio. Deus est,* &c. "It is God Which enableth us to perform." Rom. 7. 18. Phil. 2. 13.

This we find by experience to be true in things that are evil. The brethren of Joseph, when they sold him to the Egyptians, had a purpose to work their brother's hurt, but they had no power to perform their wicked attempts, for God turned their wicked purpose to good. When Paul was going to Damascus with purpose to persecute the Church, it pleased God in the way to stay his purpose so that he could not perform that evil which he intended. Thus much the Wise Man sheweth, when by an example he proveth that the strongest doth not always carry away the battle. Gen. 50. 20. Acts 9. 3-6. Eccl. 9. 11, 15, 16.

The heathen themselves say that heroical virtues are in the mind of man, but if any singular thing be done, it is

S E R M. the gods that give that power; and the Pelagian saith,
I.
——— though we be able to begin a good work, yet the accomplishment is of God.

Secondly, we are not able *facere*, no more than we were
[Joh. 15. 5.] able to effect, for so saith Christ, *Sine Me nihil potestis*
Jer. 10. 23. *facere.* The Prophet saith, *Scio quod viri non est via ejus.*
If it be not in man's power to order his way and to rule his
own steps, much less is he able to hold out to his journey's
Prov. 16. 9. end, but it is God That ordereth and "directeth man's
Rom. 7. 19. steps." Therefore St. Paul saith, "The good I would do,
I do not;" and if we do any good, that it be not effected,
yet it is the work of God in us, as the Prophet confesseth:
Isa. 26. 12. *Domine, omnia opera nostra operatus es in nobis.*

Thirdly, the inchoation or beginning of that which is good
is denied us: though we purpose in our hearts to perform
those duties of godliness that are required, yet we have not
Isa. 37. 3. the power to put them in practice. *Filii venerunt ad partum,
et non sunt vires pariendi,* "The children are come unto the
birth, and there is no strength to bring forth." If we begin
Phil. 1. 6. to do any good thing, it is *Deus Qui cœpit in nobis bonum
opus.* In consideration of which place Augustine saith of
the Pelagians, *Audiant qui dicunt a nobis esse cœptum, a Deo
esse eventum;* 'Here let them learn of the Apostle that it is
the Lord That doth begin and perform the good work.'

Fourthly, the power to speak that which is good is not in
Prov. 16. 1. us, for as the Wise Man saith, "A man may well purpose a
thing in his heart, but the answer of the tongue cometh from
the Lord." Whereof we have often experience. They that
have the office of teaching in the Church, albeit they do
beforehand prepare what to say, yet when it comes to the
point, are not able to deliver their mind in such sort as they
had purposed; as on the other side, when God doth assist
them with His Spirit, they are enabled on a sudden to deliver that which they had not intended to speak.

Phil. 2. 13. Fifthly, as the ability of effecting was attributed to God,
so is the will.

1 Cor 2. 14. Sixthly, for understanding, the Apostle saith, "The natural man perceiveth not the things that are of the Spirit
Rom. 8. 7. of God." "For the wisdom of the flesh[1] is enmity with
[¹ φρόνημα
τῆς σαρ-
κος.] God."

Seventhly, the power of thinking the thing that is pleasing to God is not in us, so far are we from understanding or desiring it, as the Apostle in this place testifieth. And therefore where the Prophet speaketh generally of all men, "The Lord knoweth the thoughts of men, that they are but Ps. 94. 11. vain;" the Apostle affirmeth that to be true of the wise men of the world that are endued only with wisdom of the world and the flesh, that "their thoughts are vain" also. 1 Cor. 3. 19, 20.

Secondly, that we should not think that the want of ability standeth only in matters of difficulty and weight, the Apostle saith not we are unable to think any weighty thing, but even that without the special grace of God's Spirit we cannot "think any thing." So Augustine understandeth Christ's words, John the fifteenth, where He saith not, *Nihil* [Tract. in *magnum et difficile,* but *Sine Me nihil potestis facere.* Joan. 81. 3.]

This is true in natural things, for we are not able to pro- [Joh. 15. 5.] long our own life one moment; the actions of our life are not of ourselves but from God, in Whom "we live, move, and Acts 17. 28. have our being." Therefore upon those words of Christ's, *Ego a Meipso non possum facere quicquam nisi quod video Patrem,* "I of Myself can do nothing but what I see My Joh. 5. 19. Father do," &c., Augustine saith, *Ei tribuit quicquid fecit, a* [Vid. *Quo est Ipse Qui facit.* Tract. in Joan. 18.]

But the insufficiency of which the Apostle speaketh, is not in things natural, but in the ministration of the Spirit. So he saith, that God of His special grace hath made them "able Ministers of the New Testament, not of the letter, but [2 Cor. 3. of the spirit:" his meaning is, that no endeavour of men can 6.] endue us with the grace of repentance, with faith, hope, and Christian charity, except the inward working of God's Spirit.

As the Apostle speaks of the gift of tongues, of the understanding of secrets, and of all knowledge without charity, *Nihil mihi prodest;* so all our endeavours are unprofitable to 1 Cor. 13. us, unless God by His Spirit do co-operate with us; for, 2, 3. " He that abideth in Me, and I in him, the same bringeth Joh. 15. 5. forth much fruit," that is, "the fruit of righteousness, the Rom. 6. 22. end whereof is eternal life."

Thirdly, the persons whom he chargeth with this want of ability, are not the common sort of "natural" men that are 1 Cor. 2. 14. not yet regenerate by God's Spirit, but he speaketh of him-

self and his fellow Apostles. So these words are an answer
to that question, Καὶ πρὸς ταῦτα τίς ἱκανός; " Unto these
things who is sufficient?" he answereth himself, Not we, for
we are not able of ourselves to think a good thought, much
less are we fit of ourselves to be means by whom God should
manifest the savour of His knowledge in every place; so that
[Joh. 15.
5.]
which Christ spake, John the fifteenth, He spake it to His
disciples, who albeit they were more excellent persons than
the rest of the people, yet He telleth them, *Sine Me nihil
potestis facere.*

The negative being general, we may make a very good use
of it : if the Apostles of Christ were unable, how much more
Gen. 32. 10. are we. If Jacob say, "I am unworthy of the least of Thy
Mat. 3. 11. blessings ;" if John Baptist say, " I am not worthy ;" if St.
1 Cor. 15. 9. Paul confess, "I am not worthy to be called an Apostle :"
much more may we say with the prodigal son that had spent
Lu. 15. 19. all, " I am not worthy to be called Thy son ;" and with the
Mat. 8. 8. centurion, " I am not worthy thou shouldest come under my
roof."

The reason of this want of ability is, for that the nature
of men cannot perform that which the Apostle speaks of,
neither as it is in an estate decayed through the fall of
Adam, and that general corruption that he hath brought
into the whole race of mankind ; nor as it is restored to the
highest degree of perfection, that the first man had at the
beginning. Adam himself, when he was yet perfect, could
not attain to this, for he was but " a living soul ;" the se-
1 Cor. 15.
45.
cond Adam was " a quickening Spirit." And it is not in the
power of nature to elevate and lift itself up to conceive hope
of being partakers of the blessedness of the life to come, to
2 Pet. 1. 4. be made " partakers of the Divine Nature," and of the heavenly substance : if men hope for any such thing, it is the
Spirit of God That raiseth them up to it.

As the water can rise no higher than nature will give it
leave, and as the fire giveth heat only within a certain compass, so the perfection which Adam had was in certain compass, the light of nature that he had did not reach so high as
to stir him up to the hope of the blessedness to come ; that
was without the compass of nature, and comes by the supernatural working of grace.

As we are corrupt, it never cometh into our minds to hope for the felicity of the life to come; "for all the thoughts of Gen. 6. 5. man's heart are only evil, and that all the day long."

That is true which the Apostle witnesseth of the Gentiles, "That they by nature do the things of the law," if we Rom. 2. 14. understand it of moral duties, for the very light of nature doth guide us to the doing of them. But as the Prophet saith, "My goodness doth not extend to Thee;" so whatso- Ps. 16. 2. soever good thing we do by the direction of natural reason, it is without all respect of God, except He enlighten us before. Therefore in our regeneration not only the corruption of our will is healed, but a certain divine spark of fire and zeal of God's Spirit is infused into us, by which we are holpen to do those duties of piety, which otherwise naturally we have no power to do.

Now follows the qualification of this general negative sentence. For where the Apostle hath said, "We are not able to think any thing of ourselves," the Scripture recordeth divers good purposes that came into the hearts of God's servants. The Lord Himself said of David: "Whereas it 1 Kings 8. was in thine heart to build an house to My name, thou didst 18. well in thinking so to do." The Apostle saith of unmarried folks, "that they care for the things that belong to the Lord, 1 Cor. 7. 32. how they may please the Lord." But the Apostle sheweth, that if we have any such thoughts at any time, they do not proceed from us.

By which words the Apostle no doubt maketh this distinction, that there are some things that come of us, and are of ourselves; again, there are other things that come from us and yet are not of us.

That is from and of ourselves, that groweth in us naturally: that is said to be from ourselves, but not of ourselves, which is engrafted in us. It is the true olive that, from itself and of itself, yieldeth fatness; and the wild olive being Rom. 11. engrafted in it doth from itself yield fatness but not of it- 17, 18. self, but as it is by insition made partaker of that fatness which naturally is in the true olive.

Figmenta cogitationis are from and of ourselves; but if any divine and spiritual thoughts come into our hearts, the Jer. 18. 6. Lord God is the "potter" that frames them in us.

S E R M.
I.
:om. 7. 18.
Rom. 7. 17.

The Apostle saith, *Scio quod in me, hoc est, in carne meá, non habitat bonum.* But " sin dwells in me :" therefore sin that dwells in us, is from us and of us; but the grace of God's Spirit, which dwells not in us but doth tarry guest-wise, is that which is from us but not of us.

Lu. 24. 38.

Jas. 1. 17.

Our Saviour saith, " Why do thoughts arise in your hearts ?" Such thoughts are from us and of us; but those thoughts that come from "the Father of lights," are from ourselves but not of us.

Ilos. 13. 9.

All that we have by the strength of nature, is said to be of ourselves and from ourselves, but the power wherewith we are endued from above to the doing of heavenly and spiritual things, is of ourselves but not from ourselves. *Perditio tua ex te, Israel*—that is from us and of us : *Tantummodo salus ex Me*—that is neither of us nor from us.

1 Cor. 15.
9, 10.

The Apostle saith, " I persecuted the Church :" that was from himself and of himself; but when he saith, "yet I laboured more than they all," he correcteth that and saith, " yet not I, but the grace of God with me ;" because that was of himself, but not from himself but from the grace of God which did co-operate with him.

Aug.

Sins are of ourselves and from ourselves, but not good actions. *Hoc piarum mentium est, ut nihil sibi tribuant,* ' This is the part of godly souls, that they attribute nothing to themselves.' It is dangerous to ascribe too little to the grace of God, for then we rob Him of His glory, but if we ascribe too little to ourselves there is no danger ; for whatsoever we take from ourselves, it cannot hinder us from being true Christians ; but if we ascribe that to the strength of our own nature which is the proper work of grace, then do we blemish God's glory.

[2 Cor. 2.
16.]

Phil. 4. 13.

The affirmative part is, " Our sufficiency is of God." So that albeit in regard of themselves he said, " Who is sufficient to these things?" yet having ability from God he is bold to say, *Omnia possum in Eo Qui me confortat.*

Tit. 1. 9.

Col. 1. 12.

The Apostle willeth Titus to choose sufficient men, such as were "able to exhort with wholesome doctrine," that is, such as God hath made able : so he speaks of all in general, that " God the Father hath made us meet to be partakers of the inheritance of the saints in light."

As none are meet but such as are made meet, so there are
none ἄξιοι, 'worthy,' but ἀξιωθέντες, "such as are made Lu. 20. 35.
worthy." The Apostle saith, "I was indeed to come to you, 2Cor. 1. 15.
that ye might receive a second grace." Whereby he sheweth
that to be true which St. Paul affirmeth, "That the grace of Tit. 2. 11.
God is manifested." And so much we are to understand by [1 Joh.
the words of the Evangelist, when he saith, "That from the Joh. 1. 16.
fulness of Christ we received grace for grace."

As Noah is reported to have "found grace in the sight of Gen. 6. 8.
God," so many do find grace with God. First, He worketh
grace in men by the means of His word, when before they
were void of grace: "The grace of God hath appeared to all, Tit. 2. 11,
teaching them." Also by the means of the cross, and by Job 33.
that He worketh a second grace that is inherent, whereby Ps. 119.
they are enabled to do the duties of holiness.   [67.]

In which respect as He is said to give grace, *Humilibus* Prov. 3. 34.
dat gratiam, so we receive grace. After God by His Spirit 2 Cor. 6. i.
hath thus enabled us, we are said to be able and meet to do
those things which we are commanded, so that though our
righteousness be but *menstrualis justitia,* He will not reject Isa. 64. 6.
it; though our zeal in godliness be but as "smoking flax"
or the "bruised reed," He will not quench nor break it; Isa. 42. 3.
and though the measure of our charity exceed not the "cup Mat. 10. 42.
of cold water," yet we shall not "lose our reward." And
though "the afflictions of this life" which we suffer for
Christ's sake "be not worthy of the glory that is to be re- Lu. 21. 36.
vealed," yet as the Evangelist speaks καταξιωθήσονται, "for Rom. 8. 17,
if we suffer together with Christ, we shall be glorified with 18.
Him."

So then, the sum of all cometh to this: Where the Apostle
exhorteth, "Let us have grace," the question is, from whence Heb. 12. 28.
we may have it? It is certain we have it not of ourselves,
for it is a divine thing, therefore we must have it from Him
That is the well of grace. If we come to Him, "out of His Joh. 1 16.
fulness we shall receive grace for grace."

He is not a well locked up, but such an one as standeth
open that all may draw out of it. Therefore the Apostle 1 Pet. 1. 13
saith that the grace of God is χάρις φερομένη. And as Solo- Prov. 12. 2.
mon saith, *Bonus vir haurit gratiam.*

The means to obtain this grace at the hands of God is by

SERM. prayer. For He hath promised to "give His Holy Spirit to
I.   them that ask it." And having received grace from God,
Lu. 11. 13.
2 Thess. we shall likewise have *bonam spem per gratiam.* He hath
2. 16. promised that "those that seek shall find."
Mat. 7. 7.

If in humility we seek for grace from God, knowing that
we have it not of ourselves, we shall receive it from God, for
1 Pet. 5. 5. He "giveth grace to the humble."

Seeing then that in us there is no ability, no not so much
as "to think any thing," and all ability cometh from God,
Lam. 5. 21. we are to learn from hence that if God say, Turn to Me,
and I will turn to you, we must pray, Convert Thou us, O
Ezek. 18. Lord, and we shall be converted. If He say to us, "Make
31. you clean hearts," because that is not in us we must pray,
Ps. 51. 10. "Create in Me a clean heart, and renew a right spirit in me."
Joh. 11. 26. When Christ saith, "Believest thou this?" forasmuch as
Eph. 2. 8. faith "is the gift of God," we are to pray with the disciples,
Lu. 17. 5. *Domine, adde nobis fidem.* When the Apostle exhorteth,
1 Pet. 1. 13. *Perfecte sperate,* we should say with the Prophet, "Lord my
Ps. 39. 7. hope is even in Thee." And where our duty is to love with
all our hearts, because we cannot perform this without the
Rom. 5. 5. assistance of God's Spirit, we are to pray that "the love of
God may be shed in our hearts by the Holy Ghost."

A

PREPARATION TO PRAYER.

SERMON II.

JAMES i. 16, 17.

Err not, my dear brethren.

*Every good giving and every perfect gift is from above, and
cometh down from the Father of lights, with Whom is no
variableness, neither shadow of turning.*

[*Nolite itaque errare, fratres mei dilectissimi.*

*Omne datum optimum et omne donum perfectum desursum est, de-
scendens a Patre luminum, apud Quem non est transmutatio, nec
vicissitudinis obumbratio.* Lat. Vulg.]

[*Do not err, my beloved brethren.*

*Every good gift and every perfect gift is from above, and cometh down
from the Father of lights, with Whom is no variableness, neither
shadow of turning.* Eng. Trans.]

As St. Paul tells us, "that we are not sufficient to think" 2 Cor. 3. 5.
a good thought, "but our sufficiency is of God;" so the
Apostle saith, It is God only from Whom "every good
giving and every perfect gift" cometh; and that we shall
err if we either think that any good thing which we enjoy
cometh from any other but from God, or that any thing else
but good proceedeth from Him; so that as well the ability
which man had by nature, as our enabling in the state of
grace, is from God. He is the fountain out of Whom, as
the Wise Man saith, we must draw grace by prayer, which [Prov. 12.
is *situla gratiæ*, 'the conduit or bucket of grace.' There- 2.]
fore He promiseth in the Old Testament to pour upon His
Church both "the Spirit of grace and of prayer," that as Zech. 12.
they sue for grace by the one, so they may receive it in by 10.

SERM.
II.

Ps. 4. 6.

Jas. 3. 11.

Hos. 13. 9.

the other.   Unto this doctrine of the Apostle in this place, even those that otherwise have no care of grace do subscribe, when they confess themselves to be destitute of the good things of this life, and therefore cry, *Quis ostendet nobis bona?*

As before the Apostle shewed that God is not the cause of any evil, so in this verse he teacheth there is no good thing but God is the author of it; if He be the fountain of every good thing, then He cannot be the cause of evil, for "no one fountain" doth out of the same hole "yield sweet and bitter water."

Secondly, if every good thing be of God only, then have we need to sue to Him by prayer, that from Him we may receive that which we have not of ourselves.   Wherefore as this Scripture serves to kindle in us the love of God, forasmuch as He contains all good things that we can desire, so it is a special means to provoke us to the duty of prayer.

This proposition hath two parts: first, an universal affirmative in these words, "Every good giving;" secondly, a prevention; for where it may be objected, that howsoever some good things come of God yet evil things also may successively come from Him, even as the heathens say that Jupiter hath divers boxes out of which he doth pour both good and evil, the Apostle preventeth that objection and saith, "that with God there is no variableness nor shadow of changing."   So that as the meaning of these words in the Prophet Osee, *Salus tua tantummodo ex Me,* is both that salvation is only of God, and that nothing else but salvation cometh from Him; so the Apostle's meaning in these words is, both that God is only the cause of good, and that He is the cause of nothing else but good, lest when we are tempted unto evil, we should make God the author of all such temptations.

The former part of the proposition called *subjectum* is, "Every good giving, &c."   The latter part called *prædicatum* is, "descendeth from above."

Where the heathen call all virtues and good qualities which they have, ἕξεις, of having, the Apostle calleth them δόσεις καὶ δωρήματα, of giving, to teach us that whatsoever good quality is in any man, he hath it not as a quality within himself, but he receiveth it from without as it is a gift.

Esau speaking of the blessings bestowed upon him saith, "I have enough;" and the rich man, *Anima*, "Soul, thou hast much good;" as though they had not received them from God: but the saints of God spake otherwise. Jacob saith, "These are the children which God hath given me." Again, when Pilate without all respect of God of Whom the Apostle saith, "There is no power but of God," said, "Knowest Thou not, that I have power to crucify and to loose Thee?" our Saviour said again, "Thou shouldest have no power over Me, except it were given thee from above." Gen. 33. 9. Lu. 12. 19. Gen. 33. 5. Rom. 13. 1. Joh. 19. 10, 11.

The consideration hereof serveth to exclude our "boasting;" that "the wise man boast not of his wisdom," seeing wisdom, strength, and whatsoever good things we have, it is the good gift of God, as the Apostle tells us, *Quid habes quod non accepisti?* Rom. 3. 27. Jer. 9. 23. 1 Cor. 4. 7.

Secondly, this division is to be marked, that of the good things which come from God some are called *donationes*, others *dona;* and to these two substantives are added two adjectives, whereof one doth answer to the givings of God's goodness, the other to the gifts of God ascribeth perfection.

The first error the Apostle willeth them to beware is, that they think not that God is the cause of any evil, because every good thing cometh from Him; the second error is, that they should not conceive this opinion, that the main benefits are from God, and the lesser benefits are from ourselves; not so, for the Apostle tells us, that as well "every good giving," as "every perfect gift, is from above."

That which the Apostle calls *donatio*, is a transitory thing; but by gift he meaneth that which is permanent and lasting.

Joseph is recorded to have given to his brethren not only corn, "but victuals to spend by the way." So by "giving," the Apostle here understandeth such things as we need in this life, while we travel towards our heavenly country; but that which he calleth "gifts," are the treasures which are laid up for us in the life to come; and thus the words are used in these several senses. Gen. 45. 21.

Y

Phil. 4. 15.

Rom. 5. 16.

Job 1. 21.

Lu. 10. 42.

1 Cor. 2. 9.

Zech. 4. 10.

2 Cor. 3. 5.

[Mat. 6. 10, 11.]

Of things transitory the Apostle saith, "No Church dealt with me in the matter of giving;" there the word is δόσις· but speaking of the good things that come to us by Christ he saith, "The gift is not as the fault," where the word is δώρημα.

By "giving" he understandeth beauty, strength, riches, and every transitory thing whereof we stand in need, while we are yet in our journey towards our heavenly country; such as Job speaks of, *Dominus dedit, Dominus abstulit.* By "gift" he meaneth the felicity that is reserved for us after this life, the kingdom of heaven, that whereof our Saviour saith to Martha, "Mary hath chosen the better part, which shall not be taken from her."

That which is a stay to us in this life is δόσις, but "the things which neither eye hath seen, nor ear heard, all which are reserved for them that love God," these are δωρήματα, and as well the one as the other come from God. So much we are taught by the adjectives that are joined to these words. "Givings" are called "good," and the "gifts" of God are called "perfect;" in which words the Apostle's purpose is to teach us that not only the great benefits of the life to come, such as are perfect, are of Him; but that even that good which we have in this life, though it be yet imperfect and may be made better, is received from Him and not elsewhere. "Who doth despise little things?" saith the Prophet.

God is the author both of "perfect" and "good things:" as the image of the prince is to be seen as well in a small piece of coin as in a piece of greater value, so we are to consider the goodness of God, as well in the things of this life as in the graces that concern the life to come, yea even in this, "to think that which is good."

Of Him are the small things as well as the great. Therefore our Saviour teacheth us to pray, not only for that "perfect gift," *ut adveniat Regnum,* but even for these lesser good things, which are but His "givings," namely, that He would "give us our daily bread."

Under "good" are contained all gifts, both natural or temporal. Those "givings" which are natural, as to live, to move, and have understanding, are good, for of them it is said, "God saw all that He made, and lo, all was Gen. 1. 31. good."

Of gifts temporal, the heathen have doubted whether they were good, to wit, riches, honour, &c., but the Christians are resolved that they are good. So our Saviour teacheth us to 1 Joh. 3. 17. esteem them, when speaking of fish and bread, He saith, "If you which are evil can give your children good things." Lu. 11. 13. And the Apostle saith, "He that hath this world's good." 1 Joh. 3. 17. For as Augustine saith, That is not only good *quod facit* [Aug. Ser. *bonum, sed de quo fit bonum,* 'That is not only good that 61. 2, 3.] makes good, but whereof is made good:' so albeit riches do not make a man good always, yet because he may do good with them they are good.

The "gift" which the Apostle calls "perfect" is grace and glory, whereof the one is in this life the beginning of perfection; the other in the life to come is the end and constancy of our perfection, whereof the Prophet speaketh, "The Lord will give grace and glory." Ps. 84. 11.

The Apostle saith, *Nihil perfectum adduxit Lex,* "The Heb. 7. 19. Law brought nothing to perfection;" that is, by reason of the imperfection of our nature, and "the weakness of our Rom. 8. 3. flesh."

To supply the defect that is in nature grace is added, that grace might make that perfect which is imperfect.

The Person That giveth us this grace is Jesus Christ, "by Joh. 1. 17. Whom grace and truth came." And therefore He saith, *Estote perfecti sicut Pater vester cœlestis perfectus est.* And Mat. 5. 48. by this grace not only our sins are taken away, but our souls are endued with inherent virtues, and receive grace and ability from God, to proceed from one degree of perfection to another all our life time, even till the time of our death, which is the beginning and accomplishment of our perfection, as our Saviour speaketh of His death. Lu. 13. 32.

In the latter part of the proposition we are to consider the place from whence, and the Person from Whom, we receive these gifts; the one is *superne,* the other *a Patre luminum.* Now he instructeth us to beware of a third error, that we look not either on the right hand or on the left hand, that we regard not the persons of great men, which are but instruments of God, if we have any good from them; all the

SERM.
II.

good we have it is *desursum*, the thoughts of our hearts that
arise in them, if they tend to good, are not of ourselves but
infused into us by the divine power of God's Spirit, and so
is whatsoever good thought, word, or work, proceeding from
us. This is one of the first parts of divinity John Baptist
Joh. 3. 27. taught: "A man can receive nothing, except it be given
him from above." This was the cause of Christ's ascending
Ps. 68. 18. into heaven: "He went up on high," and *dedit dona homini-*
Joh. 7. 39. *bus;* and the Evangelist saith, "The Holy Ghost," Which
is the most perfect gift that can come to men, "was not yet
given, because Christ was not yet ascended." Therefore, if
we possess any blessing or receive any benefit, we must not
look to earthly means but to heaven.

The thing which is here mentioned excludeth the fourth
error: we think that things come to us by fortune, or cus-
tomably; he says not that good things fall down from above,
but they descend, *et qui descendit proposito descendit.* Our
instruction from hence is, that they descend from a cause
intelligent, even from God Himself, Who in His counsel
and provision bestoweth His blessings as seemeth best to
Himself; for as the heathen men speaketh, God hath *sinum
facilem* but not *perforatum*, that is, 'a lap easy to receive and
yield, but not bored through,' to let things fall through without discretion.

Ps. 145. 16. When the Prophet saith, *Tu aperis manum*, he doth not
say that God letteth His blessings drop out of His fingers.
Christ, when He promised to His disciples to send the Com-
Joh. 16. 7. forter, saith, *Ego mittam Eum ad vos.* Whereby He giveth
them to understand, that it is not by casualty or chance that
the Holy Ghost shall come upon them, but by the deliberate
[Jas. 1. 18.] counsel of God: so the Apostle speaks, "Of His own will
begat He us by the word of truth."

The Person from Whom, is "the Father of lights." The
heathens found this to be true, that all good things come
from above, but they thought that the lights in heaven
are the causes of all good things: therefore is it that they
[Jas. 1. 17.] worship the sun, moon, and stars. St. James saith, "Be
not deceived, all good things come not from the lights,
but from the Father of lights." The natural lights were
Deut. 4. 19. made *in ministerium cunctis gentibus;* and the Angels that

are the intellectual lights, are appointed to do service unto ^{Heb. 1. 14.} the elect.

But it is "the Father of lights" That giveth us all good things; therefore He only is to be worshipped, and not the lights which He hath made to our use.

God is called "the Father of lights," first, in opposition to the lights themselves, to teach us that the lights are not the causes of good things but He That said, *Fiat lux.* Gen. 1. 3. Secondly, in regard of the emanation, whether we respect the sunbeams called *radii* shining in at a little hole, or the great beam of the sun called *jubar*, He is author of both, and so is the cause of all the light of understanding, whether it be in small or great measure. Thirdly, to shew the nature of God: nothing hath so great alliance with God as light; "the light maketh all things manifest," and the Eph. 5. 13. wicked hate the light, "because their works are evil." But Joh. 3. 19. God is "the Father of lights," because as out of light [Jas. 1. cometh nothing but light, so God is the cause of that 17.] which is good.

Again, light is the cause of goodness to those things that are good of themselves; "It is a pleasant thing to behold Eccl. 11. 7. the light." On the other side, howsoever good things are in themselves, yet they afford small pleasure or delight to him that is shut up in a dark dungeon, where he is deprived of the benefit of light. So God is "the Father of lights," for that not only all things have their goodness from Him, but because He makes them good also.

Light is the first good thing that God created for man; Gen. 1. 3. *Fiat lux.* But God is "the Father of lights," to shew that He is the First Cause of any good thing that can come to us.

Again, because He is that only cause of the visible light which at the first He created, and also of that spiritual light whereby He shineth into our hearts by "the light of the 2 Cor. 4. 4. Gospel," the Apostle saith of the whole Trinity, *Deus lux* 1 Joh. 1. 5. *est.* More particularly Christ saith of Himself, *Ego sum* Joh. 8. 12. *lux mundi.*

The Holy Ghost is called light, where He is represented Acts 2. 3. by "the fiery tongues." The angels are φλόξ πυρός. David Heb. 1. 7. also, as a civil magistrate, was called "the light of Israel." 2 Sam. 21. 17.

SERM.
II.
——
Mat. 5. 14.
Phil. 2. 15.

1 Joh. 1. 5.

John 1. 9.

[Ps. 107.
10.]
2 Cor. 4. 4.

[Lu. 9.
54.]

2 Pet. 1. 19.
Gen. 3. 8.

1 Kings 19.
11, 12.

1 Tim. 6.16.

Gen 27. 37.
1 Cor. 15.
41.

Ecclesiastical ministers are called light; *Vos estis lux mundi.* And not only they, but the people that are of good conversation are said to shine *tanquam luminaria in mundo.* All these "lights" have their being from God, and for this cause He is worthily called *Lux mundi,* and "the Father of lights." Again, this name is opposed unto darkness; "God is light, and in Him there is no darkness:" therefore the ignorance of our minds is not to be imputed unto Him. "He is the light that lighteneth every one," and "cannot be comprehended of darkness:" therefore it is not long of Him that we through ignorance are said "to sit in darkness, and in the shadow of death;" this comes of the devil, the prince of darkness, who blindeth men's eyes. God is "the Father of lights."

Furthermore, He is so called to distinguish Him from heat.

The lights which we make for these private uses, do not only give light but heat also, but God giveth light without heat; wherefore such as are of a fiery spirit as the disciples that said, "Shall we command that fire come down from heaven and consume them?" are not like God. Christ is called the "day-star," not the dog-star. God is said to have "walked in the cool of the day," not in the heat of the day. When God would speak to Elijah, He shewed Himself neither "in the strong wind, nor in the earthquake, nor in fire, but in a small still voice:" to teach men that, if they will be like God, they must be of a meek and quiet spirit. He is said to "dwell in the light," not that He is of a hot fiery nature as our lights are, but because He giveth us the light of knowledge.

In respect of the number, He is not called the Father of one light, but *Pater luminum.* It was an imperfection in Jacob, that he had but one blessing. God is not the cause of some one good thing, but as there are divers stars "and one star differeth from another in glory," so as we receive many good things and of them some are greater than others, so they all come from God, Who is the author and fountain of them all.

Our manifold imperfections are noted by the word *tenebræ,* which is a word of the plural number, and in regard thereof

it is needful that God in Whom we have perfection shall
not be *Pater luminis* but *Pater luminum.* Our miseries are
many; therefore that He may deliver us quite out of miseries, there is with the Lord *copiosa redemptio.* The sins Ps. 130. 7.
which we commit against God are many; therefore He is
the Father, not of one mercy but *Pater misericordiarum.* 2 Cor. 1. 3.
The Apostle Peter tells us that the mercy of God is *multi-* 1 Pet. 4. 10.
formis gratia. So that whether we commit small sins or
great, we may be bold to call upon God for mercy: "Ac- Ps. 51. 1.
cording to the multitude of Thy mercies have mercy upon
me." For as our sins do abound, so the mercy of God
whereby He pardoneth and is inclined to pardon us, is
exuberans gratia. Rom. 5. 17.

The darkness that we are subject to is manifold: there
is darkness inward, not only in the understanding where
the Gentiles are said "to have their cogitations darkened," Eph. 4. 18.
but in the heart whereof the Apostle speaketh, "He that 1 Joh. 2. 9.
hateth his brother is in darkness."

And there is the darkness of tribulation and affliction,
whereof the Prophet speaketh, "Thou shalt make my dark- Ps. 18. 28.
ness to be light;" and the misery which the wicked suffer
in the world to come which our Saviour calleth "utter dark- Mat. 22. 13.
ness." God doth help us and give us light in all these
darknesses, and therefore is called "the Father of lights."

As the sun giveth light to the body, so God hath provided
light for the soul; and that is, first, the light of nature,
which teacheth us that this is a just thing, *ne alii facias
quod tibi fieri non vis:* from this light we have this knowledge, that we are not of ourselves but of another, and of
this light the Wise Man saith, "The soul of man is the Prov. 20.
candle of the Lord." They that resist this light of nature 27.
Job 24. 13.
are called *rebelles lumini.* With this light "every one that Joh. 1. 9.
[2 Sam.
cometh into this world is enlightened." Howbeit this light 4. 4.]
hath caught a fall, as Mephibosheth did, and thereupon it
halteth; notwithstanding, because it is of the blood royal,
it is worthy to be made of.

Next, God kindleth a light of Grace by His word, which
is *lux pedibus,* and *lux oculis;* and that we may be capable Ps. 119.
105.
of this outward light, He lighteneth us with His Spirit; Ps. 19. 8.
because the light of the Law shined but darkly, therefore

SERM.
11.

1 Pet. 2. 9.

Ps. 97. 11.

Ps. 94. 19.

2 Thess. 2.
16.

Col. 1. 12,
13.

He hath called us into the light of His Gospel, which is "His marvellous light."

He lighteth the outward darkness of affliction by ministering comfort; "there springeth up light for the righteous, and joyful gladness for such as are true of heart." "In the multitude of my sorrows, Thy comforts have refreshed my soul." "He giveth us everlasting consolation, and good hope through grace." And that we should not be cast into utter darkness, He hath "made us meet to be partakers of the inheritance of the saints in light," yea, "He hath delivered us from the power of darkness, and hath translated us into the kingdom of His beloved Son."

From hence it followeth: first, if all good things be "gifts," we may not boast of them; if they come from God, we may not forget Him from Whom we receive them.

Phil. 4. 15.

Mat. 25. 19.

Lu. 15. 13.

Mat. 25. 27.

Secondly, because "gifts" are rather *commendata quam data,* because there is λόγος δόσεως, seeing God will come and take account of the talents, we must neither wastefully misspend them, nor have them without profit. *Ut crescit donum, sic crescat ratio donati.*

Thirdly, seeing they come from above, we must not be like blind moles, nor as swine grovelling upon the earth, which eat the acorns that fall from the tree and never look up, but it may teach us to look up: *Sursum cor, qui habes sursum caput.*

1 Thes. 5. 5.

Eph. 5. 8.

Fourthly, seeing God is *Pater luminum,* we must walk as "children of light," for we are not "darkness but light."

Fifthly, seeing God hath divers good things in His hand to give, we must desire to receive them from Him by prayer.

A

PREPARATION TO PRAYER.

SERMON III.

MATTHEW vii. 7.

Ask, and it shall be given to you; seek, and ye shall find; knock, and it shall be opened unto you.

[*Petite, et dabitur vobis; quærite, et invenietis; pulsate, et aperietur vobis.* Lat. Vulg.]

[*Ask, and it shall be given you; seek, and ye shall find; knock, and it shall be opened unto you.* Eng. Trans.]

AFTER the consideration of our own inability mentioned by St. Paul, and the examination of the manifold goodness 2 Cor. 3. 5. of God from Whom, as St. James saith, "every good giving [Jas. 1. 17.] and every perfect gift cometh;" because we see that of ourselves we cannot so much as think any good, and yet that from "the Father of lights" we may receive that grace which shall enable us to do all things; now it followeth by good order, that we repair to God for that power which we have not of ourselves. Christ will not have "holy things given to [Mat. 7. 6.] dogs," nor "pearls cast to swine," that is, to such as make no account of them; and therefore if we esteem of the grace of Christ or make any reckoning of it, we must come to Him for it. Now we cannot come to God but by prayer, as Augustine saith: *Non passibus sed precibus itúr ad Deum, et nuncius noster oratio est quæ ibi mandatum nostrum peragit quo caro nostra pervenire nequit;* 'It is not with paces but with prayers we go to God, and our messenger is prayer which there doth our errand where our flesh cannot come.' Therefore Christ saith, Do not wait as swine till the grace of

God be cast unto you, but if you will have it, "ask, and it shall be given to you."

The tenor of this Scripture hath this coherence: first, knowing our own insufficiency and the goodness of God from Whom "every good thing cometh," presently we wish with ourselves that He would admit us to be suitors unto Him. Therefore Christ in the word "Ask," tells us, that God hath His Courts of Requests, that we may be bold to put up our supplications.

Secondly, whereas earthly princes may perhaps afford a good countenance but will not grant the thing that is sought for at their hands, Christ saith that " the Father of lights" is not only affable but liberal; so that albeit we be not only Gen. 18. 27. "dust and ashes" and therefore unworthy to pray to God, but also wretched sinners unworthy to be heard, because as Joh. 9. 31. the blind man saith *peccatores non exaudit Deus,* " yet He Ps. 66. 18. will not cast out our prayers nor turn His mercy from us ;"
20. but if we " ask, it shall be given."

Thirdly, that we should not think that as in the world there are many suitors but few obtainers, so howsoever all do pray unto God yet we are not in the number of those that speed, therefore Christ addeth, " Whosoever asketh, receiveth ; whosoever seeketh, findeth ; and to him that knocketh, it shall be opened." No unworthiness of our own can exclude us from the mercy of God, for He receiveth the Lu. 18. 14. prayer not only of the Publican but of the prodigal son, and Lu. 15. 20. Lu. 23. 43. promiseth mercy to the " thief hanging on the cross," if at the last hour he seeketh it by prayer.

Of these two verses there are three parts : first a precept, *Petite, quærite, pulsate,* "Ask, seek, knock ;" secondly, a promise, " It shall be given, ye shall find, and it shall be opened ;" thirdly, an enlargement of the promise, which is made not only to such as are of just and holy conversation, [Mat. 7. 8.] but to sinners, " for whosoever asketh, receiveth."

As on God's behalf we see, first, His affability ; secondly, His liberality ; thirdly, the largeness of His liberality : so on our own parts we are taught, first, that we may boldly pour out our desires before God ; secondly, we may conceive hope to be heard in the thing we crave ; thirdly, not an uncertain hope, confounded through our own unworthiness, " For who-

soever asketh, receiveth;" and, as Christ speaketh, "Him Joh. 6. 37.
that cometh to Me, I will in no wise cast out."

In the precept four things are to be considered : first, the
necessity ; secondly, the vehemency, signified by a threefold petition which implieth an instancy, as Solomon speaks ;
" Have I not written three times to thee ?" thirdly, the cohe- Prov. 22.
rence of these three terms, asking, seeking, and knocking ; 20.
fourthly, the distinguishing of them.

Touching the first, the example of our Saviour might be
a sufficient motive to stir us up to prayer, Who " in the Mark 1. 35.
morning very early before day went into a solitary place and
there prayed," and in the evening prayed, Himself "alone in Mat. 14. 23.
the mountain."

Secondly, whereas He setteth down a form of prayer, He Mat. 6. 9.
sheweth that prayer is necessary ; but when unto both He
addeth a precept, we may not think any longer it is a matter indifferent but of necessity ; a commandment is a thing
obligatory. So when Christ commands us to pray, He doth
not leave it as a thing in our own choice, but binds us to
the performance of it ; for prayer is not only required as a
thing supplying our need—for when we feel want, we need
not be provoked to prayer—the brute beasts themselves
being pinched with hunger "do seek their meat at God," Ps. 104. 21.
and " the ravens call upon Him for food ;" but it is required Ps. 147. 9.
as a part of God's service. Anna being in the Temple,
" served God by prayer ;" by prayer the Apostles performed Lu. 2. 37.
that service to the Lord, which the Apostle calls λειτουργία. Acts 13. 2.
Therefore, so oft as we resort to the house of God to put up
our petitions to God, then we do Him service properly, and
not only when we are present at a sermon, for then God
rather serveth us and attends us, and entreats us by His
ministers " to be reconciled to Him."   2 Cor. 5. 20.

As prayer is a part of God's worship, so the neglect of
prayer is a sin, as one saith, *peccatum non orandi.* Therefore
the Prophet among other sins wherewith he chargeth the
wicked, reckoneth this to be one, that "they call not on the Ps. 14. 4.
Lord." The neglect of this duty was the beginning of Saul's
fall, as all the Fathers interpret that place where it is said
that Saul commanded the priest to "withdraw his hand" 1 Sam. 14.
from the ark. For this hath been commanded ever from the 19.

S E R M.
III.

Job 8. 5.
Deut. 10.
12.

Ps. 141. 2. beginning, that we should pray unto God; not only in the law of nature, but also in the law of Moses.

In the time of the Law, a special part of the service which the people performed to God was the offering up of incense, and therefore the Prophet compareth prayer to incense. And it is most fitly resembled to incense, for the use of incense was to sweeten those places which are unsavoury; even so the wicked imaginations and unchaste thoughts of our hearts, which yield a stinking smell in the nostrils of God, are sweetened by no other means than by prayer; and therefore to shew how the one is resembled by the other, it is said Lu. 1. 10. that while the incense was burning, the people were without upon their knees in prayer. Neither was it a thing usual in Ps. 50. 15. the Law only, but also in the Prophets. " Call upon Me ;" Ps. 81. 10. and, *Aperi os tuum et implebo.* Touching the effect and Joel 2. 32. fruit whereof it is said, " Whosoever calleth on the name of the Lord, shall be saved."

Secondly, albeit God have little commandments, as Christ Mat. 5. 19. speaks, " He that breaks one of these little commandments ;" yet this touching the duty of prayer is not a slight commandment but of great instance, and so much we are to gather from hence, that Christ is not content once to say " Ask," but repeats it in three several terms, " Ask, seek, [Retrac. 1.
19. 9.] knock ;" which, as Augustine saith, sheweth *instantissimam necessitatem.*

From the vehemency of this commandment we are to consider these three things : first, it lets us see our want and need, in that we are willed to ask; secondly, by seeking, Christ doth intimate thus much to us, that we have lost ourselves; thirdly, in that He would have us to knock, He would have us to learn that we are as men shut out of the presence of God and His kingdom, where is the fulness of joy and pleasure for ever.

The first sheweth man what is the misery of his estate, in regard whereof he is called Enoch ; secondly, his blindness, Mat. 20. 22. which is so great, that when he doth pray he asketh he knows not what. If he would pray, he knows not how to Lu. 11. 1. pray, for which cause the disciples desire Christ to teach them. Their blindness is such as they know not the way Joh. 14. 15. to come to the Father, as Thomas confesseth. Thirdly, it

sheweth our slothfulness in seeking our own good, which
appeareth herein, that we have need to have a commandment given us to stir us up to pray to God.

The third thing in the precept is the dependence of these
three words, *Petite, quærite, pulsate.* For there is no idle
word in God's book. Therefore as they that have to do with
gold will make no waste at all, but gather together the
least paring; so we must esteem preciously of God's word,
which is more precious than gold. We must be gone hence,
and there is a place whither we desire all to come, which we
cannot do except we knock; and because we know not at
what door to knock, therefore we must seek the door; but
we have no will nor desire to seek, therefore Christ willeth
in the first place that we ask it, and the thing that we must
ask is the Spirit of grace and of prayer; and if we ask It,
then shall we have ability and power not only to seek the
door, but when we have found it to knock at it.

Fourthly, as these words depend one upon another, so
they are to be distinguished one from another: they that
are suitors for any earthly benefit do occupy not only their
tongue in speaking, but their legs in resorting to great persons; they that seek do occupy not only their legs in going
up and down, but their eyes to look in every place; and
they that knock, as they use other members, so especially
they use their hands. But when our Saviour enjoineth us
the use of prayer, He expresseth it not in one word but in
three several terms, to teach us that when we come to pray
to God the whole man must be occupied, and all the members of the body employed in the service of God, for Christ
will not have pearls cast unto swine, and we may not look
to have the gifts of God cast into our mouths; but if we will
obtain, we must first " open our mouths" to ask it. Secondly, Ps. 81. 10.
they are not so easily found as that we shall stumble upon
them, but we must seek diligently with the lifting up of our
eyes; and, " to God That dwells in the heavens." Thirdly, Ps. 123. 1.
because the door is shut and locked up, therefore we must
knock: for which end we are willed " to lift up our hands Lam. 3. 41.
with our hearts to God Which is in heaven."

The lifting up of our hand is that which the people call
the "evening sacrifice." As the body, so also the soul may Ps. 141. 2.

SERM.
III.
not be idle, but occupied with these three virtues : first, it must *petere*, which noteth confidence and trust ; secondly, *quærere*, which signifies diligence ; thirdly, *pulsare*, which implieth perseverance. If we join these three virtues to our prayer, doubtless we shall be heard.

As the second cause of our life here is *sudor vultús*—for we live *arando ac serendo* ' by ploughing and sowing,'—so the second cause of our living is another *sudor vultús*, which consisteth in asking, seeking, knocking. As in the sweat of our brows we eat the bread that feeds our bodies, so by these spiritual pains and endeavours we come to the bread of life, which feedeth our souls eternally.

Job 21. 15.
Now if we ask that question that is made, " What profit shall we have if we pray unto Him ?" it is certain that God having created us, may justly command us ; but He doth not only constrain us to pray by His commandment, but allure us thereunto by His promise ; He saith, if we ask the life of grace we shall obtain it ; if we seek it, we shall find it ; thirdly, having found the way, we shall *intrare in gau-*
Mat. 25. 21.
dium Domini, " enter into our Master's joy."

Ps. 24. 5, 6.
If we ask we shall have grace, whereby it shall appear we have not received our soul in vain ; secondly, seeking we shall find the help and assistance of God's Spirit, so that we
2 Cor. 6. 1.
shall not receive " grace in vain ;" thirdly, by knocking, the
1 Cor. 15.
58.
way of entrance shall be opened unto us, so that " our labour shall not be in vain in the Lord ;" as Augustine saith, *Non dicitur quid dabitur,* ' Christ nameth not what shall be given to you :' to let us know that that gift is a thing *supra omne nomen,* ' above all that can be named.'

It is as great a gift as an earthly prince can give, to pro-
Mark 6. 23.
mise " half his kingdom," but God hath promised not half His Kingdom, but all His Kingdom ; we shall receive of God not only whatsoever we desire, (for *desiderare nostrum,* as one saith, is not *terminus bonitatis Dei,* ' our desire is not
Eph. 3. 20.
the limit or bound of God's goodness') but " above all that we can ask or think."

In the confidence of this promise, the saints of God in the time of their misery fly unto God by prayer as their only ready help. In the days of Enoch, which were full of
Gen. 4. 26.
miseries and troubles, men " began to call upon the name of

the Lord;" and Abraham in every place where he came, being
departed out of his own country and living in exile, " built Gen. 12. 8.
an altar, and called on the name of the Lord." David saith,
that his only remedy which he used against the slander and
injuries of his enemies stood herein, that " he gave himself Ps. 109. 4.
to prayer." Jehoshaphat being besieged with enemies on
every side, used this as a bulwark against them : " Lord, we 2 Chron.
have no power to withstand this great company that are 20. 12.
come against us, and we know not what to do, but our eyes
are towards Thee." The like comfort did Hezekiah find in
prayer, both when Sennacherib threatened his destruction,
and in his sickness; and it is indeed the city of refuge,
whither the godly in all times have used to fly for safeguard
from their miseries. It is *rete gratiarum et situla gratiæ,*
'the net of graces and bucket of grace,' by which a good
man draweth the grace of God. Prov. 12. 2.

The special gift that we can desire of God is Christ Himself, Who is *Donum illud Dei.* Now forasmuch as indeed Joh. 4. 10.
nothing can be a greater benefit than to enjoy the presence
of God—as the Prophet saith, " Whom do I desire in heaven Ps. 73. 25.
but Thee?" and Philip saith, *Ostende nobis Patrem, et suf-*
ficit, " Shew us the Father, and it is sufficient"—we are to Joh. 14. 8.
consider how we may come to it.

Christ saith, " I am the way," *et Ego sum ostium.* If He Joh. 14. 6.
be both the way and the door, then no doubt but if God Joh. 10.
bestow Christ on us, we shall both find the way to God, and
enter into His kingdom by Christ, Who is the door. For
the obtaining of this gift we must be instant with God in
prayer, which if we do, He will give us that we ask; therefore Augustine saith, *Domine cupio Te, da mihi solum Te,*
aut non dimittam Te, 'Lord, I desire Thee, give me Thee
alone, or else I will not let Thee go.'

In the third place our Saviour enlargeth the promise : lest
we should doubt that God will not hear all manner of persons that pray to Him, or that He will not grant all their
suits, therefore in regard of the persons Christ saith, *Quis-*
quis, " Whosoever asketh receiveth." Whosoever join these
three virtues in their prayer, confidence, diligence, perseverance, and occupy all the parts of their body in this service of God, they shall be sure to receive the thing they ask,

SERM.
III.

Mat. 7. 6.

Joh. 16. 23.

1 Joh. 5. 14.

Mat. 20. 22.

Prov. 21. 13.
Ps. 109. 7.
[S. Aug. Ser. 56. 2.]
[Lu. 11. 11, 12.]

for the promise is made only to them that perform God's commandment, *Petenti dabitur*, we must ask and we shall have it; for God useth not to cast holy things upon them that make no reckoning of them.

Touching the things themselves, He That is the truth hath said, "Whatsoever you ask My Father in My name, He will give it you." Therefore it is impossible He should lie, especially when He confirmeth it with an oath, as in that place, "Verily, verily, I say unto you, whatsoever you ask the Father in My name, He will give it you." But we must take heed what we ask; we may not αἰτεῖν ἄνευ αἰτίας, 'ask without a cause.' "If we ask any thing according to His will, He heareth us." Therefore our prayers must be grounded upon some just cause; we may not ask any childish petition of God, for He will revert them. If we like children ask we know not what, we cannot assure ourselves to be heard, for unto such prayers He answereth, "Ye ask ye know not what." Much less will He grant hurtful petitions.

As He is our physician, He will not give us cold drink when we are sick of an ague, though we cry for it never so much. They that ask vengeance of God, and would have Him to be the executioner of their wrath, "shall not be heard," but "their prayer is turned to sin." So far is it from the service of God.

If the child ask fish, the father will not give him a scorpion; no more will God hear us in those things which we ask of Him, if He know they will be hurtful.

He only is wise, and knoweth what is good for us; and if we receive not the thing which we ask, yet—as Jerome saith —*non accipiendo accepimus*, 'in not receiving we have received.' Christ saith not 'Ask and ye shall receive the thing ye ask,' but "Ask and it shall be given unto you," that is, the thing that you desire. We all desire those things that be good though outwardly we are not able to discern what is good, but God our heavenly Father as He knoweth best what is good for us so He will give us good things, though we be not able always to ask that which is good for ourselves.

Secondly, we must pray in such manner and form as He requireth; God doth hear us many times, even *quando peti-*

mus malum, inasmuch as He doth not give us the hurtful things which we ignorantly ask. But He will not hear us *cum petibus male:* "Ye ask, and receive not, because ye ask Jas. 4. 3. amiss." Therefore we must beware how we stand affected at the time of prayer: if we pray coldly, without any great desire to attain the thing we ask, we ask like swine that esteem not of pearls but trample them under their feet; if "we draw near with our lips, but our hearts be far from Isa. 29. 13. God," then it is not like we shall be heard; if we pray as Peter, and the other disciples, who "being heavy with sleep" Lu. 9. 32, asked they knew not what, we cannot receive the truth. ^{33.} But if, as Moses speaks, "we seek the Lord with all our Deut. 4. 29. heart," if we do with Paul *orare spiritu et orare mente,* then 1 Cor. 14. we may conceive hope to be heard, for the commandment to ^{15.} ask is given *cordi non pulmoni,* 'to the heart not to the lungs;' *id quod cor non facit non fit,* 'that which the heart doth not is not done.'

Secondly, touching the manner, as with fervency so we must pray with reverence, not having our heads covered, as we see many do; which behaviour, how rude and unbeseeming it is we may easily discern, as the Prophet speaks, "Offer this kind of behaviour to thy lord or master, and see Mal. 1. 8. whether he will accept it."

If thou having a suit to an earthly prince darest not speak but upon thy knees with all submission, how much more ought we to reverence the Lord God, in comparison of Whom all the princes in the earth are but crickets and "grasshoppers." Therefore the manner of our prayer to Isa. 40. 22. God must be in all reverence.

Solomon prayed upon his knees; Daniel fell down upon 2 Chron. 6. his knees: so did St. Peter, so did Paul; and not only men _{13.} Dan. 6. 10. upon earth but the glorious spirits in heaven cast themselves Acts 9. 40. and their crowns down before Him That "sits upon the Rev. 4. 10. throne;" yea, Jesus Christ the Son of God fell down upon His knees and prayed to His Father, *et exauditus propter* Lu. 22. 41. *reverentiam.* So did Paul serve God μετὰ πάσης ταπεινο- Acts 20. 19. φροσύνης. Secondly, if we would obtain any thing at God's hand, we must not only ask it, but seek for it. He that having prayed sits still without adding his endeavour, shall not receive the thing he prays for, for he must not only

z

SERM.
III.
Heb. 12. 12.
orare but *laborare; pro quibus enim orandum, pro iis labo-randum est.* To this end the Apostle would have us " to pull up our faint hands and weak knees." And when we have asked grace, we must be careful that we ourselves be not wanting unto grace, as well as we were careful that grace should not be wanting unto us.

This diligence is noted in the word *Petite,* which as it is used in the first place, so also it signifieth ' to go to,' or ' to hit and knock,' so that it containeth all the three virtues that are required unto prayer; but for our instruction, our Saviour hath expressed them in three several terms.

Thirdly, having found the way we may not rest there, there is a door whereby we must enter; and that shall not stand open for us against we come, we must knock at it.

2 Cor. 5. 20. It pleaseth God to "entreat" us, to seek and find us when
Lu. 15. 32. we are "lost;" " He stands and knocks at our door." There-
Rev. 3. 20.
[Deut. 10. fore as Moses speaks in Deuteronomy, we are to consider
12.] what He doth require at our hands.

The service that we owe Him is likewise to entreat Him, to seek for grace at Him, to knock continually till He open the gate of His mercy. If God hear us not so soon as we
1 Sam. 28. ask, we may not cease to knock as Saul did, who because
6. that " God answered him not, neither by dreams, nor by Urim, nor prophet," asked counsel of a witch. Importunity,
[Lu. 18. as our Saviour speaks in the eighteenth chapter of St. Luke,
2-5.] is a means whereby oftentimes men obtain their suits. The unjust judge will be content to hear the widow's cause at length, even because he would be rid of cumber; if she be earnest with him, she shall at last obtain her suit by importunity; so howsoever God be not inclined to do us good and have His ears open to our prayers, yet He is much delighted with our importunate suits.

[Lu. 18. If the unjust judge that neither feared God nor reverenced
5-7.] man, may be overcome with importunate suit, much more will God revenge them which give not over their suits, but
[Gal. 6. 9.] " cry to Him night and day." " Let us not be weary of well-doing; for in due season we shall reap, if we faint not."

These conditions being performed; first, that we seek in the desire of our heart and in humility; secondly, that we be not wanting to grace, but work with it; thirdly, if we do it with continuance, not giving over, then we shall find it true which Christ saith, *Omnis qui petit accipit.* [Mat. 7. 8.]

The sum is, as when God said, " Seek ye My face," David answered, " Thy face, O Lord, I will seek ;" so when Christ Ps. 27. 8. saith to us, " Ask," our answer must be, We will at least dispose ourselves thereunto, especially seeing He doth not only *præire exemplo*, but *dicere ut petas*, seeing He doth not only by His commandment *permittere*, but *præcipere ut petas.*

Lastly, seeing by His promise He doth not only allure them *ut petant*, but doth *minari si non petas*, ' threaten if thou ask not ;' for if we ask of any but from Him He is angry, as He was with the King of Israel that enquired of Baal-zebub when he should recover ; " Is there not a God 2 Kings 1. in Israel ?" And Christ was offended with His disciples for ^{2, 3.} the neglect of this duty : " Hitherto ye have asked nothing." Joh. 16. 24. And when we come to ask of God, we must not cease our suit if He grant us not our suit at the first, but say with Jacob, *Non dimittam Te.* We must be instant, as the Ca- Gen. 32. 26. naanite was ; we must be earnest, as he that came at mid- Mat. 15. night to borrow bread ; and importunate, as the widow with Lu. 11. 5. the judge ; and then we may assure ourselves of a comfort-able effect of prayers.

A

PREPARATION TO PRAYER.

SERMON IV.

Romans viii. 26.

Likewise the Spirit also helpeth our infirmities: for we know not what to pray for as we ought: but the Spirit Itself maketh request for us with sighs which cannot be uttered.

[*Similiter autem et Spiritus adjuvat infirmitatem nostram: nam quid oremus sicut oportet nescimus: sed Ipse Spiritus postulat pro nobis gemitibus inenarrabilibus.* Lat. Vulg.]

[*Likewise the Spirit also helpeth our infirmities: for we know not what we should pray for as we ought: but the Spirit Itself maketh intercession for us with groanings which cannot be uttered.* Eng. Trans.]

SERM. IV.

2 Cor. 3. 5.
Jas. 1. 17.
Mat. 7. 7
Out of St. Paul we may see, first, "that of ourselves we are not sufficient" at all to do good; and that all good comes "from the Father of lights," and that in that regard we must ask and receive at His hands from Whom it comes. Now the Apostle meeteth with another difficulty, which is, how we may pray; for as we cannot perform any good thing of ourselves unless God minister power, so we know not how to ask this grace at His hands. Therefore to answer that question of the disciples which desired that Christ
Lu. 11. 1. should teach them how to pray, the Apostle saith, that because "we know not what to pray for as we ought," therefore "the Spirit doth help our infirmities."

The Apostle begins at "our infirmities," which he lays down in such sort as we may plainly see that our defects and wants are many. For as there are infirmities of the

body which the Scripture calls "the infirmities of Egypt," Deut. 7. 15.
whereunto the saints of God are subject as well as other,
as the Apostle speaks of Timothy that he had *crebras in-* 1 Tim. 5.
firmitates; so the soul also hath certain infirmities, and that ^{23.}
is the infirmity whereof the Apostle speaketh; for albeit
our soul be the stronger part, as our Saviour speaketh when
He saith, "The spirit indeed is strong," yet it is subject to Mat. 26. 41.
many infirmities and weaknesses when it doubteth of God's
mercies, saying, "Will the Lord absent Himself for ever? Ps. 77. 7,
hath God forgotten to be gracious?" which the Prophet ^{9, 10.}
acknowledgeth to be signs of his infirmities. And as the
spirit is weak, so there is a weakness of conscience: and no 1 Cor. 8. 7.
marvel if there be such infirmities in the bodies also, for life
itself is but weak, in regard whereof it is said of God, that
hereby He is content to spare us, for that " He remembereth Ps. 103. 14.
that we are but dust," and considereth "that we are but Ps. 78. 39.
even as the wind that passeth away."

The difference is that, as Christ saith, *hæc infirmitas non* Joh. 11. 4.
est ad mortem, and the dropsy, palsy, and such like diseases
and infirmities of body, are not mortal.

The second thing which the Apostle teacheth is, that howsoever we be, as the Apostle speaketh, "compassed with in- Heb. 5. 2.
firmities," yet they are not past cure, for "the Spirit helpeth [Rom. 8.
our infirmity;" so that albeit we are subject to fall through ^{26.]}
weakness, yet "there is hope concerning this thing," and Ezra 10. 2.
our error may be healed, for there is "balm in Gilead," Dan. 4. 27.
which serveth to cure all our spiritual diseases. Jer. 8. 22.

Now the cure of the infirmities of our soul is not performed by any strength of our own nor by our own spirit,
but by the Spirit of God; for so long as our infirmities are
but bodily, the "spirit of man will sustain them," and there
is help to be found; but when the "spirit itself is wounded, Prov. 18.
then who can help it?" ^{14.}

The spirit of man must have help from a higher thing
than itself, as from the Spirit of God, Which only is able
to minister help.

The Apostle ascribeth to the Spirit of God two benefits:
first, in regard of the life to come; secondly, in respect of
this present life. For the one, as He is the Spirit of adoption, assures us of our estate in the life to come; namely,

SERM.
IV.

that as God hath adopted us to be His children, so we shall be fellow-heirs with His own Son of His heavenly kingdom. Touching the other, because we are subject in this life to fall through infirmity we have this benefit from Him, that He stays and upholds us, and therefore is called *Spiritus* ἀντιλήψεως.

As our infirmities are manifold whether we respect the body or the soul, so the weakness and defects of our souls

Gal. 5. 17.

appear not only in good things which we cannot do "because the flesh ever lusteth against the spirit so that we cannot do the things that we would," but in evil things which we should bear and are not able.

The evil things that we should bear, are not only afflic-

[2 Cor. 4. 17.]

tions and the crosses which we are subject to, which the Apostle proveth to be more tolerable because they are not worthy of the glory to come, but *dilatio boni*, wherein we need the virtue of magnanimity, because it is a great cross;

Prov. 13. 12.

as the Wise Man saith, *Spes quæ differtur affligit animam.* Touching which affliction and crosses, because in this life

Ps. 55. 6.

we cannot obtain that which the Prophet wisheth, namely, "to fly away (as it were) with the wings of a dove, that so we might be at rest," therefore we must betake ourselves to

Isa. 38. 14.

the mourning of the dove, waiting patiently when God will give us time to escape.

The means and ways whereby the Spirit doth help us are many, but he only meaneth prayer; to teach us, that howsoever it be not esteemed as it ought, yet it is the chief prop and principal pillar which the Holy Ghost useth

1 Tim. 2, 1, 2.

to strengthen our weakness. Therefore when the Apostle willeth that, "first of all, prayers and supplications should be made for Kings and all in authority," the reason is, as Augustine noteth, because both man's salvation, the honesty of life, knowledge of the truth, quietness of kingdoms, duties of Kings, and whatsoever tendeth to the public benefit, come by and from prayer; so that not only the Church and spiritual matters, but the commonwealth and temporal things, are stayed upon the pillar of prayer.

Wherefore as prayer is a special help, so we are not only exhorted by religion to use it, but nature itself binds us unto it; for so long as we can devise any help of our-

selves, or receive it from any other, so long we lean upon
our own staff; but when all help fails, then we fly to prayer
as our last refuge. And therefore when God is said to
"feed the ravens that call upon Him," that cry of theirs Ps. 147. 9.
is the voice of nature; so that albeit men for a time lean
to their stays and help, yet there is a day when all flesh
shall be made to come unto Him Who only it is That Ps. 65. 2.
heareth prayer; that is, when they lie "howling upon their Hos. 7. 14.
beds," then they shall be fain to call upon God for help.
So, howsoever Pharaoh in the pride of his heart say, "Who Exod. 5. 2.
is the Lord that I should hear His voice?" yet He made him
come to Him, when He plagued him with thundering, and
rain, and hail, which made him send to Moses and Aaron Exod. 9. 27, 28.
that they might pray unto God for him.

But here the Apostle meaneth the prayer of the spirit,
which always reckons prayer to be the first and chiefest
help in all trouble and not the last, as the prayer of the
flesh doth.

Therefore, as we must discern *simulacra virtutum* from
virtues themselves, and that which is natural from that
which is of grace, so we must distinguish the prayer of the
spirit from the carnal prayer; and be sure that the virtues
which we have, if they be any, are not natural as those in
many of the heathen, but that they proceed from grace and
the working of God's Spirit.

To the right framing of our prayer it is required that
we do not only *orare mente et spiritu,* but as the Psalmist 1 Cor. 14.
saith of the praising of God so we pray to God "with Ps. 47. 7.
understanding." Both our heart, our understanding, our
affection must concur in making intercession to God.

For a second point, if prayer be a stay to us in our infirmities, then we must be careful that our prayers be not
faint and weak, but that they proceed from the fervency and
vehemency of the spirit; for as Christ saith, "If the light Mat. 6. 23.
that is in thee be darkness, how great is that darkness!" if
our prayer be nothing else but infirmity as it is for the most
part, how great is our infirmity!

But the Apostle sheweth our weakness in prayer in that
he denieth men two things: first, that "we know not what
to pray for;" secondly, that we know not "how to pray."

SERM.
IV.
Joh. 8. 12.

[Joh. 3. 8.]

Mat. 20. 22.

Rom. 6. 19.

Mat. 20.
20—23.

For both these defects we have a double supply : for Christ, as He is the "light of the world," hath directed us what to pray for by that form of prayer which He hath prescribed unto us; and the Holy Ghost, Who is compared to the "wind that bloweth where it will," instructeth us how to pray, for that It stirreth up our affections, so that we pray with fervency of spirit, and utter our desires unto God with sighs that cannot be expressed. For, as a man that travelleth must have a knowledge of his way, so he cannot take a journey in hand, except he have a good wind to set him forward : to this end we are taught, not only by the wisdom of God the Father what to pray for, but from the power of His Spirit we have those motions kindled in us whereby our prayer is made fervent.

Touching the persons whom the Apostle chargeth with this twofold ignorance, they are not the common sort of men but even the Apostles themselves, for he includes himself in the words, "We know not." So Christ said, not to the heathen men, *Nescitis quid petitis,* but to His disciples, James and John; so that this is generally true of all men, that they know not what to ask καθὸ δεῖ, "as they ought," except God's Spirit help them.

It is true that we have a diffused knowledge of good and evil, and a desire to be partakers of the one and to be delivered from the other, (for, *Ignoti nulla cupido*) but we must have a distinct knowledge, that is, whether the thing we desire be good or no. There is an estate of life which is contemplative, and another active, and our infirmity is such as we know not which of them to take ourselves unto, but oftentimes we think that course of life to be good for us, which albeit it be good in itself yet turns to our overthrow; so that when we desire of God to place us in any such course of life we "speak after the manner of men," taking it for a contented course for ourselves, whereas it falls not out so.

This will appear more plainly, both in things temporal and spiritual. The sons of Zebedee in their suit to Christ had a desire to obtain some good thing at our Saviour's hands, and they could not bethink themselves of any thing better than to be exalted to some place of honour, and therefore desired that "one of them may sit at His right hand, and the other at His left hand:" but Christ told them "they asked they knew not what," for honour is not fit for all men; they were the disciples of Christ, and were to drink of the cup of affliction, and therefore willed them to be mindful of it and not to affect that which was not for their good.

Likewise in spiritual things we may err, and hereof we have example in St. Paul, whom a man would think to have had knowledge enough so that he would not ask the thing that was not good for him; he had "the messenger of Satan [2 Cor. 12. sent to buffet him," and he prayed that it might be removed 7.] from him, which seemeth to have been a reasonable petition, but God answered him that he asked he knew not what, it was more necessary for him to be exercised with the temptations than not; and whereas he desired to be so pure as not once to be driven to evil, God told him that His "grace was sufficient" for him, for it was His will to per- 2 Cor. 12. fect His strength in his weakness. Therefore if we have 9. any revelation from "flesh and blood" that persuadeth us Mat. 16. 17. that this or that is good for us, we must know that all such are false; and that we must suffer ourselves to be directed by God's Spirit, Who knoweth better what is good for us than we ourselves.

But to the end that we should not err the Spirit of God maketh intercession for us, and therefore we may be sure that although we know not how to pray in such sort as may please God, yet the Spirit of God Who knoweth the 1 Cor. 2. secrets of the counsel of God will make that prayer for 10, 11. us which shall be both for our good and also according to God's will.

It cannot be verified of the Holy Ghost Which is God, that He either prayeth or groaneth; but the Apostle's meaning is that He makes us to make intercession, and [S. Aug. hath that operation in our hearts that He makes us to 16, 17.] groan. So when the Apostle says that "the Spirit cries, Gal. 4. 6. Abba, Father," his meaning is, that "by It we cry, Abba, Rom. 8. 15. Father."

Again, the Spirit is said to make intercession for us, because It "sheddeth abroad the love of God in our hearts." Rom. 5. 5.

SERM.
IV.

For from the love of God proceeds this love and affection in us that we desire Him and all His blessings, and therefore make our prayer to Him to that end, which is nothing else but *explicatio desiderii;* so that we do not so soon desire any good thing, but we are ready to pray for it. So

Ps. 38. 9.

saith the Prophet, "Lord, Thou knowest my desire, and my groaning is not hid from Thee."

Likewise, when our desire is delayed, so that we obtain not the thing we would have, then we are cast into sorrow, which is wrought in us by the Spirit Which is in us, and by prayer; for it is the Spirit of God Which kindleth this

[Vid. ad
Simp. 1.
21.]

fervency of desire in prayer, as Augustine saith, *Tepida est omnis oratio, quam non prævenit inspiratio,* 'Every prayer is lukewarm which is not prevented with inspiration.'

The first thing that the Spirit of God works in us is, that He inclineth our hearts to pray to God for the good which we lack, which is a thing not in our own power; and there-

2 Sam. 7.
27.

fore David thanks God "that he found in his heart to pray;" for when we would settle ourselves to pray, *nihil tam longe abest a nobis quam orare ut decet,* 'there is nothing so far from us as to pray as we ought.'

Now being thus untoward in ourselves, the Spirit of God comes and helps our infirmity, and as the Psalmist saith, He opens our hearts to pray. By this means it comes to pass, that a man having his affection cold shall on a sudden feel

Ps. 108. 1.

in himself a desire to pray, and shall say, *Domine, paratum est cor meum,* "O Lord, my heart is ready."

Ps. 81. 10.

Secondly, whereas the Lord saith, "Open thy mouth and I will fill it," we find this infirmity in ourselves, that when we have found a heart to pray yet we cannot

Ps. 51. 15.

open our mouths, and therefore David saith, "Open Thou my lips;" and so must we sue to Christ that He will give us words to speak, for God hath a key both to our tongue and will.

Thirdly, having begun to pray, that falls out many times

Ps. 40. 12.

which David complains of, *Cor meum dereliquit me.* Our heart will be gone, and our mind will be wandering abroad, not regarding what our tongue speaks.

It falls out often, that as Abraham had his sacrifice ready,

Gen. 15. 11.

he was no sooner gone from it but the fowls of the air did

light upon it. So while we offer up to God "the calves of Hos. 14. 2.
our lips," and our course is past, it comes to pass through
our wantonness many foul thoughts be got upon our sacrifice and despoil it; and the remedy that the Spirit of God Ps. 141. 3,
affords us against this infirmity is, that It calls us home [4.]
and tells us we are kneeling before the Majesty of God,
and therefore ought to take heed what we speak in His
presence. Therefore Bernard, to keep his mind in the
meditation of God, when he would pray began thus, "Let Ps. 68. 1.
God arise, and let all His enemies be scattered;" and Augustine to the same purpose began thus, "Save me, O God, Ps. 69. 1.
for the waters overflow."

Fourthly, though we have our meditation still on God,
yet we shall find in ourselves that our spirits are dull and
heavy, and have no manner of vigour to help our infirmity;
herein the Spirit helps and puts these meditations in our
hearts, whereby It kindleth, as the Prophet saith, a fire [Ps. 39. 3.]
burning within us; so that God shall be fain to say to us
as He did to Moses, *Dimitte Me,* "Let Me alone." Ex. 32. 10.

Fifthly, albeit we pray but faintly and have not that
supply of fervency that is required in prayer, yet we have
comfort that ever when we most faint in prayer there
are of God's saints that pray for us with all instancy,
by which it comes to pass that being all but one body
their prayers tend to our good as well as their own, for
the faithful howsoever they be many and dispersed into
divers corners of the world, yet they are but one dough;
and as they are the members of one body, so they pray
not privately for themselves but for the whole body of
the Church; so that the weakness of one member is supplied by the fervent and earnest prayer of the other. Therefore when the Apostle saith, "The Spirit maketh intercession for us," *gemitibus inenarrabilibus,* Augustine asketh,
What groanings are these? are they thine or mine? No,
they are the groanings of the Church, sometime in me,
sometime in thee. And therefore Samuel, to shew that
the ministers of God do the people no less good when
they pray for them than when they teach them, said,
"God forbid I should cease to pray for you, and so sin 1 Sam. 12.
against God;" for he was a help to them not only in [23.]

SERM. preaching to them, but in offering burnt offerings for them.
IV. Therefore the people pray to Esay, " Lift thou up thy prayer
[Isa. 37. 4.] for us," for as the offering of the minister is to put the
2 Pet. 1. 12. people in mind, so they are God's remembrancers; they are
angels as well ascending upwards by their prayer in the
behalf of the people, as descending to teach them the will
of God.

But if the spirit that quails in us do quail also in the
Lu. 19. 41. whole Church, yet we have a supply from the tears which
Heb. 5. 7. our Head, Christ, shed on His Church, and from "the
strong cries" which He uttered to God His Father "in
the days of His flesh," by which He ceaseth not to make
request to God still for us; so that albeit the hardness of
our heart be such as we cannot pray for ourselves nor the
Church for us, yet we may say, *Conqueror Tibi, Domine,
lachrymis Jesu Christi.*

Lastly, because we cannot pray $\kappa\alpha\theta\grave{o}$ $\delta\epsilon\hat{\iota}$, we have two
helps also in that behalf from the Spirit; first, that the
Spirit teacheth us to submit our will unto God's will,
Rom. 6. 19. because as we are men so we "speak after the manner
of men."

This submission we learn from the example of Christ's
Mat. 26. 39. prayer to God His Father: *Transeat calix iste a Me,* "Let
this cup pass from Me, yet not My will but Thy will be
2 Sam. 15. done." So David qualified his desire: "If I have found
25, 26. favour with the Lord, He will bring me again; but if not,
let Him do what seemeth good to Himself."

Secondly, when we look back upon our prayer and see
that by reason of want of fervency and zeal it is but
Isa. 42. 3. "smoking flax," then the Spirit stirreth us up to desire
God that according to His promise " He will not quench
2 Cor. 12. it," but that His grace may be sufficient for us, and that
9. He will make perfect His strength in our weakness.

The other thing wherein the Spirit helpeth our infirmities
is, that He worketh in our hearts certain groans that cannot
be expressed, which is a plain opposition to drowsy and
[S. Aug. slothful prayer; for a devout prayer *plus constat gemitibus
Epist. 130. quam sermonibus,* it is not fine phrases and goodly sentences
c. 10.] that commend our prayer but the fervency of the Spirit
from Whom it proceeds.

It is well if we do *orare mente et spiritu*, but if our _{1 Cor. 14.} prayers do draw our sighs and groanings from our hearts ^{15.} it is the better, for then it appears that our prayer is not a breath coming from the lungs but from the very depths of the heart, as the Psalmist says of his prayer, *De profundis*, _{Ps. 130. 1.} "Out of the deeps have I cried to Thee, O Lord."

What the Apostle meaneth by "groanings which cannot be expressed" is plain, for when the grief of the heart is greatest then are we least able to utter it, as appears by the Shunamite. Notwithstanding, as it was God That _{2 Kings 4.} wakened in us the desire of good things, so though we be ^{27.} not able to utter them in words, yet He doth hear *etiam vocem in silentio*.

There are *mutæ preces et tamen clamantes*, such as are the silent prayers of Moses which he made in his heart to God though he expressed it not in words: to this God said, *Cur* _{Ex. 14. 15.} *clamas ad Me ?*

Now as Martha was loath to serve alone, and therefore would have Mary to "help her;" so the Spirit doth not _{Lu. 10. 40.} pray alone, but doth συναντιλαμβάνεται, "bears together, or helps us," whereby the Apostle gives us to understand, that man must have a co-operation with God's Spirit. So we see the saints of God, albeit they acknowledge prayer to be the work of God's Spirit in them, forasmuch as we are not able to "call Jesus Lord but by the Spirit of God," yet they _{1 Cor. 12.} are not themselves idle but do add endeavour; as David, ^{3.} "Lord, open Thou my lips," so he affirms of himself, "I _{Ps. 119.} have opened my lips, and drew in my breath." _{131.}

But that we may have the help of God's Spirit without which our endeavour is but vain, we must still think upon our own weakness and humble ourselves in the sight of God, as the Publican did. So the Spirit of God will rest upon us, _{Lu. 18. 13.} as the Lord promiseth. For this end fasting is commended _{Isa. 66. 2.} to the Church, for it hath been an use always among the faithful, "to humble their souls with fasting." _{Ps. 35. 13.}

Secondly, as we must pray in faith, so we must also be charitably affected to our brethren, first, by forgiving them, if we will have forgiveness at the hands of our heavenly _{Mark 11.} Father. Secondly, by giving them that need: this com-^{25.} mended Cornelius' prayer, that he gave alms. _{Acts 10. 4.}

If our prayer be thus qualified, we shall have God's Spirit to assist us in prayer; Whose help if we obtain and unto our prayer add a patient expectation, so that we be not in haste to obtain the thing we crave but we wait upon God's leisure, as the Prophet saith, *Qui crediderit non festinabit,* Isa. 28. 16. "He that believeth makes not haste," thus we shall find that the Lord will not cast out our prayer.

A

PREPARATION TO PRAYER.

SERMON V.

LUKE xi. 1.

And so it was, that as He was praying in a certain place,
when He ceased, one of His disciples said unto Him, Master,
teach us to pray, as John also taught his disciples.

[*Et factum est, cum esset in quodam loco orans, ut cessavit, dixit unus*
ex discipulis Ejus ad Eum, Domine, doce nos orare, sicut docuit et
Johannes discipulos suos. Lat. Vulg.]

[*And it came to pass, that, as He was praying in a certain place, when*
He ceased, one of His disciples said unto Him, Lord, teach us to
pray, as John also taught his disciples. Eng. Trans.]

WHICH words do bring us to that form of invocation, to
which by degrees we have been approaching : for, first, out
of St. Paul we learned, that "of ourselves we are not able 2 Cor. 3. 5.
so much as to think" a good thought, much more unable
to do that which is good ; secondly, from St. James, that
albeit we have no power in ourselves, yet our want may be
supplied by "the Father of lights ;" thirdly, that therefore [Jas. 1. 17.]
to the end we may obtain this ability, we are to seek for it
by prayer, as Christ counselleth ; *Petite, et dabitur vobis.* [Mat. 7. 7.]
But then we meet with another difficulty, and that is,
as Paul confesseth, that albeit grace may be obtained at
the hands of God by prayer, yet we know not how or what
to ask except "the Spirit" of God supply "our infirmities ;" Rom. 8. 26.
and therefore, as then it was said that "the Spirit of God
maketh intercession for us," so here the same Spirit doth
move the disciples to seek for a form of prayer of Christ ;

SERM.
V.
whereby we are taught, that if we know not how or what to pray for, our duty is to repair to Christ with the disciples that He would direct us.

Lu. 11. 1, 2. This text hath two parts: first, the petition of the Apostles; secondly, Christ's answer thereunto.

In the first part we are to consider, first, the occasion of the petition; secondly, the petition itself, *Domine, doce nos,* "Master, teach us."

Touching the first point, the disciples took occasion of this petition from Christ's praying; for seeing Him not only pray now but at sundry other times, presently they conceived thus within themselves, that doubtless prayer was a matter of great importance and a means of no small benefit, otherwise Christ would never have prayed so often.

Before, we considered two special motives to prayer : the first was Christ's commandment, the second Christ's pro-
Mat. 7. 7. mise, "Ask, and it shall be given you." And here again we have other two motives : first, the provocation of Christ's example, Whom the disciples found praying in a certain place; secondly, the mould and set form of prayer which He hath given us for our better direction in this duty, "Our Father, &c."

Concerning the first of these, no doubt the examples of holy men ought to move us to pray; much more when Jesus
Dan. 9. 24. Christ Himself, Who is the "Holy of Holies," doth by His own example stir us up hereunto.

King David, when he had his crown pulled off his head by his own son, and was driven out of his kingdom, said
2 Sam. 15. to the priest, "If it please God He can bring me again,
25. and shew me" both the ark and the tabernacle. Declaring hereby, that he was more careful to have the liberty to come into the house of prayer to pour out his supplication before the Lord, as he was wont, than to be restored to his crown; so great account did he make of prayer. The like account did the holy prophet Daniel make; for when by the commandment of the king it was proclaimed that whosoever made any petition to God or men save only to
Dan. 6. 7. the king should be "thrown into the lions' den," he chose rather to adventure his life than not to pray. Whereby we may gather, both how acceptable to God, and also how

necessary for us, this duty of prayer and invocation is;
so that these examples of these holy men ought to be of
no small efficacy to persuade us hereunto; and especially
if we consider the example of our Saviour Jesus Christ,
Who is greater than either David or Daniel. Of Whom
it is reported, that He went into a "solitary place" alone, Mark 1. 35.
not only in the morning but also in the evening; not for Joh. 6. 15.
an hour, but to spend "the whole night in prayer;" He Lu. 6. 12.
prayed not only in *deserto*, "in the desert," which was a Joh. 18. 1.
place of distress, but *in horto*, "in the garden," which was Lu. 22. 41.
a place of pleasure. As He prayed when He was in His Joh. 6. 15.
agony, so also when He was to be made King, to teach
us that as well in prosperity as in adversity we have need
to pray; for hereunto our Saviour doth exhort us in plain
words not only by precept, "Pray that ye enter not into Mat. 26. 41.
temptation," because prayer is a mean to keep us from evil, Lu. 22. 46.
both *a malo culpæ et a malo pœnæ*, 'as well from sin as from
all manner of plagues' which are the effects of sin—as one
saith, there would none adversity come upon us, unless
there were perversity in us—but secondly, by promise of
reward, "Pray unto your Father in secret, and He will re- Mat. 6. 6.
ward you openly."

We think it sufficient, if earthly princes will vouchsafe to
hearken to our prayer; but God promiseth us more, He will
reward us for the same. Therefore seeing God both commands us to pray, and promiseth to grant us that we pray
for; seeing He doth not only by His example teach us that
prayer is requisite, but prescribes us also a form of prayer,
we ought not to be negligent in this duty.

Besides, out of this occasion we are to consider this, that
Christ prayed though He needed nothing. As He was "the
only-begotten" Son of God, He was "full of grace and Joh. 1. 14.
truth," He had received the Spirit without "measure:" yet Joh. 3. 34.
for all that He prayed.

There are three uses of prayer: first, there is an use of
necessity; for God hath left prayer to be our city of refuge,
to the end that when all means fail we should fly unto God
by prayer. In which regard the Wise Man saith, *Turris* Prov. 18.
altissima est nomen Domini, "The name of the Lord is a 10.
strong tower." But Christians should have a further use of

SERM.
V.

Ps. 141. 2.
Rom. 12. 1.
1 Pet. 2. 5.

Job 27. 3.

Col. 1. 15.

Eph. 1. 22.

Joh. 11. 41,
42.

Lu. 10. 42.

1 Sam. 14.
19.

1 Pet. 3. 7.

this duty; for unreasonable creatures, as lions and ravens, are provoked in regard of their necessity to call upon God.

Secondly, the use of duty, for prayer is an offering; the Prophet compareth it to "incense," "a reasonable service," our "spiritual sacrifice." It is compared to "incense," which giveth a sweet smell to all our works, words, and thoughts, which otherwise would stink, and be offensive to the Majesty of God. This use of prayer we have not only for the supply of our wants in the time of adversity, but at all times, as Job saith.

Thirdly, there is the use of dignity, when a man doth abstract himself from the earth, and by often prayer doth grow into acquaintance and familiarity with God; for this is a great dignity, that flesh and blood shall be exalted so much as to have continual conference with God.

Now as Christ was the Son of God, He had no cause to pray in any of these three respects; but as He was *Principium omnis creaturæ*, "the first-born of every creature," as He was "the Head of the Church," He had use of prayer in these three respects. As He was a creature, He stood in need of those things which other creatures of God were wont to desire. Again, as He was a creature, though the chief of all creatures, He owed this duty of invocation unto God His Creator; and as He called on God in these two respects so He was heard, as Christ speaks, "I know Thou hearest Me always." But as He was in the state of a creature, the last use doth most of all concern Him; for which cause having told Martha that "one thing was needful," because the obtaining of the same is not in our power, He presently withdraweth Himself unto prayer in the beginning of this chapter, teaching us to do the like.

Before we come to the petition, these words, *ut cessavit*, are to be considered; for there are some with Saul will call for the ark, and will presently cry, Away with it; that is, will begin their prayers and will break them off in the midst upon any occasion: but the Spirit of God doth teach us to be of another mind, when He willeth us to avoid whatsoever may be a means to interrupt our prayers.

The disciples forbare to make their petitions to Christ till He had done praying, and therefore from their example we are to learn so to settle ourselves to prayer as that nothing should cause us to break off, and so to regard others that are occupied in this duty as by no means to interrupt them.

In the petition we are to consider, first, the thing that they desire; secondly, the reason why they make this petition. First, whereas they make request that Christ would teach them how to pray, they do by implication acknowledge as much as St. Paul speaketh of, that they " know Rom. 8. 26. not what to ask." Not that they were without that general institution which we have from nature, that is, to desire that which is good, but because they know not how to limit their desire.

As in temporal things, they know not whether it were good for them to be the chief men in a kingdom, which was Mat. 20. 21. the ignorance of the sons of Zebedee, so in spiritual matters they will be like St. Paul, who thought it good for him to be saved from the temptation, whereas God told him that His " grace was sufficient" for him, and yet that the temptation 2 Cor. 12. 9. should continue still.

As James and John made a request ignorantly for themselves, so they make another in the behalf of Christ : " Lord, Mat. 20. 20. wilt Thou that we command that fire come down from hea- Lu. 9. 54. ven?" and therefore were reproved by Christ for it. And as we see both by examples of Christ's own disciples that we may "pray amiss," so in the Old Testament David saith Jas. 4. 3. we may pray so as "prayer" (which is a part of God's ser- Ps. 109. 7. vice) "shall be turned into sin." For prayer is nothing else but an interpreter of our desire, as one saith, *Ea petimus quæ appetimus,* 'We pray for those things which we desire;' and as our desires are many times not only vain and unprofitable but dangerous and hurtful, so it falls out likewise that our prayers are vain, and so are turned into sin.

The disciples therefore being privy to their own infirmities in this case are stirred up by God's Spirit to seek for a perfect form of prayer of Christ, in Whom " all the treasures Col. 2. 3. of wisdom and knowledge are hid." And this they do to the end they might not fail either in the matter or manner of their prayers, and that having received a platform of prayer from Christ they might use it as a pattern and complement of all their petitions.

SERM.   The Pharisees were great prayers, but they under a pre-
V.
Mat. 23. 14. tence of long prayers did "devour widows' houses," and
therefore their prayers turned into sin. The heathen used
Mat. 6. 7. also to make long prayers, but they erred, for they thought
that they should be heard for their long babbling. There-
fore the disciples that they might not pray amiss do make
[Lu. 11. 1.] their request to our Saviour, "Lord, teach us to pray."
Which petition was therefore acceptable to Christ, because
profitable for themselves; for thus He professeth of Him-
Isa. 48. 17. self, *Ego Dominus Deus tuus docens te utilia.* Not *subtilia,*
Acts 20. 20. saith Augustine. So St. Paul confirmeth that he "withheld
nothing" from the Church "that was profitable" for them
to know.

[Mark 10.   The world is full of curious questions : the Pharisees move
2.]   questions touching matrimony.

The Sadducees asked what should come to pass after the
Mat. 22. 23, end of the world, whether we shall know one another. These
&c.   were unprofitable and curious, the inventions of flesh and
blood, not those that proceeded from the Holy Ghost. The
disciples' question is here, how they may serve God, and
how they may perform that duty for which they came into
Deut. 29. the world : curious things are those *abscondita* which "be-
29.   long to God," with which we may not meddle; we must
enquire of things which concern us. Of the sons of Cain
[Gen. 4. 20, and Abel, who were inventors of tents, some devised to
21, 22.]   work in brass and copper, others found out music, as they
thought it most profitable for the public weal. The trade
that the sons of Seth used and professed at the same time,
Gen. 4. 26. that they thought to be most profitable, was the "calling
upon the name of the Lord;" and they were occupied
therein as an art no less profitable than the building of
houses, or making of armour. And ever since, howsoever
the world do addict themselves to other things that serve
to make most for their private profit, yet the Church and
city of God are busy in studying how they may by prayer
Heb. 4. 16. "receive mercy, and obtain grace to help them in time
of need."

The reason whereby they urge their suit is, " as John
taught his disciples." Which reason, in the judgment of
flesh and blood, might seem of small efficacy ; for whereas

John confessed himself "unworthy to unloose Christ's shoe," Lu. 3. 16.
He might have took it in scorn that the disciples of John
should teach Him His duty after the example of John; but
Christ to commend His humility is content both in His
preaching and praying to follow John. John said, " Every Mat. 3.10
tree that brings not forth good fruit;" and Christ, though
He were the wisdom of God, and furnished with all manner of doctrine, yet was content to borrow that sentence
from John Baptist, as appeareth in His sermon. So He was Mat. 7. 19.
content to follow him in prayer; so that the example of
John's diligence in teaching his disciples that duty, was a
motive to Him to do the like unto him.

Whereas the disciples of Christ tell Him that John was
wont to teach his disciples to pray, they speak by experience, for divers of them were before-time disciples unto
John, as appears by John the first chapter and thirty-
seventh verse.

The ordinary prayer that was used in the Synagogue
among the Jews, was that prayer which is intituled " The Ps. 90.
Prayer of Moses;" and as Christ saith, " The Law and the Lu. 16. 16.
Prophets were until John," so that prayer of Moses continued in the Church of the Jews until John's time. When
he was come, he used another form of prayer, which endured to the coming of Christ, Who having taught His disciples a third form of prayer, John's prayer ceased. The
reason was because, as the Apostle speaketh of Moses, al- Heb. 3. 5.
beit both Moses, the Prophets, and John, were faithful in
the house of God, yet they were but servants, but Christ
was that Sun of Righteousness, and the Day-Star that was
long before promised; and therefore seeing He being come
hath taught a more perfect form of prayer, He being only
wise, all other forms ought to give place to His.

Secondly, according to the rule of John Baptist, " a man Joh. 3. 27.
can receive nothing except it be given him from above."
Then if we will obtain any thing, we must put up our supplications to God for it. But in making our prayers we may
offend, "for he that is of the earth is earthly, and speaks Joh. 3. 31.
earthly things :" therefore John, according to his own confession, may mingle some corruption with his prayer. But
Christ "That is from heaven is above all," and therefore if

SERM.
V.

Lu. 10. 27.

Joh. 1. 17.

Joh. 3. 31.

[Lu. 11.
14.]
Ps. 47. 7.
1 Cor. 14.
15.

He teach us to pray, it shall be in such sort as God shall accept it : and for this cause Christ's prayer doth excel the prayers both of Moses and John, and all the Prophets.

Touching which form of prayer, as before He had given them an abridgment of that obedience which the Law requireth, so here He doth briefly set down a form of prayer.

As it is said of Him, that "grace and truth is by Jesus Christ," so when in the other chapter He had shewed them the truth of the Law, so now He tells them that grace must be sought for of God by prayer, whereby we may be able to obey that law.

The suit of the disciples being both profitable to themselves and no subtle question, Christ is content presently to grant their request, and therefore His answer is, "When ye pray, say," &c.

Wherein we are to observe two things : first, whereas there are certain practic spirits that cross that saying of our Saviour, and tell us we may not use this prayer which Christ gave, saying, "Our Father," but that we are to frame our prayers of our own as our state shall require, these words are a contradiction to their *Ne dicite.*

Christ Himself hath commanded us to use this form of prayer, and therefore we may be bold to say, "Our Father." Whatsoever prayers we make of ourselves they have some earth, because we ourselves are of the earth, but the prayer instituted by Christ is free from all imperfection, because it was penned from Him That was "from above."

In this prayer there is not one word wanting that should be put in, nor any word more than ought to be. Therefore both in regard of the Author of it and the matter, we may safely use this form of prayer.

Secondly, these words are an opposition betwixt *Cogitate* and *Dicite.* It is not enough to think in our minds this prayer, but our prayers must be vocal ; so that as in this Christ casteth out the dumb devil, so here he casteth out the dumb prayer. It is true that the life of prayer and thanksgiving standeth herein, "that we sing praises with understanding," that we do *orare mente et spiritu.* Herein stands the soul of prayer, but as we ourselves have not only a soul but a body also, so our prayer must have a body ;

our " tongue must be the pen of a ready writer." We must Ps. 45. 1.
at the time of prayer bow our knees, as our Saviour Christ Lu. 22. 41.
did. We must " lift up our hearts with our hands." Our Lam. 3. 41.
Ps. 123. 1.
eyes must be lifted up to God "That dwelleth in the hea- Ps. 35. 10.
ven." And, as David says, all our " bones" must be exercised in prayer.

The reason why we must use this form of prayer is taken
from the skill of Him That hath penned it, and from His
favour with God.

We are not acquainted with the phrases of the Court, and
we know not what suit to make unto God. But Christ Who
is our Advocate, in Whom " all treasures of wisdom and Col. 2. 3.
knowledge are hid," He can form us a bill, and make such
a petition for us, as shall be acceptable at the hands of God ; 1 Cor. 2. 11.
" None knows the things of God, but the Spirit of God."
So none knows what pleaseth God but Christ, Who hath
received the Spirit from God ; and in this regard, as He
knows God's will best, so He is best able to frame a form of
prayer so as it may be agreeable to God's will.

Secondly, touching the authority which Christ hath with
God His Father, it was such as God proclaimed from heaven, [Mat. 17.
5.]
" This is My beloved Son ;" and Christ saith, " Thou hearest Joh. 11. 42.
Me always." So greatly was He respected with God.

In both these respects we may be bold to say, " Our
Father," &c.

We have the promise, that if we ask any thing in the Joh. 16. 23.
Name of Christ, He gives it us. Much more may we have
confidence to be heard, *si non modo in nomine Ejus, sed
verbis Ejus.*

The Apostle saith, " If I had the tongue of men and 1 Cor. 13. 1.
angels." His meaning is, that the tongues of Angels were
more glorious than the tongues of men ; and therefore that
song of the Angels, " Holy, holy, holy," is magnified in the Isa. 6. 3.
Church ; but this prayer was formed by the tongue of Christ,
Who is the Lord of Angels.

The Cherubims hid their faces before the Lord of hosts. Isa. 6. 2.
And He That made this prayer was the Lord of Hosts, of [Joh. 12.
41.]
Whom it is said, *Os Domini exercituum locutum est.* [Isa. 1. 20.]

This prayer, as one said, is δάνεισμα τῆς ἀγάπης, 'the engaging of our character and love ;' for we desire to have re-

mission of sin no otherwise than as we forgive our brethren, whereby the love of our brother is continually increased. And this prayer is *breviarium fidei*, it teacheth us to believe those things which we pray for.

Lastly, our perfection in obeying the Law, and believing those things which we ought to intreat, with such a hope by prayer : *Legem implendi, et legem credendi, lex statuit supplicandi.*

A

PREPARATION TO PRAYER.

SERMON VI.

Luke xi. 2.

*And He said unto them, When ye pray, say, Our Father which
art in heaven, hallowed be Thy name. Thy kingdom come.
Let Thy will be done, even in earth as it is in Heaven, &c.*

[*Et ait illis, Cum oratis, dicite, Pater, sanctificetur nomen Tuum.
Adveniat regnum Tuum.* Lat. Vulg.]

[*And He said unto them, When ye pray, say, Our Father Which art
in heaven, hallowed be Thy name. Thy kingdom come. Thy will
be done, as in heaven, so in earth.* Eng. Trans.]

It is the answer of our Saviour Christ to that disciple of
His, which in the name of the rest desired to be taught a
form of prayer.

Concerning prayer, among other things already noted, we
are to know that it is the doctrine of the Fathers, that God
not prayed unto on our parts, and His Holy Spirit not yet
possessing our souls, hath notwithstanding promised, "that Joel 2. 28.
He will pour His Spirit upon all flesh," as it was poured
upon the Apostles after Christ's ascension; namely, that Acts 2. 17.
Spirit Which He calls "the Spirit of grace and prayer." Zech. 12.
When He thus vouchsafeth to send "the Spirit of grace" 10.
into our souls, then from thence there do run two streams
into the two several faculties of our soul: that is, the Spirit
of grace hath a working on our understanding by the light
of faith, and secondly, in our will, by inspiring us with holy
desires; of which holy desires the interpreter betwixt us and
God is prayer, for that, as the Apostle speaks, our "requests Phil. 4. 6.
are made known to God by prayer and supplication."

Now as prayer is properly the effect of grace, so whatso-

SERM.
VI.

ever we obtain of God by prayer, it is the gift of grace; which prayer is therefore our reasonable service of God, because we do therein acknowledge not only our own wants and unworthiness, but also that as God hath in His hands all manner of blessings to bestow upon us, so Ps. 84. 11. if we sue to Him for them "He will withhold no good thing" from us.

Before we can pray for good things, it is required that we do conceive a love of them; which if it be in us, then we shall not only be inflamed with a desire of them which is an effect of love, but shall be stirred up to pray for them. But it is the peculiar work of the Holy Ghost to shed in our Rom. 5. 5. hearts the love, not only of God, but of all other good things; which work He performeth not in all indifferently, Joh. 3. 8. for He is compared to the wind that "bloweth where it will." But those whom it pleaseth the Holy Ghost to inspire with a love and affection towards good things, they do not only desire them, but withal do pray earnestly for them unto God; for as it is the work of Jesus Christ, the [Joh. 1. 9.] eternal Word, to enlighten "every one that cometh into the world," so it is the office of the eternal Spirit to inspire our hearts with holy desires.

In this answer of our Saviour, we are to consider three points: first, a time limited for prayer; secondly, the contents of the word *oratis;* thirdly, what is to be noted out of the word *Dicite.*

Touching the time limited for prayer, we have heard already that there are three uses of prayer: one was the use of dignity and perfection, when men do converse and enter into familiarity with God by abstracting their minds from human affairs, and sublevating them into Heaven by a continual meditation of God and things pertaining to the life to come, which because it is peculiar to them that have already attained to some perfection we must say of it as Mat. 19. 12. Christ did of another matter, *Qui potest capere capiat,* "He that is able to receive it let him receive it." Our weakness is such as cannot by any means come to this use; yea the Joh. 16. 12. infirmity of the disciples themselves was so great, that albeit Christ had so many other things to tell them of, yet they were not able as yet to bear them.

Therefore we are to consider the two other uses, which do more nearly concern us; whereof the one is the use of necessity, which standeth either upon fear or upon want; and when necessity lieth upon us, in either of these respects, they are so forcible that they make "all flesh to _{Ps. 65. 2.} come unto Him That heareth prayer." Of fear the Prophet saith; "Lord, in trouble they visited Thee, they poured out _{Isa. 26. 16.} a prayer when Thy chastening was upon them." And the want of outward things is so vehement a motive, as when nothing else can move men to prayer, yet they will "assemble themselves" before the Lord "for corn and oil." _{Hos. 7. 14.}

These two, the one being, as Solomon termeth it, *plaga* _{1 Kings 8. 38.} *cordis*, 'the plague of the heart,' the other, *desiderium* _{Ps. 21. 2.} *cordis*, 'the heart's desire, do point to us two times of prayer; namely, when either we are oppressed with misery as the effect of sin, or disquieted with ourselves with the conscience and guilt of sin itself, which is the cause of all our miseries.

Touching sin, the Prophet saith, "While I held my tongue my bones consumed away;" but after he had "confessed his sins unto the Lord," and craved pardon, He "forgave his wickedness;" and because it is not his case only, forasmuch as we have all sinned, his counsel is in this behalf, *Pro hoc orabit omnis pius*, "For this shall every one that is godly _{Ps. 32. 3, 5, 6.} pray unto Thee." Which being done as the Prophet speaketh, the weakest of them, that is, every sinner, shall be as David. Neither are we of necessity to pray that God will forgive the guilt of our sins past, but that He will prevent us with His grace against temptations of sins to come; for in this regard our Saviour Christ would have His disciples occupy themselves in this holy duty: *Orate*, "Pray ye that _{Lu. 22. 40.} ye enter not into temptation."

For the effect of sin, which is adversity. Then is prayer necessary in the time of affliction, when outwardly through the malice of our enemies we are in misery: in which case the Prophet saith, When the ungodly, for the love he bare _{Ps. 109. 4.} to them, requited him with hatred, then he gave himself to prayer. Or else inwardly, by reason of crosses which it pleaseth God to bring upon us, against which the only remedy is to use prayer, as the Apostle exhorts, "Is any _{Jas. 5. 13. Isa. 26. 18.}

SERM.
VI.
afflicted? let him pray." *A timore Tuo concepimus spiritum salutis.* That is, for fear.

And when we consider our own wants, the troubles that are upon us, though for a time we hold our tongues and speak nothing, yet a fire will kindle in us, we cannot long be silent, but the desire of our heart must have a vent by Ps. 39. 3. prayer, as the Prophet had experience in himself. So that as well the fear of danger to come, as present want and affliction, will lead us to prayer.

But when we are rid of all adversity, yet there is another use of prayer, which is the use of duty.

We are to pray, not in regard of ourselves, but in obedience to God, Who commandeth prayer to be made by us, as a part of His service and duty which we owe to Him.

Prayer made of duty is of two sorts, both in regard of time and place.

Job in the law of nature telleth us, that it is our duty Job 27. 10. *invocare Deum omni tempore,* "always to call upon God;" and our Saviour's charge unto His disciples is, that they Lu. 18. 1. should *semper orare,* "pray always," which the Apostle 1 Thes. 5. interpreteth by ἀδιαλείπτως, "without ceasing." But this 17. cannot be performed of us, by reason of our infirmity; therefore we must expound this otherwise and, as St. Paul Rom. 6. 19. speaks, we must "speak after the manner of men," *propter* [Vid. S. Aug. de *infirmitatem,* "because of our weakness;" and so when we Hæres. 57. et Epist. are commanded "to pray always," the meaning is, that it 130. ad is our duty to appoint certain hours for prayer; for, as Prob.] Augustine saith, *Semper orat, qui per certa intervalla temporum orat.* The reason of this exposition is, for that our Rom. 12. 1. service to God must be "a reasonable service," and the preaching of the word must not be done negligently; for 1 Pet. 2. 2. it must be λογικὸν γάλα, which cannot continually be performed of man without some respect.

Touching the set times appointed to the service of God in the Law, it is appointed and required that there should be both morning and evening sacrifice day by day, and that Nu. 28. 3, upon the Sabbath there should be twice so long service as 9, 10. upon other days.

This public service was performed by the Jews, among Neh. 9. 3. whom the book of the Law was read four times a day.

For private devotion the Prophet saith, " In the evening, Ps. 55. 17. in the morning, and at noon-day, will I call upon Thee ;" and Daniel was, for praying " three times a day," cast into Dan. 6. 10. the lions' den.

In the New Testament this duty of prayer was by the practice of St. Peter limited to " the third hour," to " the Acts 2. 15. sixth hour," to " the ninth hour," at which time " Peter Acts 10. 9. Acts 3. 1. and John went up to the temple together to pray; whose diligence and care ought to stir us up to the like.

Further, the disciples desire to be taught a right form of prayer, not only as here, as Christians, but as Apostles and Ministers sent forth to preach the Gospel; whereby we learn that prayer belongeth not only in general to every Christian, but more particularly and specially to those that have any ecclesiastical authority over others.

So that is an opinion very erroneous, that we have no other use of the Apostles of Christ and their successors, but only for preaching; whereas, as it is a thing no less hard to pray well than to preach well, so the people reap as great benefit by the intercession of their pastors which they continually make to God both privately and publicly, as they do by their preaching.

It is the part of the ministers of God, and those that have the charge of the souls of others, not only to instruct the flock but to pray for them.

The office of Levi and his posterity, as Moses sheweth, was not only to teach the people the laws and judgments of the Lord, and to instruct Israel in the Law, but also to offer " incense" unto the Lord; which " incense" was no- Deu. 33.10. thing else but a type of prayer made by the faithful. Ps. 141. 2.

Therefore Samuel confesseth that he " should sin" no less 1 Sam. 12. " in ceasing to pray for" the people, than if he were slack 23. to shew them " the good and right way."

This duty the ministers of God may learn from the example of Christ's own practice, Who " went out early in the Mark 1. 35. morning" to pray. So He prayed for Peter, " that his faith Lu. 22. 32. should not fail." Also from the example of the Apostles, who albeit they did put from them the ministration of the sacraments, yet gave themselves " continually to prayer, and Acts 6. 4. the ministry of the word."

SERM.
VI.
1 Cor. 1. 17.

In which regard Paul saith, he was "sent not to baptize but to preach the Gospel;" which they did refuse to do, not as a thing impertinent to their office, but that they might with more attention of mind and fervency of spirit apply themselves to make intercession for God's people.

Mal. 2. 7.

Thus much they are to learn from hence, that the priests are *angeli Domini exercituum.* If angels, then they must not only descend to the people to teach them the will of God, but ascend to the presence of God to make intercession for the people; and this they do more cheerfully, for that God is more respective to the prayers which they make for the people than the people are heedful to the Law of God taught by them.

Isa. 62. 6.

For this cause the priests are called the Lord's remembrancers, because they put God in mind of His people, desiring Him continually to help and bless them with things needful; for God hath a greater respect to the prayers of those that have a spiritual charge, than to those that are of the common sort. Thus the Lord would have Abimelech

Gen. 20. 7.

deal well with Abraham and deliver him his wife, because he "is a prophet, and should pray for him that he may live."

Job 42. 8.

So to the friends of Job the Lord said: "My servant Job shall pray for you, and I will accept him."

Lev. 5. 6.

This office was appointed to the priests in the law, *Orabit pro iis sacerdos,* "The priest shall pray for them." Thus

Isa. 37. 4.

Hezekiah sent for Esay; so saith he, "Lift thou up thy prayer."

Ps. 55. 17.

Men, as they are Christians, ought to pray three times a day, as David; but as they are prophets, and have a special charge, they must pray to God "seven times a day," as the same David.

Ps. 119.
164.

This day of prayer, made by the priests in the behalf of the people, was so highly esteemed, that they took order that prayer should be made continually; and because the same priests are not to do all one thing, but to pray, therefore some were appointed for the first watches, others for the second, and others for the third watches, that so while one rested the other might pray, whereof David speaketh when

Ps. 119.
148.
Lu. 12. 38.

he saith, "Mine eyes prevent the night watches." So Christ speaketh of the "second and third watches."

Touching David's diligence in performing of this duty for
the good of the people, he saith, "At midnight I will rise Ps. 119. 62.
up to give thanks to Thee." So did Paul and Silas rise Acts 16. 25.
"at midnight to sing praise to God." And it were to be
wished that the like order were taken in the Church, that
the sacrifice of prayer were continually offered among Christians as it was in the synagogues of the Jews.

Secondly, in regard of the place, we are everywhere to
"lift up pure hands;" and so the Psalmist extended this 1 Tim. 2. 8.
part of God's service to "all places" generally "of His Ps. 103. 22.
dominion." Howbeit, though it be not to be neglected in
no place, yet especially we must offer this sacrifice of prayer
and praise "in the assembly, among the faithful in the con- Ps. 111. 1.
gregation;" and so we must learn to distinguish the Liturgy
and the public service of God in the Church from that private devotion which our Saviour would have us to perform
daily when He saith, "When thou prayest, enter into thy Mat. 6. 6.
chamber." For God hath promised to accept that worship
which we tender unto Him in the place consecrated for that
purpose: "In every place where I put My name, thither Ex. 20. 24.
will I come and bless thee." *Non solum quod oratis, sed
quod ibi oratis,* that is, the public place whither the saints
of God from time to time assemble themselves to call upon
God together. In His temple doth every man "speak of Ps. 29. 9.
His praise." Our Saviour Christ did therefore tell them that
it was *domus orationis,* to teach us that the chief end of our Isa. 56. 7.
meeting there should be not to make it a public school of [Mat. 21. 13.]
divinity and instruction, but to pour out our prayers to
God; for private prayers were not enough, unless at times
appointed we meet together to pray publicly.

So the Apostle St. Peter doth teach us by his example,
who not only when he was at home "went up to the top of Acts 10. 9.
his house to pray," but "to the temple" also. Acts 3. 1.

St. Paul did not content himself to bow his knees to God
when he was at Rome and Ephesus and other places, but
he went to Jerusalem and prayed in the Temple; which Acts 21. 26.
thing as he did for himself, so no doubt he did it in behalf
of the Church of God to which he was sent to preach; and
it were to be wished, that in the Church there were *minus
oratorum et plus orantium.*

The second general point is, touching the contents of the
word *Oratis.*

Our necessities are manifold, and the grace of God which
1 Pet. 4. 10. we sue for to God is *multiformis gratia.* Besides, the Apo-
Eph. 6. 18. stle saith, "Pray with all manner of prayer:" therefore
it is meet that we should take notice how many kinds of
prayer there are, wherein the Apostle guides us when he
1 Tim. 2. 1. saith, "Let supplications, prayers, thanksgiving and inter-
cessions be made." These four contain all those sorts
of prayer which are contained in the body of the word
Orate.

Prayer or invocation consists of confession and petition;
confession is divided into *confessionem fraudis,* which the
Greeks call ἐξομολόγησις, that is, the confession of sins,
whereunto they add supplication to God for pardon, like
Lu. 18. 13. that of the Publican, "God be merciful to me a sinner."

The other kind of confession is *confessio laudis,* that is,
thanksgiving to God for His goodness in pardoning our
sins, and bestowing His benefits upon us, which kind of
confession is called ἀνθομολόγησις. This also is a part of
Phil. 1. 3. 4. prayer, and ought to go with it, as appears where the
Col. 1. 3. Apostle doth "thank God always" for the Churches "in
his prayer."

Both these the Jews gather from the words Judah and
Israel; for Judah is 'confession,' and Israel is the name of
'prevailing' in wrestling with the Angel, as the faithful do
Rom. 12. strive with God in prayer.
12.
The one they call *Tehillah,* the other *Tephillah.*

[Vid. S. They had both these, Hosanna and Hallelujah.
Aug. Ep.
ad Paul. Petition stands upon comprecation and deprecation.
149. c. 2.]
Deprecation is, when we desire that evil be removed, which
kind of prayer is δέησις and *Techinah.*

Comprecation is, when we would have our want supplied
with good things, which is προσευχὴ and *Tephillah.*

Intercession is in another kind of prayer proceeding from
charity, as the other came from faith, when we do not only
confess our own sins but the sins of others, when we pray
not only for ourselves but for others; when we praise God
not only for His goodness on ourselves, but for others.

So it was the charge which God gave by His Prophet

to them in captivity, not only to pray for themselves, but Jer. 29. 7. to pray for the prosperity of the city where they were prisoners.

As they were to have a care of the commonwealth, so the like is to be had of the Church. Therefore when Peter was in prison, "there was prayer made continually of the Church Acts 12. 5. to God for him." "Pray for all saints," saith the Apostle, "and for me especially, that utterance may be given to me," Eph. 6. &c. And as for them that have any special place in the 18, 19. Church or commonwealth, so we are bidden to pray for all such as are in misery, as David teacheth us by his example; who, when his enemies were sick, ceased not to pray for them no less than for himself, but "put on sackcloth, Ps. 35. 13. and humbled his soul with fasting."

Unto these kinds of prayer some add two more: the first is, when upon condition that God will grant us our desire, we vow that we will faithfully serve Him afterwards, as Jacob Gen. 28. prayed; the other is a simple prayer or petition uttered in 20, 21. short words, as "Lord have mercy upon me," and such like, [Ps. 6. 2.] which are nothing else but sparks of that fire which kindleth Ps. 39. 3. within us, whereof David spake, "Hear me, Lord, and that Ps. 143. 7. right soon, for my spirit faileth."

In regard of this our weakness, our Saviour hath in a short prayer comprehended whatsoever is needful for us, which brevity He used lest if He had set a large form of prayer our spirit should be dead, and our devotion key-cold before we could come to the end; and for the same purpose the Church hath prescribed Collects, prayers answerable to that short petition of our Saviour Christ.

All these kinds of prayers were used by our Saviour Christ in the days of His flesh, as He took our nature and was the Head of a body. *Factus pro nobis peccatum,* 'He 2 Cor. 5. 21. was made sin for us," and so did not only confess Himself a sinner, but suffered the wrath of God for it, which made Him cry, *Deus Mi, Deus Mi,* "My God, My God, why hast Mat. 27. 46. Thou forsaken Me?" "The rebuke of them that rebuked Rom. 15. 3. Thee, fell on Me." Ps. 69. 9.

Also He was an example to us of thanksgiving: "I Lu. 10. 21. thank Thee, O Father, &c." "I thank Thee that Thou Joh. 11. 41. hast heard Me."

B b

SERM.
VI.

Mat. 26. 39.

Joh. 17. 5.

Lu. 23. 34.

Joh. 17. 20.

For deprecation, as He was a man : " Let this cup pass from Me."

The good He prayed for at the hands of His Father was, *Pater glorifica Me eâ gloriâ quam habui apud Te, &c.,* " Father glorify Me with that glory which I had with Thee before the world was."

Touching intercession, He prayeth, *Pater ignosce eis.* " I pray not for them only, but for all them that shall believe by their preaching."

As He used all these kinds of prayer, so He set them all down in this form of prayer.

The confession of sin, and the supplication for remission, is in the five petitions ; the thanksgiving is that δοξολογία, " For Thine is the Kingdom, power, and glory ;" and the good which He desireth is, the sanctification of God's name, the accomplishment of His Kingdom, and the fulfilling of His will, as also a continual supply of all things needful for this present life.

The evil from which He prays to be delivered is, first, from sin itself; secondly, from the temptations of sin; thirdly, from evils which are the effects of sin.

The third and last point in this text is, that we observe something in this word *Dicite;* whereof the first is, that here Christ doth not say, " Say thus," as Matthew the sixth, whereof some gather, that we may frame prayers after the form of the Lord's Prayer, but not use the words themselves; but He saith to His disciples, *Dicite, Pater noster,* " Say, our Father," &c., that is, we may boldly use the very words of this prayer ; and albeit, to set forth the desire of our hearts, we use other forms of prayer, and that in more words, yet we must conclude our prayers with this prayer of Christ.

[Mat. 6. 9.]

Secondly, when He says *Dicite,* He doth not say *Cogitate,* or *Recitate,* or *Murmurate,* but *Intus dicite et cum ore,* for there is a mouth in prayer, *et non est oratio sine ore,* therefore He alloweth vocal prayer. And as He will have us express the desire of our hearts in words, so the chiefest thing is that our prayers be from the heart ; for invocation is " a spiritual sacrifice," " a reasonable service." So both the understanding and reason must be occupied, and also

1 Pet. 2. 5.

Rom. 12. 1.

the spirit or inward affection of the heart. Our Saviour requireth both in express words, "Worship Him in spirit Joh. 4. 24. and in truth." "Sing with understanding." "I will pray ${}^{Ps. 47. 7.}_{1 Cor. 14.}$ with the spirit, and I will pray with the understanding ${}^{15.}$ also."

We must not only have a spiritual fervency and zeal, but also must know what we pray for, which is belonging to the understanding; so that if both do not concur, our service is not reasonable, nor our sacrifice of praise spiritual.

As for that prayer that comes only from the lips, it may be said of it as God spake of hypocrites, "Is that the fast Isa. 58. 5. that I required?" So of assembling to hear the word, as a people useth to do, Is that this which God requireth? Ezek. 33. "Is this to eat the Lord's Supper?" 31, 32. 1 Cor. 11. It is not enough to make long prayers and use many 20. words, there is a spiritual prayer which God will have with our vocal petitions; and therefore, that we may pray with understanding, we have need to be instructed in the sense of the Lord's Prayer.

The excellency of this prayer is in regard of Him That made it, Who is come from above, Who hath mixed nothing with these petitions that savoureth of the earth; so they are all heavenly, as He Himself is heavenly. Secondly, in respect of the form, which is a most perfect form; it was compiled by Him Who was the wisdom of God, and therefore cannot be but perfect, *quia perfecta sunt opera Jehovæ*, "be- [Ps. 111. cause the works of the Lord are perfect." Thirdly, in re- 2.] gard of the excellent benefits that are procured to us by it, which are so many as can be desired at the hands of God. Fourthly, for the order which Christ keepeth.

If man did make a prayer, he would begin at daily bread; but Christ in this prayer teacheth us "first to seek the King- Mat. 6. 83. dom of God."

Our first petition must be for the glory of God, and then for our own welfare, chiefly in the world to come, and also in this life; for as we may not pray at all for things that are evil, so in things that are good and lawful we must take heed that we ask not amiss.

The petitions being seven, are divided thus: The first concerns God Himself, the other six concern us.

They concern us in a threefold estate: first, of Glory; secondly, of grace; thirdly, of nature.

In these petitions that concern us, the evil that we would have removed from us is: first, sin; secondly, temptation; thirdly, evil.

The good we desire to be granted to us is: first, that God's Kingdom may be in our hearts; secondly, that His will may be performed of us; thirdly, that He will give us things necessary for this present life.

THE LORD'S PRAYER.

SERMON VII.

LUKE xi. 2.

Our Father.

THIS prayer, penned by our Saviour Christ in the behalf of His disciples and His Church unto the end of the world, standeth first upon an invocation, then upon certain petitions.

The invocation is the style or word of salutation, wherein we call upon the Majesty of God. The petitions contain the sum of those things we seek for at the hands of God.

That which we have generally to note out of this preface is, that this is one benefit which God vouchsafeth us, that we may pray unto Him and be heard; whereby we are to conceive of Him that He is not like the great monarch to whom no man might presume to speak, except he "hold out his golden sceptre" to him, as it is in Esther. The Est. 4. 11. heavenly Majesty vouchsafeth every man this honour to speak to Him, and the golden sceptre of His word doth allure us thereunto.

Secondly, it is a greater benefit to pray to God on this manner, that is, by the name of Father; and therefore by that which He promiseth the faithful, "Before they call Isa. 65. 24. I will hear them," we are taught that we are so assured of God's goodwill and favour towards us, even before we open our mouths to ask any thing of Him, that we doubt not to call Him Father; from whence we may reason as the Apostle doth, "Seeing He hath given us His Son, how Rom. 8. 32. shall He not with Him give us all things?" So seeing God taketh us for His children, how shall He deny us any thing whereby He may shew Himself a Father?

In the first, we consider the perfection of God's goodness in these words, "Our Father." In the second, the excellency of His power, expressed thus; "Which art in Heaven."

Both these are attributed unto God, not only of the Christians but even by the heathen that are strangers to the Church, for they attribute this unto God, that He is *optimus maximus;* and therefore where these two doubts Mat. 8. 2. arise in our hearts, *Domine si vis,* "Lord, if Thou wilt," Mark 9. 22. and *Domine si quid potes,* they are both taken away by these two attributes.

By that term which setteth out the perfection of God's goodness, He assureth us that He is willing; and by that which expresseth the excellency of His power, we are taught that He is able to perform our requests.

His goodness giveth us *fiduciam,* that in regard of it we Heb. 4. 16. may "boldly come to the throne of grace."

The consideration of God's power breedeth in us devotion and reverence—for both must be joined together; neither fear without the consideration of His goodness, nor bold confidence that is not tempered with a dutiful regard of His power, is acceptable to Him.

So that which we learned *in lege credendi,* that God is the Father Almighty, is here taught again *in lege supplicandi,* where we are instructed in our prayers to ascribe both these unto God; first, that He is "our Father," secondly, "our heavenly Father."

The consideration of these two are the pillars of our faith, and there is no petition wherein we do not desire that God will either shew us His goodness or assist us with His power, and no psalm or hymn that is not occupied in setting forth one of these.

The titles which express God's goodness have two words; the one a word of faith, the other a word of hope and charity.

Of both these words of *Pater* and *noster* Basil saith, that here *Lex supplicandi non modo credendi sed operandi legem statuit,* 'The law of prayer doth not only establish and confirm the law of belief, but of working also;' for where in the word "Father" is expressed the love of God to us, it comprehendeth withal the love we bear to Him.

Where we call God "our Father," and not 'my Father,' therein is contained our love to our neighbour, whom we are to love no less than ourselves: "Upon these two hang the Mat. 22. 40. Law and the Prophets."

Again, the word "Father" is a word of faith, and "our," a word of charity; and the thing required of us in the New Testament is, *fides per charitatem operans,* "faith which Gal. 5. 6. worketh by charity."

So that in these words, "Our Father," we have a sum both of the Law and the Gospel.

Christ might have devised many more magnificent and excellent terms for God; but none were apt and fit for us, to assure us of God's favour. Our Saviour saith, that earthly Lu. 11. 13. fathers which many times are evil men have notwithstanding this care for their children, that if they ask them bread they will not give them a stone; "much more shall our Heavenly Father give us the Holy Spirit if we ask it."

Wherefore Christ teaching us to call God by the name of "Father," hath made choice of that word which might serve most to stir us up unto hope; for it is *magnum nomen sub quo nemini desperandum,* 'a great name under which no man can despair.'

There may seem an opposition to be betwixt these words "Father" and "our," if we consider, first, the majesty of God, before Whom the hills do tremble, and the Angels in heaven cover their faces; secondly, our own uncleanness and baseness, both in respect of the mould whereof we be made, which made Abraham confess himself unworthy " to speak Gen. 18. 27. unto God, being but dust and ashes;" and also in regard of our pollution of sin, in which regard we are called the slaves Joh. 8. 34, of sin, and children of the devil. 44.

Herein we find a great distance between God and us; and so are we far from challenging this honour to be the sons of God in regard of ourselves. 'Who durst,' saith Cyprian, [De Orat. 'pray God by the name of Father, if Christ our advocate did Domin. post init.] not put these words in our mouths?' He knoweth how God standeth affected towards us for all our unworthiness, and

SERM.
VII.

therefore seeing He hath framed this petition for us we may boldly as He commandeth say thus, "Our Father."

Therefore, albeit of ourselves we cannot conceive hope that God is "our Father," yet we may call Him Father by the authority of Christ, and say with Augustine, *Agnosce, Domine, stilum Advocati Filii Tui,* 'Lord, take notice of the style of our Advocate, Thy Son.'

Joh. 1. 18.

Heb. 4. 16.

We know not God's affection towards us, but by Christ we take notice of Him, for He hath "declared Him" unto us; and being taught that God in Christ vouchsafeth to admit us for His children, "we do with boldness come to the throne of grace."

Therefore we have thankfully to consider unto what dignity we that live under the Gospel are exalted, not only above the patriarchs in the time of the Law, but above the heavenly Spirits.

Gen. 18. 27.

Ex. 20. 2.

Heb. 1. 5.

Before the Law was given, Abraham saith, "Shall I speak to the Lord?" In the Law Christ saith, *Ego sum Dominus Deus tuus:* then He was not called "Father." But if we ask that question which the Apostle maketh, "To which of the Angels said He, Thou art My Son?" it will appear that God hath honoured us in a degree above Angels, for that He giveth us leave to call Him "Father."

Thus we see what pre-eminence we have from God, above, as well the saints on earth in time of the Law, as the heavenly Angels; that we may not only pray, but pray thus, "Our Father."

In the word "Father" we are further to note, not only that God is the cause of all things, for that He bringeth forth all things, but also His στοργὴ φυσικὴ, or 'natural affection,' to those things that are produced.

Job 38. 28.

Jas. 1. 17.

Ps. 138. 8.

Gen. 1. 11.

God's paternity is, first, generally to be considered in all creatures, which for that they have their being from God, He is said to be their Father: so Job called God *Pater pluviæ* "the Father of the rain." Also He is called *Pater luminum,* and this is a motive sufficient to move God to be favourable to our prayer, if there were no more, that we are His creatures: so David spake, "Despise not the work of Thine own hands." But men have another use of God's paternity; for whereas of other things God said, *Producat terra,* when man was to be created He said, "Let Us make man," giving us to understand that howsoever other creatures had their being from God mediately, God Himself would be his Father and frame him immediately with His own hand. [Gen. 1. 26.]

Secondly, when God created man according to His own image, He breathed into him life immortal, He gave him the sparks of knowledge, and indued his soul with reason and understanding, in which regard it is called "the candle of the Lord." Pro. 20. 27.

Thirdly, when man was fallen from his first estate, God opened to him a door of repentance, which favour He hath not vouchsafed to the Angels that fell; and so we may crave God's favour, not only as we are the works of God's hands, but as we are His own image.

Fourthly, God is "Our Father," as we are Christians. That which Moses saith, "Is He not Thy Father?" and, "Doubtless Thou art our Father," is to be understood of our generation; but we have a second birth, called ἀναγέννησις, or 'regeneration,' which setteth us in a degree above mankind, and makes us not only men but Christians : which if we be, then we are the sons of God, not as the rain or lights, or they that are created to the image of God, but for that we are "born of God," that is, "born again of the water and of the Spirit," without which regeneration no entrance is "into the kingdom of God." Deu. 32. 6. Isa. 63. 16. Joh. 1. 13. [Joh. 3. 3, 5.]

And our dignity in being the sons of God, in these three sorts, is to be considered : first, in that we are the "price" of Christ's blood. Secondly, we have *characterem,* that is, 'the stamp' of the sons of God, when we are "called Christians." Thirdly, we are "the temples of the Holy Ghost;" by means whereof He giveth us holy desires, and maketh us sorry that we have offended His Majesty. The assurance of this is that which the Apostle calleth "the Spirit of adoption," Which He sendeth into the hearts of Christians to certify them both that they are the sons of God, and may call Him "Father," in a double sense, both in respect of nature and grace; not only by generation, but by regeneration. 1 Cor. 6. 20. Acts 11. 26. 1 Cor. 3. 16, 17; 6. 19. Rom. 8. 1.

In the natural affection that God beareth us, we have two things; 1. the immutability of it, 2. the excellency.

SERM.
VII.

God doth teach us, that His love to us is unchangeable, in this, that He expresseth it by the name of " Father ;" *Nam pater etiamsi offensus est pater, et filius etiamsi nequam tamen filius,* ' A father though offended is a father, and a son though naught yet is a son."

The master may cease to be a master, so may a servant; the husband may cease to be a husband, so may the wife by means of divorce ; but God can never cease to be " our Father" though He be never so much offended, and we cannot cease to be His sons how wicked soever we be ; and therefore God doth by an immutable term signify unto us the immutability of His affection.

Heb. 6. 18.

And indeed, whether He do bestow good things on us, or chasten us, His love is still unchangeable, for both are to be performed of a father towards his children ; and therefore whether He afflict us, or bestow His blessings on us, we are in both to acknowledge His fatherly care, howsoever to flesh and blood " no affliction seemeth good for the present."

Heb. 12. 11.

This immutability of His love, as it ministereth comfort in time of affliction, so doth it comfort and raise us up in sin and transgression, so that notwithstanding the greatness of our sins we may be bold to seek to God for favour and say, *Etsi amisi ingenuitatem filii, tamen Tu non amisisti pietatem Patris;* ' Although, Lord, I have lost the duty of a son, yet Thou hast not lost the affection of a Father !"

The excellency of God's love appeareth herein, that He is not described to be God under the name of a King or great Lord, as Matthew the eighteenth. There we have an example of great goodness in pardoning ten thousand talents, but yet a doubt will arise in our minds except we know Him to be good otherwise than as He is a King ; for so, look what mercy He sheweth to us, the like He will have us shew to others : but we come short of this. But this is it that contents us, that He describes His goodness under the term of Father, in which regard how wickedly soever we deal, yet still we may say with the evil child, " I will go to my Father." He had cast off his father, he had spent all his patrimony ; yet for all that he resolveth to go back, and his father is glad to receive him ; he went, and met, and entertained him joyfully. Such affection doth God bear to His children.

[Mat. 18.
24, 27.]

Lu. 15. 18.

The benefits that we have by the fatherly love of God, are of two sorts : First, *fructus indulgentiæ paternæ;* secondly, *fructus liberalitatis paternæ;* that is, 'the fruit of fatherly compassion,' and 'the fruit of fatherly bounty.'

Fathers stand thus affected towards their children, that they are hardly brought to chasten them ; and if there be no remedy, yet they are ready to forgive, or soon cease punishing. *Pro peccato magno paululum supplicii satis est patri,* 'For a great offence, a small punishment is enough to a father.'

And for their bountifulness, the Apostle saith, that there is naturally planted in fathers a care "to lay up for their children." They are both in God ; for facility *ad veniam,* 'to pardon,' and readiness to forgive, makes him *Patrem miseri-cordiarum,* "a Father of mercies," not of one, for He hath "a multitude of mercies," great mercy and little mercy. [2 Cor. 12. 14.] [2 Cor. 1. 3.] [Ps. 51. 1.]

The affection of David toward Absalom, a wicked son, was such that he forgave him, though he sought to deprive his father of his kingdom ; and though we offend the majesty of God, yet He assureth us that He will be no less gracious to our offences than David was, for David was "a man after God's own heart." [2 Sam. 18. 5.] [1 Sam. 13. 14.]

Touching the care which God hath to provide for us, the Prophet saith, and also the Apostle, "Cast your care upon the Lord, for He careth for you." He careth for us, not as "He careth for oxen," but such a tender care as He hath for "the apple of His eye." He provideth for us, not lands and goods as earthly fathers, but "an inheritance immortal, incorruptible, and that fadeth not, reserved in heaven for us ;" and hath prepared for us a heavenly kingdom, whereof we are made "co-heirs with His Son Christ." And this is the fruit of His fatherly bountifulness towards us. [Ps. 55. 22.] [1 Pet. 5. 7.] [1 Cor. 9. 9.] [Zech. 2. 8.] [1 Pet. 1. 4.] [Rom. 8. 17.]

Out of these two, the immutability and excellency of God's love, shewed both in forgiving sins and providing good things, ariseth a duty to be performed on our parts. For *nomen Patris ut explicat sic excitat charitatem,* 'the name of a Father as it sheweth, so it stirreth up love;' as it sheweth *quid sperandum,* 'what is to be hoped for,' *sic quid sit præstandum,* 'so what is to be performed of us.' The name of a Father doth promise unto us forgiveness of sins, and the

S E R M.
VII. blessings not of this life only, but especially of that that is
to come; and this duty lieth upon us, that we so live as becometh children; we may not continue in sin, but at the
sa. 63. 17. least must have *virtutem redeundi*, 'the virtue of returning.'
"Why hast Thou caused us to go out of the way."

A child though he have wandered never so far, yet at
Lu. 15. 18. length will come to that resolution, "I will return to my
father."

But if we consider the dignity whereunto we are exalted,
we shall see on earth, *Si filii Dei, quodammodo dii sumus,*
'If we be sons, we are after a sort gods;' *et divinæ participes*
2 Pet. 1. 4. *naturæ,* "partakers of the divine nature," as the sons of men
are men.

1 Joh. 3. 1. But the Apostle sets down this plainly : "Behold, what
great love He hath shewed us, that we should be called
the sons of God." This dignity requireth this duty at our
Mal. 1. 6. hands, that we reverence our Father. "If I be your Father,
where is My love?" "If ye call Him Father, Who without
1 Pet. 1. 17. respect of persons, &c.," then "pass the time of your dwelling here in fear."

"Our" is a word of hope, as "Father" is a word of faith ;
for he that says *noster,* "our," includes himself, and by hope
applieth God's favour in particular to himself, which by faith
he apprehends to be common to all, neither doth appropriate
it to himself, saying, 'My Father,' but includes them with
himself; and so the word "our" is also *vox charitatis,* 'the
voice of charity.'

As the first word did teach us the Fatherhood of God, so
the word "our" implieth the fraternity we have with one
another; for God, to shew what great regard He hath of
the love of our neighbour, hath so framed and indited this
prayer, that there is neither *Ego,* nor *mi,* nor *meum,* nor
mea, neither 'I,' nor 'mine,' nor 'my,' but still the tenor
of it is, "Our Father," "our bread," "our trespasses," "us
from evil."

[Vid. Ter-
tull. de
Orat. c. 1.] Therefore one saith, that prayer is not only *breviarium
fidei,* 'an abridgement of our faith,' but δάνεισμα ἀγάπης, 'a
mutual pledge of our love' towards our brethren, which is
then especially testified when we pray to God for them.
For this prayer which our Saviour sets down for us, and all

Christians' prayers, are not the prayers of nature (*pro se orat necessitas*, 'necessity stirreth up men to pray for themselves') but the prayers of charity, when we are to commend the state of our brethren to God as well as our own, *quia pro aliis charitas*, 'for charity prayeth for others;' for in this prayer there is matter not only of supplication for the avoiding of evil, and comprecation for the obtaining of good in our own behalf, but of intercession also, to teach us that whether we desire that evil be removed or good bestowed upon us, we should desire it for others as well as for ourselves.

The use of this doctrine is of two sorts : first, against pride, for if God be not the Father of one man more than another, but all in common do call Him " Our Father," why then doth one man exalt himself above another ? " Have Mat. 2. 10. we not all one Father?" and the Apostle saith, " Ye are all Gal. 3. 26. the sons of God by faith in Christ Jesus ;" and our Saviour saith, *Vos omnes fratres estis*, " Ye are all brethren." There- Mat. 23. 8. fore we are not only to love one another as brethren, but to honour one another, because we are the sons of God ; for this end the Apostle exhorteth—" in giving honour go Rom. 12. 10. one before another." So far ought we to be from despising one another : *Cur enim non pudeat aspernari fratrem, quem Deus non aspernatur filium?* ' Why are we not ashamed to scorn him to be our brother, whom God scorneth not to be His son ?'

Secondly, it serveth against malice ; we were all in the loins of Adam when he fell, and all one in the body of Christ ; so that whatsoever He as our Head hath done or suffered, the same all men do and suffer in Him.

And lastly, we are all included in this word, to teach us that we ought to wish the same good to others which we do to ourselves ; for this is that which Christ commendeth in our Christian practice in the duty of prayer, *ut singuli orent pro omnibus, et omnes pro singulis*, ' that each should pray for all, and all for each other.'

He hath taken order that no man can pray this prayer but he must pray for others as well as for himself and so do good to all, and the mends that is made him is that they also for whom he prayed do likewise at another time pray for him ; and though we cannot always pray in such fer-

S E R M.
V II.

Rom. 8. 26.

Gal. 4. 6.

2 Tim. 2.
25, 26.

Mat. 5. 44.

[Rom. 11.
32.]

1 Thes. 4. 3.

vency of spirit as is required in prayer, yet the Holy Ghost doth "supply our infirmity" by stirring up others to pray and make intercession in our behalf *cum gemitibus inenarrabilibus,* " with unspeakable groans," even then when we cannot do for ourselves ; and this is a special benefit, which the faithful have in the communion of saints.

The Apostle saith that God, to assure us that He takes us for His sons, hath sent His Spirit into our hearts, whereby we cry " Abba, Father." The one of these words hath respect to the Jews, the other to the Gentiles, teaching that it is our duty to pray both for Jews and Gentiles, and so for all, though they be strangers to us.

Secondly, we are to pray for sinners, be their sins never so great, in hope that " God will give them the grace to repent," and to come " out of the snare of the devil," and that He will translate them out of the state of sin into the state of grace : for this life as long as it lasteth is, *tempus præstitutum pænitentiæ,* ' a time ordained for repentance.'

Thirdly, as for our brethren, so for our " enemies," as our Saviour willeth, for they also are comprehended under the word *noster;* " for God hath shut up all in unbelief, that He may have mercy upon them all."

Neither are we to pray in general for all, but for some in particular as need requireth.

Not in general for all good things, but for some special blessings.

As we are to pray generally that God's will may be done, so (for " that this is God's will, our sanctification") we may pray in particular for those things that we have need of ; as to be delivered from all temptation generally, so specially from those sins whereunto the corruption of our nature is most inclined.

THE LORD'S PRAYER.

SERMON VIII.

Which art in Heaven.

WHICH words contain the second part of this invocation; for as in the word "Father" we call upon the bowels of God's mercy, so by these words, "Which art in heaven," we do invoke the arm of His power—for so it is termed by the Prophet in the Old Testament—"Stir up Thy strength Ps. 80. 2 and help us." "Rise up, thou arm of the Lord." So that Isa. 51. as the leper's doubt is taken away by the consideration of Mat. 8. 2. God's fatherly goodness, so that when we know that this "our Father" hath His being in heaven, it takes away that doubt which we use to make of His power, *Domine, si quid potes,* "Lord, if Thou canst do us any good." For the style Mark 9. 22 of God in respect of our necessities consists of His goodness and greatness, which as they are both expressed by the heathen in the title *optimus, maximus*[1], so the power [1 Cicero of God in these words which they use, τὰ ὀλύμπια δώματ' de Nat. Deor. 2. [ἔχοντες[2]], 'dwelling in heavenly habitations.' 25.] [2 Hom. Christ willing to express the greatness of God's power Il. 1. 18.] doth it by that place where His glory and power are most manifest, and that is heaven whereof the Prophet saith, Ps. 19. 1. "The heavens declare the glory of God, and the firmament sheweth His handy work." For when we see a poor cottage, we presently guess that the dweller is no great person; but if we meet with some great house, we conjecture that some person of account dwells there; and therefore Job saith, that the baseness of man in respect of the Angels is great, for that he "dwells in the houses of clay, whose foundation Job 4. 19.

SERM.
VIII.

is of the dust." But here our Saviour tells us, that God "our Father" hath His dwelling in the stately tabernacle of heaven; whereby we may gather what is the greatness of His power.

But before we come to these things which are particularly to be considered in these words, first, we are to take heed that we run not into their error which so confine and compass God in heaven as if He had nothing to do in earth, such as they who say, "How should God know? can He judge through the dark cloud? the clouds cover Him that He cannot see." For when He is said to have His being in heaven, the Holy Ghost thereby doth not express His presence but His power; therefore we are to know that God is not so in heaven that He is not in earth also, for so doth the Old Testament witness of Him, *Cælum et terram Ego impleo.* "Behold the heaven, and heavens, and the heaven of all heavens, are not able to comprehend Thee." And the Prophet David saith, "If I go up to heaven, Thou art there; if I go down to hell, Thou art there also." Whereby it appeareth that we may not limit God's power and presence to any one place, Who is every where present, for when God is said to be in heaven, we learn thereby what His excellency is, which doth especially shew itself there; for as the glory and majesty of earthly princes doth chiefly appear in their thrones, so the glory and majesty of God doth especially shew itself in "heaven, which is His throne." He hath not His denomination from earth a place of worms and corruption, but from heaven a place of eternal glory and happiness.

Secondly, the use of this is to temper our confidence in God; for albeit we love Him as He is "our Father," yet withal we must fear Him forasmuch as He dwelleth in heaven; as we may in regard of His goodness pray unto Him with confidence, so withal considering His power we must pray with due devotion and reverence unto His majesty, for He is not as an earthly father that dwelleth in houses of clay; but His dwelling is in heaven, and therefore as He is "a Father" and consequently will be honoured, so because He is our Lord He requireth fear at our hands. "With Thee is mercy, that Thou mayest be feared." Whereby the Prophet would have us so to esteem of God's mercy, that

Margin notes:
Job 22. 13, 14.

Jer. 23. 24.
1 Kings 8. 27.

Ps. 139. 8.

Isa. 66. 1.
Mat. 5. 34.

Mal. 1. 6.

Ps. 130. 4.

withal we be bound to fear Him; and that we be not like those that contemn the riches of God's mercy, the more that He laboureth with His bountifulness and goodness to bring us "to repentance;" for as sweet things have an obstructive Rom. 2. 4. power to stop the passages which are in our bodies, and on the other side sour and bitter things do fret and consume and so open the veins, so it fareth with the soul; for it is stopped when we consider nothing but the mercy of God, and contrariwise when we cast our eyes too much upon the majesty and power of God the force thereof casts us into an astonishment and brings to desperation; and therefore, that we neither have *nimiam trepidationem*, 'too much terror,' nor *nimiam ostentationem*, 'too much security,' we must know that God is so in heaven as that yet He is Father, and as He is a Father so not an earthly but a heavenly Father; and we cannot but fear and reverence God, if we in humility consider our baseness in respect of Him; for though He be our Father, yet so long as we be on earth we are strangers and exiles from Him, and howsoever it please Him to account us sons, yet as it fared with Absalom, we cannot see 2 Sam. 14. our Father's face until He take us hence, that we may be 24. at home with Him in His kingdom of glory.

Thirdly, these words lead us also to a confidence in God, and serve to raise up our faith. There is *Paternitas* both Eph. 3. 15. in heaven and earth; there are "fathers of the flesh," and Heb. 12. 9. Fathers of the spirit. But when the Holy Ghost saith that God our Father hath His being in heaven, we are thereby to distinguish Him from other fathers. If He be a heavenly Father, He is of a more excellent nature than other fathers that are earthly and carnal, for they are mortal; as they live on earth, so by death they shall be brought *sub terris* and forsake us, but our heavenly Father is immortal, "His years Ps. 102. 27. change not;" and though our fathers and mothers forsake Ps. 27. 10. us, yet the Lord will take us up and succour us. Secondly, though earthly fathers were immortal, yet they are mutable, and their affections are turned away, either by means of some lewd parts in the children, or for that they bear not that natural affection towards their children which they ought. But God is immutable in His love; so that al-

c c

SERM.
VIII.

Isa. 63. 16.
Rom. 1. 31.

though Jacob will not acknowledge us, and Abraham will not know us, yet God will be our Father.

The Apostle saith, there are wicked parents that are ἄστοργοι, "without all natural affection." And it falleth out that sometimes a woman will deal cruelly with her own child; but though she "forget" it, yet God our heavenly Isa. 49. 15. Father "will not forget" His children, nor turn His fatherly affection from them; and therefore Tertullian saith, *Nullus pater tam pater*, 'No father so fatherly.' Thirdly, though they wish us never so well, yet many times they cannot do us that good they would for want of ability; yea though they be never so able, yet they cannot deliver from sickness and death, for the sons of princes die daily; they can give Lu. 11. 11. us "bread" and "fish," they have a care to provide and 2 Cor. 12. "lay up for their children," but it is such "treasure" as 14.
Mat. 6. 19. the "moth and rust will corrupt." But God our heavenly Father can deliver us from all evil, He can give us not only Lu. 11. 13. bread and fish, and other things necessary for this life, but His "Holy Spirit" if we ask it.

The treasure that God layeth up for us is not earthly, but 1 Pet. 1. 4. "an inheritance incorruptible and undefiled," such things Isa. 64. 4. as "neither eye hath seen nor ear hath heard." For God 1 Cor. 2. 9. is not only careful in this life for our well doing, (the knowledge of that is *spes mortua*, 'a dead hope,') but His care extendeth to the life to come; and therefore the Holy Ghost saith not, *Pater in cœlo, sed in cœlis*, "in the heavens" 1 Pet. 1. 3. whereby He "hath begotten us unto a lively hope." *Quæcunque optant vel timent homines*, 'whatsoever things men either wish for or are afraid of,' all things come from heaven, whether it be rain, drought, or contagion, or plague, and Mat. 6. 26. from the first heaven, *ubi vultures cœli*.

From this heaven St. Paul tells the heathen, that God Acts 14. 17. sends us "rain and fruitful seasons." And when Job saith Job 37. 5, 6. that God sends rain, and frosts, and snow; and thundereth, and worketh marvellous things, &c. that is done in *primo cœlo*, 'in the first heaven.' But in the second heaven are the eclipses of the sun and moon: there He works in the Job 38. 31. signs of heaven, He binds the seven stars together; whatsoever wonders are wrought there it is God That worketh them, and therefore He saith to His sons, *Nolite timere a* Jer. 10. 2. *signis cœli,* "be not dismayed at the signs of heaven;" He is in the second heaven, and will not suffer any thing to hurt them.

The third heaven is that whereunto the saints of God shall be received in the life to come, where St. Paul "heard 2 Cor. 12. 4 things that were not lawful to be uttered. So that as God will not suffer the first or second heaven to do us hurt, so He will bring us to the happiness of the third heaven, for he is *Pater noster in cœlis,* "Our Father in the heavens." Whereby we have hope and comfort not in this life only, which is but a dead hope, but a lively hope touching the life to come. For Christ doth not express God's power by an action, saying, 'Our Father Which madest heaven and Ps. 121. 2. earth,' nor, 'Which ridest upon the heavens;' but by a Ps. 68. 4. local word, to shew that as God is in heaven, so we have an interest in the same place, and that He will at the length bring us to the same place where He is.

Fourthly, this word "heaven" serveth to prepare us to prayer, to the end that we should lift up our hearts and affections from earth to heaven, seeing we speak not to an earthly father but to One That is in heaven, and this is that Ἄνω τὰς καρδίας, or *Sursum corda,* 'Lift up your hearts.' Touching which thing one saith, *Aquilarum est hoc negotium,* 'This business belongs to eagles,' which as they fly highest so they look most stedfastly upon the sun; *non talparum,* 'not belonging to moles,' nor of such as are blind and will not open their eyes; *nec milvorum,* 'neither to kites,' which albeit they fly aloft yet cast their eyes still downward to the dunghill. We must wish with the Prophet, "O that I had Ps. 55. 6. the wings of a dove," and labour more and more to fly up with the eagle into heaven, into the presence of God the Father, and His Son Who sitteth at the right hand bodily, for *ubi cadaver ibi congregantur aquilæ,* "wheresoever the Lu. 17. 37. body is there will the eagles be gathered together."

As the consideration of God's majesty Who is in heaven doth bring us down and make us "bow our knees" before Eph. 3. 14. God our Father, so it must cause us *levare manus et corda,* Lam. 3. 41. "to lift up our hands and hearts," and "to lift up our eyes Ps. 121. 1. to the hills," and to have such a continual meditation of

c c 2

SERM.
VIII.
[Ps. 16. 8.] His power that we may say with David, *Providebam Domi-num in conspectu meo semper,* "I have set the Lord always before me."

Fifthly, this word doth admonish us what things we should sue unto God for. He is a heavenly Father, therefore we must ask of Him heavenly things; His answer to the sons Mat. 20. 22. of Zebedee was, "Ye ask ye know not what;" honour and wealth are not things proportionable to Him That is in heaven, and an earthly prince will count it a disgrace if a man ask at his hands mean things, such as may be had of every man.

The gifts we are to ask of our heavenly Father are, the eternal salvation of our souls, the gift of the Holy Ghost, Lu. 11. 13. which He hath promised "to them that ask it," and "all Eph. 1. 3. spiritual blessings in heavenly places."

God is a Father, as Abraham was; and as he had move-able goods which he gave to the sons of Keturah, so he Gen. 25. 6. bestowed the inheritance which was immoveable upon his Gal. 4. 28. son Isaac. So we that are "the children of the promise as Isaac was," must seek for the inheritance of Isaac, and not content ourselves with that portion which was given to the sons of Keturah.

Prov. 30. 7. Solomon saith not amiss, "Two things have I desired of the Lord." But David saith better, *Unum petii a Domino,* Ps. 27. 4. "I have sought one thing of the Lord, that I may dwell in the house of the Lord;" that I may be partaker of grace in this life, and may be received into glory in the life to come.

Unto Martha that was troubled about many things our Lu. 10. 42. Saviour said, *Unum est necessarium,* "one thing is neces-sary;" and this is the reason why it is not said, *Qui es in terris,* 'Which art in earth,' for God sheweth Himself a Father rather in heaven than in earth; *Deus pater est in cœlis,* He is in heaven by assuring us of God's heavenly blessings, for they are the signs of God's fatherly bounty to such as are His heirs by promise. As for earthly things He sheweth Himself in them rather to the sons of Keturah than to Isaac, and in respect of this world Martha is said Lu. 10. 42. to have chosen "the better part."

Sixthly, as it teacheth us what we must pray for, so also we learn hereby that we are to judge of ourselves, and how

we are to dispose of our minds when we come to pray: if
God our Father be in heaven, then because we are yet on
earth, we must esteem ourselves as strangers and pilgrims.
This did all the Fathers acknowledge: "I am a stranger, Ps. 39. 12.
and a sojourner upon earth as all my fathers were;" and
therefore having a longing to be in our city, "Wo is me Ps. 120. 5.
that I am constrained to dwell in Mesech." The Apostles
Peter and Paul confessed the same: the one writing to the
Church of God, called them "pilgrims and strangers;" the 1 Pet. 2. 11.
other reporteth of the Fathers, that they confessed themselves strangers and pilgrims upon earth. And in saying
these things they shew that they sought a country, not the
land of Canaan from whence they came—for they had time Heb. 11. 15,
to return thither "if they had been mindful of it"—but they 16.
sought a better, that is, an "heavenly city;" and "we have Heb. 13. 14.
no abiding city here, but do look for one to come."

These shew us that albeit we have our dwelling in earth,
and be subject to many calamities, yet for all this our exile
we do *genus de cœlo ducere,* 'we take our pedigree from
heaven.' When therefore, as the Poet saith, *Os homini sub-* [Ovid.
lime dedit, it is a shame for us to have our hearts downward; Met. 1. 85.]
we must remember that we are of a more excellent nature
than other creatures, Τοῦ γὰρ καὶ γένος ἐσμὲν, "for we are Acts 17. 28.
His offspring;" we have received from God a soul and a [Vid. Wet-
spirit endowed with many heavenly qualities, which being loco.]
dissolved from the body "returneth to God That gave it." Eccl. 12. 7.

During this our exile and pilgrimage, we are not only to
consider that we look upwards with our faces, (which moved
the heathen to meditate of heaven,) but chiefly, that in our
soul we have the image of God imprinted, which ought to
move us to think of God, and to "set our minds on things Col. 3. 2.
above."

Albeit we be here in "a far country," far from our Fa- Lu. 15. 13.
ther's dwelling, yet we must not forget our Father's dwelling
house.

The portion is in heaven which our Father will give us,
and therefore we must seek to be acquainted with the laws
of that country where our inheritance lieth, that we may
guide our lives according to the same, lest being rebellious
we deprive ourselves of our right and be disinherited.

SERM.
VIII.
2 Sam. 14.
32.

Gal. 3. 26.

Ps. 42. 2.

Ps. 84. 2.

Phil. 1. 23.

Mat. 6. 19,
21.

Phil. 3. 20.

Lu. 15. 10.

1 Cor. 15.
47.
[Lu. 22.
42.]

1 Cor. 15.
48, 49.

Secondly, seeing we know that we are not in our own country, we must say as Absalom did, "Why am I come hither, if I may not see the king's face?" He, being an ungracious son, was desirous to see his Father: then it shall be a shame for us that are "all the sons of God by faith in Christ Jesus," if we have not a longing desire to come before the presence of God our Father. If we have a desire to enter into "the courts of the Lord," if with the Apostle "we desire to be dissolved and to be with Christ," the first begotten of many brethren; and if with our Father God we lay up our treasure in heaven, and count it our chief felicity to be there, then would we think upon heaven more than we do, for "where our treasure is there must our hearts be also." But because we altogether set our hearts on earthly things, therefore it falls out that our heart is as a heavy clod of earth, and unable to lift itself up to heavenly meditation.

Thirdly, as we desire to be in heaven in our Father's house, so our conversation must be πολίτευμα ἐπουράνιον, we must not live by the laws of earthly princes, and acts of parliaments, but by a heavenly law. Though we be strangers on earth, yet we are citizens of heaven, and must carry ourselves according to the laws of our country, being always desirous to do that which pleaseth our heavenly Father, though there were no human law to compel us thereunto; and whereas natural men have for the end of their civil actions, *bonum commune,* 'a common utility,' we that are spiritual must make *bonum cœleste,* 'the heavenly good,' our end; we must do well, because God will behold our well-doing favourably, and the Angels of heaven will be glad of it.

Christ, Who is "the Lord from heaven," did subject Himself to the will of God His Father; "Not My will, but Thy will be done." "And as He that is heavenly," so must they that will be "heavenly;" as we now "bear the image of the earthly," so shall we *portare imaginem cœlestis,* "bear the image of the heavenly."

He, while He lived on earth, did guide Himself by a heavenly law, and we that remain on earth must express His image by the imitation of His obedience. It is true which both our Saviour Christ and John Baptist said, that

"that is born of the flesh is flesh," and so "that that is of Joh. 3. 6, the earth is earthly, and speaketh of the earth." But there ^{31.} must be an imitation, and we must set ourselves forward to our heavenly country. But because it is not in our power to do this of ourselves, for that, as Christ saith, "No man Joh. 6. 44. can come to Me, except the Father draw him," therefore we must pray with the Church in the Canticles, *Trahe me*, Cant. 1. 4. "Draw me." And to this end doth the holy exercise of fasting and mortification serve greatly, that we may, as it were with dove's wings, fly up into heaven.

As the word " Father" doth shew us not only our dignity, but our duty also, so the word "heavenly" doth not only give us a hope of heaven, but also teacheth us that seeing our Father is heavenly we must live by the laws of heaven. As we are careful to be made partakers of the inheritance which God hath prepared for us, so we must be as careful to please Him and to do those things which are agreeable to His will. We must not only know *quid sperandum,* 'what is to be hoped for,' but *quid præstandum,* 'what is to be performed of us.' If we pray not only with confidence, because God doth take us for His sons, but also with invocation, with devotion and reverence, knowing that our Father hath His dwelling in heaven, and we are pilgrims in earth, thus shall we be *veri adoratores,* "true worshippers." As we know we Joh. 4. 23. shall have our part in heaven, so we must begin our heaven here on earth; and this shall be done if we add our endeavour to those things which we pray for at the hands of God, as Augustine prayeth: *Da, Domine, ut pro quibus oramus, pro iis laboremus,* 'Grant, Lord, that the things we pray for and crave of Thee, for them we may also labour.'

THE LORD'S PRAYER.

SERMON IX.

Hallowed be Thy Name.

HAVING ended the first part of this prayer which was called invocation, consisting upon the power and goodness of God, we come to the petitions themselves, which are seven, of which the first concerneth God, the other concern ourselves : or they may be divided as the days of the week, whereof as one falleth out to God's portion, the other to be employed in our own affairs. So, of these petitions, the first doth immediately concern the glory of God, the other six the supply of our own necessities. In the beginning we heard that it is expedient to know not only what we are to ask, but in what order; what first, and what second; touching which point we are taught by this form of prayer, that that petition which concerneth the sanctification of God's name is *caput votorum;* and that all other things that we either desire or pray for in our own behalf, ought to stand after it; and that we must both desire and pray for the sanctification of God's name before any thing that we desire, either for ourselves or for our brethren, whether it be for the removing of evil, or for the obtaining of good; for as before we learned what His love is to us, in that He vouchsafed to be our Father, so hereby we shall express our love again to Him, if when we come to pray to Him for our necessities we be carried away with such a desire of the glory of our heavenly Father, that we forget our own selves and desire only that His name may be sanctified, which duty Christ doth by His own example commend unto us.

In this form of prayer we are put in mind of that which before was required in the law of works; for, as there we learned that God is not honoured aright except He be loved above all things, because " He created all things and for His Rev. 4. 11. will's sake they all were created," so we cannot pray to Him aright, except above all things and in the first place we seek for the sanctification of His name.

In respect of God Himself there is no cause why we should make this petition on His behalf; for as the Prophet saith, "Thou hast no need of any goods." So He stands Ps. 16. 2. not in need of any thing that can come to Him by our means : if we would wish Him any profit, " the earth is His, Ps. 24. 1. and all that is therein;" if pleasure, there is with Him *tor-* Ps. 16. 11. *rens voluptatis,* " a river of pleasure." Wherefore albeit that in His own essence and nature He be perfect, yet *extrinsecus assumpsit sibi nomen,* ' He took Himself a name from without,' He calls Himself the Lord Almighty ; not that any term can sufficiently express Him and His essence, but to the end that while we have a reverend regard of His name He might receive some service at our hands.

The account that men do make of their name is such as Solomon saith, " A good name is more to be desired than [Prov. 22. great treasure ;" it is " more worth than precious ointment." 1.]
God accounts that we do not only greatly profit Him but do Eccles. 7. procure great delight and pleasure to Him, when we reve- 1. rence His holy name ; which how precious it is it doth appear hereby, that He setteth the hallowing of His Name before His kingdom.

Many of the king's subjects that are in the farthest parts of the land never see his face all their lifetime, and yet in reverence to his name are ready to make long journeys to appear when they are commanded in his name; and so it fareth with us that live on earth, for *Deum nemo vidit un-* Joh. 1. 18. *quam.* Nay, very few are admitted to see His " back parts." Ex. 33. 23. But though we cannot see His face, yet as those are counted dutiful subjects that do not only reverence the prince's person but obey such commandments as come in his name; so look, what duty we do to God's name here on earth, He reckons it to be as good service as that which is performed by the Angels in heaven that always behold His face.

SERM.
IX.
Prov. 18.
10.

1 Cor. 6. 11.

Acts 4. 12.

Eph. 1. 4, 6.

Ps. 99. 3.
Ps. 111. 9.

Lu. 1. 46,
47.
1 Cor. 6. 20.

And reason it is that we should esteem of God's name, for as in time of trouble *turris altissima nomen Domini*, "the name of the Lord is a strong tower," so being delivered once of danger, yet we are sure of the salvation of our souls, and "sanctified in the name of the Lord Jesus."

Besides, "there is no other name given under heaven by which men can be saved;" and therefore ought by good right to receive sanctification of us.

Howbeit we may not hereupon ground that error which some gather upon these words, where it is said that God "hath chosen us in Christ to the praise of the glory of His grace." Not that God is desirous of vain-glory, He is not to receive any thing from us, (but contrariwise as He is good, so He is desirous to communicate His goodness to us,) but the care that He hath for the sanctifying of His name ariseth from the duty which man oweth unto Him; in which regard such as have been most religious in all times have reared up altars, and set up temples in honour of God's name.

The account of this petition is that which maketh the difference betwixt the papists and religious people, between heretics and the true worshippers of God, that the one esteemeth highly of the name of God, the other doth not.

We usually account of men's names, according to the worth of their persons; but God Himself is holy, therefore He tells us, that "His name also is holy," as the Prophet saith, "Holy and reverend is His name;" and it is not only holy in itself, but it gives holiness unto all things that are holy.

The word of God is holy, because it is published in *nomine Dei*: wherefore the name of God being holy in itself needs not be hallowed by us, that can neither add holiness to it nor take any from it; but when God willeth us to hallow His name it is to prove us, that by glorifying His name we may shew how we glorify God Himself and what reckoning we make of Him, that God may have proof how we do with the Virgin "magnify God our Saviour," and how we do "glorify God in our bodies, and in our spirits."

The name of God must be considered in two sorts, either as it is expressed by the term of Lord, Father, Lord Almighty, or else as it is expressed in such things as bear His

name, as He speaketh of Moses, "Behold I will send My Ex. 23. 20.
Angel before thee, beware of Him, and hear His voice," &c.,
quia nomen Meum est in Eo.

Touching the expressed name of God, whether it be Ex. 23. 20.
Father which importeth His goodness, or Lord which implieth His power, as we may not account basely of them, so
we must not use them lightly and negligently but upon just
occasion.

The things that have the name of God impressed and imprinted in them, are either those persons which have their
denomination of God, either jointly as the Church which is
called *Sancta Ecclesia Dei,* or severally as the priest of whom
Moses saith, "Let thy Urim and thy Thummim be with Deu. 33. 8.
Thy holy one."

The priests are called holy, because they are consecrated
to the Lord; in which respect as in the Old Testament they
are called *viri Dei,* so in the New they are *vasa nominis Dei,*
'vessels of the name of God,' as the Lord speaks in a vision
touching Saul to Ananias, that "he was a chosen vessel to Acts 9. 15.
bear the name of God among the Gentiles."

Secondly, those places are said to be God's which are consecrated to holy uses, as the sanctuary which is *domus Dei,*
and all those places where He puts the remembrance of His
name, and whither He promiseth that He will come to bless Ex. 20. 24.
His people that are assembled there for His worship.

Thirdly, those times which are kept holy to the Lord, as
the Sabbath, which is *dies Domini.* Rev. 1. 10.

Fourthly, the word of God preached in God's name.

Fifthly, the element consecrated in the Sacrament for a
holy use, called therefore *panis Dei.* Joh. 6. 33.

In all these there is an impression of God's name, and
therefore we must not lightly account of them but shew
great reverence to them, that thereby we may testify the
high and reverend regard and estimation we have of God
Himself, for sanctification is when God is said to magnify
or glorify.

It signifies to make great and glorious. So when sanctification is given to Him, it betokeneth to make holy, but
when we are said to sanctify, that is, to account holy; when
we magnify God, that is, *magni facere Deum,* 'to esteem

SERM.
IX.

greatly of God,' and our glorifying of God is to account Him glorious. So that when we pray, " Hallowed be Thy Name," our desire is, that God's name which is holy of itself, may be so accounted of us, and be holily used by us.

And whereas He saith not, *Glorificetur*, or *Magnificetur Nomen Tuum*, ' Glorified,' or, ' Magnified be Thy Name,' but *Sanctificetur*, " Hallowed" or " sanctified be Thy Name," it is to the end that we receiving the sanctification of God's Spirit might have a holy regard of His name ; for things may be accounted great and glorious by those which are accounted neither great nor glorious, but *Sanctificetur* cannot come from any persons that are profane but only such persons as are holy ; therefore the Angels in heaven cry not,

Isa. 6. 3.

' Glorious, Glorious,' but " Holy, Holy, Holy."

The title that Aaron wore upon his breast was not 'Glory,'

Ex. 28. 36.

but " Holiness unto the Lord." And the four beasts ceased

Rev. 4. 8.

not to cry day and night, " Holy, Holy, Holy, Lord God Almighty."

The duties which pertain to the sanctifying of God's name are two : first, that against which we do *deprecari*, or pray to be removed ; secondly, that for which we do pray, or desire to be granted.

First, we are to pray that we may not use the name of God, which is wonderful and holy, either contemptuously to magic or cursing, or negligently abuse it upon any slight occasion ; because that holy things are to be separated from a common use, and are not to be used but when necessity requireth.

We see by experience that the holy name of God hath not that reverence which it ought to have, and therefore the persons which do take it in vain do oftentimes pull upon themselves the plagues and vengeance of God by that sin ; for God doth in justice punish such offenders, not because the name of God can receive any pollution by men's default, but because we do, *quantum in nobis est*, ' as far as in us

Mat. 5. 28.

lieth,' pollute the holy name of God, even as he that " looketh after a woman to lust after her, hath already committed" the sin of uncleanness, although she be not a whit the less chaste for his lust.

The heathen fail in this duty, because they do appropriate

the name of God to "four-footed beasts," and change the Rom. 1. 23.
glory of God Who is incorruptible into the similitude of
mortal man.

The Jew sinneth because he contemns the name of Jesus,
which is "a name above all names," and despiseth the name Phil. 2. 9.
of Christ, the preciousness whereof appeareth herein, by that
that it is, *oleum effusum,* "an ointment poured out."   Cant. 1. 3.

But as we are to pray against the contemptuous abuse of
God's name, so we are to pray that we do not negligently
or carelessly use it without that reverend estimation and
regard that is due to it; that we "tread not under feet the Heb. 10.29.
Son of God, nor account of the blood of the Testament,
whereby we are sanctified, as a common thing."

Secondly, Moses and Aaron were debarred from entering
into the land of Canaan, not because they polluted God's
name, but for that they did not "sanctify the Lord among Deu. 32. 51.
the children of Israel at the waters of strife."

Therefore as we pray against the contempt and negligent
use of God's name, so we must pray that we may have a
due regard of it : first, that we "sanctify" God's name "in 1 Pet. 3. 15.
our hearts." Secondly, we must not use the name of God
with our tongues but seriously, and therefore we are forbidden to take it in vain in the third Commandment.
Thirdly, in all our actions we must not begin any thing that
is extraordinary but in the "name of the Lord That made Ps. 124. 8.
heaven and earth," and men must refer the end of them to
the "glory" of His name.   1 Cor. 10.
God, Whose name is called upon by us, is holy; and   31.
Christ, of Whom we are "called Christians," is holy : there- Acts 11. 26.
fore we must sanctify God in our actions.

Neither do we pray that we ourselves only may sanctify
God's name, but that others also may do the same; for
Christ saith not, *Sanctificemus,* 'Let us sanctify,' but *Sancti-*
ficetur, "Let Thy Name be sanctified."

This is it whereunto the Prophet exhorteth, *Laudate Do-* Ps. 117. 1.
minum omnes gentes, Laudate Dominum omnes populi, "Praise
the Lord all ye nations, praise Him all ye people:" that is
for persons.

For places, "The Lord's name be praised from the rising Ps. 113. 3.
of the sun to the going down of the same."

SERM.
IX.
Ps. 113. 2.

Thirdly, for the time, " Blessed be the name of the Lord from this time forth for evermore."

But because it cannot generally be sanctified except it be known, we must desire that all may know God, and pray Ps. 67. 2. with the Prophet, " Let Thy way be known upon earth, and Thy saving health among all nations."

Secondly, not to know it only, but cheerfully to go forward in the profession of God's truth, and in the worship of Isa. 9. 3. His name : " Thou hast multiplied the people, but not increased their joy." But we are to pray that as all nations know His name, so that they may so carry and profess it as that the heathen may not have occasion to say scoffingly, Ezek. 36. *Populus Dei est iste.* We must desire of God that all that 20. profess His name may so carry themselves, that for their Rom. 2. 24. sakes "the name of God may not be evil spoken of among Phil. 2. 15. the Gentiles," but contrariwise that they may "shine as lights in the world among a froward and crooked generation ;" that Mat. 5. 16. they may " by their good works" stir up all men to " glorify 1 Pet. 3. 1. our heavenly Father," and " by their good conversation, without the word, win those that obey not the word."

We are to desire that such as have not yet cared to perform this duty may now begin, that such as have begun to sanctify God's name may go forwards, and that such as are fallen away from God and pollute that holy name, which sometimes they did highly esteem, may *resipiscere,* that being renewed by repentance they may recover themselves out of relapses, that they may be of the society of Angels that cry Isa. 6. 3. continually, " Holy, Holy, Holy."
Rev. 4. 8.

We must be careful not for ourselves only but for those over whom we have power, that they may sanctify God's name and account it holy ; that the heathen may not take occasion to pollute the holy name of the Lord, saying, Are these the people of the Lord? but that while they behold 1 Cor. 14. our good conversation they may have occasion to say, " Verily 25. God is in you."

Thirdly, *Tuum Nomen,* "Thy Name." Men are given generally to give a kind of honour to God, but in the mean time they will have themselves honoured ; but here they are taught otherwise. It is our duty to ascribe all glory to God : Ps. 115. 1. *Non nobis, sed nomini Tuo da gloriam,* " Not unto us, O

Lord, not unto us, but to Thy name give the glory." So
that all men are no less desirous of their own honour and
glory, than the builders that built Babel that said, "Let us Gen. 11. 4.
get us a name."

But such as are thus affected, and carried with the love of
themselves, are not fit to sanctify the name of God; as our
Saviour speaks, "How can ye believe, seeing ye receive Joh. 5. 44.
glory one of another, and seek not the glory which is of
God."

As we may not usurp God's honour for ourselves, so we
may not deify princes; for we see how ill that voice was
taken, *Vox Dei et non hominis,* "The voice of God and not Acts 12. 22.
of man." Neither may we give divine honour to the Apostles and Prophets of God. The heathen people said of Paul
and Barnabas, "Gods are come down to us in the shape of
men," and they would have sacrificed unto them; but the
Apostles not willing to admit this sacrilege "rent their Acts 14. 11,
clothes and cried, We are men subject to the same passions ^14, 15.^
that you yourselves be." For we are desirous to give honour,
if not to ourselves, yet to others; but here Christ tells us
that no other name is to be sanctified but the name of God,
whereof we should be so careful that we ought to pray that
God's name may be sanctified by others if not by ourselves;
though we in our own persons cannot hallow it, yet *sanctificetur Nomen Tuum,* "let Thy Name, O Lord, be sanctified."

Hereby, as we pray for the gift of "the fear of God," Isa. 11. 2.
which is one of the seven virtues which are set down because
we do truly sanctify God when we make Him "our fear and Isa. 8. 13.
dread," so we pray against the vice of pride which is the
contrary to the virtue of fear; so shall we obtain the blessings, "Blessed are the poor in spirit," &c. And upon this Mat. 5. 3,
petition is grounded not only whatsoever hymn or psalm is ^&c.^
sung of the congregation, but even the end of all assemblies
is to ascribe holiness to God, and to sanctify His name for
His benefits bestowed upon us.

And in this they acknowledge, first, their own unworthiness; secondly, they bless Him for His goodness extended
toward them; thirdly, they do not acknowledge it in themselves, but do tell it forth as the Psalmist speaketh, "O
come hither and hearken all ye that do fear God, and I Ps. 66. 16.

SERM.
IX.

Ps. 66. 8.

will tell you what He hath done for my soul." Fourthly,
to this end they lift up their voices in singing, " to the end
they make the voice of His praise to be heard."

And among other benefits, we are to praise and bless His
name for the benefits of sanctification, which we have in the
name of the Lord Jesus; secondly, for the means whereby
this sanctification is offered and wrought in us, which is

Joh. 17. 17.

Col. 1. 12.

Isa. 6. 3.

the word, as Christ saith, " O Father, sanctify them in Thy
truth." For the perfection of sanctification, that we shall
have after this life, when we shall be " partakers of the inheritance of the saints in light," when we shall continually
sing with the heavenly angels, " Holy, Holy, Holy, Lord
God of Hosts."

And howsoever, when we desire of God that His name
may be sanctified, we seem like natural children to forget our
own necessities in respect of the care we have to God's glory;
yet even then we pray no less for ourselves than for God,

1 Sam. 2. 30.

2 Thess. 1.
12.

for the Lord hath promised, " Them that honour Me I will
honour;" and Christ saith, " that if the name of the Lord
Jesus be glorified in us, we also shall be glorified in Him."
Et sanctificando nomen adveniet regnum, In sanctifying His
name His kingdom shall come, as the next petition is.

If while we remain on earth our whole desire be to sanctify
God's name, we shall at length come to the place where we

Isa. 6. 3.

Lu. 2. 14.

Rev. 4. 11.

shall day and night sing as the Cherubims do, and with the
heavenly host of Angels sing, " Glory to God on high;" we
shall fall down before His Throne, saying always, " Thou art
worthy, O Lord, to receive glory and honour and praise for
ever."

THE LORD'S PRAYER.

SERMON X.

Thy Kingdom come.

HAVING intreated of the first petition touching the holy estimation of God's Name, we are consequently to speak of those six that concern ourselves, whereof the first three are spent in praying for that which is good, in the other three we pray for the removing of evil. The first two petitions, or the sum of them, is excellently expressed by the Prophet and by our Saviour; for agreeably to the words of David and of Christ our Saviour, in the first petition we ask for "glory" Ps. 84. 11. and seek for "the Kingdom of God;" in the second, for Mat. 6. 33. grace and righteousness; in the third, for the good things of this life, which shall not be withheld from them that lead a godly life, but shall be ministered unto them that upon earth do seek God's Kingdom and the righteousness thereof.

Wherefore, as of things which concern our good, the first both in order and nature is the Kingdom of God; for the first thing in our desire ought to be the Kingdom of God according to the commandment of our Saviour, and we are to "account all things but dung" in respect of it. Here- Phil. 3. 8. unto is required "the Spirit of wisdom and understanding," Isa. 11. 2. That may teach us to contemn all earthly pleasures in respect of the heavenly Kingdom.

Here our Saviour condemneth that capital vice that reigns in those men which in the world live of their own, and take no further care but to establish for themselves a kingdom upon earth. But if, according to His direction, we fix our desire upon the Kingdom of heaven, and by despising the

D d

SERM.
X.

Mat. 5. 8.

Ex. 33. 20.

Isa. 42. 8.

Ps. 145. 13.

Ps. 99. 1.

Mat. 25. 34.

Lu. 23. 42.

world do labour for the virtue which consists in the purity of the heart, then shall we have the blessing that is promised to "the pure in heart," that is, they shall be exalted to "see God."

Now when He saith, "None shall see My face and live," they that truly make this prayer shall behold His face in the Kingdom of glory.

These two first petitions have relation to the invocation; for as God by the word "Father" doth express His love to us, and for that He is in heaven doth give us hope for a heavenly estate, so we in these petitions do first desire that whereby our love towards Him may appear, while we prefer the sanctifying of His name before the regard of our own good. Secondly, we declare our heavenly hope that may come of being partakers of His heavenly Kingdom.

Howsoever God will not have any man's name hallowed or glorified but His own, as He speaks of Himself, "My glory will I not give to another;" yet He will communicate His Kingdom to us, and therefore in our own behalf we are taught to pray, "Thy Kingdom come."

In the petition we are to consider two things; first, the Kingdom itself, secondly, the coming of His Kingdom.

Touching the first point it may be objected, how it is that Christ teacheth us to make this petition; for "God's Kingdom is an everlasting Kingdom, and His dominion endureth throughout all ages." How then is it said to "come?" For the answer of this doubt, the Kingdom of God must be distinguished. First, God hath an universal Kingdom, such a Kingdom as ever was and for ever shall be; of which it is said, "The Lord is King, be the people never so impatient; He ruleth as King, be the people never so unquiet." Secondly, there is a Kingdom of glory, that whereof our Saviour speaketh, "Come, ye blessed of My Father, inherit the Kingdom prepared for you," &c. And the thief upon the cross said, "Lord, remember me when Thou comest into Thy Kingdom." And this is the Kingdom which in the first place Christ teacheth us to pray for; we pray for this Kingdom, that it may come; we pray for our own good, for it is a Kingdom of power, and therefore able to defend us; and therefore our Saviour in the con-

clusion of His prayer addeth this, " For Thine is the King- Mat. 6. 13.
dom." According to which the Prophet David saith, " Thy Ps. 145. 10,
saints give thanks to Thee, they shew the glory of Thy 11.
Kingdom, and talk of Thy power."

The government of His Kingdom is committed to Christ,
of Whom it was said by God, " I have set My King upon Ps. 2. 6.
My holy hill of Sion." In which regard He doubteth not
to affirm of Himself, *Data est Mihi omnis potestas,* &c., " All Mat. 28. 18.
power is given Me in heaven and in earth." And notwithstanding God reigneth as King, yet that is verified which the
Prophet complaineth of, " O Lord God, other Gods besides Isa. 26. 13.
Thee have ruled over us ;" for Satan taketh upon him to be
king, and hath played the tyrant, and hath prevailed so far
as that the greatest part of the world are subdued unto him ;
in which regard our Saviour calleth him " the prince of the Joh. 14. 30.
world," and by the Apostle he is termed " the god of this
world," for that he " blindeth men's eyes," and maketh them 2 Cor. 4. 4.
subject to the kingdom of darkness.

Secondly, there is a kingdom of sin, against which the
Apostle exhorteth : " Let not sin reign in your mortal Rom. 6. 12.
bodies ;" which he meaneth when he saith, that " sin hath Rom. 5. 21.
reigned unto death."

Thirdly, the Apostle sheweth that death hath a kingdom,
when he saith, that by means of sin " death reigned from Rom. 5. 14.
Adam to Moses."

These are enemies to the Kingdom of God; for while the
devil reigneth by means of sin, as he doth so long as he
" worketh in the children of disobedience," he taketh away Eph. 2. 2.
the glory of God's Kingdom, and death takes away the
power of it.

And in regard of Satan's kingdom, he is said to be " a Job 41. 34.
king over all the children of pride." For he makes the
whole world rebel against God, so that they are not ashamed
to deny Him to His face ; and that is true not only of the
common sort of the world, but even of a great many of the
Church, of which number are those that stick not to say,
" We will not have" Christ " to rule over us." Lu. 19. 14.

Again, there are many stumbling-blocks for the hindrance Mat. 13. 41.
of God's Kingdom, that the Kingdom of God cannot come ;
and therefore we do worthily pray as well that the kingdom

SERM.
X.
Ps. 110. 1.
1 Cor. 15. 26.
Rom. 16. 20.
Heb. 2. 14. 1 Cor. 15. 28.
Lu. 17. 21.
Rom. 5. 21.
Mat. 4. 17.
Joh. 3. 3, 5.

of Satan and sin may be overthrown, as for the removing of those offences.

God having exalted His Son into the highest heaven saith unto Him, "Sit Thou at My right hand, till I make Thine enemies Thy footstool."

"The last enemy that is to be destroyed is death." Wherefore our desire is, that there may be such a Kingdom, as wherein the Law of God may be exactly kept, and that it would please God in this Kingdom to "tread down Satan under our feet," that not only death itself, but he that hath "the power of death" being destroyed, "God may be all in all."

When we behold the state of the world, and see that good men are trodden under feet, and the vessels of wrath and sin are exalted and prosper, then we may know that that is not the true Kingdom, and therefore we pray that God will set up His Kingdom in our hearts, and govern us by His Spirit.

And therefore this point doth not only concern ourselves but also God, for unless His Kingdom come, His name cannot be sanctified of us.

As there are temporal kingdoms, so there is a spiritual Kingdom, called the Kingdom of grace, whereof our Saviour speaketh, "The Kingdom of God is within you."

As before we prayed for the Kingdom of glory, so now for this Kingdom of grace; for without this we shall never be partakers of that other Kingdom.

The glory of other kingdoms is the reformation of things that were before amiss, but the glory of the Kingdom of grace is, that as during the tyranny of Satan "sin reigned unto death," so now under this Kingdom "grace may reign through righteousness by Jesus Christ."

That we may have interest in both these Kingdoms, we must hearken to that which Christ proclaimeth, "Repent, for the Kingdom of God draweth near." As it draweth near to us, so we must draw near to it, else we shall never enter into it, for "except a man be born again, he cannot enter into the Kingdom of God."

And that we may begin to draw near to it, there is an outward regiment to be used, which is a token of the grace of

God bearing rule in our hearts; we must by the Kingdom
of God within us cast out devils.   We must entreat God by
the power of His Spirit to plant in our hearts that which is
good, and to root out and remove out of them that which is Mat. 13. 48.
bad.   We must displace Satan and sin that they set not up
their thrones in our hearts, and instead of it we must set up
God's Kingdom ruling in us by His Spirit; for the Kingdom
of God stands in "righteousness, and peace, and joy in the Rom. 14.
Holy Ghost." 17.

If we find these virtues in us, they are sure pledges of the
Kingdom of grace, and we may assure ourselves that after
this life is ended we shall be received into the Kingdom of
glory.

And howsoever He hath appointed kings and rulers over
us for our outward safety and defence, yet they have their
sceptre from Him, and the end of their rule is to further
God's Kingdom, as the Apostle speaketh, "that we may 1 Tim. 2. 2.
live under them in all godliness and honesty."

Touching the coming of His Kingdom, it may be demanded why we pray that it may come to us, seeing that
it were meeter that we should come toward it.   But hereby
Christ giveth us to understand what our corruption is.   It
is with us as with the Israelites, that were so addicted to
the flesh-pots of Egypt that they cared not to go into the
promised land; likewise we are so in love with this present
world, as that we have no mind of heaven.

Besides, there are so many stumbling-blocks in our way
as that the Kingdom of God must come unto us, or else we
shall never possibly come unto it.   Therefore, as we pray
that God would lighten our blind eyes, and inflame our hard
hearts with a love of His heavenly Kingdom, so also that He
would send His "angels to gather out of His Kingdom all Mat. 13. 41.
things that offend."

The things that we pray against are the kingdom of
Satan, darkness and sin, that they may depart from us,
and that the inward Kingdom of grace may take place in
our hearts; but the principal Kingdom that we desire is
the Kingdom of glory, whereof our Saviour said, "Behold, Rev. 22. 7.
I come quickly."

This is the Kingdom which the saints desire, saying,

SERM. "Come quickly, Lord Jesus;" and all creatures do wait for
X. this Kingdom, looking when they shall be "made free from
Rev. 22. 20. the bondage of their corruption." For whereas now all
Rom. 8. 20, things are "subject unto vanity," then there shall be a
21. Kingdom that shall not perish.

It is not for the wicked to desire the coming of His
Amos 5. 18. Kingdom : "Woe be to you that desire the coming of the
Lord, it is darkness and not light." The wicked shall say
Rev. 6. 16. to the mountains, "Fall upon us;" for the wrath of the
Lord, no man is able to abide it. But to the godly it
Lu. 21. 28. is a day of comfort, "Lift up your heads, for the day of
redemption draws near."

Howsoever, He will render vengeance to the ungodly that
2 Thes. 1. 8. have not known nor obeyed the Gospel of God. Yet He
comes to make a garland to crown the godly, and to set
them in His throne; they shall be received into His Kingdom of glory, where they shall enjoy the things which
1 Cor. 2. 9. "neither eye hath seen, nor ear hath heard, nor hath ever
entered into the heart of man, which He hath prepared for
them that love Him."

Phil. 1. 23. Therefore St. Paul saith, "I desire to be dissolved, and to
Lu. 2. 29. be with Christ." Simeon's desire is, "Lord, now let Thou
Thy servant depart in peace."

Thus the remembrance of the day of our redemption is a
joyful remembrance to them, and the chief thing that they
desire, so that they are willing to depart, in regard of their
future hope, rather than to tarry here; and howbeit that
Christ defers His Kingdom and coming, yet we are to be
Lu. 21. 35. watchful, "for it will come as a snare," and when He cometh
1 Thes. 5. 2. He will rather be for us than against us.

THE LORD'S PRAYER.

Thy Will be done.

THE sum of all our desires is set down by those words of
the Prophet, where he saith, "The Lord shall give glory and Ps. 84. 11.
peace, and no good thing shall be withheld from them that
live uprightly;" and our Saviour doth excellently express the
same, "Seek the Kingdom of God and His righteousness, Mat. 6. 33.
and all other things shall be ministered."

The petitions of glory, and God's Kingdom, have already
been handled. Now in this third—which is the second of
those which concern ourselves—we are suitors for the grace
of God in this life, whereby we may be enabled to do His
will here, that so we may obtain the Kingdom of glory in
the world to come; for the Kingdom of God and of glory
is the Heaven that we desire all to arrive at, and grace and
righteousness is the gale of wind that drives us forward
thereunto, and our suit to God in this petition is, that by
doing of His will here on earth "grace may reign" in our Rom. 5. 21.
hearts "by righteousness," that so hereafter we may reign
with Him in glory.

He doth not only will us to "seek God's Kingdom," and Mat. 6. 33.
tells us that there is one "prepared for us before the founda- Mat. 25. 34.
tion of the world," but also how we may find it and attain to
it: "Not every one that saith, Lord, Lord, shall enter into Mat. 7. 21.
the Kingdom of God, but he that shall do the will of My
Father Which is in heaven."

Therefore touching the order of this prayer, as of those
things which concern our good, the first is, that God's King-

SERM.
XI.

dom may come to us, so the door whereby we must enter into the same is the doing of God's will; and therefore in the second place we are taught, that the Kingdom of God shall come, not by wishing or desiring but by doing of God's [Lu. 10. 9.] will, as Christ saith, "The Kingdom of God is come near Jas. 4. 8. you." So Christ tells us, "If we draw near to God, He will draw near to us."

Touching the will of God it may be demanded, why we should demand and ask this petition; for as the Psalmist Ps. 115. 3. saith, "Our God is in heaven, He doth whatsoever He will." Ps. 135. 6. "Whatsoever the Lord willed, that did He in heaven, in the Rom. 9. 19. earth, and in all deep places;" and, "Who hath resisted Prov. 21. His will?" "No counsel or wisdom can prevail against the 30. Lord." And if any do oppose themselves against His will, Acts 9. 5. yet they do but "kick against the pricks."

The answer to this objection is, that we pray not so much that God's will may be done, but rather that what God willeth may be our will; for there is one will of God which we may resist, another which we may not resist.

For the distinction of God's will, it is either hidden and secret, or revealed and open: the one is that which the Ps. 33. 11. Prophet calls "the counsel" or "thought of His heart;" the other is that will of His word, wherein He declareth and openeth to men what His will is.

His secret will is, *voluntas beneplaciti,* 'the good pleasure of His will;' His revealed will is, *voluntas signi,* which is disclosed to us.

God's secret will is, *voluntas quam Deus vult,* 'that will which God willeth;' His revealed will is, *voluntas quam Ipse nos velle vult,* 'that will which He willeth us to will.' The secret will of His heart is, *voluntas adoranda non scrutanda:* Prov. 25. he that curiously searcheth the glory of heavenly things, 27. shall not enter into glory. "How unsearchable are His Rom. 11. 34. judgments;" and "Who hath known the will of the Lord? or who was His counsellor?" But the open and revealed will of God is, *voluntas scrutanda et facienda,* 'both to be Eph. 5. 17. searched out, and to be done of us.' "Be not unwise, but understand what is the will of God." The knowledge of Joh. 13. 17. His will is not enough, but as Christ saith, "If ye know these things, blessed are ye if ye do them."

Of the secret will of God, that is true which the Apostle saith, "Who hath resisted His will?" and therefore we pray Rom. 9. 19. not that that will may be done.

Of His revealed will, that is verified which Christ complaineth, *Quoties volui congregare vos, et noluistis?* "How Mat. 23. 37. often would I gather you together, but ye would not?" God oftentimes willeth when we will not, and therefore we have need to pray that His revealed will may be accomplished in us.

Moses thus distinguisheth God's will: *Secreta Deo nostro,* Deu. 29. 29. *quæ autem revelavit nobis et filiis nostris,* "The things that are secret belong to God, but the revealed are for us and our children." The secret will of the Father is, "that of all that Joh. 6. 39. He hath given Me, I should lose nothing." The revealed will of Him That sent Me is, that every one that seeth the Son, and "believeth in Him, should not perish, but have [Joh. 3. everlasting life." 16.]

God's "judgments," which are the fountain of reprobation, Ps. 36. 6. are *abyssus magna;* and His mercy, extended to all that by faith apprehend the same, is *abyssus et profunditas,* 'a great Rom. 11. depth.' Therefore we are not curiously to enquire and 33. search out of God's secret touching reprobation or election, but to adore it.

His revealed will doth especially concern us, which is expressed in His Commandments, whereby He declareth whatsoever He desireth at our hands, and therefore our study must be to frame our lives and actions according to that will.

Unto both these wills we must give a *fiat,* but severally.

The first will is passive, and forasmuch as the secret will of God shall be done whether we will or no, we crave that with patience we may submit ourselves to whatsoever He in His secret will hath appointed to bring upon us.

The other will is active, and therein we desire that we may willingly practise that which He willeth in His word.

There is *voluntas de nobis,* and *voluntas in nobis:* for the first, we desire that we may approve of it, though it be done without us; in the second, we desire not only an approbation, but a co-operation.

Touching His secret will, when we say *Fiat voluntas Tua,*

SERM.
XI.
we pray that *nihil Dei displiceat nobis,* 'that nothing which God commands displease us;' and in respect of His will declared our desire is, that *nihil nostrûm displiceat Deo,* ' that nothing we do do displease God.'

Touching His secret will, so long as it is not plain — within His own counsel He will compass — we may dissent from it, for a man may *bonâ voluntate velle quod Deus nonvult,* ' he may with a good will will that which God wills

1 Sam. 16. 1. not :' so Samuel's will was good when he wept for Saul, whom God would not have him to bewail.

Secondly, we may *bonâ voluntate nolle quod Deus vult,* ' with a good will not will that which God willeth ;' as a child may be unwilling of the death of his father, whom notwithstanding God's will is shall not recover.

Thirdly, men may *malâ voluntate velle quod Deus nonvult,* ' with an ill will he may will that which God willeth not ;' the Patriarchs in a corrupt will would go into Egypt, whom God would not to go thither.

And fourthly, they may in a corrupt will be unwilling to that which God willeth : so it was God's will that Saul should be king, when as the people were unwilling to it; and this is the state of the will of the creature, so long as it is not acquainted with the will of his Creator.

But when once it pleaseth God to reveal His will, then we

Isa. 46. 10. must say with the people, *Fiat consilium Domini,* "Let the counsel of the Lord come to pass." We must not wrestle nor struggle against it, but patiently submit our wills to His, not only when God's will is *voluntas dulcis,* ' when

Gen. 24. 50. His will is to do us good,' as Bethuel spake concerning the marriage of his daughter, but when it is *amara et aversa voluntas ;* we must submit our wills to His when it pleaseth Him to cross us, either outwardly by taking away those that are beneficial to us, (in which case it was said by some that

Acts 21. 14. bewailed the departure of St. Paul, "The will of the Lord be done") or in ourselves, in which case we may say with

Lu. 22. 42. Christ, "I would have this cup pass from Me; yet, O Father, if Thy will be otherwise, not My will, but Thy will be done."

This lesson had David learned; for albeit he had complained of the great affliction that he had suffered, yet he

saith, *Tacui tamen Domine.* And as he was content to bear Ps. 39. 2.
this so he gave God thanks for them, acknowledging that
it was good for him that he had been in trouble.

We must learn Job's fruits as well as Bethuel's; and Job 1. 21.
these being joined, we shall perfectly conform our wills to
God's secret will.

Concerning the will of God declared, or the will of His
word, the Lord by His Prophet saith of His Church, "My [Isa. 62. 4.
will is in it;" but David speaks more plainly of this revealed
will, "Thou hast charged that we should keep Thy com- Ps. 119. 4.
mandments diligently."

The Apostle speaks more particularly, *Hæc est voluntas* 1 Thes. 4. 3.
Dei sanctificatio vestra; and "This is the will of God, that 1 Pet. 2. 15.
by well-doing ye should stop the mouths of ignorant and
foolish men."

This is the revealed will of God, and we must not only
take notice of it, but labour to practise that which in our
understanding we know is meet to be done.

As the Apostle saith, *Ostende mihi fidem ex operibus tuis,* Jas. 2. 18.
"Shew me thy faith by thy works," so we must shew our
desire that we have unto God's kingdom by obedience of
His will; for not they that sing or say or wish that God's
will be accomplished, but *qui fecerit,* "he which doth the Mat. 7. 21.
will" of God, "shall enter into the kingdom of God."

To the doing of God's will two things are required; first,
that we lay aside our own will, for they as will sanctify God's
name must say with David, "Not to us, but to Thy name Ps. 115. 1.
give the praise." So that God's will may be done we must
say with Christ, "Not My will but Thy will be done;" we [Lu. 22.
must abridge ourselves of our own will, that God's will may ^{42.]}
take place.

The better sort that are regenerate do assent to the law
of God that it is good, and have a delight to it, but yet they Rom. 7. 16,
see "another law in their members, which leadeth them unto ^{22, 23.}
the law of sin" and death.

Every man finds that to be true in himself, that "the flesh Gal. 5. 17.
lusteth against the spirit, and the spirit against the flesh."

The will of the flesh wills one thing, and the will of God
another: therefore that God's will may take place, we must
renounce our own will and, as Christ saith, willingly "deny Mat. 16. 24.

SERM.
XI.

Joh. 1. 13.

ourselves." We must oppose God's will to "the will of the flesh" and "the will of man."

We must pray unto God, *Converte meum nolle in Tuum velle*, 'Convert my froward and unwilling will into Thy will;' and because Thy will is the true will, *insere oleam voluntatis Tuæ oleastro voluntatis meæ*, 'ingraft the true olive of Thy will into the wild olive of my will.'

If our will be contrary unto God's will and will not be subject unto it, then we must scatter it and pull it up by the roots. *In chamo et fræno constringe maxillas meas*, saith an ancient Father; and upon the words of Christ, "Compel them to enter that My house may be full," saith he, *Compelle me Domine intrare, si vocare non est satis.*

Ps. 32. 9.
Lu. 14. 23.

Secondly, that God's will may be done in us, we must be possessed with a base conceit of our own will, and have a high and reverent opinion of God's will; we must be persuaded that our own will is blind and childish and perverse, and therefore Solomon saith, *Ne innitaris, &c.*, "Do not lean to thine own wisdom." "Every man is a beast by his own knowledge." And to express the fault of man's will, Job saith that man is *tanquam pullus asini*, "like a wild ass's colt," which of all other beasts is most foolish. But be he never so wise naturally, yet he is but a fool in heavenly things, as St. Paul witnesseth.

Prov. 3. 5.
[Jer. 10. 14.]

Job 11. 12.

1 Cor. 2. 14.

Men "speak evil of things which they know not," yea, even in those things "which they know naturally they are but beasts." All our reason and understanding hath not in itself sufficient direction for our will; and therefore Christ saith of St. Peter, that "flesh and blood did not reveal" to him that knowledge that is attained by God's Spirit; and in spiritual things St. Paul, he "counselled not with flesh and blood."

Jude ver. 10.

Mat. 16. 17.

Gal. 1. 16.

Jer. 4. 22.

Lastly, our will is wholly inclined to that which is evil: wherefore one saith truly, *Tolle voluntatem tuam, et ego extinguam infernum*, 'Take away thine own will, and I will quench hell fire.'

1 Cor. 5. 5.

Rom. 1. 24.

They that are "given over to Satan," as the incestuous Corinthian, may be restored, but those whom God giveth over to their own will, their case is desperate; and therefore we have the more cause to think the more humbly of

our own will, and willingly submit ourselves to the holy
will of God.

Touching both St. Paul saith, "The Law is holy, and the Rom. 7. 12,
Commandment is holy, and just, and good;" and, "The ¹⁴·
Law is spiritual, but I am carnal, sold unto sin."

But we must think honourably of God's will, and this we
cannot but do if we consider that His will is so perfect as it
needeth no rule to be guided by; but our will being crooked
and perverse must of necessity be directed by the rule of His
will, or else we shall swerve out of the way.

Our will is blind and foolish, but His will is full of counsel
and wisdom; our will is crooked and perverse and froward,
but His will is full of all goodness; which we are to understand hereby, that He sheweth Himself a Father to us.   If
a child be left to his own will, it is as much as his life is
worth: therefore "withhold not correction, but strike him Prov.23.13.
with the rod, and he shall not die;" and our will being
childish, we must be abridged of it, or else we shall fall
into danger.   Therefore we do pray that we may not only
submit our will to God's, but that we may utterly deny our
own will being foolish, that God's most holy will may take
place in us; but we do not only pray that we may have a
will, and desire to do God's will, but also ability and power,
for of ourselves we have no strength to do it.   That appeareth by the petition itself, *Nam quid stultius quam petere
id quod penes nos est?* 'What is more foolish than to ask
those things that are in our own power?' And the Apostle
saith, "We are not sufficient of ourselves to think" a good 2 Cor. 3. 5.
thought.   Such is our corruption, that though God will, yet Mat. 23. 37.
we will not.

We cannot speak unto God; for "no man can say that 1 Cor. 12. 3.
Jesus is the Lord, but by the Holy Ghost."

We do not find either will or ability, but it is God That Phil. 2. 13.
giveth both; and though the "spirit be willing, yet the Mat. 26. 41.
flesh is but weak."

Therefore we are petitioners for the grace of God, and
for power from Him, without which we cannot do God's
will; so that our desire is to obtain something from God
whereby His will may be accomplished in us; for it is not
said, *Faciamus,* or *Fac Tu Tuam voluntatem,* 'Let us do,'

SERM.
XI.

Joh. 3. 31.

1 Pet. 1. 13.
Tit. 2. 11.

Prov. 12. 2.
Zech. 12.
10.

Lu. 24. 49.

Isa. 26. 12.

Ps. 27. 9.

Ex. 17. 11.
Mat. 14.
29, &c.

or, Do Thou Thy will; but, *Fiat voluntas Tua,* "Thy will be done."

Wherein we are to consider, *a quo, et per quem fiat,* 'from whom and by whom it is to be done; we pray not that we of ourselves may do the will of God, for no man can rise up to heaven unless he first receive a grace from heaven; "he that is of the earth speaketh of the earth." Therefore our suit is not only for good thoughts, and heavenly desires, but also for ability of grace: but this grace is either active or passive.

The passive grace is that which proceeds from God towards us, which standeth in offering grace, as God is said to do, or when He causeth His grace to "appear to all men;" and that is not enough unless we be made capable of it, as it is in vain that light doth shine unless we have eyes to see it; and therefore as He offers grace, so He must give us grace and enable us to draw grace from Him. That He would pour grace into us, that He would sow in our hearts good thoughts, change our affections, and make them conformable to His will; and so though the thoughts of His heart seem hard to flesh and blood, may for all that please us.

And last, our desire is, *ut induamur virtute ex alto,* and He doth offer His grace, and doth pour it into us.

Then we must have that active grace, by which the will of God may be done in us, of which the Prophet saith, *Omnia opera nostra operatus es in nobis,* "Thou, Lord, hast wrought all our works in us." God must not only *sanare cogitationem et mutare affectum,* 'heal the thought and change our affection,' but *perducere ad actum,* that is, 'He must bring to pass,' that as He gives us ability to do His will, so His will may be done by us; we must say with the Prophet, "Thou art my help, forsake me not, O God of my salvation."

As He prevents us with His grace by giving us both a will and a power, so He must still follow us with His grace that we may go forward in doing of His will, for our case is compared to the state of the Israelites which in their fight with Amalek did prevail as long as "Moses held up his hand," but "when he let it down" they were put to the worse. We may see it in the case of St. Peter who was able to walk upon the water while Christ held him up, but when he was left to himself he sunk; therefore we must have not only a preventing but also an accomplishing grace that may still follow us in our works, *ne cessent in effectum,* 'that they fail not in the upshot,' whereof the Evangelist makes mention, that from Him Who is full of grace " we must receive grace Joh. 1. 16. for grace."

It was not the grace of God only that wrought in St. Paul, stirring him up to holiness, but also *gratia Dei σὺν ἐμοὶ,* "the grace of God with me." And when the Angels say 1 Cor. 15. εὐδοκία ἐν ἀνθρώποις, "toward men good will," they do $^{10.}_{Lu. 2. 14.}$ not only wish that God will shew good will towards men, but that He would accomplish it in them by infusing grace into their hearts.

Our desire therefore is, that the will of God may be done and fulfilled in us, but yet by His grace and the assistance both of His preventing and following grace. And as for sanctifying of God's name our desire was that it may be sanctified of us, but if not yet that it may be by others, so here though the will of God be not done in us, yet *ut fiat quovis modo,* 'that it be done howsoever,' that it may be done in others; but especially in our own behalf, that when we are either unwilling or unable to do His revealed will it may please Him to give us the knowledge of it, and to put into us the obedience of it, that being assured in our consciences that we have done the will of God we may have that peace and joy of the Holy Ghost wherein the Kingdom of grace standeth, which may be to us a pledge of the Kingdom of glory whereunto we shall be exalted after this life, if we be careful both to submit our wills to God's secret will, and to frame our wills and the actions of our life to that declared and open will of God which for our direction He hath revealed in His word.

THE LORD'S PRAYER.

SERMON XII.

In Earth as it is in Heaven.

WHICH words are an appendix to the three first petitions;
for though it be added to the third which concerneth the
doing of His will, yet the ancient Fathers refer it also to the
two former; so that we are to pray no less that God's name
may be sanctified in earth as it is in heaven, and that His
kingdom may be consummate in earth as it is in heaven,
than that His will be accomplished on earth as it is in
heaven.

Wherefore we may observe by this complement of the
three first petitions, that God respects not only the doing of
that which He requireth but chiefly the manner of it; for
it sufficeth not simply to do God's will as others do on
earth, but we must do it as it is done in heaven; for adverbs
please God better than verbs, and He respecteth more in the
doing of His will the manner of the doing of it than our
doing itself.

The Greeks distinguish the will of God by both the words
of θέλημα and εὐδοκία. When we do God's will without any
regard how, so it be done, that is His θέλημα, but when
God's will is done with a *sicut*, and in such sort as He requireth, that is His good pleasure, and εὐδοκία.

God's will was done of the people when they sacrificed
any beast whatsoever, but if they chose out the fittest then
the sacrifice was the more acceptable; so in this prayer we
do not only desire to do God's will *utcunque*, without regard

how, whether with willingness and cheerfulness or against our wills, but we desire to do it in the best manner, "as it is done in heaven;" wherein we offer that sacrifice or service to God which is as the fat of rams, for the sanctifying of His Name.

The Apostle saith, that "at the name of Jesus every knee Phil. 2. 10. shall bow, both of things in heaven, in earth, and things under the earth." But our desire is so to reverence the name of Jesus as the things in heaven reverence it.

Of God's Kingdom it is said, that Christ is "ruler both in Ps. 110.2,3. the midst of His enemies," and also that "in the day of His power the people shall as friends offer free-will offerings with a holy worship." But we pray that God's Kingdom may come among us not as among His enemies, but that we may willingly submit ourselves to His will and government.

Lastly, for the doing of His will the Prophet said, "What- Ps. 135. 6. soever the Lord pleased, that did He in heaven, in earth, and in the sea."

We desire that His will may be performed in us, not as in the deep places but as in heaven, for this prayer contains two *sicuts:* the one pertains to God, teaching us how to love Him : the other concerns our neighbour, where we pray so to be forgiven as we forgive our debtors; so that, as heretofore we have noted, *lege operandi lex statuitur supplicandi,* though there were no law to require the love of God and our neighbour, yet this form of prayer doth teach us how to love God, and what perfect love we owe to our neighbour.

In the thing itself we are to observe three points : first, a qualification ; secondly, an elevation of the soul ; thirdly, an application.

In the qualification we are to enquire what is meant by heaven and earth, either *tanquam continentia,* or else we may understand them as things contained therein ; then, how God's will is done therein.

Howsoever our tongue or dialect speaks of heaven singularly, yet both Greek and Latin imply a plurality of heavens, for there are three heavens : first, the air, where the birds fly, whence they are called *volucres cœli;* secondly, the hea- Mat. 6. 26. ven of heavens, where the sun, moon, and stars, are set to give light; thirdly, that which the Apostle calls "the third 2 Cor. 12. 2.

SERM. heaven," whereunto he was taken up, which is the place of
XII. blessedness, where God's majesty is especially resident.

In all these heavens which contain other bodies, in them we shall find that God's will is done.

Of the lower heaven the Prophet saith that it is obedient
Ps. 148. 8. to God's will, and fulfils His word by sending down snow and fire and wind.

1 Kings   In the second heaven, which Solomon calls the "heaven
8. 27. of heavens," God's will is done, for there at God's command-
Josh.10.13. ment "the sun and moon stood still," contrary to their usual course, "till the people of God avenged themselves of their enemies."

Thirdly, the earth itself, and things contained in it, do yield obedience to heaven; for if the heaven be favourable in
Acts 14. 17. sending down "rain and fruitful seasons," the earth answer-
Ps. 67. 6. ably "will bring forth her increase" for the good of man;
Deu. 28. 23. but if the "heaven be brass, the earth also will be iron."

Lastly, as the powers of the heavens are such as that they
Ps. 65. 10. can draw up clouds from the earth, which do distil rain upon the earth, to "water the furrows thereof," so we desire that the spiritual heaven may transform us into a heavenly nature, not setting our minds on earthly things but on things above.

For the things contained in heaven, as they are heavenly,
[Phil. 3. so we desire that we living on earth may have "our conver-
20]
Gen. 3. 19. sation in heaven," that earthly man to whom God said, *Terra es*, may by this means be made heavenly.

In the third heaven is contained, in respect of His humanity, first Christ Himself, Who is both in heaven and
Eph. 1. 22. earth; for as He is called "the Head of His Church" He is
1 Cor. 12. in heaven, but in respect of His body Which is called Christ
27. He is on earth. Therefore we pray that Christ on earth, that is, the Church, may do God's will, even as Christ the Head Who is in heaven hath done it; that as Christ our
Joh. 6. 38. Head came not "to do His own will, but the will of Him That sent Him," so the whole body of Christ may labour to fulfil the same.

Ps. 103. 20.   Secondly, in heaven thus are Angels, "which fulfil His commandment, and hearken to the voice of His word." So our prayer is, that men to whom God hath made the pro-

mise that they shall be ἰσάγγελοι, may labour to be "like Lu. 20. 36.
the Angels" in doing God's will, as they hope to be like
them in nature.

Thirdly, in heaven there is the "congregation of the first- Heb. 12.23.
born," that is, the saints departed; wherefore our prayer is,
that as they have and still do carefully fulfil God's will, so
the saints on earth and Church militant may do the same.

Again, whereas St. Cyprian out of the sixteenth Psalm and [Vid. in
second verse, and the nineteenth and first verse saith, that $\frac{Orat.}{Dom.}$]
heaven is here upon earth; for when the Psalmist saith,
"The heavens declare the glory of God," the Apostle applieth that to himself and to the rest of the Apostles, of
whose preaching he saith, "No doubt their sound went out Rom. 10.
into all lands, and their words unto the ends of the world," 18.
so that the Apostles were heavens living on earth; so our
prayer is, that as they living on earth lived a heavenly life
and began heaven here, so our carnal heart may be applied to
the meditation of heaven, that we may be "saints on earth." Ps. 16. 3.

The Wise Man saith of the body, that it being "dust," at Eccles. 12.
the hour of death "turns itself to dust from whence it came, 7.
and that the spirit returns to God That gave it." Thus
must the spirit return to God in our lifetime, and we must
while we be on earth and "bear the image of the earthly
man" seek still to be in heaven, and here labour more and
more to "bear the image of the heavenly." As the hea- 1 Cor. 15.
venly part of man, that is, his spirit, is willing and doth not 49.
only "consent that God's law is good" but "delight" in it, Rom. 7. 16,
so must we be careful to bring our flesh in subjection, that 2 Cor. 4. 16.
our old man and outward man may conform himself to the Eph. 4. 22,
inward and new man. 24.

Secondly, touching the question how God's will is done in
heaven, the answer is, that where His will is both *dulcis* and
amara voluntas, 'a sweet and bitter will,' it is there obeyed
and performed in both kinds; for the heavens do not only
at God's commandment keep a continual motion which is
agreeable to nature, but against nature sun and moon stand Josh.10.13.
still at His will, whose obedience tells us that our duty is to
do His will, not only in things agreeable with our nature,
but when His will is contrary to our liking.

This obedience was performed in Christ: "Not My will, Lu. 22. 42.

SERM.
XII.
Gen. 28. 12.

Phil. 4. 12.

Heb. 1. 14.

Ps. 103. 20.

Acts 26. 28.

Rev. 4. 11.

Joh. 6. 26.

Isa. 6. 2.

Phil. 2. 14.

Lu. 14. 18.

Joh. 21. 21.
Gal. 1. 16.
Joh. 6. 60.
Mat. 8. 29.
Hag. 1. 2.

Mark 9 26.

but Thine be done ;" and in the Angels, which at God's commandment are ready not only to ascend but also to descend, to shew that they are content not only to appear in heavenly glory which is their nature, but also to be abased according to the Apostle's rule, " I can abound, and I can want."

The heavenly bodies do service to all nations, and the Angels are " ministering spirits."

As naturally they have a desire to ascend to bear rule, so at God's commandment they are content to descend to do service here below, they do altogether " fulfil God's will ;" whereas the nature of man doth hardly grant to obey God's will in that which seemeth strange to flesh and blood, as Agrippa affirmeth of himself, " Thou somewhat persuadest me."

The saints in heaven confess to God, " Thou hast created all things, and for Thy will's sake they are and were created," and therefore refuse not to subject their will to the will of God, be it pleasant to them or not; but as our Saviour speaketh, " Ye seek Me, not because ye saw the miracles, but for that ye did eat of the loaves and were filled," so if we do that which God requireth, it is rather for our own sake with regard to our own private profit than to do God's will.

The heavenly Angels do God's will with willingness and readiness of mind, which is the fat of their sacrifice; and therefore they are said to have, every one " six wings." From whose example we must learn to " do all things" commanded of God " without murmuring or disputing," and that because it is God's will we should do it.

In earth, when God willeth anything that is not pleasant to our wills we " make excuse," or we post it off to others as Peter said to John, *Quid autem hic?* We are ready to communicate with " flesh and blood," and to say with the disciples, *Durus est hic sermo,* " This is a hard speech." If we cannot shift it off from ourselves, yet as the devil reasoned, *Cur venisti ante tempus?* And as the people say, " It is not time yet to build the house of the Lord," so we are ready to defer and prolong the doing of God's will as much as may be, when we do it ; as the unclean spirit would not come out of the child but with much crying and renting of him, so we cannot do God's will but with great murmuring and

grudging; and when men do God's will in this sort, they do
it not as it is done in heaven by the Angels and saints that
willingly obey it, but as the devils in hell which against their
wills are fain to do it.   Therefore our rule in this behalf is,
that we do God's will, not ἐκ λύπης, but ἐκ καρδίας, not 2 Cor. 9. 7.
"grudgingly," but cheerfully "from the heart," accounting it Joh. 4. 34.
our "meat" to do the will "of our heavenly Father."

Secondly, for the elevation, it is true that the qualification
is signified by ὡς, not ὅσον, and our prayer is that we may
do God's will "as it is done in heaven" but not as much,
with like readiness of mind but not in like measure—for
that is impossible for earthly men; we desire to fulfil God's
will in the manner, but not in the same degree of obedience,
which may be expressed by the words "image" and "like- Gen. 1. 26.
ness."   Our obedience may be the likeness of the Angels,
but not the image.

The character or stamp of the Angels' obedience is that
which is equal in proportion, but such obedience is not to
be found; there may be a beam of it, answerable in likeness
and quality, not in quantity.   So in likeness we are *con-* Rom. 8. 29.
formes imagini Christi, and "bear the image of the hea- 1 Cor. 15.
venly" man, as endeavouring thereunto, but yet we cannot 49.
attain to it.

But albeit it is hard for flesh and blood which our Saviour
required, "Be ye perfect, as your heavenly Father is per- Mat. 5. 48.
fect," yet there is a use of such precepts; first, *ut feramur
ad perfectionem,* "that we may be led on to perfection." Heb. 6. 1.
Secondly, we must have an heroical and "free spirit," which Ps. 51. 12.
may stir us up to wish that we could do more than we can,
which consists of aspiration and suspiration.   We must aspire
to the greatest perfection with David : *Concupivit anima mea,*
"My soul hath lusted to keep Thy righteous judgments for Ps. 119. 20.
ever."   And, "O that my ways were so directed." Ps. 119. 5.

This is an angelical perfection, which we cannot attain
unto in this life : therefore we must *suspirare,* when we consider that the Law saith, "Thou shalt not lust," and yet find [Ex. 20.
that we do lust; we are to sigh and say with the Apostle, 17.]
"Who shall deliver us from this body of death?" Rom. 7. 24.

If we consider that we cannot love our God with all our
heart and soul as we ought, then to say with the Prophet, *Væ* Ps. 120. 5.

mihi, quia prolongatus est incolatus meus in terrá! " Woe is me that my dwelling is prolonged in the tents of Kedar."

We must desire to do more than we can, and grieve that we cannot do so much as we ought; that as we do what we can, so what we cannot do we should supply it *voto, desiderio, animo,* 'with our hearty wish, desire, and mind.'

Thirdly, the supplication is of two sorts, real and personal.

1 Pet. 4. 10. Touching the first, as the grace of God is *multiformis gratia,* so the will of God being one is of many sorts, and containeth divers particulars; therefore, as we generally pray that the will of God may be done, so when by the word of God we understand what is the will of God in particular, we are to

1 Thes. 4. 3. desire no less that it may be performed : " This is the will of God, even your sanctification." Therefore our desire must be, that this will of His may be done and fulfilled in us. This is a special remedy against the temptations of the flesh, which oppose themselves against God's will.

There is another will of God for patience, for He would have us suffer for Christ's sake without murmuring, that so

1 Pet. 2. 15. " we may stop the mouths of ignorant men." Therefore we are to pray that this will of God also may be done in us.

As Joseph was careful to do God's will touching sanctification, and Job to obey God's will in suffering patiently, both which are now saints in heaven, so must we after their examples be both holy, and careful, and patient.

It may be we are willing to obey God's will in particular, but we will say, *Nondum venit hora,* 'It is not yet time;" therefore we must learn to practise the Prophet's resolution,

Ps. 119. 60. " I made haste, and prolonged not the time to keep Thy law."

When God revealeth His will to us, we must presently

Gal. 1. 16. put it in practice, and as Saul did, and not counsel with flesh and blood; and this is the real application.

The persons to whom the doing of God's will is to be applied, are not only the whole earth—which is also to be

Ps. 57. 11. wished, as the Prophet sheweth—" Set up Thyself, O God, above the heaven, and Thy glory above all the earth," but the earth or land wherein we dwell, as the Prophet speaks,

Ps. 85. 9. " that glory may dwell," *in terrá nostrá,* " in our land." So we pray that God's will may be done in all lands, but especially in our land and country, that so He may bestow His blessings upon it; but yet we are every one of us particularly to apply to ourselves, for to man it was said by God, *Terra* Gen. 3. 19. *es.* To man it was said, " Earth, earth, earth, hear the word Jer. 22. 29. of the Lord." So we desire that God's will may especially be done and fulfilled in that part of the earth whereof God hath made us, that is, that in these our earthly vessels, which we carry about with us, we may be careful to do that which God requireth at our hands.

THE LORD'S PRAYER.

SERMON XIII.

Give us this day our daily bread.

Out of the words of our Saviour, in the sixth chapter of Matthew verse the thirty-third, we have elsewhere set down the order of these three petitions which concern ourselves, for the first is the petition of glory and of God's Kingdom which our Saviour willeth us to seek in the first place. The second is the petition of grace and of God's righteousness, wherein we pray that God's will may be done. The third [Ps. 84. 11.] petition tendeth to this end, that, as the Prophet speaks, God would not withhold any temporal blessing needful for this life, but that He would give us all things that are necessary for us.

The things pertaining to glory, for which we pray in the first place, are eternal; those that concern grace are spiritual, and the blessings of this life which we desire may not be withheld from us are natural and temporal.

This is nature's prayer, for not only we but all creatures above and beneath make the same suit to God by the voice Ps. 147. 9. of nature. "The ravens" of the air call upon God that He Ps. 104. 21. would feed them; "the lions" beneath, "roaring for their prey, do seek their meat at God;" and therefore no marvel that we, inasmuch as we are creatures, do seek to God Who is the God of nature to supply the defects of nature that we find in ourselves as other creatures. And yet there is a difference betwixt us and them, for they call upon God only for corporal food that their bellies may be filled; but the prayer that we make for outward things is not without respect to things spiritual, and this petition followeth upon the other by good consequent and order; for, as the heathen man saith,

> *Haud facile emergunt quorum virtutibus obstat* [Juv. Sat.
> *Res angusta domi,* 3. 164, 5.]

so we shall be unfit to seek God's Kingdom, and to do His will, unless we have the helps of this life.

Therefore we desire that God will give us the things of this life, those things without which we cannot serve Him; that as we desire the glory of His Kingdom, and the grace of His Spirit whereby we may be enabled to do His will, so He will minister to us all things for the supply of our outward wants in this life, the want whereof hath been so great a disturbance to the saints of God in all times, that they could not go forward in godliness as they would.

Abraham, by reason of the great famine that was in Canaan, was fain to "go down into Egypt." The same Gen 12. 10. occasion moved Isaac to go down to Abimelech at Gerar; Gen. 26. 1. and Jacob, to relieve his family in the great dearth at this time, was fain to send his sons, the patriarchs, into Egypt Gen. 42. 2. to buy corn. The children of Israel, when they wanted Ex. 16. 2. bread or water, "murmured" against God and His servants; Nu. 20. 2. 3. the disciples of our Saviour were so troubled in mind because they had forgotten to take bread with them, that they understood not their master when He gave them warning to "beware of the leaven of the" Scribes and "Pharisees." Mark 8. 15. So the want of outward things doth distract our minds, and make us unfit for God's service.

Therefore, that we may in quietness of mind intend those things that go before in this prayer, our Saviour hath indited us a form of prayer to sue to God, as well for things temporal, as spiritual and eternal; for it is lawful for us to pray for them, so that we do it in order.

The first petition that the natural man makes is for his daily bread, but our care must be first for the Kingdom of God, next for the fulfilling of God's will and doing that righteousness which God requires at our hands; and after, we may in the third place pray for such things as we stand in need of during our life.

This blessing the Fathers observe out of the blessings

which Isaac pronounced upon his sons; Jacob's blessing was first "the dew of heaven" and then "the fat of the earth," shewing that the godly do prefer heavenly comforts before earthly. Esau's blessing was first "the fatness of the earth," and next "the dew of heaven," to teach us that profane persons do make more reckoning of earthly commodities than of heavenly comforts.

Therefore in regard of the spiritual account we are to make of God's Kingdom, and the doing of His will, we are to wish them in the first place, and then David's *Unum petii a Domino,* "One thing I have required of the Lord." And that which Christ saith to Martha, *Unum est necessarium,* "One thing is needful," would bring us to Solomon's two things, "Give me not poverty, nor riches, but feed me with food convenient for me, lest being full I deny Thee and say, Who is the Lord? or being poor I steal, and take the name of my God in vain." And that is it which we are bold to do by Christ's own warrant, for He hath taught us first to pray for His Kingdom, then for the working of righteousness; or, for the doing of God's will, and lastly for daily bread.

If we do first pray for the two former, then we may be bold in the third place to sue to God for the latter, for He hath promised to "withhold no good thing from them that lead a godly life;" if the doing of God's will be our meat, then *requiem dedit timentibus Se,* "He hath given rest to them that fear Him."

In the petition we are to observe, from six words, six several points: first, the thing that we desire, that is, "bread;" secondly, the attribute, "our bread;" thirdly, "daily bread;" fourthly, we desire that this "bread" may be "given" us; fifthly, not 'to me,' but *nobis,* "to us;" sixthly, *hodie,* and as long as we say, *hodie,* "to-day."

To begin with giving. Hitherto the tenor of this prayer ran in the third person: now we are to pray in the second, saying, *Da Tu,* whereupon the Church hath grounded a double dialect of prayer, which comes all to one effect; for that which the Church prayeth for, "God be merciful unto us and bless us;" is no less a prayer than if she should say in the second person, *Miserere nostri,* "O Lord, be merciful

to us, and bless us;" and that which is added, " and lift up
His countenance," is all one as if the Church speaking to
God should say, " Lift up the light of Thy countenance."

This change, or alteration of person, proceedeth from the
confidence which the saints are to gather to themselves in
prayer; for having prayed for the sanctifying of God's
name, for the accomplishment of His Kingdom, and for
grace and ability to do His will, Christ assureth us that
we may be bold to speak to God for our own wants.

Out of the word 'giving' we are to note three things :
first, our own want, for if we had it of ourselves we would
not crave it of God. This confession of our want and in-
digence is a great glory to God, that all the inhabitants of
the earth *usque ad Regem Davidem* should profess and say,
" I am poor and needy but the Lord careth for me;" they do Ps. 40. 17.
profess themselves to be His beggars, not only by the voice
of nature which they utter for outward things as other unreasonable creatures do, but by those prayers which they
make for the supply of grace, whereby they may be enabled
to do God's will, so that not only *Regnum Tuum*, "Thy
Kingdom" is God's gift, but also *panem nostrum*, "our
bread," we acknowledge to be His gift. It is from God
from Whom we receive all things, as well the "good giv- Jas. 1. 17.
ings" as the "perfect gifts;" He is the author not only
of blessings spiritual but of benefits temporal; He gives
us not only grace to obey His will, but, as the Prophet
speaketh, *dat escam*, " He giveth us meat." Ps. 136. 25.

The idolatrous people say of their idols, I will go after my
lovers that give me my bread, and my water, my oil, and my
wine; but God saith after, " It is I That gave her corn, and Hos. 2. 8.
it is My wine, and My flax, and My oil." *Ipse dat semen* 2 Cor. 9. 10.
sementi, et panem manducanti, " He ministereth seed to the
sower, and good bread for food." We are destitute of the
meanest blessings that are, it is God only from Whom we
receive all things; therefore to Him we pray, acknowledging
our own want, *Da nobis panem*, " Give us bread."

Secondly, we must consider the word *Da*, as it is set in
opposition to *Veniat*, or *Habeam panem ;* it must not content
us that we have bread, but we must labour that we may have
it of God's gift. Esau said of things temporal which he Gen. 33. 9.

SERM.
XIII.

2 Pet. 2. 15.

enjoyed, "I have enough," not acknowledging from whom. Balaam cared not how he came by promotion so he had it, and therefore he is said to have "loved the wages of unrighteousness:" but we must labour not so much to have good things as to have them from God; and Pilate is to acknow-

Joh. 19. 11.

ledge that the power which he hath was "given him from above," and not to vaunt of any usurped power.

Ps. 104. 28.
Ps. 78. 23.

It is said of God, *Tu aperis manum Tuam*, "Thou openest" "the doors of heaven." So we are not so much to labour for temporal things by our own endeavour, as that we may have them from God.

Thirdly, *Da*, opposed to rendering, teacheth us that it is not of our own endeavour, but it is of God's free bounty and liberality that we have bread and other things, which while we seek for of God's gift we confess that to be true which

Eccl. 9. 11.

Solomon saith, *Non est panis sapientis;* be a man never so wise, yet he hath not always to supply his need. As he that is highest gets not always the goal, nor the strongest

Mat. 6. 27.

man the victory, so saith our Saviour, "Which of you by taking thought can add one cubit to his stature?"

Ps. 127. 2.

All our endeavours for the things of this life are unprofitable without God's blessing: "It is vain to rise up early, and to go to bed late."

And when He blesseth our labour, then He is said to give us "bread;" and therefore we are to confess with David

1 Chron.
29. 14.

that whatsoever we have received, we have received it at His hands.

Now the means of God's giving is of four sorts: first, God giveth bread when He blesseth the earth with plenty,

Hos. 2. 21,
22.

when He gives force to the heaven; when the heaven heareth the earth, the earth heareth the corn, the wine, the oil, and they hear man.

Secondly, He gives when He sets us in some honest trade of life, and vouchsafeth His blessing to our endeavours

Ps. 128. 2.

therein, that we may get our living and "eat the labour of our hands," without which the first giving will do us no good.

Thirdly, He gives us bread not only in His blessing the earth with increase, and by blessing our honest pains in

Levit. 26.
26.

our vocation, but when He gives us *baculum panis*, "the

staff of bread;" for at His pleasure He useth to "break the [Ezek. 4. staff of bread," and to make it of no power to nourish us: 16.] then are they but beggarly elements, "when we eat and Hag. 1. 6. have not enough." Therefore our prayer is, that He would cause the earth to yield us bread, so that to the bread He would infuse a force to "strengthen man's heart," for which Ps. 104. 15. end it is ordained.

Fourthly, because Moses says, "Man lives not by bread Deu. 8. 3. only but by the word of God," therefore we pray that as our bread by His blessing is made to us *panis salubris*, so it may be *panis sanctus*, that He will give us grace to use His creatures to the end that we may the better serve Him; otherwise, howsoever they nourish our bodies, yet they will prove poison to our souls.

God performeth these three former givings to the heathen, so that their bellies are full with bread, but withal "He Ps. 106. 15. sendeth leanness into their souls." But Christian men have not only the earth to yield her fruit, God's blessing being upon their labours, and a blessing upon the creature itself that it is not in vain but nourisheth, but also it is sanctified to them, and that bread is properly theirs because they are God's children, *et panis est filiorum*, 'it is the children's bread.'

Secondly, the thing we desire to be given is "bread," concerning which because the decays and defects of our nature are many, so as it were infinite to express them severally, therefore our Saviour Christ doth here comprehend them all under the term of "bread," using the same figure which God Himself useth in the Law, where under one word many things are contained.

Howsoever our wants be many yet the heathen bring them all to these two, *pabulum et latibulum*, 'food and covering;' and as they do, so doth not only Moses in the Law, where all that pertains to this life is referred to *victum* and *amictum*, Deu. 10. 18. but also St. Paul in the first Epistle to Timothy, *Habentes* 1 Tim. 6. 8. *victum et amictum, his contenti simus.*

So then under this petition is contained, not only that God would give us bread by causing the earth to bring forth corn, and all good seasons for that purpose, but that withal He will give us health of body, and not plague us with sick- Ps. 106. 29.

ness as He did the Israelites. Then, that we may have
peace, without which these outward blessings would afford
us no comfort; and that as He fills our bellies with food,
Acts 14. 17. so He will give us *lætitiam cordis,* that is, all manner of con-
tentment in this life.

Howbeit, this petition stayeth not here, for the prayer of
Christian men must differ from the lions' roaring and the
ravens' crying. The end of their praying is that their bellies
may be filled, but we must have as great a care for the food
of our souls; therefore where we call it *panem nostrum,* we
do not mean *panem communem,* 'such bread as is common'
to us with other creatures, but that spiritual bread which is
proper to man, which consists not only of body, but of soul
and body, which must be both fed. And where we pray
that God would give ἄρτον ἐπιούσιον, we ask such bread
as is apt and meet for our sustenance; that is, not only
earthly but heavenly bread, because we consist not only of
a terrestrial but also of a celestial substance: so then our
desire is, that God would give us not only *panem jumentorum,*
Ps. 78. 25. but *panem Angelorum,* "the bread of Angels;" and our suit
Joh. 6. 50. is, as well for *panis cœli,* as for earthly bread.

The bread of the soul is God's word, which hath a great
reference to earthly bread; and therefore speaking of the
Job 23. 12. sweetness of that bread Job saith, "I esteemed of the words
of His mouth, more than my appointed food." And David
Ps. 19. 10. saith, "Thy word is sweeter than honey and the honey-
comb."

In the New Testament the Apostle, to shew the nourish-
1 Tim. 4. 6. ing force of God's word, saith that Timothy was *enutritus
verbis fidei.* And, to shew the taste or relish that it hath
Heb. 6. 4. as well as natural food, saith, *gustaverit bonum Dei verbum,*
"hath tasted the good word of God." So the food of the
soul is to be desired at God's hands as well as the bodily
food.

Amos 8. 11. There is "a famine" as well of "God's words" as of
Mat. 5. 6. bread; there is a "hungering and thirsting after righteousness:" therefore we are to pray that God would supply
the wants, not only of the body but of the soul likewise.

But there is a spiritual food both for body and soul, that
Joh. 6. 35. which our Saviour promiseth, "He that cometh to Me shall

not hunger, and he that believeth in Me shall never thirst;" that is the hidden Manna that God hath promised for us in heaven, whereof it was said, "Blessed is he that eateth Lu. 14. 15. bread in the Kingdom of God."

Thus by how much the leanness of the soul is worse than bodily famine, so much the more earnestly are we to pray for the spiritual food than for the food of the body.

Thirdly, for the first attribute, we pray not simply for "bread," but for "our bread."

The word "our" hath respect not only to use, but to property and right.

This right or property is double : first, that which was appointed in the beginning, *In sudore vultûs tui comedes panem tuum.* Our request to God is for that food which is gotten by honest pains taken in our calling, whereunto God hath made a promise, "Thou shalt eat the labour of thy hands," Ps. 128. 2. and without which we have no right to this bodily food, for *qui non laborat non manducet,* "he that laboureth not, let him 2 Thess. 3. not eat." Now we would have God supply our wants with 10. bread by right, and this right is general to all adventurers.

Secondly, as we would have made it ours by the labour of our vocation, so by the duty of invocation, that this corporal food which is common to other creatures may be proper to us by calling upon God for His blessing upon it, which if we do we have a promise it shall be truly ours. "Open Thy Ps. 81. 10. mouth, I will fill it." For "the creatures of God are sancti- 1 Tim. 4. fied to us by the word of God and prayer." 4, 5.

This puts a difference betwixt the Christian man's bread and that which the profane man eats : for first, those slothful persons whom the Apostle calls "slow bellies," cannot say Tit. 1. 12. this prayer as they ought; for they are nothing but idle upon the earth, and *fruges consumere nati,* 'born to eat and [Hor. Ep. drink;' they labour not for their living, but eat *panem ali-* 2 Thess. 3. *enum,* not *suum,* which the Apostle requires. 12.

Secondly, those that "eat the bread of violence," and feed Prov. 4. 17. upon "bread that is gotten by deceit," do not eat *panem* Prov. 20. *suum* but *subdititium;* they eat not *panem datum a Deo,* but 17. *a dæmone.*

Thirdly, "Esau having filled his belly rose without giving Gen. 25. God thanks after he had eaten, as without calling upon God 34.

for His blessing before. For the which also he is said to be "profane." So are all those that eat of God's creatures without praying to Him for His blessing, and for a sanctified use of them; which thing if they refuse to do as Atheists and profane persons, their bread may be *panis salubris*, but not *sanctus*, it may be able to nourish their bodies, but it shall bring leanness to their souls.

Fourthly, the other attribute of bread is "daily," concerning which we must consider four things.

First, from the Latin word *quotidianum*, which hath relation to the time; by which word, as we acknowledge our daily want, and God's continual care and providence for the supply thereof, (of Whom it is said, "Thou givest meat in due season,") so Christ teacheth us daily to praise and magnify God's care daily extended towards us, and to use that Psalm of thanksgiving wherein the Church confesseth God's goodness in that behalf.

Ps. 104. 27.

Ps. 145.

Secondly, from the Greek word ἐπιούσιον, which signifieth bread "apt and meet for our substance."

Now, forasmuch as man consists of body and soul, his prayer to God must not be only for such meat as is meet to nourish the body, but also for the food which agreeth with the soul; for it is in vain to have food, except it be nutritive and convenient for us.

Thirdly, the Syriac word used by our Saviour signifieth *panem necessitatis meæ*, which hath relation to the quality of the bread, teaching us not to pray for dainty meat but such as is fit to relieve our hunger. *Tribue victui meo necessaria,* not meat which is above my estate; *Da panem necessitatis non lasciviæ,* 'bread of necessity not wantonness.'

[Pro. 30. 8.]

The Israelites lusted after the flesh-pots of Egypt; and therefore God gave them quails from heaven, but—which was the heavy judgment of God upon them—they perished "while the meat was in their mouths."

Ps. 78. 30, 31.

The Apostle willeth us therefore not to set our minds upon superfluity; but contrarily, ἔχοντες τροφὴν καὶ σκεπάσματα, "food and raiment, let us therewith be content."

[1 Tim. 6. 8.]

Prov. 30. 8.

Fourthly, the Hebrew word used, Proverbs the thirtieth, hath relation to the quantity; for it signifieth *panem dimensi mei non gulæ*, and it teacheth us not to seek abund-

ance, but to desire of God to measure us out so much as He
knoweth to be meet for us, and (as Christ speaketh) "to give Lu. 12. 42.
us our portion of meat in due season." For the Scripture
telleth us what inconvenience cometh of abundance of meat:
Dilectus Meus impinguatus recalcitravit, "My beloved, when Deu. 32. 15.
he waxed fat, spurned with his heel;" and the sin of Sodom
was "fulness of bread," and the people by excessive eating Ezek. 16.
and drinking of wine "made themselves sick." Therefore Hos. 7. 5.
Christ diligently warneth His disciples to take heed of "sur-
feiting and drunkenness" for this cause, *ne graventur corda,* [Lu. 21. 34.]
"that your hearts wax not heavy."

Fifthly, in the word *nobis* we must consider two things:
first, a reason; secondly, a limitation. For the first, we desire that this bread should be given us.

First, because we are God's creatures; He refuseth not
to hear the lions and ravens in this behalf, when they cry
to Him. And our Saviour saith, that our "heavenly Father Mat. 6. 26.
feedeth" the fowls of the air. And therefore we, in regard
we are His creatures as well as they, we may by right make
this prayer to Him.

Secondly, inasmuch as we are men, we may be bold to
crave that favour at His hands which He sheweth indifferently to all men, for He suffereth the "sun to shine on the Mat. 5. 45.
evil and on the good." And as David saith, *Oculi omnium
suspiciunt in Te,* "The eyes of all wait and look up to Thee," Ps. 145. 15.
therefore we are to pray that God will give bread not only
nobis animalibus but *nobis hominibus,* not only as to 'living
creatures' but as 'to men.'

Thirdly, "the Gentiles" and heathen people, which only
"seek after these things," do obtain them at God's hands; Mat. 6. 32.
much more will God grant them to us, which profess ourselves Christians and His children.

Secondly, for the limitation, it is not *mihi, non meum,* but
"Give us," and "Give our." The reason is that, as Solomon Prov. 5. 16.
says, "our wells may flow out abroad," and that there may
be "rivers of waters in the streets," and that not only we
may not be burdensome to others but that we "may have to Eph. 4. 28.
give to them that have need."

Sixthly, for the word *hodie,* our Saviour teacheth us to
pray, "Give us bread this day," and as the Apostle speaks, Heb. 3. 13.

SERM. *dum dicitur hodie :* the reason is, because life is but only
XIII. *dies,* not *sæculum.* And the Wise Man saith, "Talk not
[Prov. 27.
1.] of to-morrow, for thou knowest not what a day may bring
Lu. 12. 19. forth." We may not say to our soul, "Soul, thou hast store
of goods laid up for many years." We see by his example
what may fall out. Forasmuch as the continuance of our
life is uncertain, our desire must be that God would give us
sufficient for our present want.

Howbeit, this makes not for them that are careless for
Prov. 30. the time to come, for such are sent to learn wisdom of the
25.
ant, which provides for winter ; and not only the saints at all
times have been careful and provident for outward things,
Gen. 41. as Joseph who counselled Pharaoh beforehand to lay up
35, 36.
corn to feed him for seven years' space during the famine,
but our Saviour Himself gives charge that that which re-
Joh. 6. 12. maineth should be saved, and "nothing lost." And it was
His pleasure that Judas should bear the bag for His and
their provision, to teach us that He alloweth provident care
for things earthly.

But by this word "daily" our Saviour condemneth μερίμ-
ναν, or immoderate care for worldly things, whereby the soul
1 Tim. 5. 8. is rent and divided, and not that πρόνοια which is required
of every man for "his own household," and is both lawful
and honest.

Here ariseth an objection, how a man having filled his
belly, or being ready to leave this world, may say this
[S. Aug. prayer. The answer is, first, *Multi dormierunt divites qui*
Ser. 61.
10.] *surrexerunt pauperes ;* therefore, our desire is, that as we
have enough now, so we may be preserved in this estate,
and that God would not change plenty into poverty. Again,
though we have bread, and it continue with us, yet it is
nothing without that *beata pax :* therefore, though we have
the thing itself, yet we are to desire that which is the life
of bread, which is a power to nourish ; then, that God will
give us the sanctified bread, which is the heavenly manna,
and grace, that as we work for bread in our vocations, so
we remember to sanctify it by invocation ; for else it is
usurped bread.

THE LORD'S PRAYER.

SERMON XIV.

And forgive us our debts.

AUGUSTINE interpreting our Saviour's words of "the shut- Lu. 4. 25. ting of heaven in Elias' time," compared prayer to a key [Vid. in Append. that hath power to open heaven from whence all blessings tom. 5. 63.] descend unto us, and to shut the bottomless pit of hell from whence all evils proceed. Prayer is a means not only to draw all grace from God, but it is *obex mali, et flagellum* Prov. 12. 2. *dæmonis :* as the name of Christ is *oleum effusum*, because Cant. 1. 3. by it we receive all good, so the name of the Lord is *turris* Prov.18.10. *fortissima*, for that it saves and defends us from all evil.

As these are both truly affirmed of God's name, so by the invocation of the name of God we have this double benefit, that we do not only receive all good by it, but also are delivered from all evil.

In the three former petitions our Saviour hath taught us to draw grace from God ; in these three latter we are taught to use that kind of prayer that concerns the removing of all evil, called *Techinah, δέησις,* and deprecation.

The evil is of three sorts, of sins past, and to come, and of the evil of punishment.

In the first of these three petitions we pray against the guilt of sins past, that God would not charge us with them ; in the second, against the running issue of sin to come, that God would not suffer us to sin hereafter; in the third, that God would turn away from us all those plagues that our sins deserve, both in this life and in the life to come : and these three petitions are fitly opposed to the three former.

F f 2

SERM.
XIV.

To the Kingdom of glory we oppose our sins; to the doing of God's will, temptation; to natural good things, the evil of the world to come, and the miseries of this life; from both which we desire to be delivered when we say, "Deliver us from evil."

The petition consists of debts and forgiveness: but before we handle them we are to speak, first, of the necessity of this petition; secondly, of the goodness of God That penneth the petition for us.

What need we have to pray God for remission of our sins appears hereby, because our sins do make a partition between God and us, the effect whereof is that our misdeeds do turn God's blessings from us, and do keep "good things" from us.

Isa. 59. 2.

Jer. 5. 25.

Now having already desired at God's hands the glory of God's Kingdom, the good of grace for the doing of His will, and all outward good things necessary for this life, we are of necessity to pray that God will forgive us our sins, which otherwise will hinder us of these good things; and as our sins do hinder God's graces that they cannot come to us, so they hinder our prayers that they cannot come to God, for our sins are as it were "a cloud" to hide God, so that "our prayers cannot go through." So that except we desire the forgiveness of our sins, we shall in vain pray for the three former good things.

Lam. 3. 44.

Besides, our sins are a plain hindrance to God's Kingdom, for none shall come thither but such as are "uncorrupt," and void of sins in the whole course of their life: *et nihil impurum ingreditur illuc,* "no unclean thing shall enter thither." Therefore the Prophet saith, *Hic est omnis fructus ut auferantur peccata.*

Ps. 15. 2.

Rev. 21. 27.

Isa. 27. 9.

Secondly, the goodness of God appeareth herein, that He hath indited us a prayer to ask remission, telling us that it is possible to obtain remission of sin. It is true that by our sins we have made ourselves incapable of all good things, but yet we see the goodness of God, that as we have still *dona,* so He teacheth us to say, *Condona.*

Where He teacheth all men to pray for good things, we learn that we are all *mendici Dei;* but in that we are taught to ask forgiveness of sin, we see that we are *malefici Dei,*

' the malefactors of God,' such as have need of pardon; and the goodness of God towards us appears to be the greater in this behalf, because there is no Angel nor spirit to whom He vouchsafeth this favour, to have their sins remitted, save only to man.

Of them it is said, He found no truth in His Angels; in His servants, and in "His Angels" there was "folly;" Job 4. 18. that is, they had trespasses, but yet God will not forgive them, nor receive any supplication for pride; but contrari- 2 Pet. 2. 4. wise, He keepeth "the Angels that sinned in everlasting [Jude ver. 6.] chains to the judgment of the great day." He That is "the Nu. 27. 16; God of the spirits of all flesh," will not hear the spirits that 16. 22. sinned against Him; but, "Thou That hearest prayers, to Ps. 65. 2. Thee shall all flesh come."

There is a way for man to escape the danger of sin, if he ask pardon; but the sins of the wicked Angels shall not be forgiven. The elect Angels do make the three first petitions as well as we, and the petition for the supply of natural defects is common to all living creatures, but this which prayeth for pardon of sins is proper only to man; so we see how God exerciseth His goodness and sheweth it, not only in exercising of liberality to them that have need, but His long-suffering in pardoning them that have sinned against Him.

To come to the petition itself. By "debts" our Sa- viour meaneth "sins," expressly so called, Luke the eleventh [Lu. 11. 4.] chapter and fourth verse, and sinners are called "debtors," Luke the thirteenth chapter and fourth verse; for the Scrip- [Lu. 13. 4. *marg*] ture speaks of them, Matthew the eighteenth chapter and [Mat. 18. 24.] twenty-fourth verse. One was brought that "owed ten thou- sand talents," that is, which had committed a great number of sins; and, Luke the seventh chapter and forty-first verse, [Lu. 7. 41.] a lender had two debtors, by which are meant sinners; the [S. Aug. de Ser. Dom. 2. 8.] reason hereof is because there is a resemblance betwixt "sins" and "debts."

In the affairs of men the case is thus, that if the condition be not performed they are bound to endure the penalty, and so become double indebted: so it is between God and us, the sin that we commit by the breach of God's Law is *chiro- graphum contra nos*, " a hand-writing against us." So they Col. 2. 14.

SERM.
XIV. are called in the Old Testament, "Thou writest heavy or
hard things against" us, and our sins are compared to "a

Job 13. 26.
Ezek. 2. 9,
10.
book" written on both sides; for we are bound to keep
God's commandments because He made us, and not only so
but He still doth nourish and preserve us: therefore we

Mat. 25.
15, &c.
ought to do His will. He gives us "talents," which we
ought to employ to His glory; He gives us dwelling-places
in the world, as to the Israelites He gave the land of the

Ps. 105. 45. heathen, "that they might keep His statutes, and observe
His laws." If we fulfil them we discharge our duty to God
and are free from all penalty, but if we do it not there is an

Deu. 27. 26.
[Gal. 3.
10.]
obligation. "Cursed is every one that continueth not in all
things that are written, to do them." If He place us in the

Mat. 21.
33, 34.
Lu. 19. 23.
"vineyard," He will look to "receive fruit of it." If He
give us talents, He will have us so to employ them as that
He may reap gain thereby. The gifts and graces that God
bestows upon us must be employed in hallowing His name,
in enlarging His kingdom, in accomplishment of His will;
if we fulfil this, the penalty of the Law takes no hold on us,
but if we do not only not use them to His glory, but abuse
them and turn them to the breach of the Law by serving sin,
then are we in a double sort indebted to God, and make

Ps. 90. 11. ourselves guilty of His wrath, *Et quis intelligit, &c.* "Who
understandeth the power of His wrath?"

If we consider how grievous plagues God threatened for
the breach of the Law, we would be more careful and heedful that we do not offend Him; which because we consider
not, we become indebted to God.

Rom. 8. 12. We are "debtors" to the flesh to provide for it, only so
much as is meet for the relieving of it; and the rest of our
care must be for the spirit. But because all our care is for
the flesh, to satisfy it, in fulfilling the lusts thereof, and [we]
are careless of our spirits, therefore we become indebted to
God in a third sort by breaking His commandments in that

Rom. 1. 14. which concerns ourself; but this the Apostle saith, "I am
debtor to the wise and the unwise." That is, we must be

Gen. 4. 9. careful of others, as God said to Cain, "Where is thy bro-

Phil. 2. 21. ther?" But because *omnes quæ sua sunt quærunt,* "all seek
their own," and seek not the good of others, therefore they
grow further indebted to God.

These " debts" or sins are properly said to be " ours," because they proceed from us—for there is no member of our body that is not guilty of some sin—and not in that sense that bread is said to be ours which cometh to us and is made ours by God's gift. And when we pray, " Forgive us our debts," we learn that it is our duty to crave forgiveness for others as for ourselves; for as the Apostle by these words, " The rebukes of them that rebuked Thee, fell upon Me," Rom. 15. 3. sheweth that Christ was carried with the same zeal against sin committed against God as if it had been against Himself, so he teacheth that we must be moved with the like compassion towards others, when we consider their sins, that we find in ourselves for our own ; and that we ought no less to pray for them than for ourselves, and to suffer others to pass over the bridge of God's mercy as well as we.

In the word " debts" three things are to be noted : first, where Christ teacheth His Apostles, that were baptized and the most perfect Christians that ever were, to pray for remission of sins, it should work in our nature a humiliation, for they in making this prayer acknowledge themselves sinners ; much more ought we.

The Apostle Peter confesseth of himself, " I am a sinful Lu. 5. 8. man." St. Paul saith of himself, *Peccatorum primus sum ego,* 1 Tim. 1. " I am the chief of sinners." St. James, including himself, Jas. 3. 2. and the rest of the Apostles, saith, *In multis offendimus omnes,* " In many things we sin all." St. John saith, " If we say we 1 Joh. 1. 8. have no sin, we deceive ourselves :" he saith not, *Exaltamus nos,* as the Apostle spake of modesty, or *Non humiliamus nos,* ' we do not humble ourselves,' but *Decipimus nos,* and " if we deny it the truth is not in us." Seeing it is so, we must not say with the Pharisee, " I am not as this man," but with Lu. 18. 11, the Publican, " God be merciful to me a sinner." 13.

Secondly, we are not only sinners but daily sinners, as appeareth by this, that we are taught no less to pray daily for forgiveness of our sins than for bread. To confirm this Solomon saith, *Septies in die cadit justus,* " The just man Prov.24.16. falls seven times a day ;" and as man eateth and drinketh every day, so " he drinks iniquity like water." Job 15. 16.

Thirdly, we run into such debts as we are not able to discharge; for if we were, we needed not to say, *Dimitte nobis,* "Forgive us our debts;" but, "Have patience with me, and I will pay Thee all."

Mat. 18. 29.

To signify to us the greatness and number of our sins, one

Lu. 7. 41.

was brought that owed "five hundred pence," and another

[Mat. 18. 24.]

that owed "fifty," and another that owed to his master "ten thousand talents." By which we perceive that we cannot make satisfaction to God: therefore He must remit them.

The consideration whereof ought to work in us humiliation: first that, as Job says, our hearts do not excuse us,

[Job. 9. 20.]
Levit. 26. 40.
Ps. 32. 5.
1 Joh. 1. 9.

and that we seek not to "justify" ourselves; that as God requireth, we "confess our misdeeds," that we acknowledge our sins to God, and hide them not: for "if we confess our sins, God is faithful to forgive our sins."

Ps. 38. 18.

Secondly, that we do not only confess, but "be sorry for" them; that while we are in danger to God for our sins, we go and humble ourselves, and entreat Him, and suffer not our

Prov. 6. 4.

eyes to sleep, till we be sure how we may obtain forgiveness.

Ps. 102. 4.

The consideration of sin made David "forget to eat his bread;" so greatly was he disquieted till he was assured of pardon.

For the second point, if our sins be "debts," they must be

[Rom. 13. 8.]
Job 9. 3.

paid. "Owe nothing to any:" but we are not able to "answer one of a thousand," and for the penalty of male-

Ps. 90. 11.

diction we are not able to endure it. "Who knoweth the power of His wrath?" Therefore our prayer must be to God, that our misery may prevail more with God to move Him to compassion than our unworthiness to stir up His

Col. 2. 14.

indignation, and that He will "cancel the hand-writing;"

Jer. 31. 20.

which thing, for that He is full of the "bowels" of compassion, He is moved to do when He seeth us sorry for our sins. Howbeit His justice must be satisfied, else His mercy cannot take place: but Christ by His death having done that, God

Job 33. 24.

saith of the sinner, "Deliver him, for I have received a re-

Gal. 5. 3.

conciliation." *Qui circumcisus est, debitor est totius Legis:* but Christ was circumcised, and therefore fulfilled the Law

[Mat. 5. 26.]

for us *ad ultimum quadrantem,* "to the utmost farthing;"

Ps. 69. 4.

and not only so, but He saith of Himself, *Exsolvi quæ non rapui,* "I restored that which I took not." He not only perfectly fulfilled the Law, but suffered the curse of the Law, which He had not deserved, with this condition, *Sinite*

istos abire, " Let these go," that is, He was content to be Joh. 18. 8.
the reconciliation for us, that He might draw us out of the
hands of God's justice.

The estate of our debts may be compared with the widow's
state that was left in debt by her husband ; for as the Lord 2 Kings
blessed her oil in such sort as she did not only pay her debts ^{4. 7.}
but had enough to live on after, so Christ is our *oleum effu-* [Cant. 1.
sum, " our oil poured out," that is of power not only to ^{3.]}
satisfy God's wrath for our sins, but also to give us an estate
in the Kingdom of heaven ; and for His sake it is that we
may be bold to pray for remission of sins, and are taught
to believe that for His merits our sins are forgiven ; so that
is true, *Legem operandi et legem credendi lex statuit supplicandi,* ' The law of prayer stablished both the law of obeying
and believing.'

Out of *Dimitte* arise three things for our comfort : first,
that even these sins which we commit after baptism, after
our calling, and when we are come to the knowledge of the
truth, are remissible.

In teaching the Apostles to pray He assureth them of this
favour, that the same party that saith *peccata nostra,* " our
sins," is taught to say, *Pater noster,* " Our Father." Our
comfort therefore is, that still we are the children of God,
though great sinners ; for though we lose the dutiful affection of children, yet God cannot lose *viscera Patris,* ' the
tender bowels of a Father.'

David, to a rebellious son, could not but shew a fatherly
affection : " Do good to the young man Absalom." So though 2 Sam.18.5.
the prodigal son had offended heinously, yet the father is
ready to receive him.   Lu. 15. 20.

Secondly, another comfort, that albeit we commit sin daily,
yet He will daily forgive us ; for God should mock us, saith
Augustine, if bidding us pray for forgiveness, He should for
all that shut up the bowels of His mercy. He bids us pray
for pardon of our sins, putting no difference whether they
be penny debts, or talents ; whether fifty, or a thousand ; if
we ask forgiveness, He tells us He is ready daily to remit
them.

Thirdly, that be our sins never so great, so great as cannot
be satisfied by us, yet He will forgive them *propter Seipsum,*

SERM.
XIV.
Isa. 48. 11.
1 Joh. 2. 2.

Levit. 26.
40, 42.
Job 33. 26.
Ps. 32. 5, 6.

1 Kings 8.
49.
Mat. 18. 32.

Acts 8. 22.

Ps. 80. 4.

Rom. 6. 3.

1 Pet. 4. 1.

2 Cor. 12. 9.
Heb. 10. 26.
Gal. 5. 24.

"for His own sake." Christ hath made Himself "a satisfaction for the sins of the whole world."

We must labour how we may soundly apply His satisfaction to ourselves; and among other means whereby we apply the satisfaction of Christ to ourselves, prayer is one: "They shall confess their iniquities; then I will remember My covenant." "He shall pray unto God, and He will be merciful unto him." "I confessed my sins unto the Lord, and Thou forgavest the wickedness of my sin." *Propter hoc orabit omnis sanctus,* "For this cause shall every one that is holy pray," &c.

By virtue of this prayer Solomon saith, that the people having committed any sin, if they come into the house of the Lord and pray for pardon, God Who is in heaven will hear them. But this is more plain in the New Testament: "Did I not forgive thee" *quia rogasti Me?* and to Simon Magus, "Pray to God, if He will forgive thee the thoughts of thy heart;" that is, if we confess and be sorry for our sins, and ask pardon, He will forgive us. "How long wilt Thou be angry with Thy people that prayeth to Thee?" But we must be of the number that is meant by *Nobis,* that is of the Apostles, that is, such as are "baptized into Christ's death." We must die unto sin, as He died for sin; *ut, sicut Is dimisit peccata,* so we must *dimittere peccata,* "He hath suffered in the flesh and hath ceased from sin," so must we. We must have a care that hereafter we fall not into sin, more than our infirmity compels us: for sins of infirmity God's "grace is sufficient." But "if we willingly sin" after remission, "there is no more sacrifice for sin." We are therefore "to crucify the flesh with the lusts and affections" thereof, if we will be "Christ's," and receive benefit by His satisfaction.

THE LORD'S PRAYER.

SERMON XV.

As we forgive them that trespass against us.

In this treatise it hath been noted, that there is a double *sicut* annexed to two several petitions: the one concerning God, and our duty we owe to Him, in the third petition; the other concerning our neighbour, and the charity that we ought to shew towards him, in this fifth petition; wherein we are to consider this, that as this law of prayer which our Saviour prescribeth to us doth establish the law of works and faith, so these two *sicut*s do comprehend the sum of the Law and the Prophets. The Law saith, "Thou shalt not hate thy Levit. 19. brother in thy heart;" and the same is confirmed by this [17.] petition, wherein we are taught that if we desire to have our sins forgiven of God, we must not only not hate our brother without cause, but if he offend we must likewise forgive him. Neither doth this petition concern our neighbour and brethren only but ourselves likewise, for hereby we have a pledge of remission of sins if we acknowledge that we have forgiven others; and as the taking away of our sins is the great fruit and benefit we desire of God, so the subordinate means that God hath appointed for the end is the forgiving others that offend us. Now God hath laid upon us this blessed necessity of forgiving one another, not only that He might establish peace in earth among men, but that by this means glory might redound to God on high.

In respect of ourselves, this is our estate before we become true Christians, To be "hateful, and to hate one another;" Tit. 3. 3. and that hath a sorrowful effect, for "if we bite and devour Gal. 5. 15.

one another, we shall be consumed of one another." To prevent this, God's will is that we should not hate but forgive one another, which unless we do we cannot live peaceably; so that this petition hath a respect to our benefit also as well as our neighbour's, and God Himself also hath His part in it; for when we have forgiven our brethren and purged our hearts of all hatred, we are more fit for His service; and contrariwise, as without forgiving others we cannot live peaceably one with another, so neither can we live devoutly towards God; and therefore our Saviour chargeth, "If thou bring thy gift to the altar and rememberest that thy brother hath ought against thee, leave there thy gift at the altar and go thy way first and be reconciled;" and the Apostle gives express charge that man and wife should live quietly, *ne interrumpantur preces,* "lest their prayers be interrupted."

Mat. 5.
23, 24.

1 Pet. 3. 7.

Thus it pleased the wisdom of God in this petition to add this *sicut,* not for our neighbour's sake only, nor for ourselves only, but also in regard of God.

The first *sicut* pertaineth to the imitation of the saints in heaven : this doth not imply an imitation (for God forbid that God should no otherwise forgive us than we forgive our brethren) but it is a mere condition, teaching us that if we forgive those that are indebted to us, we shall obtain forgiveness of God; for we do not always subscribe to God's commandment, "Forgive one another, as God for Christ's sake forgave you." But by saying this petition we bind ourselves to this condition, so as we would no otherwise be forgiven than as we forgive them.

Eph. 4. 32.
Col. 3. 13.

At the first we became bound to keep His Law, which He did deliver in ten commandments, and for not fulfilling of it we fall into the penalty of *Maledictus.*

Ex. 20.
1, &c.
Deu. 5.
6, &c.
Deu. 27.

Now, because we have not obeyed the Law, we are to undergo the penalty, and therefore it is said to be *chirographum contra nos.*

God having the obligation in His own hands, might require the forfeiture of us; but it pleaseth Him to enter bond to us by another obligation, wherein He binds Himself to forgive our sins upon this condition, that we forgive others; for if we forgive not then His bond is void, as appeareth by the parable wherein our Saviour sheweth that if we will have forgiveness of God we must forgive our brethren, and have compassion on our fellow-servants as God hath pity Mat. 18. 33. on us.

It is Christ That freeth us both from the obligation of the ten commandments and of the twelve curses, and therefore [Deu. 27. as he that receiveth a benefit doth as it were become bound ¹⁵⁻²⁶.] to be thankful, so we enter into a new bond of thankfulness unto God, the condition whereof is that we should forgive our brethren, even as we desire to be forgiven of God.

By the words of this petition, we see what our estate is, to wit, *Quilibet homo est debitor habens debitorem,* 'Every man is a debtor, having a debtor;' for so it appeareth by the Mat. 18. parable, wherein as one was brought that owed a great many ²⁴, ²⁸. "talents" to God, so he had another that "owed a hundred pence:" but there is a great difference. The debts that man oweth to God are great sins, but the debts that man oweth to man are of small value; we are debtors to God not only to keep the whole Law but also to undergo the curse of God, which is due even to the least breach of the same. Deu. 27.

Secondly, we are indebted not only for not using His ²⁶. talents to His glory, but for abusing them in the service of sin; even so we are debtors one to another, not only when Rom. 1. 14. we neglect the duties of charity and justice, but when we of purpose do wrong one to another.

Now we can be content that others should forgive us, and therefore if we will have forgiveness of God for the debts that we owe Him we must forgive our brethren, for "what Mat. 7. 12. you would that men should do to you, and in what measure, even so do to them."

Therefore our Saviour in penning this petition tells us, that if we make to our brethren a release of our debts, He will release us of His; and this condition is very reasonable; for Cain hath no reason to hope for favour of God, though he serve Him never so devoutly one day, when notwith-standing he hath a purpose "to kill his brother" the next, Gen. 4. 5, 8. neither is it reasonable that he should say to God *Dimitte mihi* that will not say to his brother *Dimitto tibi.*

The difference between God's forgiving and ours is, first in the persons that forgive. When we forgive, then one "fellow-servant" forgives another, as duty binds them; but when God forgives us, there *Dominus dimittit servum.*

Again, as I have a debtor of my fellow-servant, so I may be indebted to him, and therefore I ought rather to forgive him; but God cannot be indebted to us, but we are all deeply in His debt, and therefore it is a reasonable condition that He requires at our hands.

Secondly, in the things to be remitted the number of God's debts are thousands, ours are but hundreds; His, talents, ours are but pence. The condition therefore is reasonable on God's behalf, if we consider the excellency of His person and the vileness of ours; if we regard how greatly we are indebted to God more than our brethren can be to us, *ut pudeat aliâ lege petere remissionem,* 'that we may be ashamed under any other condition to ask forgiveness.'

Then we may not think much that He requireth this forgiveness at our hands, but magnify His mercy, that having forfeited our first bond it hath pleased Him to remit it, and only to tie us to this; we are to thank Him that He vouchsafeth *accipere stipulam pro margaritis,* 'to accept our stubble for His pearls,' for the forgiveness of our sins (which was bought at so dear a rate) to accept the forgiveness we shew to our brethren.

Some would give "thousands of rams, and ten thousand rivers of oil" for this great benefit: much more ought we condescend to God, when He offereth us so great a benefit upon so easy a condition. And thus we see that to be true in some part, which some of the heathen have observed *de utilitate capiendâ etiam ab inimicis;* it is not altogether for our hurt that they wrong and injure us, for unless there were some to offend us we should not have occasion to exercise this part of our mercy in forgiving; and therefore, where David compares his enemies to "bees" and not to wasps, the reason is, for that albeit bees have stings yet they yield honey also, and so no doubt David received great comfort inwardly by means of his enemies, though outwardly they persecuted him with all the malice they could; for he, that can master his own affections so far as quietly to put up a wrong offered by an enemy and to forgive the same, may be assured that his sins are forgiven of God.

Wherein we are to consider the goodness of God That vouchsafeth to set men in His own place, and to give men a power to forgive even as He Himself doth forgive; whereby it cometh to pass that one man is to another even in God's place, so that if we would know whether God do remit our sins or no, we need not to "climb up to heaven" to be certified of it, nor "to go down into the deep, for the word is near, even in our heart and in our mouth." Rom. 10. 6-8.

If thy heart tells thee that thou forgivest thy brother, doubt not but God doth likewise forgive thee; and it is His mercy that He vouchsafeth to frame His pardons after our pardons, to assure us that as we forgive one another in earth so God forgives us the sins that we have committed against Him; and He layeth this necessity upon us, not only to shew that He is careful to have peace among men, but also that He would have us to be perfect as Himself; for God is said to be *proclivis ad misericordiam, tardus ad iram et vin-* Ps. 145. 8. *dictam,* "prone to mercy, slow to wrath and revenge."

So Christ, requiring of us that we should forgive our brethren that offend us, willeth us to be slow to anger, and long-suffering, as God is, for it is not as man judgeth an honourable thing to be revenged. Wicked Lamech thought it an honour to take revenge "seventy times seven times" Gen. 4. 24. of any that offended him, but contrariwise Christ tells St. Peter that it should be a greater honour for him to forgive until "seventy times seven times." Therefore it becomes a Mat. 18. 22. Christian rather to follow Christ than wicked Lamech; for as Christ says, It were better to lose the right eye, and the right hand, than to have "the whole body cast into hell- Mat. 5. 29. fire," so it were better for us to suffer wrong for righteousness than for worldly honour seek to deprive ourselves of the remission of our sins, which cannot be obtained of God except we be content to put up injuries offered to us.

If we will have true honour, let us imitate our heavenly Father; He is so far from taking revenge of them that offend Him, that He lets "His sun shine upon them." So Mat. 5. 45. let us account it the greatest honour for us to aspire more and more to resemble our Father herein, for the nobler sort of creatures are not desirous of revenge but only those that are vilest and of lowest power; and of all creatures unreason-

SERM. able none so angry as flies and wasps and bees, and of them
XV.   that have reason women are more testy and fretting than
men; and of men, none more subject to anger than such
as are sick; in their greatest weakness then are they most
angry, which is no sign of an honourable quality.

Let us therefore count it a shame to be like the weakest
things in this behalf, and rather let us imitate the nobler
creatures which are more slow to anger.

If we will be honourable, let us learn to get it by the example of such as have true honour. Joseph in the court of
Pharaoh no doubt was an honourable man, and yet he placed
not honour in taking revenge of his brethren that had re-
Gen. 50. warded him evil, but in forgiving them and doing them good
21.   for evil. David was an honourable man, and yet he placed
2 Sam. 19. honour in pardoning Shimei, and to do good to Mephibo-
23.
[2 Sam. 9. sheth the son of Saul, that was his deadly enemy. Solomon
7.]   knew, no doubt, what was true honour, and yet he gives us
Prov. 24. counsel not to seek honour by revenge: " Say not, I will do
29.   to him as he hath done to me." And the honourable king
that was angry with the unmerciful servant, thought it more
Mat. 18. 27. honour to draw near the honour of God in pardoning than
in revenging.

The benefit that ensueth upon this condition is of two
sorts; first, outward, for by virtue of it we have a covenant
on God's part, wherein He binds Himself to us that He will
forgive us if we forgive our brethren; so that we may be
bold to challenge Him for His promise, so that we keep the
condition.

Secondly, inward, for when we love the brethren, "not
in word and tongue only but in deed and truth," that is
1 Joh. 3. 18, a means for us "to persuade our hearts before Him." If
19.   we forgive our brethren from our hearts, we may be assured
that God will forgive us. So our Saviour affirmeth of the
Lu. 7. 47. woman, because "she loved much, she had many sins forgiven her."

Some when they came to this petition left out this *sicut*,
and so passed on to the next petition; but we must use this
prayer orderly, Christ is not mocked, He penned the prayer
for us Himself, and therefore He can quickly espy if we leave
out any of His words, and to teach us that we should pray

in true charity He hath not only enjoined us to forgive our
brethren as we would be forgiven, but willeth us before we
begin to pray to bethink ourselves whether we forgive: *Cum
stabitis ad orandum,* "When ye stand to pray, forgive." Mark 11.
Secondly, as we must use this *sicut,* so not with our lips ^{25.}
only but with our heart, for otherwise we do *imprecari nobis,*
'we pray for vengeance against ourselves,' and Christ may
say to us, *Ex ore tuo te judicabo, serve nequam.* We cannot Lu. 19. 22.
curse ourselves more bitterly than if we say to God, "Forgive us as we forgive our debtors," unless we do indeed
forgive them.

As we run in debt with God daily, and so need daily forgiveness, the same measure of charity we are to shew to
others that offend us by forgiving them their trespasses.

We must not think it enough to forgive them till "seven [Mat. 18.
times," but "until seventy times seven times;" and as we ^{21, 22.]}
would not have a counterfeit forgiveness of God so we must
be careful to forgive our brethren from our heart, otherwise
He will call back His word and promise made to us touching Mat. 18. 34.
the remission of our sins.

Whereas some count it a sufficient forgiveness to forgive
only though they do not forget, they must know that it is
only *semiplena remissio,* 'a forgiveness by halves;' for we
desire God by the Prophet, that He will not only forgive
but forget our sins, and "remember not our old sins:" Ps. 79. 8.
therefore we must perform the same measure of charity in
this behalf to our brethren. And whereas "the messenger 2 Cor. 12. 7.
of Satan" doth so "buffet" us, and our own corruption so
prevails with us, that we cannot utterly forget an injury, yet
so long as we shew not a revenge in deed nor in word nor
in look but strive to master our corrupt affection, we shall
be accounted "according to that we have and not according 2 Cor. 8. 12.
to that we have not."

As for that which some object, that so the law of justice Rom. 3. 31.
is overthrown by this kind of mercy, it is not so, for "mercy Jas. 2. 13.
triumpheth over justice."

Now as prayer is a means to apply Christ's benefits and
mercy to our souls, as Christ sheweth, "I forgave thee, Mat. 18.
because thou prayedst Me," so that is not enough unless ^{32, 34.}
we use charity and mercy; to *Dimitte Tu,* we must add,

G g

S E R M. *Nos dimittimus,* the want whereof caused the king to deal so
XV.
—— severely with the unmerciful servant.

Now mercy, which is the second means of application,
stands in giving and forgiving : *Quicquid præstatur indigenti
eleemosynæ est.* Therefore, because these have need of forgiveness which offend, we should do a work of mercy in
forgiving them when they do us wrong; and both those
kind of alms and mercy are alike accepted of God, and
therefore in the Law He ordained as well peace-offerings
as meat-offerings.

That mercy is a means to us to apply this benefit unto
ourselves which Christ offereth, appeareth by these places :
[Prov. 16. Proverbs the sixteenth chapter and sixth verse, " With mercy
6.]
[Isa. 58. 7.] and faithfulness sins are forgiven;" [a] Isaiah the fifty-eighth
[Dan. 4. chapter and seventh verse; [b] Daniel the fourth chapter and
27.]
[Lu. 11. twenty-seventh verse; and Luke the eleventh chapter and
41.] the forty-first verse, *Date eleemosynam, et omnia sunt munda.*

This is that which maketh both prayer and fasting acceptable before God, and without which all prayer is rejected as
hypocritical. Thus must we have oil from Him, and the
Mat. 6. 16. vessel to receive it in us, *Dimitte, et dimittitis,* that is, both
prayer and mercy.

As we pray to God for pardon of our sins, so we must
forgive others. Now Christ maketh choice of that kind of
mercy which standeth in forgiving, because it is common to
poor and rich, for all cannot give; but the poor may *forg*ive
as well as the rich, and therefore it is the duty of us all to
forgive one another if we will be forgiven of God.

Secondly, He maketh choice of this mercy as the greatest
and excellentest, for nature will move us to give to him that
is in need, and we cannot in such case hide ourselves from
our own flesh; but when we do not only forgive him that
hath done us wrong, but also offer kindness to him that did
provoke us to anger, that is a supernatural work.

[a] [Isa. 58. 6. "Is not this the fast
that I have chosen? to loose the bands
of wickedness, to undo the heavy burdens, and to let the oppressed go free,
and that ye break every yoke?
7. " Is it not to deal thy bread to the
hungry, and that thou bring the poor
that are cast out to thy house? when
thou seest the naked, that thou cover

him; and that thou hide not thyself
from thine own flesh?"]
[b] [Dan. 4. 27. " Wherefore, O king,
let my counsel be acceptable unto thee,
and break off thy sins by righteousness,
and thine iniquities by shewing mercy
to the poor; if it may be a lengthening
of thy tranquillity."]

Thirdly, it is the fittest mercy, for we desire to be remitted, and therefore the fittest means to obtain remission is that mercy which standeth in remission and forgiving of others.

The mercy that we shew in this behalf is active mercy; that which God promiseth us, if we forgive our brethren, is a passive mercy.

Of the active mercy our Saviour saith, "Blessed are the merciful, for they shall obtain mercy." But contrariwise, "there shall be judgment merciless to him that sheweth no mercy." Wherefore we must so deal with those which offend us that we may say to God, *Ecce misericordiam activam, præsta mihi passivam,* 'Behold my active mercy, perform to me Thy passive mercy.' Mat. 5. 7.

Jas. 2. 13.

And to shew you the necessity of this duty on our parts, Christ having penned this petition upon this condition is not contented therewith, but having ended the prayer He returns to the same matter, and sheweth why we should forgive our debtors: "For if ye," saith He, "forgive men their trespasses, your heavenly Father will forgive you yours, but if you will not, neither will God forgive you;" and hereof He hath given an example in the parable of the king who, to shew to us what we are to look for at God's hands, is said to have been loving and merciful at the first to him that was indebted so far unto him; but when the same party having the debt which he owed pardoned would notwithstanding have present payment of his fellow-servant, then the king's affection was turned and he became severe and rough and committed him till he had paid all that was due. [Mat. 6. 14, 15.]

Mat. 18. 27, 34.

THE LORD'S PRAYER.

SERMON XVI.

And lead us not into temptation.

SERM.
XVI.

Rom. 3. 25. THIS is the petition that concerns sin to come; for "remission," which was the thing we prayed for last, is referred to "sins past," and we are no less to desire of God that He will give us ability to resist sin to come, than to be gracious to us in pardoning our sins already committed. Thus much we are given to understand by this, that this petition is chained to the former with the copulative "and," as if that were not perfected without this. No more indeed is it, for as God lets go His hold so must we let go ours; and if we will have God to remit our former sins, we must beware that we do not willingly sin against His Majesty afresh, but that we strive against temptations to come; for as the Ps. 66. 18. Psalmist speaks, "If I incline to wickedness in my heart, the Lord will not hear me;" if I purpose still to continue in sin, I shall in vain pray, Forgive me my sins. But contrariProv. 28.
13.wise, he that doth not only "confess but also forsake his sins, he shall have mercy."

If, accounting it sufficient that we have spent the time of our life past in sin we shall resolve henceforth to live so 1 Pet. 4. 2, 3. much time as remaineth for us in the flesh after "the will of God," then may we assure ourselves that God will be merciful unto us, and will remember our sins and iniquities no more. And that which we are to perform in this behalf is the second part of remission, which is opposed both to retention and intention; that is, as we would have God not to retain our sins but freely to pardon them, so our care must

be that sin be more remiss in us; for whereas in the last
petition we considered a double debt, one of duty, another of
forfeiture, our desire was, not to have both forgiven, but we
desired to be forgiven *quia non prestitimus, non ne præstemus,*
'because we perform it not, not that we might not at all
perform it.'

Howsoever our prayer to God is, that He would not lay
upon us the penalty which we have run into by not keeping
His Law, yet we are still bound to do our duty.

Now, whereas the Prophet saith, *Hic est omnis fructus ut* Isa. 27. 9.
auferatur peccatum, we may not think that sin is taken away
when God for His part doth remit the guilt of our sins past;
for sin consists not only of an offence or guilt, but of an issue
or inclination to sin, so that our care must be as well that we
pray that this running issue may be stopped, as that punishment due to us for sins past be remitted; and to this end
both parts of repentance are required of us, that is, sorrow
for sins past, and a provident care to avoid sin to come; we
must by prayer seek for grace of God, *non modo quo deleatur
debitum, sed ne contrahatur debitum,* 'not only that our debt
may be done away, but that it may not be contracted.' As
the widow by the blessing of God had sufficient oil not only
to pay her creditors withal but also to live upon afterward, 2 Kings 4. 7.
so we must seek of Christ the oil of His grace, both for the
discharging of our sins and for a holy life.

As we would be glad to hear this voice from Christ, *Re-* Lu. 7. 48.
missa sunt tibi peccata, so we must be content with this, *Vade
et noli amplius peccare,* "Go thy way and sin no more."   Joh. 8. 11.

As God on His part doth covenant with us that He "will Jer. 31. 34.
remember our sins and iniquities no more," so that which
He requireth of us is, *Hæc est via, ambulate in eâ.* For it is Isa. 30. 21.
not enough for us to "confess our sins and be sorry" nor Ps. 38. 18.
yet to perform our active mercy by giving and forgiving, except we have a resolute purpose to forsake the sins we have
heretofore committed; for if being washed from our old sins
we shall wallow in the mire like swine and return to our
vomit, then shall "our latter end be worse than our begin- 2 Pet. 2.
ning." This is one reason why this copulative conjunction 20, 22.
is set before this petition.

Another is in regard of the fickleness of our estate: we

SERM.
XVI.

may not think ourselves secure, when we have forgiveness of our sins. The Apostles of our Saviour Christ having received the sacrament, which as Christ told them was a seal of the remission of sins purchased by the shedding of His blood, fell into a sleepiness, so as they were not able in time of greatest peril to watch with their Master one hour; therefore

Mat. 26. 41. He was fain to warn them, " Pray, that ye enter not into temptation." The reason is, because the devil is most malicious against them that are recovered out of his thraldom;

Mat. 12. for " when the unclean spirit is gone out of a man," he is

43 44. never quiet till he " return" again, and that he may he will use all the means he can. So that they of all others are in most danger and most subject to the malice and rage of the devil, that are restored out of the state of sin into the state of grace; and therefore we pray that as God in His mercy doth vouchsafe to pardon our sins past, so it will please Him to strengthen us with His grace that we may withstand the temptations of Satan.

The petition hath two things to be considered, the "temptation," and the " leading." Temptation (that "we may

Mat. 20. 22. know what we ask") is a trial or proof, and is of two sorts, δοκιμασία and πειρασμὸς, the one good, the other evil; the one is made by God, the other by Satan.

God is said to tempt us when He maketh " trial of our

1 Pet. 1. 7. faith," which trial is " more precious than gold," as in Abra-

Jas. 1. 3. ham, or when He trieth our " patience," as in Job; for

1 Cor. 4. 9. while we live in this world, we are *spectaculum Angelis et hominibus.*

God therefore in His wisdom thinks it good to try our faith and patience, by laying affliction upon us; that albeit He know us sufficiently, yet that both men and Angels may have a proof of our faith, He trieth us; for as the dross is consumed with fire and the pure gold remaineth behind, so the pureness of our faith is tried with the fire of affliction. This is that " fan" which Christ is said to have " in His

Mat. 3. 12. hand," whereby " He purgeth His floor," and separateth the good corn from the chaff.

The other proof or trial is that which Satan makes; for as

Gen. 22. 1. " God tempted Abraham" for his good, so Satan tempted

Gen. 3. 1, Adam, but not for his good, but only to draw him away
&c.

from his God. As Christ hath His fan, so Satan hath his;
" Satan hath desired to sift and winnow you." The differ- Lu. 22. 31.
ence is, that whereas God by affliction thinketh good to prove
how steadfastly we believe in Him and how willingly we will
undergo the cross for His sake, the devil's purpose is that by
all means he may quench our faith and dash our patience.

The devil's trial therefore is, *tentatio ad detrimentum non ad
experimentum.* God's temptation maketh us happy, " Blessed Jas. 1. 12.
is he that endureth temptation ;" but the devil's temptation
brings us to misery, and this latter is that against which we
pray, and it is of two sorts : first, that which the Apostle
calls *tentatio humana,* " such as is incident to the nature of [1 Cor. 10.
man ; secondly, *tentatio Satanica.*   13.]

Human temptations are such as are necessary and cannot
be avoided by reason of the corruption of nature; of which
the Prophet speaketh when he prayeth, *Libera me de necessi-* Ps. 25. 17.
tatibus meis. The Apostle doth more plainly express it when
he calls it " the infirmity of the flesh," and the " sin that Rom. 6. 19.
dwells in us," which causeth this necessity, that while we re- Rom. 7. 20.
main in the body the " flesh will ever lust against the spirit." Gal. 5. 17.
But there is another kind of temptation which is devilish,
when we do not sin of infirmity or through the necessary
weakness of the flesh but of malicious purpose, that whereof
the Prophet speaketh, " Be not merciful to them that tres- Ps. 59. 5.
pass of malicious wickedness," and, " Keep Thy servant from Ps. 19. 13.
presumptuous sins." These sins proceed not from that necessity of sinning which doth accompany our nature, but
from that corruption of nature which the Apostle doth call
the " superfluity of wickedness." These proceed not from Jas. 1. 21.
sin that dwells in us, but from that sin which reigneth in us. Rom. 6. 12.
And as we desire that God will pardon our necessary temptations, so especially we are to pray that we may not fall
into these superfluous sins, as the Prophet doth pray, " Keep Ps. 19.
Thy servant from presumptuous sins, that they get not the
dominion over me." And, " Order my steps in Thy word," Ps. 119.
ne dominetur mihi omnis iniquitas.   133.

For the better understanding of this point we are to consider what are the temptations, and *tentamenta,* that is, the
things whereby we are tempted.

The temptations are either without us or within us.

Without, first the devil, that is, "the tempter;" secondly, the "corruption that is in the world through lust." The tempter within us is our "own concupiscence," without which the outward tempters should not only not hurt us but also greatly profit us; for the devil shall in vain tempt us, and the evil examples of the world shall not allure us, unless we in the lusts of our hearts do suffer ourselves to be overcome; and therefore one saith well, *Teipsum vince, et victus est mundus et Satanas;* if there be neither covetousness in us, nor the lust of the flesh, the devil shall not be able to prevail against us, but we shall stand unconquered both of worldly lusts and of the lusts of the flesh.

The things whereby the devil tempteth us are Massah and
Meribah, whereby is understood prosperity and adversity. One while as a serpent he allureth us by pleasures, and if he prevail not that way then like a roaring lion he terrifieth with violent danger; and that he may have his will of us by
one of these means he "bewitcheth" our understanding, so that we either make great account of those things which indeed are of least value, or else judge the danger which he threateneth to be more terrible than it is.

From this petition we are to acknowledge that, where we pray that God will deliver us from temptation, first in regard of ourselves we are unable to encounter with these temptations and to withstand the least temptation, and yet the grace of God is sufficient for us, so that albeit in the light of our own understanding we cannot discern what is true pleasure or what is indeed to be feared, yet as the Prophet
speaks, *In lumine Tuo videbimus lumen,* "In Thy light we shall see light," and though the messenger of Satan buffet us never so much yet God's grace shall make us to have the victory, without which we are not able to resist the first temptations.

Which considerations serve to keep us from pride, and to work in us humility.

Secondly, in regard of our tempters, we are to acknow-
ledge that the devil, much less any thing else, cannot be able to tempt us without God's permission: so he was not able to touch Job until he had leave of God, nor the herd of swine till Christ had permitted him to enter.

Thus we see that Satan is chained by God so that he cannot go further than God will give him leave, which maketh for our comfort.

Temptation is necessary, and therefore we pray not *ne tentet nos Satanas,* but *ne Deus nos inducat ;* for it is God's will to use Satan's service in this work, and that if we feel that our corruption doth yield to sin, we are to say with the Prophet, " Let God arise," and, " Save me, O God." Also Ps. 68. 1. with Hezekiah, *Domine vim patior, responde pro me,* " O ^{Ps. 69. 1.} Isa. 38. 14. Lord, I suffer oppression, comfort Thou me."

Touching the leading into temptation, we desire not to be led, which hath two expositions; first, that God Who knows our weakness will not give leave to the devil to tempt us at all by any of those means, because the issue of temptation is doubtful, for many excellent men even the saints of God have been overcome thereby.

Secondly, at the least *ne inducat,* " that He lead us not" into them, which have three differences : first, in respect of God, that albeit the devil's desire be " to sift" us, yet *ne* Lu. 22. 31. *inducas Tu ;* though the " lying spirit" be ready to entice us 1 Kings 22 that we might fall, yet that God would not command him to ^{22.} go forth, yet that He would not deliver us over into Satan's hand, and leave us to ourselves.

Secondly, in regard of us, that we commit not sin that leads thereunto, for *qui ducitur volens ducitur ;* but that if we needs must yield to temptations, it may rather lay hold on us by violence against our wills than lead us. So the Apostle speaks, *Tentatio vos non apprehendit,* " Temptation hath not 1 Cor. 10. taken hold of you :" and when our Saviour saith to His dis- ^{13.} ciples, *Orate ne intretis in tentationem,* " Pray that ye enter [Lu. 22. not into temptation," His meaning is, that willingly and wit- ^{40.]} tingly, and of delight, of yourselves, otherwise than as the infirmity of your flesh doth compel you; for if any willingly enter into temptation, these God suffers to be led into it so as they cannot get out any more; that is, the Gentiles, till they be effectually called are said to " commit all unclean- Eph. 4. 19. ness with greediness." So we do not devour the temptations that are incident to our nature, and that as the Syriac word used by our Saviour is, we take not pain to satisfy the temptations of Satan, as it were to climb up into a high tree.

SERM.
XVI.

Thirdly, in respect of the nature of the Greek word, which is rather *Ne inferas,* than *Ne inducas.*

Mat. 4. 1.

Of Christ's leading into temptation it is said, Ἀνήχθη, that is, so led as that He was brought back again ; but our leading by the devil is, so to be carried into temptations as that withal we are left there to ourselves.

Christ's temptation had an issue, *nostra non habet exitum,* 'ours hath no issue;' but our prayer is not only that it be against our will, if at any time we be tempted, but that in the temptation He would so hold us by the hand that we may get out of it, that albeit we be led into it that we may be brought back again.

From whence this question ariseth, Whether God lead any into temptation so as they never get out of it again ? The answer is that there are some such, but they are those that first suffer themselves to be led, even as He hardeneth no man's heart but his that first hardeneth his own heart.

Ex. 7. 12.

Of Pharaoh it is said, that albeit " Aaron's rod ate up the enchanters' rods," that yet " he hardened his heart." After,

Ex. 8. 19.

when the sorcerers told him, *Digitus Dei hic est,* " This is the finger of God," yet he hardened his own heart, and then

Ex. 11. 10.

God seeing his obstinacy, *induravit cor ejus,* " hardened his heart."

1 Kings 21. 20.
1 Kings 22. 22.
Hos. 8. 11.

So when Ahab had first " sold himself to work wickedness," then it pleased God to deliver him to the " lying spirit" to deceive him that he might fall. " Because Ephraim would have many altars" to serve, God gave them many altars.

That we be not led into temptation, the means that we are

Ezek. 14. 3.

to use is, that we put from before our face the " stumbling-blocks of iniquity," that we restrain our eyes and mouths from beholding or speaking that which is evil, that we restrain

Prov. 5. 8.

our feet as the Wise Man saith, " Keep thy way far from her,

Prov. 6. 27.

and come not into the door of her house." " For can a man take fire in his bosom, and his clothes not be burnt ?"

Therefore, if we will not be led into temptation, we must not lead ourselves, nor tempt ourselves, nor grope for sin, for the devil's temptation cannot hurt us, it shall be a means to grace us, if we withstand it ; but if we will be drawn away of our own lusts, then we cannot but be led.

As we must forbear the occasion of sin, so must we use the means that may keep us from it, that is, prayer.

We must make " a covenant with our eyes," so we shall Job 31. 1. not be tempted.

As we prayed that God's will touching " sanctification" 1 Thes. 4. 3. and suffering may be done of us, so we are to pray not generally to be delivered from the temptations of sin, but particularly from the temptation of any several sin whereunto we are inclined : if to "worldly lusts," that He would keep Tit. 2. 12. us from them; if to " the lusts of the flesh," that He will not 1 Pet. 2. 11. suffer us to be tempted of them neither; that as our temptation increaseth, so His strength may increase, and if not increase then that He will cause His temptation to decrease.

THE LORD'S PRAYER.

SERMON XVII.

MATTHEW vi. 13.

But deliver us from evil.

THIS last petition concerneth the last of those three evils
which we desire to have removed from us; under which we
comprehend all miseries and calamities of this life, for that is
it which our Saviour understandeth by "the evil of the day"
in the last verse of this chapter.

So there is a plain opposition betwixt this petition and
the fourth.

As there by "daily bread" we understood all things necessary for this present life, so when we say, "Deliver us
from evil," we seek to be delivered from all such things as
are laborious and troublesome to us in the same.

There are that make but six petitions of this prayer,
saying that the two last are but one, but they have no
warrant for it.

The ancient Church hath always divided it into seven, and
this division they grounded upon the motive which caused
our Saviour Christ to pen this prayer, which was the avoiding of that ταυτολογία used by the heathen, into which they
cannot choose but fall which affirm that these two last petitions contain but one thing; wherein they are deceived, for
temptation and evil are not of one scantling.

Every evil is not temptation, neither is every temptation
evil.

Some things are evil in their own kind, as wolves and
kites; other things are not only evil in themselves, but

bring forth evil effects, for our sins are not only evil but the calamities and miseries which our sins bring upon us are also evil; and therefore we are to pray no less against the one than against the other.

Touching the misery of this life, we are to pray as the Prophet wills us, for the deliverance from them, "Call upon Me in the day of thy trouble." Ps. 50. 25.

That this and the former cannot be one petition, is manifest: for when we pray that we be not led into temptation, we desire that we may do no evil; when we pray that we may be delivered from evil, our desire is that we may suffer no evil.

In the first we pray against *malum culpæ*, 'the evil of sin,' in the second against *malum pœnæ*, 'the evil of punishment.'

The first is an evil of our own doing, the other of God's doing, as the Prophet speaks, *Non est malum in civitate quod* Amos 3. 6. *non fecit Dominus*, "There is no evil in a city but the Lord hath done it."

As before sin committed we desired *non induci*, 'not to be led into it,' so here when we have committed sin our desire is that God would not deliver us to our ghostly enemy that he may afflict us in this life with temporal plagues, nor in the life to come keep us in eternal torments.

When we desire that God will deliver us from the miseries of this life and of the life to come, we have these things to consider: first, that the case of Christian men is not like the state of the heathens, for they had Joves, white gods, from whom they received good things, and black gods, whom they called *depulsores malorum*, 'deliverers from evil;' but Christians have but one God to fly to, Whom they acknowledge to be both Δωτῆρα and Σωτῆρα, a God That doth not only give us good things but takes from us those that are evil. So God testifieth of Himself to Abraham, that He is not Gen. 15. 1. only his "exceeding great reward," but also his "shield," both which we are to consider in this, that in Scripture He is compared to a rock.

Secondly, that the devil hath a desire to carry us away into sin and transgression, to the end he may endanger our souls; and if he cannot hurt us that way, then he will

labour to do us some outward mischief; if he cannot prevail as a tempter, he will endeavour that he may hurt us
as a tormentor.

So he dealt with Job, who for that he was a just and
perfect man, so as Satan could not tempt him to sin against
God, therefore his desire was that he might touch his body
and torment him with outward losses, for his delight is evermore in doing of mischief; if he can no longer vex the soul
Lu. 8. 32. of man, yet he will crave this leave that he may torment the
poor hogs.

Thirdly, that we have two kind of helps against this evil:
first, that precaution which our Saviour telleth us of in the
former petition, that before we commit sin we pray *non induci*, 'not to be led into it,' that neither temptation come at
us nor we at it. Secondly, that albeit we by sin are fallen
into evil, yet there is a θεραπεία or 'salving' to be looked for
of God, Who will deliver us after that we are delivered into
the hands of our adversary. As in the first petition we pray
that we may not fall into evil by yielding to temptation,
so here if we be fallen yet God would deliver us out of it.
Both these helps are ascribed to God.

Of the first it is said to him, he that maketh his prayer
Ps. 89. 22. for His help, "The enemy shall not be able to do him
hurt, and the son of wickedness shall not come nigh him."
Ps. 69. 15. Of the other, "Let not the waterflood drown me, nor the
deep swallow me up, and let not the pit shut her mouth
upon me."

[S. Chrys.
in loc.] Touching the evil from which we desire to be delivered,
Chrysostom and the rest of the Greek Church expound it of
the devil, who is *lerna malorum*, or the greatest evil that can
befall us, which exposition is grounded upon the article ἀπὸ
τοῦ. But this exposition is too narrow, for the holy word is
best expounded when it is most enlarged; so that we shall
have a full understanding of this matter if under the word
"evil" we include whatsoever is evil, and so desire generally
to be delivered from it; but if we desire to be delivered from
[Serm.
182. 4, 5.] whatsoever is evil, then from ourselves, saith Augustine; for
we are evil, and so we have need to pray. For as, when we
ask forgiveness of sins, it is from those sins unto which our
lust hath already drawn us away into sin, so when we say,

Libera nos a malo, "Deliver us from evil," it is from that
infirmity of the flesh and necessity of sinning which doth
accompany our nature, in regard whereof the Apostle saith,
Quis me liberabit de hoc corpore mortis? "Who shall deliver Rom. 7. 24.
me from this body of death?"

So Augustine under the word "evil" doth include not
only τὸν πονηρὸν but πονηρίαν.

But Cyprian's exposition is, when we pray, *Libera nos a* [De Orat.
malo, "deliver us from evil," we desire not to be delivered Dom.]
from this or that evil, but generally from all evil, by which
he meaneth not πονηρὸν nor πονηρίαν but πόνον, that is, all
manner of trouble and calamity, and whatsoever turns away
good from us, especially that evil which keeps us from God
Which is the chiefest good thing. So then our desire is
not only to be delivered from the devil who is the beginning
of all evil, as that which is opposed to our chief good, but
from that which may turn away from us the meanest blessing which we stand in need of outwardly, which also are
bona data, "good gifts." Lu. 11. 13.

If we understand by evil, Satan, then we pray to be delivered from him not only when he playeth the subtle serpent, and changeth himself into "an Angel of light," but 2 Cor. 11.
when he playeth the "lion." First, to be delivered from 14.
his jaws, that he swalloweth us not down—for then there 1 Pet. 5. 8.
is no help for us—that is, that God would save us from "the Ps. 86. 13.
nethermost hell," that which is called "the second death," Rev. 20. 6.
and αἰωνία κόλασις.

Secondly, from his claws, under which are comprehended
all temporal calamities; first, the loss of life, against which
the Apostles being in a great tempest pray unto Christ that
He would save them, "Master, carest thou not that we Mark 4. 38.
perish?"

Secondly, of good name, whereof the Prophet saith, *Libera* Ps. 120. 2.
me a contrariis hominibus.

Thirdly, the loss of goods, concerning which, when the
Lord had formed grasshoppers to destroy their fruit, the
Prophet prayed, "O Lord God, spare, I beseech Thee." And Amos 7. 2.
this is the remedy in all outward afflictions, as Solomon
saith: If there be dearth in the land, through blasting, 1 Kings 8.
caterpillar, or grasshopper, then if the people come into the 37-39.

SERM.
XVII.

[Rev. 6.
6, 10.]

Ps. 119.
134.

Prov. 30.
8, 9.

2 Kings 6.
27.

temple and say, *Libera nos a malo*, "Deliver us from evil," God will hear their prayers and deliver them. Therefore in that dearth which is spoken of, Revelations the sixth, where corn was given by measure and weight, the remedy they had was prayer; "How long, Lord, dost thou defer to avenge our blood?" The reason why we pray to be delivered from these miseries is, that we may the better intend God's service: so said David, "Deliver me from the slanders of men, that I may keep Thy commandments."

Christ doth not expressly name tribulation, affliction, and calamity, though they be comprehended under the word "evil," wherein we are to observe that in this petition as in the rest He tempers His style with great wisdom; for outward trouble may co-operate to our good, and therefore He teacheth us not to pray that God will deliver us from them absolutely, but from that evil which is in them; and in this sense we may pray to be delivered *a malo panis*, 'from the evil of plenty,' as well as *a malo famis*, 'from the evil of scarcity;' for bread, which of itself is good, may turn to our hurt; and therefore Solomon prayeth, "Give me not riches, lest I be full, and say, Who is the Lord? neither give me poverty, lest through want I be driven to steal, and take the name of my God in vain."

There is both evil and good in both, and therefore we pray to be delivered from the evil; for if God see that it is good for us to be humbled with want, then we are not to pray against it.

Where we desire to be delivered, first, we acknowledge how little we are able ourselves. A hair or a crumb of bread oftentimes is enough to cast away a man; for the meanest creatures are able to hurt us except God deliver us, and as we cannot help ourselves so if we look about us there is none to succour us. So will the King himself tell us, who of all others seemeth most able to help; "If the Lord do not succour thee, wherewith can I help thee?"

Wherefore we may not trust to ourselves, nor to any other foreign help or power, but to God the great Deliverer, to Whom Christ hath taught us to pray, *Libera nos a malo*, "Deliver us from evil."

Secondly, herein we acknowledge our desire, which is to

be delivered. The word is ῥῦσαι, which implieth such a deliverance which doth rid us from bondage or captivity; wherefore we use this word as a motive that God will the rather deliver us, because if the evil which lieth upon us continue long it will make us the devil's bond-men. Now we are God's servants, and desire that the devil may not take us "captives at his will," but that we may come out of "his snare" to do God service; and not only so, but that our service may be done freely and with cheerfulness, for that we are His children and He our Father, that is, as the Prophet speaks, "When God hath set our hearts at liberty, we may run the way of His commandments." 2 Tim. 2. 26.

Ps. 119. 32.

But if we will be delivered from the devil indeed, we must have this freedom of Christ the Son of God, of Whom it is said, *Si Filius vos liberaverit, vere liberi eritis,* "If the Son shall make ye free, ye shall be free indeed," for He only is able perfectly to save us out of the thraldom of Satan. Joh. 8. 36.

The devil indeed is subtle and playeth the serpent, but Christ is the Wisdom of God, and knoweth well enough to keep us from temptation.

The devil is cruel, and roareth like a lion; but Christ, Who is "the power of God," is able to free us from evils, to save us from him. 1 Cor. 1. 24. 2 Pet. 2. 9

The means and ways whereby the Son of God, Who is His wisdom and power, doth free us from evil, are first, *non inducendo,* that is, not to suffer us to be tempted at all, for so we should be freed both from the evil of sin and from the evil of punishment which is the effect of sin; but forasmuch as there is none upon whom the devil hath not at least laid his nails, and as it were scratched with his claws by outward afflictions, we are not to look for that means of deliverance; the Apostles themselves had not this privilege, for St. Paul that was "a chosen vessel" had the "messenger of Satan to buffet him," even the corruption of his flesh which did still tempt him to sin. And for outward affliction, it is the case of all Christians generally, "All that will live godly in Christ Jesus, shall suffer persecution." [Acts 9. 15.] 2 Cor. 12. 7.

2 Tim. 3. 12.

So that the godly may not look for their paradise on earth, Christ hath foretold, "In the world you shall have trouble; as for their joys and comfort, it is elsewhere to be Joh. 16. 33.

SERM.
XVII.

Mat. 5. 12.
Ps. 73. 5.

[Ps. 17.
14.]

Rev. 3. 8.

Ps. 30. 5.

Joh. 16. 16.

2 Cor. 4. 17.

Gen. 41. 51.

Ps. 94. 19.

2 Cor. 1.
3, 4.

had, *Merces vestra magna est cœlis,* "Your reward is great in heaven." But if they be without tribulation in this life, if they be in the state of those that come "into no misfortune like others," it is an evil sign, and they little differ from the world "which have their portion in this life," whereas the troubles and miseries of this world are to the godly a pledge of the joys that are to come. And yet sometimes He giveth them a taste of His future mercy, by blessing them on earth, "I have set before thee an open door, because thou hast a little strength."

But we pray here for a deliverance after we are fallen into evil, and this deliverance is performed four ways: first, when God doth quickly take the evil from us, and not suffer it to continue to our utter overthrow. Such a deliverance is that when He suffereth His wrath to endure but a little season, when, "though He send heaviness over night, yet He causeth joy to come in the morning."

It was a great cause of grief to the Apostles, that Christ speaking of His departure from them said, "A little while, and ye shall not see Me;" but He delivered them out of this grief by comforting them with the hope of His speedy return, when He said, "And yet a while, and ye shall see Me again;" and, as St. Paul saith, this is a great means to deliver us out of our afflictions, when we know that it is but τὸ παραυτίκα ἐλαφρὸν τῆς θλίψεως, "a tribulation that as it is but light in itself so it is but momentary."

Secondly, God doth deliver us from evil when He doth mix some comfort with our affliction, that may make us to bear it the better. Such comfort it pleased God to mix with Joseph's trouble, who was first sold to be a slave by his own brethren, after cast into prison by means of his wicked mistress; but in the midst of his affliction God did not only bring him out of prison, but brought him into favour with Pharaoh, which made him forget all his labour and travail. Wherefore he called his first son Manasseh, of forgetting.

Thus God tempered the afflictions of David, as himself confesseth: "In the multitude of the sorrows of my heart Thy comforts have refreshed my soul." And the Apostle saith, "Blessed be God, for He giveth us comfort in all our tribulation, so as we are able to comfort others with the same comfort that He ministered to us."

Thirdly, when He gives us patience to endure our affliction, which is a greater benefit than the former; for if we suffer wrong and take it patiently, then there is thanks with God, and we follow the example of Christ Who suffered for us "though He had done no sin;" and as it is a thing 1 Pet. 2. 20. "thank-worthy with God," so the Prophet saith, "Blessed Ps. 94. 12, is the man whom Thou chastisest, O Lord, that Thou mayest 13. give him patience in the time of adversity."

Wherefore the Apostle exhorteth, "Let patience have its Jas. 1. 4. perfect work, that we may be perfect and entire, lacking nothing."

Christ was for a time forsaken of His Father, that He might comfort Himself with patience; and so it is required of us, that in our afflictions we "possess our souls with Lu. 21. 19. patience," for so we shall apply ourselves to be found in faith and the love of God, and to be lacking in no duty which God requireth at our hands.

Fourthly, when out of evil He brings good, and turns the evils that are come upon us to our greater good; for to this end God afflicteth His children, and therefore Christ saith not, Deliver us from calamity or tribulation, but from evil; for God in His wisdom doth so dispose of the afflictions of the godly, that they shall have cause to "rejoice and glory Rom. 5. 3. in tribulations." 2 Cor. 7. 4.

Now, they have cause to rejoice in their tribulations in two respects.

First, *quando crux liberat a cruciatu,* 'when the cross delivereth from anguish or vexation;' for so the Apostle saith, that "God doth chasten His children in this life, 1 Cor. 11. that they should not be condemned with the world." 32.

Secondly, *quando crux convertitur in coronam,* 'when their cross is turned into a crown;' for so St. Paul saith, "That 2 Cor. 4. 17. the afflictions of the godly, which they suffer here, are but light and momentary, and yet procure unto us a surpassing and everlasting weight of glory, such as cannot be expressed." And the same Apostle saith, "I have made my Rom. 8. 18. reckoning, and now find that the afflictions of this life are

SERM.
XVII.

Ps. 116. 16;
143. 12.

Lu. 17. 10.

Lu. 16. 1.

Ps. 138. 8.

Gen. 1. 26.

[1 Cor. 6. 20.

1 Pet. 1. 19.]

[2 Cor. 4. 7.]

Dan. 9. 18.

Rom. 12. 5.

Eph. 1. 21, 22.

Lu. 23. 33.

1 Pet. 2. 19.

not worthy or comparable to the glory that shall be revealed in the world to come."

Now, we may not limit God to any one of these ways of deliverance; but our desire must be, that He will deliver us from evil that way which seemeth best unto Him.

Lastly, seeing it is God's will that we shall undergo the cross in this life, our prayer to God must be, that of the crosses that were on Mount "Calvary" ours may be like to Christ's cross, that we may suffer innocently for the name of Christ; "For this is thankworthy, if a man for conscience towards God endure grief, and suffer wrong undeserved."

Secondly, if not innocently, yet that our suffering may be like the good thief that confessed he suffered worthily, for he repented of his sin, and by faith conceived comfort that albeit his body were crucified yet his soul should be received with Christ into glory; but in any ways our desire must be, that we suffer not like the wicked and reprobate thief that blasphemed Christ, and died without repentance.

The persons to be delivered are expressed in the word *nos*, "us," which implieth a twofold reason, first in regard of the word *libera*, "deliver." We are Thy servants, therefore make us free, and suffer us not to be slaves to Satan. So the Prophet reasoneth.

Secondly again, "deliver us," for we are Thy children, those whom Thou hast taught to call Thee Father; therefore though we be Mephibosheths for our deformity, and Absaloms for our ungraciousness, yet shew Thyself a Father to us; and of servants, though we be not only "unprofitable," but evil and wasteful, yet because we are Thy servants, "deliver us."

Thirdly, we are Thy workmanship, therefore "despise not the works of Thine own hands."

Fourthly, we are Thy "image."

Fifthly, the "price" of Thy Son's "blood."

Sixthly, "vessels" to carry Thy name: we are they "upon whom Thy name is called," therefore "deliver us," else we shall be a reproach to them that are about us.

Seventhly, we are the "members" of Thy "Church," which is the "body" of Christ Jesus our Saviour, our "Head."

The other reason is from the word *malo,* "evil :" the devil as he is our enemy so he is God's, and he hateth us because we are Thine, and therefore laboureth to draw us from Thee; but save Thou us that we fall not from Thee, as he hath done.

Lastly, "us," for we may not pray for ourselves alone, but for our brethren also, that God will be good to them likewise; and though we be out of trouble, yet because we be of the body, we may truly say, "Deliver us," when we pray in the behalf of our brethren that are under the cross.

Until the "last enemy, death, be destroyed," we shall never be fully freed, but have one evil or other. Therefore we are to pray for that time "when we shall hunger and thirst no more, when God shall wipe all tears from our eyes;" at the least, if He take us not presently out of the world, yet "to keep us from the evil of the world," till that day when there shall be "no more death, nor sorrow, nor crying, nor pain," but God shall be all in all to us for ever.

1 Cor. 15. 26.

Rev. 7. 16, 17.

Joh. 17. 15.

Rev. 21. 4.

THE LORD'S PRAYER.

SERMON XVIII.

For Thine is the Kingdom, Power, and Glory, for ever and ever.

SERM.
XVIII.
1 Cor. 14.
40.
Mat. 3. 15. ST. PAUL willeth that "all things" in the Church "be done orderly," which no doubt he took from Christ, Whose answer to John the Baptist was, *Sic enim decet,* "for so it becometh," whereby we see that both Christ and His Apostles have always observed a decorum or decency in all things.

So touching prayer, our Saviour Christ, to shew that it is an indecent thing for any having done his petitions to break off suddenly, or to begin his prayer without any introduction, hath not only made an entrance to His prayer wherein He acknowledged God's goodness, but also addeth a conclusion wherein He confesseth His "Kingdom, Power, and Glory," which the Fathers call δοξολογία, and He took the pattern of this conclusion out of the Old Testament, 1 Chron.
29. 11. where King David acknowledgeth, "Thine, O Lord, is greatness, power, and glory, and victory, and Thine is the Kingdom."

In the beginning we heard that all prayer and invocation is nothing else but a testimony and confession. The petitions that are severally made in this prayer are, confession of our weakness, want, need, and unableness to do any thing that may please God. The beginning and end of it are, an acknowledgment of God's riches, power, and goodness, whereby He is inclined to supply our wants, for that He is not only willing as a Father but able as a King; so that whatsoever prayer we make, whether *Techinah* or *Tehillah,* whether we pray that we may receive some good thing of

God, or praise Him for good received, it is a confession, and
both these confessions make for God's glory; not only to
him that was to make confession of his sin, it was said *Da
gloriam Deo,* "Give God the glory," but the blind man that Josh. 7. 19
had received a benefit by the recovery of his sight was said
"to give glory to God."   Joh. 9. 24.

The beginning of this prayer was a confession of God's
goodness; the end, of His power, for unto doing of good is
required not only willingness but power and ability.

To shew that God is willing, we are taught to call upon
Him by the name of "Father," for any father is willing to
do his child good; but with this willingness there must concur an ability to do good, which howsoever it be wanting in
earthly Fathers, yet it is not wanting in our heavenly Father;
for whereas nothing doth more express power than the name
of a king, Christ acknowledgeth God to be such a Father as
hath "Kingdom, Power, and Glory," and therefore is able
to do us whatsoever good He will. So God Himself affirmeth
of Himself, "I am a great King;" He is called "King of Mal. 1. 14
Kings and Lord of Lords;" so that if we will pray to God Rev. 19. 16.
the Father, we have cause to conceive hope that He will hear
our petitions and help us, because He is not only willing
as a Father, but able as a mighty, glorious, and powerful
Prince.

Secondly, if to God the Son, His dying for us doth assure
us of His good will and readiness to do us good; and His
rising again from the dead, when He hath broken the iron
bars, doth assure us of His power.

Thirdly, if to the Holy Ghost, we shall not need to doubt
of His willingness, for He is the essential love of God
"which is shed in our hearts." Besides, He is the Spirit Rom. 5. 5.
operative, by Whom God worketh all good things in the
hearts of His people, and therefore able to do whatsoever
good for us; and those two, to wit, the assurance of God's
goodness and power, are the two parts of "the anchor" of Heb. 6. 18,
our hope, and they give us not only *audaciam petendi* but 19.
also *fiduciam impetrandi,* 'not only boldness to ask but also
assurance to obtain.'

To make requests in our own behalf, and acknowledgment
to God of His love and power, are both confessions, but the

SERM.
XVIII.

principal is the acknowledgment of His goodness and Kingdom and power; for to make request to God for good things that we want concerns men, but to confess God's power and goodness is that wherein the heavenly Angels are occupied; they feel no want of any good thing, and therefore they have no need to make petition to God as we on earth, and therefore all the confession that they make is of God's goodness and power, whereof they cry continually, " Holy, Holy, Holy, Lord God of hosts, the earth is full of His glory." The same is done by the saints in heaven : " Blessing, and glory, and wisdom, and thanks, and honour, and power, and might, be unto our God for evermore."

Isa. 6. 3.

Rev. 7. 12.

Whereby we learn that we, concerning whom Christ saith, "that we shall be" ἰσάγγελοι, " equal or like to the Angels," ought while we live on earth not to speak only with the tongue of men but of Angels, not only to confess our own wants and to crave a supply from God, but to acknowledge God's riches, goodness, and power.

Lu. 20. 36.

Again, the petitions that we make for ourselves is a taking; but the sanctification of His name, by ascribing "Kingdom, Power, and Glory" unto God, is a giving, and therefore as the Apostle saith, " It is a more blessed thing to give than to receive," so the confession of God's goodness and power is a better confession than that which we make of our own weakness and poverty, and this is the only thing which God receives from us for the manifold benefits that we receive from Him.

Acts 20. 35.

Neither is this confession and acknowledgment left to our own choice as a thing indifferent, but we must account of it as of a necessary duty which may in no wise be omitted, seeing God enters into covenant that He will hear us and deliver us out of trouble " when we call upon Him." Therefore God challengeth this a duty to Himself by His servants, "Ascribe unto the Lord worship and strength, give unto the Lord the glory due unto His name." "All nations whom Thou hast made shall come and worship Thee, and glorify Thy name."

Ps. 50. 15.

[Ps. 29. 1, 2.]

Ps. 86. 9.

Therefore our Saviour commends the Samaritan because he returned to give glory to God for the benefit received, wherein He blames the other nine that being cleansed of their leprosy were not thankful to God in that behalf. For

Lu. 17. 18, 19.

God for this cause doth hear our prayers and grant our petitions, that we should glorify and honour His name.

But this is not all that we are to consider in these words, for they are not only δοξολογία but αἰτιολογία, not only an astipulation but an allegation, wherein as we acknowledge God's goodness and power That hath heard and granted our requests, so we allege reasons why He should not only hear us but also relieve and help us with those things that we crave for at His hands; we do not only say, Hear our petitions, for so shalt Thou shew Thyself to be a King, a mighty and glorious King, and we for our parts shall acknowledge the same; but we use this confession as a reason why our former requests are to be granted, for it is in effect as much as if we should say, Forgive Thou our sins, Deliver Thou us from evil; Hallowed be Thy name; Thy kingdom come; " For Kingdom, Power, and Glory is Thine," and not ours.

The reason why we would have our requests granted, is drawn from God Himself in two respects: first, that we may by this humble confession make ourselves capable of the graces of God, which do not descend to any but those that are of an humble spirit, " For He giveth grace to the 1 Pet. 5. 5. humble."

If we would have our desires granted because it is the nature of God to be good and gracious, to be of power to do what He will for the good of His people, we must desire Him to be gracious *propter Semet Ipsum*, " for His own Isa. 43. 25. sake;" our motive unto God must be, " For Thy loving Ps. 115. 1. mercy and Thy truth's sake." " Help us for the glory of Ps. 79. 9. Thy name, deliver us, be merciful unto our sins for Thy name's sake." By these motives we must provoke and stir up God to hear us. This is the difference that is betwixt the prayers of profane men and those that are sanctified. Heathen and profane men refer all to their own glory: so saith Nebuchadnezzar, " Is not this great Babel which I Dan. 4. 30. have built by my great power, and for the honour of my majesty?" Such a man thinketh himself to be absolute lord, and will say, " Who is the Lord over us?" Therefore Ps. 12. 4. are they called the sons of Belial. But the Patriarchs that were sanctified, frame their prayers otherwise: Jacob acknowledged, " I am not worthy of the least of Thy mercies;" by Gen. 32. 10.

SERM.
XVIII.

Dan. 9. 8.

which humility he made himself capable of mercy. "To us belongeth shame," saith Daniel, "but to Thee belongeth compassion and forgiveness, though we have offended." So Christ Himself in this place doth teach His disciples to pray that God will give them the things they desire, not for any thing in themselves, but for His name's sake: "For Thine is the Kingdom, Power, and Glory;" whereby we perceive that humility is the means to obtain at God's hands our suits.

The other respect is in regard of God, for He maketh His covenant with us "that He will be our God, and we His people." And when the Prophet stirreth up the faithful "to worship the Lord, and to fall down before the Lord our Maker," he addeth this as a reason, "For He is the Lord our God, and we are His people, and the sheep of His pasture." Wherefore one saith, *Commemoratio est quædam necessitas exaudiendi nos, quia nos Ipsius sumus, Ipse noster est;* 'It is a necessary motive to God to hear us, because we are His and He ours.'

[Jer. 31. 33.]

Ps. 96. 6, 7.

Therefore in all the prayers and psalms which the saints of God make, they ground their petitions upon this: in regard of God the Father, Who is the Creator, they say, We are Thy workmanship created by Thee; therefore "despise not the works of Thy own hands." Besides, we are the "likeness" of God's "image;" therefore suffer not Thine own image to be defaced in us, but repair it.

Ps. 138. 8.

Gen. 1. 26.

Secondly, in regard of Christ, we are the price of Christ's blood. *Empti estis pretio,* "Ye are bought with a price;" therefore suffer not so great a price to be lost, but deliver us and save us. Again, we carry His name, for as He is Christ, so we are of Him called Christians. Seeing therefore that "Thy name is called upon us," be gracious to us, and grant our request.

1 Cor. 6. 20.

Dan. 9. 19.

Thirdly, in respect of the Holy Spirit, the breath of His Spirit is in our nostrils, which is "the breath of life" which God breathed in us at our creation. Again, the same Spirit is to us a Holy Spirit, and sanctifieth us; we are not only *vaginæ Spiritûs viventis,* 'the sheaths of the living Spirit,' but *templa Spiritûs Sancti,* "the temples of the Holy Spirit." And therefore for His sake we are to entreat Him to be gracious to us.

Gen. 2. 7.

1 Cor. 6. 19.

We are God's kingdom, and therefore it belongeth to Him to seek our good. All the world is His Kingdom by right of inheritance, but we that are His Church are His Kingdom by right of purchase; we are λαὸς εἰς περιποίησιν, "a peo- 1 Pet. 2. 9. ple peculiar," or gotten by purchase; He hath redeemed us to be λαὸς περιούσιος, "a peculiar people," and the price Tit. 2 14. whereby we are purchased "is His own blood." He saith, 1 Pet. 1. 19. "He will be our God and we His people," He will be our Lev. 26. 12. Acts 20 28. Father and we His children, He our Lord and we His ser- 2 Cor. 6. 18. vants. Therefore we may challenge at His hands that favour which kings vouchsafe to their subjects, which fathers shew to their children; that is, to love them, to defend them, and to wish them all the good things they need.

If He have purchased us to Himself by His blood, then we pertain to Him, and we may say to Him as His disciples said to Christ, "Carest Thou not for us" that pertain to Mark 4. 38. Thee, "but sufferest us to perish?"

These words, "Kingdom, Power, and Glory," being jointly considered, are a representation of the Trinity.

As Moses, speaking of the Author of our creation, reckons up the name of God three times; as in the blessings of the Gen. 1. 27. Law the name of God is thrice repeated; and as the Angels Num. 6. cry there, "Holy, Holy, Holy," to teach that there are three Isa. 6 3. 24-26 Persons in the Godhead, which the heathen themselves have compassed, so Christ in the New Testament doth by these words, "Kingdom, Power, and Glory" signify those three Persons, Which afterwards He expresseth by the name of "Father, Son, and Holy Ghost." Mat. 28. 19.

If we consider them severally, although they may all be ascribed to any Person of the Deity, yet "the Kingdom" is to be ascribed unto Christ, "Power" to the Holy Ghost, 1 Cor. 15. and "Glory" to the Father; that we setting ourselves in Rom. 15. 25 Christ's "Kingdom," that is, His Church, by the "Power" Rom. 6. 4. 13. of the Holy Ghost, may be partakers of that "Glory" which God the Father hath prepared for us.

Again, these words are set to distinguish God's Kingdom from earthly kingdoms. Each king hath not power, as the king of Israel saith: "If the Lord do not succour thee, how 2 Kings 6. can I help thee?" But God's Kingdom is a Kingdom of 27. power.

SERM.
XVIII.

Secondly, there are kingdoms of might, but not of glory : such was the kingdom of David, he had a kingdom of might but not of glory, for he spent all his time in troubles ; but the kingdom of Solomon his son was both a powerful and a glorious kingdom, and there was a figure of the perfect Kingdom of Christ.

Wherefore we are taught by these words, that as the Kingdom is the Lord's, so He hath not only a Kingdom of power whereby He is able to defend, but of glory whereby He can also reward His servants and subjects. Moses desired of God that He would " shew him His glory," but he that is of Christ's Kingdom shall see the glory which Christ had from the beginning with the Father.

Ex. 33. 18.

Joh. 17. 5.

To consider these words severally. Upon these words of the Prophet, " Knit my heart unto Thee," one saith, *Religio dicitur a religando :* as there is a mutual bond between the king and his people, so there is between God and us. The king's duty is to defend his subjects from injury and wrong, and to bestow on them all manner of benefits. The duty of subjects is to be dutiful, and yield all ready service to their prince : so God for His part is ready not only to defend us from all danger, but to bestow all good things upon us ; and therefore we are bound to be religious and dutiful to Him, as to our King and Sovereign ; we must not only love Him as a Father, but fear Him as our Lord and King. And this mixture shall keep us in the way of salvation, we shall neither too much despair, nor presume of His goodness ; this fear we must testify both by a reverend regard of His Law and of His officers. He is no good subject that rebelleth against the laws of his prince, no more are we when no more can be gotten at our hands but " by the precepts of men :" when " the statutes of Omri are kept" for fear of temporal punishment, and the laws of God are had in no price, then it is a sign that we are not so dutiful and loyal to our heavenly Prince as we ought to be.

Ps. 86. 11

Mal. 1. 6.

Isa. 29. 13.

Mic. 6. 16.

Secondly, we must testify our fear of God by a reverend regard of His prophets and priests, which are the ministers and officers in His kingdom. When the Jews " mocked the messengers of God, and misused His prophets," they shewed their contempt of God Himself, and therefore " the wrath of

2 Chron.
36. 16.

the Lord arose against that people." Contrariwise, if we
have an honourable conceit of them, and "receive them as Gal. 4. 14.
the angels of God," then we shew ourselves to be dutiful
vassals to our heavenly Lord and King.

Next, for "Power." As St. Peter saith, God is able both 2 Pet. 2. 9.
to respect the righteous, and to shew vengeance upon the
wicked, so whether we respect the power of His grace inward
whereby He worketh all good things in the hearts of His
people, or the outward power whereby He defendeth them
from evil; whether it be the power of His Holy Spirit, or of
His right hand, we must confess with the Saints that "all Rev. 7. 12.
power and strength and might" belong to God. And therefore whatsoever power we have, whether inward or outward,
we must employ it all in His service. *Fortitudinem meam ad* Ps. 59. 9.
Te servo, "I will keep my strength," or "reserve it unto
Thee." So we must not spend our strength in thoughts of
vanity, but employ it to His use and to the setting forth of
His glory to Whom only all power belongeth.

Thirdly, Christ teacheth us to ascribe all glory to God,
that whatsoever praise or commendation doth come unto us
by any thing we do, we should make a surrender of it to
God, to Whom all glory is due, and say with the Church,
Non nobis Domine, etc., "Not unto us, O Lord, not unto Ps. 115. 1.
us, but to Thy Name give all glory." For, as the Prophet
saith, the Church is a place wherein "the voice of gladness"
is heard, "and the voice of them that sing, Praise the Lord Jer. 33. 11.
of Hosts, for He is loving, and His mercy endures for ever."

The faithful are taught to return all glory to God, which
is given to them. God Himself saith, *Gloriam Meam alteri* Isa. 42. 8.
non dabo, "My glory will I not give to another." If He
giveth His glory to any other, it is to such as deserve it, and
have all power of themselves; but there is no creature which
hath any power but what is given of God, and therefore God
doth by right reserve His glory to Himself, and we ought
willingly yield all glory to Him alone, because He promiseth, 1 Sam. 2.
"Them that honour Me, I will honour;" that we glorifying 30.
Him here with a verbal glory, we may be "glorified" of Him 2 Thes. 1.
with a real glory, when He cometh to judge the world; and, 2 Cor. 4. 17.
"with an exceeding weight of glory." 12.

But yet we do not fully see wherein the glorious Kingdom

of God differeth from the kingdoms of this world; for both power and glory may be ascribed to an earthly prince, and it is certain that Solomon had them all; and therefore as He is distinguished from earthly fathers, for that He is said to be "in heaven," so He differeth from earthly kings, in that His Kingdom is said to endure "for ever and ever."

There is another difference implied in the article. Earthly princes have *a* kingdom, a kingdom of power, and a certain glory in this world, but it is not "*the* kingdom."

This prepositive article imports two things, a generality and a superiority: for the first point, he that hath but a piece of the earth to bear rule in, is not an universal king; but Ps. 47. 2. "God is King over all the earth." Therefore, if we be so careful to behave ourselves aright in the presence of an earthly king whose kingdom is limited within certain bounds, which if he exceed he is no more king, much more ought we to glorify Him Whose Kingdom is universal.

Secondly, for the superiority of God's Kingdom, there are a great number of kings on earth; but of this King it is Ps. 72. 11. said, "All kings shall fall down before Him, all nations R .. 19 15. shall worship Him." "For He is said to be King of kings, and Lord of lords."

Touching the other difference, signified by the words "for ever." Though a man had all the earth for his kingdom, yet it could not be a kingdom "for ever and ever." No prince ever reigned the whole age of a man, and so long time as a man naturally may live, which the philosophers say is the space of an hundred years; but His Kingdom endureth not only the age of a man, but *in sæculum*, "for ever and ever." "Thy Kingdom, Power, and Glory" endureth "for ever and ever," whereas man's kingdom, power, and glory, lasteth but a few years, and sometimes but a few days.

Jezebel had a glorious kingdom, but within a few years it 2 Kings 9. was said of her, *Ubi est illa Jezabel?* "Where is that Jeze-
37. bel?" when it was fulfilled which the Prophet Jeremiah fore-
[Jer. 13. told, "Tell the king and queen, Humble yourselves, for your
18.] dignity shall be taken away, and the crown of your glory shall fall down." And the like is the greatness of all earthly kingdoms; and therefore Christ teacheth us to direct our Ps. 145 13. petitions to Him, "Whose Kingdom is everlasting," Whose

power endureth " for ever and ever;" not to a mortal king,
but to God *Qui solus habet etc.*, " Which only hath immor- 1 Tim. 6.
tality;" Who being Himself an everlasting King, and in- 16.
corruptible, is able to bestow upon us both " a crown," and 1 Pet. 5. 4.
an "inheritance incorruptible, and that fadeth not." This 1 Pet. 1. 4.
is our hope and the perfection of our desires, and therefore
as the Creed hath his period in life everlasting, so last of all
we are taught to pray for glory everlasting.

THE LORD'S PRAYER.

SERMON XIX.

Amen.

WE are now come to the last word of the Lord's Prayer, the power and efficacy whereof at this time is to be considered, for there is in it every way matter worthy of our consideration, and we cannot perfectly accomplish our duty in prayer, except we understand this word aright; for after we have laid out our several petitions to God, and made our allegation to God why we desire to be respected by Him, namely, because we are of His kingdom and jurisdiction, for that we have no power of ourselves to do any thing; and lastly, because that we confess that all glory is to be ascribed to Him, then it remaineth that we desire of God that those petitions and allegations made by us may by Him be ratified, which is done in the word "Amen."

Wherein the ancient writers consider two things: first, Jerome saith it is *signaculum consensûs nostri,* that by it we acknowledge that whatsoever we can desire is contained in this form of prayer.

Secondly, as St. Cyprian saith, it is *votum desiderii nostri,* that as we allow of this form of prayer and the petitions made therein, so we desire that it will please God to perform and accomplish them; so in this word is implied the consent of our mind to allow of the things which we are taught to pray for in this prayer, and secondly the desire of our heart for the obtaining of the same.

The one is the seal of our faith, inasmuch as we acknowlege those things to be true. The other is the seal of our love, whereby we testify our desire for the accomplishment of

these petitions. The one is referred to truth, the other to the
fervency of the spirit; in which two things, as our Saviour Joh. 4. 24.
affirmeth, the right worship of God consisteth. Concerning
which word, to be added in the end of our supplications,
there is an absolute commandment, not only in the Old
Testament, " Let all the people say Amen," but in the New, 1 Chron.
as appeareth by St. Paul's question, who to shew the neces- Ps. 106. 48.
sity of this word, he saith, " How shall the unlearned say 1 Cor. 14.
Amen to thy thanksgiving?" For, indeed, it concerneth ^{16.}
every one, as he will answer the transgression of *Dicet omnis*
populus, " All the people shall say," which is a flat commandment, not to be omitted, to add this word to their prayer.
The word itself is originally Hebrew, but used by the Evan-
gelists, and retained still in every language and tongue, without translation or alteration either in Greek, Latin, or any
other. The reason of the retaining of it is, that it might
appear that the synagogue of the children of Israel, and the
true congregation of the Church of Christ, gathered out of
all nations, is but one mystical body, whereof Christ is the
Head. The same we are given to understand by this, that
"the spirit of adoption" is said to "cry" not only "Abba"
in the hearts of the Jews, but also Πατὴρ and " Father" in Rom. 8. 15.
the hearts of the Gentiles. Therefore our Saviour would
not have His name to be either entirely Hebrew, as Jesus,
Messias; or entirely Greek, as Χριστὸς, Σωτὴρ, but the one
in Hebrew, the other in Greek, Jesus Christ, to shew that
" He is our peace, Who of two had made one," Who hath Eph. 2. 14,
reconciled us both in one body, and that He is the corner- ^{21.}
stone, whereby the Church consisting both of Jews and
Gentiles is coupled together, and "groweth to be one holy
temple to the Lord." Though they be, as the Apostle
speaketh, *congregatio primogenitorum,* "the congregation of Heb. 12.
the first-born," yet we are the Church of God as well as ^{23.}
they, we, I say, that are born after them; we that are of
the Gentiles have none other law for our direction than that
which the Jews had, as the Apostle saith, "I write no new 1 Joh. 2. 7.
commandment, but an old commandment which you have
heard from the beginning." We have no other faith, but
as the Apostle saith, *eumdem spiritum fidei habentes,* "having 2 Cor. 4.13.
the same spirit of faith." The same grace is offered to us

SERM.
XIX.
Acts 15. 11.
that was offered to the Fathers, "For we believe to be saved by the faith of Jesus Christ as well as they." And we have no other Sacraments than those which the Jews

1 Cor. 10.
3, 4.
had, of whom St. Paul saith, "They all did eat the same spiritual meat, and drank the same spiritual drink;" and therefore it is meet likewise that we should make the same prayer that they made; and indeed there is no petition in the Lord's Prayer which is not found in the Old Testament, used by the Church of the Jews. For that which the Pro-

Ps. 57. 5.
Ps. 67. 2.
phet prayeth, "Lift up Thyself, O God, above the heavens, and Thy glory above all the earth," "that Thy way may be known upon earth," &c. is nothing else but the hallowing of God's Name.

Ps. 106.
4, 5.
Secondly, "Remember me, O God, that I may see the felicity of Thy chosen." It is nothing else but an exposition of the second petition, where we pray, "Thy kingdom come."

Ps. 143. 10.
Thirdly, these words of the Prophet, "Teach me to do the thing that pleaseth Thee," is a full comprehension of the third petition, where we desire that His "will be done."

Ps. 145. 15.
Prov. 30. 8.
Fourthly, "The eyes of all things do look upon Thee, and Thou givest them meat in due season;" and the prayer of Solomon, "Give me not poverty, nor riches, but feed me with food meet," is a full expressing of the fourth petition.

Ps. 65. 3.

[Ps. 7. 4, 5.]
Fifthly, "My misdeeds prevail against me, O be merciful to our sins," is a sum of the fifth petition, and the condition of this petition is found Psalm the seventh, wherein the Prophet saith, "If I have done any such thing, or if there be any wickedness in my hands; if I have rewarded evil to him that dealt friendly with me (yea I have delivered him that without a cause was my enemy), then let my enemy persecute my soul;" whereby he desireth no otherwise to be forgiven of God, than as he doth forgive his brother.

Ps. 119. 37.
Ps. 141. 3.
Sixthly, that which the Prophet prayeth, "Turn away my eyes, that they behold not vanity," and "Set a watch before my mouth, and keep the door of my lips," is that which Christ teacheth us to pray, "Lead us not into temptation."

Ps. 25. 22.
Seventhly, "Redeem Israel from all trouble," in effect is as much as, Deliver them from all evil, which is the seventh petition.

Lastly, look what reason Christ teacheth us to use here, 1 Chron. 29. 11.
the same doth David use.

Therefore having the same prayer that the Jews had, it is meet that we should have the same conclusion that they had, and the same is; they said " Amen," and so do we.

Touching the use of this word, it is found in Scriptures to have two seats or places, and accordingly two several expositions, to wit, in the beginning and in the end, before and behind. In the beginning as in the doctrine of the Sacrament of Baptism, concerning which our Saviour saith, Joh. 3. 5. " Amen, Amen, except a man be born of the water and of the Spirit, he cannot enter into the Kingdom of God." And touching the Sacrament of the holy Eucharist, " Verily, Joh. 6. 53. verily, except ye eat the flesh of the Son of man, and drink His blood, ye have no life in you." And touching the effect of prayer Christ saith also, " Verily, verily, I say Joh. 16. 23. unto you, Whatsoever ye shall ask the Father in My name, He will give it you."

In those places the word " Amen" is used, and thereby our Saviour laboureth to express the truth of that which He doth teach. In the end likewise it is said, " Praised Ps. 41. 13. be the Lord for evermore. Amen, Amen." And in the Ps. 72. 19. Ps. 89. 52. New Testament, when the Apostle sheweth that of the Jews " according to the flesh came Christ, Who is over Rom. 9. 5. all, God blessed for ever. Amen." Here the word is used, and set behind, to signify that we desire that that may be performed, which God before by His Amen hath affirmed to be true. Therefore David, having received promise from the Lord by the hand of Nathan, saith, "Let the thing that Thou hast promised be Amen." Let there 1 Chron. 17. 23. be an accomplishment of the same. So when the Prophet Hananiah had prophesied in the name of the Lord, "I have Jer. 28. 2, broken the yoke of the king of Babel, and after two years 3, 6. will I bring again, into this place, all the ornaments of the house of the Lord," Jeremy the Prophet said, "Amen, the Lord do as thou hast said."

As in the beginning it ratifieth the truth of God's promise, so being set in the end it signifieth the desire of our hearts for the accomplishment of the same, and this desire always followeth and is grounded upon the promise of God and the

SERM.
XIX.
Ps. 119. 49.

Joh. 16. 23.

Isa. 65. 16.

Rev. 3. 14.

2 Cor. 1. 20.

truth thereof; in which regard the Prophet saith, "Remember me, O Lord, concerning Thy word, wherein Thou causest me to put my trust;" and therefore to Christ's "Amen" in the beginning, where He promiseth, "Verily, verily, whatsoever ye ask in My name," we may boldly add our "Amen" in the end, that His "Amen" may be performed; and by right do we ground our "Amen" upon God's "Amen," for He is called "Amen," that is, "truth." So the Apostle expresseth it, when speaking of Jesus Christ he saith, "Thus saith Amen, the faithful and true witness."

Therefore St. Paul saith of Christ, that "in Him all the promises are made to us yea" in the beginning, "and Amen" to us in regard of the certain accomplishment.

The reason of our "Amen" is, because not only faith but trust and confidence doth proceed from the truth of God; *fides* had relation to God's truth, but *fiducia* or confidence is settled upon God's faithfulness, and both are affirmed of God.

Deu. 32. 4.
Isa. 49. 7.
Heb 10. 23.
Heb. 11. 11.
['She.']

Rom. 4. 21.

1 Thess. 5.
24.

Moses saith of God that He is *verus* and *fidelis*, and Esay, "The Lord is faithful." Paul in the New Testament, "He is faithful That promised." "He[1] deemed Him faithful That promised." For there are two things required in faithfulness, without the which a man cannot be said to be faithful: the one is ability, of which Abraham doubted not of God's faithfulness, "being fully persuaded that what He promised He was able to perform;" the other is will and readiness to do, touching which the Apostle saith, "Faithful is He That called you," *et Ipse faciet.*

Joh. 14. 6.
[Joh. 15.
26.]
1 Joh. 5. 6.
Rom. 3. 4.
2 Tim. 2. 13.

Isa. 54. 10.

Mat. 5. 18.

These are the parts of faithfulness, and they are both found in God, and therefore not only God the Father is true, but Christ is said to be "the truth," and the Holy Ghost is called "the Spirit of truth." So that albeit men deal so untruly that it is verified of them, "All men are liars," yet God "abides faithful, and cannot deny Himself."

So much the Prophet teacheth when he saith, "The mountains shall be removed," but the thing which He hath spoken shall not fail. And our Saviour saith, "Heaven and earth shall pass, but one jot of My word shall not pass," that is, in regard of His power and ability.

For the other part of His faithfulness, which is His will

and readiness, He is said to be "a faithful Creator," that will have care of the souls committed to Him; and to this purpose serveth that which St. John affirmeth, "Behold what love the Father hath shewed us, that we should be sons of God." 1 Pet. 4. 19.

1 Joh. 3. 1.

There is in God that faithfulness that is in a mother towards her children, for as a woman cannot but pity her own child and "the son of her womb," so the Lord "will not forget" His own people. As His arm is not shortened but is still able to help, so His affection towards us is such that He is most willing to help. 1 Isa. 49. 15.

In this regard, as hath been observed, He is both a King and a Father, the one shewing His power, the other His willingness and good will towards us; upon both these we do ground our "Amen," and do learn not only *credere Vero*, 'believe God Which is true,' but *fidere Fideli*, 'trust Him Which is faithful.' Upon this faithfulness we may ground all our petitions: if we seek forgiveness of our trespasses, as Christ teacheth us to pray, then "God is faithful to forgive us our sins;" if we will pray against temptation, the Apostle saith, "God is faithful and will not suffer us to be tempted above that we are able to bear;" if to be delivered from evil, which is the last petition, the Apostle tells us, "The Lord is faithful, and will stablish us, and keep us from all evil." 1 Joh. 1. 9.

1 Cor. 10. 13.

2 Thess. 3. 3.

Thus we see both what is our "Amen," and whereupon it is grounded.

The last thing is, the right saying of this word, which is a thing to be enquired; for the Apostle, as though he took care for the right saying of it, saith, "How shall the unlearned say Amen?" teaching us that it is not enough to say "Amen" unless it be said in right form and manner. 1 Cor. 14. 16.

The right saying is reduced to four things: first that, as the Apostle says, "We pray with the spirit." For of the four evil Amens which the Hebrews note, one is, when our "Amen" doth not come from an earnest desire: We must "pour out our hearts before Him." So our "Amen" must come from the heart, we must be so disposed that we may say, "As the hart brayeth for the rivers of waters, so thirsteth my soul after Thee, O God." "My soul thirsteth for 1 Cor. 14. 15.

Ps. 62. 8.

Ps. 42. 1.

Ps. 63. 1.

SERM.
XIX. Thee in a barren and dry land where no water is." Without this "Amen" our "Amen" is *exanime*, a dead " Amen."

Secondly, a man may desire a false thing: so did the Pro-
Jer. 28. 6. phet give his "Amen" to the false prophecy of Hananiah, but we must be careful that it be true that we pray for;
1 Cor. 14. 15. therefore the Apostle saith, he will not pray "with the spirit" only but with his "understanding" also. So our
Joh. 4. 24. Saviour tells us we must "worship" God not in spirit only, but "in spirit and truth," that is, we must have understanding that our petitions be true and agreeable to God's will;
Ps. 47. 7. for as in thanksgiving it is requisite that we "sing praise with understanding," so the like must be done in prayer; they are both good, both to pray with the spirit and with the mind: therefore it is better to pray with both, than with but one alone. Therefore it is a marvel that any should think it enough to pray with the spirit, though they do not know in their mind what they pray for, but pray in an unknown tongue as the Church of Rome doth, seeing the
1 Cor. 14. 15. Apostle saith he "will pray both with the spirit and with the understanding," and this understanding is not of the words only but of the matter that we pray for.

We may understand the words wherein the prayer is made, and yet not understand the thing that is prayed for.

The sons of Zebedee prayed in their own language, and
[Mat. 20. 22.] yet our Saviour tells them, "Ye know not what ye ask."

The eunuch that was reading the Prophet Esay, no doubt understood the language of the Prophet, and yet when Philip asked him, "Understandest thou what thou readest?" he
Acts 8. 28, 30, 31. answered, "How can I, except I had a guide?" Therefore we must pray not only *intelligenter* but *scienter;* we must
1 Joh. 5. 14, 15. know what we ask, we must be careful that "whatsoever we ask be according to His will," for then may we be assured
Joh. 16. 23. that He will hear us; we must ask "in Christ's name."

Lastly, to a good end, for otherwise our prayers shall not
Jas. 4. 3. be heard: "Ye ask and receive not, because ye ask amiss."
But this is not all that is required, that ye may pray with the mind and understanding; for we must intend the thing that we may pray for with our heart, that the Lord may
Isa. 29. 13. not have cause to complain of us, as of the Jews, "that honoured Him with their lips while their heart was far from

Him." That we may with more attention of heart address ourselves to pray, our Saviour bids us to gather ourselves from all things that may carry away or distract our minds, and to "enter into our chamber," there to pray to our "Fa- Mat. 6. 6. ther" Which is in heaven. This did not St. Peter observe when he prayed, "Master, let us make here three taber- Lu. 9. 33. nacles;" and therefore the Evangelist saith "he knew not what he said."

Thirdly, that we may say "Amen" aright, we must not only understand in our mind and desire in our spirit the thing that we pray for, but must confidently look for the performance of that we desire; for unto this confidence there is a promise made on God's part, of Whom the Prophet saith, that "The Lord is nigh to all that call upon Him in Ps. 145. 18. truth," that is, in faith and confidence that they shall obtain the thing that they pray for. Therefore our Saviour saith, Mark 11. "Whatsoever ye pray for, believe and it shall be done;" and 24. the Apostle saith, If we will obtain our requests, we "must Jas. 1. 6. ask in faith, without wavering;" or else we shall be like the waves of the sea, that are tossed with the wind, and carried about with violence. And we shall not need to doubt but we shall be heard if we pray in a right manner, if we pray for a right end, that we may say, *Tua est gloria.*

This confidence and trust hath certain limitations: first, we may assure ourselves that God will grant our requests, if it be expedient for us; and therefore we must not limit God, nor appoint Him His time, but as the Psalmist saith, we must "direct our prayers early to Him," and wait for Ps. 5. 3. His pleasure. We must "tarry our Lord's leisure." Ps. 27. 14.

Secondly, though He grant not the same thing we desire, yet He will grant us a better. The Apostle prayed Christ that "the prick in the flesh, the messenger of Satan, might 2 Cor. 12. be taken from him;" but he had another answer, "My 7-9. grace is sufficient for thee:" that was better than if God had said, *Apage Satanas.* For if we pray to God in such manner and sort as He requireth, we may assure ourselves our prayers "shall not return into our own bosoms," but He Ps. 35. 13. will either grant the thing we desire or else that which shall be better for us.

Fourthly, that our "Amen" be indivisible, that is, we

must say Amen to every petition of the Lord's Prayer; for naturally our corruption is such that we can be content to desire the accomplishment of some of them but not of others. We do willingly say "Amen" to "Thy Kingdom come;" but as for "Hallowed be Thy name," we give no "Amen" to that, as appears by the whole course of our life, which is nothing else but a profaning and polluting of God's most glorious and fearful name.

We would gladly pray for "daily bread," but as for doing of God's "will," and obeying His commandments, we agree not to that.

We like well of the last petition, "Deliver us from evil," but as for that goes before it, "Lead us not into temptation," we will not subscribe to that; for we do seek by all means to tempt ourselves, and to draw ourselves unto sin.

We can be content to pray that He will "forgive us our trespasses," but as for the condition which is the forgiving of "those that trespass against us," we give no "Amen" to that, as is clear by the wrathful and revenging spirit that carrieth most men into all manner of outrages, while they will not learn to put up wrong, as they are taught by God's word. Therefore in regard of this petition, and the condition annexed, our Saviour saith, Take heed ye say "Amen" to this entirely; "except ye forgive one another, your heavenly Father will not forgive you."

Mat. 6. 15.

Therefore we must have a care as well to hallow God's name in this life, as to be partakers of His Kingdom in the life to come; we must labour as well for the fulfilling of His will, as for the obtaining of daily bread.

If we will be freed from evil which is the effect of sin, we must take heed that we do not tempt ourselves; and as we would be forgiven of God, so we must forgive our brethren.

Lastly, we must say "Amen" to the reason which our Saviour useth in the conclusion of the prayer. As the Apostle saith, "How shall the unlearned say Amen to thy thanksgivings?" For there are many that will say with the lepers, "Jesus, Master, have mercy upon us;" but being cleansed, few or none will return to give God thanks, and to say as our Saviour teacheth, "Thine is Kingdom, Power and Glory." We must not only pray to Him when we lie

1 Cor. 14. 16.

L... 17. 13.

sick upon our beds, that it would please Him to comfort us
"and to make our bed in our sickness," but to sing praises Ps. 41. 3.
to Him when He saveth us from adversity, and "delivers us Ps. 106. 10.
out of our enemies' hands;" our Hallelujah must be sounded
as loud as Hosanna.   The saints in heaven have no other
prayer but thanksgiving; they cry, "Amen, blessing, and Rev. 7. 12.
glory, and wisdom, and honour, and power, be to God."   All
their song is "Amen, Hallelujah."   Rev. 19. 4.

Therefore if we will come where they are, we must sound
out the praises of God as they do; if we will be like the
heavenly Angels, we must speak with the tongue of Angels;
if we say "Amen" to His praise and honour, He will ratify
His word towards us, so that His promise to us shall be
"Yea and Amen."   [2 Cor. 1. 20.]

SEVEN SERMONS

ON THE

WONDERFUL COMBAT,

FOR GOD'S GLORY AND MAN'S SALVATION,

BETWEEN

CHRIST AND SATAN.

DELIVERED BY THE REVEREND FATHER IN GOD,

DR. ANDREWES,

BISHOP OF WINCHESTER, DECEASED.

JAMES i. 12.

Blessed is the man that endureth temptation; for when he is tried, he shall receive the crown of life, which the Lord hath promised them that love Him.

SEVEN SERMONS

TEMPTATION OF CHRIST IN THE WILDERNESS.

SERMON I.

MATTHEW iv. 1.

Then was Jesus led aside of the Spirit into the wilderness, to be tempted of the devil.

[*Tunc Jesus ductus est in desertum a Spiritu, ut tentaretur a diabolo.* Lat. Vulg.]

[*Then was Jesus led up of the Spirit into the wilderness, to be tempted of the devil.* Eng. Trans.]

OUR Saviour Christ by His nativity took upon Him the Gal. 4. 4. shape of man; by His circumcision He "took upon Him" Phil. 2. 7. and submitted Himself to the degree "of a servant." By the first He made Himself in case, and able to perform the work of our redemption; by the second He entered bound for the performing of it. All was to this end, that He might restore the work of God to his original perfection. In the bringing of which to pass it was decreed by God in the beginning as a thing necessary, that the head of the serpent, [Gen. 3. by whose means it was violated and defaced, should be 15.] bruised. And "for this cause," saith St. John, "appeared 1 Joh. 3. 8. the Son of God, that He might loose the works of the devil," whereof this was the first. For in Genesis, the third chapter, we read that his first work after his fall was enviously to tempt our first parents, and thereby to overthrow all man-

SERM. kind. And here, straight after our Saviour was baptized, he
I.
— with like envy setteth on Him. Christ therefore first be-
ginneth with the overcoming of that; and for that purpose
He is here led forth to be tempted, that so being tempted
He might overcome.

Our Saviour makes this question upon their going out to
Mat. 11. 7. see John Baptist; "What went ye out to see?" As if He
should have said, They would never have gone out into the
wilderness, except it had been to see some great and worthy
matter: and behold a greater and worthier matter here. If
there be any thing in the wilderness worthy the going out to
behold, this is a matter much worthy of it. Or if there be
any matter worthy the hearing, it is worthy our attention to
Jude ver. 9. hear, not "Michael the Archangel disputing about the body
of Moses with the devil," but our own matter argued by two
such cunning adversaries; to see the combat betwixt our
1 Pet. 5. 8. grand enemy, who "goeth about like a roaring lion seeking
Ἀρχηγὸν. to devour" us, and our Archduke—for so He is called in Hebrews the twelfth chapter, and second verse; to see our
Ps. 74. 12. "King of old," the pawn of our inheritance, and our prince
Joh. 14. 30. of new, or prince by usurpation, "the prince of this world,"
Joh. 3. 14. enter the lists together; to see the wisdom of the New Ser-
Rev. 12. 9.
1 Pet. 5. 8. pent match the craftiness and subtlety of "the old ser-
Rev. 5. 5. pent;" to see "the Lion of the tribe of Judah" combating
with the "roaring lion." If any thing be worthy the sight,
it is this.

Though there should come no profit to us by the victory,
yet were it worth the sight in this respect, only to behold
how these champions behave themselves; that so we may be
warned beforehand by seeing the strength of our adversary,
and that also seeing the manner of his fight and of our Saviour's defence we may be instructed how to arm ourselves,
and how to ward accordingly. For let us be sure that since
the devil spared not to tempt our Saviour, he will be much
more bold with us; if he have done this to the "green tree,"
Lu. 23. 31. what will become of "the dry?" If he have sought our
overthrow in Christ, how much more will he do it in our-
Job 7. 1. selves? If our days here be but as "the days of an hireling,"
2 Tim. 2. 4. and our whole life be but as a continual warfare, then is it
behoveful for us to have some intelligence of our enemy's

forces and drifts. It is said his "darts" are "fiery." Here Eph. 6. 16.
we may see the manner of his casting them, that so Satan 2 Cor. 2. 11.
should not circumvent us. Let us mark how our Saviour
wardeth and defendeth Himself, that so we may be "armed 1 Pet. 4. 1.
with the same mind." Let us therefore go out into the [Matt. 11.
7.]
wilderness to see it.

"Then Jesus." This is the description of the entry into
the temptation, and it containeth as a weighty history many
circumstances importing great matters, which may be reduced to seven branches or heads. First, the two champions; first Christ, and secondly, Satan; thirdly, the leader
of Jesus into the lists, who is said to be the Holy Ghost;
fourthly, the end, which was the conflict itself, that is, "to
be tempted;" fifthly, the day of the battle, expressed under
the word "then;" sixthly, the lists themselves, that is, "the
wilderness;" seventhly, Christ's preparation to it, that is,
His fasting.

I. First, for the party defendant Christ, Who as God
"giveth food" to every living creature, and as God and man Ps. 136. 25.
with five loaves and two fishes fed "five thousand men be- Mat. 14. 21.
sides women and children." He That is said to be the very Joh. 6. 51.
meat itself, whereby we live eternally, is here said to be
hungry. He before Whom "thousand thousands" are said
to "minister," and ten thousand thousands are said to stand Dan. 7. 10.
before Him, hath here for His companions "the wild beasts"
—for so saith Mark, chapter the first, verse the thirteenth.
He to Whom "the Angels minister" is here assailed with Mat. 4. 11.
devils, which offer unto Him matter of great indignity; and
the indignity which He suffered leads us to the consideration
of the grievousness of our sins and of the greatness of His
love, both which are measured by the greatness of those
things He suffered for us; as that He was cast out from
among the company of Angels—for so Mark, chapter the
first, verse the twelfth, hath it—into the desert, to be a companion of beasts, and so led forth to be tempted; where He
suffered in His body hunger, in His soul temptation : what is
it else but a proclaiming of His great love towards us? As
if He should exulting say, What is it that shall separate Me
from the love of men? Shall temptation? shall solitariness?
shall hunger? shall wearisome labour, and travail? shall

SERM.
I.

watching? shall anguish of mind, and bloody sweat? shall mocks? shall whips? shall nails? shall spears? shall principalities? That we also might use the same challenge which Paul doth in the eighth chapter of his epistle to the Romans, the thirty-fifth verse: " What shall separate us from the love of Christ? shall tribulation? shall anguish or persecution?" These two profitable points grow out of the consideration of the person of the defendant.

II. Secondly, the party assailant is the devil, who is so called by reason of his foul mouth in defaming; for so doth the word *diabolus* import, whereby we have occasion to detest the sin of infamy; and it sheweth what name they deserve, and how to be esteemed of, in whom that quality is found. St. Paul foretold that in the latter days there should be men-devils, foul-mouthed men, evil speakers; and in the first Epistle to Timothy, the third chapter and eleventh verse, he speaketh of women-devils, because of their calumnious speeches. In the tongue wherein Christ spake these words, namely the Syriac, the fittest word that He could find to signify the devil's name, is a word that signifies *divulgator;* so that ' a publisher of infamous reports' is good Syriac for 'the devil;' as when a man lightly conceives a reproach, either forging it himself by misconstruction, or credulously receiving it upon the report of others, and then is not sorry for his brother's ill, but rather insulteth, not considering that he himself may fall into the like temptations; and so becomes "puffed up," and at last falls a blazing his brother's imperfections. These come right to the devil's quality, they take upon them the abetting of the devil's quarrel.

2 Tim. 3. 3.

Mat. 5. 22.
Gal. 6. 1.
1 Cor. 5. 2.
3 John
ver. 10.

It is the devil's occupation to defame us first with God, as he did Job, as if he had been a hypocrite and had served God only for gain; and so stands he continually accusing us. And he also defameth God with us, as if He were a God That did envy our good; and so he here defameth God to Christ, as if He were careless in providing for Him, in suffering Him to be hungry. And from these two defamations proceeds all evil whatsoever, as well that which the divines call *malum pœnæ* (as Job the first chapter and eleventh verse, accusing Job that he would curse God if He handled him roughly, and so got power over his goods) as that which they

Job 1. 9.
Rev. 12. 10.
Gen. 3. 1,
&c.

call *malum culpæ.* For his defaming God with us was the cause of all sin ; and every where still we see he laboureth to persuade us that God is an unkind God, that so we may burst forth into those terms, This good did I get at God's hand, to wit, hunger. To this doth he tempt Christ. And as to desperation, so sometimes to the contrary, presumption ; as verse the sixth, " Cast Thyself down," &c., by bringing us to have a base conceit of God, defaming Him as if He were a God of clouts, not to be reckoned of ; as if He were a man to wait upon us, and to take us up as oft as we list to throw ourselves down, that we may say in our hearts as they that were frozen in their dregs did, " He neither doth good nor hurt," it is all one to serve Him and not to serve Him. He tells us that he will " give" us all this if we will " fall down and worship" him, as though he were very liberal in rewards, and as though God were unkind or ungrateful, not once regarding us for all our service, but suffers us even to starve. Which brought men to that pass as to say, that " It is but in vain to serve God, what gain is in His service ?" If he cannot prevail this way against us, then he will try another way ; for when, seeing that this temptation succeeded not, the devil left Christ, he departed not for altogether, but went to come again—as appeareth in Luke, the fourth chapter and thirteenth verse—" he departed for a time." Christ was too cunning for him in disputing : he meant therefore to take another course ; for, as James noteth, there be two sorts of temptations, one by enticement as a serpent, another by violence as a lion ; if he cannot prevail as a serpent, he will play the lion. He had also another hour at Christ in the garden, " the hour of darkness ;" there he bruised His heel.

III. Thirdly, we are to consider the leader : " He was led by the Spirit." In which we are to note five things ; not making any question but that it was the good Spirit, for so it appeareth in Luke the fourth chapter, and first verse.

First, that the state of a man regenerate by baptism is not a standing still. " He found others standing idle in the market place, and He said to them, Why stand ye idle all day ?" We must not only have a mortifying and reviving but " a quickening" and stirring " spirit," which will move

Margin notes: 2 Kings 6. / 33. Mat. 4. 3. / Zeph. 1. 12. / Mat. 4. 9. / Mal. 3. 14. / Jas. 1. 14. / Lu. 22. 53. / Mat. 20. 6. / 1 Cor. 15. 45.

SERM.
I.

Phil. 3. 16.
1 Cor. 4. 20.

us and cause us to proceed; we must not lie still like lumps of flesh, laying all upon Christ's shoulders. We must "walk" forwards, for "the kingdom of God" consists "not in word but in power."

Secondly, as there must be a stirring, so this stirring must not be such as when a man is left to his own voluntary or natural motion: we must go according as we are led. For having given ourselves to God, we are no longer to be at our own disposition or direction; whereas before our calling we 1 Cor. 12. 2. were "Gentiles," and were carried into errors, we wandered up and down as masterless or careless, or else gave heed to 1 Tim. 4. 1. "the doctrines of devils," or else "led with divers lusts;" 2 Tim. 3. 6. but now being become the children of God we must "be led Rom. 8. 14. by the Spirit of God," "for so many as be the sons of God," are led thereby. We must not be led by the spirit whence the revelation came, the sixteenth chapter of Matthew and twenty-second verse, from whence revelations of flesh and blood do arise; but by the Spirit from whence the voice [Mat. 17. came, "This is My beloved Son, in Whom I am well 5.] pleased." It came not by the Spirit That ministered wise counsel, but by that which came down upon them.

Thirdly, the manner of leading is described to be such a kind of leading as when a ship is loosed from the shore, as ἀνήχθησαν Luke the eighth chapter, and twenty-second verse; it is called launching forth: so in the eighteenth chapter of the ἀνήχθη Acts, the twenty-first verse, Paul is said to have sailed forth. Joh. 3. 8. The Holy Ghost driving us is compared to a gale of "wind," which teacheth us that as when the wind bloweth we must be ready to hoist up sail, so must we make us ready Heb. 6. 19. to be led by the Spirit. Our "hope" is compared to an "anchor," which must be haled up to us; and our faith to the sail, we are to bear as great a sail as we can. We must also look to the closeness of the vessel, which is our conscience; for if we have not a good conscience, we may 1 Tim. 1. make "shipwreck" of faith, religion, and all. And thus are 19. we to proceed in our journey towards our country, the spiri- Acts 20. 22. tual Jerusalem, as it were sea-faring men. "Now behold, I go bound in spirit to Jerusalem;" to which journey "the 2 Cor. 5. 14. love of Christ" must "constrain" us.

Fourthly, that He was "led to be tempted." His tempta-

tion therefore came not by chance, nor as Job speaketh, Job 5. 3.
" out of the dust," or out of the earth, nor from the devil,
[for he had no power without leave[a],] not only over Job's
person, but not so much as over his goods. He had no Job 1. 12.
power of himself, no not[b] so much as over the hogs of the
Girgashites, who were profane men. Hence gather we this Mat. 8. 31.
comfort, that the Holy Ghost is not a stander by, as a
stranger, when we are tempted, *tanquam otiosus spectator*,
but He leads us by the hand, and stands by as a faithful
assistant. He makes an issue out of all our temptations,
and " will not suffer us to be tempted beyond[c] our strength." 1 Cor. 10.
And He turneth the work of sin and of the devil too unto
our " good," so that all these shall make us more wary after Rom. 8. 28.
to resist them : and hell, by fearing it, shall be an occasion
unto us to avoid that might bring us to it; and so they
shall all be fellow-helpers to our salvation. So that temptations, whether they be, as the Fathers call them, rods to
chasten us for sin committed, or to try and sift us, and so
to take away the chaff, the " fan" being[d] in the Holy Ghost's Mat. 3. 12.
hand; or whether they be sent " to buffet" us against
" the prick of the flesh;" or whether they be as matters 2 Cor. 12.
serving for our experience, not only for ourselves that we
may know our own strength and to " work patience" in Rom. 5. 3.
us, but to the devil also that so his mouth may be stopped,
as in Job the second chapter and third verse : " Hast
thou marked My servant Job, how upright he is, and
that in all the world there is not such an one ?" howsoever
they be, the devil hath not the rod or chain in his hands,
but the Holy Ghost, to order them as they may best serve
for His glory and our good ; and as for the devil, He bindeth
him fast. Rev. 20. 2.

Fifthly, by the Greek word here used is set forth the ἀνήχθη
difference between the temptations of the saints and repro-
bates. In the Lord's Prayer one petition is, " Lead us not εἰσενέγκῃς
into temptation;" but there the word importeth another
manner of leading than is here meant. We do not there
pray against this manner of leading here, which is so to
lead us as to be with us and to bring us back again; but Heb. 13. 20.

---

* added in A. [b] *no not* omitted A. [c] *above* A. [d] *is* A.

we pray there that He would not cast or drive us into temptations, and when we are there leave us by withdrawing His grace and Holy Spirit, as He doth from the reprobate and forsaken.

IV. The fourth point is the end, that is, the conflict, as it concerneth Christ, insomuch that He was "led to be tempted." In which temptation Augustine saith, *Habemus et quod credentes veneremur, et quod videntes imitemur ;* ' There be two things for faith to adore, and two things for imitation to practise.'

First, for faith, that the temptations of Christ have sanctified temptations unto us ; that whereas before they were curses like unto hanging on a tree, now since Christ hath been both tempted and hanged on a tree, they be no longer signs and pledges of God's wrath but favours. A man may be the child of God notwithstanding, and therefore he is not to receive any discouragement by any of them.

Secondly, besides the sanctifying, it is an abatement, so that now when we are tempted they have not the force they had before ; for now the serpent's head is bruised, so that he is now nothing so strong as he was to cast his darts. Also the head of his darts are blunted, " Death, where is thy sting ? Hell, where is thy victory?" For as His death and resurrection had a mortifying force against the " old man" and a quickening force toward the "new man," so hath His temptation a dulling force to the devil, and a strengthening force to us.

1 Cor. 15. 55.

For our life and imitation there are also two.

First, compassion ; for Christ knowing in what sort we were tempted, as having felt by experience both how strong the assailant was who " thrust sore at Him that He might fall," and how feeble our nature is to make resistance being nothing but " dust," He is moved thereby to lay away severity, and to put on the bowels of compassion. So that now, " we have not a High Priest which cannot be touched with our infirmities, but was tempted in like sort." So we, which were before stony judges, and too rough for physicians, ought in like sort, having been tempted ourselves, to look upon others' defects with a more passionate regard.

Ps. 118. 13.

Ps. 103. 14.

Heb. 4. 15.

The second thing we are to imitate[e], Christ is our fellow-helper in all our necessities and temptations; Who, as He sheweth us his sleights and darts, so He teacheth us how to Eph. 4. 14. avoid them. This is no small comfort to us, when we consider that He is with us, and will be, "till the end of the Mat. 28. 20. world," Who hath "overcome the world" and the devil; if Joh. 16. 33. any temptation happen, that He will bear us out, we may be of good cheer. This was it that did so animate Job: Do Job 17. 3. Thou but take my part, and who shall touch me? When as both Christ and we draw together in one "yoke," what can Mat. 11. 29. hurt us? Yet if we be afraid for that we see the enemy coming, let us call for the help of our Assistant, and as it is said in Psalm the sixty-eighth, verse the first, we shall see "God will arise, and His enemies shall be scattered;" they [Ps. 68. shall vanish like "smoke," and melt like "wax." When 1, 2.] they are ready to attack us, let us say, "Save me, O God, Ps. 69. 1. for the waters are entered even into my soul." When we are feeble, then let us say with Hezekiah, "O Lord, it hath Isa. 38. 14. oppressed me, comfort me." Or though they have wounded us, let us say with David, "Bring out Thy spear, and stop Ps. 35. 3. the way against them that persecute me; say yet to my soul, I am thy salvation." So that we have not only an example but a comfort too.

V. The fifth point is the day and time when this was done, in which we are to note two things. The word "then" relateth as well to the end of the chapter next going before, as to the present instant.

First then, when as Christ was but newly come out of the water of baptism, and immediately after the heavens had opened unto Him, and the Holy Ghost descended upon Him in the likeness of a dove, and while He was yet full of the Holy Ghost, did the devil set upon Him. When as the voice from heaven had pronounced, "This is My beloved Son in [Mat. 3. Whom I am well pleased," the devil straight addeth, In 17.] Whom I am ill pleased; and so addresseth himself against Him. And it is God's property to look for much at his hands, to whom He hath given much. When He gives a man

---

[e] [This passage seems to require emendation. Two conjectural readings are therefore given.
"The second thing we are to imitate.
Christ" &c.
"The second thing. [He] we are to imitate, Christ," &c.]

SERM.
I.
a large measure of grace, He gives the devil withal a large patent. Our Saviour had great gifts, and the devil is like a thief, that will venture most for the greatest booty.

Secondly, in regard of the present, we are to note that in thirty years the devil did nothing to our Saviour; but now, when He goes about to "gird" Himself with our salvation, (according to Psalm the forty-fifth, verse the third) then doth the devil gird on his sword also; that is as much to say as, the better the work is the more resistance it shall have. Ten repulses did the Israelites suffer, before they could get possession of the promised land of Canaan; and as many did David endure, before he was invested in the promised kingdom. Many lets came before the temple was re-edified, as is to be seen in Ezra and Nehemiah. Yea, saith the devil, [Ps. 45. 7.] hath God "anointed Him with the oil of gladness above His fellows?" I will see if I can anoint Him with the oil of sadness above His fellows. Hath He been baptized of water and the Holy Ghost? I will provide another baptism for Him, namely of fire. Hath God sent down the Holy Ghost upon Him in likeness of a dove? I will cause tribulation, and a crown of thorns to light upon His head. Hath a voice [Mat. 3. 17.] come down from heaven, saying, "This is My beloved Son?" I will provide a voice for Him that shall ascend from the [Mat. 27. 40.] foot, that shall say, "If Thou be the Son of God, come down from the cross."

VI. The sixth is the place, the lists, to wit, the wilderness, that so He might be alone, and that there might be no fellow-worker with Him in the matter of our salvation, that He Isa. 63. 3. alone might have the treading of the "wine-press." So in Lu. 9. 36. the[f] transfiguration in the Mount He "was found alone," so in the garden in His great agony He was in effect alone, for Mat. 26. 40. His disciples slept all the while, that unto Him might be ascribed all the praise.

Secondly, we will note here, that there is no place privileged from temptations. As there be some that think there be certain places to be exempt from God's presence—as was noted in the dream of Jacob—so the monks and hermits thought that by avoiding company they should be free from temptations: which is not so. For although Christ were

---

[f] *His* A.

alone in the wilderness and fasting too, yet was He tempted we see. And yet it is true, that he that will live well must shun the company of the wicked.

When the Angels had brought Lot and his family out of Gen. 19. 17. the doors, they charged them not to tarry, nor to stand still, nor once to look back. So after the cock had crowed, and put Peter in mind of his fall, he went out of the doors and "wept bitterly;" his solitariness was a cause to make his re- Mat. 26. 75. pentance the more earnest, and helped to increase his tears : and company is commonly a hindrance to the receiving of any good grace, and to the exercising and confirming us in any good purpose. But as true it is that temptations are, and may as well be, in the deserts as in public places : not only in the valleys but in the mountains; and not only in Mat. 4. 8. the country but even in "the holy city;" yea, and some- Mat. 4. 5. times full, and sometimes fasting; yea, in paradise, and in heaven itself, for thither doth the devil come and accuse us before God. We are therefore always to stand upon our guard; for in Luke the eleventh chapter, verse the twenty-fourth, he is said to "walk through dry places," lest haply some might be escaped from him thither; and though we could go whither he could not come, we should not be free, for we carry ever a tempter about with us. And when we pray to be delivered from temptation, it is not only from the devil but from ourselves; we carry fire within us. Nazianzen and Basil were of that mind once, that by change of the place a man might go from temptation; but afterward they recanted it, affirming that it was impossible to avoid temptation, yea though he went out of the world, except he left his heart behind him also.

SEVEN SERMONS

TEMPTATION OF CHRIST IN THE WILDERNESS.

SERMON II.

MATTHEW iv. 2.

And when He had fasted forty days, and forty nights, He was afterward hungry.

[*Et cum jejunasset quadraginta diebus, et quadraginta noctibus, postea esuriit.* Lat. Vulg.]

[*And when He had fasted forty days, and forty nights, He was afterward an hungred.* Eng. Trans.]

SERM.
II.

Now come we to the seventh and last circumstance. It may seem strange that being about to present Himself to the world as Prince, Priest, and Prophet, that He would make His progress into the wilderness, and begin with a fast; for this was clean contrary to the course and fashion of the world, which useth when any great matter is in hand to make a preface or *præludium* with some great solemnity. As when Solomon came first to his crown he went to the chief city and gathered a solemn convent, so Christ should rather first have gone to Jerusalem the holy city, and there should have been some solemn banquet. But Christ from His baptism began His calling, and fasted forty days and forty nights. This His fast by late[a] writers is called the entrance into His calling; by the ancient[b] writers it is called the entrance into His conflict.

[a] *the new* A.   [b] *old* A.

The manner of the Church hath always been, that at the first institution or undertaking of any great and weighty matter there hath been extraordinary fasting. So Moses, Deu. 9. 9. when he entered into his calling at the receiving of the Law, fasted forty days. So Elias, at the restoring of the same 1 Kings 19. Law, did the like. And so when they went about the re- 8. edifying of the Temple, as appeareth from Ezra, the eighth chapter and twenty-first verse. So in the New Testament, at the separation of Paul and Barnabas. And, as Jerome Acts 13. 3. reporteth, St. John would not undertake to write the divine [Commen. sup. Mat. work of his Gospel, until the whole Church by fasting had Præf. ad Euseb.] recommended the same unto God.

So likewise, at the entrance into a conflict, for the obtaining of some victory, as Jehoshaphat did when he overcame 2 Chron. the Amorites. So did Esther when she went about the de- 20. 3. liverance of the Jews; as in Esther, the fourth chapter, and sixteenth verse. And Eusebius reporteth that when Peter [Vid. S. was to enter disputation with Simon Magus, there was fast- Aug. Ep. 36. 21. ad ing throughout the whole Church generally. Casulan.]

Whether at the entrance into a calling, or to resist the devil, St. Peter's rule, mentioned in his first Epistle and [1 Pet. fifth chapter, ought to take place, we must use prayer and 5. 8, 9.] fasting.

And as at all times we are to use watchfulness and carefulness, so then especially, when we look that the devil will be most busy; and the rather, for that in some cases there is no dealing without fasting, as Mark, the ninth chapter, and twenty-ninth verse, there is a kind of devil that will not be cast out without "prayer and fasting."

As for the number of days wherein He fasted, just forty, curiosity may find itself work enough; but it is dangerous to make conclusions when no certainty appeareth.

Some say there is a correspondency between these forty days and the forty days wherein the world was destroyed by the deluge. But it is better to say, as Moses fasted forty days at the institution of the law, and Elias forty at the restoration, so Christ here. And because He came but in the shape of a servant, He would not take upon Him above His fellow-servants. Contrary to our times, wherein a man is accounted nobody except he can have a quirk above his

SERM. II. fellows. But it is more material to see how it concerneth us. It is a thing rather to be adored by admiration, than to be followed by apish imitation.

Acts 10. 9, 30. This fast here was not the fast of a day, as that of Peter and of Cornelius, but such as Luke the fourth chapter, and second verse describeth, " He did eat nothing all that time."

Mat. 3. 4. St. John the Baptist, though his life were very strict, " did eat locusts and wild honey." Ours is not properly a fast, but a provocation of meats, and therefore there can be no proportion between them. But as it is, what is to be thought of it?

[Socrat. lib. v. 22.] [Apud. Euseb. lib. v. 24.] Socrates and Irenæus record that at the first the Church did use to celebrate but one day in remembrance of Christ's fast, till after, the Montanists—a certain sect of heretics, who thereupon are called Encratitæ—raised it to fourteen days. The zeal of the clergy after increased it to forty, after to fifty; the monks brought it to sixty, the friars to seventy; and if the Pope had not there stayed it, they would have brought it to eighty, and so have doubled Christ's fasting[c].

When the Primitive Church saw the heretics by this outward show go about to disgrace the Christians by this counterfeit show of holiness, they used it also; but, saith Augustine and Chrysostom, they held it only a positive law, which was in the Church to use or take away, and not as any exercise of godliness.

Only a doubt resteth now, because of the hardness of men's hearts, whether it were better left or kept. Some would have abstinence used, and one day kept for the sabbath, but left to every man's liberty what time and day, and tied to no certainty; but that were, upon the matter, to have none kept at all.

Notwithstanding, the reformed Churches, as that of France, have used their liberty in removing of it, for that they saw an inclination in their people to superstition, who would Lu. 18. 12. think themselves holier for such fasting, like the Pharisees. The Church wherein we live useth her liberty in retaining it, and that upon good reasons: for since God hath created the fishes of the sea for man, and giveth him an interest in Gen. 9. 2. them also as well as in the beasts; since the death of fish was a plague wherewith God plagued Pharaoh, and so contrariwise the increase of fish is a blessing; God will have fish to be used, so that He may have praises as well for the sea as for the land. *Ps. 104. 25.*

If we look into the civil reason, we shall see great cause to observe it. See, Numbers the eleventh chapter and twentieth verse, the abundance of flesh that was consumed in one month. The maintenance of store then is of great importance, and therefore order must be taken accordingly. Jerusalem had fish-days, that Tyrus and such like living upon navigation might have utterance for their commodities; *Neh. 13. 16.* for Tyrus was the maritime city, till after Alexander annexed to it another city and made it dry.

The tribe of Zabulon lived by navigation, which is a thing necessary both for wealth, (and[d] made Solomon richer than any other king) and also for munition; that tribe therefore had need of maintenance. And therefore our Church and commonwealth have taken order accordingly, and the rather for that our times require it, for the times that forbade marriage and the abstinence of meats [are past; we rather live in the age of self-love, in intemperance, and filthy pleasure[e].] There is more fear of a pottingerful of gluttony, than of a spoonful of superstition. This is no fast, but a change of meat. *Gen. 49. 13. 2 Chron. 9. 20. Isa. 23. 4. [Vid. Homily on Fasting Part 2.] [1 Tim. 4. 3.] 2 Tim. 3. 2—4.*

"Then came to Him the tempter," &c. Before we come to the particular temptations, we have four general points to be considered. First, the changing of the devil's name from "devil" to "tempter;" secondly, that it is said he "came unto Him;" thirdly, that he came when He was fasting; fourthly, the diversity and order of the temptations. *ver. 3.*

I. First, in James the first chapter and thirteenth verse, it is said that "God tempteth no man;" and yet in Deuteronomy the thirteenth chapter and third verse, it appeareth that "God doth tempt some:" we must then make a difference between [temptations—between[f]] God's temptations and the devil's. The devil indeed tempteth us, but God, as our English translation hath it, trieth us. The latter is to commend us, or rather that our tribulation may bring forth "patience, and patience hope." It makes us know *Rom. 5. 3, 4.*

---

[d] *which* A.   [e] added in A.   [f] added in A.

SERM. that to be in ourselves which before we knew not, as we see
II.   in Job. So the Lord proved the Israelites, to see if they
Deu. 13. 3. loved Him or no. The devil's temptation is to know our
corruption; for knowing the innocency of Adam, he went
Exod. 16. about to corrupt him. It is like the Israelites' proving of
20.
1 Pet. 1. 7. manna, to try conclusions. God's is like the trial of "gold,"
which the oftener it is tried the purer it waxeth; the devil's
like that of manna, which stinketh and corrupteth by trial.
Mat. 3. 12. God's is like the trial of the "fan;" the devil's like that of
Lu. 22. 31. the sieve, which lets go the flour and keeps the bran.

II. Secondly, the devil hath two shapes: in the one he
tempteth and allureth, and in that he came down to our
Eph. 6. 11. Saviour; in the other he assaileth us, that is, by assault and
Mat. 22. 17. violence. The first is the temptation of hypocrites: "Shall
Joh. 6. 70. we pay tribute to Cæsar?" The second of Judas, who in
Joh. 18. 3.
the garden assaulted our Saviour. So Satan sets on Christ
by violence. He came unto Christ by casting sparks of fire
into Him, for He was devoid of any wicked and vain thoughts
coming forth of Him.

Lu. 24. 38. Two ways may a man be tempted; either by doubts aris-
Joh. 13. 27. ing in our hearts out of us, or by a "sop" entering into us.
Christ could not be tempted the first way, for He was devoid of any wicked and vain thought coming forth of Him.
To us the devil needs bring but a pair of bellows, for he
shall find fire within us; but to Christ he was fain to bring
fire too.

III. Thirdly, he then came to Him when He was fasting,
which discovereth the devil's desperate boldness, as also his
craftiness, in that he waited his time, to stay till He was
hungry. Notwithstanding Christ was new come from His
baptism, and was full of the Holy Ghost, and even now in
His exercise of mortification, yet had the devil courage to
set upon Him. There is no place so holy, nor exercise so
good, as can repress his courage, or give a stay to the boldness of his attempts; as we see Mark the fourth chapter,
and fifteenth verse. The word is no sooner sown but Satan
comes immediately and takes it out of their hearts: which
must needs be done in the church. For the word is out
before they be out of the church; so that he is not afraid of
hearing the word, but can abide it well enough, yea, better

than many. And though they carry the word out of the
church he will wait on them home, and "choke the word"
with cares and riches and voluptuous living, like the seed Mark 4. 19.
that fell among thorns.

And no more doth he care for the exercise of prayer; for
even then, immediately after the repetition of forgiveness,
when we have made even with all the world, when God hath
forgiven us, and we others, then doth the devil give us occasion to say, "Lead us not into temptation," as standing by
there ready to tempt us.

And as little cares he for the Sacraments; for presently
after they had received the Sacrament and sung the hymn,
Christ tells them they shall "all be offended in Him that Mat. 26.
night." Thus we see his courage serves him at all times, ^30, 31.
nothing is able to quail it.

As this ought not to discourage the children of God, having so faithful an Assistant to take their part; so it giveth
them this *caveat*, that they be at no time secure, but always
to keep a sure guard. St. Bernard in the midst of a sermon
was solicited to vain glory because he thought he pleased his
auditors, and thereupon brake off his speech and turned it
to the devil, saying, *Non propter te hoc opus cœptum est; nec
propter te, nec in te finitur.*

And as he is courageous, so he is subtle; for, notwithstanding his eager desire, he stayed the fittest time, wherein
consisteth a chief point of wisdom. So when he tempted
Eve he stayed till her husband was away, and till he could [Gen. 3. 1.
shew her the fruit which was so pleasing to the eye. So ^&c.]
when David lay with Bathsheba, Uriah's wife, he tempted 2 Sam. 11. 2.
him in the evening, and after his sleep, a very fit time for
the purpose. So when they were asleep, "the enemy sowed Mat. 13. 25.
tares."

And as he is wary in choosing his time, so is he as cunning in choosing the means, observing the dispositions of
men. For wanton and voluptuous men he hath the "daugh- Nu. 25. 1.
ters of Moab," a bait fit for their humours, whereby to
tempt them to idolatry. For men secure and careless he
hath a net that sufficeth to throw over them, and snare 2 Tim. 2. 26.
them in. For others, that have more care to seek and enquire into things, he hath quills to blow them up, as "know- 1 Cor. 8. 1.

SERM. ledge" which "puffs up." Yea, even the best things can
II. he make serve for his purpose, and to be occasions of temptations, so that he may find better entertainment for the
good exercises' sake that come with him. He will come
sometimes shrouded in the necessity of nature, as here;
for when a man is hungry, nature requireth somewhat to
assuage it.

Prayer no man doubteth to be a godly exercise, yet there-
by he tempted them that loved "to pray in the synagogues,"
Mat. 6. 5, 7. and make much babbling and repetition. In like sort doth
Mat. 16. 22. he abuse the name of good counsel, as in Peter to Christ,
who as a friend wished Him to spare Himself and live out
His time.

Thus can he put on a fair show, the sooner to beguile.
And for good reason, for if he should come unmasked in
his own likeness he would be rejected; as, if Jehoram the
2 Kings king of Israel had come himself without Jehoshaphat, Elisha
3. 14. would not have looked on him: so by a good pretence the
temptation shrouds and insinuates itself, otherwise it would
not be looked on.

IV. Now we are to consider the diversity and order of
the temptations, and then will we handle them particularly.
And first we are to note that, though there are but these
three recorded, yet He endured divers others. His whole
life was full of temptations, as may appear by Luke the
twenty-second chapter and twenty-eighth verse. It is said,
Luke the fourth chapter, and second verse, that He was
"tempted forty days of the devil," whereas these three
temptations here set down were not till after the end of
forty days. These only are mentioned, but there were other
Joh. 20. 30. not written, as divers of His miracles are unwritten. Only
so much was written as was expedient.

These three are a brief abridgment of all His temptations.
As it is true that Paul saith, that Christ resembled Adam,
and was made a " quickening Spirit," as Adam was " a living
1 Cor. 15. soul," (and the bringing of the children of Israel out of Egypt
45. by being called out of Egypt) so may Christ and Adam be
Mat. 2. 15. compared in these three temptations. For they both were
1 Joh. 2.16. tempted with " concupiscence of the flesh, concupiscence of
the eye, and pride of life." In Adam the devil first brought

him into a conceit that God envied his good, [and of purpose kept him hoodwinked lest he should see his good[g],] as
we see, falconers put hoods over hawks' eyes, to make them
more quiet and ruly. Secondly, he lulls him on to a proud
conceit of himself, by persuading him that by eating he
should be like God. Thirdly, he sheweth the fruit, which
was pleasant. So in Christ's temptation: first, he would
have brought Him to murmur against God; secondly, to
presume; and thirdly, to commit idolatry; all which are set
down in the first of Corinthians, the tenth chapter, and
seventh, ninth, and tenth verses. And under these three Exod. 16.
heads come all temptations. 2; 17. 2,
7; 32. 6.

To some of these extremes will the devil seek to drive one. Num. 16.
1. &c. 21.
First, by distrust he will seek to drive us to use unlawful 4, 6.
means for the obtaining of necessary things, as bread is when
a man is hungry. Or if we be in no such want, that that
temptation cannot take place, then through superfluity he
will tempt us to wanton and unnecessary desires, as to throw
ourselves down that the Angels may take us up; and having
prevailed so far, then he carrieth us to the devil and all.
"All this will I give Thee:" there is his "all." "Fall down
and worship me:" there is the devil with it. So that in this
respect it may well be said, that "the way of a serpent is over Prov. 30.
a stone." He goeth so slily that a man seeth him in, before 19.
he can tell what way or how he got in. First he wraps himself in necessity and thereby winds himself in unperceived,
then he brings us to make riches our god.

Now let us see his darts. The first is, of making stones
bread: this may well be called the hungry temptation. The
stream of the doctors make Adam's offence the sin of gluttony, but Bucer thinks that this temptation is rather to be [Enar. in
referred to distrust and despair. There is small likelihood Mat. iv.]
that one should sin in gluttony, by eating bread only. The
devil's desire was only that the stones might be turned into
bread, and that after so long a fast; and then, if the temptation had been to gluttony, Christ's answer had been nothing
to the purpose, the devil might well have replied against the
insufficiency of it. For gluttony is to be answered by a text
willing sobriety, whereas this text which Christ answereth

[g] added in A.

SERM. by containeth rather an assertion of God's providence, and
1. therefore our Saviour should have seemed very unskilful
in defending Himself. The temptation therefore is to
distrust.

This standeth well with the devil's cunning in fight; for
by this he shooteth first even at the throat, and at that
1 Joh. 5. 4. which is the life of a Christian, to wit, his "faith"—as a
man would say, *Jugulum petit*—even at that which "over-
cometh the world." He tempted Him to such a distrust as
Ex. 17. 7. was in the Israelites, when they asked if God were with
them or no? So he made Adam think, God cared not for
him; so here the devil premiseth a doubt to shake His faith,
wherein Christ made no doubt, *Si Filius Dei es.*

Indeed You heard a voice say, You were the "beloved
Son" of God, but are You so indeed? or was it not rather
a delusion? You see You are almost starved for want of
bread : well, would God have suffered You so to be, if You
had been His *Filius dilectus?* No, You are some hunger-
starved child. So, Luke the twenty-second chapter, and
thirty-second verse, Christ prayed that Peter's "faith might
1 Pet. 5. 8. not fail :" it was that the devil shot at. He is a "roaring
1 Thes. 3. 5. lion, seeking to devour" us, whom we must resist by faith.
It is our faith that he aims at; for having overthrown that,
disobedience soon will follow. Having abolished the esta-
Rom. 3. 31. blisher of the law, the breach of the law must needs follow.
He hath then fit time to set us awork about making stones
into bread, that is, to get our living by unlawful means.
First, shipwreck of faith, then of obedience.

The devil here seeing Him in great want and hunger,
would thereby bring in doubt that He was not the Son of
God : which is not a good argument. For whether we respect the natural tokens of God's favour, we see they happen
not to the wisest, and men of best and greatest knowledge,
as appeareth in Ecclesiastes, the ninth chapter and eleventh
verse, or the supernatural favour of God. We shall see
Gen. 12. Abraham forced to fly his country into Egypt for famine.
10.
Gen. 26. 1. So did Isaac; and Jacob likewise was in the same distress.
Gen. 43 1. Notwithstanding that God was called "the God of Abraham,
[Exod. 3.
6.] Isaac, and Jacob," yet were they all three like to be hunger-
starved. Yea, not only so, but for their faith many were

burned and stoned, "of whom the world was not worthy." Heb. 11. 38.
So fared it with the Apostles : they were hungry, naked, and 1Cor. 4. 11.
athirst. But what do we speak of the adopted sons of God,
when as His own natural Son suffered as much, nay, far
more? Here we see He was hungry, also He was "wearied" Joh. 4. 6.
with travel, and fain to rest; He had no house to hide His Lu. 9. 58.
head in, whereas "foxes have holes."

"If Thou be the Son of God," &c. The heathens have
observed, that in rhetoric it is a point of chiefest cunning,
when you would outface a man or importune him to do a
thing, to press and urge him with that which he will not or
cannot for shame deny to be in himself : as by saying, If you
have any wit, then you will do thus and thus; If you be an
honest man, or a good fellow, do this. So here the devil, not
being to learn any point of subtlety, comes to our Saviour
saying, "If Thou be the Son of God,"—as it may be doubted,
You being in this case—then "make these stones bread."
No, no, it follows not; a man may be the son of God, and
not shew it by any such art. So when Pilate asked who
accused Christ, they answered, "If He had not been a male- Joh. 18. 30.
factor, we would not have brought Him before thee." They
were jolly grave men, it was a flat flattery : and in John the
twenty-first chapter and twenty-third verse there is the like.
This ought to put us in mind, when we are tempted in like
manner, that we take heed we be not outfaced.

In the matter itself, we are to consider these points : first,
the devil sets it down for a ground that, follow what will,
bread must needs be had. Therefore Christ first closeth with
him. Admit He had bread, were He then safe? No, We
live not "by bread only;" so that bread is not of absolute
necessity. Well, what follows of that? Bread You must
needs have, You see Your want, God hath left off to provide
for You. Then comes the conclusion : Therefore shift for
Yourself as well as You can. First, he soliciteth us to a
mutinous repining within ourselves, as Hebrews the third
chapter and eighth verse : "Harden not your hearts, as in
the day of temptation," &c. whereby he forceth us to break
out into such like conceits as, Psalm the one hundred and
sixteenth and eleventh verse, "I said in my distress that all
men be liars;" and, Psalm the thirty-first, and twenty-second

SERM.
II.

2 Kings 6.
33.

1 Sam. 28.
7, 19.

Mat. 7. 9.

Gen. 43. 12.

1 Thes. 4.
6.

Prov. 4. 17.
Prov. 20.
17.

verse, "I said in my haste, I am cast off." Thus closely he distrusted God, in saying His prophets prophesy lies, till at last we even open our mouths against God Himself, and say, "This evil cometh from the Lord: shall I attend on the Lord any longer?" hunger and shame is all we shall get at God's hands. And so, casting[h] off God, betake themselves to some other patron, and then the devil is fittest for their turn. For when we are fallen out with one, it is best serving his enemy, and to retain to the contrary faction. Then we seek a familiar (with Saul) to answer us.

But what did the devil then tell him? did he bring comfort with him? No: he tells him that to-morrow he and his sons should die. So here doth the devil bring a stone with him. "What father," saith Christ, "if his son ask him bread, would give him a stone?" Yet the devil doth so; Christ was hungry, and the devil shews Him stones.

Here is the devil's comfort. Here be stones for Thee: if Thou canst devise any way to make these stones bread, Thou art well. Whereas we do not use to make bread of stones, but of wheat, to work it with the sweat of our brows; to get it so, we learn from Genesis the third chapter and nineteenth verse.

By extortion and usury we may make stones into bread— that is the devil's alchemistry; or haply we may make bread of nothing, when a man gets a thing by another's "oversight." Or else, what and if we can overreach our brother in subtlety, and go beyond him with a trick of wit or cunning? "Let no man defraud or oppress his brother in any matter; for the Lord is avenged of all such." The one is called "the bread of violence" and oppression; the other, "the bread of deceit."

They are indeed both made of stones, for they still retain their former property, as the event will declare. For though in the beginning such bread be pleasant, yet after, his mouth is but filled with gravel. After which will consequently follow gnashing of teeth.

[h] *having cast* A.

SEVEN SERMONS

UPON THE

TEMPTATION OF CHRIST IN THE WILDERNESS.

SERMON III.

MATTHEW iv. 4.

But He answering said, It is written, Man shall not live by bread only, but by every word that proceedeth out of the mouth of God.

[*Qui respondens dixit, Scriptum est, Non in solo pane vivit homo, sed in omni verbo quod procedit de ore Dei.* Lat. Vulg.]

[*But He answered and said, It is written, Man shall not live by bread alone, but by every word that proceedeth out of the mouth of God.* Eng. Trans.]

IT was a good service that Elisha did, to tell the king of the trains laid for him, when they lay in ambush against him. And even this is the first use that we have of our Saviour's temptations.

It warns us aforehand of the devil's coming, so that we may have time to prepare ourselves accordingly. For as at that time the devil came upon Christ when hunger pinched Him, so where we are in any distress we are to look for temptations.

This temptation hath two parts: first comes *Si*, a distrust; secondly follows unlawful means. Having laid this foundation, that bread is necessary to be had when one is hungry, he inferreth that God helpeth not nor supplieth the want:

L l 2

SERM.
III.

Mat. 7. 9.

therefore God is not Thy Father, and therefore depend no longer on Him, but shift for Yourself. This is the effect of the devil's argument.

Eph. 6. 16.

The Fathers upon the words, "Take the shield of faith, to quench all the fiery darts of the devil," do note that about every one of the darts or temptations of the devil there are, as it were, balls of wildfire. For being to assault our obedience, and knowing that faith is our shield, to that end he useth the arrow-head, which is distrust in God, about which is fire; to wit, the using of unlawful means to consume our obedience, which will consume our shield of faith, and so make way for the dart to kill or wound us. So that his drift is, to bring our adoption or son-ship to a *Si*.

There is no doubt but Christ was able to have turned stones into bread: but why would He not then follow the devil's advice? The devil by saying, "Say unto these stones," seemeth to acknowledge that He had the force to have done it, even by His bare word: for even stones are said to hear the voice of God and obey His commandment,

1 Kings 13.
5.

and not only God's but even God's servants; as when the man of God had pronounced that the altar should rent in

Mat. 27. 50,
51.

sunder, it did so. And "when Jesus cried out with a loud voice, the veil of the temple rent in twain, the earth did quake, and the stones were cloven." The dead men are worse than stones, yet they in their graves heard His voice.

And not only was He able to turn stones into bread, but

Mat. 3. 9.

into men also; as "children to Abraham, of stones." If therefore it had pleased Him, He was as well able at this

Joh. 2. 10.

time to have turned stones into bread, as after He turned water into wine.

It was no less possible to Him, no doubt, to have saved

Mat. 27. 42.

"Himself" when the Jews scoffingly bade Him, as to have "saved others;" and to have "come down from the cross" being alive, as it was after for Him, not only being dead and buried, but a great stone being over Him, to remove it and

Mat. 28. 2.

come out of the grave. He had power to both, but not will alike to both.

But why would He not here use His power for the satisfying of His hunger, and follow the devil's advice? In setting down the history of turning water into wine it is thus fur-

ther said, that He did it that His disciples might believe in Joh. 2. 11.
Him. That was the reason that moved Him to the working [S. Aug.
of that miracle, and because there was no such cause here 2.] Ser. 123.
He did it not. For the devil would not believe in Him, He
knew, though He had done it. The devil desired Him but
to have Him shew what He could do for a need only, for
a vaunt of His power: wherein we see the humour of pride,
that made him at the first to fall.

It is the same temptation that his kinsfolks used: "No [Joh. 7.
man doth any thing secretly, that seeketh to be famous. If 4.]
Thou dost these things, shew Thyself to the world." But
see how unfitly the temptation hangeth together. He should
rather have said, If You be hungry, than, "If You be the
Son of God;" and then rather have bid Him fast forty days
more, than turn the stones into bread. If it had been to
have made a son of God, Christ would have done it; but not
to have shewed Himself to be the Son of God.

But it may be asked, Why did Christ vouchsafe to give
him any answer at all, whereas He might have commanded
him to silence, and tormented him "before his time," and [Mat. 8.
have punished him for his sauciness? When Peter tempted 29.]
Him, He cut him up very sharply, saying, "Come behind Mark 8. 33.
Me, Satan." Why did He not answer the devil so? He
might have enjoined him, and thrown him into the bottom- Lu. 8. 31.
less pit, or at the least bidden him, "Avoid, Satan." Lu. 4. 8.

Augustine answereth this doubt, that Christ answered in
the like time to teach us to answer; willing us thereby, as
Abimelech did his soldiers, to do as he had done before. Ju. 9. 48.
So Christ is our example, and bids us to do as He had done. Joh. 13. 15.
Christ is our captain, He hath gone before us and shewed us
how to behave ourselves in fight. When the devil assaulteth
us with distrust, then are we to ward it off with a text of
God's providence; and so of the rest, as He hath done before us. Our Saviour's shield whereby, we see, He beareth
off all the devil's darts, is covered all over with *Scriptum est.*
We have here a brief view of the Church's armoury, of "the Cant. 4. 4.
tower of David," built for defence. Here be the shields
wherewith Solomon's temple was hanged, and which Paul
calleth "the weapons of our warfare, not carnal, but mighty 2 Cor. 10. 4.
through God to cast down holds."

SERM.
III.

Ps. 39. 3.
Mat. 26. 41.

Joh. 6. 35.

Isa. 12. 3.

Heb. 4. 12.
Prov. 30. 5.

Eph. 6. 16.

Ps. 62. 11.

[1 Sam. 3.
5.]
1 Thes. 2.
13.

Ps. 58. 5.

1 Pet. 5. 8.

[Gen. 1.
26.]

They are in number five: first, a preparation of ourselves by the use of God's sacraments, that we may be the more strong to sustain and bear off temptations, and to hold out to the end without fainting; secondly, a withdrawing ourselves into the desert, or some other solitary place, there by meditation to kindle good thoughts; thirdly, fasting; fourthly, watchful prayer; fifthly, the perfecting ourselves in the Scriptures. These be the five shields wherewith Solomon's temple was hanged.

Now as for the Scripture, we are to note that where God speaketh of any good that we are to receive out of it, it is recommended to us as a storehouse whither we are to make our resort for the bread of life and the water of life, whereof he that tasteth shall never thirst. And from thence are we to draw the waters of comfort, "out of the fountains of salvation." When there is any ill spoken of which we are to resist, then it is commended to us as an armoury, whence we may fetch any kind of weapon which we shall need, either offensive as "a sword," or defensive as "a shield."

The Scripture is the broad plate that is to bear off "the darts;" our faith is the braces or handle whereby we take hold, and lift it up to defend ourselves withal. For the Scripture is a shield, *non quod dicitur, sed quod creditur.* *Dicitur*—there is the strong and broad matter, fit to bear off; and *creditur*—that is the handle or braces to it, "God spake once, or twice I have heard it, power belongeth unto God." So that it sufficeth not that it be spoken only by God, but we must hear it too; neither must we hear it as the voice of a man (as Samuel at the first did, who when God called him thought it the voice of Eli) but as the voice of God, that we which were dead in our sins He hath quickened, and forgiven us all our trespasses. This is the perfection of our faith.

Generally of the Scriptures this is Christ's opinion, confirmed by His own practice, that if the devil come as a serpent, here is a charm for him; or if he come as "a lion," here is that is able to prevail against him. And that the devil knows well enough, as appeareth by his malice that he hath always borne it, before it was Scripture, when it was but only *dictum.* For so soon as God had said, "Let Us

make man in Our likeness," that word was straight a whetstone to the devil's envy.   And after the fall, when the
"Seed" was promised, that was and is the cause of all the Gen. 3. 15.
devil's "enmity;" so when the promise was reiterated, that Gen. 22. 18.
was the cause he so turmoiled all the patriarchs.

But when the word was to be written, and to become
Scripture, then his malice began to grow very hot, insomuch
that he caused it for anger to be broken.   For the Fathers Ex. 32. 19.
are of opinion, that all the devil's busy endeavour in making
the Israelites to commit idolatry with the golden calf was to
the end that he might so heat Moses in his zeal, as that in
his anger he should break the tables of the Law by casting
them hastily out of his hands.   We are to note therefore,
that there is a forcible sound in the word, which the devil
cannot abide; and not only the sound, but the sight also.

It is written of Augustine, that lying sick on his bed he [Vit. S.
caused the seven penitential psalms to be painted on the wall $\frac{August.}{Lib 8.}$
over against him in great letters; that if after he should c. 11.]
become speechless, yet he might point to every verse when
the devil came to tempt him, and so confute him.   Blessed [Ps. 127.
is he that hath his quiver full of such arrows, they shall not 5.]
be ashamed.   Blessed is he that hath the skill to choose out
fit arrows for the purpose, as the Fathers speak out of Esay,
the forty-ninth chapter and second verse.

Christ saith affirmatively of the Scriptures, that "in them Joh. 5. 39.
is eternal life."   Negatively, that the cause of error is the Mark 12.
not knowing of them.   David saith it was that that "made $\frac{24.}{Ps. 119. 98,}$
him wiser than his enemies," than "his teachers," and than 99, 100.
"the ancients."   Knowledge of the truth is the way to 2 Tim. 2. 25.
amendment after a fall.   There is much calling now-a-days
for the word, and others find fault as fast that it is no better
hearkened unto.   For as the want of obedience and all other
abuses (which are so much cried out against) proceed not
only from the not hearing of the word, but as well from
the not mingling of "faith" with it, without which mixture Heb. 4. 2.
it is nothing worth, it profiteth not, so the error of the
former times was in yielding too far to the devil's policy,
by sealing up the Scriptures, and locking the storehouse
and armoury of the people.   It is the policy Christ tells
us of, in the eleventh chapter of Luke's Gospel, verse the

SERM.
III.

1 Sam. 13. 19.

Isa. 29. 11.

Deu. 8. 3.

Lu. 12. 19.

twenty-second.   A strong man puts "the strong armed man" out of his house and "takes away his armour from him;" then he needs not fear him.

The like policy we read of, in the first book of Samuel, the thirteenth chapter and nineteenth verse, when the Philistines had taken away all smiths and armour: then they thought they were safe.   So, in the time of darkness, the devil might let them do their good works and what they list, and yet have them still under his lure, for he might offend them at his pleasure that had no armour to resist him.   All the children of God had a right and property in the Law of God, as appeareth by Christ's words, John, the tenth chapter and thirty-fourth verse.   He answereth them, that is, the common people, "Is it not written in your Law?"   As though He should say, The Scripture is yours.   To the young man (in the tenth chapter of St. Luke's Gospel, and twenty-sixth verse) that asked Christ what he should do to be saved?   Christ answereth, "What is written in the Law? how readest thou?"   Whereunto to answer that we cannot read, or that the book is "sealed" up, is as the devil would have it.   Then hath he a fit time to offer us stones to make bread of.   But this answer with our Saviour Christ will not be allowed of.

Now come we to the special point of Christ's answer, "It is written, Man lives not by bread only," &c.   There is no better kind of reasoning, than that when one grants all that hath been said by his adversary, and proveth it to make on his part, and upon a new conceit avoids all that his adversary said.   Here our Saviour might confess all that the devil objected, as that He is the Son of God, and admit the stones were made bread, and that bread were of absolute necessity, and that it were so to be come by, which is untrue: were we then in good case?

This indeed is the devil's position, wherewith he would persuade all those that have *animam triticeam*, as the Fathers call it, that those external things are necessary to be had, and that if they have enough thereof they are well enough; as we see it to be the mind of the rich man.   This man having a wheaten soul, having corn enough, bade his soul take rest, and live merrily "for many years."   But Christ goeth further, and saith, Though the stones be made bread, it will not avail; except it please God by the blessing of His word to give virtue, and as it were life unto the bread, there is no difference between it and a stone.

It is not the plenty or quality of victuals, howsoever some dote upon such external means, as they did which "sacrificed to their net, and burnt incense to their yarn, because Hab. 1. 16. by them their portion was fat, and their meats plenteous." For what saith Job? "If I had rejoiced because my sub-Job 31. 25, stance was great, this had been an iniquity." So that our 28. life is not maintained by bread only, descended out of the mould of the earth.

The nature of bread and stones are not much unlike, they come both out of one belly, that is to say the earth, and of Job 28. 5, 6. themselves the one of them hath no more power than the other unto life; for we know that the Israelites died even "while the flesh of quails was in their mouths," and manna, Nu. 11. 33. heavenly fare, being far better than our bread. It is the devil's crafty policy to bury a man's life under a loaf of bread, and as it were to fetter the grace of God to the outward means; whereas they of themselves are of no more efficacy without the operation and grace of the word, than a hammer and a saw without a hand able to employ them.

David saith, "The eyes of all things wait on God for their Ps. 104. 27, meat in due season, and Thou fillest them:" With what? 28. with bread? No, but "with Thy blessing and goodness." Our hearts must be "stablished with grace, not with meats." Heb. 13. 9. It is God's prerogative, that as all things had their "begin-Col. 1. 18. ning" from Him, so He supporteth and sustaineth them. Heb. 1. 3.

This is a further point than all philosophy teacheth us. For they having laid down the four elements, bare and simple essences, *tanquam materiam,* by compounding and[a] tempering of them, they bring forth a certain quintessence or balm full of virtue. But divinity leadeth us to a quintessence, without which all the quintessences and balms in the world can do us no good.

To the question that Jeremiah propoundeth, "Is there no Jer. 8. 22. balm at Gilead? Is there no physician there?" the answer may be, Man's health is not recovered by balm or physic

[a] *or* A.

SERM. III.

2 Chron. 16. 12.

Ps. 20. 7.

Levit. 26. 26.

Lu. 12. 19.

1 Kings 17. 14, 15. [Mat. 14. 17, 21.]

only, "but by every word that proceedeth out of the mouth of God," if we weigh Christ's argument aright. For we may see, Asa died for all his "physicians" that were about him. So if it be asked, Are there no horses nor chariots in Gilead? we may answer, Warlike victory consisteth not in warlike furniture only, but "in remembering the name of the [b] Lord God." A horse is a vain thing to save, without the power of this word. And so when a man thrives not or prospers not in his actions, it is not often for want of labour or care. Psalm the hundred and twenty-seventh and first verse tells him, "Except the Lord build the house," &c. Augustine adviseth his auditory to believe it in time, lest by woful experience they find it to be true, when as they shall have such a consumption that no meat shall do them any good, or such a dropsy that no drink shall avail them.

The power and virtue of this word is called "the staff of bread," and it is meant of a chief staff, such a one as is set in the midst to bear up all the tent. The plainest similitude I can use to make you understand the force thereof is this: When we go to physic for any disease, we are bidden seethe such herbs in running water, and then to drink the water; we know it is not the water which helpeth, but the decoction or infusion. So it is not the bread (considered barely in itself) that nourisheth us, but the virtue and grace of the word infused into it. We are not therefore to stick to the means like the glutton, but to pray for this blessing. And to this end God, in the establishing of nature, hath thereout reserved four special prerogatives to His word.

As first, with a very little of the means to go far in operation, with a little oil and a little wheat He fed Elias, the poor widow, and her son, a great while. And, Matthew the fourteenth chapter and seventeenth verse, Christ made "five loaves and two fishes" serve "five thousand" persons. The heathen man thought no certain proportion was to be set down for a family, because when a heavenly hunger cometh on men they eat more at one time than at another. But whatsoever the heathen have spoken wisely, we have far more wisely uttered by the Holy Ghost in one place or other. In Psalm the seventeenth and fourteenth verse this

[b] *our* A.

is set down, where there is mention made of a certain
"hidden treasure" wherewith men's "bellies be filled;" and
Haggai, the first chapter and sixth verse, saith, "Men eat
much, yet have not enough; drink much, but are not filled."
This is the first prerogative.

His second is, He takes order as well for the quality as for
the quantity: coarse meats and fine are all one with Him,
for the Israelites, notwithstanding their quails and manna
died; and Daniel and his fellows that fed with coarse meats,
"looked better than all the children that were fed upon the Dan. 1. 15.
king's own diet."

Thirdly, without means He worketh sometimes. There-
fore Asa had said little or nothing to the purpose if he had 2 Chron.
said, "God helpeth by many or few"—if he had not put in 14. 11.
too—"and sometimes by none." For there was "light" Gen. 1. 3.
before any sun or moon, though after it pleased God to Gen. 1. 14.
ordain them as instruments. And so the earth was fertile,
when as then no "rain" had fallen on the earth, nor any Gen. 2. 5.
such ordinary means. Let Moses be on the mount and but
hear God, and he needeth no bread.

The fourth is, that He can bring His purpose to pass even
by those means whose natures tend to contrary effects, as
to preserve by stones. Coloquintida, being rank poison, in 2 Kings 4.
eating whereof is present death, was by the Prophet made 40.
matter of nourishment. So Christ, by those things which
were fit to put out a seeing man's eyes, as dust, made a Joh. 9. 6.
blind man recover his sight. And so doth He make "light 2 Cor. 4. 6.
to shine out of darkness," one contrary out of another.
Thus we see the devil answered. Now let us apply these
things to ourselves.

Christ's answer doth import two words, and so two mouths,
and two breaths or spirits; and these two be as two twins.
He that will be maintained by the one, must seek after the
other. The first word is the same decree whereby the course
of nature is established, according to Psalm the one hundred
and forty-seventh, and fifteenth verse: "He sendeth forth
His commandment upon the earth, and His word runneth
very swiftly; He giveth snow like wool," &c.

Secondly, the other is that whereof James speaketh, to Jas. 1. 18.
wit, "the word of truth," wherewith "of His own will He

SERM.
III.

Ps. 33. 9.

Jer. 15. 19.

Ps. 104. 29.

Gen. 22. 2.

[Gen. 22.
7, 8.]

[Gen. 22.
14. marg.]

Ex. 14. 21.
[Ps. 78.
24, 25.]

Deu. 8. 4.

[Ps. 78.
20.]

Ps. 34. 9.

begat us." The one proceedeth from the mouth of God's
providence, creating and governing all things, "He but
speaking the word, and it was done;" the other proceedeth
out of the mouth of God's Prophets, who are as it were
His mouth, "Thou standest before Me, as if thou wert My
mouth."

From the first word all things have their beginning and
being; as when He sent forth His spirit or breath they were
created and had their beginning, so He teacheth us that so
soon as "God hides His face, they are troubled. And if He
takes away their breath, they die and return to dust."

The other Spirit, that is, the sanctifying Spirit, ministereth unto us supernatural life. Now therefore to set them
together, every man is thus to think with himself: If I get
my living contrary to God's word, that is, by any unlawful
means, surely God's other word will not accompany such
gotten goods. That is, these two words be twins: if we get
not our goods by the one word, we shall want the blessing
of the other word, and then we were as good eat stones; it
will be but gravel in our mouths or quails. We are then to
use the means according to the second word.

Abraham, we see, went forth to sacrifice according to
God's appointment, the word was his direction; therefore
when Isaac asked, Where was the sacrifice? he might boldly
answer, God would "provide" one; as we see even at the
very pinch He did. Whereupon it came to be a proverb,
that even *In monte Jehova providebit.*

The Israelites went out of Egypt by the warrant and
appointment of God's word. How then? First, they had
a way made them, where never was any before, through
the Red Sea; they had bread downwards out of the clouds,
whereas it useth to rise upwards out of the earth; their garments in "forty years" never "waxed old;" they had water
whence water useth not to come; by striking the rocks "the
water gushed forth." So that it is true which the Prophet
David saith, "There is no want to them that fear God."

Though God peradventure will not use the same means
He did for the Israelites, yet the children of God walking
after His will shall have some way of relief always. And
therefore Christ would not distrust the providence of God,

for He knew He was in the work and way of God. For we read that He was "led into the wilderness by the Spirit," and therefore could not lack; as indeed He did not, for the "Angels came and ministered unto Him," as it followeth in the eleventh verse of this chapter. So either the crows shall minister to our wants as they did to Elias; or our enemies, as the Egyptians did to the Israelites; or else the Angels themselves, as they did here.

But to grow to a conclusion. "Let us seek the Kingdom [Mat. 6. of God, and all other things shall be ministered unto us." [33.] And in all like temptations we may learn a good answer out of Daniel, the third chapter and seventeenth verse: "That God That we serve is able to relieve and deliver us, even from the burning fire." But, if it should not be His will so to do, yet we will not use unlawful means, or fall to idolatry, or turn stones into bread.

In this answer, again, Christ would teach us here to be resolute, howsoever God's blessing doth not concur with our gettings, as it doth not when we get them by indirect means, contrary to God's word. To goods so gotten, God will add sorrow; for "the blessing of the Lord maketh rich, Prov. 10. and He doth add no sorrow with it." When God gives [22.] riches, He gives quietness withal; but if God give them not, we were as good be without them, whether they be gotten by oppression or "violence," or by fraud and "deceit;" for Prov. 4. 17. these two be the quicksilver and brimstone of the devil's [Prov. 20. 17.] alchemistry. God will add sorrow to them, for though they be "pleasant at the first," and money gotten by stinking Prov. 20. means smells like other money, as an emperor said, and [17. Juv. Sat. 14. 204.] bread so gotten tastes like other bread, yet in the end a plain conclusion and experiment will make it manifest that it was made of stones, and had sorrow mingled or added to it. And therefore it shall be either an occasion or matter of the disease called the stone; or it shall "turn his meat in Job 20. 14. his bowels, and fill him with the gall of asps;" or as Asa's oppression by delicacy became an occasion of the dropsy or [2 Chron. gout; or else shall "the extortioner catch all that he hath, 16. 12.] Ps. 109. 11. and the stranger spoil him;" or "spend them upon phy- Mark 5. 26. sicians" or on lawyers; or else, though God suffer them to enjoy them quietly all their lifetime, and even to die by their flesh-pots, yet on their deathbed they shall find such a grudging and torment in their conscience, that they will wish that they had starved for hunger before they had begun to use any such means. Or if God in His judgment, for their greater torment, suffer them to die in their beds, without any remorse of conscience, like blocks, or like an ox dying in a ditch, at the last day they shall feel a gnashing in their teeth, and then they will know it was made of stones.

SEVEN SERMONS

TEMPTATION OF CHRIST IN THE WILDERNESS.

SERMON IV.

MATTHEW iv. 5, 6.

Then the devil took Him up into the holy city, and set Him
on a pinnacle of the Temple,
And said unto Him, If Thou be the Son of God, cast Thy-
self down; for it is written, that He will give His Angels
charge over Thee, and with their hands they shall lift Thee
up, lest at any time Thou shouldst dash Thy foot against a
stone.

[*Tunc assumpsit Eum diabolus in sanctam civitatem, et statuit Eum*
super pinnaculum Templi,
Et dixit Ei, Si Filius Dei es, mitte Te deorsum. Scriptum est enim,
Quia Angelis Suis mandavit de Te, et in manibus tollent Te, ne forte
offendas ad lapidem pedem Tuum. Lat. Vulg.]

[*Then the devil taketh Him up into the holy city, and setteth Him on a*
pinnacle of the Temple,
And saith unto Him, If Thou be the Son of God, cast Thyself down;
for it is written, He shall give His Angels charge concerning Thee,
and in their hands they shall bear Thee up, lest at any time Thou
dash Thy foot against a stone. Eng. Trans.]

THE manner is, after one hath taken a foil, his courage
will fail. The Angel would have been gone, when he saw
he could not prevail over Jacob. But it is not so here Gen. 32. 26.
with the devil; for when he saw that his first temptation

SERM.
IV.

Job 2. 5.

[1 Sam. 17.
37, 50.]

Ex. 17. 7.

Deu. 6. 16.

Ps. 78. 20.

would not prevail, he trieth another. And even so he played with Job; for when he could do no good upon his first patent, by taking away all he had, he comes and sues for a new commission, that he might "touch his flesh and bones;" and thereby he giveth us to learn that it is not one foil that can make him give over.

He is one of those, whom a Father saith to have courage above their strength; and of that nature be many in our days, whose daring is above their skill, and have courage to undertake much more than their ability is to perform. Not like David, who did as much as he undertook in killing Goliath; nor like him of whom Esay speaketh in the seventh verse of his third chapter, that when they would have made him prince he had "no bread nor clothing," and therefore refused; but they will take it upon them, though they have not wherewithal, and thereby become authors of trouble, wanting ability to go through withal. But as Augustine saith, Is it not all one not to be able to answer, nor to be able to hold their peace? We see here the devil is a great undertaker.

Secondly, he is not only content to take a foil, but even out of the same thing wherewith he was foiled maketh he matter of a new temptation, a new ball of fire. Out of Christ's conquest he makes a new assault; that is, since He will needs trust, he will set Him on trusting, He shall trust as much as He will. As the former tempted him to diffidence, so this shall tempt Him to prefidence. As before the devil brought Him to the waters of Meribah, where the children of Israel did murmur and tempt God, so now he brings Him to the temptation of Massah, that is, to presumption, wantonness, and delicacy; for then with bread they were not content, but they must have "flesh" and other dainties. As the first might be called the hungry temptation, so this may be called the wanton temptation. That which was in the Old Testament the temptation of Meribah, is here in the New Testament the temptation of the wilderness; and that which was there the temptation of Massah, is here the temptation of the pinnacle.

In the first, by want of things necessary, he thought to drive them to vexation and bitterness of spirit, and to distrust

God's power and goodness. In the second, by unnecessary matters, he draweth us on to wantonness, and to put God to try what He can do, and to set Him about base services. By the one he driveth us unto unlawful means, by the other he draweth us from the use of things lawful. By the one he brings us to this conceit, that we are so abjected of God that if we trust in Him He will in the end fail us; by the other to think we are so dear in God's eyes, and such darlings, as throw ourselves into any danger and He will not forsake us. By the one he puts us in fear, as Augustine saith, *Deum defuturum etiam si promisit;* by the other in hope, *Deum adfuturum ubi non promisit.* By the one he slandereth God unto us, as if He were a God of straw, of base condition, and subject to our beck; by the other as if He were a God of iron, that would not incline, though we requested Him.

Now to the temptation, wherein we are to consider three things: first, the ground the devil chose for the working of this temptation; secondly, the temptation itself, to wit, the devil's speech; thirdly, Christ's answer to it.

In the place, three things are to be noted. first, the place itself; secondly, the devil chose it; thirdly, that our Saviour followed him thither.

For a new temptation he makes choice of a new place. Indeed, for a temptation to presumption, the wilderness was not a fit place: first, it was not high enough, and then it was not populous enough. It was a melancholy place: when a man is under the cross in affliction, or in some anguish and sorrow for want, death of friends, or otherwise, and generally for all solitary men, the hungry temptation is fitter than this of presumption. As long as Noah was in the ark in the midst of the waters, he had in him no presumptuous thought, but sitting under the vine in his vineyard he was overcome therewith. And "just Lot," in Sodom, had no fit time or 2 Pet. 2. 7. place to be presumptuous; but when he dwelt in the mountain in security, then he committed incest with his daughters, being made drunk by them. David, so long as he was persecuted by Saul, and tossed up and down from post to pillar, had no leisure to be presumptuous; but in the top of his 2 Sam.11.2. turret, when he was at rest in his palace, presumption gave him a blow. So here the wilderness was no fit place, but the

M m

SERM.
IV.
—————

pinnacle is a very fit place for one to be presumptuous on. It is as good as a stage to shew himself upon, to see and to be seen.

In the wilderness there was small warrant for one that would be presumptuous; but from the pinnacle he might discern far and near, both the inner court and outward court, and see a whole cloud of witnesses, and have some warrant of example of all estates, high or low, wise or noble. For what abuse soever be in him, be he never so presumptuous, he shall see some as proud, stout, and as high-minded as himself; be his hair never so long, or his ruffs never so great, he shall find some as far gone therein as himself.

If we mark the four gradations that it hath, we shall find it to be a very fit place. As first, before he could come to the pinnacle, He must go out of the wilderness into the city; secondly, not any city, but the holy city; thirdly, into the temple of the city; and fourthly, out of the temple up to the pinnacle.

First, having got Him to leave the wilderness, he brought Him into the city, that there he might say unto Him, You see such and such grave men, how they behave themselves; why should You seek to be holier than they? This was a good civil temptation : he brought Him not to Cæsarea or Samaria, but even to Jerusalem, "the holy city;" for that addition is given it, Matthew the fourth chapter and fifth verse, and Daniel the ninth chapter and twenty-fourth verse. Thirdly, he brought Him into the temple, where even the very ground was holy. Fourthly, not to any other place of it, but the very top and pinnacle, which was over the *sanctum sanctorum*.

Who would not tread hard there, and take upon him, being in such a place? where if a man will be carried away with example, he may see Ananias the high-priest renting his clothes at the hearing of things that sounded like blasphemy, and yet buying his bishopric for money. Who will not then be bold to do the like? And Herod a prince, such a one as heard John Baptist preach, yea and with much delight, to commit adultery. Who would fear to do the like? There he may see the Pharisee, under show of great holiness, "tithe mint and cummin," and under colour of long prayers

Mark 14. 63.

Mark 6. 20.

Mat. 23. 14. 23.

"devour widows' houses;" bringing in by extortion, and sending out by excess.

And so in this city one may see some men, both great frequenters of sermons, and yet great usurers, gentlewomen misshapen in their attire. Seeing this, who will not be as bold as they, the place being so holy? And being thus warranted by example, surely we must needs commend the devil's wit for his choice.

Out of this arise two notes. First, against some fantastical spirits who say, Can that be a holy city where there be "dumb dogs?" There were so in Jerusalem. Where the "leaders be blind?" They were so where Judas ministered the Sacrament. Where there is division and debate amongst themselves? Can this, they say, be the holy city? And thereupon they forsake the fellowship. Whereas they, notwithstanding the former abuses, and notwithstanding the eleven tribes were apostates, did yet name it "the holy city." *[Isa. 56. 10. Mat. 15. 14.]* *[Phil. 4. 2.]* *[Heb. 10. 25.]*

Secondly, on the other side we are to be instructed, that though a man be on the battlements of the Church yet hath he no sure footing, or cause to be secure, but rather to fear the more; for even there doth the devil stand at his elbow, watching his overthrow. There is no place we see privileged from temptations, no desert so solitary but the devil will seek it out; no pinnacle so high but the devil is a bishop over it, to visit and overlook it.

To conclude, though in Jerusalem sits the "abomination of desolation" whereof Daniel spake, yet it is "the holy city" still. And though the place be never so holy, yet is that no cause of privilege, but even there may sit "the abomination of desolation." Both are proved out of Matthew, the twenty-fourth chapter and fifteenth verse. *[Dan. 12. 11.]*

The second thing that we observed in the circumstance of place is, that the devil assumpted Christ; which, to those that are weak (as Gregory also collecteth) may be offensive, in giving them to think that the devil had such power over Christ as to carry Him whither he listed. But when they shall consider that even the limbs of the devil haled and harrowed him to and fro; from Annas to Caiaphas, from Caiaphas to Pilate, from Pilate to Herod, and from him back again to Pilate; and how spitefully and contemptuously He *[In Evan. Lib. 1. Hom. 16. init.]*

SERM.
IV.
[1] [S. Greg.
ubi sup.]

Lu. 22. 53.

Phil. 2. 8.

Mat. 3. 15.

Lu. 9. 51.

1 Tim. 3.
16.

Ps. 69. 22.

1 Cor. 8. 1.

was used in all these places, and at last carried to execution; what marvel will it be to see Him, as Augustine[1] speaketh, *in montem duci a capite, Qui a membris traditur, &c.* These things do indeed, as all other His sufferings, set forth the greatness of the love of God towards us. Of God the Father, that He would give His only Son, yea appoint Him this work of our salvation, and give the devil such a "power" over Him; of God the Son, that He would be content to suffer such indignity, as to be "obedient to the death of the cross."

The reason of all these His sufferings, as also that He would be baptized of John a weak and sinful man was, as Himself declareth it, to "fulfil all righteousness." So here He was to suffer it, else God's righteousness would not have been fulfilled, nor the work of our salvation. And as He suffered this assumption, so afterwards His second assumption was to go to Jerusalem to suffer; and so at the last He came to His third and last assumption, to be "received up into glory." And by the very same steps and degrees must we be assumpted. And this is His assumption of suffering, which brought Him to glorifying.

The third thing is, that our Saviour followed; whereby we are to mark not so much His courage that durst encounter with the devil in any place wheresoever he list to carry Him, and that He was not only the God of the valleys, but a God of the mountains also, contrary to their surmise, the first book of Kings, the twentieth chapter and twenty-third verse. That, I say, is not so much to be marked, as that our Saviour would at all stand upon a pinnacle.

There be some that would make us believe, it is a sin to stand upon a pinnacle; but then, if that had been so, Christ would never have stood there. And since Christ stood there, it is no more sin for any man else to stand there, than it is to stand in the wilderness; for it is lawful for us to follow His footsteps, and to tread wheresoever He hath trod before us: yet such places be not privileged. For, as it is true that many men's "table" and wealth is their "snare," even so the good gifts and graces of God be turned to a man's hurt; as "knowledge" may serve for a quill to "puff him up" and make him swell. Nay, even that godly sorrow which is so much to be wished for, hath in it matter of temptation, lest men " be swallowed up with too much heaviness." 2 Cor. 2. 7.

The Scriptures themselves, we see, are subject to the abuse of the devil; whereby it should follow that they are to be refused, if every thing be to be refused which brings matter of temptation. But as Augustine saith, *Non est laus stetisse in pinnaculo, sed stetisse et non cecidisse :* in every place to answer the devil is praiseworthy. Indeed it is dangerous for Isa. 51. 22. one that hath a light and giddy brain, for such as are " drunk, though not with wine," to stand so high. Job could stand Job 31. 37. there without falling, for he had a more settled brain. Such places are for the wisest and sagest men. St. Paul stood not there, but yet he could have stood there, for he had the trick or skill of it, as himself confesseth : " I can be abased, and I Phil. 4. 12. can abound," &c.

Now come we to the temptation itself, which hath three general heads : first, the ball of wildfire which is to consume His faith ; secondly, the dart, " Cast Thyself down," which is to pierce the soul ; thirdly, he tempereth the head of his dart with some stronger metal, which is, *Scriptum est.*

I. First, *Si Filius Dei es.* This is a great mote in the devil's eye, he useth the same term in the former temptation, and here he is up with it again. And all is to this end, that by often bringing it into question whether He be the Son of God, he may at last make it out of question or doubt that we are not the sons of God ; that by and from *Si sis* he may bring it to *Ne sis,* and so we may be like himself. For to this end is all his " compassing of sea and land, to Mat. 23. 15. make one proselyte" like himself, according to the endeavour of the Pharisees, who did in like sort ; and when he is made, " ye make him twofold more the child of hell than yourselves." As on the other side, Christ would have us the sons of God like Him. But see what a dexterity the devil hath in making things serve for his purpose ; he maketh one self-same thing serve for two several, yea contrary purposes. What a goodly grace he hath in the first temptation ! He useth it there, to procure us to desperation ; he maketh it here, to serve for presumption.

But indeed there be two manner of *Si es,* or *Ifs :* the one is a questioning or doubting *Si,* as, If Thou be the Son of Mark 8. 11.

SERM.
IV.
Mat. 8. 2.
Phil. 3. 11.

God, shew us a sign, "Lord, if Thou wilt, Thou canst make me whole;" the other is a plain affirmation, as, "If by any means I might attain to the resurrection of the dead," where we are sure he made no doubt thereof. So here the devil saith, "If Thou be the Son of God," as I now grant indeed; I was in some doubt, but now I confess Thou art; I am of the voice's mind, that pronounced Thee so at Thy Baptism.

The devil, in the former temptation, came out like a malecontent or a murmurer; here he comes like a flattering parasite, he will *pinguare caput Ejus oleo*, 'make His head even swim in the oil of ostentation.' But though it be not the same temptation, yet it is the same devil in both places. For both by the one and the other he seeketh the downfall and destruction of man; and though his two *Ifs* be contrary in themselves, yet are they both also contrary to the will and word of God: for He would not in any case we should distrust Him, neither would He that at any time we should cast ourselves down. And therefore hath He caused battlements to be made on every house-top, that none might be slain with falling down. Now he would have Him shew Himself thereby to be the Son of God, for He is now in the sight of all Jerusalem.

Deu. 22. 8.

It is said that Christ comes now to put to a spark of fire, that is, of faith; and that His will was, it might burn and be maintained. The devil, on the other side, labours by all means possible to quench and put it out; and seeing water would not do it in the former temptation, he goeth now about to see if he can make the very oil itself to put it out, even that very thing whereby it was to be maintained: as indeed it will, if we pour out too great a quantity. Or, if he cannot quench it either with water or oil, he will see if he can blow it up with gunpowder. As, seeing the water of distrust will not extinguish His faith, but that He would trust in God, he endeavoureth now by Scriptures (that magnify the providence of God, and the confidence we are to put in Him) to set Him as far gone in the other extreme, by presuming or trusting too much, that so the fire which before he would have quenched may now so flame out as not to keep itself within the chimney, but to set the whole house on fire. This is the ball of wildfire of this second temptation; and so both, we see, tend to the consuming and nullifying of our faith.

II. The dart itself is, " Cast Thyself down :" which consisteth of two points. First, the casting down; secondly, that He Himself was to cast down Himself.

For the first, it is general, the neglect of ordinary means, as here. Whereas the ordinary way was down the stairs, he would have Him leap or throw Himself over the battlements. And here a man may see to what end the devil's exalting cometh; he brings a man up by little and little to some high place, that so he may send him at once with his head downward. All the preferments that he bestoweth on a man is not to any other intent but that he may do as the devil himself did, (who being on high did cast himself down) and so be like him; that is, "from beneath," not from above; who Joh. 8. 23. fell "from heaven like lightning." So that howsoever in Lu. 10. 18. outward show he may seem to befriend us, yet this is his inward intention and scope. As the Edomites in time of the prosperity of the Israelites pretended great good will to them, but in the day of their calamity they were they that cried, " Down with them, down with them." Ps. 137. 7.

God's manner is, when He meaneth to exalt a man, He Mat. 23. 12. will first humble him, and make him low. The devil's manner is, we see, clean contrary; to lift them up to " the clouds," Isa. 14. 14. that he may bring them down to the grave, yea to " the Ps. 86. 13. lowest grave." He carrieth them the higher, to throw them down with the greater violence. He lifteth up Adam with a conceit to be like God, to the very top of perfection, to the intent he might be " like the beast that perisheth." Ps. 49. 20.

The second hath some matter of comfort : the devil is here a suitor to Him, to do it Himself. Why doth not the devil cast Him down ? First, it was not in his power; or, if it had, yet would not that have served his turn : then there had been no sin of presumption in it. There must be two persons that must concur in our downfall : well may the devil induce, and move us to it; but unless we ourselves be consenting, and cast ourselves down, there can be no downfall to hurt us. For as Chrysostom saith, *Nemo læditur nisi a seipso ;* so, *Nullum præcipitium nisi voluntarium.* The devil did not cram Eve with the forbidden fruit; but when " she Gen. 3. 6.

SERM. saw it, she took it, and ate it." So the devil, when he enter-
IV. eth into the soul of a man (which he counteth his palace)
he doth not break open the door, no nor so much as draw
Lu. 11. 25. the latch; but "when he cometh, he findeth it swept
and garnished," and so goeth in. There must therefore
be a reaching out of the hand, and an opening of the door
by ourselves, and so a casting down of thyself, or else
Ps. 118. 13. though the devil thrust sore at thee that thou mayest fall,
the Lord will help thee. In Deuteronomy the twenty-se-
cond chapter and eighth verse, God hath caused battlements to be made on every house-top, by which we may
Job 1. 10. stay ourselves. The devil tells God that He had made "a
hedge" about Job, so that unless Job step over it or break
it down, he is safe.

III. The devil's dart is, "Cast Thee down;" but he bestoweth some great cost on this. With the self-same armour
that Christ bare off the other dart, doth the devil sharpen
and harden this: he doth not so in any other of the temptations, therefore we are to look for some great matter; he
bringeth Scripture, that he may be the better credited. He
speaks not now after the manner of men, so that it is not he
1 Cor. 9. 8. now that speaketh but Scripture, as Paul reasoneth there.
You see, saith he, I counsel You to nothing but that the
Psalms will bear you out in.

The devil knew well by his own fall how dangerous the
sin of presumption is, it cost him dearly; and so did it
David likewise, and therefore of all other he prayeth God to
Ps. 19. 13. keep him "from presumptuous sins." He knew also what
Rom. 2. 4. it was to abuse "the goodness, patience, and long-suffering
of God." Therefore he avoucheth it by Scripture; he tells
Him it will be long to go down the stairs, and teacheth Him
a nearer way, but to jump or to cast Himself down, and to
fear no hurt, for the Angels have charge of Him.

And even so he persuadeth men now-a-days; that they
need not go down fair and softly, in fear and trembling, but
to defer all till their dying hour, and then commend themselves to God, and throw themselves upon God's mercy, and
that fiery chariot that took up Elias shall come and fetch up
them; or else, an Angel shall carry them up, let them be
sure they shall have no harm, for they be God's darlings, and

God doth so dote on them, that He will not suffer them in
any case to receive the least hurt that may be.

If ever the devil came in his likeness, it was here. In the
first of Samuel, chapter the twenty-eighth, and fifteenth
verse, he came but in the guise of a Prophet; so that instead of saying, "Is Saul among the Prophets?" it might [1 Sam.
have been said, What is the devil among the Prophets? But 10. 11.]
here he hath used himself so cunningly, that if ever he was
"transformed into an Angel," here it is verified. For he 2 Cor. 11.
cometh here like a white devil[1], or like a divine; he comes 14.
with a Psalter in his hand, and turns to the place, and shews 1 [See Lu-
our Saviour the ninety-first Psalm, the eleventh and twelfth ther on
Gal. 1. 4,
6.]
verses. Wherein first we are to note that the devil readeth
Psalms as well as we, and hath the words of Scripture in his
mouth. And, the first of Samuel, the twenty-eighth chapter, [1 Sam. 28.
he counterfeited Samuel so right, and used the very words 15, &c.]
that he had used, that they could not know him from Samuel.
So here he counterfeited the voice of David.

This will make us shake off security, considering that God Acts 19. 15.
doth, for our trial, sometime deliver the adversary the key
of the armoury, whereby he is able to hold argument with Jude ver. 9.
an Archangel, yea with Christ Himself, as we see here. How
careful therefore had we need to be, to find out a fit answer
for him! For only to assault us, doth he read the Scriptures; yea, but not to any good end, but even thereby to
deceive the simplicity of men; as here, to make them put
their souls in adventure to the last hour.

He hath indeed a grace with some vain youths of the
court, and ungodly atheists, to set them a scoffing at the
Scripture, as Esay the twenty-eighth chapter, and twenty-
second verse. But with others that have the Scriptures in
more high reverence, he goeth another way to work, making
it to them the savour of death. Rom. 7. 10.

The words which he useth in the name of Samuel, he
useth to make Saul despair; and here he useth David's
words to cause presumption, and to make them our bane.
And not every Scripture; but if there be any Scripture more
full of heavenly comfort than another, that of all other will
the devil abuse; as indeed the Psalms are; and of all the
Psalms, this ninety-first especially; and in that part, if any

SERM. IV. one sentence be sweeter than another, that of all other will the devil abuse.

Mark the eleventh verse here cited : " He shall give His Angels charge over Thee, to keep Thee in all Thy ways." These last words the devil leaves out, because they make not for his purpose. " They shall bear Thee in their hands, that Thou dash not Thy foot against a stone." And we shall see nothing can be spoken more comfortable ; as first, in that it is said, that " the Angels have charge over us in all our ways." " Behold, I send My Angel before thee, to guide thee in the way ;" and to comfort, and confirm us (as when Jacob was in fear of his brother Esau, the Angels " met him") and to defend us in all dangers, and succour us in all necessities, spreading their wings over us, and pitching their tents about us.

Ex. 23. 20.

Gen. 32. 1.

Ps. 34. 7.

Secondly, this charge not only concerneth our head and principal members, but also our feet ; yea, God's providence reacheth even to " the hairs of our head," for they " are numbered."

Mat. 10. 30.

Thirdly, this charge of theirs is not only to admonish us when danger cometh, but they are actually to help us, as it were putting their hands between the ground and us. They shall take the rubs and offences out of the way.

Fourthly, this do they not of courtesy, as being creatures given by nature to love mankind ; but by special mandate and charge they are bound to it, and have a *Præcipe* for it, yea, the very beasts and stones shall be in league with us.

This Psalm, and these verses, containing such comfort, hath the devil culled to persuade men, that being such sweet children of God they may venture whither and upon what they will ; for the Angels attend them at an inch. He bids them put the matter in adventure, and then but whistle for an Angel, and they will come at first. He carrieth them up to the top of the pinnacle, and shews them their own case in Annas and Herod, and tells them God will require no more of them than He did at their hands ; and all the way as they go up, he singeth them a Psalm of the mercies of God ; he carrieth them up with a song, that " God's mercy is above all His works." And with Psalm the one hundred and third, and eighth verse, " How gracious and long-suffering God is,

Ps. 145. 9.

[Ps. 103. 8, 10.]

Who rewardeth us not according to our deserts;" and Psalm the one hundred and thirty-sixth, " That His mercy endureth [Ps. 136. for ever." God therefore, being so full of mercy, will take all ^{passim.]} things in good part. But this mercy the devil tells them of, differeth from the mercy David meant. For the mercy David speaketh of, is coupled with judgment. " I will sing mercy Ps. 101. 1. and judgment to Thee, O Lord ;" and, " Mercy and truth Ps. 85. 10. are met together, justice and peace have kissed each other." Thus, I say, they shall have music all the way, and if any at the height think it a great way down, No, saith the devil, you need but a jump from your baptism into heaven, you shall need no stairs at all.

SEVEN SERMONS

TEMPTATION OF CHRIST IN THE WILDERNESS.

SERMON V.

MATTHEW iv. 7.

Jesus said unto him, It is written again, Thou shalt not tempt the Lord thy God.

[*Ait illi Jesus, Rursum scriptum est, Non tentabis Dominum Deum tuum.* Lat. Vulg.]

[*Jesus said unto him, It is written again, Thou shalt not tempt the Lord thy God.* Eng. Trans.]

SERM.
V.

Jas. 4. 5.
Joh. 10. 35.
Eph. 6. 17.

Neh. 6. 10,
12.

Heb. 4. 2.

CONSIDERING that St. James saith, "The Scripture speaketh nothing in vain," and that as our Saviour Christ saith, "No scripture can be disappointed," it may seem strange that the devil coming armed with "the sword of the Spirit" —for so is the word of God termed—Christ gives not place, but opposeth Himself to answer. We see that a message coming in the name of the Lord, this very name abashed Nehemias at the first hearing, till he perceived it was contrary to the law of God, and so came not from Him. Which here we see to be the cause, why Christ doth not yield by and by upon the hearing of the word, but sets Himself to make answer; forsomuch as the word is not of force *quia dicitur* only, but *quia creditur*, as Augustine noteth. If there be not the mixture of "faith" with it, whereof Paul speaketh, it is nothing worth. And therefore the bad spirit was nothing abashed or daunted at the hearing of the bare names of Jesus and Paul, but answered, "I know them, Acts 19. 15. but who are ye?" They did not believe, and therefore could do them no good, but were wounded themselves; glorious names would not serve the turn. So was it here used without faith.

When the Scripture is here urged against one, a man would think it were not to be answered by citing another place of Scripture, but by some "tradition of the elders," or Mark 7. 3. some gloss or other shift: but we see our Saviour answereth here, no way but by Scripture.

Because the wolf comes sometimes disguised in a sheep's skin, it is no reason that therefore the very sheep should lay away their fleeces. So here, because the devil useth the word as "the slaying letter," or as the sword to kill men 2 Cor. 3. 6. with, it is no reason why Christ may not therefore use it in His own defence. Why then, will some say, one of these two inconveniences will follow, that hereby we shall think the Scripture is of the devil's side, as well as of Christ's side, and so divided; as in like sort they make a division of 1 Cor. 1. Christ, when one holds with Paul, another with Apollos. 13. No, it is not so, Christ allegeth not this Scripture in that sort, as one nail to drive out another; but by way of harmony and exposition, that the one may make plain the meaning of the other. For, albeit the devil sheweth himself to be the devil in citing that text so as might best serve for his purpose, in that whereas the Psalm whereout he taketh it hath it thus, "That He might keep Him in all His ways;" which words he leaveth out. For if he had cited that, he could not thereby have enforced any casting down. For the Angels have no charge over a man, but in his ways; and from the top of the pinnacle there was no way, but down the stairs on his feet. He was not, relying on the Angels, to cast himself down with his head forward. But the devil hath a wrest to make the string sound high or low as he list; or if that will not serve, he hath a rack to stretch them out, as some did St. Paul's 2 Pet. 3. Epistles. He can set them on the tenters, to prove that 16. down the stairs or over the battlements all is one, the Angels shall safeguard him.

Though this, I say, be the devil's corruption, which the

SERM.
V.

late writers have well spied, yet Christ we see is not willing to take advantage of that, but useth a wiser course (for so are we to think that He went the best way to work) that is, the conference of Scripture with Scripture, which Christ here practiseth, and commendeth unto us.

In every art all propositions are not of a like certainty, but some be grounds and principles so certain as that no exception is to be taken against them. From them are others derived by a consequence called deduction, not so certain as the other : from these again others, to the twentieth hand. So is it in divinity. Christ here reduceth the devil's argument and place to a place most plain to be confessed. For the Jews, valuing of the means, had to consider that God "fed them with manna which they knew not," to

Deu. 8. 3.

teach them that "Man liveth not by bread only," contemning the same; and in Deuteronomy the sixth chapter and sixteenth verse bade them, "they should not tempt the Lord their God, as in Massah," when they cried for bread.

Jer. 17. 5.

The Lord curseth him that "maketh flesh his arm, and

Habak. 1. 16.

withdraweth his heart from God." They "sacrificed unto their yarn, because their portion was plentiful." Job con-

Job 31. 24.

demneth the making "gold our hope," or "the wedge of gold our confidence." As then we must not deify the means, attributing all-sufficiency to them, so we may not nullify them and think too basely of them, but use them that we tempt not God according to His word.

Out of these two grounds may every question be resolved, for every proposition must be proved out of the ground. So that, as we may not think the arm of God to be so shortened that He cannot help without means, so are we not to think basely of God for ordaining means.

Secondly, we heard that the devil's allegation was taken out of the Psalm, and one of the most comfortable places of all the Psalm. Christ, by not standing in disputation about the words and meaning of the text, commendeth to us the safest and wisest way to make answer in such like cases. Our Saviour would warn us, that the ninety-first Psalm is not fit matter for us to study on when we are on the top of the pinnacle; He therefore chooseth a place of a contrary kind, to counterpoise Himself standing in that fickle place.

The Law, we know, is a great cooler to presumption. If one tamper much with the Psalms, being in case of confidence, he may make the fire too big. Faith is the fire which Christ came to put on the earth, and it is seated between two extremes, distrust, and presumption. Distrust is as water to it, which if it be poured on in abundance, it will make it to be smoking flax, or utterly quench it. Presumption, on the other side, is as gunpowder to it, which being thrown into it it will blow it up, and make it fly all about the house. Christ was to take heed of overheating his faith. Luther upon the Galatians saith, The ninety-first Psalm is no meet study for many men's humours in our days; they had more need of a corrosive, to eat out the sore from the root and bottom.

Now to the answer, which consisteth of six points. First, what it is to tempt God; secondly, wherein; thirdly, the manner how; fourthly, this proposition, "Thou shalt not tempt;" fifthly, the reason why we may not; sixthly, though He be our God, and we on the pinnacle, these be no arguments for us to presume.

I. First, whosoever will not use such ordinary means as God hath appointed, tempteth God if he use extraordinary, as here the devil would have Christ do: when nobody went about to thrust Him down, wilfully to have cast Himself down were great madness. Or, when a man hath a fair pair of stairs to go down by, to call for "a cherub" to carry him, Ps. 18. 10. or for "the wind" to fly down, were as great wantonness.

There is an humour in man that we are all given unto by nature, to be marvellously desirous to try conclusions in matters that are rare and unknown unto them; contemning things common, and to be fond after strange novelties. It was told them as plain as could be, that they should not reserve of the manna till morning, and they needed not to have reserved it, they had fresh every day; and yet forsooth they would needs keep it, if it were but for an experiment sake, to try whether it would stink or no. And Ex. 16. 20, though they were forbidden to gather on the Sabbath day, 27. and on the even had enough for two days, and it was told them they should find none, yet they must needs try. When a thing cannot be had without great difficulty, it is our man-

SERM.
V.
———
2 Sam. 23.
15.

ner to have a vehement longing after it; as when David was in a hold, and the garrisons of the Philistines were in Bethlehem, then being thirsty no water would serve his turn but that in Bethlehem. But when three mighty men had broken into the host of the Philistines, and had brought him of it, he cared not for it.

II. For the second we are to know, that where need is— as the heathen speaketh—there a man may commit himself to the providence of God, and rely upon Him. For we have heard that where the means fail us, God hath yet in store His four prerogatives. Therefore when it comes to a dead lift, as we say, then to have a strong confidence in God is thankworthy; and it is the practice and property of faith to say boldly with Abraham when he saw nothing present,

Gen. 22. 14.
[marg.]

that even "on the hill God will provide." When our enemies are behind us and the Red Sea before us, then to look for a way through the sea, and to expect manna out of heaven, and water out of the rock, is much worth. So our Saviour, when He and His company were in the desert where no meat was to be had, fed them miraculously; but being near to the town where they might have it, He dis-

1 Kings
19. 5.

missed them. When Elias was in distress, and all meats failed him, then the Angel brought him meat. When Hagar

Gen. 21. 17.

and Ishmael were in the wilderness, and the water in the bottle spent, and she in great heaviness, then God comforted

Ex. 23. 20.

her from heaven. When the Israelites were in the desert,

Dan. 3. 25,
28.

then they had "an Angel" to lead them. When Shadrach, Meshach, and Abednego, were cast bound into the fiery furnace, then God sent them an Angel to be their deliverer. And so when Daniel was thrown into the lions' den—not

Dan. 6. 22.

when he put himself in—"God sent His Angel to stop the lions' mouth." When we are *deserti in deserto*, and all

[Job 1. 22;
2. 10.]
Heb. 13. 5.

means fail, it is time to trust in God, as Job did.

Our "conversation" therefore must be "without covetousness, and we must be content with those things that we

[Deut. 31.
6.]

have;" for He hath said, "He will not fail us, nor forsake us." This is out of the compass of tempting God, and this is as much as the Psalm could warrant Him to look for. Look upon it, and you shall see that it expresseth such dangers as could not be prevented by man's care and industry; as, "from the snare of the hunter," who useth to Ps. 91. 3, 5. lay it so as we cannot see it to avoid it. "Thou shalt not fear the arrow that flieth by day." An arrow, we know, will reach a man far off, before he be aware. And so, throughout the Psalm, they are things out of our defence, therefore they had need of Angels' help; but when we have means to help ourselves, God's omnipotency is for the time discharged. Eutychus, that fell out of a window by heaviness of sleep, Acts 20. 9. was restored to life by Paul. This then is Christ's answer. If there were no stairs and He must needs go down, it were a good Scripture to meditate on.

III. Thirdly, as it is a point of God's power to help without means, so hath He in His wisdom appointed means; there be degrees whereby we ascend to the effect, they are as a pair of stairs. Where these are we must use them, but when He offereth us a strange sign, it is scrupulous and foolish niceness to refuse it. As when God bade Ahaz "ask Isa. 7. 11. a sign," and he would not for tempting God, he was too precise, he was but a hypocrite. Moses asked a sign and had it, and God was well pleased with it. And so did Gideon also, to assure himself of delivering Israel by him.   Judg. 6. 36, &c.

In great, weighty, and extraordinary callings, it was allowable to request a sign: but when there is no need, or when there be otherwise sufficient, as Matthew the sixteenth chapter and first verse, where many miracles were daily done before their eyes, and where — though they had never so many more — yet they would not have believed on Him. Such were the Scribes and Pharisees, that for every trifling occasion must have "a sign from heaven." Thus to grate upon God's omnipotent providence, is saucy malapertness. For ordinary matters there be ordinary means to serve our turns; and for extraordinary there be extraordinary ways and means reserved, that we need not let fall our trust in matters corporal. We all confess there be means, as they which "will not work may not eat." In warfare there is 2 Thes. 3. no victory to be hoped for without fight, building of ram- 10. piers, and making of darts and shields: only in spiritual 2 Chron. matters we think to do well enough, though we never put 23. 9, 10. to our endeavour; we lay all upon God, and trouble not ourselves.

N n

SERM.
V.

Rom. 10.
14.

2 Pet. 1.5,6.

[Num. 23.
10.]

Prov. 7. 22.

[Eccl. 12.
1.]

There is but one degree or step in all Christianity, it is no more but out of the font to leap straight into heaven; from predestination we leap straight to glorification, it is no matter for mortification, there be no such mean degrees. But St. Paul tells us, it is so high that we had need of a ladder in which be many steps; insomuch as he puts a "How shall" to every step. "How shall they call on God on Whom they have not believed?" &c. There must be calling on God, believing on Him, hearing His word. There must be ordinary means, and there is a ladder of practice as well as of speculation or contemplation. "Join virtue with your faith, and with virtue knowledge, and with knowledge temperance; and so patience, godliness, brotherly kindness, and love. For if these things be in you, you shall not be idle and fruitless in the knowledge of Christ:" for he that hath not these things is blind, he goeth blindfold to the wood, and may chance hap beside heaven, or step besides the ladder. A great many say as Balaam did, "O let my soul die the death of the righteous;" but they care not for living the life of the righteous. He went but blindfold, he knew not the Angel that stood with a sword drawn in the way, but would have gone upon it if his ass had been so foolish. A great many think that presumption in being secure of their salvation is good divinity. Balaam thought he went well, when he went on the point of a naked sword. So one enticed by the flattery of a harlot thinks he goes to a place of great pleasure, but he goeth as one that "goeth to the slaughter, and as a fool to the stocks." Those whom it pleaseth God to have partakers of His Kingdom, He puts them in mind, "To remember their Creator in the days of their youth, before the evil days come." He giveth the grace of timely repentance, and suffereth them not to defer it till the last cast, and then to think that with the turning of a pin, as it were, they shall with a trice be in heaven, with Elias in a whirlwind. Augustine saith, 'We may in some cases advise men to have great hope that they shall be saved, but in no case give them warrant of security.' So in Ephesians, the fifth chapter, and fifth verse: "This we know, that no whoremonger, nor unclean person, hath any inheritance in the kingdom of heaven." "Let no

man deceive you through vain words: he that doth right- 1 Joh. 3. 7,
eousness is righteous, and he that doth unrighteousness, is [Eph. 5. 6.]
of the devil."

 Now therefore, to neglect the hearing of the word, or
when he cometh to hear it to clap down in his place without
desire or mind to bear it away, thereby to be bettered in his
life; and without purpose after by meditating on it to chew
it, and so to kindle a fire within himself whereby it may be
digested and turned into the substance of the mind; this is
to tempt God. So also, to bear a greater countenance, and
make more show of holiness than indeed is in one, is to
lay a greater "yoke" on himself than he need; as Acts,
the fifteenth chapter, and tenth verse, is a tempting of God.
Again, he that sinneth must look for evil to follow. He Ps. 91. 9, 10.
therefore that sinneth, and yet thinketh to escape punishment, tempteth God.

 They that by often experience have found that such and
such things have been to them occasions of sinning, and yet
will presume to use the same again, tempt God; and those
which "set up their idols in their heart, and put the stum- Ezek. 14. 3.
bling-block of iniquity before their face," and think not they
sin, such tempt God. He that comes to ask forgiveness of
God, and will not perform the condition of the Lord's Prayer,
that is, forgive others, tempts God. Generally, he that seeketh for good of God, and will not perform that which he is
to do; or doth evil, thinking to escape scot-free, without
endeavouring to avoid or resist it, both these tempt God·
And to these two may all other be referred.

 IV. The fourth is, we must not at all tempt God at no
hand; we must not think but God is able to bring water
even out of a rock, when there is nothing but rocks and Nu. 20. 11.
stones; but when we may hope to find it, we must dig for
it. So, when the soil will bear corn, we must till it. When
Elisha was in a little village, not able to defend him from
the Assyrians, he had "chariots and horses of fire" to de- 2 Kings 6.
fend him; but when he was in Samaria, a strong walled city, 17.
then when the king of Israel sent to fetch his head, he said
to those which were with him, "Shut the door." Christ in 2 Kings 6.
the wilderness miraculously fed many; in the city He sent 32.

SERM.
V.

"His disciples to buy meat," as John the fourth chapter and the eighth verse.

In the beginning, when the Gospel was published, there wanted sufficient men for the purpose; the Apostles had the power, as appeareth from Acts the eighth chapter and nineteenth verse, that on whomsoever they laid hands he received "the Holy Ghost," and was straight able and meet to preach the Gospel: but after, every man to his study, 1 Tim. 4. 15. "These things exercise," &c. We see that notwithstanding Paul was told by an Angel that there should be no loss of any man's life in the ship, yet he caused the mariners to Acts 27. 23, "cut the ropes," and to cast anchor; nay, when some would 24, 29—32. have gone out by boat, he would not let them. So here Christ answereth that howsoever Angels attend on Him He may not tempt God.

V. Now follow the reasons why we may not tempt God. There be two sorts of tempting; the one by ignorance, the other by unbelief. It is the manner of chirurgeons, when they are to dress a wound, and know not how far nor which way it goeth, to tent it. In the same manner is God, after the manner of men, said to tempt us; sometimes "to prove what is in our hearts, and whether we will keep His commandments," as He did the Israelites forty years. To this Deut. 8. 2, 3. end He both "made them hungry, and fed them with manna." We sometimes tempt God as if the arm of His power had received a wound, or His eye a hurt, as if He could not help or discern our wants as well[a] as before, be- Nu. 20. 10. cause He brings us not "water out of the rock." But such miracles now are not agreeing with His will, which must Rom. 9. 18. content us. "He will have mercy on whom He will have Rom. 2. 4. mercy." And we must not "despise the riches of His boun- teousness, and patience, and long-suffering, which leadeth to [Isa. 59. 1.] repentance." "The Lord's hand is not shortened that He cannot save, nor His ear heavy that it cannot hear;" be- Ps. 50. 21. cause He doth not reprove us, "we think Him like us." When God holds His peace, we think His tongue is cut; Mal. 4. 6. But I will not always hold My peace, saith God. But "how shall I know this," say men now-a-days? as Zacharias

a *now* added in A.

knew his wife was with child, who, when he would not be- _{Lu. 1. 18.} lieve the Angel that told him so but would needs have a sign, was stricken dumb. "Behold thou shalt be dumb till [Lu. 1. 20.] the day." Here is a sign for incredulity; he had been as good have believed without a sign.

The second kind of tempting proceedeth of over-much familiarity, when as we think we may be bold with God, and that He will take it in good part, and therefore we will put Him to it, as we say; we will try both Him and His Angels, what metal is in them and what they can do. We are to think upon the name of God as of a heavy and weighty thing, that is not upon every small occasion to be taken up and removed. We are not to account it as a feather that we may lightly toss up and down at our pleasure; and even so are we to esteem of the mercy of God. It is not to be advocated upon every vain trifle, for that were to use God as _{Ex. 7. 11.} we are wont to use our jugglers. Come on, let us see what you can do, shew us a miracle, say they. So Herod " de- [Lu. 9. 9.] sired to see" Christ, that he might see "some miracle" of Him, as in Luke the twenty-third chapter and eighth verse. It is a heavy case when men stand thus affected toward God, when afterwards in Luke the twenty-second chapter and sixty-fourth verse they blindfolded Him, and bade Him read who struck Him. We ourselves would not be so used, we could not endure to see our friends used so. How much less ought we to use God in that manner! especially that attribute, quality, or property of God, which of all others He would have to be most magnified, that is, His mercy!

He must needs take it very heinously to see that abused, since of all the rest He makes most account of it. Howsoever He could be content to "serve," yet would He not be a servant to our "sins" in any case, especially not to be _{Isa. 43. 24.} made a packhorse, if I may so say, for our sins to load on even till His back ache. He saith, that He "is pressed _{Amos 2. 13.} under us, as a cart is pressed that is under sheaves." Let us not make a dungcart of God's mercy, let us forbear Him that service of all other.

VI. The sixth is, that none of these *Dominum Deum tuum*, neither Lord nor God, nor that He is thine, are fit arguments to prove that we may presume upon Him. The devil

SERM.
V.
belike had perceived that there was some acquaintance between Christ and God, and peradventure had said unto Him,
You may be bold with Him and with His Angels. What?
He is Your Father, and as Cæsar's daughter answered, that
though he forget himself to be Cæsar, yet do not You forget
to be His Son. No, saith Christ, these be no good arguments to make one presume. As for *Dominus*, we will all
grant I am sure there is small matter of presumption in
that. In *Deus* there may be some more colour, but yet very
little. It is no good dealing with one that is mightier than
ourselves, lest he happen not to take it in good part, but
fall to earnest and so we feel the smart. We were not best
[Judg. 16. to make sport with Samson, lest he pull the house about our
25, 29, 30.]
ears and so make us pay dearly for our pastime. Paul saith,
1 Cor. 10. "Do we provoke the Lord to anger? Are we stronger than
22.
He?" If we will needs tempt, we were best tempt with our
matches. There is no dealing with fire, for it will burn all
Heb. 1. 7. that toucheth it; His Angels and "ministers" are a "flame
of fire:" but Hebrews the twelfth chapter and twenty-ninth
verse it is said, "Our God is even a consuming fire." Indeed, if He were like Dagon, the Philistines' god, He might
be set up and taken down, and we might break His neck
and hands at our pleasure; but being the strong and mighty
God of Hosts, we were best take heed how we deal with
Him.

Tuum, what say we to that? An ungracious child might
make that an argument of presumption, but whosoever is of
a[b] good nature will make it an argument of the contrary.
Isaac was Jacob's father, but was Jacob more bold to abuse
him for that? No, but rather more timorous. "My father,"
Gen. 27. 12. saith he, "may chance feel me, and so I shall seem to him
a mocker, and so bring a curse on me, and not a blessing."
Ps. 130. 4. Is God merciful? Yea truly, "mercy is with Thee, but that
Thou mayest be feared;" we may not abuse His mercy, as
Rom. 6. 1. to "sin that grace may abound." Is He bountiful and long-
suffering? We must therefore the more fear to displease
Him. When the Pharisees tempted Him, and would adven-
Mar. 8. 12. ture their souls in seeking a sign, it is said, "Christ sighed."
And why did He sigh? Because God "sware in His wrath

^b *any* A.

that they should never enter into His rest," whose fathers Ps. 95. 11.
tempted Him in the wilderness. What rest? He doth not
mean the rest in the land of Canaan only, but that which Heb. 3. 11;
shall be in the kingdom of God. 4. 9.

These two temptations of the devil may fitly be compared
to those two rocks between which Jonathan was to pass,
which are said to be "sharp." One is called "Bozez," 1 Sam. 14. 4.
which signifieth dirt; the other "Seneh," which signifieth
a bramble, or some sharp prick; between which, he and his 1 Sam. 14.
armour-bearer were fain to clamber up. Between two such 13.
rocks lieth our way, that is, presumption and desperation:
therefore blessed is he that so loveth God, that he can be
content to creep on hands and feet to Him.

SEVEN SERMONS

TEMPTATION OF CHRIST IN THE WILDERNESS.

SERMON VI.

MATTHEW iv. 8, 9.

Again, the devil taketh Him up into an exceeding high moun-
tain, and sheweth Him all the kingdoms of the world, an
the glory of them;
And saith unto Him, All these things will I give Thee, if Thou
wilt fall down and worship me.

[*Iterum assumpsit Eum diabolus in montem excelsum valde, et ostendit*
Ei omnia regna mundi, et gloriam eorum;
Et dixit Ei, Hæc omnia Tibi dabo, si cadens adoraveris me. Lat.
Vulg.]

[*Again, the devil taketh Him up into an exceeding high mountain, and*
sheweth Him all the kingdoms of the world, and the glory of them;
And saith unto Him, All these things will I give Thee, if Thou wilt
fall down and worship me. Eng. Trans.]

SERM.
VI.

AT the first overthrow, we had the first " again;" and
when Christ overthrew him then also, yet would not the
devil leave then neither, but he cometh with his second
" again;" he comes " again" and " again." The first " again"
was an argument of his courage and stomach; this second is
an argument of his importunity.

The first repulse could not drive him away, nor the second
neither; no, nor this third for altogether; for Luke saith,
Lu. 4. 13. " he departed for a season." So that as Christ saith, " After
Joh. 16.16. a while ye shall see Me, and after a while you shall not see
Me;" so saith the devil also, After a while you shall not see

me, and again, after a while you shall see me. Which teacheth us this lesson : that it is not enough to have prevailed
against his temptations twice or thrice, and so become secure; but we are alway to stand upon our guard, knowing
how the devil will successively every turning of a hand be
with us, and that while we live we shall never be at rest
with him; or if he tempt us not, we shall be in as bad or
worse case. For so long as the Lord left other nations
among the Israelites "to prove them by," and to be pricks Judg. 3. 1.
to their sides, it went well enough with them; but when
they began to live in some security (having for the most
part subdued them) then grew they to mutual dissension. It
is the greatest temptation to be without temptation. Therefore Paul had "the messenger of Satan to buffet him;" for 2 Cor. 12. 7.
then follows the pressing of God by prayers. But whether
we join hands with Satan or resist him, we shall be sure he
will set upon us and try by fair means what he can do. Or
if we say nay, yet in the end he will weary us, as Delilah
did Samson, who, because she was importunate, "his soul Judg. 16.
was pained to the death," and then he told her. Or if we 16.
will be obstinate in rejecting his temptations, giving him at
the first a peremptory refusal, then he will go another way
to work, as to imagine some device against us, and "smite Jer. 18. 18.
us with the tongue;" he will be rough with us. If none of
these will prevail, he will persuade us we must be like other
men, and that is as profitable or pleasant to us; and then
say Samuel what he can, "we will have a king." And when 1 Sam. 8. 19.
we have yielded once, "then goes he" to fetch company, "and Lu. 11. 26.
takes unto him seven worse spirits than himself." So "the
last state of that man is worse than the first." Give but an
inch, and he will take an ell; if he can get in but an arm, he
will make shift to shove in his whole body. As we see, if the
point of a nail have once made entry the rest will soon in.

We see an example of his encroaching even in David. 2 Sam. 11.
After he had once made him commit adultery by some mean 4.
degrees with Bathsheba, see how he draws[a] him on from one
wickedness to another. She was with child; her husband,
being in the service of God and the king, was by the king
murdered to hide her shame and satisfy his lust. So did he

[a] *tolls* A.

draw on Peter: first he made him follow aloof off; secondly, flatly to deny Christ; thirdly, to forswear Him; and fourthly, to curse himself if he knew Him.

The Hebrew writers note, that the devil's name Beelzebub signifieth a great flesh-fly, or a master-fly : flap him away never so often, he will still fly thither again.   So the devil will never cease molesting us, till "the smoking flax" be quite quenched, and "the bruised reed" clean broken.

Isa. 42. 3.

First, he twists certain small threads together, and so makes a little "cord of vanity," to draw us unto him; afterward with a "cart-rope" or cable of iniquity he seeks to bind us fast unto him for starting, either by the vice of lust, or of envy, or at least covetousness.   But if all should fail, pride is sure to hold : "O Lord, I thank thee, I am not like" such and such, nor "like this publican"—a degree farther—nor like this Pharisee.

[Isa. 5. 18.]

Lu. 18. 11.

This may be a good *caveat* unto us that we stand alway upon our guard, and that we be sure that we make strong resistance in the beginning, and break it if we can while it is but a whipcord.   And to use the like policy in a good matter that the king of Egypt did in a bad, who took order that every male child should be killed to keep the Israelites down betimes; and against the succession of temptation, to entertain the succession of prayer.

Now to the matter.   The devil deals as with a city.   In the first he tells Him He must be famished, except He can turn stones into bread.   Secondly, he comes to make a train of Scripture to entrap Him.   Now he comes to the ordinary means of dealing, that is, when men strive about any thing, and both parties are loath to yield, there will be some parley of composition and sharing between them.   So here, the devil seeing that he cannot overthrow His faith, offereth Him to compound; and on his part he is content to give Christ all the kingdoms of the world, if our Saviour for His part will but fall down and worship him.

The devil before came disguised in the shape of a malecontent, as that Christ should be in such hunger.   Next, he came in the habit of a divine, and that very demurely, with his Psalter in his hand.   Now he comes in all his royalty, "like the prince of this world," as he is so called.   He doth

Joh. 14. 30.

not stand peddling[b] with Christ, but goes roundly and frankly
to work; he offers all that he hath (and that is no small
matter) to bring Christ but to one sin, that so he might
overthrow all mankind.

He comes no more now with *Si Filius Dei es;* for that we
see is here left, he would not have Him think on it; he
would have Him now *filius sæculi.* This is called by St.
Paul the bewitching temptation, whereby men become " so Gal. 3. 3.
foolish" as that after they have " begun in the Spirit," they
will end in "the flesh." Where the devil cannot prevail
either by our own concupiscence or by his enticings, he will
see what he can do with his dragon's tail, and by that means,
say the Fathers, he did more hurt than by the other. Secondly, "his tail" is said to draw down "the third part of Rev. 12. 4.
the stars of heaven, and to cast them to the earth."

We are here to consider, first, the preparation that the
devil makes, by taking Him up to a " high hill," to make Mat. 4.
the offer; secondly, the temptation itself; thirdly, our Sa- 8—11.
viour's answer, and the shield He opposeth to it; fourthly,
the issue of the conflict, the victory.

In the first we are to consider, first, the devil's " method;" Eph. 4. 14.
secondly, the place and ground; thirdly, his policy, in not
only telling what he would give, but in shewing thereof;
fourthly, the things themselves which he offers, which are
two; "the kingdom of the earth, and the glory thereof."

I. First, of his "method." We are warned not to be
wavering, and " carried about with every wind of doctrine, ibid.
by the deceit and craftiness of men, whereby they lie in wait
to deceive." Craftiness and deceit then be the instruments
which the devil useth; he brings Christ from the wilderness
to the temple, and from the temple to the mountain, to destroy the temple, which mountain is prosperity. So in adversity we vow to God that we will serve Him, but after help
we break it.

II. Secondly, the lists where this temptation was used was
the mountain. The reason why he chose this place rather
than any other, is the fitness of it in regard of the prospect.
The wilderness, we know, was a melancholy place, and in
no wise fit for this temptation: so neither was the pinnacle;

[b] *pelting* A.

SERM.
VI.

for besides that it might have hindered the working of this temptation, being the pinnacle of the temple, the prospect was not good enough. For though it were high, yet there were divers hills about Jerusalem which would have hindered the sight of many things. And though Sion were a mountain, yet in respect of mount Hermon and Libanus it is said to be "a little one." And, Psalm the sixty-eighth and fifteenth verse, Basan is said to be the "great hill." Therefore as God chose a convenient hill, both for height and nearness, where Moses might "behold the whole land of Canaan," so here the devil chose "an exceeding high mountain," where a high mind might best take view and contemplate; such, where His horizon might be as spacious as was possible, and where His sight might not be hindered by any mean object.

Ps. 42. 6.
[marg.]

Deu. 32. 49.

III. Thirdly, he sets before His eyes "all the kingdoms of the earth." There is nothing so soon enticed and led away as the eye; it is the broker between the heart and all wicked lusts that be in the world. And therefore it was great folly in Hezekiah to shew his robes and treasure, as he was told by the Prophet; it stirreth up such coals of desire in them that saw them, as could not be quenched till they had fetched away all that he had, and all that his ancestors had laid up even till that day.

Isa. 39. 2.

It is the wisdom that is used now-a-days, when men would have one thing for another, to shew the thing they would so exchange; as the buyer sheweth his money, and the seller his wares in the best manner that he can, each to entice the other by the eye to the desire of the heart.

It is the devil's ancient sleight; he would not go about to persuade the matter in words, till he might withal present the thing to the eye.

Gen. 3. 6.

So he dealt with Eve. First he shewed her how "pleasant" the fruit was, and "the woman saw it." So the cause of the deluge was, that "the sons of God saw the beauty of the daughters of men." Ahab's seeing of Naboth's vineyard, for that "it lay near his house," was the cause of all the mischief that followed. This same foolish vanity of apparel, whereof I have given so often warning out of this place, comes from hence: "I saw a fine Babylonish garment, and

Gen. 6. 2.

1 Kings
21. 2.

Josh. 7. 21.

desiring it I took it" saith Achan. So the seeing of the bribe "blindeth the eyes of the judge." So still the sight of the eye allureth the heart to desire. ^{Deut. 16. 19.}

The heathen man therefore wished that virtue and honesty might as well be seen with bodily eyes, for then he thinketh that *admirabiles amores excitarent sui.* So if we could as well see that which God hath for us as that the devil here offereth us, we would not regard the devil's largess. Moses and the other Patriarchs saw Him Which is invisible, Which had provided a better thing for them: "Therefore he refused to be called the son of Pharoah's daughter, and to enjoy the pleasure of sin." [Cicero de Off. lib. i. c. 5.] ^{Heb. 11. 24, 25.}

But you are not so to take it, as though it were a thing simply ill to behold such things, or to look on a cupboard of plate, or to stand on a pinnacle: it is dangerous, but no sin; especially it is unfit for an unstayed and an ungoverned eye. Therefore Lot and his wife were forbidden to "look back" at the destruction of Sodom. To Abraham it was left at large, without any restraint, for that he was a man of better ruled affections. For, as there must be one without to take view and to entice, so must there be one within to hearken to it and to condescend. Be sure of that within that it be upright, and then thou mayest the better look with that which is without. But ever be wary, for the tinder of thy nature will soon take fire. ^{Gen. 19. 17.}

Job said, "he made a covenant with his eyes; why then should he think on a maid?" and that he had not "been deceived by ^c a woman," and that "his heart had not walked after his eyes." Paul knew "how to use want, and how to use abundance" or plenty, how poverty; "both to be full, and to be hungry:" he had stayed affections. ^{Job 31. 1. Job 31. 9. Job 31. 7. Phil. 4. 12.}

IV. *Omnia regna.* This was no small offer, but even all the wealth and honour that may be; two such things as are most vehemently desired of all men. So that, as Jerome saith, *Præ auri sacrá fame nihil sacrum.* The desire thereof also is so unsatiable that it is like the dropsy, which the more liquor is ministered to it the more it thirsteth; it is perpetual and unnatural. The less time a man hath to live, and so needs the less, the more he covets to abound. These

^c *with* A.

SERM.
VI.

two do never wax old; of all vices, gray hairs do never grow on these. This is the bait the devil laid for Christ, and lays for youth, and minds lasciviously given; he lays a bait on live flesh. To choleric natures he ministereth matters that may increase their wrath; for melancholy he lays baits of envy: and so for every one, according to their natural inclinations and humours, such baits as may entice them soonest. Which if he can get them once to swallow, his hook that is within, it will hold them sure enough, and by his line he will draw them to him when he list, so that he cares not to let them play with the line. Then, though he go to twenty sermons, it is no matter: with an apple he caught Adam and Eve, and all their posterity.

Well, we must be as children, "weaned" from this world, though it bring weeping with it.

Ps. 131. 2.
Gen. 27. 38.

When Eve was lady and mistress of all the world, yet because there was a godship, a higher degree than hers, she was not content. Princes, because they can go no higher by any earthly dignity, aspire to be gods, and so would be

[Acts 12.
22.]

accounted; as was said to Herod, that it was "the voice of God, and not of man." But, as they that are above can abide to have no equals, but will be alone by themselves, so they that be below can abide no superiors. As when Saul was chosen by lot from amongst the Israelites to be king

1 Sam. 10.
27.
2 Sam. 15.
4.

over them, some wicked men said, There is a goodly wise king; nay, I would I were king, I would they might come to me for justice.

Every one hath this conceit of himself, that he is worthier to bear rule than they which are in authority. Not so much

Judg. 9. 15.

as the silly furze-bush, but it thought itself a fit person to make

2 Kings 14.
9.

a king, and "the thistle" would have "the cedar's daughter" married to his son. The spider, a silly poisonful thing, would

Prov. 30.
28.
Jonah 4. 6,
10.

yet be in the top of "the king's palaces;" the gourd starts up in one night, and was gone in the next. Goodly Zebedee's wife could find no less thing to ask of Christ for her two

Mat. 20. 20,
21.

sons, that came the last day from the cart, but that "the one might sit at Christ's right hand and the other at the left in

Nu. 22. 23,
25, 27.
[Acts 1. 6.]

His kingdom." Balaam could never think his ass went half fast enough, when he rode towards preferment; the disciples also longed for the kingdom of Israel to be restored.

The devil did not shew all his kingdoms to Saul when he was coming from keeping his father's sheep, and Samuel 1 Sam. 9. 24. feasted him; nor after Saul was chosen king, and he fol- 1 Sam. 11. 5. lowed his cattle; neither did he shew them to the king bidden to Absalom's sheep-shearing, nor at such time as princes 2 Sam. 13. withdraw themselves to be private. But he shews them at Dan. 6. 18. such times as they are in their greatest glory and ruff, when kingdoms were grown to the top of jollity and majesty, as the kingdom of Israel was in Solomon's time; and chooseth such a time as when they were in most triumph and pomp, as they were wont to be at the day of the king's birth, or Hos. 7. 5. inauguration, or at a coronation, or at the receiving of am- Cant. 3. 11. bassadors; or at the entertaining of foreign states, as when "the Queen of Sheba" was in Solomon's court. To con- 1 Kings 10. clude, he sheweth them not when they are in a base estate, 1. but when they are in greatest "pomp." Acts 25. 23.

Now come we to the second point, to wit, the temptation itself: *En hæc omnia Tibi dabo.* Having prepared Christ's Mat. 4. 9. mind, as he thought, by shewing Him that he would give Him, now he comes in with a short and pithy oration; "All this will I give Thee." Here Thou seest all Thou canst wish for; "without Thee shall no man lift up his hand or his foot Gen. 41. in all Egypt," as Pharaoh said to Joseph, so as He might 1 Sam. 22. "make all captains," and "give to every one fields and vine- 7. yards," that He might say to every one what He list: Speak- est thou to Me? "Seest thou not that I have power to Joh. 19. 10. crucify thee, or to let thee go?" that His favour might raise a man so high as Haman was exalted "above all the princes," Est. 3. 1; and His disfavour, or the least word of His mouth quite over- 7. 10. throw him, as Haman was, by picking some small quarrel against him.

But this is not all neither; for the same gayish apparel wherein many do delight, is contained under this *Hæc omnia.* Not only embroidered with gold, but even "gold" itself, and Ps. 45. 8, 9. smells of the finest scent. And as for the delights of the flesh, if He can see any that delight Him better than other, it is no more than with David to send for her and have her, she was straight at His command. Neither must any say it was unlawful; no, not John Baptist, if he love his head. Mark 6. 17, He may command what He list: if any gainsay it He may 25, 27.

SERM.   despatch him out of the way, for He may kill and wound
VI.   whom He list. He may command all men's tongues, that
Dan. 5. 19.
2 Sam. 14. they dare not once open their mouth to speak against Him.
10.   Nay, He shall have all men's tongues and pens ready to ex-
2 Sam. 14. tol all that He doth, and say, "The king is like an Angel of
20.
Acts 12. 22. God," or that "it is the voice of God, and not of man."

Why then to have all men's hands, feet, bodies, faces,
tongues, and pens, this may be well said "All :" to have not
only one kingdom, but all; to have all the power and glory
of those kingdoms ; here is even all the kingdom, the power,
and the glory. He comes not after a pelting manner, he
1 Tim. 6. 6. shews himself a frank chapman ; he saith not that "Godliness is great gain," and a mind content with his lot, and wills
1 Tim. 6. 8. Him to be "content with food and raiment." He comes not
with *Illa*, which we shall not once behold till another world
come ; and whether there be any such or no, many doubt.
Heb. 12. 18. He shews Him "a mount that may be touched," he comes
with *hæc*, that is, with ready money in his hand ; he not only
offers but stakes down : and whereas God saith that in the
Gen. 3. 19. "sweat of our forehead we shall eat our bread," the devil
requires no such thing. This is a donative, *Hæc omnia dabo.*
What say ye now ? Shall Christ take it or no?

[Vid. Cic.   The heathen man saith, If a man be to violate his faith for
de Offic.
lib. iii.   any thing, it is for a kingdom. Christ hath here offered
c. 21.]   Him all kingdoms, a very enticing bait : but is there never a
hook hidden under it ? The woman was fine and brave, and
Rev. 17. 4. had "a cup of gold in her hand," but it was "full of abominations." So here, for all these fair shows, if you will gain
any thing by the devil, you must worship him—that is the
condition annexed to the grant ; it is no absolute gift, the
devil is not so kind as to part from all that for nothing. It
is such a gift as the lawyers call *excambium*, that is, 'exchange:' I will give you this, if you will give me that.

But yet one would think it a very large offer, to give so
great a lieu for so small a service ; it is but a little external
reverence, the bowing of the knee, you may notwithstanding
in heart think what ye list. Well, we may think there was
somewhat in it, that the devil offered so much for so little,
and yet Christ refused it. Indeed Christ had great reason
to refuse it, for He should have been a loser by the bargain.

I will stand to it, He had been better to have yielded to either
of the two former temptations than to this; He should full
dearly have bought all His kingdoms, He had been better to
have cast Himself down from the pinnacle. For that which
the devil here demandeth in lieu, is as much worth as both
the glory of God and the redemption of man.

Of His glory God saith, that He will not "give it to Isa. 42. 8.
another." If to no other, then not to the devil of all other.
And therefore the Angel would not have "a burnt offering" Judg. 13.
offered to him, but to God. The Angel would not let John ^{16.}
fall down and worship him, but bade him "worship God." Rev. 19. 10.
For he knew that God was very jealous of His honour, and
stood precisely upon that point. If He would not impart
this honour with the Angels, much less would He with the
devil: for there are degrees in idolatry. It is not so ill to
turn "the glory of God into the image of a man," as into Rom. 1. 23.
"birds and beasts."

Secondly, if we look into the desire that he had to satisfy
his ancient envy by the destruction of mankind, we must
needs commend the devil's wit in making such a bargain. It
had been the best pennyworth that ever was bought. For if
we mark how Christ rateth one only soul, we may see how
he, that to gain all the kingdoms of the world shall "lose Mat. 16. 26.
his own soul," makes but a foolish bargain. Then what rate
shall be made of all men's souls, if one be worth kingdoms?
All which had been lost, if Christ had consented to that
which the devil here requireth; for then He could not have
said, "I restored that which I took not." By His death He Ps. 69. 4.
paid the price for the sins of the whole world; He should
then have had a score of His own to have paid, and His
death could have been sufficient but for Himself only. If He
had fallen down and worshipped him, He could not have
said that "the prince of this world had nothing" to say Joh. 14. 30.
against Him.

Now let us apply this to ourselves.

But we will peradventure say the devil never made us any
such offer, and therefore what needs any admonishment in
this behalf? But I answer, Though the devil come not in
person to us as he did to Christ, yet he comes by his instruments. When Balak sent to Balaam to "come and curse" Num. 22.
^{17.}

SERM.
VI.

Acts 8. 18.

Mark 6. 23.

Mat. 26. 15.

Ezek. 13.
19.
Prov. 28.
21.
Amos 8. 6.

the Israelites, and promised him great rewards, it was not Balak's messengers that spake, but the devil used them as instruments to speak. So when Simon Magus would have bought the Holy Ghost with money, the devil therein tempted the Apostles with simony; Simon was but the trunk, through which the devil spake.

Again, there be some that will say, they were never tempted with kingdoms. It may well be, for it needs not, when less will serve. It was Christ only That was thus tempted; in Him lay a heroical mind, that could not be allured with small matters. But with us it is nothing so, we esteem far more basely of ourselves; we set our wares at a very easy price, he may buy us even dagger-cheap, as we say; he need never carry us so high as the mount, the pinnacle is high enough; yea, the lowest steeple in all the town would serve the turn. Or let him but carry us to the leads or gutters of our own houses, nay let us but stand in our window or in our doors, if he will give us but so much as we can there see he will tempt us throughly, we will accept it and thank him too. He shall not need to come to us with kingdoms, one kingdom is too much; what say ye to "half" a one? No, will the devil say, I will give ye half a one. If He would come to us but with "thirty pence," I am afraid many of us would play Judas. Nay, less than so would buy a great sort, even "handfuls of barley and pieces of bread." Yea, some will not stick to "buy" and sell "the poor for a pair of shoes," as Amos speaketh.

When he cometh then to tempt us, he may abate a great deal of this that he offers Christ; he may strike out *omnia* and *hæc* too, and instead thereof put in *hoc*, and say, Hold, ye shall have this to worship me, I will give ye no more. I fear me, we will make short work, and take it; *hoc aliquid*, a matter of half-a-crown or ten groats, a pair of shoes, or some such trifle, will bring us on our knees to the devil.

Is there a pretty commodity to be had? It makes no matter for breaking faith and promise. This is that that makes the devil so good a husband and thrifty, and to go near hand; what need he give more, when so little will serve? Whereas, if we will stand hucking with him, we might get a great deal more.

In this temptation, as in the former, there is both fire to consume our faith, and a dart to wound our consciences. The fire is the motion of discontent, that God is either a poor God, not able sufficiently to reward those that serve Him; or else an unkind God That will not reward the duties that are performed by those that serve Him. By this we come to say, " Who is the Almighty, that we should serve Him?" Job 21. 15. The wicked are they that prosper and increase in riches. " I have cleansed my heart in vain, for daily have I been Ps. 73. 13, punished." Then this dart makes us weary of well-doing; ^{14.} and then follows, that we will serve the devil. Being discontent with God's service, we undertake the service of His enemy; he requireth nothing but a little falling down, and then if Simon shall come and require any unlawful thing at our hands, we are ready with Judas to meet with him and say, " What will ye give me, and I will do it?" though it be to Mat. 26. 15. the betraying of Christ. The devil here opens his meaning in this temptation plainly, that he would have Him fall down and worship him, with a bare and bold face : before, he came disguised, and spake in parables. His meaning is not, when he saith *dabo*, to give them, but to barter or exchange one thing for another. It is no gift, but a flat bargain, men use not to account it a gift, except it be without rendering back either money or service. If he render here service back, he may well think, I have sold my soul for *hoc aliquid.* He Mat. 16. 26. may think, as " Esau sold his birth-right for a mess of pot- Heb. 12. 16. tage," so hath he sold his soul, his birth-right, and freedom; for we were " all bought with a price," the same great High- 1 Cor. 7. 23. Priest redeemed us all with His blood. No sins are so carefully to be taken heed of as these that have annexed to adoration, donation; he hath *malum* with a jointure. If He should have cast Himself down from the pinnacle, here is all He should have had, they would have talked of it, and have wondered a while at it.

Well, we must be thus persuaded, that God is as well able and willing to reward us for any service as the devil, and better too. It is He indeed That reigneth over the king- Dan. 5. 21. doms of men, and placeth in them whom pleaseth Him; but when He giveth or disposeth, He giveth indeed freely, exact- Jas. 1. 5. ing nothing back again, unless it be such things as He were

SERM.
VI.

to have without any such gift; such things as are due of mere right, without any stipulation or hire. The devil's *dabo* is as offices and parsonages are given amongst us; that is, as usually sold as horses in Smithfield. But if we could be content to give indeed, let that heroical mind that was in Abraham be in us, that as he would not take any thing of Melchizedek[d], so we will not be "a shoe-latchet" the richer by the devil. If he offer to make us wealthy, let us answer him *Pecunia tua tecum pereat.*

Gen. 14. 23.

[Acts 8.
20.]

[d It was the King of Sodom, and not Melchizedek.]

SEVEN SERMONS

TEMPTATION OF CHRIST IN THE WILDERNESS.

SERMON VII.

MATTHEW iv. 10, 11.

*Then Jesus saith unto him, Get thee hence behind Me, Satan;
for it is written, Thou shalt worship the Lord thy God, and
Him only shalt thou serve.*

*Then the devil leaveth Him, and behold the Angels came, and
ministered unto Him.*

[*Tunc dicit ei Jesus, Vade Satana; scriptum est enim, Dominum
Deum tuum adorabis, et Illi soli servies.*

*Tunc reliquit Eum diabolus, et ecce Angeli accesserunt, et minis-
trabant Ei.* Lat. Vulg.]

[*Then saith Jesus unto him, Get thee hence, Satan; for it is written,
Thou shalt worship the Lord thy God, and Him only shalt thou
serve.*

*Then the devil leaveth Him, and behold Angels came, and ministered
unto Him.* Eng. Trans.]

THE answering of this temptation, if some had had the
answering of it, would have been *facto*, 'by the doing' of the
thing that the devil required; and not in words, standing
upon terms in disputation. Insomuch, as they would never
have cared for a cushion to kneel on, but have fallen down
straight on their very faces, and have thanked him too.

SERM.
VII.
Num. 22.
17.

If Balak should say unto one of them, "I will promote thee to great honour," an Angel standing in the way should not hinder him from going. The manner of flesh and blood is, in cases of preferment, to respect nothing that may bring them out of their conceived hope or desire thereof; and therefore whatsoever it is that stands in their way, be it never so holy, down it shall for haste to make the way nearest.

Gen. 37. 5.

2 Sam. 16.
11.

2 Kings
11. 1.

2 Kings
10. 8.

In regard of this, one brother respects not another. When Joseph had had "a dream" of his brethren, and "told it" them, all brotherly affection was laid aside. The son and subject Absalom forgetteth his duty as to his father, and allegiance as to his prince, seeking his life. "The mother of Ahaziah, Athaliah, when she saw her son dead," makes no more ado but "destroys all the king's seed." Jehu makes no bones, nor is abashed at the sight of "heaps" of dead men's heads, of the king's sons that he had caused to be slain, but adds more murders to them. What's a basketful of heads to a kingdom? And Herod stuck not to kill all the male-born children in Bethlehem. So that Gregory might well say, *Ambitio est vita cui etiam innocentes nocent:* such is the vehement desire of a kingdom.

Mat. 2. 16.

[Mat. 16.
23.]

Jer. 2. 27.
1 Tim. 5.
15.

So that a great many would have made no scruple at the matter, neither would they have counted it a temptation, but good counsel. Neither would so have cut up Peter as Christ did, to bid him go behind Him, and turn their backs on him; but they would rather "have turned their backs" to God, and their faces "after Satan." And indeed it must needs be, that either our Saviour was unwise in refusing so good an offer, or else the world in these days is in a wrong bias.

Our Saviour, we see, doth not only refuse the thing, but also gives him hard words for making the offer and motion. For He doth not only confute him here by saying, *Scriptum est;* but He adds words of bitter reprehension, saying, "Avoid, Satan!" He might have given fair words, as He did before; but here He seemeth to have left His patience. The reason why He was more hot in this than in the former is, for that this toucheth the glory of God, and the redemption of mankind: the former temptations touched but Himself in particular, as the turning of stones into bread, but for miracle; and the casting Himself down was but to try God what care He had of Him. But this so much toucheth the glory of God, as He can hold no longer. Also His longing to redeem man caused the same. Neither did He only answer the devil so, but when His blessed Apostle who meant friendly to Him moved Him to the like matter, He rebuked him sharply.

Two causes there are wherein Christ is very earnest: one in counsel ministered to Him, tending to the impairing of God's glory; the other in practices tending to the impairing of God's Church: there He was not only vehement in words, Joh. 2. 15. but made a whip to scourge them out. And so in the Old Testament it is said of Moses, that "he was a meek man, Num. 12. 3. above all the men of the earth;" yet when he came to a case of idolatry, it is said, "he threw the tables out of his Exod. 32. hands, and brake them." And so far did he lose his natural 19, 28. affection to his people and countrymen, that he caused a great number of them to be slain.

And so in a case of the Church, when Korah rebelled, Num. 16. then Moses waxed very angry; for, "Glory be to God on [Lu. 2. 14.] high, and peace on earth," is the Angels' song and joy, and the devil's grief; as on the other side, the dishonour of God, and dissension of the Church, is the devil's joy, and grief of the Angels.

Now, besides that He doth in words rebuke him sharply, He doth no less in gesture also; as by turning His back upon him (as it is most like He did in saying "Avoid, Satan") which is such a despiteful disgrace, as if that one should offer us the like, we would take it in very great disdain. Which is to us an instruction, that as there is a time when we are to keep the devil before us, and to have our eye still upon him, and his weapon or temptation, for fear lest unawares he might do us some hurt, so is there a place, a time, and a sin, that we are to turn our backs on, and not once to look at his temptation.

In affliction, patience is to be tried; there "resist the Jas. 4. 7. devil," stand to him, "and he will fly from ye." Here we are to set the devil before us. But in a case of lust, or 1 Cor. 6. 18. filthy desire, then do ye fly from him. So in the second

Epistle to Timothy the second chapter and twenty-second verse, we are exhorted to "fly from the lusts of youth, and to follow justice;" there is no standing to gaze back on the devil and his temptations.

Now to the answer, *Scriptum est.*

The disputing or deciding of the devil's title, that is, whether the kingdoms of the earth were his to give or no, Christ stands not upon; nor upon this, whether the devil were a man of his word or no. Indeed, it might well have been doubted, whether the devil be as good as his word; his [2 Cor. 1. 20.] promises are not "Yea and Amen," as the promises of God are. We may take example by Eve, to whom he promised, that if they did eat of the forbidden fruit, that they should be like gods; but were they so indeed, after they had eaten? No, but like the beasts that perish. And as true it is that the kingdoms are his.

If the kingdom of Israel had been at his disposition, we may be sure David should never have been king; as well appeareth by the troubles he raised against him. No, nor Hezekiah neither, of all other he would never choose such. Job 2. 7. We may see his good will in Job; he could not only be content to spoil him of all that he had, but also he must Mat. 8. 30, afflict his body: and so upon the Gergesenes' hogs. 32.

The kingdoms are none of his, but they are committed to him in some sort to dispose, as himself saith, Luke the fourth chapter, and sixth verse. He hath, as it were, an advowson of them, to present unto them; but yet, not as he there saith, to give to whom he list, but to whom he is permitted.

[Job 1. 12.] God must first put all that Job hath in his hands, or else Judg. 9. he can do nothing. Abimelech and Herod came to their 1, &c. Mat. 2. kingdoms by the devil's patent, they be the devil's officers. 1, &c. So we see daily in our days, that he bestows offices, and presents to Churches. So that, as Brentius saith, many have *panem quotidianum* that cannot come by *Da nobis,* they come not to it by God's gift; yet all the interest that the devil hath, is but to present *pro hâc vitâ tantum.* As therefore it may be true, that in some sort they may be given him, so yet not to dispose as he will.

It is God only That can say so, for His only they are

absolutely. "The earth is the Lord's, and all the fulness Ps. 24. 1.
thereof, the round world and all that dwell therein." It is
He, "the most high God, That divided to the nations their Deut. 32. 8.
inheritance." "By Him kings reign, and princes have do- Prov. 8. 15.
minion." He brought Nebuchadnezzar to know that "the Dan. 5. 21.
most high God bare rule over the kingdoms of men." He
indeed may well say, *Cui voluero, do ea;* and to whomsoever God giveth, "He giveth liberally, and reproacheth no Jas. 1. 5.
man."

The devil, we see, exacteth more than the thing is worth,
and restraineth the benefit of his grant with unjust cove-
nants. But Christ goes not about to answer the devil that
way, but by flying to the Scriptures as to His surest hold.
Therefore David prays that his mind may be inclined to Ps. 119. 36.
God's law, "and not to covetousness."

For there is a medicine for every disease, and power as
well against this temptation of covetousness as against the
former; the law of God can as well keep a man from covetousness, as from desperation; "Heaven and earth shall pass, [Mat. 5.
but no one jot" of this. Let therefore *Hæc omnia* give place ¹⁸·]
to *Scriptum est:* marry, *Omnia illa,* which both we now
enjoy, and which are laid up for us hereafter, are come to
by *Scriptum est.* So that *Omnia hæc* is not all we must care
for; there be things to come, besides these things which we
lay hands on, far more precious. Though here be all the
kingdoms of the earth, yet they are said to be shewed in the
twinkling of an eye; so cannot the other kingdom of exceeding glory. All the power of all the princes on the earth
have not power over one silly soul to destroy it. All the Mat. 10. 28.
glory of them is called but a great big fan, or "pomp." Acts 25. 23.
Solomon was the most glorious prince that ever was, yet he Mat. 6. 29.
was not clothed like a lily. Nor all the lilies in the field,
nor stars in heaven, nor the sun and moon itself, are comparable to one soul.

The Scripture whereby Christ answereth the devil, is in
Deuteronomy the sixth chapter and thirteenth verse. "Thou
shalt fear the Lord thy God, and serve Him." If any fantastical spirit oppose itself against Moses, let it be accursed.

There is in this answer two things set down, worship and
service, both which are due to God only. Covetousness

endeth in idolatry, and fitly is so termed : if Christ had been covetously minded, then He must needs have fallen down and worshipped the devil, for covetousness and idolatry being joined together, we would not have parted from so great a benefit.

Christ hath here changed a word which the *Septuaginta* translator hath ; which signifieth a service with an open testi-
Rom. 10.
10.
mony. So that, will ye know if a man do believe? "He believeth unto righteousness with the heart, that with the mouth confesseth to salvation." Such as glorify God, as well
1 Cor. 6. 20. in their members as in their spirits. As St. James saith of
[Jas. 2. 18.] faith, "Shew me thy faith by thy works," so may it be said of fear. You say you have fear, can you shew me your fear? If it be not a dead fear, it is to be seen; as Daniel the third chapter, and seventh verse, it must be shewed by falling down and worshipping.
Mat. 18. 26. The servant that feared, "fell down" and besought his master. Do you fear? then where is the outward reverence?
1 Kings 19. The inward affection must appear by the outward action :
18.
religion is outward as well as inward.

There be two ways whereby we may have traffic with the devil, either of both will serve his turn : first, homage; secondly, service of the body; and both these doth God
Ezek. 8. 12. require, even when we are "in the dark," or in our chamber. Indeed, might the devil say, this mountain is very open; but how say ye? will ye be content closely in a corner to worship me? If ye will not wear my cognisance on your forehead, yet ye may take my mark in your hand; then shutting your hand, nobody can perceive it. If ye will not take "the
Rev. 13. 17, mark," yet take "the number of the beast's name," that
18.
is, "six hundred threescore and six." Will ye do none
Rom. 16. of these? What then? will ye "serve" me? Thus ye see
18.
what glorious terms he useth; but if one should seem to do one of these on courtesy, he will not be content till he do it of duty.

Now let us see first what it is to worship. It is that
Acts 10. 25. which Cornelius did to Peter; he "met him, fell down at his feet, and worshipped him." And that which John did
Rev. 19. 10. to the Angel; that is, he "fell down before his feet to worship him." It is when one on the knees doth a bodily worship.

I will shew it you in David's words, for I cannot tell it ye better. When Michal scoffed at David for being bare-headed before the ark, he saith, "I will be more vile than thus, and 2 Sam. 6. will be low in mine own sight." A man can never be too ^{20, 22.} reverent to God; we think it a great disgrace, and debasing of ourselves, if we use any bodily worship to God. It may be said to them as it was to him that feared to do too much reverence to Cæsar, *Hic homo timet timere Cæsarem.* Our religion and *cultus* must be uncovered, and a bare-faced religion; we would not use to come before a mean prince, as we do before the King of kings, and Lord of lords, even the God of heaven and earth.

"The four-and-twenty elders fell down before Him That [Rev. 4. sat on the throne, and worshipped Him That liveth for ever, ^{10.]} and cast their crowns before His throne."

The wandering eye must learn to be "fastened on Him," Lu. 4. 20. and "the work of justice" and "peace." The worship of Isa. 32. 17. the "knees" "to bow," and "kneel before the Lord their Eph. 3. 14. Maker." Our feet are to "come before His face; for the Ps. 95. 6. Ps. 95. 2, 3. Lord is a great God, and a great King above all gods." Jacob, though he were not able to stand or kneel, yet, because he would use some corporal service, "leaned upon his staff, and worshipped" God, as appeareth from Genesis the forty-seventh chapter and thirty-first verse, and Hebrews the eleventh chapter and twenty-first verse. This must be done as duty due unto God, and in regard of those that be strangers.

Secondly, what it is to "serve." This is to bow the soul, as the other is to bow the body. For the king "to serve and 1 Kings 12. speak kindly to the people," that they may "serve him for ^{7.} ever after," is not the service he meaneth, nor to do all that 2 Sam. 15. the king commands. For God must be above all; and "of 2 Pet. 2. 19. whomsoever a man is overcome, to him he is in bondage." We must serve God with our sacrifices, but not with our Isa. 43. 23, sins, nor weary Him with our iniquities. We may not make ^{24.} a dungcart of Him, to load Him with our sin and filth; and Amos 2. 13. when He comes again, to have as much more for Him.

"Only." The devil himself would grant, that God is to be served; his meaning was, that a man might serve God and him too: but Christ saith, "God only." But it may be

SERM.
VII.

said, this word "only" is not in the Scripture whence Christ citeth this sentence, and so Christ hath added to the word of God.   Indeed, in Deuteronomy the sixth chapter and thirteenth verse "Alone" is not; but in the next verse it is said, "Do not follow after other gods," which is in effect, "God only."

The Papists ask where we find "only" in justification by faith? Indeed we do not find it, but we do find that "by faith" and nothing else we are "justified," and so we may well collect it by faith only. "By grace we are saved through faith; and that not of ourselves, it is the gift of God."   And on this warrant have many of the ancient Fathers been bold to add the word "only;" as Origen upon Romans the third chapter, and twenty-eighth verse. Hilary upon Matthew the ninth chapter, and divers others say, "Faith only justifieth."

Rom. 3. 28.
Eph. 2. 8.

[Commen.
in Mat.
c. 8. § 6.]

God is only to be worshipped and served, and none besides Him. Zephaniah prophesieth against them "that serve the host of heaven upon the house-top, and swear by Malcham." But "Jacob sware by the fear of his father Isaac;" and it is said, "they feared the Lord, and served their idols also."

Zeph. 1. 5.

Gen. 31. 53.
2 Kings 17.
41.

It is the property of Aaron's rod, that being turned into a serpent, if the magicians turn theirs also into serpents, Aaron's will devour the rest. Bring the ark into the temple of Dagon, Dagon will fall down and break his face; and though it were lifted up again, yet it fell down again. The stories bear witness that the gods of the Hebrews would not come into Pantho. Samuel bade the people, "If they were come again to the Lord with all their hearts, to put away their strange gods from amongst them." If there were any other beside Him that were able to help up, we might have some reason to serve other; but since it is He That must help us in all necessities, we must worship Him alone. Otherwise, when we pray to Him, He may send us to "the gods which we have chosen" to serve, for our help. If we could find an equal, or a better than God, we had some reason to make him a partner in His worship; but if none be worthy once to be named with Him (so far is all beneath Him) we shall offer Him too much disgrace and injury in so doing.

Ex. 7. 12.

1 Sam. 5. 2,
3, 4.

1 Sam. 7. 3.

Judg. 10. 14.

It is an embasing of gold to have any other metal joined

with it, yea though it be silver. "The son," saith Malachi, Mal. 1. 6.
"honoureth his father, and the servant his lord : if I be your
Father, where is the honour which you do Me? if your Lord,
where is your reverence?" Whether we account of God as
of our Lord and Master, [a man can have but one Lord and
Master[a] ;] or whether we take Him for a Father, a man can [Mal. 2.
have but one father except he be a bastard and so be *filius* 10.]
populi : if for a "husband," not two husbands, for He is a Isa. 54. 5.
jealous God, and cannot abide that. "No man can serve [Mat. 6.
two masters, but he must love the one, and despise the 24.]
other ; no man can love God and Mammon."

"Then the devil left Him." "Blessed is the man," saith Mat. 4. 11.
St. James, "that endureth temptation ; for when he is tried, Jas. 1. 12.
he shall receive the crown of life." Christ hath endured the
temptation : now follows the blessing. Jacob would not let
the Angel depart (with whom he strove) before he had Gen. 32. 26.
"blessed" him. Job after his afflictions received his twofold Job 42. 10.
blessing. The woman of Canaan first heard herself accounted [Mark 7.
a dog, but at last she heard, *Fiat tibi.* Paul was first buf- [2 Cor. 12.
feted by the prick of the flesh, and after heard, "My grace 7, 9.]
is sufficient for thee."

So here at last, when the devil saw it was bootless to stay
any longer, there was no good by him to be done, he leaves
our Saviour ; but yet he went not away willingly of himself,
but was sent away with an Avaunt. Which is a comfort to
us, to think we stand not at the devil's courtesy, and that he
shall not attempt us so long as he list ; for God hath the Rev. 20. 2.
devil in a chain, and will not suffer him "to tempt us above 1Cor.10.13.
our strength." "For the rod of the wicked shall not rest Ps. 125. 3.
on the lot of 'the righteous, lest the righteous put forth their
hand to wickedness." To have the devil not to come to us,
is a great favour ; but to have him come and go away conquered, is exceeding mercy. "For tribulation brings pa- Rom. 5. 3,
tience, and patience experience, and experience hope, and 4, 5.
hope makes not ashamed." As God said of Job, "Hast thou Job 2. 3.
marked My servant Job, who keepeth still his integrity?"

"And behold, the Angels came, and ministered unto [Mat. 4.
Him." And as Luke saith, "There is joy with the Angels Lu. 15. 10.
in heaven, upon the conversion of every sinner." "For we 1 Cor. 4. 9.

a added in A.

574   *Seven Sermons upon the Temptation of Christ.*

SERM. are made a spectacle unto men and angels." Before God
VII.
Dan. 7. 10. are said to stand, "ten thousand Angels, and to minister
before Him." He hath a greater pre-eminence, "but we
2 Pet. 1. 4. are also herein partakers of the Divine nature;" either be-
1 Kings 19. cause we are fed by Angels as Elias was, or defended by
5.
them, or watched of them.

Isa. 28. 16. But saith Esay, "He that believeth makes not haste."
Christ was not hasty, but stayed God's good time; He
would not make His own bread, but stayed till the "Angels
Lu. 22. 43. ministered unto Him." Then "there appeared an Angel to
comfort Him."

Job 33. 33. This wisdom must we learn by holding our tongue: otherwise one of these two extremes shall we come to; either,
Lu. 16. 25. *Extremum luctûs gaudium occupat*, or, *Extrema gaudii luctus
occupat* [b], saith Bernard.

Judg. 4. 19, The world is like Jael, who meets Sisera and entertains
21.
him at first very friendly; she allures him to her, and gives
him drink, and lays him down; but so soon as he was asleep,
she smites a nail into his temples. The world begins with
milk, and ends with a hammer. But our Saviour's mean-
Joh. 2. 10. ing is clean contrary. The world first uttereth "good wine,
and when men have well drunk, then that which is worst."
But Christ "hath kept back the good wine till now." As
Mat. 13. 41, Matthew saith, "The Son of man shall send forth His
42.
Angels, and they shall gather out of His Kingdom all things
that offend, and them which do iniquity, and shall cast them
into a furnace of fire, where [c] shall be weeping and gnashing
of teeth. Then shall the just shine as the sun, in the Kingdom of their Father." Our Saviour's method is, to give
bitter first, and sweet afterward. Wherefore we are to
wish, that here we may suffer affliction, that we may after
be crowned by Him.

[b] [Dom. in Ram. Palm. Serm. 1. init. In Vigil. Apost. Pet. et Paul. Serm.
circa med.]   [c] *there* A.

The following variations, in the Nineteen Sermons UPON
PRAYER IN GENERAL, AND UPON THE LORD'S PRAYER IN PAR-
TICULAR, distinguished by italics, are given as exhibiting the
differences between the Editions of 1641 and 1642.

p. 301 l. 21 differently pointed. A period at 'place.' The following
sentence begins, *For whereas* &c. There is a colon at
' hope.'
302 — 23 *this* saying.
— — 32 *So while* &c.
304 — 11 'not' is omitted.
313 — 5 *speak* otherwise.
— — 10 'again' is omitted.
— — 14 *are* the good gifts.
— — 20 doth *add* to the givings.
325 — 7 *parings*.
— — 15 *Which if we ask*.
326 — 27 be given to *us*.
332 — 15 ' do' is omitted.
333 last line but one, *it* assures us.
335 — 22 *prayers*.
— — 25 *and* our affections.
336 — 36 *might* sit.
— — 40 *He* willed.
340 — 37 The Latin is translated. There is then a period, and the
next sentence begins, Such *were* &c.
341 — 9 as David *prayed*.
348 — 3 the like unto *His*.
358 — 16 *the* prevailing.
— — 26 'in' is omitted.
383 — 8 *it* ought.
390 — 18 *So* the.
391 — 4 *we* shall be exalted.
— — 37 *when* we pray . . . and a comma at ' come.'
398 last line but one, ' that' is omitted.
399 — 2 'that' is omitted.
406 — 33 *which may be considered* either . . . . or else as things . . .
The words ' we may understand' which follow ' else' are
omitted.
409 — 30 ' as Peter said to John, *Quid autem hic ?*' omitted.
410 — 33 a period at *suspirare*. ' When' begins another sentence.
— — 37 If we *find* &c.
411 — 29 'and' is omitted.
— — 40 apply *it*.

p. 414 l. 19 *in his* time.

418 — 27 *where he saith* after the word 'Timothy.'

419 — 22 *he* hath tasted.

421 — 18 Tribue *mihi victum necessarium.*

428 — 4 as *well as* for.

— — 24 as *if* the Apostle spake.

432 — 25 *the* peace.

438 — 11 *so* the same measure.

444 — 14 corruption of *our* nature.

— — 37 what are the temptations, and *what the.*

446 — 4 a period at ' work.' The following sentence begins, *There-*
 fore.

— — 19 *nor* deliver us over.

— — 33 that *as* the Gentiles &c. and then a comma at ' greediness.'

447 — 9 *yet* we may be.

— — 17 ' that' omitted.

— — 29 *and* that we *also.*

— — 35 *but* it shall be a means.

448 — 9 and if *it* not increase.

469 — 14 ' It' is omitted.

It has not been thought necessary to point out the instances in which the Latin is translated in the edition of 1641, and not in that of 1642 ; for the only difference between the two editions in this respect is, that the former more generally translates than the latter, though neither one nor the other does so invariably.

Made in the USA
Columbia, SC
20 October 2022

69776763R00324